M000073716

Bernard LUCE

DICTIONNAIRE
GASTRONOMIQUE
FRANÇAIS / ANGLAIS

DICTIONARY OF
GASTRONOMIC
TERMS
FRENCH / ENGLISH

La Maison du Dictionnaire
98, Bld du Montparnasse F-75014 PARIS
Tél : (+33) 1 43 22 12 93 Fax : (+33) 1 43 22 01 77

Hippocrene Books, Inc
171 Madison Avenue, New York, NY, 10016
Tel : (212) 685-4371 Fax : (212) 779-9338

©LA MAISON DU DICTIONNAIRE PARIS 1997

Le code de la propriété intellectuelle du 1er juillet 1992 interdit en effet expressément la photocopie à usage collectif sans autorisation des ayants droit. Or cette pratique s'est généralisée notamment dans les établissements d'enseignement, provoquant une baisse brutale des achats de livres, au point que la possibilité même pour les auteurs de créer des oeuvres nouvelles et de les faire éditer correctement est aujourd'hui menacée.

En application de la loi du 11 mars 1957 (articles 40 et 41; Code pénal, article 425), il est interdit de reproduire intégralement ou partiellement le présent ouvrage, sur quelque support que ce soit, sans autorisation de l'Editeur ou du Centre Français d'Exploitation du Droit de Copie, 3 rue Hautefeuille, 75006 Paris.

Dépôt légal :
ISBN : 2-85608-088-X
Code livre : 3.67.12.103
Printed in France

The distribution of this book is being handled in the USA by : HIPPOCRENE BOOKS INC.
171 Madison Avenue
ISBN : 0-7818-0555-4
NEW YORK N.Y 10016 USA

DICTIONNAIRE
GASTRONOMIQUE
FRANÇAIS / ANGLAIS

Table des matières

DICTIONARY

OF

GASTRONOMIC

TERMS

FRENCH / ENGLISH

Contents

DICTIONNAIRE

GASTRONOMIQUE

FRANCAIS / ANGLAIS

Avant-propos :

Le but de cet ouvrage est de répondre aux besoins de traduction de Français en Anglais des MENUS pour restaurants / limonadiers / glaciers, mais il peut être également utile à toutes les professions des métiers de bouche en général :
(boucherie, boulangerie, charcuterie, épicerie, pâtisserie, poissonnerie, fruits et légumes, etc...../ ainsi qu'aux publicitaires), qui ont à faire avec la langue anglaise.

Notre ambition est de permettre à des utilisateurs ayant peu de connaissance de la langue anglaise, de pouvoir néanmoins par eux-mêmes réaliser une traduction acceptable, tout comme étiqueter leurs produits de façon non équivoque.
Nous avons travaillé avec " LE LAROUSSE GASTRONOMIQUE " pour la partie technique, mais avec de nombreux dictionnaires pour la partie traduction - O.A.L.D.O.C.E / COLLINS / THE CONCISE OXFORD FRENCH DICTIONARY / ainsi que / CHAMBERS THESAURUS / des ouvrages spécialisés en anglais en ce qui concerne les viandes, les poissons et les champignons.

« Nous remercions particulièrement Monsieur RENAUD, boucher au marché central de La Rochelle pour sa participation en ce qui concerne les termes de boucherie » .

Nous recommandons les grammaires suivantes:
a) - pour non anglicisants :

" La grammaire anglaise de l'étudiant "
(S. BERLAND-DELEPINE / OPHRYS Paris)

b) - pour anglicisants :

" A Practical English Grammar "
A.J.THOMSON / A.V.MARTINET / OXFORD U.P.)

" Practical English Usage " (MICHAEL SWAN / OXFORD U.P.)

" Dictionary of English Phrasal Verbs " (COLLINS)

Comment traduire vos MENUS

Nous avons travaillé sur le sujet dans deux directions différentes, d'abord en vous traduisant les termes de base de la cuisine, d'autre part en vous donnant des traductions utilisables immédiatement.

- **1° Partie** - Références rapides classées en ordre alphabétique, et comprenant :

a) Liste des mots ou termes <u>étrangers</u>, admis dans le <u>langage</u> courant en anglais :
" Thesaurus "

b) Mots < <u>Uncountable</u> > qui ne prennent pas le pluriel par eux-mêmes

c) Termes généraux de base les plus usuels, avec notation < Uncountable > - < <u>Adjectif</u> > - < <u>v.t / adjectif</u> > - < <u>attributif adjectif</u> >; ces trois dernières notations font considérer le mot ou le terme comme " adjectif ".

d) Termes généraux pour les poissons, avec des notations similaires; < Uncountable > - < <u>Pluriel inchangé</u> > dans ce dernier cas le mot reste sans changement au pluriel, cette notation peut être indiquée également en a) ou en c).

e) Les viandes boeuf, gibier, mouton, porc, veau, volaille, avec des notations comme en b) / c) / d)

- **2° Partie** - Dictionnaire classé en ordre alphabétique reprenant aussi bien les références rapides de la première partie, que les termes de cuisine ou les traductions directement utilisables.

Pour trouver ce dont vous avez besoin, il vous suffit de consulter le dictionnaire en ordre alphabétique qui vous indique entre parenthèse le mot ou la phrase correspondante en anglais :
- exemple = 1) - Salicorne saltwort

2) - Hamburgers de poisson
fried hamburgers made of egg, crumbs, coalfish, and onion; topped with a fried egg.

" **Nota** " - Toutefois lorsque plusieurs termes sont identiques, avec un sens différent ces derniers sont indiqué comme suit:
- Cerise { liqueur } : cherry brandy
- Cerise { tomate } : tomato variety eaten raw with salt

FRENCH / ENGLISH

DICTIONARY

OF

GASTRONOMIC TERMS

Foreword :

This reference work is intended primarily to address the translation needs of restaurants / cafes / ice cream vendors of menus from French into English, but it could equally be of use to all those involved in the food industry (butchers, bakers, delicatessens, grocers, patissiers, fishmongers, greengrocers, etc., along with the associated publicity sector) who need to use the English language.

Our ambition is to enable users with minimal knowledge of English to be able nonetheless to produce their own acceptable translations, and to label their products appropriately.
We have worked with " LE LAROUSSE GASTRONOMIQUE " for the technical part, but with a number of different dictionaries for the translation part: O.A.L.D.O.C.E., COLLINS, THE CONCISE OXFORD FRENCH DICTIONARY, and the CHAMBERS THESAURUS, and also with specialised English language reference works dealing with meats, fish and mushrooms.

" <u>We would particularly like to thank Mr. RENAUD, the butcher in the central market at La Rochelle</u> for his help with butchery terms. "

We recommend the following grammars:
a) - in French:

" La grammaire anglaise de l'étudiant "
(S. BERLAND-DELEPINE / OPHRYS Paris)

b) - in English:

" A Practical English Grammar "
A.J.THOMSON / A.V.MARTINET / OXFORD U.P.)

" Practical English Usage " (MICHAEL SWAN / OXFORD U.P.)

" Dictionary of English Phrasal Verbs " (COLLINS)

How to translate your menus

We have approached the subject in two ways, firstly translating the basic culinary terms, then providing translations that can be used immediately.

- 1st Part - Ready references classified in alphabetical order, comprising :

    a) List of <u>foreign</u> words or terms used in <u>everyday</u> English. " Thesaurus "

    b) < <u>Uncountable</u> > words which have no plural

    c) The most usual basic general terms, with the notation < Uncountable > - < <u>Adjectif</u> > - < <u>v.t / adjectif</u> > - < <u>attributif adjectif</u> >; the final three notations assign the word or term to the category " adjective".

    d) General terms for fish, with similar notations: < Uncountable > - < <u>Plural unchanged</u> >; in the latter case, where the word remains unchanged in the plural, this notation may be signalled in (a) or in (c).

    e) Meats (beef, game, mutton/lamb, pork, veal, poultry), with notations as in (b), (c) and (d).

- 2nd Part - Dictionary classified in alphabetical order and including the ready references in the first part, as well as straight culinary terms or translations ready for use

To find what you need, simply consult the dictionary in alphabetical order, which will indicate in brackets the corresponding English word or phrase:
- example = 1) - Salicorne saltwort

        2) - Hamburgers de poisson fried hamburgers made of egg, crumbs, coalfish, and onion; topped with a fried egg

" Note " - When more than one term is indicated, each with a different meaning, these are indicated as follows:
- Cerise { liqueur } : cherry brandy
- Cerise { tomate } : tomato variety eaten raw with salt

Situation de Menus dans les
crêperies et les brasseries

BUCKWHEAT PANCAKES
Crêpes de blé noir

Au beurre (pancake with butter)

" composez vous-même votre garniture " *compose yourself your garnish*

a) **" une garniture ou la première garniture "** *one garnish or the first garnish*
b) **" toute garniture supplémentaire** " *for each garnish added*

Jambon campagne	country ham
Andouille	large sausage filled with chitterlings
Bacon	bacon
œuf	egg
Tomates	tomatoes
Oignons	onions
Champignons	mushrooms
Camembert	camenbert
Gruyère	gruyère

Autre schéma de vente possible:

Une garniture au choix   with a chosen garnish (**1**)

Deux garnitures au choix   with two chosen garnishes (**1**)

Trois garnitures au choix   with three chosen garnishes (**1**)

For more garnishes , the bill is charged accordingly " pour d'autres garnitures le prix sera majoré en conséquence "

(**1**) - garnishes : either jambon (ham) - etc.......

CAFETERIA (coffee)

Irish coffee	drink made with wiskey more coffee, topped of whipped cream
Café express *	espresso coffee
Café décaféiné *	decaffeinated coffee
Café (grand)	large cup of coffee
Café décaféiné (grand)	large cup of decaffeinated coffee
Café crème	coffee with milk
Café crème (grand)	coffee with milk (large)
Café crème décaféiné	decaffeinated coffee with milk
Café crème décaféiné (grand)	decaffeinated coffee with milk (large)

* < after 13.30 BST > " prix après 14.30 heure d'été "

HOT DRINKS
Thés et Boissons chaudes

Thé	tea
Infusion	infusion
Thé parfumé	flavoured tea
Lait chaud	hot milk
Supplément < lait > < citron >	milk or lemon
Grog < citron >	Grog flavoured with lemon - etc
Chocolat au lait	chocolate in milk

inclusive of service " service inclus "

COCKTAILS D'APERITIF

Bloody Mary

APERITIFS

Campari
Vermouths 5 cl
Supplement kirsch or Gin
Porto 5 cl (port)
Pineau des charentes 5 cl (unripe grape juice added of cognac)

WISKIES

THE CELLAR I OR I WINE LIST
La Cave

wines in carafe   1/4 of litre   1/2 litre

BLANC :

ROSE :

RED WINE :

Beaujolais A.O.C *
Bordeaux A.O.C *

VERRE (wines by a glass 15 cl; from the same list then in carafe above)

WINES IN BOTTLE   Bottle   1/4 of bottle

Red wine   11° vol.
Beaujolais   A.O.C *
Bordeaux   A.O.C *
Côtes du Rhône   (Rhône valley) A.O.C *

* V.D.Q.S = quality wine   **A.O.C** = high quality wine

Mineral water (half a bottle)
inclusive of service " service inclus "

11

COMPOSED SALADS
Salades Composées

RAW VEGETABLES AND HORS D'ŒUVRES
Crudités et Hors d'œuvres

Salade verte (green salad)

PORK BUTCHERY

Charcuterie

Jambon de campagne (country ham)

CHEESES
fromages

Camembert (camembert)

inclusive of service " service inclus "

COMPOSED MEALS BY UNIT OF PLATE
Assiettes composées

Pâtes fraîches (fresh pasta with grated cheese and tomato purée)

MEAT
Viandes

(all garnished with chips)
" pour l'indication - toutes garnies frites "

- supplement for other garnishes below :

« pour l'indication - supplément pour autres garnitures ci-dessous »

< Beignets >	fritters
< Pâtes >	fresh pasta with butter
< haricots >	haricot beans
< Epinards >	spinach
< Brocolis >	cabbage-sprouts
< Lentilles >	lentils
< Haricots verts >	french beans
< Salade verte >	green salad

HAMBURGERS
Les Burgers

BEEF
bœuf

Entrecôte maître d'hôtel   grilled entrecôte, served with parsley butter

---

PORK
Porc

Boudin	polony
Andouillette	small sausage filled with chitterlings
Saucisse	sausage

HELPING OF GARNISH OR VEGETABLES
Portion de garniture ou de Légumes

Frites	chips
Lentilles	lentils
Haricots verts	french beans

DESSERTS

" Le mot a le même sens en anglais "

Salade de fruits   fruit salad
Fruits   fruits according to the supplies, ask the waiter
             for those availables

" Le texte en anglais indique - les fruits sont ceux approvisionnés
sur le marché, demander au serveur ceux qu'il peut vous servir "

< have a look to the pages " pancakes " and " ice-creams " >
" Le texte en anglais indique que les crêpes ou les glaces peuvent être demandées en dessert "

inclusive of service
" service compris "

Autre exemple:

  Dans cet exemple nous avons attribué un numéro à chaque article, de
façon que le serveur puisse faire la relation sans équivoque entre la
commande du client et son choix, contrairement à ce que nous avons fait
par ailleurs.

Fromage ou Dessert parmi<1> profiterolles, <2> tarte maison, <3> fruit, <4>glace, <5>
sorbet (Cheese or dessert among<1> profiteroles, <2> home made tart, <3> fruit, <4> ice
cream<5> sorbet).

MIXED ICE-CREAMS IN CUPS
Nos coupes composées

Pêches melba (vanilla ice-cream topped with halved peaches poached in syrup ; <1> covered
with raspberry purée)

Café liègeois <café viennois> :
 - a) café (coffee mixed with cream and chilled / or / coffe ice crream)
 - b) entremets glacés (strong coffee, more coffee ice cream of sugar, topped with sugared
whipped cream) / or / (ice cream of sugar, cream and coffe extract, topped with sugared whipped
cream)

Chocolat liégeois (chocolate ice cream with sugared whipped cream)

- our cups may be served without sugared whipped cream
" Le texte anglais indique - nos coupes peuvent être servies sans
crème chantilly "

HIGH QUALITY ICE CREAMS AND SORBETS
Glaces et Sorbets de marque

- **cup with 2 balls** : " coupe avec 2 boules "
- **cup with 3 balls** : " coupe avec 3 boules "

chosen among : " choisis parmi "
          < vanille > (vanilla) - etc.....

- **coupe de crème chantilly** (cup of sugared whipped cream):
- **supplement crème chantilly** :

FOR THE DOG
" Menu du chien "

CIDER
cidre

Verre	by a glass
Grand verre	by a large glass
Cidre doux en bouteille	soft bottled cider, by a bottle
Cidre brut en bouteille	very dry bottled cider, by a bottle

inclusive of service " service inclus "

BEER
bières

- **< pression >** draught beer
- **< distingué >** beer mug of half a litre
- **Supplement for < limonade >** lemonade, or **< sirop >** syrup

----

REFRESHMENTS
Rafraîchissements

- Chilled, tea **< thé >**, or coffee **< café >**, or chocolate **< chocolat >**
- Supplement **crème Chantilly** / sugared whipped cream
- **< Limonade 1/4 l >** (lemonade 1/4 litre)
- **< Eau minérale 1/4 l >** (mineral water 1/4 litre)

- Supplement syrup **< sirop >**, or slice of lemon **< tranche >**
- **Lait froid** (chilled milk)
- **Chocolat froid** (chilled chocolate)

ALCOHOLS / BRANDIES / LIQUEURS
alcools, digestifs, liqueurs

- **Poire** (pear brandy), or **Framboise** (raspberry brandy) 4 cl

- **Cognac** *** 2.5 cl " two years old cognac "
- **Armagnac** *** 2.5 cl " one year old armagnac "
- **Cognac** V.S.O.P (five years old) 3 cl
- **Calvados** 2.5 cl

- For other drinks 4 cl, **ask the waiter :** " *La phrase anglaise indique - pour d'autres boissons demandez au serveur* "

EVENING COCKTAILS
coktails de soirée

- **Bloody Mary** (Bloody Mary) - etc ....

inclusive of service
" service inclus "

STEAK TARTARES
Même sens en anglais

- **All are garnished with chips and salad -**
" Tous garnis frites et salade "

GALETTES élaborées
(elaborated pancakes)

NOTRE GRILL
(other dishes and grillings)

Les Salades (salads)

Les Assiettes Froides (cold meat)

Les œufs(eggs)
L'œuf plat I ou I L'omelette Nature 3 œufs (either fried eggs or plain omelette of three eggs)

L'omelette garnie (omelette with a chosen filling) **(1)**

(1) either <fines herbes> (herbs) - etc...

Nos Grillades (grillings I ou I grillstones)

- All our meat are served with a garnish of chips and green salad -
" Toutes nos viandes sont servies avec une garniture frites et salade "

Le Steak à cheval (œuf) (steak topped with a fried egg) **(2)**
Le Steak grillé (grilled steak) **(2)**

Légumes en supplément (extra vegetables) :
 - **haricots verts** (french beans) - etc.....

Cuisson (cooking state) **(2)**
 - **cuit à point** (well cooked I or I done I or I done to a turn)
 - **bleu** (underdone I ou I rare)

CREPES AU FROMENT
(pancakes)

Au sucre (with icing sugar)
Beurre, sucre (with butter and icing sugar)
Une garniture au choix (with one chosen garnish) **(1)**
Deux garnitures au choix (with two chosen garnishes) **(1)**
Trois garnitures au choix (with three chosen garnishes) **(1)**

Suppléments (extras) :

 - **flambés** (flamed) see **(4)**
 - **fruits** (fruits) see **(2)**
 - **glace** (ice-cream) see **(3)**

(1) garnitures au choix (chosen garnishes):
 - miel (honey)
 - fraise (strawberry jam) - etc.....

(2) fruits (fruits) :
 - framboises (raspberries) - etc....

(3) glaces (ice-creams) :
 - vanille (vanilla) - etc....

(4) alcool (alcohol and fruits in alcohol) :
 - raisins au rhum (raisins in rum)
 - calvados (calvados) - etc..

NOS CREPES PARFUMEES
(flavoured pancakes)

GLACES GOURMANDES
(ice-cream list)

LES PARFUMS (flavoured ice-creams) :

Sorbets (sorbets - different flavourings see under)

- **fraise** (strawberry) - etc.........

- **crèmes glacées** (ice-creams - different flavourings see under)

- **vanille** (vanilla) - etc......

- **Une boule au choix** (one ball according to your choice)

- **Deux boules au choix** (two balls according to your choice)

- **Trois boules au choix** (three balls according to your choice)

- **Chantilly supplément** (extra whipped cream)

- **Chantilly coupe** (cup of whipped cream)

LES SORBETS RAFRAICHIS
(chilled sorbets)

_ **Supplément chantilly** (extra sugared whipped cream)

- **La Coupe des sorbets 10 parfums** (sorbets' cup with ten different flavourings)

LES GOURMANDES
(for the connoisseurs) " pour les connaisseurs "

BIERES (beer)

BOUTEILLES (bottles)

Françaises (french beer)

Belges (belgian beer)

Allemandes (german beer)

Hollandaises (dutch beer)

Danoises (danish beer)

Irlandaises (irish beer)

Anglaises (british beer)

LES FRAPPES
(chilled coffee or chocolate)

- **Café** (coffee) | or | **Chocolat** (chocolate).(with cane sugar, crushed ice, mixed in the shaker)

LE CELLIER
(wine list)

EN CARAFE (in carafe)

- **Rouge** (red wine) / **Rosé** (vin rosé) / **Blanc** (vin blanc)
- **Muscadet** (muscatel wine)

CELLIER (from the cellar)
1/2 B. (half a bottle) **Bout**. (bottle)

- **Champagnisé** (sparkling wine)

ALCOOLS (alcohols 2,5 cl)

- **Rhum** (rum), **Calvados** (calvados), **Marc** (marc), **Armagnac** (armagnac), **Gin** (gin) etc..

Liqueurs diverses :

Crème de banane (crème de banane) /
Cherry brandy (cherry brandy) / Curaçao (Curaçao) / Peppermint (peppermint) etc..
Cointreau (cointreau) / Chartreuse (chartreuse)

COCKTAILS

- **Alexandra** (cocktail of cream, cognac, and cream of cacao)
- **Side car** (sidecar)

- **Gin Fizz** (gin fizz)
- **Bloody Mary** (bloody mary)

WINE LIST

VINS BLANCS SECS : a bottle   half bottle

- **Muscadet sur lie -** (muscatel wine)

- **Sancerre** (white wine from Loire valley, " sauvignon " variety of wine)

VINS BLANCS D'ALSACE :

- **Riesling**

- **Gewurztraminer** (high quality wine from Alsace area, " traminer " variety of wine)

- **Edelzwicker** (wine from a mixing of good varieties of wine)

VINS ROSÉS : a bottle   half bottle

- **Côtes de Provence** (high quality wines from vineyards located between Marseille and Nice)

- **Listel** (high quality fruity rosé wine from Languedoc area)

VINS ROUGES : a bottle   half bottle

- **From different locations:**

- **Haut Poitou** (quality wine from Poitiers area)

- **Mareuil rouge** (red wine from Vendée area)

- **Loire**

- **Saumur Champigny** (quality red wine from " cabernet franc " variety of wine)

- **St Nicolas de Bourgueil** (high quality red wine from " cabernet franc " variety of wine

- **Bordeaux :** (a bottle, half bottle)

- **Fronsac** (among the best red wines fom Fronsac near Libourne)

- **Gd Cru St Emilon** (high quality red wine from St Emilion)

- **St Estèphe** (high quality red wine from Médoc)

- **Bourgogne** (BURGUNDY)

CHAMPAGNE : (a bottle, half bottle)

- **Moët et Chandon** ...

PARTIE B

Words and phrases for menus / Récapitulation des termes ou phrases pour menus

- **Autres plats et grillades** (other dishes and grillings)

- **Boissons chaudes** (hot drinks)

- *Café :* Ce mot ne doit pas être utilisé seul comme titre :

a) S'il a le sens de boisson il faut le traduire (coffee)
b) En anglais le mot désigne un établissement ou l'on peut
   consommer du thé, certains plats comme les omelettes, mais
   pas de boissons alcoolisées.
c) Enfin comme enseigne, il conserve son sens dans tous les
   autres pays d'Europe, même pour un anglais.

- *Cafetaria***:** Si le mot indique la vente de cafés, boissons, et nourritures servies sur un plateau, il peut être utilisé tel que en anglais. Si au contraire il signifie le service des différentes sortes de café, il doit être traduit (coffees)ou (coffee-bar)

- **Cartes de crédit et chèques** acceptés à partir de 100 francs
(all the credit cards and cheques are accepted, only from a sum of 100 FF)

- **Carte des vins:** Conventionnellement la traduction est (wine list) toutefois si dans le menu l'intitulé est " La Cave " vous pouvez très bien traduire par (The Cellar),
en anglais c'est l'endroit ou un particulier conserve ses vins, la traduction reste dans l'esprit.

- **Cidre pression au goblet** (draught cider in goblet)

- **Cidre pression le litre** (draught cider by one litre)

- **Deuxième partie (Part II)**

- **Différents parfums**, voir ci-dessous (different flavourings, see under)

- **Entrées froides** (cold hors d'œuvres)

- **Etat de cuisson** (cooking state):
    - cuit à point (well cooked I or I done I or I done to a turn)
    - bleu (underdone I ou I rare)
    - trop cuit (overdone)
    - pas assez cuit (underdone)

- **Garnitures possibles** (available garnishes)

- **Hors d'œuvres de poissons froids** (cold hors d'œuvres of fishes)

- **Hors d'œuvres chauds** (hot hors d'œuvres)

- **Indication des prix en anglais:** " Dans ce cas la virgule du prix en français est remplacée par un point " ; exemple 12,50 devient 12.50 FF

- **Jetez un regard à nos cocktails, desserts et glaces** (Look at our list of cocktails / desserts / ice-creams)

- **La Cave** (wine list)

- **L'heure du thé** (tea break)

- **Les légumes** (vegetables)

- **La marée** (food from the sea or fishes)

- **Les pâtisseries** (pastries)

- **Menu à la carte** (menu à la carte / à la carte / from the menu)

- **Menu à prix fixe** (set menu / fixed price menu / net price menu)

- **Menu pour le chien** (for the dog)

- **Menu pour enfants** (menu for the kids)

- **Menu rapide** (quick meal)

- **Menu du jour** (today's menu)

- **Menus prix nets / vins non compris** (menus net prices - wines not included)

- **Muscadet 1/2 bouteille ou bouteille** (muscatel wine 1/2 bottle or bottle)

- **Nous n'acceptons pas les chèques en paiement** (we do not accept the cheques in payment)

- **Nos poissons** (our fishes)

- **Pâtisserie du jour** (sweet of the day or pastry of the day)

- **Première partie** (Part I)

- **Prix nets** (net prices)

- **Prix net** (net price)

 - **Plats italiens** (italian dishes)

- **Plats garnis < viande >** (meat dishes)

- **Possibilité supplément chantilly**
  (possibility to order extra sugared whipped cream)

- **Prix modulés à partir d'une certaine heure:**

a) en heure d'été si elle est en vigueur -
< exemple après 14,30 > (after 13.30 BST), soit une heure de
moins que l'heure locale, mais ne pas oublier la mention " BST "

b) en heure d'hiver ou heure française s'il n'y a pas de
changement d'heure -
< exemple après 14,30 > (after 13.30 UT), soit une heure de moins
que l'heure locale, mais ne pas oublier la mention " UT ".

- **Repas léger** (light meal or snack)

- **Supplément pour autres garnitures ci-dessous**
  (supplement for other garnishes below)

- **Service compris** (inclusive of service)

- **Sur le pouce** (light meals)

- **Salades comme hors d'œuvres** (salads as hors d'œuvres)

- **Tous les plats sont servis avec une garniture**
  (all the dishes are served with a garnish)

- **Tous les plats sont garnis** (all the dishes are garnished)

- **Toutes nos viandes sont servies avec frites et salade verte**
  (all our meat are served with a garnish of chips, and green salad)
  " Si la ou les garnitures sont différentes remplacer **< chips >**
  ou **< green salad >** "

- **Tous garnis frites** (all garnished with chips)

- **Vins en carafe par 1/4 ou 1/2 litre**
  (wines in carafe by 1/4 of a litre or 1/2 litre)

- **Valable suivant approvisionnements ou arrivages**
  (available according to the supplies)

- **Voir page suivante** (look next page for.....)
« nom anglais de la chose / ou / pour renvois <3> <4> par exemple ».

LISTES DES TERMES ACCEPTES
en ANGLAIS dans le langage courant

1) Alcools et Boissons / Alcohols and Beverages

Français	Anglais	Français	Anglais
Absinthe	Absinth(e)	Aguardiente	Aguardiente
Akvavit	Akvavit	Amontillado	Amontillado
		< xérès >	
Anisette	Anisette	Apple-jack	Apple-jack
Aquavit	Aquavit	Arak	Arak
Armagnac	Armagnac		
Beaujolais	Beaujolais	Beaune	Beaune
Bénédictine	Benedictine	Bichof	Bishop
Black vel	Black velvet	Bloody Mary	Bloody Mary
Bourbon	Bourbon	Bucelas	Bucellas
Bourgogne	Burgundy		
Calvados	Calvados	Campari	Campari
Catawba	Catawba	Chablis	Chablis
Chambertin	Chambertin	Champagne	Champagne
Chartreuse	Chartreuse	Cherry brandy	Cherry brandy
Chianti	Chianti	Chicha	Chicha
Cidre	Cider	Claret	Claret
Cobbler	Cobbler	Cognac	Cognac
Cointreau	Cointreau	Constantia	Constantia
Cordial	Cordial		
Daiquiri	Daiquiri		
Eau de vie	Eau de vie	Egg-nog	Eggnog
Fine < eau de vie >	Fine	Fino < xérès >	Fino
Flip	Flip		
Genevrette	Genevrette	Gimlet	Gimlet
Gin	Gin	Gin-fizz	Gin-fizz
Ginger wine	Ginger wine	Glögg	Glogg
Grappa	Grappa	Graves	Graves
Grog	Grog		
Hermitage	Hermitage		
Johannisberg	Johannisberger		
Képhir	Kéfir	Kirsch	Kirsch
Kéfyr	Kefir	Kummel	Kümmel
Manzanilla	Manzanilla	Marasquin	Maraschino
Marc	Marc brandy	Marsala	Marsala
Martini	Martini	Médoc	Médoc
Mirabelle < eau de vie >			Mirabelle

Alcools et Boissons (suite) / Alcohols and Beverages (foll.)

Français	Anglais	Français	Anglais
Moselle < vin >	Moselle	Muscat < vin >	Muscat
Muscadet < vin >	Muscatel		
Eau de noyau	Noyau		
Oloroso	Oloroso	Ouzo	Ouzo
Pastis	Pastis	Peach brandy	Peach brandy
Pernod	Pernod	Perry	Perry
Persicot	Persico(t)	Pilsener	Pils(e)ner
Pombé < bière de mil >		Pombe	
Porto	Port	Pousse café	Pousse-café
Pulque	Pulque	Punch	Punch
Purl	Purl		
Quetsche <eau de vie >		Quetsch	
Ratafia < liqueur >	Ratafia	Retsina	Retsina
Riesling	Riesling	Rioja	Rioja
Rhum	Rum	Rye <whisky>	Rye
Rye < whiskey >	Rye-whiskey		
Saké	Sake	Sangaree	Sangaree
Sangria	Sangria	Sauternes	Sauterne(s)
Schiedam	Schiedam	Schnaps	Schnapps
Scotch	Scotch	Sherry	Sherry
Sherry-cobbler	Sherry-cobbler	Schrub	Schrub
Sidecar	Sidecar	Slivovitz	Slivovitz
Sloe gin	Sloe gin	Sour <cocktail>	Sour
St Julien < Médoc >	St Julien	Stingo <G.B>	Stingo
I			
Tafia		Taffia	Tafia
Tarragona <vin>	Tarragona		
Tequila	Tequil(l)a	Toddy <cocktail>	Toddy
Tokay	Tokay	Tom Collins	Tom Collins
Vermouth	Vermouth	Vin blanc	Vin blanc
Vin du Rhin	Rhine-wine	Vin ordinaire	Vin ordinaire
Vin rosé	Rosé	Vin rosé	Vin rosé
Vinho verde	Vinho verde	Vodka	Vodka
Whiskey	Whiskey	Whisky	Whisky
Xérès	Xeres		

2) Fromages / Cheeses

Français	Anglais	Français	Anglais
Bel paese	Bel paese	Bleu d'Auvergne	Bleu d'Auvergne
Blue vinny	Blue vinny	Boursin	Boursin
Brie	Brie		
Caboc	Caboc	Caerphilly	Caerphilly
Camembert	Camembert	Carré	Carré
Cheddar	Cheddar	Cheshire	Cheshire
Chevrotin	Chevrotin	Colwick	Colwick
Coulommiers	Coulommiers	Crowdie	Crowdie
Danish blue	Danish blue	Derby	Derby
Dolcelatte	Dolcelatte	Dorset Blue	Dorset Blue
Double Gloucester	Double Gloucester	Dunlop	Dunlop
Edam	Edam	Emmental	Emmental
Emmenthal	Emmenthal	Esrom	Esrom
Ewe-cheese	Ewe-cheese		
Feta	Feta	Fynbo	Fynbo
Gammelost	Gammelost	Gjetost	Gjetost
Gjetost	Getost	Gloucester	Gloucester
I			
Gorgonzola	Gorgonzola	Gouda	Gouda
Grana	Grana	Gruyère	Gruyère
Handkäse	Handkäse	Havarti	Havarti
Herrgardsost	Herrgardsost	Herve	Herve
Huntsman	Huntsman	Hushallsost	Hushallsost
Islay	Islay		
Jarslberg	Jarslberg		
Killarney	Killarney	Kryddost	Kryddost
Lancashire	Lancashire	Leicester	Leicester
Limbourg	Limburg	Limburger	Limburger
Lymeswold	Lymeswold		
Mouse-trap	Mouse-trap	Mozzarella	Mozzarella
Munster	Munster	Mysost	Mysost
Neufchâtel	Neufchâtel		
Parmesan	Parmesan	Petit suisse	Petit Suisse
Pipo crème	Pipo crème	Pont l'évêque	Pont l'Eveque
Port Salut	Port Salut	Port Salut	Port du Salut

2) Fromages (suite) / Cheeses (foll.)

Français	Anglais	Français	Anglais
Prästost	Prästost	Provolone	Provolone
Pultost	Pultost		
Raclette < fondue >	Raclette	Red Windsor	Red Windsor
Reggiano	Reggiano	Ricotta	Ricotta
Romadur	Romadur	Roquefort	Roquefort
Sage derby	Sage derby	Saint Paulin	Saint Paulin
Samsoë	Samso	Schabzieger	Sapsago
Stilton	Stilton	Stracchino	Stracchino
Tilsit	Tilsit	Tilsit	Tilsiter
Vacherin	Vacherin		
Wensleydale	Wensleydale	Wexford	Wexford

3) Herbes et Epices / Herbs and Spices

Français	Anglais	Français	Anglais
Ail	Garlic	Aneth	Dill
Armoise	Wormwood		
Cannelle	Cinnamon	Chicorée frisée	Endive
Ciboulette	Chive	Civette	Chive
Clou de girofles	Cloves	Colza	Rape
Coriandre	Coriander	Cresson	Watercress
Cumin	Cum(m)in	Curcuma	Turmeric
Estragon	Tarragon		
Fenouil	Fennel	Fenouil bâtard	Dill
Fenugrec	Fennugreek		
Gaulthérie	Wintergreen	Genièvre	Juniper
Gentiane	Gentian	Gingembre	Ginger
Hysope	Hyssop		
Macis	Mace	Marjolaine	Marjoram
Menthe	Mint	Menthe poivrée	Peppermint
Moutarde	Mustard	Muscade	Nutmeg
Myrrhe	Myrrh		
Origan	Oregano		

3) Herbes et Epices (suite) / Herbs and Spices (foll.)

Français	Anglais	Français	Anglais
Paprika	Paprika	Persil	Parsley
Pourpier	Purslane		
Raifort	Horseradish	Réglisse	Liquorice
Romarin	Rosemary	Rue	Rue
Safran	Saffron	Safran des Indes	Turmeric
Sarriette	Savory	Sauge	Sage
Séneçon	Groundsel		
Thym	Thyme		
Vanille	Vanilla	Verveine	Verbena

4) Nourriture et Plats / Food and Dishes

Français	Anglais	Français	Anglais
Ange à cheval	Angel on horseback		
Blanquette	Blanquette		
Borchtch	Borscht	Bouillabaisse	Bouillabaisse
Boudin	Polony	Beignet	Fritter
Berlingot	Humburg	Biscotte	Zwieback
Biscuit complet	Graham crackers	Boule de gomme	Gumdrop
Bubble and squeak	Bubble and squeak	Burgoo	Burgoo
Cake	Fruit cake		
Cannelloni	Cannelloni	Carbon(n)ade	Carbon(n)ade
Cassoulet	Cassoulet		
Charlotte russe		Charlotte russe	
Chateaubriand	Porterhouse (steak)	Chowder	Chowder
Chili con carné	Chili con carné	Chop suey	Chop suey
Cock-a-leeckie	Cockaleekie	Cocktail de fruits	Fruit cocktail
Colcannon	Colcannon	Consommé	Consommé
Copeaux de chocolat	Chocolate vermicelli		
Craquelin	Water-biscuit		
Crème anglaise	Egg-custard	Crème aux œufs	Flummery
Crêpe	Flapjack	Crépinette	Faggot
Croquette de poisson	Fishcake		
Cake au fruits	Fruit cake	cuit très dur	Hardbake
Choucroute	Sauerkraut		
Dariole	Dariole	Doughnut (beignet)	Doughnut
Dragée	Dragée	Dumpling	Dumpling
Diplomate (à l'anglaise)		Trifle	
Eccles cake	Eccles cake	Eclair	Eclair
Enchilada	Enchilada	Escalope	Escalope

4) Nourriture et Plats (suite) / Food and Dishes (foll.)

Français	Anglais	Français	Anglais
Escalope à la viennoise		Wiener schnitzel	
Escargot	Escargot		
Farce	Forcemeat		
Fedelini (pâtes)	Fedelini	Fettucine (pâtes)	Fettucine
Fishball	Fishball		
Flan	Flan or custard tart	Foie gras	Foie gras
Fondant	Fondant	Fondue (fromage)	Fondue
Fraise	Fraise	French toast	French toast
Fricandeau	Fricandeau		
Fricassée	Fricassee	Fritto misto	Fritto misto
Friture	Friture	Fromage bleu	Danish blue
Fudge	Fudge		
Galantine	Galantine	Game chips	Game chips
Gâteau	Gateau		
Gâteau sec au gingembre		Ginger nut	
Gâteau sec au gingembre		Gingersnap	
Gaspacho		Gazpacho	
Gaufrette	Wafer	Gaufre	Waffle
Ghee	Ghee		
Gnocchi	Gnocchi		
Goulache	Goulash	Goulasch	
Gruau	Gruel	Gruau d'avoine	Grits
Guacamole (sauce)	Guacamole		
Hachis parmentier		Shepherd's pie	
Haggis	Haggis	Halva	Halva(h)
Hamburger	Hamburger	Hot-dog	Hot-dog
Huîtres de claire		Prairie oyster	
Kedgeree	Kedgeree		
Langoustine	Scampi		
Macédoine de fruits	Fruit cocktail		
Maïs bouilli	Hominy	Matelote	Matelote
Millefeuille	Millefeuille(s)	Minestrone	Minestrone
Mous(s)aka	Moussaka		
Navarin	Navarin		
Olla-podrida	Olla-podrida	Opsonium	Opsonium
Paella	Paella	Panade	Panada
bread soup			
Pain de régime	Diet-bread	Pain blanc	French bread
Pain spécial	Fancy bread	Pain d'épice	Gingerbread
Pain complet	Graham bread	Pain complet	Wholemeal bread
Pain de Gênes	Genoa cake	Pain de seigle noir	Pumpernickel
Pemmican	Pem(m)ican		
Pilaf	Pilaf	Pilau	Pilau

4) Nourriture et Plats (suite) / Food and Dishes (foll.)

Français	Anglais	Français	Anglais
Pirojki	Pirozhki	Pizza	Pizza
Plum-pudding	Plum-pudding	PLum-pudding	Plum-duff
Ploughman's lunch		Ploughman's lunch	
Polenta	Polenta		
Pot-au-feu	Pot-au-feu	Potage à la tortue	Turtle soup
Profiterole	Profiterole	Prosciutto	Prosciutto
Pudding aux raisins de Corinthe		Spotted dick	
Pumpernickel	Pumpernickel		
Quenelle	Quenelle	Quiche	Quiche
Ragoût		ragout ou Hotpot	
Ramequin	Ramekin	Ratatouille	Ratatouille
Ravioli	Ravioli	Rémoulade	Remoulade
Risotto	Risotto	Rissole	Rissole
Sabayon	Zabaglione		
Sachertorte	Sachertorte	Salmigondis	Salmagundi
Salmis	Salmi(s)	Saltimbocca	Saltimbocca
Salade de fruits			Fruit salad
Sauce blanche	White sauce		
Sauce hollandaise			Sauce hollandaise
Sauce vinaigrette			French dressing
Saucisse de Francfort			Frankfurter
Scampi ou langoustine			Scampi
Schnitzel	Schnitzel	Smorbrod	Smorbrod
Smögarsbord	Smorgasbord	Soufflé	Soufflé
Spaghettis à la bolognaise			Spaghetti (alla)
			Bolognèse (suite
Stroganoff	Stroganoff	Succotash	Succotash
Sukiyaki	Sukiyaki	Sundae	Sundae
Sushi	Sushi	Syllabub	Syllabub
Tabasco	Tabasco	Tablette	Tablet
Taco	Taco	Tamal	Tamal(e)
Tandouri	Tandoori	Tapioca	Tapioca
Timbale	Timbale		
Toad-in-the-hole			Toad-in-the-hole
Torte	Torte	Tortellini	Tortellini
Tortilla	Tortilla	Tutti-frutti	Tutti-frutti
Velouté sauce	Velouté sauce	Vermicelle	Vermicelli < U >
Vichyssoise	Vichyssoise	Vol-au-vent	Vol-au-vent
Welsh rarebit			Welsh rabbit ou welsh rarebit
Worcestershire sauce			Worcestershire sauce
Yaourt	Yoghurt		
Yorkshire pudding			Yorkshire pudding
Zabaglione	Zabaglione		

Taille des bouteilles / Bottle sizes

Français	Anglais	Français	Anglais
Balthazar 16 bout.	Balthasar	Jéroboam 4 bout.	Jeroboam
Magnum 2 bout.	Magnum	Mathusalem 8 bout.	Methuselah
Nabuchodonosor 20 Bout			Nebuchadnezzar
Réhoboam 6 bout	Rehoboam	Salmanazar 12 bout.	Salmanazar

Nota:

- Dans ces tableaux, lorsque plusieurs traductions sont possibles,
elles sont séparées soit par : (/), soit par / or /.

- < **uncountable** > indique les mots anglais qui ne prennent pas le
pluriel lorsqu'ils sont utilisés isolèment, la seule possibilité
étant la construction d'une phrase pour indiquer le nombre:
exemple = deux tasses de café (**two cups of coffee**)
= trois choppes de bière (**three mugs of beer**)

- les mots anglais qui ne changent pas au pluriel ou sont
invariables
sont notés < **pluriel inchangé** > ou < **invariable** >

- pour certains mots anglais l'orthographe du pluriel est indiquée

- les verbes transitifs conjugués au participe passé qui ont valeur
d'adjectif sont notés < **v.t adjectif** >

- les verbes qui ont l'attributif d'un adjectif sont notés < **adjectif** >

A

abattis	terme général (giblets)
- de volaille	giblets of poultry
- de gibier à plume	giblets of game fowl
abats	offal < uncountable >
abricot	apricot
aeglé	Indian grapefruit
affinage	refining
agneau	lamb
agnelet	lambkin / or / small lamb
agnelle	lamb
aigre	bitter / or / sour
aigre-doux	middling sweet and sour
aiguillette - volaille	thin slice of poultry breast
- steak	thin slice of steak
ail	garlic < uncountable >
aile	wing
aileron	pinion
aillé	with garlic < uncountable >
airelle	bilberry - < pluriel > (bilberries)
	whortleberry - < pluriel > (whortleberries)
airelle rouge	cranberry - < pluriel > (cranberries)
alcool	alcohol < uncountable > / or / spirit
	< uncountable >
alkékenge	physalis / or / winter-cherry
allonger (sauce)	to thin a sauce
allongé	diluted
alouette	lark / or / skylark
aloyau	sirloin
alterne	alternate
alterné	alternately
amande	almond
amande d'un fruit	kernel
ambré	amber-coloured
amourette	amourettes / or / calf's marrow
amuse-gueule	snack / savoury
ananas	pineapple < uncountable >
anchois	anchovy < pluriel > (anchovies)
andouillette	andouillette
angélique	angelica < uncountable >
angostura	angostura brandy
anguille	eel
animelles < mouton >	testicles of lamb /
< boeuf >	testicles of bull
anis	aniseed < uncountable >
anisette	anisette
apéritif	aperitif
aquavit ou akavit	akavit
arête	fish bone
arachide	ground-nut / pea-nut
arlequin (décoration)	motley
armillaire couleur de miel	honey fungus - < pluriel > honey fungi
armoise	artemisia / or / wormwood < uncountable >
aromate	aromatic
aromatisé	flavoured with

arquebuse < liqueur >	arquebus liquor
arroche ou arroche bonne dame	orache
arrosé < en général >	sprinkled / or / moistened
< viande >	basted
arrow-root	arrow-root < uncountable >
artichaut	globe artichoke
asiago < fromage >	asiago cheese
asperges	asparagus < uncountable >
aspic	aspic < uncountable >
assa-fœtida	asafoetida
assaisonné	seasoned / or / seasoned with
aubépine	hawthorn / whitethorn
aubergine	aubergine
au gratin	cheesed / au gratin
auriculaire oreille de judas	black mushroom
autruche	ostrich
avec	with
aveline	filbert
avocat	avocado / or / avocado pear
avoine	oat / or / oatmeal
azyme	unleavened

Poissons :

ablette	bleak / or / ablet
actinie	sea anemone
aiglefin	haddock < pluriel inchangé >
alose	shad / allis shad / thwaite shad
	< tous plur. inchangé >
amande de mer	kind of queen scallop
anchois	anchovy (plur.) anchovies
anchois de norvège	sprat
anémone de mer	starfish
ange de mer	angel fish
anguilles	eels
anguille de mer	conger eel
apron	small perch
araignée de mer	spider crab < cuisine uncountable >

B

baba	sponge cake
badigeonner	to brush with
ballottine	poultry meat loaf
bambou " cuisine "	bamboo shoots
banane	banana
barbadine	passion fruit
barbotine - tanaisie	the aromatic herb tansy
bardane	burdock
bardé	larded
barde	larding
baron de boeuf	baron of beef
baron de lapin	saddle of rabbit
baron d'agneau	saddle of lamb
barquette	pastry-boat
basilic	basil < uncountable >
bâtonnet - viande	lamella
battre	to whisk / or / to whip
bavarois	Bavarian mousse
bavaroise	drink of tea, milk and alcohol
bavette	lower part of sirloin
beaujolais	Beaujolais
beaune	Beaune
bécasse	woodcock < pluriel inchangé >
becfin ou becfigue	warbler
beignet	fritter
bénédictine - liqueur	Benedictine
bette	beet
betterave	beetroot
beurre	butter < uncountable >
beurré	buttered < v.t adjectif >
biche	a female deer < pluriel inchangé >
bière	beer < uncountable >
bifteck de cheval	horse-meat steak
bifteck haché	hamburger
bigarade	Seville / bitter orange
biscotte	rusk
biscuits à la cuillère	sponge fingers
bisque	bisque
blanc de volaille	white meat < uncountable >
blanc d'oeuf	white of egg
blanquette	blanquette
blé	wheat / wheat-flour < tous uncountable >
bolet	boletus
bombe glaçée	ice-pudding
bonbon	a candy < pluriel candies > / sweet
bordé de	accompanied with / surrounded by
borchtch	borsch / borscht / bortsch < tous uncountable >
botte ou botillon	bunch / bundle
bouchée (patisserie)	patty - < plur.- patties >
boudin - forme	roll
boudin blanc	white pudding
boudin noir	black pudding < pluriel normal >/ or / polony < uncountable >

bougie	candle
bouillabaisse	bouillabaisse
bouillant	boiling / or / scalding
bouilleture	matelote of eels
bouilli	boiled < v.t adjectif >
bouillie	porridge < uncountable >
bouillon	stock / broth / soup < tous uncountable > - stew
bouillon de poisson	fish stock
boulette de pâte ou boulette de pâte cuite avec un fruit à l'intérieur	dumpling
boulette	ball / croquette
bourbon	bourbon < uncountable >
bourgogne	burgundy < uncountable >
boyau	bowel
braisé	braised
brandy	brandy < pluriel > brandies
brebis	ewe
brioche	brioche
broche	skewer / or / spit
brochette	skewer / or / kebab
brocoli	broccoli
broyé < état >	crushed / pounded
brugnon	nectarine
brunoise	thinly diced vegetables / thinly diced ... < nom du légume >
brunoise de légumes braisés	braised thinly diced vegetables / braised thinly diced < nom du légume >

Poissons :

baliste	trigger fish
bar	sea bass / or / sea perch < tous plur. inchangé >
barbarin	surmullet
barbeau	barbel
barbillon	young barbel
barbue	brill
baudroie	angler fish
bécasse de mer	surmullet
becfigue des eaux	sea smelt
belon	Belon oyster
bélouga ou béluga	caviar / or / caviar from beluga sturgeon
bernacle	barnacle
bernique	limpet
besugo	sea bream < pluriel inchangé >
bigorneau	winkle
blanchaille	whitebait < uncountable >
blennie ou cagnette	blenny < pluriel : blennies >
bogue	bogue fish
bonite	bonito
brême	bream < pluriel inchangé >
brême de rochers	black bream < pluriel inchangé >
brême argentée	silver bream < pluriel inchangé >
boucs ou crevettes grises	shrimps
brochet	pike < pluriel inchangé >
brocheton	pikelet / pikeen / pickerel < tous plur. inchangé >
buccin ou ran ou bulot	whelk

C

cacao	cocoa / or / cacao < tous uncountable >
cacahouète	peanut
caillé - lait	curds / or / curdled milk
caille - oiseau	quail < pas de "S" au pluriel >
cajou	cashew-nut
cake	fruit cake
calas - noix pilées	crushed nuts
calamar	squid
calvados	calvados
camomille	camomile / or / chamomile < tous uncountable >
camembert	camembert
canapé	canapé / or / savoury < pluriel; savouries >
canard	duck < viande > uncountable
caneton	duckling
cannelle	cinnamon < uncountable >
cannelloni	cannelloni
câpres	capers
caramel	caramel / or / burnt sugar < substance uncountable >
caramélisé	caramelized
carapace - tortue, etc...	carapace
carafe	carafe
carbonnade	carbonnade
cardamome	cardamom < uncountable >
cardon	cardoon
cari	curry
carotte	carrot
carpe	carp < pluriel inchangé >
carré	square
carré d'agneau	loin of lamb
carvi	caraway seeds
casserole	casserole
cassis	blackcurrant / or / blackcurrant liquor
cassolette	cassolette
cassonade	brown sugar
cassoulet	cassoulet
caviar	caviar < uncountable >
cayenne	cayenne pepper < uncountable >
cédrat	cedrate / or / citron
céleri	celery < uncountable >
céleri-rave	celeriac
centilitre	centilitre / cl.
cépage	variety of vine
cèpe	boletus
cerise	cherry < pluriel cherries >
cerneau de noix	green walnut
cerf	stag / or / deer (1) / or / red deer (1) < (1) uncountable >
cerfeuil	chervil < uncountable >
cervelas	saveloy / or / cervelat
cervelle	brains
chair à saucisse	sausage meat
chambertin	chambertin
chamois	chamois

champagne	champagne
champignon	mushroom
chapelure	breadcrumbs / crumbs
chapon (coq castré)	capon
charcuterie	pork butchery < uncountable >
charlotte	charlotte
charlotte russe	charlotte russe
chartreuse	chartreuse (liqueur)
chataîgne	chestnut
chateaubriand - viande	chateaubriand / or / porter's house steak
chaud-froid	chaudfroid
chausson	turnover
chayote	gourd
cherry brandy	cherry-brandy
chester	cheshire cheese
chèvre	goat
chevreau	kid
chevreuil	roebuck / or / roe-deer / or / roe
chicorée sauvage	chicory / or / succory < tous uncountable
chicorée cultivée ou frisée	légume (endive) - café (ground chicory)
chiffonnade	chiffonade
chinchard	horse mackerel < plur.in
chipolata	chipolata (sausage)
chips	potato crisps
choesels	testicles of bull
chou	cabbage < cuisine uncountable >
chou à la crème	cream puff
choux de bruxelles	brussels sprouts
chou-fleur	cauliflower
chou-fleur au gratin	cauliflower cheese
choucroute	sauerkraut < uncountable >
ciboule	ciboule / welsh onion
ciboulette	chive (s)
cidre	cider < uncountable >
cigale	cicada
citron	lemon
citrouille	pumpkin
cive	chives
civelles	baby eels
civet	jugged hare / or / jugged rabbit / or / jugged venison en général < jugged >
clafoutis	clafoutis
coco	coconut
cocotte	cast-iron casserole
cœur de palmier	heart of palm
coffre de homard	lobster's frame
cognac	cognac
coing	quince
cointreau	cointreau
colin	hake < pluriel inchangé >
composé	composed with
compote	compote / or / stewed fruit
concentré	concentrate
- bouillon	concentrate / or / stock extract
- bouillon de boeuf concentré	beef extract
- lait condensé ou concentré	condensed milk
- concentré de tomates	tomato purée
concombre	cucumber

condiment	condiment / seasoning
cône	cone
confit - fruits	preserved / or / candied
- d'oie , canard etc ...	conserve of goose " oie " / duck " canard "
confiture	jam < uncountable >
confitures d'oranges	marmalade < uncountable >
congélateur	freezer / or / deep freeze
consommé	consommé
contre filet	hind brisket
convive	guest
coq	cock
coq de bruyère	capercaillie
coquelicot	wild poppy
corail - homard	creamy lobster's meat
- st jacques	yellow part from scallop
coriandre	coriander
cornichon	gherkin
corolle	corolla
côtes de boeuf	ribs
côtelette d'agneau	cutlet of lamb
côte de porc	chop of pork
côte de veau	veal chop
couenne	rind <1> (of pork or bacon) / crackling < (1) - uncountable >
coulis	purée
courgette	courgette
courge	gourd / or / marrow
court-bouillon	court-bouillon
couscous	couscous
couteau - coquillage	solen / or / razor shell
crapaudine (en)	flattened (chicken , etc...)
crème	cream < uncountable >
crème - patisserie	custard
crème anglaise	egg-custard
crème bavaroise	bavarian cream
crème frangipane	almond-flavoured cream
crème de menthe	crème de menthe
crème - sauce	sauce
crème de cassis	black-currant liqueur
crêpe	pancake
crépine	caul (of veal, pork, etc...)
crépinette	crépinette / or / flat sausage
cresson	watercress / or / cress < tous uncountable >
crête de coq	cockscomb
creton	melted fat
croquettes	croquettes
croquignole	cracknel
crosne	Japanese artichoke
croustade	croustade
croûte - hors d'oeuvre	slice of bread
- entremets	slice of savarin or brioche
croûte (en)	in pastry case
croûton	crouton / or / sippet
cru	raw < adjectif > / or / uncooked < v.t adjectif >
cru - vin	vintage
crustacés	crustaceae / or / crustaceans
cuit à la vapeur	steamed < v.t adjectif >
cumin	cumin / or / cummin

curaçao	curaçao
cygne	swan

Poissons :

cabillaud	fresh cod < cuisine uncountable >
cabot	miller's thumb / or / bullhead
cagnette	blenny < pluriel > (blennies)
caille de la manche	sea smelt
calamar	squid
capelan	capelin / or / caplin
capitaine	African sea bass < pluriel inchangé >
caramote	large prawn
cardine	flounder
carpe	carp < pluriel inchangé >
carpeau ou Carpillon	young carp < pluriel inchangé >
carrelet	plaice < pluriel inchangé >
casserons	small squids
caviar	caviar < uncountable >
caviar blanc ou Boutargue ou Poutargue	mullet roes, dried and pressed
céteaux	small soles
chabot	bullhead
chevaine ou chevesne ou chevenne	chub / or / dace < uncountable >
chevrettes - crevettes roses	prawns
chien de mer	dogfish / or / smooth hound
chinchard	mackerel < pluriel inchangé >
chipirons	squids
cigales de mer	mantis shrimps
civelles	baby-eels
clam	clam
clovisse	small clam
coelacanthe	coelacanth
coffre	coffer fish
colin	hake < pluriel inchangé >
colineau ou Colinot	codling
congre	conger eel / or / sea eel
coque - fruits de mer	cockle
coquillages	shellfishes / or / shells
coquille st jacques	scallop
courbine	kind of sea-bass < pluriel inchangé >
couteau - mollusque	solen / or / razor -shell
crabe	crab
créas ou créat	sturgeon
crevette	shrimp / or / prawn
crevette rose	prawn
crevette grise	shrimp
crustacés - pluriel	crustaceae / or / crustaceans
cyprin	cyprinoid
cyprin doré	goldfish

D

darne	steak of cod " morue " / salmon " saumon "/. hake " colin "
datte	date
décalotter	to uncap
décoquiller	to shell
décoration	decoration
décorer	to decorate
décortiqué	decorticated
délayer	(poudre) to mix - (sauce) to thin down
demi glace	reduced stock
démouler	to remove from mould / to turn out (cake, etc ..)
dénoyauter	to stone < fruit >
dépecé	carved up < v.t adjectif >
désossé	boned < viande > - filleted < poisson > < tous adj. >
dessert	dessert / or / sweet course
diablotin	sippet spreaded with cheese and browned
digestif	digestive
diplomate	trifle
dinde	turkey < viande uncountable >
dindon	turkey cock < viande uncountable >
dindonneau	turkey-chick / or / turkey-poult < viande uncountable >
distributeur	vending machine
dôme	dome
dorer - cuisine	to glaze
dragée	dragée
dresser	to lay, laid, laid
dur	hard
duxelles	chopped mushrooms cooked with butter and chopped shallots

Poissons :

daurade	dorado
denté ou Denti	kind of sea bream
diable de mer - lotte	angler
- rascasse	scorpion fish
- chabot	bullhead
dorade	dorado
doucet	yellow gurnard

43

E

eau	water < uncountable >
eau minérale	mineral water
eaux minérales - carte	minerals
eau de cologne	eau de cologne
eau gazeuse	soda water
eau de vie	eau de vie / or / brandy
écailler < huître >	to open
< poisson >	to scale
echalote	shallot
échine de porc	chine of pork
éclair	éclair
écrevisse	crayfish
émincer	to slice thinly
émulsion	emulsion
endive	chicory < uncountable >
enfiler sur des brochettes	put on skewers
enflammé	fiery
ensacher	to put into (sacks, etc...)
entouré	surrounded
entrelarder	to lard
entremets	sweet / or / dessert
enveloppe d'un fruit	casing
épinards	spinach < uncountable >
escalope	escalope
escargot	escargot / or / snail
escarole	endive
estragon	tarragon < uncountable >
et	and
étoffé	stuffed
étouffée (à l')	to steam / or / to braise
étuver	to steam (à l'étuvée = braised)
évider	to hollow out
évidé	hollowed out
extrait	extract

Poissons:

écrevisse	crayfish < plur. > (crayfishes) / or / (crawfish)
églefin ou Aiglefin	haddock < plur. inchangé >
encornet	squid
éperlan - mer -	sea-smelt / or / sand-smelt
éperlan - rivière -	river smelt
épinoche	stickleback
équille	sand eel
espadon	swordfish
esprot	sprat
esturgeon	sturgeon
esturgeon de la baltique	Baltic sturgeon
étrille	small crab
exocet	flying fish

F

faire revenir de la viande	to brown meat
faisan	pheasant < viande uncountable >
faîne	beech-nut
farce	stuffing / or / forcemeat
farci	stuffed
fariné	floured / or / flour coated
farine	flour < uncountable >
- complète	wholemeal-flour / wholewheat-flour < tous uncountable >
- d'avoine	oatmeal
- de blé	wheat-flour < uncountable >
- de maïs	cornflour < uncountable >
- de sarrasin	buckwheat-flour < uncountable >
- de seigle	rye-flour < uncountable >
- de son	bran-flour < uncountable >
farineux	farinaceous / or / starchy
faux-filet	sirloin steak < uncountable >
fécule	fecula / or / starch < tous uncountable >
feuilleté	in puff-pastry
feuilleton	multi-layers of.....
fenouil	fennel < uncountable >
fermenté	fermented
feu de bois	wood fire
fève	shell bean / or / broad bean
figue	fig
filet	fillet
filet mignon	fillet mignon
fine champagne	high quality cognac
flageolet	flageolet / or / kidney bean
flambé	flamed
flamber des plumes de volailles	to singe
flan	flan
fleurs d'acacia	acacia flowers
fleur d'oranger	orange blossom < uncountable >
fleur de lys	lily
flocons de maïs	cornflakes
foie	liver
foie gras	foie gras
fondant	fondant
fond d'artichaut	artichoke heart
fondue < plat >	fondue
fouetté (crème)	whipped
fouetté	whipped up
four	oven (au four baked / roasted in the oven)
- (à four vif)	in a hot oven
- (à four doux)	in a slow oven
fourré	stuffed
fraise	fraise / strawberry
framboise	raspberry
frappé	iced / or / chilled
fretin	fry

fricandeau	fricandeau
fricassée	fricassee
friture	friture
fromage blanc	soft white cheese
fromage râpé	grated cheese
fruit	fruit
- au sirop	preserved fruits
- confits	candied fruits / or / crystallized fruits
- de la passion	passion fruit
- exotiques	exotic fruits
- rafraîchis	fruit salad
- sec	dried fruit
fruit de mer	sea food
fumé	smoked
fumet - cuisine	arome (aroma)
- fumet de champignons	mushroom stock
- fumet de poisson	fish stock
- vin	bouquet / or / aroma

Poissons :

fausse dorade	red sea-bream < pluriel inchangé >
favouille	small spider crab
fine de claire	oyster
flet	flounder
flétan	halibut < pluriel inchangé >
fretin	fry

G

galantine	galantine
galette - gâteau	flat cake
galette - crêpe	buckwheat pancake
gamba	large prawn
garni	garnished
garniture	garnish

- garni avec	served with a garnish of	(1)
	garnished with	(2)
	covered with	(3)

énumérations

< description du plat plus, (1) (2) (3) ou rien et description de la garniture >

(2) - **choron** (potato-balls and artichoke hearts stuffed with peas or asparagus tips)

　　- **foyot** (covered with béarnaise sauce added of the gravy)

　　- **laguipière** (covered with a sauce, and sprinkled with a julienne of truffle macerated in Madeira)

(2) - **cavour** (large mushrooms stuffed with mashed chickens' livers and sliced truffle)

(1) - **condé** (mashed red beans)

(2) - **du Barry** (cauliflower in a sauce of cream, egg-yolk and grated cheese)

(2) - **meyerbeer** (fried eggs)

(1) - **rossini** (truffles and sliced foie gras)

(2) - **anversoise** (hop stalks in cream or butter)

(2) - **argenteuil** (asparagus in purée or in tips)

(2) - **nantua** (crayfishes)

　　- **clamart** (voir texte dictionnaire)

(2) - **périgueux** (truffles and sometimes foie gras)

(3) - **bordelaise - poissons/viandes blanches** (white wine sauce)
　　- **viandes rouges** (red wine sauce)
　　- **grand veneur** (covered with a peppery sauce added of redcurrant jelly and cream, plus mashed chestnuts)

(2) - **batelière** (poached mushrooms, fried eggs, crayfishes and fried onions)

(2) - **commodore** (fish quenelles, croquettes of crayfish tails)

- **mussels,** more a sauce thickened of crayfish purée)

(1) - **bouquetière** (vegetables laid in bunches)

- **jardinière** « ne pas utiliser l'en tête garni avec »
  (cooked with vegetables)

gâteau	gateau / cake / tart / disc / round piece / dessert pastry
gaufre	waffle
gaufrette	wafer
gélatine	gelatine
gélatineux	gelatinous
gelée	jelly / or / aspic (in aspic) < tous uncountable >
genièvre	juniper berry / (gin) < uncountable >
génoise	genoese sponge
germe	germ
gésier	gizzard
gibier	game < uncountable >
gibelotte	rabbit ragout in white wine
gigot - mouton	leg of mutton / leg of lamb -
- cheval	hind leg of horse
gin	gin < uncountable >
gin fizz	gin fizz < uncountable >
gingembre	ginger < uncountable >
girofle	clove < clou de girofle > clove
girolle	chanterelle mushroom / edible agaric
gîte à la noix	silverside of beef
gîte	shin
glacé	adj (glazed)
- fruit	glacé / or / candied / or / crystallized fruit
- café	iced coffee
- chocolat	iced chocolate
- légumes	glazed
- viande	glazed
- boisson	icy / or / ice-cold
glucose	glucose
glutamaté	gluten extract
godiveau	forcemeat balls
gonfler	(pâte) to rise
- riz, lentilles,etc...	to swell up (in water, etc...)
gonflé	risen / or / swelled up
goulash	goulash
gourilos	endives
grain de raisin	grape
graisse	grease / or / fat / or / cooking fat
- de porc	lard
- végétale	vegetable fats
gras double	tripe < uncountable >
gratin	cooked au gratin
graves	graves
grenade	pomegranate
grenouille	frog
grillade	grilling / or / grilled meat
grillé	grilled
grog	grog < uncountable >
gros sel	coarse salt

groseille	redcurrant
gruyère	gruyère cheese / or / swiss cheese

Poissons :

gamba	large prawn
galathée	squat lobster
gobie	goby
gougeon de mer	goby
goujon	freshwater gudgeon
gastrochère	small shellfish
grondin	gurnard / or / red gurnet
gade	gadoid
gymnote	electric eel
gardon	roach

H

haché	chopped / or / minced
hacher	to chop / to hack / to mince / to hash / to cut up
hachis	hash / or / mincemeat / or / forcemeat
hachis parmentier	shepherd's pie
hamburger	hamburger
haricot	bean
haricot vert	french bean
herbe	herb
hérisson	hedgehog
hirondelle	swallow
hirondelle de mer	tern
honneur (en l')	honoured
hot-dog	hot-dog
houblon	hop
huile	oil
- d'amande	almond oil
- d'arachide	peanut oil
- de colza	rape oil
- de faîne	beech-nut oil
- de maïs	corn oil
- de noix	nut oil / or / walnut oil
- d'olive	olive oil
- de soja	soya oil
- de tournesol	sunflower oil
- de palme	palm oil
huître	oyster
hydne sinué	spreading hydnum
hysope	hyssop

Poissons :

haddock	smoked haddock < pluriel inchangé >
hareng	herring
hénon - coque	cockle
hippocampe	seahorse / or / long nose seahorse / or / short nose seahorse
homard	lobster < cuisine uncountable >
huître	oyster
huître de claire	prairie oyster / or / fattened oyster

I

inciser	to incise
incrusté ("avec" ou "de")	incrusted with
infusion	infusion
igname	yam
imprégné	steeped / or / to be impregnated
izarra	yellow or green liqueur from Basque area

J

jambon	ham < uncountable >
jambon blanc	cooked ham / or / boiled ham
jambonneau	small ham < uncountable >
jarret de boeuf	shin of beef / leg of beef
jarret de porc	hock of pork
jarret de veau	knuckle of veal
jaune d'oeuf	egg-yolk
jujube	jujube
julienne	julienne
jus	juice
jus d'orange	orange juice < uncountable >
jus de viande	gravy < uncountable >

Poissons :

jean doré ou john dory	john dory
julienne - poisson vendu en filets	ling fillets
- vendu entier	ling

K

kaki - fruit	Japanese persimmon < fruit >
kari	curry
karité - beurre	butter from tropical fruit
ketchup	ketchup < uncountable >
kirsch	kirsch < uncountable >
kiwi	kiwi fruit
kummel	caraway seed liqueur

Poissons :

kipper - hareng	kippered herring

L

lactaire	orange brown lactarius
lait	milk < uncountable
laitance	milt < uncountable > / or / soft roe of fish
lait de poule	eggflip
lama	llama
lambick	very strong Belgian beer
lamelle	lamella
lanière	lamella
langue de chat	finger biscuit
lapereau	young rabbit
lapin	rabbit
lapin de garenne	wild rabbit
laquer	to lacquer
lard	pork fat / or / fat pork / or / streaky bacon
lard fumé	smoked bacon
lardé	larded
lardon	lardon / or / lardoon
laurier	laurel
lavande	lavender
lentilles	lentils
levain	leaven
levure	yeast
liant (un)	a binder
lie	lees / or / dregs
lié	thickened with < v.t adjectif >
lieu jaune	pollack
lieu noir	saithe / or / coalfish
liqueur	liquor
liquoreux - vin	sweet / or / liqueur-like
longe - veau	loin of veal / or / < porc > (loin of pork)
losange	lozenge
lotte	angler / or / conger eel

Poissons :

lamproie	lamprey
lamproie de rivière	river lamprey / or / brook lamprey
lamproie de mer	sea lamprey
lançon	sand eel / or / sand lance / or / grig
langue d'avocat	sole
langouste	spiny lobster / or / rock lobster / or / crayfish
langoustine	Norway lobster / or / Dublin bay prawn
langoustines frites	scampi < nom pluriel >
large loche	weatherfish
lavagnon ou lavignon	false clam
lavaret	Coregonus / or / freshwater herring
lieu jaune	pollack
lieu noir	saithe / or / coalfish)
limande	dab / or / lemon sole

limande sloop ou limande salope	flounder
limande sole	lemon sole
limule	horseshoe crab
lingue	ling
lisettes " petits maquereaux "	small mackerel < pluriel inchangé >
loche	loach
lotte des lacs	burbot / or / eel pout
lotte de mer	angler fish / or / devilfish
lotte de rivière	burbot / or / eel pout
loubine < sur côte atlantique " bar " >	sea bass " pluriel inchangé "
loup - bar -	sea bass / sea perch / sea dace
	< tous plur. inchangé >

M

macaroni	macaroni < uncountable >
macarons	macaroons
macédoine	fruit salad / or / vegetable salad
macérer	to macerate
macéré	macerated
mâche	corn-salad
macis	mace < uncountable >
madeleines	kind of sponge-cake
madère	Madeira
maïs	maize / or / corn < tous uncountable >
malaxage	mixing / or / kneading
malaxer du beurre	to cream butter
mandarine	mandarin orange / tangerine
mangue	mango (plur.) mangos
manié ou malaxé	kneaded
manioc	manioc / or / cassava < tous uncountable >
marasquin	maraschino
marc	marc
marcassin	young wild boar
marjolaine	sweet marjoram
marron	chestnut
marinade - sauce -	marinade / pickle / brine
mariné (e) - viande -	marinated meat / soused meat
- poisson -	marinated fish / soused fish
marmelade	jam < uncountable >
mayonnaise	(adj) in mayonnaise, (nom) mayonnaise
	< uncountable >
matelote	matelote
médaillon	< cuisine > thin slice / or / round slice
	(of meat etc...) / or / < beurre > (pat of butter)
melon	melon
menthe	mint < uncountable >
meringue	meringue
mie	crumb < uncountable >
miel	honey < uncountable >
mignonnette(poivre)	ground pepper
mijoter	to simmer
mil	millet
millefeuille	millefeuille < dessert >
mimosa	mimosa flower < edible >
minestrone	minestrone < uncountable >
mirepoix	mixture of diced vegetables
mis en purée	mashed < v.t adjectif >
moelle	bone-marrow < uncountable >
moisissure	mouldiness
moka	mocha < uncountable >
mondé	skinned < v.t adjectif >
morille	morel
morue	salt cod < uncountable >
mou	lungs of sheep, etc..
mouiller	added to

mouillé	moistened of.< v.t adjectif >
moule	mussel
moule à bordure	edge mould
moulu	ground / or / powdered < v.t adjectif >
mousse - crème	mousse
mousseline	creamed
mousseline de pommes de terre	creamed potatoes
mousseron	button-mushroom
moutarde	mustard < uncountable >
mouton	sheep / mutton
mûre - fruit	mulberry
muscade	nutmeg < uncountable >
muscadet	muscatel wine / or / muscadet wine
myrtille	bilberry / or / whortleberry

Poissons :

maigre - poisson	meagre
maquereau	mackerel < pluriel inchangé >
margate	cuttle fish
mendole	picarel / or / mendole / or / cackerel
merlan	whiting < pluriel inchangé >
merluche	hake < pluriel inchangé > / or / (stockfish)
merlu	hake < pluriel inchangé >
merlus	hake < pluriel inchangé > / or / stockfish
mérou	grouper
meuille	grey mullet / mullet / thick-lipped mullet / thin-lipped mullet
morue	salt cod / or / cod
morue d'eau douce	burbot
motelle ou mustelle	rockling
moule	mussel
muge	thick-lipped mullet
mulet	grey mullet / mullet / thick-lipped mullet / thin-lipped mullet
murène	moray eel / or / Muraena / or / sea lamprey
mye	type of clam

N

napper	to cover
nappé avec	covered with < v.t adjectif >
nature	natural / or / plain / or / without garnish / or / unseasoned / or / unmixed ; with nothing added
navarin	navarin
navet	turnip
nectarine	nectarine
nèfle	medlar
nid d'hirondelles	bird's nest < potage > bird's nest soup
noisette - fruit	hazelnut
- cuisine	small round piece of ..
- d'agneau	noisettes of lamb
- de mouton -	noisettes of lamb
- de beurre	knob of butter
nouilles	noodles / or / ribbon vermicelli < uncountable >
nouillettes	small noodles
noix	nut / or / walnut
noix de coco	coconut
noix de muscade	nutmeg < uncountable >
noix de veau	cushion of veal

Poissons :

nonnat < prêtre ou faux éperlan ou aphya >	transparent goby / or / nonnat

O

oeuf	egg
oeufs au miroir	eggs fried in butter
oeufs brouillés	scrambled eggs
oeuf à la coque	soft-boiled egg
oeuf dur	hard-boiled egg
oeufs moulés - en général	moulded eggs with a hash of parsley, ham and truffle
- autre recette	moulded eggs with...
oeuf mollet	soft boiled egg
oeuf poché	poached egg
oie	goose < viande uncountable >
oignon	onion
- trop d'oignon	too much onion
oiseau	bird
olive	olive
omelette	omelette / omelet
onglet - boeuf	body thick skirt of beef
orange	orange
orangeade	orangeade
- boisson faite avec jus d'orange	orange juice < uncountable >
orge	barley < uncountable >
ortolan	ortolan
ortie	nettle
os	bone
os à moellle	marrowbone < uncountable >
oseille	sorrel
oursin	sea urchin / sea hedgehog
ovale	oval

Poissons :

oeufs de poisson	roes / or / spawn
omble-chevalier	char / or / hill-trout / or / grayling
ombre	grayling
orlong	spined sea scorpion
ormeau	ormer / or / haliotis / or / sea ear
orphie	garfish / or / sea-pike / or / sea needle / or / horn-fish
oursin	sea urchin / or / sea hedgehog

P

pain	bread < uncountable >
pain d'épice	gingerbread
paleron	shoulder blade / or / chuck / or / blade bone
palet	quoit
palombe	wild pigeon
pamplemousse	grapefruit
panade	panada / or / bread soup
panais	parsnip
paner	to coat with breadcrumbs / to dress with breadcrumbs
pané	coated with breadcrumbs / fried in breadcrumbs
papier aluminium	aluminium paper < uncountable >
papier à fioritures	paper frills
papier sulfurisé	greaseproof paper < uncountable >
papillotte (en)	in buttered paper
paprika	paprika
parfumé	flavoured
paraffine	paraffin < uncountable >
parfait	parfait
parfumer - cuisine	to flavour
- liquide	to lace with
parmesan	parmesan cheese
parsemer	to sprinkle
pastèque	watermelon
pastis	pastis
patate douce	sweet potato
pâte	dough / or / paste / or / batter
pâte (nouille)	macaroni < uncountable > / or / noodle < pour la soupe > / or /pasta < uncountable >
pâte brisée	short pastry
pâte à choux	choux pastry
pâtes de fruits	fruit jelly
pâté en croûte	pie in pastry case
pâte feuilletée	puff-pastry / or /flaky-pastry
pâtisserie	pastry.
paupiette	veal olive / or / small ball of veal
peau < fruits >	rind < uncountable >
pêche	peach
pédoncule	peduncle
peluche - général	shredded material
- cerfeuil	shredded chervil
- autres	shredded
perdreau	young partridge < uncountable >
perdrix	partridge < uncountable >
perdrix rouge	red-legged partridge < uncountable >
pernod	Pernod
persil	parsley < uncountable >
petit déjeuner	breakfast
petit-four	petit-four
petit lait	whey < uncountable >
petit pain	roll

petit pâté	patty
petit pois	pea < pluriel : peas>
petit salé	streaky bacon / salt pork
petit suisse cheese	petit suisse
pièce montée - ornement	tiered cake
- mariage	wedding cake
pied de mouton - champignon	hedgehog fungi / or / pied de mouton mushroom
- viande	lamb trotter
pigeon	pigeon / or / dove
pignon	pine-kernel
pilaf	pilaff < uncountable >
pilé	pounded / or / crushed
piment / or / capsicum	pimento < uncountable > / or /(red pepper)
	< uncountable >capsicum
piment doux	pepper < uncountable >
pimenté (e)	hot (adj.); (verbe) to put chillis in
pintade	guinea fowl < plur. inchangé > / or / guinea hen
pintadeau	guinea-chick
piqué - cuisine	larded / studded / pitted / spotted
pissenlit	dandelion
pistache	pistachio
pistil	pistil
pizza	pizza
poché	poached
poêlé	fried
poire	pear
poireau	leek
pois	pea
pois chiches	chick peas
poitrine (boucherie) : - boeuf	brisket of beef < uncountable >
- mouton	breast of lamb
poivre	pepper < uncountable >
poivre de cayenne	cayenne-pepper < uncountable >
poivré	peppered < v.t adjectif >
poivron	capsicum
poivron rouge	red pepper < uncountable > capsicum
poivron vert	green pepper < uncountable > capsicum
polenta	polenta
pomme	apple
pomme de terre	potato
pommes paille	fried julienne of potatoes
porc	pork < viande uncountable >
portion - nourriture	helping
porto	port < uncountable >
pot en grès	earthenware pot
potage	thick soup
pot au feu	pot au feu
potée - bœuf	stew of boiled beef
- porc	stew of pork
- légumes	stew of vegetables
potiron	pumpkin
pouding	plum pudding
poudre	powder
poudré	powdered < v.t adjectif >
poularde	fattened pullet
poulet	chicken < viande uncountable >
pourpier	purslane
pousse de soja	soya shoot

praline	burnt almond / or / praline chocolate almonds
praliné	praline paste
pressé	squeezed / or / pressed
primeurs - fruit	early fruits
- légume	early vegetables
profiteroles	profiteroles
prune	plum
pruneau	dried plum
prunelle	prunella / or / sloe
pulpe - fruit	pulp
punch	punch < uncountable >
purée	purée
pyramide	pyramid

Poissons :

pageot ou pageau ou Rousseau ou pagre	kind of dorado
palourde	clam
patagos	cockles
patelle	limpet
perche marine	sea-bass (perch / or / freshwater bass) < pluriel inchangé >
perche noire	black sea-perch < pluriel inchangé
pétoncle	queen scallop
pholade	pholas / or / stone-borer
pibales	baby eels (piranha)Plie
pilchard	plaice < plu. inchangé > pilchard / or / sardine
piranha	piranha
poisson	fish
poisson chat	horned pout / or / catfish / or / Danubian catfish
poisson épée	swordfish
poisson lune	moonfish / or / opah
poisson scie	sawfish
poisson torpille	torpedo fish
poisson volant	flying fish
portugaise < huître >	Portuguese oyster
portune	small crab
poulpe	octopus
praire	small clam

Q

quartiers	pieces
quatre-épices	fennel flower
quenelle	quenelle
queue	tail
queue de bœuf	oxtail
quiche	quiche

R

râble (lièvre)	saddle of hare
(lapin)	saddle of rabbit
radis	radish
ragoût	ragout
rafraîchi (e)	cooled < v.t adjectif > / or / chilled < v.t adj. >
raie < décoration >	line
raifort	horse-radish < uncountable >
raisin	grape
raisins de corinthe	currants
raisins secs	raisins
raisins de smyrne	sultanas
raisins de malaga	malaga raisins / or / scraped
rassis - général	stale
- pain	stale bread
râpé - général	grated
ratatouille	ratatouille
raves	hors d'œuvre dish, rapesravier
ravioli	ravioli < pluriel inchangé >
réchauffé	reheated / warm up / warm up again
recette < cuisine >	recipe
risotto	risotto
rissolé	browned / or / sautéed
romarin	rosemary < uncountable >
rosé	rosé / vin rosé / rosé wine
rôti - état de cuisson	roasted < v.t adjectif >
rôti - adj. ou plat	roast
roux	roux
royale	moulded custard
rye	rye whisky

poissons :

raie	ray / or / skate
raie blonde	blonde ray
raie bouclée	thornback ray
- autres raies	cuckoo ray; eagle ray; ray; thornback ray; undulate ray; spotted common skate; common stingray
raiteau	small ray / or / small skate
rascasse	scorpion fish / or / sea-scorpion / or / short-spined sea scorpion / or / long-spined sea scorpion
rémora	remora / or / small headed sucker / or / cornish sucker / or / sucking fish

requin	shark
- autres requins : < requin bleu 3-4m >	blue shark
< requin de 6m >	tresher
< requin bleuté 3m >	mako (dangereux)
rogue - de morue	roe of cod
- de hareng	roe of herring

rotengle
rouget
roussette - poisson

roach < pluriel inchangé >
red mullet / or / red gurnard
dogfish

S

sabayon	zabaglione
safran	saffron
saindoux	pork fat / or / lard
saison	season / in season
< ce n'est pas la saison >	out of season
salade	salad
salade de saison	salad in season
salamandre - grill	grill
- poêle	slow combustion stove
salamis	salami < uncountable >
salangane - hirondelle	salangana
salé	salted < v.t adjectif >
salpêtre	salpetre
salpicon	culinary stuffing
salsifis	salsify < uncountable >
sang	blood
sanglier	wild boar
sangria	sangria
sarcelle	teal < pluriel inchangé >
sarment de vigne	vine shoot
sarrasin	buckwheat < uncountable >
sarriette	savory < uncountable >
sauce	sauce
sauce béarnaise	béarnaise sauce
sauce béchamel	béchamel sauce
sauce bolognaise	bolognèse sauce
sauce chaud-froid	chaudfroid sauce
sauce hollandaise	sauce hollandaise
sauce mornay	béchamel sauce with egg-yolks and grated gruyère
saucière	gravy-boat
saucisson	large sausage
sauge	sage < uncountable >
saumure	brine / or / pickle < tous uncountable >
saupoudrer	sprinkled with
sauté (e) - plat	sauté of
- adjectif	sauté

Nota:

Si par contre le terme " **sauté** " est pris au sens " **ragoût** " il faut traduire (**ragout of** ...)

sauté de veau	ragout of veal
sauter (verbe transitif)	to sauté
sauté (v.t adjectif)	sauté
savarin	savarin cake
scarole	endive
sel	salt < uncountable >
semoule	semolina < uncountable >
sirop	syrup < uncountable >

socle	socle
soja	soya
sorbet	sorbet / or / sherbet
soufflé	soufflé / or / soufflé dish
soupe	soup < uncountable >
soupière	soup-tureen
spaghetti	spaghetti < uncountable >
spaghetti à la bolognaise	spaghetti à la bolognèse
stérilisé	sterilized
sucre	sugar < uncountable >
sucré	sweetened < v.t adjectif > / or / sugared < v.t adjectif >
sucre de canne	cane sugar < uncountable >
sucre semoule	granulated sugar < uncountable >
sucre vanillé	vanilla sugar < uncountable >
successivement	successively
suprême	supreme

Poissons :

sabre	silvered Mediterranean fish
saint pierre	john dory
sandre	pike-perch < pluriel inchangé >
sardine	sardine / or / pilchard
saumon	salmon / or / Atlantic salmon < tous uncountable >
saumon blanc	coalfish / or / hake < pluriel inchangé > / or / saithe
saumon rose	pink salmon < uncountable >
saurel	mackerel < pluriel inchangé >
scampi	scampi < nom pluriel >
scare	scarus / or / parrot fish
sciène	sciaena
scombridés	scombridae / or / scombrids
scorpion - poissson -	scorpion fish
seiche / or / sépia / ou / supion poisson	cuttlefish
sélacien	selachian
séteau < sole Vendée / Charentes >	sole
silure	silurus / or / sheat-fish
sole	sole / or / common sole
sole limande	dab sole
solen	solen / or / razor shell
solette	solenette
sourdons verts	cockles
sprat	sprat
sterlet	sterlet
stockfisch	dried cod
surmulet	surmullet
surmulet rouget	red mullet
syngnathe	pipefish / or / syngnathus

T

tafia	tafia
taillé	cut < attributif adjectif >
tamis	sieve
tamiser	to sieve
tapioca	tapioca < uncountable >
tarte	tart
tartelette	small tart / or / tartlet
terrine - récipient>	a rectangular earthwarecooking-dish
- plat cuisiné	terrine (pâté)
thé	tea < uncountable >
thym	thyme < uncountable >
tiède	lukewarm / or / tepid
tige	stalk / or / stem
tilleul	lime-tree flowers
timbale	timbale
tisane	herbal tea
tomate	tomato
tomate - apéritif	aniseed aperitif, coloured with pomegranate syrup
topinambour	Jerusalem artichoke
torsade	twisted cord
tortue - terre	tortoise
- mer	turtle
tournedos	tournedos / fillet-steak
tournesol	sunflower
tourte	pie
tourtière	pie-dish / or / baking-tin
tranche	slice
tremper	to steep
trempé	steeped < v.t adjectif >
truffe	truffle
truffé	garnished with truffle
turban	turban

Poissons :

tanche	tench
tarpon	tarpon
taupe	porbeagle
thon	tuna / or / tunny-fish < pluriel inchangé / or / tunnies >
thonine	Mediterranean tunny
tomate de mer	red sea anemone
torpille	torpedo
tourteau (crabe)	large crab
tremble < poisson torpille >	torpedo fish
trigle	gurnard / or / gurnet
truie de mer	hog-fish
truite	trout / or / brook trout < pluriel inchangé >
truite brune	brown trout < pluriel inchangé >
truite arc en ciel	rainbow trout< pluriel inchangé >
truite de mer	sea trout < pluriel inchangé >

truite saumonée
turbot
turbotin

sea trout < pluriel inchangé >
turbot < pluriel inchangé >
young turbot < pluriel inchangé >

V

vanille	vanilla < uncountable >
vapeur (à la)	boiled < v.t adjectif > / or / steamed < v.t adj. >
veau - viande	veal < uncountable >
velouté - sauce	velouté sauce
verjus	unripe grape juice / verjuice
vermicelle	vermicelli < uncountable >
vessie de porc	pork bladder / or / pork blister
vin blanc	vin blanc / or / white wine
vin ordinaire	vin ordinaire
vin rosé	vin rosé / rosé / rosé wine
vinaigre	vinegar < uncountable >
vinaigrette	vinegar sauce / oil and vinegar dressing / French dressing
vodka	vodka < uncountable >
volaille	poultry " nom collectif "
vol-au vent	vol-au-vent

Poissons :

vairon	minnow
vandoise	dace < pluriel inchangé >
vénus	cockle
vernis	venus shell
vieille	sea wrasse / or / rock fish
vive	weever
vras	wrasse

Y

yaourt	yoghourt < uncountable > traduire le pluriel par : (...with some yoghourt)

Z

Zeste	(peel / or / rind) < tous uncountable >
- fruits :	
- citron	(lemon peel) < uncountable >
- orange	(orange peel) < uncountable >
- cuisine	(peel) < uncountable >
	(zest) < uncountable >
- avec un zeste de citron	(with a piece of lemon peel)

Récapitulation des mots anglais les plus usuels qui sont « UNCOUNTABLE »

A : alcohol / aluminium paper / aniseed / asparagus / aspic

B : barley / basil / beer / bone-marrow / borsch / brine / broth / buckwheat / burgundy / butter

C : camomile / caramel / cardamom / caviar / cayenne pepper / cider / innamon / cocoa / corn / cream / cress / crumb

D : duck < inchangé quand il est utilisé comme nom collectif

F : flour

G : game / garlic / gin / gin fizz / ginger / gravy / greaseproof paper / grog

H : ham / horse-radish

J : jam / jelly

K : kirsch / ketchup

L : lavender

M : macaroni / mace / maize / marmalade / marrow-bone / mayonnaise / milt / minestrone / mint / mocha / mustard

N : nutmeg

O: offal / orange blossom / orange juice

P : parsley / partridge / pepper / peel / pickle / pilaf / pimento / pork / pork butchery

R : rind / rosemary / rye flour

S : salami / salsify / salt / salt cod / sage / savoury / semolina / small ham / soup / spirit / starch / stock / succory / sugar / syrup

T : tapioca / tarragon / thyme / tripe / turkey

V : vanilla / veal / vermicelli / vinegar / vodka

W : water / watercress / wheat-flour / whey / wormwood

Y : yoghourt / young partridge

- *CORPUS* -

DICTIONNAIRE

GASTRONOMIQUE

Français / Anglais

- *CORPUS* -

French / English

DICTIONARY of

GASTRONOMIC

Terms

A

Abaisse ⇒ rolled-out pie crust

Abalone *-[mollusque]-* ⇒ abalone or ormer

Abats
- **bœuf, porc, etc ...** ⇒ offal < *uncountable* >
- **volaille** ⇒ giblets of ...
  a) **abats blancs**
    - **amourettes** ⇒ amourettes
    - **veau** ⇒ calf's marrow
    - **boeuf** ⇒ beef's marrow
    - **mouton** ⇒ mutton's marrow
    - **animelles** ⇒ testicles
    - **cervelle** ⇒ brain
    - **fraise** ⇒ caul
    - **pieds** ⇒ trotters
    - **ris** ⇒ sweetbread
    - **tête** ⇒ head
  b) **abats rouges**
    - **cœur** ⇒ heart
    - **foie** ⇒ liver
    - **langue** ⇒ tongue
    - **poumons** ⇒ lungs
    - **rate** ⇒ spleen
    - **rognons** ⇒ kidneys

Abattis
- **terme général** ⇒ giblets
- **de volaille** ⇒ giblets of poultry
- **de gibier à plume** ⇒ giblets of game fowl

Abattis à l'anglaise ⇒ giblets of poultry cooked with sautéed onions and potatoes, plus parsley

Abattis babylas ⇒ giblets of poultry browned with chopped onions, then cooked in stock with mushrooms, cream and mustard

Abattis bonne femme ⇒ giblets of poultry sautéed in goose fat with lardoons, onions, potatoes and garlic, then cooked in white wine and stock

Abattis à la bourgeoise ⇒ giblets of poultry sautéed in goose fat with lardoons, onions, carrots and garlic, then cooked in white wine and stock

Abattis à la bourguignonne ⇒ giblets of poultry sautéed in goose fat with lardoons, onions, mushrooms and garlic, then cooked in burgundy red wine and stock

Abattis chasseur ⇒ sautéed giblets of poultry with mushrooms, chopped shallots, plus white wine and tomato sauce added

Abattis de dinde aux navets ⇒ browned diced lardoons and giblets of turkey cooked in stock with onion, clove and turnip < *autres recettes de légumes possibles, dans ce cas remplacer « turnip » par le légume approprié* >

Abattis en fricassée ⇒ giblets of turkey and duck, plus chive, basil, garlic, clove and mushrooms; cooked in stock, thickened of egg-yolk and cream

Abattis en ragoût ⇒ giblets of poultry braised and stewed with garlic, white wine, stock and vegetables; served on timbales

Abbaye de morgeot ⇒ Burgundy wine either red or white

Abegnades ⇒ goose's tripe cooked in its blood

Abignades ⇒ goose's tripe cooked in its blood
Ablette ⇒ bleak or ablet
Aboukir
- **entremets** ⇒ sweet made with layers of Genoese sponge and chestnut purée, then coated of coffee custard and pistachio
- **amandes** ⇒ petits fours decorated with an almond
Abricot ⇒ apricot
Abricot-brandy ⇒ brandy
- **pluriel** ⇒ brandies
Abricot du japon ⇒ persimmon fruit
Abricot de st Domingue ⇒ sapodilla
Abricot pays ⇒ Caribbean apricot
Abricot sec ⇒ dried apricot
Abricots condé ⇒ crown of rice cooked in milk, garnished of halved apricots and decorated of angelica; served with apricot sauce flavoured of kirsch
Abricots chantilly ⇒ mashed apricots with cream and sugar, served cold
Abricots au miel ⇒ gateau with apricots cooked in honey and moistened of kirsch plus melted butter
Abricots à l'ancienne ⇒ poached apricots in syrup laid on a pastry, moistened of rum and covered with apple jam; then sprinkled of chopped almonds plus sugar and browned
Abricots bourdaloue ⇒ poached apricots in syrup, laid on semolina, covered with crushed macaroons and granulated sugar; then browned in the oven
Abricots Colbert ⇒ poached apricots in syrup, stuffed with rice cooked in milk, then coated and fried; served with a sauce flavoured of kirsch
Abricots confits à l'eau de vie ⇒ preserved apricots in eau de vie, vanilla and rum
Abricots flambés ⇒ poached apricots flamed with kirsch
Abricots au sirop ⇒ stoned apricots preserved in syrup
Abricots au sirop congelés ⇒ stoned apricots preserved in syrup and stored in the freezer
Abricots stérilisés au naturel ⇒ sterilized stoned apricots
Abricoter ⇒ to brush with apricot jam
Absinthe ⇒ asinthe or absinthe
Abusseau ⇒ transparent goby
Acacia
- **fleur** ⇒ acacia flower
- **miel** ⇒ acacia honey
Accolade (en ...) ⇒ two pieces of « either poultry or other meat of same nature » laid closed together
- **la première ligne est la définition « pour l'utilisation en texte, voir ci-dessous »** ⇒ two pieces of ... « nom anglais de la viande » laid closed together
Accommodé ⇒ seasoned with ... < v.t adjectif >
Acra ⇒ spicy fritter of vegetable or fish
Accra ⇒ spicy fritter of vegetable or fish
Acétomel ⇒ syrup of honey and vinegar
Achard de légumes au citron (ou Achar ...) ⇒ seasoning of preserved macerated lemons plus carrots, capsicums, cucumbers, french beans, cabbage and cauliflower; chopped onions, ginger, cayenne pepper, saffron and olive oil added
Achard ⇒ Indian seasoning
Achar ⇒ Indian seasoning
Achatine -[escargot]- ⇒ tinned snails
Ache de montagne ⇒ lovage
Ache des marais ⇒ wild celery
Ache large ⇒ alexanders or horse parsley

Ache odorante ⇒ celery < *uncountable* >
- pour le pluriel utiliser les phrases suivantes en mettant le nombre devant sauf pour
« **a bunch** » ⇒ ... sticks of celery or ... heads of celery or a bunch of celery
A cheval -[*steak, hamburger, entrecôte*]- ⇒ ... topped with a fried egg
Acide ⇒ acid
Acidifier ⇒ to acidify
Acide (*devient ...*) ⇒ to become sour
Aciduler ⇒ flavoured slightly with lemon juice
Açorda -[*Portugal*]- ⇒ soup of bread steeped in oil and added of pounded garlic
Acquette ⇒ liqueur based on cinnamon, cloves and nutmeg
Acra -[*légume*]- ⇒ edible root
Actinia ⇒ kiwi fruit
Actinie ⇒ sea anemone
Adant -[*sucre*]- ⇒ squared sugar
Adjem pilaf -[*Turquie*]- ⇒ mutton shoulder roasted and diced; added of chopped onions
Adjersandal -[*Russe*]- ⇒ aubergines baked with tomatoes and fried onions
Admirable de courtiller -[*raisin*]- ⇒ variety of grape
Adotz -[*poisson*]- ⇒ haddock
Adoucir ⇒ to soften
- **adouci** ⇒ softened < *v.t adjectif* >
Advocaat ⇒ dutch liquor
Aeglé ⇒ Indian grapefruit
Aération -[*bouquet du vin*]- ⇒ bouquet
Afchain -[*bêtise*]- ⇒ sweet made of cooked sugar flavoured with mint
Affinage ⇒ refining
Affriander ⇒ to tempt or to make attractive
Affrioler ⇒ to tempt or to entice
Africaine (*à l' ...*) ⇒ ... with a garnish of potatoes sautéed in butter, plus aubergine and cucumbers
Agar-agar ⇒ agar or agar-agar
Agaric couleur de miel ⇒ honey fungus or bootlace fungus
Agaric visqueux -[*gomphide « champignon »*]- ⇒ glutinous gomphidius
Agarvan -[*vins du Canada*]- ⇒ Canadian wine
Agave ou Agavé ⇒ agave
Agneau ⇒ lamb
Agneau (*Pascaline ...*) ⇒ rolled meat of lamb stuffed with lamb meat, egg-yolks, breadcrumbs; seasoned of chopped herbs and cooked in open fire
Agneau de Paulliac ⇒ Paulliac lamb
Agneau de pré-salé ⇒ salt marsh lamb
Agneau aux pruneaux, au thé et aux amandes ⇒ braised diced lamb meat, simmered with cinnamon, almonds, granulated sugar and orange blossom; plus stoned dried plums steeped in tea
Agneau de lait farçi ⇒ lamb stuffed with rice and its offal, then roasted on a skewer; served with watercress and quartered lemons
Agneau de lait rôti ⇒ lamb stuffed with its offal, then roasted on a skewer but sprinkled with melted butter; served with early vegetables
Agneau de lait à la kurde ⇒ roasted lamb, stuffed with its offal, rice and dried apricots
Agnelet ⇒ lambkin or small lamb
Agnelle ⇒ lamb

Agnès Sorel
   1) garniture ⇒ ... with a garnish of ...
      - **omelette** ⇒ omelette filled with ...
      - **veau poêlé** ⇒ fried veal garnished with ...
      - **veau braisé** ⇒ braised veal garnished with ...
      - **suprême de volaille** ⇒ supreme of poultry garnished with ... diced mushrooms, white meat and oxtongue
   2) potage ou crème Agnès Sorel ⇒ soup thickened with julienne
Agnolotti ⇒ kind of ravioli
Ago glain *-[Afrique noire]-* ⇒ crab ragout with rice
Agrafaou *-[Grèce]-* ⇒ Greek cheese
Agraz ⇒ sorbet from unripe grape juice and almonds
Agrumes ⇒ citrus fruits
Aguardiente ⇒ aguardiente
Ahi moha *-[Tahiti]-* ⇒ Tahitian dish of roasted wild goose and other meat
Aïda *-[filets de poissons]-*
      - **Barbue** ⇒ brill fillets ...
      - **Turbot** ⇒ turbot fillets ... served with spinach, and covered with a béchamel sauce added of egg-yolks, gruyère, and paprika
Aigle de mer *-[poisson]-* ⇒ eagle ray
Aiglefin ⇒ haddock < *pluriel inchangé* >
Aiglefin fumé *-[haddock dans le commerce]-* ⇒ haddock < *pluriel inchangé* >
Aïgo bouïdo ⇒ Provencal garlic soup served on slices of bread
Aïgo boulido ⇒ Provencal garlic soup served on slices of bread
Aïgo boulido aux œufs pochés ⇒ poached eggs in a stock made of garlic, sage and thyme; plus tomatoes, fennel, saffron, and sliced potatoes
Aïgo bullido ⇒ Provencal garlic soup served on slices of bread
Aïgo sau d'iou ⇒ Provencal fish soup with garlic, potatoes, onions and tomatoes
Aigre ⇒ bitter or sour
Aigre-doux ⇒ middling sweet and sour or bitter sweet < *adjectif* >
Aiguebelle ⇒ syrup or liquor or fruit paste
Aiguillat *-[requin]-* ⇒ dogfish
Aiguillat commun *-[poisson]-* ⇒ picked dogfish or spurdog
Aiguille *-[poisson]-* ⇒ garfish
Aiguille *-[haricot vert]-* ⇒ french bean
Aiguille de pin ⇒ pine needle
Aiguillette
      - **boucherie** ⇒ thin slice of meat or aiguillette
      - **volaille** ⇒ thin slice of poultry ou aiguillette
Aiguillette *-[poisson]-* ⇒ garfish
Aiguillette baronne *-[bœuf]-* ⇒ aiguillette from the rump of beef
Aiguillettes de bœuf en gelée ⇒ thin slice of beef cooked in the oven with calf trotter, carrots, tomatoes, garlic and pepper; served cooled in the cooking jelly
Aiguillettes de canard glacées rouennais à l'orange ⇒ cooled thin slices of roasted duck, with a mousse made of its thigh's meat, plus oranges and jelly flavoured of port
Aiguillettes de canard au vinaigre de miel ⇒ grilled thin slices of duckling, basted of a sauce made with shallot, honey and vinegar; served with potatoes and rice, or carrots and turnips
Aiguillon *-[boucherie]-* ⇒ spicy pork-butchery
Ail ⇒ garlic < *uncountable* >

Ail blanc ⇒ garlic < *uncountable* >
Ail d'Espagne -*[rocambole]-* ⇒ garlic < *uncountable* >
Ail rose ⇒ garlic < *uncountable* >
Ail rôti sur la braise -*[Charente]-* ⇒ garlic roasted on charcoal
Ail rouge des Provenceaux -*[rocambole]-* ⇒ garlic < *uncountable* >
Aile ⇒ wing
Aileron -*[volaille]-* ⇒ pinion
Ailerons de requin ⇒ shark fins
Ailerons de dinde en gelée ⇒ turkey's pinions stuffed and braised; served cooled, covered with
    Madeira jelly
Ailerons de dindonneau farçis braisés ⇒ duckling's pinions stuffed with a forcemeat and larded,
    sautéed and baked with onions, carrots, white wine and stock; served with a garnish
    or braised vegetables
Ailerons de dindonneau farçis en chaud froid ⇒ duckling's pinions stuffed with a forcemeat and
    larded, cooled and covered of chaudfroid sauce; served with jelly and white of eggs
Ailerons de dindonneau à la fermière ⇒ duckling's pinions stuffed with a forcemeat and larded;
    baked with a garnish of buttered vegetables
Ailerons de dindonneau en fricots ⇒ braised duckling's pinions, marinated in olive oil, lemon juice,
    pepper and parsley; then steeped in dough and fried
Ailerons de dindonneau ste Ménéhould ⇒ braised duckling's pinions with aromatics, sprinkled of
    breadcrumbs and butter, then browned in the oven
Aïllade
    - provence ⇒ garlic sauce
    - autres régions ⇒ dishes based on garlic
Aillade à la toulousaine ⇒ garlic mayonnaise mixed with pounded walnuts
Aillé ⇒ with garlic < *uncountable* >
Aillée ⇒ seasoning made of crumbs, crushed almonds and stock
Ailloli ⇒ garlic and oil mayonnaise
Aïoli ⇒ garlic and oil mayonnaise
Airelle ⇒ bilberry < *pluriel bilberries* > or whortleberry < *pluriel whortleberries* >
Airelle rouge ⇒ cranberry
Aïtïou -*[Afrique noire]-* ⇒ dish of maize porridge and a ragout
Ajiaco -*[Colombie]-* ⇒ stew of poultry, maize, potatoes, avocado, and capsicum
Ajonjoli -*[sésame]-* ⇒ sesame
Akra ⇒ spicy fritter of vegetable or fish
Akkra ⇒ spicy fritter of vegetable or fish
Akvavit ⇒ akvavit
Aquavit ⇒ akvavit
Albacore -*[thon]-* ⇒ yellowfin tuna or tuna or tunny-fish < *pluriel tunnies ou inchangé* >
Alberge ⇒ kind of apricot
Albert -*[sauce au raifort chaude]-* ⇒ sauce made of grated horse-radish, stock, mustard and
    vinegar; thickened with egg-yolks
Albigeoise (*à l'* ...) -*[garniture]-* ⇒ ... with a garnish of stuffed tomatoes and potato croquettes
Albuféra (*à la d'* ...)
    - Canetons à la d'Albuféra ⇒ ducklings baked in butter with ham, onion, clove and Malaga
        wine; garnished with ham lamellas and mushrooms in the gravy
    - then poached in stock; garnished of oxtongue, sweetbread and mushrooms, covered with a
        supreme sauce added of butter and capsicum
Alcamo -*[Sicile Sardaigne]-* ⇒ Sicilian wine

Alcazar ⇒ sweet made of sugared paste, apricot jam and almond paste
Alcool ⇒ alcohol or spirit < *tous uncountable* >
Al dente -*[cuisson]*- ⇒ crisp or crunchy
Ale -*[bière]*- ⇒ ale
Alcatico di Puglia ⇒ flavoured Italian wine with 15 alcohol
Alevins ⇒ fry < *Nota fry est un nom pluriel* >
Alexandra -*[cocktail]*- ⇒ cocktail of cream, cognac, and crème de cacao
Alexandra -*[cuisine]*-
    1) **consommé de volaille** ⇒ poultry consommé
    2) **potage parmentier garni de brunoise** ⇒ potato soup added of braised diced vegetables
    3) **filets de sole** ⇒ sole fillets ... and 3a or 3b
        - **poulet sauté** ⇒ sauté chicken ... and 3a or 3b
        - **cailles en cocotte** ⇒ quail braised and simmered ... and 3a or 3b
        - **noisettes** ⇒ noisettes of lamb ... and 3a or3b
        - **tournedos** ⇒ tournedos ... and 3a or 3b
    3a) lorsqu'ils sont nappés de sauce blanche ⇒ ... covered with white sauce and garnished of truffle lamellas, plus asparagus tips
    3b) lorsqu'ils sont nappés de sauce brune ⇒ ... covered with brown sauce and garnished of quartered artichoke hearts
    4) **cocktail** ⇒ cocktail based on crème de cacao
Alexandrine-douillard ⇒ variety of pear
Algérienne *(à l' ...)* ⇒ ... with a garnish of sautéed or fried sweet potatoes shaped in quoits, plus crushed tomatoes flavoured with garlic
Alginate -*[gélatine]*- ⇒ gelatine
Algue ⇒ seaweed
Algue brune ⇒ brown algae
Algue rouge ⇒ red algae
Alica ⇒ semolina
Alicante *(vins de ...)* ⇒ red wines from Alicante area
Alicot ou Alicuit ou Alycuit ⇒ giblets and wings of poultry or goose, stewed with garlic, carrots and potatoes
Aligot ⇒ mashed potatoes added of Cantal cheese and garlic
Aligot au pain ⇒ thick purée mixture of crumbled bread simmered in milk with butter and cheese
Aligot sucré ⇒ mashed potatoes added of Cantal cheese, garlic and sugar; then flamed with rum
Aligot *(marinette ...)* ⇒ purée made of potatoes, pounded garlic and cheese
Aligoté ⇒ light Burgundy white wine
Alise ⇒ service-apple
Alise pâcaude ⇒ bread paste enriched of butter, eggs and sugar; flavoured with orange blossom
Alize pâcaude ⇒ bread paste enriched of butter, eggs and sugar; flavoured with orange blossom
Alkékenge ⇒ physalis or winter-cherry
Alkermès ⇒ Italian digestive
Alberge ⇒ kind of apricot
Alléluia ⇒ small cake flavoured with cedrate
Allemande -*[sauce]*- ⇒ Sauce allemande
Allemande -*[velouté]*- ⇒ velouté sauce added of nutmeg
Allemande -*[pour poissons]*- ⇒ sauce based on fish stock
Allemande -*[pour abats, volailles pochées, légumes et œufs]*- ⇒ sauce based on veal or poultry stock
Allemande -*[grasse]*- ⇒ velouté sauce added of egg-yolks, and butter
Allemande -*[maigre]*- ⇒ fish stock and velouté sauce, added of egg-yolks and butter

Allemande *(à l' ...)*
    1) avec sauce allemande ⇒ ... with a sauce based on fish stock or veal stock
    2) cuissot de chevreuil ⇒ leg of roebuck ...
        - selle de chevreuil ⇒ saddle of roebuck ...
        - râble de lièvre ⇒ saddle of hare ...
        - râble de lapin ⇒ saddle of rabbit ,.. roasted on the vegetables of the marinade; served
        with the gravy added of the marinade, cream and vinegar
Alliès ⇒ hash of mutton meat, mutton kidneys and fat, added of brown sugar plus lemon peel; wrapped
        in pastry dough and baked
Allongé ⇒ diluted
Allonger *-[sauce]-* ⇒ to thin a sauce
Allumettes *-[pâtisserie]-* ⇒ flaky pastry fingers
Allumettes au cumin ⇒ puff-pastry lamellas, covered of cumin seeds and baked
Allumettes au fromage ⇒ cheese straws or cheese sticks
Allumettes glacées ⇒ flaky pastry fingers covered with sugar icing, white of egg and lemon juice
Allumettes au gruyére ⇒ small sticks made of flour, butter, grated cheese, salt and cayenne-pepper
Allumettes à la toscane ⇒ puff-pastry lamellas, covered with a culinary stuffing of ham, poultry and
        chopped truffles; sprinkled with grated parmesan, then baked
Allumettes salées *-[différentes sortes]-*
    1) aux anchois ⇒ puff-pastry lamellas covered with anchovies and baked
    2) à l'andalouse ⇒ puff-pastry lamellas covered of a forcemeat of poultry, plus a culinary
        stuffing of ham and onions; then baked
    3) à la châlonnaise ⇒ puff-pastry lamellas covered of a forcemeat of poultry with the
        cockscombs, kidneys and mushrooms added; then baked
    4) à la chavette ⇒ puff-pastry lamellas covered of a forcemeat of fish, plus a garnish of crayfish
        tails; then baked
    5) à l'écarlate ⇒ puff-pastry lamellas covered of a forcemeat of veal and oxtongue; then baked
    6) à l'écossaise ⇒ puff-pastry lamellas covered of a forcemeat of smoked haddock, thickened
        with béchamel sauce; then baked
    7) à la florentine ⇒ puff-pastry lamellas covered of spinach, thickened with béchamel sauce,
        sprinkled of grated cheese; then baked
    8) à la toscane ⇒ puff-pastry lamellas with grated cheese; then baked
Almond cake *-[cake]-* ⇒ almond cake
Alose ⇒ shad or allis shad or thwaite shad < *tous pluriel inchangé* >
    - à BORDEAUX grillée ⇒ grilled shad
    - à NANTES à l'oseille ⇒ shad cooked with sorrel
Alose de l'adour ⇒ shad baked with ham and a sorrel stuffing
Alose étoffée à la mode de cocherel ⇒ shad stuffed with a forcemeat of whiting, egg, pepper, grated
        nutmeg and cream; cooked on a skewer and served with potatoes in butter, plus
        quartered artichoke hearts
Alose frite ⇒ bits of shad, steeped in milk and flour, then fried
Alose farçie à l'oseille ⇒ shad stuffed with sorrel or sorrel purée
Alose grillée à l'oseille ⇒ shad marinated in oil, lemon juice, parsley, thyme and laurel; then grilled
        and served with parsley butter, plus a garnish of braised sorrel
Alose au plat ⇒ shad stuffed with kneaded butter and parsley, cooked in the oven
Alose à la provençale ⇒ shad stuffed with kneaded butter and parsley, cooked in the oven
Alose à la bonne femme ⇒ shad stuffed with kneaded butter and parsley, cooked in the oven
Alouette ⇒ lark or skylark
Alouette de mer ⇒ sandpiper
Alouettes en brochettes ⇒ barded larks, grilled on a skewer

Alouettes en croûte ⇒ boned larks, stuffed with a forcemeat of foie gras and truffles, sprinkled of melted butter and cooked in the oven; then they are encrusted in a loaf of bread hollowed out, and served with the cooking juice added of Madeira

Aloumere -[pholiote]- ⇒ changeable agaric

Aloxe-corton ou Corton ⇒ high-quality Burgundy wine

Aloyau ⇒ sirloin of beef

Aloyau à la d'albuféra ⇒ braised sirloin accompanied with a ragout made of white wine, basil, ham, onions, carrots, butter, sweetbread escalopes, oxtongue and mushrooms; served with a garnish of rabbit fillets and cockscombs

Aloyau avec les côtes de boeuf ⇒ loin and ribs of beef

Aloyau braisé ⇒ braised sirloin studded with lardoons marinated in cognac, pepper, parsley, carrots and onions; served with a garnish

Aloyau composé (avec filet et faux-filet ...) ⇒ sirloin

Aloyau composé (du filet [faux filet] rumsteak ...) ⇒ rump and loin of beef

Aloyau rôti ⇒ roasted sirloin served with watercress and vegetables in butter

Alphonse Lavallée -[raisin]- ⇒ variety of black grape

Alsaciennne (à l' ...)
  - **garniture** ⇒ ... with a garnish of sauerkraut, sausages, ham, salted breast, potatoes and pork roasted or braised
  - **timbales** ⇒ timbales ...
  - **pâté en croûte** ⇒ pie in pastry case ...
  - **terrine** ⇒ terrine ... with foie gras
  - **tarte** ⇒ fruit tart covered with a custard added of eggs

Alterne ⇒ alternate

Alterné ⇒ alternate

Alternatif ⇒ alternate

Alternative ⇒ alternating

Altesse -[vin de Savoie]- ⇒ white wine from Savoy area

Alumelle -[omelette]- ⇒ omelette or omelet

Alumette -[omelette]- ⇒ omelette or omelet

Alupka -[vin d'URSS]- ⇒ rosé wine from USRR

Alycuit ⇒ giblets and wings of poultry or goose, stewed with garlic, carrots and potatoes

Amande ⇒ almond
  - **amande d'un fruit** ⇒ kernel
  - **en amande** ⇒ almond shaped

Amande de mer ⇒ kind of queen scallop

Amande de terre -[souchet]- ⇒ galingale or sedge

Amande douce -[huile]- ⇒ almond oil

Amandes Aboukir ⇒ petits fours decorated with an almond

Amandes grillées ⇒ almonds browned in the oven

Amandes hachées ⇒ chopped almonds

Amandes mondées ⇒ skinned almonds

Amandes salées ⇒ fried skinned almonds, sprinkled with salt

Amandine
  a) **tart** ⇒ tart
    - **tartelette** ⇒ tartlet ... in sugared paste, garnished with a mixing of eggs, sugar, almond powder, flour, and melted butter; then flavoured with rum
  b) **pâtisserie moulée** ⇒ moulded pastry of sugar, egg-yolks, vanilla, almond powder, flour, whipped white of eggs, and butter; glazed with fondant

Amandines en beignets *-[petits choux]-* ⇒ small fritters made of choux pastry and skinned almonds

Amandines à la duchesse ⇒ flat cakes covered with a preparation of butter, semolina, almond powder and kirsch; plus redcurrant jelly added, then baked

Amanite *(voir les variétés ...)*
  1) **Amanite des Césars** ⇒ egg mushroom or orange agaric or orange milk mushroom or imperial mushroom
  2) **Amanite jonquille** ⇒ jonquil mushroom
  3) **Amanite vaginée** ⇒ scheathed agaric
  4) **Amanite rougeâtre** ⇒ blusher

Amarelle *-[cerise]-* ⇒ cherry

Amaretto ⇒ Italian liquor made of apricot kernels and aromatics

Amatriciana *(all' ...)* *-[spaghetti]-* ⇒ spaghetti < *uncountable* >

Amauguette ⇒ dish made of offal of mutton, boiled with aromatics

Amauguète ⇒ dish made of offal of mutton, boiled with aromatics

Ambassadeur
  - **garniture grosses pieces de boucherie** ⇒ ... with a garnish of artichoke hearts stuffed of chopped mushrooms, plus fried balls of mashed potatoes, eggs and butter
  - **potage** ⇒ soup of fresh beans

Ambassadrice
  - **garniture grosses pieces de boucherie** ⇒ ... with a garnish of artichoke hearts stuffed of chopped mushrooms, plus fried balls of mashed potatoes, eggs and butter
  - **potage** ⇒ soup of fresh beans

Ambigu *-[buffet froid]-* ⇒ buffet supper

Ambré ⇒ amber-coloured

Ambre gris *-[bonbon]-* ⇒ sweet

Ambrette *-[musc]-* ⇒ musk

Ambroisie
  - **liqueur** ⇒ liquor
  - **thé** ⇒ infusion of ambrosia leaves, and ambrosia flowers

Amelette *-[omelette]-* ⇒ omelette or omelet

Amer *-[apéritif]-* ⇒ bitters drinks

Américaine *(à l' ...)*
  - **poissons** ⇒ ... with a garnish of lobster lamellas, and lobster sauce
  - **sauce** ⇒ sauce based on lobster stock
  - **oeufs, volailles, viandes grillées** ⇒ ... with a garnish of tomatoes and bacon

Américano *-[apéritif]-* ⇒ bitters drinks

Américano *-[cocktail]-* ⇒ cocktail of Campari, Martini, Vermouth, and lemon peel

Amerise *-[merise]-* ⇒ wild cherry

Amertume *-[bière]-* ⇒ beer < *uncountable* >

Améthyste *-[clitocybe]-* ⇒ clitocybe mushroom or flavoured edible mushroom

Amiral *(à l' ...)* ⇒ ... with a garnish of oysters, mussels, crayfish tails, mushrooms, truffle; covered with béchamel sauce added of mashed crayfishes, cognac, and cayenne pepper

Amontillado *-[xérès]-* ⇒ amontillado

Amoroso *-[Xérès]-* ⇒ xeres

Amour-en-cage *-[alkékenge]-* ⇒ physalis or winter-cherry

Amourette ⇒ amourettes OR « veau » calf's marrow OR « bœuf » beef's marrow OR « mouton » mutton's marrow

Amourettes en fricots ⇒ amourettes macerated in olive oil and lemon juice, then plunged into batter and fried; served with tomato sauce

Amourettes au gratin ⇒ browned amourettes on a layer of chopped mushrooms, sprinkled with lemon juice, covered of sauce and breadcrumbs

Amoureuses *-[chambolle-musigny]-* ⇒ Burgundy wine

Amphitryon ⇒ host

Amuse-gueule ⇒ appetizer or cocktail snack

Amygdalin *-[poisson]-* ⇒ spurdog

Anacardier *-[noix de cajou]-* ⇒ cashew nut

Ananas ⇒ pineapple < *uncountable* >

Ananas des iles ⇒ pineapple, bananas, cream, sugar and kirsch mixed together, then laid in the pineapple casing; served cold

Ananas glacé à la bavaroise ⇒ pineapple first hollowed out of its pulp, then filled with a culinary stuffing of rum, pineapple, and gelatine

Ananas glacé à la bourbonnaise ⇒ pineapple first hollowed out of its pulp, then filled with rum, ice, and pineapple pulp macerated in rum

Ananas glacé à la chantilly ⇒ pineapple first hollowed out of its pulp, then filled with vanilla ice-cream, macerated pineapple, plus whipped cream

Ananas glacé à la créole ⇒ pineapple first hollowed out, then filled with pineapple ice-cream, plus a culinary stuffing of preserved fruits macerated in rum

Ananas glacé à la parisienne ⇒ pineapple first hollowed out, then filled with pineapple macerated in rum, banana ice-cream, and almonds

Ananas en surprise

    1) **glacé** ⇒ pineapple first hollowed out, then filled with a culinary stuffing of pineapple macerated in rum, plus fruits in season

    2) **crème** ⇒ pineapple first hollowed out, then filled with diced pineapple macerated in granulated sugar and rum; plus a custard of milk, vanilla, egg-yolks and cream

Ancho ⇒ variety of pimento

Anchoïade

    - **draguignan** ⇒ paste made of mashed anchovies, onion and egg-yolks

    - **provence** ⇒ mashed anchovies added of crushed garlic and olive oil

Anchois ⇒ anchovy

    - **pluriel** ⇒ anchovies

Anchois de Norvège ⇒ sprat

Anchois congelés ⇒ freezed anchovies

Anchois frits ⇒ anchovies steeped in milk and floured, then fried; served with quartered lemons

Anchois marinés ⇒ anchovies marinated in oil, onion, garlic, salt, thyme, laurel and pepper

Anchovy sauce ⇒ anchovy sauce

Anchoyade

    - **draguignan** ⇒ paste made of mashed anchovies, onion and egg-yolks

    - **provence** ⇒ mashed anchovies added of crushed garlic and olive oil

Anchoyade corse aux figues ⇒ anchovies pounded with figs and garlic, served on slices of bread

Ancienne *(à l' ...)*

    - **fricassée** ⇒ fricassee ...

    - **blanquette** ⇒ blanquette ... garnished with onions and cultivated mushrooms

Andalouse *(à l' ...)* ⇒ ... with a garnish of sauté capsicums, tomato, aubergines and chipolatas

Andouille ⇒ large sausage filled with chitterlings

Andouille de Jargeau ⇒ dry sausage made with shoulder and breast of pork; cooked before to be eaten

Andouillette ⇒ andouillette or small chitterlings sausage

Andouillettes à la lyonnaise ⇒ andouillettes fried in pork fat with browned onions and vinegar

Andouillettes à la tourangelle ⇒ andouillettes moistened of armagnac, on a layer of mushrooms flavoured of lemon juice, sprinkled with Vouvray wine and baked

Âne -[viande]- ⇒ donkey meat

Anellini -[pâtes alimentaires]- ⇒ pasta < uncountable >

Anémone de mer ⇒ sea anemone

Aneth ⇒ dill

Ange de mer ⇒ angel fish or angel shark

Angélique ⇒ angelica < uncountable >

Angélique confite ⇒ diced angelica preserved in syrup, then dried

Angelot
- **fromage** ⇒ cheese < uncountable >
- **pont l'évêque** ⇒ pont l'évêque

Angels on horseback ⇒ angels on horseback

Anges à cheval ⇒ angels on horseback

Anglaise -[cerise]- ⇒ cherry

Anglaise (à l' ...)
1) **légumes** ⇒ boiled vegetables or English name of the vegetable served with parsley and butter
2) **viande** ⇒ poached meat or steamed meat
3) **poissons et viandes panées** ⇒ nom de a viande ou du poisson coated with breadcrumbs then fried or sautéed
4) **poisson grillé** ⇒ nom du poisson brushed with oil or melted butter, then grilled

Angostura ⇒ angostura brandy

Anguille ⇒ eel

Anguilles en brochettes à l'anglaise ⇒ bits of eel marinated in oil, lemon juice, pepper and parsley; then grilled on a skewer alternated with ham

Anguille à la bonne femme ⇒ poached bits of eel with onions, pepper and white wine; served on sippets, plus sautéed potatoes

Anguille au court-bouillon ⇒ eel cooked with onion, carrots, garlic and wine

Anguille à la diable ⇒ eel cooked in a white wine court-bouillon, then covered of mustard plus melted butter and grilled

Anguilles frites orly ⇒ eel escalopes steeped in batter and fried in oil; served with parsley and tomato purée

Anguille à la provençale ⇒ bits of eel simmered with onions, pepper, crushed tomatoes, garlic and white wine

Anguille au vert ⇒ bits of eel simmered with chopped spinach and sorrel, white wine, parsley, tarragon, plus sage; then thickened with egg-yolks

Anguille au vert ⇒ eel served cold with green sauce

Anguille de mer ⇒ conger eel

Anguillette ⇒ baby eel

Anguille à la beaucaire ⇒ eel braised in wine and cognac, then stuffed with a forcemeat of fishes and laid on shallots, onions plus mushrooms

Animelles ⇒ testicles

Animelles à la crème ⇒ testicles cooked in butter and cream

Animelles frites ⇒ testicles steeped in vinegar, tarragon, olive oil, plus thyme, laurel, onion and parsley; then fried

Anis ⇒ aniseed < uncountable >

Anis -[anisette]- ⇒ anisette

Anis -[faux]- ⇒ caraway

Anis -[étoilé]- ⇒ star anise

Anisé -[champignon]- ⇒ aniseed agaric

Anisette ⇒ anisette
Anna ⇒ sliced potatoes cooked in butter
Annette ⇒ julienne of potatoes cooked in butter
Annrisse -*[tripes]*- ⇒ tripe < *uncountable* >
Anone ⇒ anona or custard-apple
Antiboise *(à l' ...)* ⇒ ... with cheese, and garlic
    - si vous ajoutez tomates et sardines utilisez la phrase suivante ⇒ with cheese, garlic,
        tomatoes and sardines
Anticucho -*[cœur]*- ⇒ heart of an animal
Antillaise *(à l' ...)*
    1) poissons, volailles ⇒ with a garnish of rice covered with either vegetables cooked in their
        own liquid or pineapple or bananas
    2) desserts ⇒ sweets with exotic fruits and rum
Antilope ⇒ antelope
Antipasto ⇒ Italian hors d'œuvre
Anversoise *(à l' ...)* ⇒ ... with a garnish of hop shoots braised in butter or cream
    - **sur tartelettes, supprimer « ... with a garnish of » et ajouter après « cream »** ⇒ laid on
        tartlets
    - **sur fonds d'artichauts id** ⇒ laid on artichoke hearts
Anneaux de saturne ⇒ fritter of dough-pastry cut in rings
Aoucou *(à l' ...)* -*[tourin]*- ⇒ onion soup cooked with conserve of goose thigh
Apéritif ⇒ aperitif
Aphtonite -*[boudin noir]*- ⇒ polony
Apollo -*[pomme de terre]*- ⇒ potato
A point
    - **viande rôtie** ⇒ done to a turn
    - **steak grillé** ⇒ medium
    - **fruit** ⇒ ripe
Appareil à la bombe
    1) glace préparée avec jaunes d'œufs, sirop et crème fouettée ⇒ preparation for ice-cream
        made of egg-yolks, syrup and whipped cream
    2) glace préparée avec jaunes d'œufs, sirop, crème fouettée et kirsch ⇒ preparation for
        ice-cream made of egg-yolks, syrup, whipped cream and kirsch
Appareil à la charlotte froide ⇒ preparation for charlotte made of gelatine, egg-custard, cream and
    vanilla
Appareils à condés ⇒ paste made of chopped almonds, sugar, vanilla and egg
Appareil à la Maintenon
    1) Côtes d 'agneau ⇒ lamb chops served with ...
      - **Ris de veau** ⇒ calf sweetbread served with ...
      - **Omelette fourrée** ⇒ omelette stuffed with ...
      - **oeufs pochés** ⇒ poached eggs with ...
      - **Pommes de terre farçies** ⇒ potatoes stuffed with ... a mixing of mushrooms, onions
        and white sauce; plus sometimes a culinary stuffing made of truffle, oxtongue and
        white meat
    **2) Ris de veau à la maintenon, braisés et dressés sur des croûtons surmontés d'une
        lame de truffe, garnis d'une purée soubise et d'un cordon de sauce
        suprême** ⇒ braised calf sweetbread laid on sippets and topped of truffle lamella;
        garnished with a purée of rice and onions, plus supreme sauce
Appareil à matignon
    - **au maigre** ⇒ carrots, celery and onions braised in butter; added of thyme, laurel and Madeira

- **au gras** ⇒ carrots, celery and onions braised in butter; added of thyme, laurel, Madeira and diced ham

Appareil à la pomme duchesse ⇒ mashed potatoes mixed with salt, pepper and butter, added of egg

Appellation d'origine contrôlée *-[A.O.C]-* ⇒ very high quality wine or certified description of wine

Appenzell ⇒ swiss cheese

Appétits *(ciboule, ciboulette, petits onions ...)* ⇒ ciboule, chive, and small onions

Apple-brandy ⇒ calvados

Apple-pie ⇒ apple-pie

Apple-jack *-[calvados]-* ⇒ apple-jack

Apple pudding *(ou pudding aux pommes à l'anglaise ...)* ⇒ sort of large turnover made of flour, kidney grease, and granulated sugar; filled with slices of apples flavoured with sugar, lemon peel and cinnamon, pour le pudding aux poires, mettre « pear » à la place de « apple » dans le titre et le texte

Apron ⇒ small perch *< pluriel inchangé >*

Aquavit ⇒ akvavit

Aquilon *-[petit pois]-* ⇒ pea

Arachide ⇒ natural peanut

Araignée *-[boeuf]-* ⇒ meat for grilling

Araignée de mer ⇒ spider crab or spinous spider crab *< cuisine uncountable >*

Arak ⇒ arak

Aralia *-[ginseng]-* ⇒ root from a Korean plant

Arapède ⇒ limpet

Arbolade
  1) **crème** ⇒ sugared custard with eggs
  2) **omelette** ⇒ omelette sugared or salted
  3) **recette ménagier de Paris** ⇒ omelette filled with ache, tansy, sage, beets, spinach, lettuce, and mint; sprinkled of grated cheese

Arboulastre
  1) **crème** ⇒ sugared custard with eggs
  2) **omelette** ⇒ omelette sugared or salted
  3) **recette ménagier de Paris** ⇒ omelette filled with ache, tansy, sage, beets, spinach, lettuce, and mint; sprinkled of grated cheese

Arbouse ⇒ arbutus-berry

Arbre à pain
  1) **arbre** ⇒ breadfruit tree
  2) **fruit à pain ou pain bois** ⇒ breadfruit

Archiduc *(oeufs, soles, volailles ...)* ⇒ ... cooked with onion, paprika, plus sauce flavoured of cognac, or whisky, or Madeira, or port

Ardennaise *(à l' ...)* ⇒ ... with juniper berries

Arek ⇒ alcohol from vegetal fibres

Arepa *-[Colombie]-* ⇒ maize flat cake

Arête ⇒ fish bone

Argenté des champs *-[lapin]-* ⇒ breed of rabbit

Argenteuil ⇒ ... garnished with asparagus in purée or in tips

Argentin *-[poisson sabre]-* ⇒ frostfish

Argentine *-[poisson]-* ⇒ sand smelt or atherine

Ariègeoise *(à l' ...)* ⇒ ... with cabbage leaves, salt pork and potatoes

Arlequin *-[décoration]-* ⇒ motley

Arlésiennne *(à l' ...)* ⇒ ... with a garnish of tomatoes garlic, aubergines fried in olive oil, braised courgettes and fried onions

Arlésiennes ⇒ stripes of puff-pastry glazed with egg and sprinkled of sugar

Armagnac ⇒ armagnac

Armenonville ⇒ ... with a garnish of sliced potatoes cooked in butter, and morels in cream; thickened with cognac or Madeira, plus a sauce

Armillaire couleur de miel ⇒ honey fungus
- **pluriel** ⇒ honey fungi

Armoise ⇒ artemisia *or* wormwood < *uncountable* >

Américaine *(à l' ...)*
- **poissons** ⇒ ... with a garnish of lobster lamellas, and lobster sauce
- **sauce** ⇒ sauce based on lobster stock
- **oeufs, volailles, viandes grillées** ⇒ ... with a garnish of tomatoes and bacon

Armottes ⇒ maize porridge filled with cooked goose fat

Aromate ⇒ aromatic

Aromatisé ⇒ flavoured with OR flavoured

Arôme ⇒ aroma OR flavour OR flagrance

Arquebuse -*[liqueur]*- ⇒ arquebus liquor

Arrabia *(all' ...)* -*[macaroni]*- ⇒ macaroni < *uncountable* >

Arrières de veau ⇒ hind 1/4 of veal

Arroche ⇒ orache

Arroche bonne dame ⇒ orache

Arroséla ⇒ grilled sea bream stuffed of chopped capsicum, sprinkled of oil flavoured with garlic

Arrosé
- **gâteaux** ⇒ sprinkled OR moistened
- **viande** ⇒ basted

Arrow-root ⇒ arrow-root < *uncountable* >

Arsinoé -*[vin de Chypre]*- ⇒ white wine from Cyprus

Artagnan *(à la ...)* ⇒ ... with a garnish of boletus, stuffed tomatoes and potatoes

Artichaut ⇒ globe artichoke

Artichaut à la barigoule ⇒ artichoke stuffed with mushrooms and ham, then braised in olive oil and wine

Artichauts bouillis ⇒ boiled artichokes, served hot or cold with a sauce

Artichauts braisés farçis au gras ⇒ boiled artichokes stuffed with sausage-meat, onions and parsley; then larded and simmered with white wine, plus veal stock

Artichauts à la bretonne ⇒ boiled artichokes, plus a creamy sauce and butter

Artichauts clamart ⇒ early spring artichokes, cooked with peas and lettuce; served with butter

Artichauts crécy ⇒ early spring artichokes and carrots, cooked in butter

Artichauts à la diable ⇒ artichokes stuffed with a forcemeat of crumbs, garlic, capers and pepper; cooked sprinkled of olive oil

Artichaut de Jerusalem -*[Pâtisson]*- ⇒ kind of gourd

Artichauts à la lyonnaise ⇒ boiled quartered artichokes, braised in oil and butter plus stock; served with parsley, butter and lemon juice

Artichauts mirepoix ⇒ early spring artichokes cooked in chopped vegetables, diced ham, white wine and stock

Artichauts des murailles -*[joubarbe]*- ⇒ houseleek

Artichauts en ragoût ⇒ artichokes first boiled, then braised in oil with potatoes and diced streaky bacon

Artois *(d' ...)*
- **potage** ⇒ soup of haricot beans
- **garniture** ⇒ ... with a garnish of potato croustades filled of peas and served with Madeira sauce

Asado ⇒ roasted piece of beef
Asapao ⇒ stew of chicken
Ashcake ⇒ ashcake
Asiago -[*fromage*]- ⇒ asiago cheese
Asperge ⇒ asparagus < *uncountable* >
Asperges à la Fontenelle ⇒ asparagus served with melted butter and a soft-boiled egg
Asperges à la flamande ⇒ asparagus served hot with hard-boiled egg-yolks and melted butter
Asperges à la crème ⇒ asparagus with cream
Asperges congelées ⇒ frozen asparagus
Asperges au gratin ⇒ boiled asparagus, laid on a dish and covered with a sauce, plus grated parmesan;
    then browned
Asperges à la polonaise ⇒ bunches of asparagus boiled in water, served in a dish sprinkled of hard
    boiled egg-yolk, and parsley
Asperges servies chaudes ⇒ cooked asparagus, served hot with melted butter and lemon juice, or an
    other sauce
Asperges servies tièdes ⇒ cooked asparagus, served tepid with a mayonnaise, or an other dressing
Aspergé ⇒ sprinkled or sprinkled with
Aspic ⇒ aspic < *uncountable* >
Aspic d'asperges ⇒ asparagus tips with mashed foie gras, covered with jelly
Aspic de cabillaud ⇒ ratatouille of tomatoes, aubergines, courgettes, onion, thyme and basilic; topped
    with fresh cod fillets baked in butter and white wine, covered of jelly
Aspic de crabes ⇒ crabs in elaborated aspic
Aspic de crevettes ⇒ shrimps in elaborated aspic
Aspic de homard ⇒ lobster in elaborated aspic
Aspic de langouste ⇒ spiny lobster in elaborated aspic
Aspic de foie gras ⇒ foie gras and truffles in aspic
Aspic de jambon et de veau ⇒ diced ham and veal meat in aspic
Aspic de volaille ⇒ chicken in aspic
Aspic d'oeufs de caille au caviar ⇒ quail eggs and caviar in aspic; served with a mousse made of
    tomato purée, cream and armagnac
Aspic de poisson ⇒ fish in elaborated aspic
Aspic de saumon fumé ⇒ smoked salmon in aspic
Assa-fœtida ⇒ asafoetida
Assaisonné ⇒ seasoned or seasoned with
Assam -[*thé*]- ⇒ tea
Assation ⇒ food cooked in its own juice
Assiette ⇒ plate
Assiette à potage ⇒ soup plate
Assiette à salade ⇒ salad plate
Assiette anglaise ⇒ assorted cold meat
Assiette de crudités ⇒ assorted raw vegetables
Assiette plate ⇒ dinner plate
Assiette (*à l' ...*) -[*service*]- ⇒ served by unit of plate or sold by unit of plate
Assmannshaüsen -[*vin du Rhin*]- ⇒ red wine from Rhine valley
Assortiment de coquillages farçis ⇒ various stuffed shellfishes
Asti ⇒ Italian wine
Asti spumante ⇒ muscat sparkling wine
Athénienne (*à l' ...*) ⇒ poultry or lamb or brochettes prepared with olive oil and onion; garnished of
    aubergines, capsicums and rice
Athérine ⇒ atherine

Atokiko -[*Afrique noire*]- ⇒ mango's kernel
Attendri ⇒ tenderized
Attente (*en ...*) -[*cuisson de l'esturgeon*]-
- **servi froid** ⇒ sturgeon cooked in a court-bouillon, served chilled with parsley, mushrooms, olives, crayfish tails, shredded horse-radish, lemon and gherkins
- **servi chaud** ⇒ sturgeon cooked in a court-bouillon, served with tomato purée added of crayfish butter

Attereau (*préparation ...*) ⇒ pieces of meat, fish or vegetables, coated with crumbs
Attereaux d'ananas ⇒ diced pineapple on a skewer, covered with breadcrumbs and fried
Attereaux de foie de volaille à la mirepoix ⇒ diced sauté chicken's liver, diced ham and mushrooms on a skewer; covered with chopped vegetables and breadcrumbs, then fried
Attereaux d'huitres ⇒ poached oysters and sauté mushrooms on a skewer, covered with breadcrumbs and fried; served with quartered lemons

Attereaux de moules ⇒ cooked mussels coated of mustard, plus mushrooms on a skewer, covered with breadcrumbs and fried; served with quartered lemons
Attereaux à la niçoise ⇒ stoned olives, bits of tunny and anchovy fillets on a skewer, covered with breadcrumbs and fried
Attereaux à la piémontaise ⇒ squares of polenta on a skewer, covered with breadcrumbs and fried; served with tomato purée
Attereaux pompadour à l'abricot ⇒ slices of bun and apricots on a skewer, steeped in a cream flavoured with rum or kirsch and fried; served with an apricot sauce
Attignole ⇒ ball made of meat, bread in milk, eggs, pepper, and onion; cooked in the oven
Attriau ⇒ fried crépinettes made of pork liver, veal meat, herbs and onion
Aubépine ⇒ hawthorn or whitethorn
Aubergine ⇒ aubergine
Aubergines à la crème ⇒ aubergines sliced and sautéed in butter, mixed with cream
Aubergines au cumin ⇒ diced aubergines cooked in a court-bouillon with lemon, coriander, and caraway seeds; served chilled
Aubergines farçies ⇒ aubergines hollowed out and filled with a culinary stuffing of chopped black olives, crushed anchovy fillets, aubergine pulp, and garlic; cooked in the oven
Aubergines farçies à la catalane ⇒ aubergines hollowed out and shaped in boat, stuffed with aubergine pulp, hard boiled egg, garlic and parsley; covered of breadcrumbs and browned in the oven
Aubergines farçies à l'italienne ⇒ aubergines hollowed out and filled with a culinary stuffing of aubergine pulp, risotto, parsley and garlic; covered with breadcrumbs and browned in the oven
Aubergines au gratin à la toulousaine ⇒ sauté slices of aubergines and tomatoes, covered with breadcrumbs and garlic, then browned in the oven
Aubergines au gratin à la languedocienne ⇒ sauté slices of aubergines and tomatoes, covered with breadcrumbs and garlic, then browned in the oven
Aubergines iman bayildi ⇒ aubergines hollowed out and filled with a stuffing of aubergine pulp, onion, tomato, rice, raisins, spices and aromatics; served chilled
Aubergines sautées ⇒ diced aubergines, sautéed in olive oil
Aubergines soufflées ⇒ aubergines hollowed out and filled with a culinary stuffing of aubergine pulp, béchamel sauce, egg and nutmeg, then baked
Aubergines soufflées à la hongroise ⇒ aubergines hollowed out and filled with a culinary stuffing of aubergine pulp, béchamel sauce, egg, nutmeg, onion and paprika; then baked
Aubun -[*oeuf*]- ⇒ white of egg
Au four ⇒ baked or roasted in the oven

Au gratin ⇒ au gratin
Au jus ⇒ roasted meat served in its own gravy
Ail ⇒ garlic < *uncountable* >
Aumale *(à la d' ...)*
 - **poularde** ⇒ fattened pullet, garnished with croustades filled of a culinary stuffing comprising tongue, foie gras and Madeira sauce
 - **oeufs brouillés** ⇒ scrambled eggs, added of crushed tomatoes and kidneys sautéed in Madeira
Aumonière *(en ...)* ⇒ dessert made of fruits where the seeds is replaced by sugar, then rolled in short-pastry and cooked in the oven; served with apricot hot sauce and garnished with chopped grilled almonds
Auréole ⇒ variety of peas
Auriculaire oreille de judas ⇒ black mushroom
Auronne ⇒ vervain
Aurore *-[dans un consommé ou une sauce]-* ⇒ added of tomato purée
Aurore *-[sauce]-* ⇒ velouté sauce, added of tomato purée, and butter
Auslese ⇒ white wine from Riesling vine
Ausone *-[vin]-* ⇒ red wine from St Emilion area
Autrichienne *(à l' ...)*
 - **avec paprika** ⇒ seasoned with paprika
 - **avec paprika, onions frits, fenouil ou crème aigre** ⇒ with paprika, fried onions, fennel or sour cream
Autruche ⇒ ostrich
Auvergnate *(à l' ...)*
 - **potée** ⇒ ... with streaky bacon, pork fat and ham
 - **soupe** ⇒ ... with cheese
 - **aligot et truffade** ⇒ ... with Cantal cheese
Auxerre *-[vins de]-* ⇒ wines from Chablis neighbourhood
Auxerrois *-[Cahors]-* ⇒ variety of wine from Cahors area
Auxey-Duresses ⇒ Burgundy wines from Côtes de Beaune
Avec ⇒ with
Aveline ⇒ cob-nut
Avgolemono ⇒ consommé of eggs and lemon juice, thickened with rice
Avizine Koze ⇒ porridge of fermented oat flakes
Avocat ⇒ avocado or avocado pear
Avocats à la coque ⇒ stoned avocado, served with french dressing, chopped shallots and lemon juice, or an other sauce
Avocats farçis au crabe ⇒ avocado husks, filled with a mixture of mayonnaise, cayenne pepper, crab and avocado pulp diced or pounded
Avocats farçis aux crevettes ⇒ avocado husks, filled with a mixture of mayonnaise, cayenne pepper, prawns and avocado pulp diced or pounded
Avocats farçis à l'américaine ⇒ avocado husks, filled with a mixture of diced pineapple, soya germs and mayonnaise; plus avocado pulp flavoured of lemon juice and pepper
Avocat vinaigrette ⇒ avocado with french dressing
Avocette *-[échassier du littoral]-* ⇒ avocet
Avoine ⇒ oats or oatmeal
Avolas ⇒ flat dragées
Axonge *-[saindoux]-* ⇒ pork fat
Ayu
 - **grillé** ⇒ grilled Japanese fish
 - **terme général** ⇒ ayu sweetfish

Ayu (suite)
- **séché** ⇒ yakiboshi
- **fermenté** ⇒ sushi

Azeito ⇒ Portuguese ewe cheese

Azérolier ⇒ azarole tree
- **baie azérole** ⇒ azarole or Neapolitan medlar

Aziminu ⇒ Corsican bouillabaisse from Corte

Azuki ⇒ small red beans

Azure ⇒ pudding made of chick-peas, rice, flour, milk, sugar, preserved fruits, and orange blossom

Azyme ⇒ unleavened

B

Baba ⇒ sponge cake

Baba Kanouy -*[Liban]-* ⇒ aubergine or broad bean purée thickened with sesame oil

Baba au rhum ⇒ rum baba

Baba rapide ⇒ sponge cake moistened with rum sauce

Baba économique ⇒ sponge cake made of flour, sugar, eggs, milk and yeast; then cooked in the oven

Babarin -*[rouget]-* ⇒ red mullet

Babeurre ⇒ buttermilk

Babine -*[liqueur]-* ⇒ sparkling drink made with avocado-pear tree leaves

Babka ⇒ kind of brioche

Babylas *(abattis ...)* ⇒ giblets of poultry simmered in stock with chopped onions, mushrooms and cream

Bacalan ⇒ variety of green cabbage

Bacalao ⇒ salt cod served with tomatoes, onions, capsicums and hard boiled eggs

Bacalhau ⇒ salt cod

Bacile ⇒ voir criste marine

Bacioli ⇒ biscuit flavoured with lemon

Backenoff ⇒ ragout of marinated meat, potatoes, onions and condiments

Bacon ⇒ bacon or smoked lean bacon or smoked lean pork fillet

Badiane ⇒ star anise

Badigeonner ⇒ to brush with

Badoise *(à la ...)*
  - **petites piéces de gibier** ⇒ ... sautéed and garnished of stoned cherries, plus a sauce of cream and pepper
  - **grosses piéces de gibier** ⇒ ... with a garnish of braised cabbage, pork fat, and potato purée

Baekenofe ⇒ ragout of marinated meat, potatoes, onions and condiments

Bagels ⇒ small rolls of bread

Bagnes -*[fromage pour fondue, râclette]-* ⇒ pressed cow's milk cheese

Bagration
  1) **soupes** ⇒ soups ...
      - **salade** ⇒ salad ...
      - **oeufs** ⇒ eggs ... with a preparation based on macaroni
  2) **langouste** ⇒ spiny lobster ...
      - **filets de sole** ⇒ sole fillets ... with vegetable salad in mayonnaise 3
      - **avec purée de volaile ou salpicon de truffe et langue écarlate** ⇒ ... with mashed poultry or culinary stuffing of truffle and oxtongue

Baguette -*[pain]-* ⇒ a long stick of bread or French stick

Baguette laonnaise ⇒ cow's milk cheese shaped in parallelepiped

Baguette thiérarche ⇒ cow's milk cheese shaped in parallelepiped

Bahuri ⇒ ragout made of pork, salted fish, pineapple and mango

Baie ⇒ berry

Baies rouges ⇒ red berries

Baies roses ⇒ rose berries
  liste des baies utilisées en cuisine
  - **grain** -*[raisin]-* ⇒ grape
  - **groseille** ⇒ redcurrant
  - **bouquet** -*[sureau]-* ⇒ elder

Baies roses ⇒ rose berries (follow)
- **baies sauvages** *(airelle ...)* ⇒ bilberry, pluriel bilberries
- **arbouse** ⇒ arbutus-berry, pluriel arbutus-berries
- **aubépine** ⇒ hawthorn
- **épine vinette** ⇒ berberis
- **fraise des bois** ⇒ wild strawberry, pluriel wild strawberries
- **framboise** ⇒ raspberry, pluriel raspberries
- **merise** ⇒ wild cherry, pluriel wild cherries
- **mûre** ⇒ mulberry, pluriel mulberries
- **myrtille** ⇒ whortleberry, pluriel whortleberries
- **ronce** ⇒ blackberry, pluriel blackberries
- **sureau** ⇒ elderberry, pluriel elderberries

Baiser ⇒ twin petit four sticked with custard

Bajoue ⇒ cheek or chop or chap

Baking powder *-[levure]-* ⇒ yeast

Baklava ⇒ triangular pastry stuffed with grilled almonds, pistachio, chopped walnuts, and sugar; sprinkled with honey or syrup

Balai *-[clavaire jaune]-* ⇒ tiny yellow hands

Bamancés ⇒ mixture of chocolate, eggs and sugar in pots

Balaou
- **chinchard** ⇒ horse mackerel
- **orphie** ⇒ saury

Baleine ⇒ whale

Balisier ⇒ canna

Baliste ou Fanfré
- **méditerranée** ⇒ kind of tuna
- **amérique** ⇒ triggerfish or filefish

Balkenbrij ⇒ pig's head gateau, served with apple compote

Ballotine ⇒ galantine
- **de viande** ⇒ ... of meat
- **de volaille** ⇒ ... of poultry
- **de gibier** ⇒ ... of game
- **de poisson** ⇒ ... of fish ou nom anglais du poisson

Ballottine chaude d'anguille ⇒ eel stuffed with a forcemeat of fish, poached in white wine, and cooked in the oven

Ballottine chaude d'anguille à la bourguignonne ⇒ eel stuffed with a forcemeat of whiting and parsley, cooked in a red wine court-bouillon; covered with burgundy sauce of red wine, fish, onion, mushrooms and butter

Ballottine chaude de lièvre à la périgourdine ⇒ meat loaf of hare plus larding, stuffed with a forcemeat of wild rabbit, truffles and foie gras; sprinkled with cognac and braised in Madeira plus aromatics

Ballottine d'agneau à la gelée ⇒ meat loaf of lamb's boned shoulder, filled of galantine forcemeat mixed with a stuffing of oxtongue, ham and olives; cooked in jelly

Ballottine d'agneau braisée ⇒ braised meat loaf of lamb's shoulder stuffed with sausage meat, parsley, garlic, onions and butter

Ballottine d'anguille froide ⇒ eel stuffed with a forcemeat of fish, poached in white wine, and cooked in the oven; then cooled

Ballottine de faisan à la gelé e ⇒ meat loaf of pheasant, stuffed with a forcemeat of foie gras, red-legged partridge, egg-yolks and herbs; cooked in jelly with Madeira

Ballottine de porc ⇒ braised meat loaf of pork's shoulder stuffed with sausage-meat, parsley, garlic, onions and butter

Ballottine de poularde à brun ⇒ meat loaf of fattened pullet, stuffed with a forcemeat of pork, veal, ham, egg-yolks, cognac and pepper; cooked in jelly with calf trotters and Madeira

Ballottine de poularde à la gelée ⇒ meat loaf of boned fattened pullet, stuffed with a forcemeat of ham, oxtongue, pork fat, sausage meat, veal, egg-yolks, cognac and truffles; cooked in a jelly with Madeira

Ballottine de poularde en chaud froid ⇒ meat loaf of fattened pullet, stuffed with a forcemeat of pork, veal, ham, egg-yolks, cognac and pepper; covered of chaudfroid sauce

Ballottines d'oie au Savigny-lès-Beaune ⇒ meat loaf of goose

Ballottines de veau ⇒ meat loaf of boned veal's shoulder, filled of galantine forcemeat mixed with a stuffing of oxtongue, ham and olives; cooked in meat jelly

Ballottines de volailles *(petites ...)* ⇒ meat loaf of poultry thighs, stuffed with a forcemeat; cooked in a jelly and Madeira

Balthazar ⇒ balthasar

Bamboche *(en ...)* ⇒ with fried salt cod, plus sometimes fried eggs added

Bambou-cuisine ⇒ bamboo shoots

Bamia ⇒ Egyptian vegetable

Bamya ⇒ Egyptian vegetable

Banana split ⇒ splitted banana topped with ice-cream and chocolate sauce or American banana split

Banane ⇒ banana

Banane bourdaloue ⇒ poached bananas laid on semolina, covered with crushed macaroons and granulated sugar; then brown in the oven

Banane flambée ⇒ banana cooked in butter, and flamed with rum, armagnac and cognac

Banane plantain ⇒ large banana for cooking

Bananes à la créole gratinées ⇒ pieces of banana rind, stuffed with rice and crystallized fruits, covered of banana pulp macerated in lemon; browned in the oven

Bananes à la crème ⇒ banana lamellas, sprinkled with sugar, moistened of kirsch and cream

Bananes au beurre ⇒ bananas sprinkled with melted butter and sugar; cooked in the oven

Bananes au four *(en lamelles ...)* ⇒ banana lamellas with raspberry jelly, cooked in the oven

Bananes au four *(avec beurre et sucre ...)* ⇒ bananas cooked in the oven; served with butter and sugar or redcurrant jelly

Bananes au lard ⇒ larded bananas, browned in olive oil; served with rice, plus raisins, peanuts and ginger

Bananes au rhum ⇒ bananas macerated in rum, then coated with breadcrumbs and glazed in butter; served with red-currant jelly

Bananes beauharnais ⇒ bananas sprinkled with sugar, rum and cream; cooked in the oven

Bananes chantilly ⇒ mashed bananas moistened of kirsch, then mixed with cream; accompanied of sponge fingers

Bananes grillées ⇒ grilled buttered bananas, covered of sugar and cream

Bananes soufflées ⇒ mashed bananas mixed with butter, sugar, flour, milk and eggs; cooked in the oven

Banc d'huitres ⇒ oyster bed

Bandol *-[vin]-* ⇒ Provencal wine

Bannette *-[dolic]-* ⇒ bean

Bannocks *(GB ...)* ⇒ bannocks

Banon ⇒ cylindrical Provencal cheese wrapped in chestnut-tree leaves, steeped in eau de vie

Banon au pèbre d'aï ⇒ cylindrical Provencal cheese wrapped in chestnut-tree leaves, steeped in eau de vie, and flavoured with savoury

Banquière *(à la ...) -[garniture]-*

a) volaille ⇒ poultry ...
- **ris de veau** ⇒ calf sweetbread ...
- **croûtes garnies** ⇒ pastry boats ...
- **timbale** ⇒ timbale ...
- **vol au vent** ⇒ vol-au-vent ... with a garnish of mushrooms, truffle lamellas, and poultry quenelle; covered with supreme sauce added of Madeira and truffle

b) tournedos ⇒ tournedos ...
- **noisettes d'agneau sautées** ⇒ sauté noisettes of lamb ... laid on croutons, with a garnish of poultry quenelles and truffle lamellas covered with the gravy thickened of Madeira

Banuyls -*[vin]-* ⇒ sweet natural wine from Collioure area

Bar-poisson ⇒ sea bassor sea perch < *tous pluriel inchangé* >

Bar à huitres -*[restaurant]-* ⇒ oyster bar < *comptoir ou sont servies les huitres dans un restaurant* >

Bar à la dugléré ⇒ chopped onions, shallots, parsley, garlic, mushrooms, plus tomato pulp and a sea-bass; cooked in the oven

Bar à la livournaise ⇒ sea-bass laid on butter, tomato pulp and sprinkled with breadcrumbs; cooked in the oven

Bar à la meunière ⇒ floured sea-bass, fried in butter

Bar à la portugaise ⇒ sea-bass moistened of white wine, cooked in the oven

Bar à la provençale ⇒ floured sea-bass browned in olive oil first; then covered with a sauce plus breadcrumbs and cooked in the oven

Bar braisé ⇒ braised sea-bass, with browned onions, shallots and parsley

Bar frit ⇒ sea-bass watered in milk, then floured and fried in oil

Bar grillé ⇒ sea-bass brushed with olive oil and grilled

Bar poché chaud ⇒ sea-bass poached in a court-bouillon; served with a sauce and vegetables

Bar poché froid ⇒ chilled poached sea-bass, plus lemon, artichoke hearts and tomatoes; served with a mayonnaise and french dressing

Bara brith -*[GB]-* ⇒ bara brith

Barack ⇒ apricot eau de vie

Barack Palinka ⇒ apricot eau de vie

Baraquilles ⇒ triangular puff-pastry patties, filled with a culinary stuffing of game fillets, truffles, mushrooms, calf sweetbread, and foie gras; thickened with sauce added of Madeira

Barbacoa -*[barbecue]-* ⇒ barbecue

Barbadine ⇒ Caribbean fruit

Barbaresco -*[Italie vin]-* ⇒ red wine from Piedmont

Barbarosso -*[corse vin]-* ⇒ red wine from Corsica

Barbe à papa ⇒ sticks covered with coloured sugar in filaments

Barbe de bouc -*[salade; salsifis]-* ⇒ wild salsify

Barbe de bouc -*[hydne]-* ⇒ imbricated hydnum

Barbe de bouc -*[clavaire]-* ⇒ tiny yellow hands

Barbe de chèvre -*[clavaire]-* ⇒ tiny yellow hands

Barbe de chèvre -*[hydne]-* ⇒ spreading hydnum

Barbe de vache -*[hydne]-* ⇒ spreading hydnum

Barbe de capucin-chicorée sauvage ⇒ chicory or succory

Barbeau
- **poisson** ⇒ barbel
- **botanique** ⇒ cornflower

Barbecue ⇒ barbecue

Barbentane -*[aubergine]-* ⇒ variety of aubergine

Barbera -*[Italie vin]-* ⇒ Italian wine from Piedmont

Barbillon ⇒ young barbel

Barboton ⇒ sliced potatoes, tomatoes, and aromatics; cooked in stock thickened of flour

Barbouche ⇒ couscous of tripe simmered with oil, garlic, cummin, caraway seeds, beans, and beef dried sausage

Barbouille *(en ...)*
- **Nivernais** ⇒ rabbit cooked in red wine with its blood added
- **Berry** ⇒ cock or fattened pullet cooked in red wine with the blood added

Barbue ⇒ brill

Barbue à la bercy ⇒ brill cooked in the oven with shallots, parsley and white wine

Barbue à la bonne femme ⇒ brill moistened with white wine; cooked in the oven on a layer of parsley and mushrooms

Barbue à la brancas ⇒ brill cooked in the oven on a julienne of onions, leeks, celeriac, mushrooms and potatoes

Barbue à la dieppoise ⇒ brill cooked with white wine in the oven; plus a garnish of crayfish

Barbue à la fermière ⇒ brill cooked in the oven with carrots, onions, leeks, celeriac, butter and white wine

Barbue à la florentine ⇒ brill fillets poached in a white wine court-bouillon, covered with sauce, grated cheese and butter; browned in the oven on a layer of spinach

Barbue à la provençale ⇒ floured brill browned in olive oil; then covered with a sauce plus breadcrumbs and cooked in the oven

Barbue au Champagne ⇒ brill and mushrooms cooked in Champagne; served with a garnish of sole fillets

Barbue au chambertin ⇒ brill and mushrooms cooked in Chambertin, covered with butter

Barbue braisée ⇒ brill braised in the oven with carrots, onions, celeriac, parsley and thyme

Barbue cardinal ⇒ stuffed brill poached in white wine; served with round slices of lobster

Barbue chérubin ⇒ braised brill with tomato pulp, diced truffles and a julienne of red-peppers

Barbue farçie saumonée ⇒ brill stuffed with a forcemeat of salmon, poached in the oven on a layer of julienne

Barbue grillée ⇒ brill brushed with oil or butter and grilled

Barbue pochée ⇒ brill poached in stock, and served with a sauce

Bardane ⇒ burdock

Bardatte ⇒ cabbage stuffed with hare or rabbit, cooked in a terrine with stock; served with braised chestnuts and roasted quail

Barde ⇒ larding or bard

Bardé ⇒ larded or barded < *v.t adjectif* >

Bardière ⇒ pork back fat

Barigoule *(à la ...)* ⇒ artichokes stuffed with a forcemeat of ham and mushrooms, then braised

Barin double *(gigot et filet de mouton ...)* ⇒ hind 1/4 of lamb

Barley broth ⇒ scotch broth

Barman ⇒ bartender

Barolo -*[Italie vin]*- ⇒ red wine from Barolo in Piedmont

Baron
- **mouton** ⇒ saddle of mutton
- **agneau** ⇒ saddle of lamb
- **bœuf** ⇒ baron of beef

Baron d'agneau ⇒ saddle of lamb

Baron d'agneau à la périgourdine ⇒ roasted saddle of lamb with tomatoes and chestnuts; browned in goose fat

Baron de boeuf ⇒ baron of beef

Baron de lapin ⇒ saddle of rabbit

Barons de lapereaux à la menthe ⇒ boned saddles of young rabbits, steamed in a court-bouillon, plus slices of tomatoes and courgettes browned in the oven; covered with mint leaves

Barquette ⇒ pastry-boat

Barquette à la bouquetière ⇒ pastry-boat filled of vegetable salad thickened with béchamel sauce, plus asparagus tips

Barquette aux abricots ⇒ pastry boat filled with apricots, cooked in the oven and covered of apricot jam

Barquettes à l'américaine ⇒ pastry-boats filled with a culinary stuffing of crustaceae, covered with breadcrumbs and cooked in the oven

Barquettes Bagration ⇒ pastry-boats garnished of poultry purée plus a layer of white meat and truffles; covered of jelly

Barquettes Beauharnais ⇒ pastry-boats filled with a banana purée, lemon juice and rum, cooked in the oven; covered with crumbs of buns plus melted butter

Barquettes au fromage (*chaudes ...*) ⇒ pastry-boats filled of béchamel sauce mixed with sauté mushrooms and swiss cheese; moistened of melted butter, then browned

Barquettes aux champignons, chaudes ⇒ pastry-boats filled of chopped mushrooms and scrambled eggs, warm up in the oven

Barquettes aux crevettes froides ⇒ pastry-boats filled of mayonnaise mixed with avocado pulp; covered with prawns

Barquettes aux framboises ⇒ pastry-boats filled with custard, raspberries and redcurrant jelly

Barquettes aux laitances (*chaudes ...*) ⇒ pastry-boats filled with poached soft roes, sauté mushrooms and béchamel sauce; covered of grated cheese then browned

Barquettes aux marrons ⇒ pastry-boats filled of chestnut cream, covered with a custard

Barquettes aux oeufs brouillés et aux asperges (*chaudes ...*) ⇒ scrambled eggs, covered of asparagus tips and melted butter; warmed in the oven

Barquettes aux oeufs de poisson ⇒ pastry-boats filled with fresh cod roes, diced lemon and butter

Barquettes chaudes aux anchois ⇒ pastry-boats filled of sauté mushrooms thickened with béchamel sauce and anchovy fillets; cooked in the oven

Barquettes d'huitres à la normande ⇒ pastry-boats filled with poached oysters, mussels, mushrooms, shrimps and sauce

Barquettes d'huitres chaudes ⇒ pastry-boats filled with a sauce, plus poached oysters, then covered of breadcrumbs

Barquettes d'huitres froides ⇒ pastry-boats filled with poached oysters and mayonnaise; covered of truffles

Barracuda -*[poisson]-* ⇒ barracuda

Barsac ⇒ Sauternes white wine

   - **chateaux ö Climens** ⇒ Coutet, Broustet, Caillou, Doisy-Daène, Doisy-Védrines, Myrat, Nairac, Suau

Barszcz -*[Pologne]-* ⇒ beetroot soup

Barszcz wigilijny -*[Pologne]-* ⇒ soup of beetroot juice and mushrooms

Bartavelle ⇒ rock partridge < *uncountable* >

Bas de carré -*[veau]-* ⇒ rack of veal

Bas morceaux -*[bœuf]-* ⇒ cheap cuts of beef

Bas morceaux ⇒ the cheap cuts or meat for dishes braised or boiled

Basco béarnais -*[fromage]-* ⇒ pressed ewe-cheese

Baselle ⇒ Basella or Malabar nightshade

Basilic ⇒ basil < *uncountable* >

Basma -*[Kounafa]-* ⇒ pastry made of browned dough, crushed almonds and crushed hazelnuts; sprinkled with syrup

Basmati -*[riz]-* ⇒ variety of rice

Basquaise *(à la ...)*
- **omelette** ⇒ omelette with tomato, capsicum, garlic and ham
- **poulet sauté** ⇒ sauté chicken with tomato, capsicum, garlic and ham
- **garniture** ⇒ ... with a garnish of sauté boletus, plus sliced potatoes cooked in butter

Basquaise *-[bouteille]-* ⇒ shaped flat bottle for armagnac

Bas-rond *-[baron]-*
- **mouton** ⇒ saddle of mutton
- **agneau** ⇒ saddle of lamb
- **bœuf** ⇒ baron of beef

Basse côte à braiser ⇒ braising steaks

Basse côte avec une partie de l'épaule ⇒ steak meat

Basse côte ou Côte découverte *-[veau]-* ⇒ Middle neck of veal

Basses côtes ⇒ steak meat

Bassi salté ⇒ couscous based on millet

Bastella ⇒ Corsican turnover ... filled with vegetables and meat

    variantes *(toutes avec viandes ...)*
- **inarbrittate** ⇒ ... filled with beets or spinach plus meat
- **inzuccate** ⇒ ... filled with gourd or pumpkin plus meat
- **incivulate** ⇒ ... filled with onions and meat

Bastella *-[pastilla]-* ⇒ puff-pastry stuffed of poultry, seafood or vegetables

Bastion ⇒ dish shaped as a tower

Bastion d'anguilles ⇒ eels stuffed with a forcemeat of whiting; poached in white wine and aromatics

Ba-ta-clan ⇒ gateau made of pounded almonds, eggs, sugar, rum and flour; covered with vanilla custard

Batata ⇒ Spanish word for potato or potato

Batavia ⇒ Webb lettuce

Bath bun ⇒ bath bun

Batida *-[cocktail]-* ⇒ mixing of sugar-cane, eau de vie, and lemon

Battre ⇒ to whisk or to whip

Bâtard *-[pain]-* ⇒ bread < *uncountable* >

Bâtard-montrachet *-[vin]-* ⇒ Burgundy wine either red or white

Bâton de jacob ⇒ eclair filled with custard and covered of sugar

Bâton ou Bâtonnet
- **pâtisserie** ⇒ small pastries shaped in small little sticks
- **légumes** ⇒ nom anglais ... shaped in small sticks

Bâtonnet *(viande ...)* ⇒ lamella

Bâtonnets au chocolat ⇒ sticks made of almonds, sugar, cocoa, vanilla and white of eggs; cooked in the oven

Bâtonnets au cumin ⇒ sticks of dough with cumin seeds added; cooked in oven

Bâtonnets aux amandes ⇒ sticks made of crushed almonds, sugar, white of eggs and rum; cooked in the oven

Bâtons aux amandes ⇒ sticks made of butter, eggs, sugar, flour and chopped almonds

Bâtons feuilletés glacés ⇒ puff-pastry sticks, glazed with a preparation of sugar, white of eggs and lemon juice

Bâtons glacés à la vanille ⇒ sticks made of almond powder, sugar, white of eggs and vanilla; cooked in the oven

Bâtons salés ⇒ sticks made of milk, butter and flour; slightly salted

Bâtonnets salés ⇒ sticks made of milk, butter, flour, salt and egg

Baudroie ⇒ angler fish

Baudruche ⇒ gold-beater's skin
Bavarois ⇒ bavarois
Bavarois à la créole ⇒ layers of Bavarian mousse, and culinary stuffing of bananas flavoured with rum; covered of whipped cream
Bavarois à la crème ⇒ Bavarian mousse made of milk, gelatine, egg-yolks and sugar; covered with a cream
Bavarois à la cévenole ⇒ Bavarian mousse, plus chestnut cream flavoured with kirsch; covered of whipped cream
Bavarois à la normande ⇒ Bavarian mousse flavoured with calvados, plus apple jam, gelatine and whipped cream
Bavarois aux fruits ⇒ Bavarian mousse made of gelatine, syrup, lemon juice, fruit purée plus whipped cream
Bavarois rubanné au chocolat et à la vanille ⇒ Bavarian mousse in layers with a preparation of vanilla and chocolate
Bavaroise *-[boisson]-* ⇒ a beverage based on tea, milk and alcohol
Bavette
  - bifteck ⇒ undercut for steak
  - pot-au-feu ⇒ undercut for pot-au-feu
Bavette à l'échalote ⇒ lower part of sirloin, fried with chopped shallots
Bavette de boeuf à l'échalote ⇒ beef lower part of sirloin, fried with chopped shallots in butter
Bavette de boeuf grillée ⇒ undercut for steak brushed with oil, covered of chopped herbs and grilled
Bavette grillée ⇒ lower part of sirloin brushed with oil, covered of chopped herbs and grilled
Bayonnaise *(à la ...)* *-[jambon]-* ⇒ dried ham rubbed with salt, pepper and aromatics
Bazine ⇒ Muslim dish made of a dough with semolina, yeast and oil
  - Ramadan ⇒ ... served with butter, honey and lemon juice during Ramadan
  - jours ordinaires ⇒ ... served with fish soup, or raisins and sauté meat
  - autres recettes sans levure mais avec bouillon de poulet ⇒ Muslim dish made of a semolina dough cooked in poultry stock, and served with scrambled eggs
  - sans levure et formé en boule ⇒ Muslim dish made of a semolina dough shaped in ball, and cooked in stock
Béa ⇒ new potato
Béarnaise *(à la ...)* ⇒ dish from Béarn recipe
Béatilles
  - pour vol au vent ⇒ vol-au-vent ...
  - bouchées ⇒ patties ...
  - tourte ⇒ pie ... with a garnish of cockscombs, kidneys, lamb sweetbreads, diced foie gras and mushrooms; thickened with velouté
Béatrix
  1) grosses piéces de boucherie ⇒ ... served with a garnish of braised morels, carrots and quartered artichoke hearts, plus potatoes in butter
  2) salade ⇒ composed salad made with white meat, potatoes, asparagus tips, mayonnaise, and truffle lamella
Beaucaire
  1) salade composée ⇒ salad composed with a julienne of celery and celeriac, chicory, ham, apples, beetroots and potatoes
  2) soupe ⇒ soup made of cabbage, leek and celery cooked in stock with butter, basil and sweet marjoram; garnished of pearl barley, diced poultry liver, and grated cheese

3) anguille ⇒ eel stuffed with a forcemeat of fish, laid on shallots, onions and mushrooms; then braised with white wine, and cognac

Beaucuit ⇒ buckwheat

Beaufort
- **fromage** ⇒ cow's milk cheese from the Alps
- **râclette** ⇒ râclette made with Beaufort cheese

Beauharnais
- **petites pièces de boucherie grillées ou sautées** ⇒ ... served with a garnish of mushrooms stuffed with a gratin forcemeat, plus sauté artichoke hearts, and Madeira sauce
- **œufs** ⇒ soft boiled eggs laid on artichoke hearts
- **apprêts sucrés** ⇒ sugared preparation based on banana and rum

Beaujolais -[*vin*]- ⇒ Beaujolais < *uncountable* >

Beaumes de venise -[*Provence*]- ⇒ sweet wine from Vaucluse

Beaune -[*vin*]- ⇒ Beaune < *uncountable* >

Beaune-les-grèves ⇒ Burgundy wine

Beauvaisienne (*à la ...*) -[*truite*]- ⇒ trout sprinkled with pepper seeds, then roasted

Beauvilliers -[*gâteau*]- ⇒ gateau made of crushed almonds, sugar, butter, eggs and rice flour

Beauvilliers (*garniture pour grosses pièces de boucherie braisées ...*) ⇒ ... with a garnish of braised salsify, tomatoes stuffed with mashed brain, and fried spinach

Bécasse ⇒ woodcock < *pluriel inchangé* >

Bécasse à la Souvarov ⇒ woodcock stuffed with foie gras, truffle and cognac; then baked with truffles, plus game stock added of Madeira

Bécasse à la fine champagne ⇒ cuts of a woodcock cooked in a cast-iron casserole; moistened with the cooking juice, brandy and lemon juice

Bécasse à la riche ⇒ woodcock cooked in the oven, laid on a large slice of bread and forcemeat; covered with a sauce made of brandy, foie gras and butter

Bécasse de mer
- **orphie** ⇒ garfish
- **très petits rougets barbets surnommés bécasses de mer** ⇒ red mullet

Bécasse en casserole à la périgourdine ⇒ woodcock stuffed with a forcemeat of foie gras and truffles, cooked in a cast-iron casserole; moistened with armagnac

Bécasse en casserole ou en cocotte ⇒ woodcock cooked in a cast-iron casserole, moistened of stock flavoured with cognac

Bécasse en cocotte à la crème ⇒ woodcock stuffed with a forcemeat of foie gras and truffles, cooked in a cast-iron casserole; moistened with armagnac and cream

Bécasse froide à la diane ⇒ roasted woodcock cut in fillets, reconstituted with a forcemeat and truffles macerated in brandy; covered with a jelly of game

Bécasse rôtie sur canapé ⇒ larded woodcock, roasted on a high flame and laid on a canapé with a forcemeat of foie gras, butter, mustard, cognac, lemon juice, and egg-yolk

Bécasse sautée à l'armagnac ⇒ cuts of woodcock, cooked in a cast-iron casserole; covered with a purée made of armagnac, cooking juice, and cayenne-pepper

Bécasse sautée Brillat-Savarin ⇒ cuts of woodcock, cooked in a cast-iron casserole, laid on a flan paste; garnished with a culinary stuffing of truffles and foie gras

Bécasse truffée rôtie ⇒ woodcock stuffed with a forcemeat and truffles; cooked in the oven, moistened with cognac

Bécasseau ⇒ young woodcock < *pluriel inchangé* >

Bécassine ⇒ snipe < *pluriel inchangé* >

Beburi -[*fraise*]- ⇒ variety of fraise or variety of strawberry

Becfigue ⇒ warbler

Becfigue des eaux -[*Eperlan*]- ⇒ sea smelt

Becfigue en brochettes à la landaise ⇒ warbler, wrapped in vine-leaves and larded, then set on a skewer with sippets, and grilled basted of goose fat; served with grapes in armagnac

Becfigues poêlés ⇒ warblers seasoned and fried in butter

Becfigues rôtis ⇒ roasted warblers laid on sippets

Béchamel ⇒ béchamel sauce

Beef-tea ⇒ beef-tea

Beefalo ⇒ cross-breeding of bison and cow

Beefsteak ou Beef-steak ⇒ beefsteak or beef-steak

Beerenauslese *-[vin du Palatinat]-* ⇒ sweet white wine

Beguso *-[poisson]-* ⇒ sea bream

Beigne *-[beignet]-* ⇒ fritter

Beignet ⇒ fritter

Beignet venteux ⇒ fritter made with choux-pastry

Beignet viennois ⇒ fritter filled with apricot jam

Beignets d'oranges ⇒ fritters with bits of orange macerated in liquor

Beignets à l'ananas ⇒ fritters with slices of pineapple, plus sugar and rum

Beignets à l'imbrucciata ⇒ fritters of dough, with slices of Corsican ewe cheese

Beignets à la banane ⇒ fritters with bits of banana macerated in sugar and kirsch

Beignets à la confiture ⇒ fritters with thick jam macerated in kirsch

Beignets à la créole ⇒ fritters filled of dates stuffed with rice flavoured of curaçao

Beignets à la florentine ⇒ fritters filled with a spinach purée, thickened of béchamel sauce and grated cheese

Beignets alsaciens ⇒ fritters made of flour, sugar, butter milk and yeast; cooked in pork-fat

Beignets au riz ⇒ fritters made of rice cooked in milk; flavoured with rum or cognac and whipped eggs

Beignets aux abricots ⇒ fritters with apricots macerated in rum

Beignets aux cerises ⇒ fritters with cherries macerated in rum

Beignets aux fleurs d'acacia ⇒ fritters flavoured with acacia flowers

Beignets aux fraises ⇒ fritters with bits of fraise macerated in liquor

Beignets aux pommmes ⇒ fritters with slices of apple macerated in sugar and rum

Beignets aux pêches ⇒ fritters with peaches macerated in rum

Beignets belges ⇒ fritters of dough made with egg, sugar, cinnamon and butter; cut in squares

Beignets bernois ⇒ fritters filled with swiss cheese, ham and béchamel

Beignets d'anchois ⇒ fritters filled with anchovies, egg-yolks, butter and parsley

Beignets d'artichauts ⇒ fritters filled with pieces of artichoke macerated in lemon, pepper and oil

Beignets d'aubergines ⇒ fritters filled with aubergines marinated in oil, lemon juice, parsley, salt and pepper

Beignets d'huitres ⇒ fritters filled of poached oysters macerated in oil, lemon juice and pepper

Beignets de banane ⇒ fritters made of flour, mashed bananas, sugar, rum and cinnamon

Beignets de bouillie ⇒ fritters made of dough prepared with flour, eggs, milk, sugar and lemon juice

Beignets de cervelle ⇒ fritters filled with poached brains marinated in oil, parsley and lemon juice

Beignets de champignons ⇒ fritters filled with mushrooms, egg-yolks, butter and parsley

Beignets de dattes ⇒ fritters filled of dates, plus custard flavoured with kirsch

Beignets de figues ⇒ fritters filled with figs macerated in eau de vie

Beignets de foie de raie ⇒ fritters filled of skate's liver marinated in salt, pepper, oil, and lemon juice

Beignets de foie de volailles ⇒ fritters filled of poultry's liver, egg-yolks, butter and parsley

Beignets de foie gras à l'ancienne ⇒ fritters filled with pancake covered of foie gras and truffles; flavoured with brandy

Beignets de fromage ⇒ fritters filled of béchamel sauce thickened with grated cheese, parsley and pepper

Beignets de gourilos ⇒ fritters filled of endives macerated in oil, lemon juice and pepper
Beignets de laitances ⇒ fritters filled of poached soft roes marinated in oil, lemon juice, pepper, and parsley
Beignets de langoustines ⇒ fritters filled of poached Norway lobsters macerated in oil, plus lemon juice
Beignets de langue ⇒ fritters filled of oxtongue macerated in oil, pepper and parsley
Beignets de pomme de terre ⇒ fritters made of mashed potatoes, salt, butter and egg
Beignets de ris de veau ⇒ fritters filled of calf sweetbread; served with lemon and tomato purée
Beignets de salsifis ⇒ fritters filled with salsify, egg-yolks, butter and parsley
Beignets de sardines ⇒ fritters filled with sardines
Beignets de saumon au coulis de pommes ⇒ fritters of egg-yolks, cream, maïzena, cider and diced salmon; served with an apple purée
Beignets de semoule ⇒ fritters filled with semolina sweet, plus raisins in rum
Beignets en couronne ⇒ fritters made of flour, salt, sugar, egg and butter
Beignets mont-bry ⇒ fritters filled of apricot jam diluted in rum, plus a culinary stuffing of nuts and figs
Beignets nanette ⇒ fritters filled of slices of bun covered with a cream, plus a culinary stuffing of raisins macerated in kirsch
Beignets secs ⇒ fritters made of eggs, cream, salt, kirsch, sugar and flour
Beignets soufflés
    a) aux anchois ⇒ fritters made of choux-pastry and diced anchovy fillets
    b) à la hongroise ⇒ fritters made of choux pastry, braised onions, and paprika
    c) au fromage ⇒ fritters made of choux pastry, grated parmesan, and nutmeg
    d) à la toscane ⇒ fritters made of choux pastry, ham, and white truffle
Beignets soufflés à la toscane ⇒ fritters made of choux-pastry, parmesan, ham and truffles
Beignets soufflés fourrés aux cerises ⇒ fritters filled of cherries in syrup, flavoured with kirsch
Bélier ⇒ ram
Bel Paese -[fromage]- ⇒ Bel Paese
Belle angevine -[poire]- ⇒ variety of pear
Belle de Boskoop -[pomme]- ⇒ variety of apple
Belle-Hélène
    1) tournedos ⇒ grilled tournedos with a garnish of potatoes shredded in straw and fried, plus watercress, and mushrooms filled with supreme sauce
    2) suprêmes de volailles sautés ⇒ chicken in supreme sauce laid on asparagus croquettes, topped with truffle lamella
    3) grosses pièces sautées ⇒ ... served with a garnish of grilled mushrooms filled with crushed tomatoes, peas in butter, shaped carrots and potato-croquettes
    4) entremets ⇒ sweet of fruits, ou nom anglais du fruit, poached in syrup and chilled, then laid on vanilla ice-cream; covered with chocolate sauce
Bellet -[fromage]- ⇒ Provencal cheese
Bellet -[vin]- ⇒ Provencal wine from Nice area
Bellevue
    1) général -[crustacé, poisson, volaille]- ⇒ ... in jelly
    2) homard ⇒ lobster
      - **langouste** ⇒ spiny lobster, thin slices of ... in jelly
    3) bécasse ⇒ woodcock
      - **caille** ⇒ quail
      - **grive** ⇒ thruh ... stuffed and poached in game stock, then chilled and covered of chaudfroid sauce plus jelly

Bellevue (en ...)
    1) général -[*crustacé, poisson, volaille*]- ⇒ ... in jelly
    2) homard ⇒ lobster
        - langouste ⇒ spiny lobster ... thin slices of ... in jelly
    3) bécasse ⇒ woodcock
        - caille ⇒ quail
        - grive ⇒ thrush ... stuffed and poached in game stock, then chilled and covered of chaudfroid sauce plus jelly
Belon ⇒ Belon oyster
Bélouga -[*caviar*]- ⇒ beluga caviar
Belrubi -[*fraise*]- ⇒ variety of fraise or variety of strawberry
Béluga -[*caviar*]- ⇒ beluga caviar
Bénédictine (à la ...)
    - avec morue et pommes de terre ⇒ ... served with a purée of salt cod and potatoes
    - avec morue ⇒ ... served with mashed salt cod
Bénédictine -[*liqueur*]- ⇒ Benedictine liqueur
Bengale -[*thé*]- ⇒ variety of tea
Bengkuang -[*Indonésie*]- ⇒ kind of big turnip
Benincase ⇒ kind of gourd
Benoiton -[*pain*]- ⇒ buckwheat bread added of currants
Beoerewors -[*Afrique du sud*]- ⇒ beef sausages
Bequis ⇒ biscuits
Berdonneau -[*poisson*]- ⇒ turbot < *pluriel inchangé* >
Bergamote
    - poire ⇒ bergamot pear
    - orange ⇒ bergamot citrus
    - sucre d'orge ⇒ barley sugar
Bergerac ⇒ high quality sweet wine from Bergerac area
Bergerette -[*fromage*]- ⇒ goat's milk cheese
Bergeron -[*abricot*]- ⇒ variety of apricot
Bergues -[*fromage*]- ⇒ Flemish's cheese
Berle -[*chervis*]- ⇒ skirret or water-parsnip
Berline ⇒ fritter made of flour, butter, eggs, yeast and milk, stuffed of jam or almond paste; served hot with egg-custard, or a sauce made of apricot pulp, syrup and brandy
Berliner weisse -[*bière*]- ⇒ white beer from Berlin
Berlingolette -[*Poitou*]- ⇒ cracknel
Berlingot -[*bonbon*]- ⇒ humburg sweet
Bernacle ⇒ barnacle
Bernardht (Sarah ...) -[*criste marine*]- ⇒ Crithmum or rock samphire
Bernique ⇒ limpet
Berny
    1) croquettes ⇒ croquettes of potatoes, coated with almonds and fried
    2) garniture de gibier ⇒ ... served with a garnish made of potato croquettes, and tartlets filled with mashed lentils
Berrichonne (à la ...)
    1) grosses pièces de boucherie ⇒ ... with a garnish of braised cabbage, poached chestnuts, onions and bacon

2) fricassée de poulet ⇒ chicken fricassee; served with a garnish of carrots and potatoes cooked with onions plus lardoons

Besugo ⇒ sea bream < *pluriel inchangé* >

Besugo de noil ⇒ sea bream stuffed of chopped capsicum, sprinkled of oil flavoured with garlic, and grilled

Bétel ⇒ betel

Bête de compagnie ⇒ wild boar

Bête rousse -*[sanglier]*- ⇒ young wild boar

Bêtise -*[bêtises de cambrai ou sottises de valenciennes]*- ⇒ sweet made of cooked sugar flavoured with mint

Bette ⇒ beet

Bettelman ⇒ small cake of crumbs steeped in milk with vanilla, sugar, egg-yolks, preserved orange, eggs, stoned cherries, kirsch, and cinnamon

Betterave ⇒ beetroot

Betteraves à l'anglaise ⇒ slices of beetroots, cooked and served with butter

Betteraves à la crème ⇒ cooked beetroots, sliced and steamed in butter; served with warmed cream

Betteraves à la lyonnaise ⇒ cooked beetroots, sliced and steamed in butter plus onions; served with stock thickened of butter

Betteraves en salade à la polonaise ⇒ slices of cooked beetroots, served in a french dressing with chopped hard-boiled eggs and parsley

Bettes à l'italienne ⇒ beets simmered in an Italian sauce, seasoned and covered with basil

Bettes à la béchamel ⇒ sauté beets with béchamel sauce

Bettes à la crème ⇒ beets cooked in butter and cream

Bettes à la polonaise ⇒ cooked beets, served with chopped hard-boiled eggs and parsley

Bettes au beurre ⇒ beets sautéed in butter

Bettes au gratin ⇒ beets prepared in béchamel sauce, sprinkled with grated cheese and melted butter, then browned

Bettes au gratin au verjus ⇒ dish of beets, whipped cream, unripe grape juice, egg-yolks, parsley, and pepper; covered with grated cheese, then browned

Bettes au jus ⇒ beets simmered in stock; served with the cooking juice and butter

Beugnet ⇒ apple fritter

Beugnon -*[beignet]*- ⇒ fritter shaped in ring

Beugnon -*[vin]*- ⇒ Chablis wine

Beurre -*[haricot vert]*- ⇒ french bean

Beurre

    - nom ⇒ butter < *uncountable* >

    - verbe ⇒ buttered < *v.t adjectif* >

Beurre à la bourguignonne ⇒ composed butter added of chopped shallots, parsley and garlic

Beurre à la colbert ⇒ parsley butter added of meat juice and tarragon

Beurre bercy ⇒ poached bone-marrow mixed with shallots, white wine, butter and pepper

Beurre blanc ⇒ vinegar and chopped shallots added of butter

Beurre chivry ⇒ butter mixed with herbs

Beurre composé

    1) général ⇒ composed butter

    2) froid pour viandes et poissons grillés, allumettes ⇒ cold butter added with ... < *autres ingredients* >

        - anchois ⇒ anchovy

        - ail ⇒ garlic

        - échalote ⇒ shallot

        - estragon ⇒ tarragon

        - raifort ⇒ horse-radish

        - moelle pochée ⇒ poached bone-marrow

        - champignons hachés ⇒ chopped mushrooms

3) **chaud pour certaines sauces telles que beurre cardinal** ⇒ melted butter added of crushed lobster carapace, then sieved

  - **beurre Nantua** ⇒ melted butter added of crushed crayfish carapace, then sieved

Beurre d'ail ⇒ mashed garlic mixed with butter

Beurre d'amandes ⇒ powdered almonds mixed with butter

Beurre d'anchois ⇒ anchovy paste

Beurre d'escargot ⇒ composed butter added of chopped shallots, parsley, and garlic

Beurre d'estragon ⇒ tarragon butter

Beurre d'échalote ⇒ poached bone-marrow mixed with shallots, white wine, butter, and pepper

Beurre d'écrevisses ⇒ crayfish paste

Beurre d'érable ⇒ butter from maple syrup

Beurre de cacahouètes ⇒ peanut butter

Beurre de cacao ⇒ cocoa butter

Beurre de crevettes ⇒ shrimp paste

Beurre de Gascogne *(pour accompagner les grillades, apprêts panés et les légumes à l'anglaise ...)* ⇒ paste of veal fat, and mashed garlic

Beurre de homard ⇒ composed butter added of lobster's eggs orlobster butter

Beurre de karité ⇒ butter from tropical fruit

Beurre de mangoustan *-[beurre de kokum]-* ⇒ mangosteen seed paste

Beurre de Montpellier ⇒ paste of butter, parsley, chervil, cress, chives, spinach, shallots, gherkins, capers, anchovy fillet, garlic, and egg-yolk

Beurre de muscade ⇒ nutmeg paste

Beurre de noix de coco ⇒ coconut butter

Beurre de pistache ⇒ pistachio paste

Beurre de poivron rouge ⇒ red pepper cooked slowly in olive oil

Beurre de pomme ⇒ apple sauce

Beurre demi-sel ⇒ slightly salted butter

Beurre doux ⇒ unsalted butter

Beurre en pommade ⇒ butter whipped in paste

Beurre fondu ⇒ melted butter

Beurre marchand de vin ⇒ butter added of shallots, red wine, consommé, parsley, and lemon juice

Beurre maitre d'hotel ⇒ butter kneaded with parsley or parsley butter

Beurre mousseux ⇒ frothy butter

Beurre noir ⇒ browned butter added of capers, chopped parsley and vinegar

Beurre noisette ⇒ butter cooked lightly

Beurre ravigote ⇒ composed butter with chopped shallots, herbs and mustard

Beurre rose ⇒ butter added of cream and compote of bilberries

Beurre salé ⇒ salted butter

Beurre vert ⇒ butter added of spinach juice

Beurreck ⇒ fritters made of béchamel sauce and cheese quenelles, wrapped in batter

Beurré *-[beurre]-* ⇒ buttered < *v.t adjectif* >

Beurré-hardy *-[poire]-* ⇒ variety of pear

Beurrée *-[laitue]-* ⇒ variety of lettuce

Beursaudes ⇒ cooked pieces of pork fat, salted and chilled

Bi-thanh ⇒ steamed gourd hollowed out, filled with chicken, lotus seeds, mushrooms, ham, crab and ginger

Bibace *-[nèfle du Japon]-* ⇒ Japanese medlar

Bibasse *-[nèfle du Japon]-* ⇒ Japanese medlar

Biche ⇒ female deer < *pluriel inchangé* >

Bichof
    1) général ⇒ drink made of wine, citrus and spices
        - **Liqueur d'évêque** ⇒ drink made of Bordeaux wine, citrus and spices
        - **Liqueur de cardinal** ⇒ drink made of white wine, citrus and spices
    2) Bichof classique *(ou Bishop à l'anglaise ...)* ⇒ bishop or drink made of sugar in syrup,
            orange and lemon peel, cinnamon, clove, plus Bordeaux wine
Biden *-[Afrique du sud]-* ⇒ South African vegetable
Bierküse *-[Weisslücker]-* ⇒ cubic German cow's milk cheese
Bierwurst ⇒ variety of sausage
Bife com batatas ⇒ steak covered with mashed garlic and pepper; served with grilled ham and sauté
            potatoes
Bifteck ⇒ beefsteak or steak
Bifteck à l'allemande ⇒ hamburger
Bifteck à l'américaine ⇒ chopped beef meat, egg-yolk and seasoning
Bifteck à l'andalouse ⇒ steak of chopped beef meat, onion and garlic, cooked in oil; served on sauté
            tomatoes, plus rice, and sprinkled with xeres
Bifteck à l'hambourgeoise ⇒ hamburger
Bifteck de cheval ⇒ horse-meat steak
Bifteck de cheval ⇒ horse-meat < *utilisé seul est uncountable* >
Bifteck haché ⇒ hamburger
Bifteck poitevin ⇒ hamburger thickened with bone-marrow, eggs, crumbs, onions, and white wine
Bigarade
    - **fruit** ⇒ Seville orange or bitter orange
    - **garniture** ⇒ garnished with bitter orange
Bigarreau *-[cerise]-* ⇒ cherry
Bigeye *-[thon]-* ⇒ tunny
Bigne *-[beignet]-* ⇒ fritter
Bignet *-[beignet]-* ⇒ fritter
Bignon *-[beignet]-* ⇒ fritter shaped in ring
Bigorneau ⇒ winkle
Bigos ⇒ sauerkraut first boiled with apples and onions, then cooked in the oven on alternate layers of
            pork fat and meat, moistened with the cooking stock
Bigoudens ⇒ flat cakes made of flour, sugar, cream, butter, eggs, chopped almonds, and eau de vie
Bijane *-[Anjou]-* ⇒ soup from Anjou recipe
Bikaver *-[vin]-* ⇒ Hungarian red wine
Billy by ⇒ mussels cooked in white wine with onions, parsley, celery and fish stock
Biltong ⇒ dried meat from beef, mutton or antelope
Bilva *-[aeglé]-* ⇒ Indian grapefruit
Birchermuesli ⇒ mixing of cereals, dried fruits and fresh fruits, sprinkled with milk
Bireweck ⇒ bread added of fruits
Birthday cake ⇒ birthday cake
Biscotte ⇒ rusk or zwieback
Biscottes de Pons ⇒ rusks
Biscottin ⇒ Provencal pastry
Biscottin ⇒ pastry from Aix
Biscuit ⇒ biscuit
Biscuit à l'italienne ⇒ cake made of sugar, vanilla sugar, egg-yolks, flour and fecula; cooked in the
            oven

Biscuit aux amandes ⇒ cake made of sugar, vanilla sugar, egg-yolks, flour and almonds; filled with raspberry jelly

Biscuit complet ⇒ Graham crackers

Biscuit glacé
1) **glace** ⇒ dessert shaped in brick and made of layers from different ice creams
2) **gâteau** ⇒ gateau shaped in ring or square made of meringue and sorbet; decorated with whipped cream, preserved fruits and chocolate vermicelli

Biscuit mousseline ⇒ sponge cake

Biscuit mousseline à l'orange ⇒ cake filled with a layer of curaçao and marmalade; covered of marmalade

Biscuit roulé ⇒ almond biscuit sprinkled with syrup, covered of apricot jam and rolled; decorated with grilled almonds

Biscuit sec ⇒ biscuit

Biscuits à la cuillère ⇒ sponge fingers

Biscuits au cassis ⇒ cake made of sponge-biscuits steeped in a syrup and redcurrant liqueur, mixed with a whipped cream

Biscuits au citron ⇒ small cakes made of sugar, eggs, lemon peel, flour and fecula; baked in the oven

Biscuits d'avoine ⇒ oatcakes

Biscuits de Reims ⇒ small sticks made of whipped eggs and granulated sugar, plus flour and vanilla sugar

Biscuits de dames ⇒ biscuits made of flour, butter, sugar, eggs, yeast, vanilla powder, plus currants macerated in rum

Biscuits de savoie ⇒ cake made of sugar, vanilla, egg-yolks, flour, fecula, whipped white of eggs; cooked in the oven

Biscuits fins ⇒ small cakes made of dough, plus a culinary stuffing of orange peel

Biscuits genevois ⇒ small cakes made of sugar, lemon peel, eggs, butter, crushed almonds and flour; cooked in the oven

Biscuits italiens ⇒ small cakes made of sugar, eggs and flour; cooked in the oven

Biscuits punch ⇒ small cakes made of semolina, eggs, rum, flour and butter; flavoured with orange and lemon extract

Biscuits soufflés au chocolat ⇒ macaroons made of chocolate, eggs and sugar; baked in the oven

Bishop à l'anglaise ⇒ bishop

Bismarck -*[hareng]*- ⇒ herring marinated in vinegar and aromatics

Bison ⇒ bison

Bisque ⇒ bisque

Bisque d'écrevisses ⇒ crayfishes sautéed in a mixture of diced vegetables and ham, then peppered and flamed with cognac; garnished of mashed rice, cooked in stock or crayfish bisque

Bisque de homards ⇒ lobsters sautéed in a mixture of diced vegetables and ham, then peppered and flamed with cognac; garnished of mashed rice cooked in stock or lobster bisque

Bisque de langoustines ⇒ Norway lobsters sautéed in a mixture of diced vegetables and ham, then peppered and flamed with cognac; garnished of mashed rice cooked in stock or Norway lobster bisque

Bistecca ⇒ entrecôte steak grilled with olive oil

Bistorto -*[Roussillon]*- ⇒ brioche shaped in ring

Bistouille ⇒ mixing of coffee and eau de vie

Bistrouille ⇒ mixing of coffee and eau de vie

Bitoke ⇒ preparation of chopped beef meat, butter, pepper, grated nutmeg, sautéed in butter; served with fried onions and sauté potatoes

Bitter -*[boissons]*- ⇒ bitters drinks

Bière ⇒ beer < *uncountable* >
Bière à la pression ⇒ draught beer
   - un verre de bière à la pression ⇒ a glass of draught beer
Bière de mil ⇒ millet beer
Black bass ⇒ black bass
Black pudding ⇒ black pudding
Black velvet *-[cocktail]-* ⇒ black velvet
Blaff ⇒ marinated fish, simmered in a court-bouillon with onion, thyme, parsley and clove; served with rice and red beans
Blagny ⇒ red wine from Côte de Beaune
Blanc *(à ...)*
   1) croûtes cuites à vide pour garniture ultérieure pour vol-au-vent ⇒ case
     - en forme ⇒ pastry boat
   2) désigne souvent cuisson au blanc ⇒ voir au blanc
Blanc *(au ...)* ⇒ cooked in a court-bouillon of water and flour
Blanc
   - viande ⇒ white meat
   - poisson ⇒ fish fillet
Blanc cassis ⇒ blackcurrant liqueur mixed with dry white wine
Blanc d'oeuf ⇒ white of egg
Blanc de blanc *-[vin]-* ⇒ white wine made only of white grapes
Blanc de champignons ⇒ stock made of butter, lemon juice, salt and mushrooms
Blanc de cuisson ⇒ stock made of water, flour, and lemon
Blanc de noirs *-[vin]-* ⇒ white wine made of white and black grapes
Blanc de poulet ⇒ white meat or breast of chicken
Blanc de turbot ⇒ turbot fillet
Blanc de volaille ⇒ white meat < *uncountable* >
Blanc de volaille farçi de boursin ⇒ white meat stuffed with Boursin cheese
Blanc manger *(entremets sucré ...)* ⇒ almond jelly or blanc-mange
Blanc pour abats et viandes ⇒ stock made of flour, water, salt, kidney suet, carrot, onion and clove
Blanc pour légumes ⇒ stock made of flour, water, salt and kidney suet
Blanchaille ⇒ whitebait < *uncountable* >
Blanchots *-[Chablis]-* ⇒ high quality Chablis wines
Blancos *-[vin]-* ⇒ Spanish white wines
Blancs de pintade aux pommes de terre Alex-Humbert ⇒ white meat of guinea-fowl cooked in a cast-iron casserole, with butter, chopped shallots and breadcrumbs; served with potatoes in butter
Blancs de st pierre au velouté de whisky servi avec sa julienne de légumes ⇒ john dory fillets, cooked in the oven with shallots, butter, white wine, whisky and cream; served with potatoes and julienne
Blanquette de Limoux ⇒ effervescent white wine from Limoux
Blanquette de langoustines et de lotte aux artichauts ⇒ blanquette of Norway lobsters and angler, with artichokes
Blanquettes de filets de soles ⇒ blanquette of sole fillets
Blarney *-[fromage]-* ⇒ Blarney
Blatina rouge ⇒ Yugoslavian red wines
Blended *-[bourbon; thé]-*
   - bourbon ⇒ mixing of straight and alcohol
   - thé ⇒ mixing of several varieties of tea

Blended scotch whisky ⇒ blended scotch whisky
Bleu *(au ...)*
   - **général** ⇒ cooked in red wine
   - **Bleu d'Auvergne** ⇒ bleu d'auvergne
   - **poisson** ⇒ fresh fish cooked in a vinegar court-bouillon
Bleu *-[fromage]-* ⇒ blue cheese
Bleu d'Auvergne *-[fromage]-* ⇒ bleu d'auvergne
Blé noir ⇒ buckwheat
Bloater *-[hareng]-* ⇒ bloater
Bloater *-[corégone]-* ⇒ whitefish
Blondir ⇒ to turn golden
Bloody mary *-[cocktail]-* ⇒ bloody Mary
Bloody red ⇒ variety of grapefruit
Blue Vinny *-[fromage]-* ⇒ Blue Vinny
Blue cheddar ⇒ blue cheddar
Blue cheshire ⇒ blue cheshire
Bluefin *-[thon]-* ⇒ tunny
Boal *-[madère]-* ⇒ Madeira wine
Boboti ⇒ chopped beef added of spices, onions, and almonds; baked with whipped eggs
Bochyn ⇒ Russian drink based on raisins, yeast, whey, sugar, and hop extract
Bock ⇒ quarter-litre glass of beer
Bockbier ⇒ strong German beer
Bockwurst ⇒ German sausage
Bodrost ⇒ Russian drink made of whey, sugar and raisins; flavoured with burnt sugar, and beetroot juice
Boeuf à la diable ⇒ slices of boiled beef steeped in mustard, breadcrumbs and melted butter; then grilled
Boeuf à la mode ⇒ larded beef macerated in cognac, spices, red wine, olive oil, onions, sliced carrots and garlic; cooked in stock and its marinade with boned calf trotter, plus strips from rind of pork or stewed beef with carrots
Boeuf à la mode de beaucaire ⇒ dish made with layers of streaky bacon, plus slices of beef studded with lardoons and marinated in vinegar, onion, cognac, plus olive oil; cooked with red wine, capers and clove
Boeuf bouilli ⇒ bones of beef, beef's meat and vegetables cooked together; served with coarse salt, gherkins and mustard
Boeuf braisé ⇒ beef roasted first, then braised with onions, carrots, necks of pullet, pig trotter, tomatoes, white wine, and stock
Boeuf braisé à la créole ⇒ diced beef studded of lardoons, marinated in spices and cognac; then braised with pork fat, onions, tomato purée, crushed garlic, thyme, parsley and saffron
Boeuf braisé à la guardiane ⇒ larded beef, braised in olive oil with onions, garlic, cloves, nutmeg, basil, laurel, rosemary, thyme and savoy
Boeuf braisé Dumaine ⇒ beef roasted first, then braised with onions, carrots, necks of pullet, pork's trotter, tomatoes, white wine, red wine and stock
Boeuf braisé Porte Maillot ⇒ beef studded with lard lamellas, marinated in oil, cognac, herbs, chopped garlic and pepper; braised in white wine, marinade stock, turnips, carrots, and served with french beans
Boeuf cuit ⇒ pressed boiled beef
Boeuf gros sel ⇒ bones of beef, beef's meat and vegetables cooked together; served with coarse salt, gherkins and mustard
Boeuf haché *-[viande hachée]-* ⇒ mince beef

Boeuf miroton ⇒ slices of boiled beef covered with a sauce made of steamed onions, flour, vinegar and white wine; then browned

Boeuf pressé ⇒ pressed beef

Boeuf salé ⇒ pickled beef cooked in water and served with cabbage, or sauerkraut, or other vegetable

Boeuf stroganov ⇒ beef lamellas marinated in white wine, onions, shallots, carrot, laurel and thyme; then sautéed and served with sauté mushrooms, plus a sauce made with the marinade added of cream

Bogue -*[poisson]*- ⇒ bogue

Bogue -*[chataigne]*- ⇒ chestnut burr

Bohémienne ⇒ ratatouille

Bohémienne *(à la ...)*

- **Oeufs mollets à la bohémienne ou Oeufs pochés à la bohémienne** ⇒ poached eggs on foie gras croustade, covered of velouté sauce and topped with a julienne of ham in Madeira
- **Poulet sauté à la bohémienne** ⇒ chicken sprinkled of paprika and sautéed in oil, cooked with capsicums, tomatoes, onion, fennel and garlic; served with the gravy thickened of white wine, stock and lemon juice, accompanied with rice
- **Salpicon à la bohémienne** ⇒ culinary stuffing of foie gras, truffles, Madeira sauce, butter and paprika
- **utilisé pour garnir bouchées** ⇒ patties
- **croustades** ⇒ croustades
- **œufs pochés** ⇒ poached eggs
- **tartelettes** ⇒ tartlets
- **Sauce à la bohémienne** ⇒ béchamel sauce added of egg-yolks, oil, and vinegar flavoured with tarragon

Boichée ⇒ gingerbread

Boichet ⇒ gingerbread

Bois d'Inde ⇒ Caribbean wood

Boisson gratuite -*[réception]*- ⇒ a free drink

Boisson marquise ⇒ drink made of sugar, water, white wine, soda water, and slices of lemon

Bol ⇒ bowl

- **bol rempli** ⇒ bowlful

Bolet -*[cèpe]*- ⇒ boletus

Bolet à chair jaune ⇒ red cracked boletus

Bolet annulaire ⇒ brown-yellow boletus

Bolet blafard ⇒ lurid boletus

Bolet bronzé ⇒ edible black boletus

Bolet granulé ⇒ granulated boletus

Bolet orangé ⇒ orange cap boletus

Bolet rude ⇒ shaggy boletus

Bolet élégant ⇒ elegant boletus

Bolée -*[ou moque]*- ⇒ mug

Bolée -*[cidre]*- ⇒ cider bowlful

Bollito misto ⇒ pot-au-feu of various meat and vegetables; served with cucumbers, capers, onions in vinegar, salad and mustard

Bolognaise *(à la ...)* ⇒ with bolognèse sauce

Bombe Alhambra ⇒ ice-pudding of strawberries, coated of an icing flavoured with vanilla; decorated of strawberries macerated in kirsch

Bombe archiduc ⇒ praline paste coated with an icing of strawberries

Bombe bourdaloue ⇒ anisette ice-pudding, coated with an icing of vanilla

Bombe cardinal ⇒ praline paste flavoured of vanilla; coated with an icing of strawberries

Bombe Chateaubriand ⇒ vanilla ice-pudding, and crystallized fruits macerated in maraschino; coated with an icing of apricot

Bombe de kirsch ⇒ spherical bottle of kirsch

Bombe diplomate ⇒ maraschino ice-pudding, plus macerated crystallized fruits; coated with an icing of vanilla

Bombe Doria ⇒ vanilla ice-pudding, mixed with chestnut bits macerated in rum; coated with an icing of pistachio

Bombe Grimaldi ⇒ kümmel ice-pudding, coated with an icing of vanilla

Bombe Monselet ⇒ ice-pudding made of port, plus orange peel macerated in brandy; coated with an icing of tangerine

Bombe duchesse ⇒ pear ice-pudding, coated with an icing of pineapple

Bombe glacée au yaourt ⇒ ice-pudding made of beans, sugar, vanilla, yoghourt and honey; served with a purée of strawberries, plus pears macerated in wine and sugar

Bombe glacée montmorency ⇒ cherry-brandy ice-pudding, mixed with cherries macerated in kirsch; coated with an icing of kirsch

Bombe tutti frutti ⇒ tutti-frutti ice-pudding ½ ou ½ elaborated ice-pudding based on crystallized fruits and kirsch; coated with an icing of pineapple

Bombine ⇒ roast of pork cooked with stock, onions, potatoes and garlic; served with grilled black pudding and dried sausage

Bondard ⇒ cylindrical cheese

Bondart ⇒ cylindrical cheese

Bonde ⇒ cylindrical cheese

Bondon ⇒ cylindrical cheese

Bondon de Neuchâtel ⇒ cylindrical cheese

Bonne femme ⇒ without sophisticated recipe ou simmered dish of ...

Bontemps ⇒ cider and mustard sauce

Borasus -[*ou Rônier]*- ⇒ Asian palm tree

Borchtch ⇒ borscht or borsch or bortsch < *tous uncountable* >

Borchtch ukrainien ⇒ Ukrainian borscht

Bordelaise *(à la ...)*

- **poissons et viandes** ⇒ ... with white wine sauce

- **viande rouge** ⇒ ... with red wine sauce

Bordure ⇒ edging

Bordure d'oeufs Brillat-Savarin ⇒ forcemeat of veal shaped in an edge, filled with scrambled eggs and truffles, sprinkled of grated cheese, then browned in the oven

Bordure d'oeufs princesse ⇒ forcemeat of veal shaped in an edge, filled with scrambled eggs and bits of asparagus or shrimps, sprinkled of grated parmesan, then browned

Bordure de cervelle à la piémontaise ⇒ risotto cooked in an edge-mould; served with calf brains and mushrooms

Bordure de farce de poisson

    1) au ragoût de fruits de mer ⇒ forcemeat of whiting poached on an edge-mould; served with a ragout of mussels, oysters, clams, scallops, Norway lobsters, and sauté mushrooms

    2) aux médaillons de homard à l'américaine ⇒ forcemeat of whiting poached in an edge-mould; served with round slices of lobster

Bordure de farce de veau

    1) à la cervelle de veau ⇒ forcemeat of veal cooked in an edge-mould; served with calf brains and mushrooms

2) aux amourettes ⇒ forcemeat of veal cooked in an edge-mould; served with amourettes and mushrooms

Bordure de riz à la créole ⇒ rice or risotto cooked in an edge-mould, filled with slices of pineapple in syrup and angelica

Bordure de riz à la montmorency ⇒ rice cooked in an edge-mould, filled with custard flavoured of kirsch, and cherries poached in syrup, then sprinkled of crushed macaroons

Bordure de riz garnie ⇒ rice or risotto cooked in an edge-mould, filled with a ragout of shellfishes, poultry, offal, slices of lobster and shrimps

Bordure de semoule aux fruits ⇒ semolina plus a culinary stuffing of preserved fruits cooked in an edge-mould, filled with fruits poached in syrup; flavoured of rum or kirsch

Bordures de sole à la normande ⇒ forcemeat of fish and cream poached in an edge-mould, filled with a ragout of shellfishes plus a sauce; served with sole fillets poached in white wine

Bori-bori ⇒ Uruguayan stew of meat, vegetables, cheese, and corn

Bosaka ⇒ cockerel fried in palm oil

Bossons macérés ⇒ goat's milk cheeses macerated in olive oil, white wine, marc and aromatics

Boterkoek ⇒ cake based on butter

Botermelk *(ou lait battu ...)* ⇒ preparation of milk, pearl barley, brown sugar, honey and dried fruits

Botillon ⇒ bunch or bundle

Botte ⇒ bunch or bundle

Bottereaux ⇒ fritters shaped in square or lozenge, flavoured with eau de vie or liquor

Botvinia ⇒ cold soup made of beet leaves, spinach and sorrel, garnished either of cucumbers or smoked fish

Boubliki ⇒ Russian bread

Boucan

    1) viande séchée ⇒ smoked meat

    2) cuisine créole ⇒ mutton stuffed with duck and bird meat, onions plus spices; cooked on charcoal

Boucanage

    1) général ⇒ process for the smoking of meat

    2) produits, brésil ⇒ smoked beef served in lamellas

       - charqui *(le ...)* ⇒ smoked beef or mutton or llama served in lamellas

       - pasterma ⇒ smoked mutton

Boucaud *(crevette grise ...)* ⇒ shrimp

Bouché *(cidre, vin ...)*

    - vin ⇒ bottled wine

    - cidre ⇒ bottled cider

Bouchée à la dieppoise ⇒ patty filled with mussels, shrimps and a white wine sauce

Bouchée au chocolat ⇒ sweet filled or wrapped with chocolate

    - variantes régionales ⇒ cabaches de châlons, chardons des alpes, granits de Semur en auxois, guignes de Bordeaux, joyaux de Bourgogne, mojettes du poitou, quernoux d'Angers, muscadins Nantais

Bouchée fourrée au chocolat ⇒ sweet filled or wrapped with chocolate

    - variantes régionales ⇒ cabaches de châlons, chardons des alpes, granits de Semur en auxois, guignes de Bordeaux, joyaux de Bourgogne, mojettes du poitou, quernoux d'Angers, muscadins Nantais

Bouchée salée ⇒ patty with a garnish of culinary stuffing; served hot

Bouchée sucrée ⇒ petit four garnished with custard or jam

Bouchées à l'abricot ⇒ patties made of sugar, eggs, flour, melted butter and rum, then baked; filled with apricot jam and topped of grilled almonds

Bouchées à l'américaine ⇒ puff-pastry patties, filled with a culinary stuffing of lobster or crawfish or monkfish

Bouchées à la bouquetière ⇒ patties, filled with vegetable salad and béchamel sauce

Bouchées à la bénédictine ⇒ puff-pastry patties, garnished with salt cod and truffles

Bouchées à la financière ⇒ puff-pastry patties, filled with a culinary stuffing of veal, chicken's cockscombs and kidneys, plus mushrooms

Bouchées à la julienne

1) **légumes** ⇒ puff-pastry patties, filled with a julienne of early spring vegetables thickened in cream

2) **légumes et jambon** ⇒ puff-pastry patties, filled with a julienne of vegetables thickened in cream, plus diced ham

Bouchées à la moelle ⇒ puff-pastry patties, filled with diced bone-marrow poached in a court-bouillon, thickened with Madeira sauce

Bouchées à la périgourdine ⇒ puff-pastry patties, filled of a culinary stuffing of foie gras and truffles, thickened with Madeira sauce

Boucles aux champignons ⇒ puff-pastry patties, filled with morels in cream or a culinary stuffing of mushrooms thickened of cream

Bouchées aux crevettes ⇒ puff-pastry patties, filled with a ragout of crayfish tails

Bouchées aux fruits de mer ⇒ puff-pastry patties, filled with a ragout of shellfishes

Bouchées aux laitances ⇒ puff-pastry patties, filled of soft roes poached in a court-bouillon and thickened with cream

Bouchées aux écrevisses à la Nantua ⇒ puff-pastry patties, filled with a ragout of crayfish tails, plus béchamel sauce added of mashed crayfishes, cognac, and cayenne pepper

Bouchées d'huîtres à la Denis ⇒ puff-pastry patties, filled with foie gras and an oyster

Bouchées de lotte au chou nouveau ⇒ angler fish fillets wrapped in cabbage leaves, then steamed in a court-bouillon of herbs, tarragon, fennel and thyme; served with a sauce based on tomatoes, capsicums and lemon juice

Bouchère *(à la ...)*

1) **consommé au chou émincé** ⇒ cabbage consommé served with slices of bone marrow

2) **oeufs mollets** ⇒ soft boiled eggs served with slices of poached bone marrow

3) **oeufs pochés** ⇒ poached eggs served with slices of poached bone marrow

4) **omelette** ⇒ omelette filled with diced bone marrow

5) **côtes de veau** ⇒ veal ribs macerated in oil and grilled, served with vegetables in season

Bouchot *-[moule de]-* ⇒ bred mussel

Boucs ou crevettes grises ⇒ shrimps or brown shrimps or common shrimps

Boudin d'écrevisses ⇒ crayfish polony

Boudin du Poitou ⇒ black porridge

Boudin *-[forme]-* ⇒ roll

Boudin antillais ⇒ polony made of pork's blood, crushed bread, milk, chopped onions braised in pork fat, chopped garlic, pimento, chives and pepper; poached in water

Boudin aux pruneaux ⇒ white pudding baked with stoned dried plums

Boudin blanc grillé ⇒ grilled white pudding; served with creamed potatoes or compote of apples or mashed celery

Boudin de volaille à la Richelieu ⇒ small puddings made of chicken's forcemeat, served with supreme sauce

Boudin noir à la normande ⇒ slices of apples plus bits of black pudding sautéed in butter

Boudoir ⇒ variety of dry biscuit

Bouffi *-[hareng]-* ⇒ bloater

Bougie ⇒ candle

Bougnette
1) bougnette de Castres ⇒ crépinette made of chopped pork fat and panada added of eggs, cooked in grease
2) bougnette des cévennes ⇒ kind of fritter
3) bougnette d'auvergne ⇒ pancake
Bougon ⇒ goat's milk cheese
Bougros ⇒ high quality Chablis wine
Bouillabaisse créole ⇒ fishes, crabs, crawfish tails, cooked with braised onion, tomatoes, crushed garlic and pimento in olive oil, plus thyme, laurel, nutmeg and pepper
Bouillabaisse d'épinards ⇒ chopped spinach, cooked with potatoes, pepper, saffron, chopped garlic and fennel; plus eggs added at the end of the cooking
Bouillabaisse de morue ⇒ bouillabaisse made of salt cod, onions, leeks, tomatoes and crushed garlic
Bouillabaisse de sardines ⇒ bouillabaisse made of onion, leeks, tomatoes, crushed garlic, fennel, orange peel, potatoes and sardines
Bouilleture angevine ⇒ matelote made of eels, red wine, shallots, butter, cognac, mushrooms, onions and dried plums
Bouillie ⇒ porridge < *uncountable* >
Bouilloire ⇒ kettle
Bouillon de noces *-[périgord]-* ⇒ pot-au-feu made of four various meat, vegetables, fried onions, and vermicelli
Bouillon de poisson ⇒ fish stock
Boukha ⇒ fig eau de vie
Boukhra ⇒ fig eau de vie
Boule de Berlin ⇒ fritter made of flour, butter, eggs, yeast and milk, stuffed of jam or almond paste; served hot with egg-custard, or a sauce made of apricot pulp, syrup and brandy
Boulaouane *-[vin gris du Maroc]-* ⇒ Moroccan rosé wine
Boulaud *-[rabotte]-* ⇒ whole apple or pear wrapped in short pastry, and baked
Boule de Berlin *-[krapfen]-* ⇒ fritter made of flour, butter, eggs, yeast and milk, stuffed of jam or almond paste; served hot with egg-custard, or a sauce made of apricot pulp, syrup, and brandy
Boule de Lille *-[mimolette]-* ⇒ Dutch cheese
Boule de gomme ⇒ gumdrop
Boule-ponche *-[punch]-* ⇒ bowl-punch
Boulette *-[pâtisserie]-* ⇒ cake added of almonds and walnuts
Boulette de cambrai *-[fromage]-* ⇒ cow's milk cheese flavoured of parsley, tarragon, and chive
Boulette de pâte ⇒ dumpling
Boulette de pâte cuite avec un fruit à l'intérieur ⇒ dumpling
Boulettes d'Avesnes ⇒ cheese shaped in cone, added of parsley, tarragon and spices
Boulettes de Charleroi ⇒ Belgian cheese made of spiced curds
Boulettes de harengs à la suèdoise ⇒ fried small balls made of hashed herring fillets, mashed potatoes, onion, pepper and nutmeg
Boulettes de roquefort ⇒ small balls made of Roquefort cheese, butter, cayenne pepper and cognac; coated with breadcrumbs
Boulotchki ⇒ Russian bread made of flour and milk, sprinkled with crumbs
Boulghour ⇒ crushed germinated wheat ...
    - cuit à l'eau additionné de beurre ⇒ ... cooked in water and added of butter
    - cuit à l'eau additionné de vinaigre, et servi avec raisins ⇒ ... cooked in water added of vinegar; served with raisins, chickpeas and meat balls
Boumania ⇒ ratatouille served with rice
Bouquet *-[crevette rose]-* ⇒ prawn or common prawn
Bouquet du vin ⇒ bouquet

Bouquetière *(à la ...)*
  1) **garniture** ⇒ ... surrounded by a garnish of vegetables laid in bunches
  2) **salade** ⇒ vegetable salad thickened with béchamel sauce
Bouquin *-[lièvre mâle]-* ⇒ hare
Bourdaine ⇒ buckthorn
  - miel ⇒ buckthorn honey
Bourdelot ⇒ apple or pear hollowed out, filled with sugar, calvados, plus butter; wrapped in paste and
      baked
Bourekakia ⇒ small pastry filled with vegetables, meat or fish, Feta cheese, and herbs

Bourg *-[Bourgeais]-* ⇒ wines from vineyards of the Gironde right bank
Bourgeais ⇒ Bordeaux wine red or white
Bourgogne
  1) **moutarde de Dijon** ⇒ mustard flavoured with unripe grape juice
    - cassis de Dijon ⇒ blackcurrant liquor
    - pain d'épice de dijon ⇒ gingerbread
    - jambon persillé ⇒ cooked ham with jelly and parsley
    - saumon au chablis ⇒ salmon cooked with chablis wine
  2) **préparations à la bourguignonne ou en meurette**
    - escargots cuits en meurette ⇒ snails cooked in red wine sauce with mushrooms,
      onions and lardoons
    - fromage de chèvre bourguignon ⇒ goat's milk cheese preserved in marc
    - st florentin ⇒ burgundy cheese
    - soumaintrain ⇒ burgundy cheese
    - flan aux courges ⇒ flan with gourds
    - corniottes ⇒ burgundy sweets
Bourgueil ⇒ red wine and rosé wine from Tours area
Bourguignon ⇒ ragout of beef meat
Bourguignotte *(à la ...) -[sauce pour poissons]-* ⇒ sauce made of eel, onions, mushrooms, garlic,
      shallots, spices, anchovy, Volnay wine, and crayfish tails
Bouribout ⇒ salmi of duck and raisins
Bourride sétoise ⇒ bits of angler fish boiled in a court-bouillon of white wine, leek, onions, carrots,
      chopped garlic, orange peel and pepper; served on slices of bread with a sauce
Bourriol *-[Quercy]-* ⇒ thick pancake of mashed potatoes, buckwheat-flour, wheat-flour, and milk
Boursadas ⇒ boiled chestnuts
Boursin *-[fromage frais]-* ⇒ Boursin
Bout de poitrine ⇒ brisket
Bout de poitrine désossé ⇒ boneless brisket
Boutargue *(fausse ...) -[cabillaud]-* ⇒ fresh cod
Boutargue *-[caviar blanc]-* ⇒ mullet roes dried and pressed
Boutehors ⇒ dragées made of spices and preserved fruits
Bouteille ⇒ bottle
Boutifar ⇒ black pudding containing pork fat and milk
Boutifare ⇒ black pudding containing pork fat and milk
Boutifaron ⇒ black pudding containing pork fat and milk
Bouton de culotte ⇒ small goat's milk cheese
Bouvard *-[hareng]-* ⇒ herring or spawning herring
Bouvillon ⇒ steer or bullock
Bouzigue *(la ...) -[huitre]-* ⇒ oyster from Than

Bouzourate
- **boisson** ⇒ drink made with melon seeds
- **glace** ⇒ sorbets or granitas

Bouzy rouge ⇒ red wine from champagne area « not sparkling »

Bowl-punch ⇒ bowl-punch

Boxties ⇒ boxties

Boyau
- **général** ⇒ bowel
- **enveloppe saucisson, etc ...** ⇒ gut dressing

Brabançonne (à la ...)
- **grosses pièces d'agneau ou de mouton rôti -[baron, carré, gigot]-** ⇒ ... served with a garnish of brussels-sprouts or chicory or hop shoots
- **tournedos et noisettes sautées** ⇒ ... laid on tartlets, and covered of béchamel sauce added of egg-yolks and gruyère; served with potatoes shaped in olive and baked with butter, or potato croquettes

Braiser ⇒ to braise

Braisé ⇒ braised < V.t adjectif >

Braisé -[jambon]- ⇒ variety of ham

Bragance
1) **garniture pour tournedos ou noisette d'agneau** ⇒ ... with a garnish of potato croquettes and braised tomatoes filled with béarnaise sauce
2) **entremets** ⇒ pastry made of Genoese sponge moistened with orange syrup, then filled of egg-custard and decorated with preserved orange peel

Brambory -[Tchécoslovaquie]- ⇒ potatoes

Brancas ⇒ ... with a garnish of sliced potatoes cooked in butter and lettuce chiffonade in cream

Brandevin ⇒ wine's eau de vie

Brandade ⇒ brandade

Brandade à la provençale -[sauce]- ⇒ velouté sauce with egg-yolks, grated nutmeg, pepper, garlic, lemon juice, and olive oil

Brandade de morue nîmoise ⇒ purée of poached salt cod, cooked in olive oil and milk

Brandy ⇒ brandy < pluriel brandies >

Brandza ⇒ Romanian ewe's milk cheese

Brassadeau ⇒ ring of sugared paste cooked in water, coloured with saffron, then baked

Brassado ⇒ ring of sugared paste cooked in water, coloured with saffron, then baked

Brayaude
1) **omelette brayaude** ⇒ omelette with ham, potatoes, cream and cheese
2) **soupe brayaude** ⇒ vegetable soup
3) **gigot brayaude** ⇒ leg of mutton studded of garlic, braised in white wine with potatoes or other vegetables

Bread sauce ⇒ bread sauce

Breakfast ⇒ breakfast

Bregott ⇒ mixing of cream and vegetal oil

Bressandes ⇒ wine from Beaune area

Bressane (à la ...)
- **poularde** ⇒ fattened pullet stuffed with foie gras and mushrooms, then braised
- **flan ou gâteau** ⇒ flan or gateau made of poultry livers
- **Feuilletés et salades composées** ⇒ voir recettes

Bresse -[bleu]- ⇒ blue cheese

Brestois
  1) **aux amandes** ⇒ gateau made of Genoese paste, crushed almonds, lemon extract and orange liquor
  2) **aux confitures d'abricot** ⇒ gateau made of Genoese paste, then sliced and filled of apricot jam, garnished of almonds
Breton
  1) **pièce montée** ⇒ wedding almond cake
  2) **gâteau** ⇒ gateau based on butter and egg-yolks
Bretonne *(à la ...)*
  1) **garniture de gigot et d'épaule** ⇒ ... with a garnish of haricot beans
  2) **sauce pour oeufs et filets de poisson** ⇒ ... with a sauce based on vegetables and cream

Brewis *(potage ...)* ⇒ brewis
Bréjaude ⇒ soup made of pork fat, cabbage, leeks, rape, and potatoes
Brèdes ⇒ herbs plus vegetable leaves, cooked with bacon and spices; served accompanied of rice
Bred *(la ...)* ⇒ mixing of boiled manioc leaves, fish, and coconut
Brèdes d'épinards ⇒ spinach cooked with browned pork fat, onion, garlic and crushed tomato; served with rice
Brèdes de cresson ⇒ watercress cooked with browned pork fat, onion, garlic and crushed tomato; served with rice
Brèdes de laitues ⇒ lettuce cooked with browned pork fat, onion, garlic and crushed tomato; served with rice
Brême à la vendangeuse ⇒ bream baked with butter, chopped shallots, thyme, laurel and white wine; served with the cooking sauce, thickened of lemon juice and grape
Brême argentée ⇒ silver bream
Brick ⇒ cheese from the Wisconsin
Brick à l'œuf ⇒ pasta filled with egg and herbs, then fried
Brik ⇒ triangle made of folded pancake, filled with an egg and fried
Brioche antillaise ⇒ brioche first hollowed out, then filled with a stuffing made of its crumbs, buttered diced pineapple, and banana slices, plus pineapple syrup flavoured with rum
Brioche aux fraises des bois ⇒ brioche hollowed out and moistened with kirsch; filled of wild strawberries and whipped cream
Brioche aux framboises ⇒ brioche hollowed out and moistened with kirsch; filled of raspberries and whipped cream
Brioche aux fruits ⇒ brioche filled with diced fruits in season macerated in brandy, sugar and lemon juice
  - avec cerises ⇒ filled with custard and stoned cherries
Brioche aux pralines ⇒ brioche made of flour, yeast, sugar, eggs, butter, plus burnt almonds
Brioche avec cerises ⇒ brioche hollowed out and moistened with kirsch; filled with custard and stoned cherries
Brioche bordelaise ⇒ brioche made of dough and chopped preserved fruits, decorated with crushed sugar and preserved fruits
Brioche de gisors ⇒ brioche made with flour, yeast, eggs and butter
Brioche mousseline ⇒ brioche brushed with whipped egg
Brioche parisienne ⇒ shaped brioche with a large part topped of a small ball
Brioche parisienne individuelle ⇒ small shaped brioche
Brioche polonaise ⇒ brioche moistened of kirsch, stuffed with preserved fruits added of confectioner's custard and covered with meringue
Brioche roulée aux raisins ⇒ brioche shaped in roll, made of paste, custard, and raisins swelled up; flavoured with rum
Brioches au foie gras ⇒ small brioches hollowed out and filled with crumbs, foie gras, and butter

Brioches au fromage ⇒ small brioches hollowed out and filled with crumbs, diced ham, plus a sauce made of cream, egg-yolk and grated cheese

Brioches aux anchois ⇒ small brioches hollowed out and filled with crumbs, plus anchovy paste

Brioches aux champignons ⇒ small brioches hollowed out and filled with crumbs, chopped mushrooms, and béchamel sauce

Brisse -[garniture]- ⇒ ... with a garnish of onions stuffed with a poultry forcemeat, plus tartlets filled with stuffed olives

Bristol -[garniture]- ⇒ ... with a garnish of risotto, kidney beans in butter, small potatoes sautéed in butter with lardoons

Broche -[outil]- ⇒ skewer or spit

Brochet au beurre blanc

   1) au court-bouillon ⇒ pike cooked in a court-bouillon; served with a sauce based on vinegar, shallots and butter

   2) en marinade ⇒ pike cooked in a marinade of onions, shallots, garlic, thyme, laurel, pepper and white wine; served with a sauce made of kneaded butter and shallots

Brochet au bleu ⇒ pike in a court-bouillon with vinegar; served with potatoes or other vegetables

Brochet au vinaigre ⇒ pike fillets milked and floured, braised in butter and oil, plus browned onions and vinegar; covered of sauce thickened with cream and vinegar

Brochet du meunier ⇒ bits of pike, floured and milked, braised in butter and oil, plus browned onions and vinegar; served with sippets browned in butter

Brochet rôti à la mode du bugey ⇒ pike stuffed with a forcemeat of whiting, cream, truffle and butter; grilled on a skewer and sprinkled with cream, then served garnished of crayfish tails and truffles

   autres recettes

   - **carpe** ⇒ carp

   - **saumon** ⇒ salmon

   - **omble-chevalier** ⇒ char

   - **sandre** ⇒ pike perch

   - **truite saumonée** ⇒ sea trout < *remplacer « whiting » dans le texte anglais, par l'un de ces poissons* >

Brocheton ⇒ pikelet or pikeen or pickerel < *tous pluriel inchangé* >

Brochette de colin à la fondue de poireaux ⇒ hake grilled on a skewer, served with leeks stewed in their own liquid

Brochettes d'agneau ⇒ bits of lamb's fillet, lardoons and sometimes mushrooms, sprinkled with melted butter, then grilled on a skewer

Brochettes d'anguilles ⇒ bits of eel and lardoons macerated in olive oil, herbs and garlic; grilled on a skewer

Brochettes d'huitres à l'anglaise -[angels on horseback]- ⇒ angels on horseback

Brochettes d'huitres à la villeroi ⇒ poached oyster grilled on a skewer, and served with a sauce of stock added of truffle extract, and a purée

Brochettes d'ortolans ⇒ larded ortolans, plus sippets put on skewers and baked; served with watercress and lemon

Brochettes de cigales de mer au safran ⇒ mantis shrimps macerated in saffron, olive oil, lemon juice, and garlic; grilled on a skewer

Brochettes de coquilles st jacque et d'huîtres -[à la villeroi]- ⇒ scallops and oysters first poached, then fried on a skewer

Brochettes de filet de boeuf mariné ⇒ diced beef fillet and lardoons macerated in oil, plus diced capsicums and onions; grilled on a skewer

Brochettes de foie d'agneau ⇒ diced lamb's liver and diced capsicums, grilled on a skewer

Brochettes de foie de porc à l'italienne ⇒ larded diced pork's liver plus bits of bread, grilled on a skewer

Brochettes de foie de veau ⇒ macerated diced calf liver and capsicums, grilled on a skewer; basted with vinegar, plus chopped shallots

Brochettes de foies de volaille ⇒ macerated poultry's livers, plus mushrooms and lardoons, grilled on a skewer; served with rice and Indian sauce

Brochettes de foies de volailles à l'italienne ⇒ larded poultry livers, onions and sage, macerated in oil, pepper and thyme; grilled on a skewer, served with lemon and salad

Brochettes de fruits de mer ⇒ poached shellfishes macerated in olive oil, lemon juice, herbs, garlic and thyme; grilled on a skewer with mushrooms

Brochettes de fruits en papillotes ⇒ sliced bananas, quartered oranges, diced pears and apples, macerated in sugar plus brandy; laid on skewers and wrapped in buttered paper, then baked

Brochettes de lotte ⇒ diced angler fish and sliced aubergines, macerated in olive oil, lemon juice, herbs, garlic, and thyme; grilled on skewers

Brochettes de moules *(nahmias ...)* ⇒ mussels, bits of pork fat and tomatoes, grilled on skewers

Brochettes de moules ⇒ mussels poached in wine and shallots, then coated of mustard plus breadcrumbs and grilled on skewers

Brochettes de porc aux pruneaux ⇒ larded dried-plums and diced pork, macerated in oil, chopped shallots, nutmeg and pepper; then grilled on skewers

Brochettes de queues de langoustines ⇒ Norway lobster tails macerated in olive oil, lemon juice, garlic and herbs; grilled on a skewer

Brochettes de ris d'agneau ⇒ diced lamb sweetbread, lardoons, and quartered tomatoes; grilled on a skewer

Brochettes de ris de veau ⇒ diced calf sweetbread, lardoons and quartered tomatoes, grilled on a skewer

Brochettes de rognons ⇒ lamb kidneys, oiled and peppered, then grilled on a skewer

Brochettes de saumon au foie de canard frais ⇒ diced salmon plus diced duck's liver put on skewers, cooked in the oven on a layer of julienne; covered with a sauce of white wine, shallots, cream, truffle and egg-yolks

Brochettes de sole aux champignons ⇒ diced sole fillets covered with a forcemeat of egg-yolks, crumbs and parsley; grilled on a skewer with mushrooms in butter

Brocoli à la crème ⇒ broccoli cooked with garlic, then chopped and sautéed in butter plus cream; served with meat or fish

Brocoli à la vendéenne ⇒ stew of salt-pork, broccoli, garlic and potatoes; served warmed up again in butter for the meat plus vegetables, and in a soup tureen with bread for the stock

Brouet ⇒ stock made of eggs, milk and sugar

Brouet de st jacques aux épinards crus ⇒ scallops poached in stock thickened of cream, then added with spinach, egg-yolks and lemon juice; served with diced tomatoes

Broufado de boeuf ⇒ marinated beef braised in olive oil, onion, marinade, wine, gherkins and anchovies; served with potatoes

Brouillade de truffes ⇒ timbales of scrambled eggs, mixed with diced truffles browned in butter

Broulaï ⇒ dish of fish, potatoes or manioc, tomato purée, onion, capsicum and rice

Brousse *-[fromage]-* ⇒ ewe's milk cheese

Broutart
- **agneau** ⇒ young lamb
- **veau** ⇒ young veal

Broye béarnaise ⇒ porridge of flour and vegetable stock; served chilled and fried in slices

Broyé poitevin ⇒ flat cake made of sugar, egg, butter, flour and rum; then brushed with egg-yolk and cooked in the oven

Brunch ⇒ brunch

Brûlot
- **alcool** ⇒ alcohol flamed before to be drink

- **sucre dans café** ⇒ sugar moistened with brandy, flamed before to be poured in the coffee
- **café-brûlot** ⇒ rum warmed with sugar, cinnamon, orange and lemon peel, mixed with coffee
Brie -*[fromage]*- ⇒ Brie
Brillat-Savarin -*[fromage]*- ⇒ cow's milk cheese from Forges les Eaux
Brindinettes de Douai ⇒ kind of biscuit covered with chocolate
Brinzen ⇒ Hungarian ewe-cheese
Briouats -*[Maroc]*- ⇒ turnovers filled with meat or almonds or honey
Briquettes ⇒ kind of biscuit covered with chocolate

Briscat (*garbure ...*) ⇒ stew based on maize
Brisolée ⇒ grilled chestnuts eaten with cheese
Broccio ⇒ Corsican ewe-cheese
Bromi ⇒ rice alcohol
Broodkaas ⇒ pasteurized Dutch cow's milk cheese
Brouilly ⇒ Beaujolais wine
Brousse -*[Provence]*- ⇒ Provencal soft white cheese
Brown Betty ⇒ American pudding
Brownies ⇒ American pastries with chocolate
Broyé -*[action]*- ⇒ crushed or pounded < *tous v.t adjectif* >
Brudu ⇒ Tunisian soup
Brune kager ⇒ dried biscuits flavoured with spices, almonds, and brown sugar
Brunoise ⇒ thinly diced vegetables or thinly diced ... < *nom du légume* >
Brunoise de légumes braisés ⇒ braised thinly diced vegetables or braised thinly diced ...
Bruxelloise (*à la ...*)
- **petites et grosses pièces de boucherie** ⇒ ... served with a garnish of steamed brussels-sprouts, braised chicory, and small potatoes sautéed in butter with lardoons
- **oeufs** ⇒ ... garnished with brussels-sprouts or chicory
Bréhan
- **garniture pour grosses pièces de boucherie** ⇒ ... served with artichoke hearts filled of mashed broad beans, cauliflower covered with sauce hollandaise, and boiled potatoes sprinkled of parsley
Brögenwurst ⇒ sausage made of bacon, pig's brain, oatmeal, and onion
Brünsli ⇒ cakes made with almonds, hazelnuts, and chocolate
Bubble-and-squeak ⇒ bubble-and-squeak
Bucelas-vin ⇒ bucellas
Buchteln ⇒ cake filled with jam
Bückling ⇒ smoked herring or bückling
Buccin ou Ran ou Bulot ⇒ whelk
Buffet
- **liquide** ⇒ refreshments
- **mets** ⇒ supper
Buffet dînatoire ⇒ buffet supper
Buffet froid ⇒ cold buffet
Buffle ⇒ buffalo
Bufflonne ⇒ buffalo
Bugey
- **blanc** ⇒ bugey white wine
- **rosé** ⇒ bugey rosé
- **rouge** ⇒ bugey red wine

Bugnes lyonnaises ⇒ fritters made of flour, sugar, eggs and rum
Buisson d'asperges en croustade ⇒ croustade filled with asparagus; topped with asparagus tips in
mayonnaise, shaped in bush
Buisson d'écrevisses ⇒ poached crayfishes shaped in bush
Bulgogi ⇒ marinated beef
Bulghur ⇒ crushed germinated wheat ...
    - **préparations, cuit à l'eau additionné de beurre** ⇒ ... cooked in water and added of butter
    - **cuit à l'eau additionné de vinaigre, et servi avec raisin secs, pois chiches et boulettes**
        de viande ⇒ ... cooked in water added of vinegar; served with raisins, chickpeas and
meat balls
Buns ⇒ buns
Burgoo -[Amérique du nord]- ⇒ burgoo
Buriello -[fromage]- ⇒ Italiao cheese garnished in the centre with a ball of buffalo butter
Busecca ⇒ thick soup of veal's tripe and vegetables
Buttariga ⇒ dried tunny eggs
Butterine ⇒ Australian mixing of butter and vegetal oil
Bâton de jacob ⇒ eclair filled with custard and covered of sugar
Bâtonnet -[viande]- ⇒ lamella
Bête de compagnie ⇒ wild boar
Bêtise -[bêtises de cambrai ou sottises de valenciennes]- ⇒ sweet made of cooked sugar flavoured
with mint
Bündnërfleisch ⇒ smoked beef

C

Caballo -[*cocido*]- ⇒ Spanish meal made of various dish
Cabardès ⇒ red wine and rosé from Languedoc
Cabassol
   - **Albi** ⇒ ragout made of ewe's head simmered in white wine
   - **Lodève** ⇒ ragout made of trotters, sweetbread and head of lamb, plus ham and veal's knuckle
   - **Rouergue** ⇒ stock of lamb
Cabécou ⇒ small cheese from a mixing of goat's milk and cow's milk
Cabernet -[*raisin*]- ⇒ cabernet grape
Cabessal (*en ...*) ⇒ stuffed hare cooked in a baking-tin
Cabillaud ⇒ fresh cod < *cuisine uncountable* >
Cabillaud à l'anglaise ⇒ slices of fresh cod coated with breadcrumbs, and fried in butter
Cabillaud à l'indienne ⇒ fresh cod cooked with braised onions, tomatoes, curry and white wine; served with rice
Cabillaud à la boulangère ⇒ fresh cod baked with sliced potatoes, onions, pepper, thyme and laurel; sprinkled with melted butter
Cabillaud braisé à la flamande ⇒ slices of fresh cod braised in butter with shallots, parsley, and white wine
Cabillaud frit ⇒ thin slices of fresh cod, milked and floured, then fried in oil; served with parsley, and quartered lemons
Cabillaud grillé ⇒ slices of fresh cod, oiled and buttered, then grilled; served with lemon and parsley
Cabillaud poché chaud ⇒ fresh cod poached in a court-bouillon, and served with a sauce
Cabillaud poché froid ⇒ fresh cod poached in a court-bouillon, then chilled; served with lettuce, hard-boiled eggs, plus mayonnaise or a sauce
Cabillaud rôti ⇒ fresh cod marinated in oil, pepper and lemon juice, then roasted; served with its cooking juice added of white wine
Cabillaud sauté à la crème ⇒ fresh cod braised in butter and cream
Cabillaud étuvé à la crème ⇒ diced fresh cod braised in butter with chopped onions, white wine, and cream
Cabiros ⇒ young goat
Caboc -[*fromage*]- ⇒ Caboc
Cabot ⇒ miller's thumb 1/2 or 1/2 bullhead
Cabrales -[*espagne*]- ⇒ goat's milk cheese
Cabri ⇒ young goat
Cabus -[*chou pommé*]- ⇒ common cabbage
Cacahouette ⇒ peanut 1/2 or 1/2 ground nut
Cacahouète ⇒ peanut 1/2 or 1/2 ground nut
Cacahuète ⇒ peanut 1/2 or 1/2 ground nut
Cacao ⇒ cacao 1/2 or 1/2 cocoa < *tous uncountable* >
Caccavelli ⇒ Corsican pastry topped with eggs
Cacao ⇒ crushed green olives from Provence area
Cachat -[*brebis*]- ⇒ Provencal ewe's cheese
Cachat -[*chèvre*]- ⇒ Provencal goat's cheese
Cacher -[*kasher*]- ⇒ kosher
Cachiman -[*anone*]- ⇒ anona or custard-apple
Cachir ⇒ kosher
Cascher ⇒ kosher
Cacik ⇒ cucumber with yoghourt

Cacio e pepe *(a ...)* ⇒ spaghetti with cheese and pepper
Caciocavallo ⇒ Italian cheese
Cadgery *-[kedgeree]-* ⇒ kedgeree
Cadillac ⇒ Bordeaux wine, white and sweet
Cadran *-[oronge]-* ⇒ egg-mushroom
Caerphilly *-[fromage]-* ⇒ Caerphilly cheese
Café *(grand ...)* ⇒ large cup of coffee
Café ⇒ coffee
Café allongé ⇒ diluted coffee
Café arabe ⇒ coffee, made of finely ground arabica coffee and granulated sugar boiled together
Café au lait ⇒ coffee with hot milk
Café au marc de bourgogne ⇒ coffee mixed with sugar and burgundy marc, poured on ice cube
Café calva ⇒ coffee added of calvados
Café crème ⇒ coffee with milk
Café décaféiné ⇒ decaffeinated coffee
Café express ⇒ espresso coffee
Café filtre ⇒ filter coffee
Café glacé ⇒ chilled coffee
Café liègeois *-[Café viennois]-*
    a) **café** ⇒ coffee mixed with cream and chilled 1/2 ou 1/2 coffee ice cream
    b) **entremets glacé** ⇒ strong coffee, plus coffee ice cream, topped with sugared whipped cream
        ice-cream of sugar, cream and coffee extract, topped with sugared whipped cream
Café noir ⇒ small black coffee
Café turc ⇒ Turkish coffee
Cafeine ⇒ caffeine
Caffé *-[Café]-* ⇒ coffee
Caffuts *-[boulettes de Cambrai]-* ⇒ cow's milk cheese flavoured of parsley, tarragon and chives
Caghuse ⇒ hock of pork with onions and butter; cooked in the oven
Gagnette *-[blennie]-* ⇒ blenny < *pluriel blennies* >
Cagouille ⇒ snail or escargot
Cagouilles à la vigneronne ⇒ shelled snails sautéed in garlic and shallots; then wrapped in dough
        added of chive and fried
Cahoat *-[café]-* ⇒ coffee
Cahors ⇒ red wine from cahors
Cahouet *-[café]-* ⇒ coffee
Caïeu-ail ⇒ clove of garlic
Caille ⇒ quail < *pluriel quail* >
Caille de la manche *-[eperlan]-* ⇒ sea smelt
Caille en casserole aux raisins ⇒ quail wrapped in vine leaves and barded, browned in butter; then
        baked with grapes, and sprinkled with the cooking juice flavoured of armagnac or
        cognac or calvados
Caillebotte
   - **fromage frais Aunis, Saintonge** *-[vache]-* ⇒ fresh cow's milk cheese
   - **fromage frais Saintonge, Poitou** *-[chèvre]-* ⇒ fresh goat's milk cheese
Caillebottes poitevines ⇒ cooked curdled milk, added of fresh milk, and topped with sugar plus cream
Cailles à la minute ⇒ quail braised in butter with onion; served with a sauce made of the gravy,
        chopped mushrooms and cognac
Cailles à la romaine ⇒ quail baked with onions, diced ham, peas, and butter
Cailles au riz ⇒ quail cooked in butter; served on timbales with rice, plus the cooking juice added of
        cognac and game stock

Cailles aux cerises ⇒ stoned cherries cooked in sugar and redcurrant jelly, plus browned quail with their gravy

Cailles en caisse Mont-Bry ⇒ quail stuffed with a forcemeat of poultry and chopped truffle, cooked in a cast-iron casserole; served with the cooking juice added of champagne

Cailles en casserole ⇒ browned quail in butter, plus a sauce with cognac

Cailles en casserole à la bonne femme ⇒ quail cooked in butter with potatoes and pork fat

Cailles en casserole à la grecque ⇒ browned quail in butter, plus the gravy added of white wine; served on a layer of rice

Cailles en casserole cinq mars ⇒ browned quail in butter, xérès, a julienne of carrots, onions and celery, plus a julienne of mushrooms and truffle; then baked with the gravy added of cognac

Cailles en chemise ⇒ quail stuffed with a forcemeat and poached; served with a consommé added of aromatics

Cailles farçies à la financière ⇒ quail cooked in casing, sprinkled with their gravy added of madeira; served laid on ... croutons or croustades decorated of truffle lamellas, plus a ragout thickened of madeira sauce added of truffle extract

Cailles farçies à la gourmande ⇒ sauté quail stuffed with butter, ham and truffle; served in their gravy added of champagne, plus sauté boletus or chanterelle mushrooms

Cailles farçies à la lamballe en caisse ⇒ quail stuffed with a forcemeat, cooked in butter; served in shaped boat paper with a julienne of mushrooms in cream, plus the cooking juice added of port

Cailles farçies à la périgourdine en gelée ⇒ quail stuffed with foie gras and truffle, poached in meat stock and madeira; served in jelly

Cailles farçies à la souvarov ⇒ quail stuffed with a culinary stuffing of foie gras, truffle, salt and cognac, cooked in butter with truffles; then basted with the cooking juice added of madeira sauce, and baked

Cailles farçies au nid ⇒ quail stuffed, then poached in madeira; served on a nest of potatoes, covered with the cooking juice

Cailles farçies en caisses ⇒ quail stuffed with a forcemeat, and cooked in butter; served in paper case with their gravy thickened of madeira < *autres préparations suivant la sauce, à l'italienne, à la mirepoix, à la périgueux, à la strasbourgeoise* >

Cailles farçies lucullus ⇒ quail stuffed with foie gras and truffle, served on croustade, covered with the cooking juice thickened of chopped truffle and madeira

Cailles farçies monselet ⇒ quail stuffed with foie gras and truffle, poached in stock and Madeira; then baked with artichoke hearts, truffle and cream

Cailles grillées ⇒ quail brushed with oil and aromatics or melted butter, then grilled

Cailles grillées petit duc ⇒ quail brushed with melted butter and crumbs, then grilled; served on sliced potatoes baked in butter, and grilled mushrooms; then basted with game stock added of Madeira

Cailles rôties ⇒ quail wrapped on vine leaves and barded, grilled on a skewer; served with watercress, and quartered lemons

Caillettes
- **général** ⇒ crépinettes made of minced pork and greenstuff, then baked
- **caillettes tricastines** ⇒ crépinettes made of minced pork and truffle, then baked
- **caillettes de Soyans** ⇒ crépinettes made of minced pork and spinach, then baked
- **caillettes de Chabeuil** ⇒ crépinettes made of minced pork and green vegetables, then baked
- **caillettes de Valence** ⇒ crépinettes made of pig liver and beet, then baked
- **caillettes à la pugétoise** ⇒ crépinettes made of pig liver, then baked
- **caillettes de Cornouailles** ⇒ crépinettes made of minced pork and baked; served with mustard sauce and mashed potatoes

Caillettes ardéchoises ⇒ crépinettes made with a forcemeat of chopped beet, spinach, dandelions, nettles, wild poppies, pork liver, lung, pork fat, onion and garlic; then baked

Caillettes provençales ⇒ crépinettes made with a forcemeat of chopped beet leaves, spinach, sausage-meat and garlic; baked and served ...

    - chaud ⇒ ... hot with a tomato purée

    - froid ⇒ ... chilled with a salad

Caillé ⇒ curds or curdled milk

Caillou -[Barsac]- ⇒ quality Bordeaux wine from Barsac area

Cailloux -[dragées]- ⇒ dragée

Cairanne ⇒ wine from Vaucluse area

Caisse

    - cuisine ⇒ hot hors d'oeuvres of culinary stuffing or ragout, in boat shaped casing « paper, pastry, etc ... »

    - patisserie ⇒ sponge cakes, etc ... laid in boat shaped paper

Caissette -[Champagne]- ⇒ biscuit with meringue

Caissette

    - cuisine ⇒ hot hors d'oeuvres of culinary stuffing or ragout, in boat shaped casing « paper, pastry, etc ... »

    - patisserie ⇒ sponge cakes, etc ... laid in boat shaped paper

Caissette en papier ⇒ small box in paper

Cajasse ⇒ sweet made of pancake dough and fruits, flavoured with rum

Cajou ⇒ cashew nut

Cake ⇒ fruit cake

Cake au gingembre ⇒ cake made of ginger, butter, eggs, rum, sugar, flour and yeast

Cake au miel et aux cerises confites ⇒ cake made of butter, granulated sugar, honey, yeast, flour, eggs, rum and preserved cherries; decorated with preserved cherries and angelica

Cake aux fruits ⇒ fruit cake

Cakes du yorkshire -[petits]- ⇒ small cakes made of yeast, milk, butter, sugar, flour, eggs, diced fruits and ginger; then baked

Caladon ⇒ pastry from Nîmes area

Calalou -[Antilles]- ⇒ thick purée flavoured with herbs, pork fat, batata leaves, sorrel, ketmias, cucumber, Caribbean cabbage, etc ...

Calamar ⇒ squid or calamaro

Caldeirata -[Portugal]- ⇒ Portuguese bouillabaisse flavoured with coriander

Caldereta -[Espagne]- ⇒ Spanish soup from Asturia area

Caldo verde ⇒ soup made of olive oil, potatoes, cabbage, and dried sausage

Calebasse ⇒ calabash

Californie -[variétés de vins]- ⇒ varieties of wines < *gamay red wine, grenache rosé, riesling white wine, champagne* >

Calisson ⇒ sweet made of almonds and preserved fruits, plus syrup and orange blossom extract

Calissoun ⇒ sweet made of almonds and preserved fruits, plus syrup and orange blossom extract

Callune -[miel de Callune]- ⇒ honey from Landes area

Calmar ⇒ squid or calamaro

Calmars à l'andalouse ⇒ squid lamellas browned in olive oil, cooked with capsicums, tomatoes and white wine; covered with a sauce made of bread, parsley, garlic, saffron, almond powder and oil, then served hot with rice

Calmars farçis à la marseillaise ⇒ squids stuffed with a hash of onions, bread, garlic, parsley, crushed tomatoes, egg-yolks and pepper; cooked in the oven with garlic, onion and white wine, then browned

Calmars frits ⇒ squids braised in olive oil with garlic and parsley

Calmars sautés ⇒ squids braised in olive oil with garlic and parsley

Calmars sautés à la basquaise ⇒ browned lamellas of squid and capsicum, plus onions and tomatoes; sprinkled with parsley

Calon-ségur -*[st estèphe]-* ⇒ high quality Bordeaux red wine from Médoc

Calvados ⇒ calvados

Calvi -*[Corse; vins de]-* ⇒ Corsican wine from Balagne area

Calville -*[pomme]-* ⇒ variety of juicy apple

Cambridge favourite -*[fraise]-* ⇒ strawberry from Loire valley

Cambridge -*[sauce]-* ⇒ Cambridge sauce

Cameline -*[sauce]-* ⇒ sauce made of bread steeped in wine, spices, and vinegar

Camembert ⇒ camembert

Camérani ⇒ voir garniture ou potage

Camino -*[abricot]-* ⇒ variety of apricot

Camolino -*[riz]-* ⇒ variety of rice

Camomille ⇒ camomile or chamomile < *tous uncountable* >

Campanili -*[brioche]-* ⇒ Corsican brioche

Campari ⇒ Campari

Camus de Bretagne -*[artichaut]-* ⇒ variety of artichoke

Canada -*[vins du]-* ⇒ Canadian wines

Canadian whisky ⇒ Canadian whisky

Canapé ⇒ canapé or savoury < *pluriel savouries* >

Canapés à l'anguille fumée ⇒ canapé with mustard butter or horse-radish butter, topped with smoked eel, plus egg-yolk and chive

Canapés à l'écarlate ⇒ canapés with composed butter added of paprika and cayenne pepper, garnished of a slice of beef

Canapés à la bayonnaise ⇒ buttered canapé garnished with a slice of ham and jelly

Canapés à la bordelaise ⇒ canapés with shallot butter, topped of a culinary stuffing of boletus and ham, plus pimento butter

Canapés à la danoise ⇒ canapés with horse-radish butter, garnished of salmon and smoked herring lamellas, plus salmon eggs or lemon

Canapés à la langouste ⇒ canapés with spiny lobster butter, garnished of spiny lobster tails and parsley

Canapés à la langouste ⇒ canapés with spiny lobster butter, garnished of spiny lobster tail, and parsley

Canapés à la moelle ⇒ canapés garnished with bone-marrow from pot-au-feu

Canapés à la parisienne ⇒ canapés with chervil butter, garnished with poultry meat and mayonnaise

Canapés à la russe ⇒ canapés with butter and herbs, covered with Russian salad, and jelly

Canapés arlequins ⇒ canapés garnished in motley of various hashed items

Canapés au caviar ⇒ buttered canapés, topped with caviar and chive, sprinkled of lemon juice

Canapés au crabe ⇒ buttered canapés topped of bits of crab mixed with béchamel sauce and saffron; browned and decorated with slices of lemon

Canapés au cresson ⇒ canapés with cress butter, cress leaves, and chopped hard-boiled egg

Canapés au fromage ⇒ canapés covered with grated cheese and browned

Canapés au homard ⇒ canapés with lobster butter, garnished of lobster tail, and parsley

Canapés au jambon ⇒ canapés with butter and herbs, garnished of slices of ham, and jelly

Canapés au saumon fumé ⇒ buttered canapés, garnished with smoked salmon, and lemon

Canapés aux anchois ⇒ buttered canapés, topped with anchovy fillets and chopped hard-boiled egg

Canapés aux asperges ⇒ canapés with mayonnaise, topped of asparagus tips and capsicum

Canapés aux champignons ⇒ canapés garnished with chopped mushrooms added of béchamel sauce, sprinkled with crumbs and melted butter, then browned

Canapés aux crevettes ⇒ canapés with prawn butter, garnished of prawn tails and parsley

Canapés aux harengs à la hollandaise ⇒ canapés buttered of mashed soft roes, garnished with smoked herring fillets, chopped egg-yolk and sprinkled of lemon juice

Canapés aux laitances ⇒ buttered canapés garnished with soft roes, and lemon juice

Canapés aux rillettes ⇒ canapés with rillettes, served hot

Canapés de foie de morue ⇒ buttered canapés garnished with salt cod liver and lemon

Canard ⇒ duck < *viande uncountable* >

Canard à l'agenaise ⇒ duck filled of stoned dried plums, cooked with lardoons, diced carrot, onion, and Bordeaux wine flavoured of herbs; served with the cooking juice added of armagnac, plus dried plums

Canard à l'alsacienne ⇒ duck browned in butter, then cooked with white wine and poultry stock; served with sauerkraut, sausage, and its cooking juice

Canard à l'ananas ⇒ duck flamed in rum and cooked with pineapple syrup, lemon juice and pepper; served with slices of pineapple browned in butter

Canard à l'orange ⇒ duck in orange sauce

Canard à l'orange Lasserre ⇒ duck braised in butter with Grand Marnier brandy; served with sauté quartered oranges, plus the cooking sauce added of orange juice, and apricot liqueur

Canard à la chipolata ⇒ duck browned in butter, then cooked with white wine and poultry stock; served with browned chestnuts, onions, lardoons, and chipolatas

Canard à la presse ⇒ duck of which the fillets are braised in red wine and the thighs are grilled, the rest is pressed and the juice added of cognac plus butter for the cooking of the fillets

Canard aux feuilles de thé ⇒ duck cooked with ginger, cinnamon, aniseed and basted of xeres; then baked on a layer of tea leaves, and browned

Canard aux fleurs de citronnier ⇒ duck floured with lemon blossom and grilled on a skewer

Canard aux mangues ⇒ duck brushed with pork fat, roasted accompanied of carrots, celery, thyme, and laurel; served with stewed mangos and the cooking juice

Canard aux olives ⇒ duck with a sauce made of onions, carrots, stock, tomato purée, thyme and laurel; baked with browned lardoons, and stoned olives

Canard aux petits pois ⇒ duck braised in butter with onions, lardoons and peas

Canard aux pieds de porc et au cidre ⇒ pig trotters plus duck fillets, simmered in cider with carrots, leeks, celery, onion and garlic

Canard braisé ⇒ duck browned in butter, then cooked with white wine and poultry stock; served with peas and its cooking juice

Canard braisé aux olives ⇒ duck browned in butter, then cooked with white wine and poultry stock; served with stoned olives

Canard cornille ravi ⇒ roasted duck, served with a sauce made of giblets of duck, onion, carrot, stock, chocolate and stoned olives

Canard de Barbarie ⇒ Muscovy 1/2 or 1/2 musk duck

Canard farçi à la rouennaise ⇒ duck stuffed with its liver, chopped onions, plus pork fat, then roasted with onion, carrots and celery, basted with Madeira; served with the cooking juice

Canard laqué ⇒ duck lacquered with a sauce, marinated and roasted on a skewer; served with lettuce, leeks, and gherkins

Canard rouennais au porto ⇒ duck cooked in casserole with butter, and served with its cooking juice thickened of port

Canard rouennais braisé ⇒ braised duck ...
- **à la bigarade** ⇒ ... with a garnish of orange
- **aux cerises** ⇒ ... with stoned cherries and Madeira
- **au champagne** ⇒ ... with champagne and veal stock
- **au Chambertin** ⇒ ... with Chambertin, plus lardoons and mushrooms in butter

Canard rouennais en chemise ⇒ duck stuffed with a forcemeat of onion, pork fat, poultry livers, pepper, and fennel flower, roasted in the oven; then wrapped in a pork bladder, and poached

Canard rôti ⇒ roasted duck

Canard rôti aux pêches ⇒ roasted duck, served with poached peaches, and its cooking juice

Canard sauvage ⇒ wild duck

Canard sauvage à la tyrolienne ⇒ wild duck stuffed with apple jam, cinnamon and mace; roasted on a skewer and served with its cooking juice added of redcurrant jelly

Canard sauvage à la walter scott ⇒ wild duck cooked in the oven with apples; served with sippets spreaded of foie gras, topped with the apples, and marmalade diluted in whisky, plus the cooking juice apart

Canard sauvage au Chambertin ⇒ roasted duck, served with its cooking juice and a sauce added of Chambertin wine, plus mushrooms and truffle

Canard sauvage au porto ⇒ roasted wild duck, served in thin slices, with the cooking juice thickened of port and butter

Canard sauvage aux poires ⇒ roasted fillets of wild duck, served with a sauce made of caramel, red wine, cinnamon, coriander, pepper, and orange peel; plus pears cooked in the sauce

Canard voisin ⇒ timbale made with layers of roasted duckling fillets, sauce of meat jelly and truffle lamellas

Cancalaise (*à la ...*)

    1) **poisson** ⇒ nom du poisson ... garnished with poached oysters and shrimp tails, then covered with creamy sauce or white wine sauce

    2) **soupe** ⇒ fish consommé with tapioca, garnished of poached oysters; sometimes sole fillets or quenelles of pike are added

Cancoillote ⇒ preparation made of cheese, salted water and butter, flavoured with white wine; eaten tepid

Candi

    - **adjectif** ⇒ candied

    - **fruit** ⇒ candied fruit 1/2 or 1/2 crystallized fruit

    - **sucre** ⇒ sugar-candy

Cane -[*volaille*]- ⇒ female duck

Caneton ⇒ duckling

Caneton à la bigarade ⇒ duckling braised in butter covered with a sauce made of its cooking juice, white wine, meat juice, caramel, orange juice, lemon juice, bitter orange peel, and lemon peel

Caneton Montmorency ⇒ fried duckling with aromatics, garnished of cherries poached in Bordeaux wine; covered with the gravy added of cherry brandy

Caneton au miel de lavande et au citron ⇒ duckling braised in butter, served in thin slices, covered with a sauce made of duckling giblets, diced vegetables and ham, white wine, lemon juice, lavender honey, and butter

Canetons à la d'Albuféra ⇒ ducklings baked in butter with ham, onion, clove and Malaga wine; garnished with ham lamellas and mushrooms in the gravy

Canette -[*petite cane*]- ⇒ female duckling

Canissoun ⇒ sweet made of almonds and preserved fruits plus syrup and orange blossom extract

Canissoun ⇒ sweet made of almonds, preserved fruits and syrup, laid on unleavened bread

Canja -[*Portugal*]- ⇒ poultry consommé garnished with lemon, mint, and sometimes almonds, ham, plus sliced onion

Canne à sucre ⇒ sugar-cane

Canneberge ⇒ cranberry

Cannelle ⇒ cinnamon < *uncountable* >

Cannelloni ⇒ cannelloni

Cannelloni à la béchamel ⇒ cannelloni with a mixture of béchamel sauce, chopped onions, ham, chicken, and grated cheese; browned in the oven

Cannelloni à la florentine ⇒ cannelloni garnished with a preparation of hard boiled eggs, béchamel sauce, spinach, cream, and grated parmesan; browned in the oven

Cannelloni à la viande ⇒ cannelloni garnished with bolognèse sauce, and grated cheese; browned in the oven

Cannelloni aux fruits de mer ⇒ cannelloni garnished with a forcemeat of crab, and béchamel sauce; covered with a sauce of cream and calvados; then browned

Cannoli -[*Sicile, Sardaigne*]- ⇒ gateau stuffed with cream cheese, and preserved fruits

Cannolicchi ⇒ pasta cubes stuffed with meat, and herbs

Canole ⇒ small dried cake made of flour and eggs

Canotière (*à la ...*)

    1) poissons pochés ⇒ freshwater fishes poached and covered with a sauce

    2) carpe farçie ⇒ stuffed carp baked in white wine and browned; served with the cooking juice added of butter, plus crayfishes in court-bouillon

    3) matelote ⇒ matelote thickened with butter; and garnished of crayfishes

Cantal -[*fromage*]- ⇒ Cantal cheese

Cantalet -[*cantal*]- ⇒ Cantal cheese

Cantalon -[*cantal*]- ⇒ Cantal cheese

Cantaloup -[*melon*]- ⇒ cantaloup melon

Caoliang ⇒ sorghum alcohol

Caouanne -[*tortue*]- ⇒ turtle

Cap Corse -[*apéritif*]- ⇒ Corsican aperitif

Capelan (*capelin or caplin ...*) -[*Capelan de méditerranée*]- ⇒ poor cod

Capelletti -[*Italie*]- ⇒ pasta stuffed with a hash of chicken, cheese, and egg

Capillaire -[*sirop de capillaire*]- ⇒ maidenhair fern

Capilotade (*en ...*) ⇒ reduced to pulp

Capilé ⇒ drink made of capillaire, and grated lemon peel

Capitaine -[*poisson*]- ⇒ threadfin

Caponata ⇒ diced aubergines fried in oil, plus diced olives, celery, anchovies, and capers; mixed with a sauce of browned onion, tomato purée, and vinegar

Capone -[*rascasse*]- ⇒ scorpion fish

Cappon magro -[*Italie*]- ⇒ successive layers of bread rubbed with garlic, cooked vegetables, fish from court-bouillon, plus mayonnaise flavoured with herbs; served with olives, shrimp tails, hard boiled eggs, and anchovy fillets

Cappucino -[*café*]- ⇒ strong coffee topped with cream, and chocolate powder

Câpres ⇒ capers

Caprice de Buffon -[*truite à la Montbardaise*]- ⇒ trout stuffed with spinach and shallots, then cooked in a court-bouillon

Capucin -[*tartelette*]- ⇒ salted tartlet garnished with choux-pastry

Capucine ⇒ nasturtium

Capun -[*Suisse*]- ⇒ stuffed beet leaves

Caqhuse ⇒ hock of pork with onions and butter; cooked in the oven

Caracol -[*escargot*]- ⇒ snail

Carafe ⇒ carafe

Carago -[*escargot*]- ⇒ snail

Carambole ⇒ carambole fruit

Caramel ⇒ caramel or burnt sugar < *sens de substance, uncountable* >

Caramel à napper ⇒ burnt sugar for covering purpose

    - nappé avec caramel ⇒ ... covered with burnt sugar

Caramel à sauce ⇒ caramel cooked slowly, and becoming amber-coloured or amber-coloured caramel
Caramel dur ⇒ toffee
Caramel dur au café ⇒ toffee flavoured with coffee extract
Caramel dur au chocolat ⇒ toffee flavoured with honey and cocoa
Caramel mou ⇒ caramel or 1/2 fudge
Caramel mou à la crème ⇒ caramel made of sugar, cream, coffee extract and honey 1/2 ou 1/2 fudge
    made of sugar, cream, coffee extract and honey
Caramel mou au beurre ⇒ caramel made of sugar, milk, honey, vanilla and butter 1/2 ou 1/2 fudge
    made of sugar, milk, honey, vanilla and butter
Caramote ⇒ large prawn
Caramélisé ⇒ caramelized
Carapace -[*tortue, etc ...*]- ⇒ carapace
Caraque -[*cacao*]- ⇒ best quality cacao
Carasuolo di vittoria -[*Sicile, Sardaigne*]- ⇒ perfumed Italian wine
Caravane -[*thé*]- ⇒ variety of tea
Carbonada criolla -[*Argentine*]- ⇒ ragout simmered in gourd bark
Carbonade ⇒ carbonnade OR 1/2 carbonade
Carbonade à la flamande ⇒ carbonade
Carbonade -[*viande grillée*]- ⇒ meat grilled over charcoal
Carbonara (*alla ...*) ⇒ spaghetti served with a sauce made of lardoons, cream, butter, grated parmesan
    and egg-yolks
Carbonnade ⇒ carbonnade or carbonade
Carbonnade ou Carbonade -[*viande grillée*]- ⇒ meat grilled over charcoal
Carcasse -[*viande*]- ⇒ carcase
Carcaulada -[*escargot*]- ⇒ snail
Cardamone ⇒ cardamom < *uncountable* >
Carde ⇒ chard
Cardinal -[*cocktail*]- ⇒ mixing of red Beaujolais wine, and blackcurrant liqueur
Cardinal -[*raisin*]- ⇒ variety of black grape
Cardinal
    1) **poisson de mer** ⇒ sea fish, ou nom du poisson, covered with lobster escalopes, escalopes de
        homard, or sometimes truffle lamellas, lamelles de truffes, or sea fish, ou nom du
        poisson, covered with a sauce added of lobster purée
    2) **entremets glacés aux fruits rouges** ⇒ bombe cardinal voir définition
    3) **desserts aux fruits** -[*fruits froids crus ou pochés*]- ⇒ ... laid on vanilla ice cream, and
        covered with strawberry or raspberry purée
      - **desserts aux fruits** -[*tièdes*]- ⇒ nom du fruit, poached ... served tepid and covered
        with its cooking juice added of blackcurrant liqueur
Cardinal -[*poire*]-
    1) **froides** -[*fruit cru*]- ⇒ raw pear laid on vanilla ice cream, and covered with strawberry 2
      - **froides** -[*fruit poché*]- ⇒ poached pear laid on vanilla ice cream, and covered with
        strawberry or raspberry purée
    3) **tiède** ⇒ poached pear served tepid and covered with its cooking juice added of blackcurrant
        liqueur
Cardinaliser ⇒ cooking into a court-bouillon of the crustaceae
    - **crustacés cardinalisés** ⇒ crustaceae cooked into a court-bouillon
Cardine -[*poisson*]- ⇒ megrim
Cardon ⇒ cardoon
Cardons à la béchamel ⇒ cardoons simmered with butter and béchamel sauce
Cardons à la crème ⇒ cardoons simmered with cream

Cardons à la lyonnaise ⇒ cardoons simmered with onion, and white wine sauce
Cardons à la moelle ⇒ braised cardoons, served with bone-marrow, and a creamy sauce
Cardons au beurre ⇒ braised cardoons in butter, sprinkled with parsley or mint
Cardons aux fines herbes ⇒ cardoons simmered in a sauce with herbs
Cardons frits ⇒ cardoons marinated in olive oil, lemon juice and parsley; then coated of dough, and fried
Cardons Mornay ⇒ braised cardoons covered with creamy sauce, grated parmesan, and melted butter; then browned
Caret -[*tortue*]- ⇒ tortoise
Cargo -[*riz*]- ⇒ variety of brown rice
Cargolade ⇒ grilled snails flavoured with garlic and oil mayonnaise, plus parsley
Cari ⇒ curry ou curry-powder
Cari à l'anglaise ⇒ ragout of meat, plus flour, curry, and stock
Cari à l'indienne ⇒ ragout of tomatoes, curry and spices, plus braised diced meat
Cari à la chinoise ⇒ diced meat marinated in curry and soya sauce, then braised in pork fat
Cari d'agneau ⇒ bits of lamb macerated in ginger, saffron, olive oil and cayenne pepper; then braised in pork fat with crushed tomatoes, onions, curry, garlic, apple and coconut milk, served with rice, plus in separate hors-d'oeuvre dishes, cashew-nuts, raisins, diced pineapple, and diced bananas
Cari de lotte à la créole ⇒ angler fish simmered with onions, tomatoes, saffron, ginger, curry, garlic, and pepper; served with rice
Cari de poulet ⇒ bits of chicken simmered with chopped browned onions, ham, and apples; seasoned of garlic, thyme, laurel, cinnamon, mace and cardamom; then cream, lemon juice, curry and coconut milk are added in the cooking process, before they are served in timbale with rice
Cari de volaille ⇒ curried chicken ou chicken curry
Carignan (*à la ...*)
    1) viande ⇒ small round pieces of lamb or fillet steak of beef sautéed first, then laid on sauté potatoes, covered with a sauce of port and gravy; garnished of asparagus tips in butter, and fried moulded eggs filled of foie gras purée
    2) dessert ⇒ sweet of pear, peach or apple, hollowed out and filled with chocolate ice-cream, laid on Genoese sponge; then covered of vanilla fondant
Carmen
    1) consommé ⇒ consommé with tomato or capsicum, and a spicy garnish
    2) oeufs ⇒ eggs with tomato or capsicum, and a spicy garnish
    3) filets de sole ⇒ sole fillets with tomato or capsicum, and a spicy garnish
    4) salade ⇒ salad made of rice, diced white meat, capsicums and peas, in a dressing of oil, vinegar, mustard and tarragon
Carmélite (*à la ...*)
    1) volaille ⇒ breast and wing fillets of poultry, covered of chaudfroid sauce and decorated with truffle lamellas; laid on a crayfish mousseline, plus crayfish tails
    2) oeufs ⇒ soft boiled eggs laid on a pastry case, garnished of mussels in cream, and covered with white wine sauce
Carmin ⇒ carmine
Carnar -[*escargot*]- ⇒ snail
Carnaval -[*crêpes et pâtisseries énumération*]-
    - **crespets des landes** ⇒ voir traduction
    - **merveilles et bottereaux** ⇒ voir merveilles
    - **faverolles de ste ménéhould** ⇒ voir faverolles
    - **beugnons solognots** ⇒ voir beugnon

Caroline ⇒ small éclairs eaten as a hors d'oeuvre 1/2 or 1/2 small éclairs

Carolines à la hollandaise ⇒ éclairs stuffed with a culinary stuffing of herring fillets, egg-yolks, and butter

Carolines à la mousse de foie gras ⇒ éclairs garnished with a preparation of foie gras, butter and cognac

Carolines joinville ⇒ éclairs garnished with a béchamel sauce, plus shrimp tails flamed in marc

Carotte ⇒ carrot

Carottes à l'anglaise ⇒ boiled early spring carrots, sprinkled with melted butter and parsley

Carottes à la crème ⇒ boiled carrots covered with cream

Carottes à la forestière ⇒ carrots and mushrooms braised in butter, sprinkled with parsley

Carottes glacées ⇒ carrots cooked with sugar, butter and salt, then served with a creamy or buttered sauce

Carottes râpées ⇒ grated carrots

Carottes râpées aux anchois ⇒ grated carrots mixed with mayonnaise flavoured of lemon juice and anchovies; served with stoned olives, and slices of lemon

Carottes râpées aux raisins ⇒ grated carrots in french dressing, plus currants macerated in lemon juice

Carottes vichy ou à la vichy ⇒ slices of carrots cooked in water added of sugar; served with butter and parsley

Caroube ⇒ carob-bean 1/2 or 1/2 locust-bean

Carouby de Maussane -[pois gourmand]- ⇒ green peas

Carpaccio ⇒ hors d'oeuvre made of thin slices of beef; served with french dressing and chopped onions

Carpe ⇒ carp < *pluriel inchangé* >

Carpe à l'alsacienne ⇒ carp stuffed with forcemeat balls in cream, then baked in court-bouillon and white wine; served on a layer of sauerkraut surrounded of boiled potatoes

Carpe à la bière ⇒ carp baked in beer on a layer of onions, diced gingerbread, celery and butter; served with the cooking juice

Carpe à la chinoise ⇒ bits of carp, cooked in a sauce of onions, vinegar, sugar, ginger, xeres, and pepper

Carpe à la polonaise ⇒ carp in jelly with a sauce of horseradish and cream

Carpe Chambord ⇒ carp stuffed with a forcemeat of fish meat, then larded and baked in red wine; coated with a roux added of tomato purée, then served with mushrooms, plus a sauce of fish stock and vegetables, moistened with red wine

Carpe farçie à l'ancienne ⇒ carp boned first, then reconstituted with a forcemeat of carp fish-meat, eel, anchovies, truffle, mushrooms, and covered of breadcrumbs plus egg-yolk; baked with melted butter

Carpe frite ⇒ carp milked and floured, then fried in oil; served with parsley and lemon

Carpe grillée à la maître d'hôtel ⇒ carp brushed with oil, then grilled; served with parsley, lemon and butter

Carpe juive ⇒ carp braised in white wine, garlic and parsley

Carpe rôtie à la mode de Bugey ⇒ carp stuffed with a forcemeat of whiting, cream, truffle and butter; grilled on a skewer and sprinkled with cream, served garnished of crayfish tails and truffles

   - autres recettes brochet ⇒ pike

   - saumon ⇒ salmon

   - omble-chevalier ⇒ char

   - 1/2 sandre ⇒ pike perch

   - truite saumonée ⇒ sea trout < *remplacer whiting dans le texte par l'un de ces poissons* >

Carpeau ⇒ young carp < *pluriel inchangé* >

Carpillon ⇒ young carp < *pluriel inchangé* >

Carrelet ⇒ plaice < *pluriel inchangé* >

Carreteria *(a la ...)* ⇒ spaghetti with mushrooms and tunny

Carré de 1 *-[mouton]-* ⇒ best end neck of lamb

Carré de 1 *(paré et manche fait ...)* *-[mouton]-* ⇒ rack of lamb

Carré de 1 *(paré et raccourci ...)* *-[mouton]-* ⇒ rack of lamb larder trim

Carré de 1 *(séparé ...)* *-[veau]-* ⇒ best end split and chined

Carré *-[agneau]-* ⇒ loin of lamb

Carré *-[porc]-* ⇒ loin of pork

Carré *-[fromage]-* ⇒ carré

Carré avec caprin, ficelé *-[boeuf]-* ⇒ beef forerib boneless

Carré d'agneau ⇒ loin of lamb

Carré d'agneau à la bonne femme ⇒ loin of lamb baked with onions, potatoes and lardoons

Carré d'agneau à la bordelaise ⇒ loin of lamb baked with potatoes and boletus

Carré d'agneau à la boulangère ⇒ loin of lamb studded of garlic, baked with potatoes and onions

Carré d'agneau à la languedocienne ⇒ loin of lamb baked in goose fat with onions, ham, garlic and boletus

Carré d'agneau à la niçoise ⇒ loin of lamb baked in butter and oil with diced courgette, quartered tomato, plus potatoes

Carré d'agneau La Varenne ⇒ loin of lamb coated of breadcrumbs and whipped egg, then cooked in butter; served with a culinary stuffing of mushrooms and cream

Carré d'agneau clamart ⇒ loin of lamb basted with melted butter and baked with peas

Carré d'agneau en crépine ⇒ loin of lamb cooked in butter, then covered with a forcemeat of pork and diced truffles

Carré d'agneau grillé ⇒ grilled loin of lamb, served with watercress or early spring vegetables

Carré d'agneau parmentier ⇒ loin of lamb cooked in butter with diced potatoes; served with its cooking juice added of white wine, and stock

Carré d'agneau rôti ⇒ loin of lamb basted of melted butter and roasted, served with the gravy added of white wine

Carré de 1 et filet double *-[veau]-*

- **avec os, mais paré** ⇒ chine and end of veal « trimmed »

- **avec ses rognons** ⇒ chine and end of veal

- **sans ses rognons** ⇒ chine and end of veal « ex kidney »

Carré de 7 côtes préparé pour cuire ⇒ seven bone rib « oven prepared »

Carré de Lannoy ⇒ Carré cheese from Lannoy

Carré de côtes de porc ⇒ pork best end of neck

Carré de côtes découvertes ou côtes premières *-[mouton]-* ⇒ chops

Carré de côtes premières

- **« talon os de culotte » prêt à trancher** ⇒ forerib « oven prepared »

- **« talon os de culotte »** ⇒ forerib « carvery cut »

Carré de côtes secondes de boeuf ⇒ ' Scotch cut ' forerib

Carré de l'est ⇒ Carré cheese from Lorraine area

Carré de mouton ⇒ loin of mutton

Carré de porc ⇒ loin of pork

Carré de porc à l'alsacienne ⇒ loin of pork baked with sauerkraut, bacon and sausages, plus boiled potatoes

Carré de porc à l'ananas ⇒ loin of pork cooked in butter and oil, plus browned bits of pineapple and apple; served with the cooking juice flavoured of rum

Carré de porc à la languedocienne ⇒ roasted loin of pork, studded of garlic, and served with sauté potatoes

Carré de porc au chou rouge ⇒ roasted loin of pork, served with braised red cabbage and potatoes or chestnuts

Carré de porc bonne femme ⇒ loin of pork baked in butter with potatoes, and onions

Carré de porc rôti et ses garnitures ⇒ roasted loin of pork, served with various vegetables

Carré de premières côtes de boeuf ⇒ forerib of beef

Carré de veau ⇒ veal best end of neck

Carré de veau froid ⇒ roasted loin of veal covered in jelly and served with artichoke hearts, watercress and asparagus tips

Carré double 1 -*[veau]-* ⇒ best end of veal

Carré double avec selle et côtes découvertes -*[mouton]-* ⇒ chine and end of lamb « long »

Carré double de côtes 1 avec peau -*[mouton]-* ⇒ best end of lamb « split and chined »

Carré double sans selle et côtes découvertes -*[mouton]-* ⇒ chine and end of lamb « short »

Carré découverte -*[mouton]-* ⇒ middle neck of lamb

Carré désossé, ficelé -*[boeuf]-* ⇒ forerib « boned and rolled »

Carte ⇒ menu

Carte *(à la ...)* ⇒ menu à la carte

Carte à prix fixe ⇒ set menu or ... F.Fr menu

Carte des vins ⇒ wine list

Carte du jour ⇒ today's menu

Carte gastronomique ⇒ gourmet's menu

Carte touristique ⇒ economy-price menu

Carthagène ⇒ grenache wine added of wine eau de vie

Carthame ⇒ bastard saffron

Cartilage d'épaule et côte basse ⇒ back ribs

Carvi ⇒ caraway

Carvi -*[cari]-* ⇒ curry or curry powder

Casarda -*[tadorne]-* ⇒ sheldrake OR shelduck

Cascamèche *(à la ...)* -*[Berry]-* ⇒ fried gudgeons marinated in a spicy marinade

Caséine ⇒ casein

Casher ⇒ kosher

Cassate ⇒ Neapolitan ice cream or cassata

Cassate aux fraises ⇒ cassata made of ice-cream flavoured with strawberries, vanilla, plus whipped cream added with a culinary stuffing of preserved fruits macerated in eau de vie

Casse ⇒ various bits of pork cooked with spices and chopped onions

Casse rennaise ⇒ dish of membrane from calf's intestine, calf trotters, rind of pork, and pie sprinkled with their cooking stock; topped with a loin of pork studded of garlic, and baked

Casse-croûte ⇒ snack

Casse-museau ⇒ hard small cake from almond and cheese

Casse-pierre ⇒ Crithmum or rock samphire

Casserole *(en ...)*
- **général** ⇒ dish braised and simmered
- **faire un poulet á la casserole** ⇒ to casserole a chicken
- **veau à la casserole** ⇒ casserole of veal

Casserole
- **ustensile** ⇒ stewpan or saucepan
- **méthode de cuisson** ⇒ in casserole

Casserole *(préparation ...)* ⇒ cassolette or timbale ... made of rice or mashed potatoes with a garnish of ...
- **de mousses** ⇒ ... mousses
- **de salpicons** ⇒ ... culinary stuffing
- **de hachis** ⇒ ... hash
- **de purée de gibier** ⇒ ... game purée
- **de ris de veau** ⇒ ... calf sweetbread
- **de ris d'agneau** ⇒ ... lamb sweetbread
- **d'escalopes de foie gras aux truffes** ⇒ ... truffle flavoured foie gras escalopes
- **autres garnitures** ⇒ voir à la sagan, à la vénitienne, à la bouquetière, à la régence, à la Nantua

Casserole au riz à l'ancienne ⇒ rice cooked in casserole with stock and browned in the oven; served with a sauce

Casserolette ou casserole ⇒ rice in timbale or shaped in casserole; with a garnish ...
- **garnitures à la sagan, à la vénitienne, à la Nantua, à la bouquetière, à la régence, etc** ⇒ voir textes

Casseron ⇒ small cuttlefish

Casserons ⇒ small squids

Cassé *-[sucre de pomme]-* ⇒ apple sugar

Cassis
- **fruit** ⇒ blackcurrant
- **liqueur** ⇒ blackcurrant liqueur

Cassis de Dijon ⇒ blackcurrant liquor

Cassissine ⇒ sweet made of blackcurrant paste and blackcurrant liqueur

Cassolette ⇒ cassolette
- **cassolettes salées** ⇒ dish made of culinary stuffing, plus various ragouts thickened with a sauce
- **cassolettes sucrées** ⇒ custards flavoured with aromatics, plus poached fruits

Cassolette de pétoncles à la crème de noix ⇒ cassolette of queen scallops in walnut liqueur

Cassolettes de St jacques aux endives ⇒ cassolettes of braised chicory bits, topped with fried scallops; covered with a sauce of port, lemon juice, and butter

Cassonade ⇒ brown sugar

Cassoulet ⇒ cassoulet

Cassoulet Prosper Montagné ⇒ cassoulet made of beans cooked with bacon, rind of pork, carrot, onions, clove and garlic; plus chine of pork, and loin of pork braised in pork fat; served on alternate layers of meat and beans, which are browned in the oven

Cassoulet de Castelnaudary ⇒ cassoulet made of haricot beans, pork, sausages, conserve of goose, plus a hash of bacon and garlic

Cassoulet toulousain ⇒ cassoulet made of haricot beans, rind of pork, carrots, garlic, goose meat, and tomatoes

Castagnatti *-[Corse]-*
- **beignets** ⇒ fritters ...
- **gaufrettes** ⇒ waffers ...
- **flan** ⇒ flan ... based on chestnut dough

Castagnatti *(appelé Castanhet ...)* *-[Cévennes]-* ⇒ cake made of chestnut purée, eggs, and butter

Castanhet *-[Corse]-*
- **beignets** ⇒ fritters ...
- **gaufrettes** ⇒ waffers ...
- **flan** ⇒ flan ... based on chestnut dough

Castanhet *(appelé Castanhet ...)* *-[Cévennes]-* ⇒ cake made of chestnut purée, eggs, and butter

Castello del monte *-[vin de Pouille]-* ⇒ Italian wine

Castiglione *(à la ...)*
    a) Petites pièces de boucherie ⇒ sauté ..., laid on slices of aubergine, then topped with bone-marrow, and mushroom head, stuffed of risotto
    b) Sole ⇒ sole
        - filets de poisson ⇒ fillets ... glazed in white wine; garnished with mushrooms, lobster escalopes, and steamed potatoes
Castillane *(à la ...)*
    1) noisette ⇒ sauté noisettes of lamb ...
    2) tournedos ⇒ sauté tournedos ... topped with crushed tomatoes thickened of olive oil, plus potato croquettes, and slices of fried onions
Castor ⇒ beaver
Casu marzu *-[Sicile, Sardaigne]-* ⇒ Sardinian cheese with a strong smell
Catalane *(à la ...)*
    1) Poulet sauté ⇒ sautéed chicken ...
        - Sauté d' agneau ⇒ sauté of lamb ...
        - Sauté de veau ⇒ sauté of veal ... served with a garnish of quartered tomatoes sautéed in butter, poached chestnuts, chipolatas and stoned olives
    2) Grosses pieces de boucherie ⇒ ...; served with a garnish of diced aubergines and pilaf
    3) Tournedos ⇒ fillet steak of beef ... or tournedos ...
        - Noisettes ⇒ noisettes of lamb ... laid on artichoke hearts, surrounded by grilled tomatoes
Catawba *-[Canada vins du]-* ⇒ Catawba
Catherine *-[prune]-* ⇒ variety of plum
Catigau ⇒ matelote of river fishes
Catigot ⇒ matelote of river fishes
Cauchoise *(à la ...)*
    1) Râble de lièvre ⇒ saddle of hare ...
        - Râble de lapin ⇒ saddle of rabbit ... marinated in white wine and aromatics, then baked and covered with the gravy thickened of cream and mustard; served with apples sautéed in butter
    2) Sole ⇒ sole braised with cider in the oven, covered with the cooking juice added of butter; served with a garnish of crayfishes, plus sometimes sauté mussels poached oysters, fried sea smelts or mushrooms
    3) Salade ⇒ salad of sliced apples, celery and chopped ham; seasoned with cream, cider vinegar and chervil
Caudière de Berck ⇒ kind of bouillabaisse
Caudrée ⇒ kind of bouillabaisse
Causalade *(à la ...) -[oeufs]-* ⇒ eggs fried with slices of ham
Cavagnats de Menton ⇒ pastries shaped in basket, and filled with eggs dyed in red
Cavendish *-[banane]-* ⇒ variety of banana
Caviar ⇒ caviar < *uncountable* >
Caviar blanc ⇒ mullet roes dried and pressed
Caviar d'aubergine ⇒ pulp of aubergines firstly baked in tomato and onion, then thickened with oil; decorated of hard boiled eggs and slices of tomatoes
Cavim ⇒ Brazilian cassava eau de vie
Cavour
    1) escalopes ou ris de veau ⇒ escalopes or sweetbread of veal sautéed and laid on polenta pancakes, garnished with grilled mushrooms, livers and truffle
    2) grosses pièces de boucherie ⇒ ... with a garnish of semolina croquettes and ravioli
Cawcher *-[kascher]-* ⇒ kosher
Cayenne ⇒ cayenne pepper < *uncountable* >

Cazu marzu ⇒ Sardinian cheese with a strong smell
Cebiche ⇒ Peruvian dish of fish marinated in lemon juice
Cédrat ⇒ cedrate or citron
Cédratine ⇒ cedrate liquor
Celeri au beurre ⇒ celery cooked in butter and stock
Céleri en branche ⇒ celery < *uncountable* >
    - **pour le pluriel utiliser les phrases suivantes en mettant le nombre devant sauf pour**
    « a bunch » ⇒ ... sticks of celery or ... heads of celery or a bunch of celery
Céleri en rémoulade ⇒ grated celeriac seasoned with remoulade
Céleri farçi à la paysanne ⇒ celeriac stuffed with diced carrots and onions, covered of butter, grated
    cheese and stock, then baked
Céleri-branche à la milanaise ⇒ alternate layers of celery and grated cheese, sprinkled of melted
    butter, then browned
Céleri-rave ⇒ celeriac
Céleris à la crème ⇒ baked celery served with the cooking juice added of béchamel sauce, cream and
    butter
Céleris à la sauce béchamel ⇒ celery braised in butter and covered with béchamel sauce
Céleris braisés *-[au gras ou au maigre]-* ⇒ celery in bunch, cooked in butter, rind of pork, onions,
    carrots and stock
Célestine
    a) **poulet** ⇒ sauté chicken with mushrooms and skinned tomatoes, flamed in cognac; then
      moistened of white wine and sprinkled with garlic powder plus chopped parsley
    b) **consommé** ⇒ poultry consommé thickened with tapioca, garnished of pancakes in julienne,
      poached white of meat and chervil
    c) **omelette** ⇒ omelette garnished with a julienne of white of meat, cream sauce, chervil; then
      topped with an other omelette
Cendre *(sous la ...)*
    - **cuire quelque chose** ⇒ to cook something in the embers
    - **pommes de terre cuites** ⇒ potatoes cooked in the embers, served with slightly salted butter
    - **truffes cuites** ⇒ truffles moistened in cognac and wrapped in aluminium paper; then cooked in
      the embers
Cendré *-[fromage, bourgogne, orléanais, champagne]-* ⇒ yellow cow's milk cheese, shaped in
    disc
Cent vignes *-[Beaune]-* ⇒ vintage from Beaune area
Centilitre ⇒ centilitre or cl
Cépage ⇒ variety of vine
Cèpe ⇒ boletus
Cèpes à la bordelaise ⇒ boletus sautéed in oil and lemon juice; served with chopped parsley
Cèpes à la hongroise ⇒ boletus braised in butter with chopped onion, pepper and paprika; then
    covered with cream
Cèpes à la mode béarnaise ⇒ boletus studded with garlic and grilled; served with a sauce made of
    oil, crumbs, garlic, and parsley
Cèpes à la provençale ⇒ braised boletus in olive oil with chopped garlic
Cèpe à pied rouge *-[Bolet à chair jaune]-* ⇒ red cracked boletus
Cèpe de Bordeaux *-[Bolet]-* ⇒ boletus
Cèpe de mélèzes *-[Bolet élégant]-* ⇒ elegant boletus
Cèpes au gratin ⇒ boletus umbrellas garnished with a stuffing of shallots, chopped boletus stems, and
    crumbs; moistened with oil, and browned
Cèpes en terrine ⇒ terrine of bacon, plus boletus sautéed in olive oil with garlic and shallots
Cèpes grillés ⇒ grilled boletus sprinkled with melted butter or oil

Cèpe jaune -[*bolet annulaire*]- ⇒ brown-yellow boletus
Cèpes marinés à chaud ⇒ boletus marinated in a hot preparation of olive oil, vinegar, fennel, lemon peel, laurel, thyme, and pepper
Cèpe noir -[*Bolet bronzé*]- ⇒ edible black boletus
Cèpe pleureur -[*Bolet granulé*]- ⇒ granulated boletus
Céréale ⇒ cereal
Cerf ⇒ stag or deer 1 or red deer 1 or hart < *1 pluriel inchangé* >
Cerfeuil ⇒ chervil < *uncountable* >
Cerise -[*liqueur*]- ⇒ cherry brandy
Cerise -[*tomate*]- ⇒ tomato variety eaten raw with salt
Cerise ⇒ cherry < *pluriel cherries* >
Cerises à l'anglaise ⇒ cherries boiled in water and sprinkled with sugar
Cerises à l'eau de vie ⇒ cherries preserved in eau de vie and sugar
Cerises au vinaigre à l'allemande ⇒ stoned cherries preserved in a preparation of vinegar, sugar, clove, cinnamon, and nutmeg
Cerises condé ⇒ rice cooked in milk, covered with poached cherries, angelica and almonds, plus a sauce of syrup and cherries
Cerises confites fourrées à la pâte d'amandes ⇒ preserved cherries stuffed with almond paste
Cerise d'hiver -[*alkékenge*]- ⇒ physalis or winter cherry
Cerises déguisées dites « marquises » ⇒ preserved cherries coated in fondant melted with kirsch
Cerises flambées à la bourguignonne ⇒ stoned cherries cooked in water and sugar, then flamed with burgundy marc
Cerises jubilé ⇒ cherries cooked in syrup and arrow-root, flamed with kirsch
Cerisette
　　- **boisson** ⇒ drink made of cherries
　　- **bonbon** ⇒ stuffed sweet
Cernaux de noix au verjus ⇒ green walnuts sprinkled with unripe grape juice and herbs, then served with cold meat
Cerneau ⇒ green walnut
Cernier -[*mérou*]- ⇒ grouper
Cérons -[*vin*]- ⇒ Graves white wine
Cerveja -[*bière*]- ⇒ beer
Cervelas
　　- **saucisse** ⇒ saveloy or cervelat sausage < *pluriel saveloys* >
　　- **terrine** ⇒ fish terrine of pike with potatoes, butter and eggs
Cervelas à la lyonnaise ⇒ saveloy added of truffle and pistachio
Cervelas en salade ⇒ salad of sliced cervelats, cucumbers, celery, plus artichoke hearts, in french dressing and mayonnaise
Cervelas farçis aux épinards ⇒ spinach cooked in butter, served with cervelats stuffed of scrambled eggs
Cervelle au beurre noisette ⇒ brains cooked in a court-bouillon, then sautéed in butter with lemon juice, vinegar, and capers
Cervelle d'agneau ⇒ lamb brain
Cervelle de bœuf ⇒ ox brain
Cervelle de bœuf à l'indienne ⇒ ox brain cooked in a court-bouillon, then sautéed in butter; served with rice and curry sauce
Cervelle de canut ⇒ soft white cheese added of chopped shallots, herbs, cream, white wine, and oil
Cervelle de veau ⇒ calf brain
Cervelle de veau à l'allemande ⇒ calf brain poached in court-bouillon, then braised in butter and served on sippets with sauce

Cervelle de veau à la hongroise ⇒ calf brain escalopes sprinkled with paprika and sautéed in butter; served on sippets plus a culinary stuffing of mushrooms and hard boiled eggs

Cervelle de veau à la poulette ⇒ calf brain poached in a court-bouillon, then warmed up in a sauce of egg-yolks, stock and lemon juice

Cervelle de veau en fritots ⇒ diced calf brain macerated in oil and lemon juice, then steeped in dough and fried; served with tomato sauce

Cervelle de veau en meurette ⇒ calf brain poached in a sauce made of carrot, onion, garlic, burgundy red wine and burgundy marc; served with kneaded butter and sippets

Cervelle de veau en panier ⇒ tomatoes studded with calf brain escalopes poached in a court-bouillon, macerated in olive oil and lemon juice; served with anchovy sauce

Cervelle de veau frite à l'anglaise ⇒ calf brain escalope macerated in oil and lemon juice, then fried; served with tomato purée

Cervelle sautée à la provençale ⇒ brains cooked in a court-bouillon, then floured and sautéed in olive oil; served with black olives, basil and tomato purée

Cervelles ⇒ brains

Cervelles à la meunière ⇒ brains browned in butter, and served with parsley, plus lemon juice

Cervelles de veau en matelote ⇒ calf brains cooked in a red wine court-bouillon, plus sauté mushrooms and onions; served with the cooking juice

Cerveza -[*bière*]- ⇒ beer

Cervoise ⇒ barley beer

Céteaux ⇒ small soles

Cévenole (*à la ...*)
- **avec marrons** ⇒ ... with chestnuts
- **avec marrons glacés** ⇒ ... with glazed chestnuts
- **avec purée de marrons** ⇒ ... with chestnut purée

Ceviche ⇒ Peruvian dish of fish marinated in lemon juice

Chabessal (*en ...*) -[*cabessal*]- ⇒ stuffed hare cooked in a baking-tin

Chabichou ⇒ goat's milk cheese

Chablis ⇒ Chablis wine

Chablis ⇒ chablis

Chablis de Californie ⇒ Californian wine from chablis vine

Chaboisseau ⇒ tiny freshwater fish

Chabot -[*poisson*]- ⇒ bullhead

Chabrol -[*soupe*]- ⇒ to add red wine in the plate of soup

Chabrot -[*soupe*]- ⇒ to add red wine in the plate of soup

Chachadi ⇒ Indian middling sweet and sour ratatouille, with mustard and coconut

Chachlik ⇒ bits of marinated lamb grilled on a skewer; served with rice

Chadrons -[*oeufs d'oursin*]- ⇒ eggs of sea-urchin

Cha gio ⇒ small Vietnamese pancake of rice and eggs, stuffed with shrimps plus crab; seasoned, rolled and fried

Chair ⇒ meat or animal flesh

Chair à saucisse ⇒ sausage-meat

Chakchouka ⇒ ragout made of potatoes and onions cooked in oil, seasoned with pimentos, capsicum purée, and tomato sauce; topped with eggs and sprinkled of dried mint

Chaleuth ⇒ sugared sweet made with a mixing of crumbs, sliced apples, eggs, sugar, rum, raisins and cinnamon; baked and served tepid or sweet made of sliced apples cooked with sugar and cinnamon in paste

Chalonnaise (*à la ...*) ⇒ ... with a garnish of kidneys, cockscombs, truffle lamellas, plus mushrooms in supreme sauce

Chalumeau -[*pour boissons ou glaces*]- ⇒ straw

Chalwa -[*halva*]- ⇒ halva ou halvah
Chambertin ⇒ Chambertin
Chambolle-Musigny ⇒ Burgundy wine
Chambord
   - **carpe** ⇒ carp ...
   - **saumon** ⇒ salmon ...
   - **sole** ⇒ sole ... stuffed and braised in red wine, garnished with fish quenelles, sole fillets, sauté
        milt, mushrooms, truffles and crayfishes
Chambrer -[*vin*]- ⇒ to bring wine to room temperature
Chameau ⇒ camel
Chamois ⇒ chamois
Chamois -[*hydne*]- ⇒ spreading hydnum
Champagne -[*cocktail*]- ⇒ crusta
Champagne (*en addition des longs drinks ...*) -[*vin*]- ⇒ champagne
Champagne flip ⇒ cocktail of champagne, egg-yolk, lemon peel, and nutmeg
Champagne -[*plats*]-
   1) **potée champenoise** ⇒ stew of bacon, smoked ham, sausage, cabbage and other vegetables
   2) **salade de pissenlits au lard** ⇒ dandelion salad with streaky bacon
   3) **matelote** ⇒ matelote of freshwater fishes in white wine
   4) **brochet en blanquette** ⇒ pike in blanquette
      - **brochet à la sauce blanche** ⇒ pike in white sauce
      - **brochet farçi au jambon** ⇒ pike stuffed with ham
   5) **les écrevisses à la nage** ⇒ crayfishes poached in court-bouillon flavoured with herbs
      - **les écrevisses au marc** ⇒ crayfishes cooked in marc
   6) **escargots de vignes farçis à l'ail** ⇒ snails stuffed with garlic
   7) **pâtés de gibier** ⇒ game pie
   8) **terrines de gibier** ⇒ terrines of game
   9) **jambons en croUtes** ⇒ ham in croustade < *revoir Champagne-Ardennes pour autres détails
        si besoin est* >
Champignon ⇒ mushroom
Champignon à bague -[*coulemelle*]- ⇒ parasol mushroom
Champignon de couche ⇒ cultivated mushroom
Champignon des bruyères ⇒ horse mushroom
Champignon des fées ⇒ fairy ring mushroom
Champignon des prés ⇒ field mushroom
Champignons à l'anglaise ⇒ sippets garnished of mushrooms and butter, then baked
Champignons à la crème ⇒ mushrooms sautéed in butter and simmered with cream
Champignons à la hongroise ⇒ mushrooms braised in cream, lemon juice, paprika, and pepper
Champignons à la poulette ⇒ mushrooms braised in a sauce of egg-yolks, stock, and lemon juice
Champignons au beurre ⇒ sliced mushrooms sautéed in butter with herbs and onions
Champignons de Paris ⇒ cultivated mushrooms
Champignons en garniture ⇒ sauté mushrooms, plus a sauce with Madeira and stock
Champignons exotiques ⇒ dried black mushrooms
Champignons farçis ⇒ mushrooms stuffed with a forcemeat, sprinkled of olive oil and crumbs, then
      browned
Champigny ⇒ rectangular puff-pastry filled with apricot jam
Champoreau ⇒ black coffee added of cognac, or calvados, or marc
Champvallon -[*côtelettes mouton*]- ⇒ mutton chops baked in butter with onions, garlic, thyme,
      sliced potatoes, stock and pepper

Chanachur -*[Inde]*- ⇒ snack of various items, split peas, peanuts, lemon, pimentos, and lentil flour; fried separately

Chanciau ⇒ thick pancake, sugared or salted

Chanfaïna -*[Antilles]*- ⇒ fried slices of liver, covered with fried quartered tomatoes, crushed garlic, and pimentos

Chanfaïna d'Espagne -*[sauce pour volaille, escalope, viande blanche ou homard]*- ⇒ sauce made of diced onions, capsicums and vegetables; cooked in hot oil with mint, parsley, cumin, and pepper

Chanoinnesse (à la ...)

    1) Poularde ⇒ poached fattened pullet, surrounded of tartlets filled with crayfish tails thickened of supreme sauce

    2) Potage ⇒ velouté added of crayfish tails and suprême sauce

    3) Ris de veau ⇒ calf sweetbread ...

        - **Oeufs mollets** ⇒ soft boiled eggs ...

        - **Oeufs pochés** ⇒ poached eggs ... served with a garnish of small carrots in cream, plus truffles covered with a sauce added of xeres

Chanterelle -*[champignon]*- ⇒ chanterelle

Chanterelle brune ⇒ involute paxillus

Chanterelle grise ⇒ chanterelle Grise mushroom

Chantilly ⇒ whipped cream or sugared whipped cream

Chanturgues -*[vin]*- ⇒ red wine from Clermond Ferrand area

Chao chen -*[thé]*- ⇒ green tea

Chao xing ⇒ Chinese rice alcohol

Chaource ⇒ cow's milk cheese shaped in cylinder

Chapati ⇒ Indian pancake

Chapeau chinois -*[patelle]*- ⇒ limpet

Chapelle Chambertin -*[Gevrey Chambertin]*- ⇒ Chambertin

Chapelure ⇒ breadcrumbs or crumbs

Chapon -*[pain]*- ⇒ bread seasoned with garlic, sprinkled with olive oil, and vinegar

Chapon -*[rascasse rouge]*- ⇒ large-scaled scorpion fish

Chapon -*[coq castré]*- ⇒ capon

Charbon de bois ⇒ charcoal

Charbonnée

    - **général** ⇒ meat grilled on charcoal

    - **Berry** ⇒ jugged pork thickened with blood

    - **Ile de France** ⇒ ragout of beef, cooked in red wine plus onions, carrots and aromatics, thickened with blood

Charbonnier -*[hygrophore]*- ⇒ march mushroom

Charbonnier -*[russule]*- ⇒ russula

Charcuterie ⇒ pork-butchery < *uncountable* >

Charcutière (à la ...)

    - **sauce** ⇒ with a sauce made of onions, white wine and gherkins

    - **côtes** ⇒ sauté ribs of pork « carré », or roast of pork « rôti » or crépinettes, or floured culinary stuffing « cromesquis » fried in hot oil

    - **œoeufs** ⇒ poached eggs laid on sauté crépinettes, then covered with a sauce of onions and white wine

Chardonnay -*[vin]*- ⇒ variety of vine

Chardonnette ⇒ wild artichoke flower

Charentais -*[melon]*- ⇒ variety of melon

Charentaise *-[porée]-* ⇒ leeks braised in butter, then cooked in fish stock, cream, salt, and pepper, with turbot fillets, scallops, and Norway lobsters; served with the cooking juice thickened of egg-yolk and sprinkled with chervil

Chariot ⇒ trolley

Charlemagne *-[corton charlemagne]-* ⇒ quality white wine from Côtes de Beaune

Charleston *-[pain]-* ⇒ variety of bread from Aude area

Charlotka *-[charlotte glacée]-* ⇒ voir charlotte glacée au cassis, aux marrons, à la vanille

Charlotte ⇒ charlotte

Charlotte à la chantilly ⇒ charlotte made of sponge fingers, and whipped cream added of preserved fruits

Charlotte à la crème fouettée ⇒ trifle

Charlotte à la valentin ⇒ charlotte made of sponge fingers and raspberry purée sealed together; decorated with almonds and meringue

Charlotte au chocolat ⇒ charlotte made of melted chocolate, egg-yolks, cream, sugar, and sponge fingers

Charlotte aux deux fruits ⇒ charlotte made with slices of bread with alternate layers of apricot jam, apple jam, and sliced apples

Charlotte aux fraises ⇒ charlotte made of sponge fingers, eggs, sugar, and a Bavarian mousse of strawberries

Charlotte aux framboises ⇒ charlotte made of sponge fingers flavoured with raspberry syrup, whipped cream added of sugar, vanilla, and raspberry purée

Charlotte aux framboises *-[bistrot du port N.D]-* ⇒ charlotte made of a syrup added with raspberries and cream, plus sponge fingers steeped in kirsch; served with egg custard

Charlotte aux marrons ⇒ charlotte made of sponge fingers moistened of whisky and syrup, plus a preparation of chestnut purée, whisky, gelatine, and whipped cream flavoured with vanilla

Charlotte aux poires *-[Boutier]-* ⇒ charlotte made of sponge fingers, plus a preparation of gelatine, pear pulp, diced pears, eau de vie, and eggs; served with raspberry purée

Charlotte aux poires *-[Mauduit]-* ⇒ charlotte made of sponge fingers, plus a preparation of egg-custard, liqueur, and whipped cream; in alternate layers with sliced pears

Charlotte aux pommes ⇒ charlotte made of apples sautéed in butter with vanilla and lemon peel, then moulded with sponge fingers and baked; covered with apricot compote

Charlotte aux pommes à la cassonade brune ⇒ charlotte made of buttered slices of bread, plus a preparation of quartered apples and brown-sugar, cooked in butter, and flavoured of calvados; served with egg-custard

Charlotte aux pommes et au riz ⇒ charlotte made of rice cooked in milk, filled with apple jam

Charlotte aux rougets ⇒ charlotte made of fried red-gurnard fillets, plus a preparation of aubergine pulp, lemon juice, butter, and red-gurnard livers

Charlotte de chou aux olives ⇒ charlotte made of mashed cabbage, egg-yolk, grated cheese, and stoned black olives

Charlotte de légumes ⇒ charlotte made of asparagus, tomatoes, eggs, and cream

Charlotte glacée à la vanille ⇒ charlotte made of sponge fingers and vanilla ice-cream

Charlotte glacée au cassis ⇒ charlotte made with alternate layers of blackcurrant ice-cream and sponge fingers moistened of blackcurrant syrup

Charlotte glacée aux marrons ⇒ charlotte made of sponge fingers, a syrup of sugar and lemon juice, chestnut purée, and egg-custard

Charlotte majestic ⇒ charlotte made of preserved fruits, finger biscuits, ice-cream with any flavouring

Charlotte russe ⇒ charlotte russe

Charmes *-[Gevrey Chambertin]-* ⇒ high quality Burgundy red wine from Côtes de Nuits

Charmes *-[Chambolle-Musigny]-* ⇒ high quality Burgundy wine from Côtes de Nuits

Charmoula ⇒ sauce made with a ragout of onions, pimento and spices, added of vinegar, honey, raisins and sometimes carrots, celery plus shallots

Charognard -*[saumon non consommable]*- ⇒ salmon
Charolais -*[bœuf]*- ⇒ Charolais or Charollais
Charolaise -*[pot au feu]*- ⇒ chunk of beef for pot au feu
Charollais -*[fromage]*- ⇒ goat's milk cheese
Charqui *(le ...)* ⇒ smoked beef, or mutton, or llama, served in lamellas
Chartres *(à la ...)*
    1) **côtes d'agneau** ⇒ lamb's cutlets braised with tarragon
    2) **tournedos** ⇒ tournedos sautéed and covered with the gravy added of tarragon
    3) **garniture pommes de terre sautées au beurre avec lardons** ⇒ garnished of small
        potatoes sautéed in butter with lardoons
        - **garniture champignons farçis et laitue braisée** ⇒ garnished of stuffed mushrooms,
        and braised lettuce
        - **garniture purée de pois** ⇒ garnished of mashed peas
Chartreuse -*[plats]*-
    1) **viandes et gibiers** ⇒ successive layers of braised cabbage and meat or game, shaped in dome
        2
        - **perdrix** ⇒ partridge with cabbage
    3) **poissons** ⇒ successive layers of fish and lettuce with sorrel
    4) **oeufs** ⇒ successive layers of eggs, braised cabbage, and other vegetables
Chartreuse -*[liqueur]*- ⇒ chartreuse
Chartreuse à la parisienne en surprise ⇒ moulded dish, decorated with truffles cooked in
    champagne plus crayfish tails, filled of chicken fillets, blanquette and mushrooms
Chartreuse de perdreau ⇒ moulded dish of cabbage braised in goose fat, forcemeat of veal,
    partridge, turnips, and carrots
Chäshappen ⇒ fried spirals of pasta made of Appenzell cheese, milk, flour, yeast, and eggs; served
    with a salad
Chassagne-montrachet ⇒ Burgundy wine either red or white
Chasse ⇒ dish of roasted game
Chasselas -*[Gutetel]*- ⇒ ordinary but quality wine from Alsace area
Chasseur -*[saucisson]*- ⇒ dried sausage of pork and beef
Chasseur -*[plats]*-
    1) **rognons** ⇒ kidneys ...
        - **médaillons** ⇒ round slices of meat ...
        - **escalopes** ⇒ escalopes ...
        - **côtes de veau** ⇒ veal's chops
        - **poulet** ⇒ chicken ... sauté with a sauce of mushrooms, shallots, white wine and tomato or
        hunter's ... et le nom anglais de la viande
    2) **oeufs pochés** ⇒ poached eggs ...
        - **oeufs sur le plat** ⇒ fried egg ... served with a sauce of mushrooms, shallots, white wine,
        tomato and sauté poultry livers
    3) **omelette** ⇒ omelette filled with a sauce of mushrooms, shallots, white wine, tomato and sauté
        poultry livers
    4) **potage** ⇒ soup
        - **bouchées** ⇒ patties ...
        - **oeufs cocotte** ⇒ eggs baked in butter ... with mashed game
Chataîgne ⇒ chestnut
Chataîgne d'eau -*[macre]*- ⇒ water-caltrop or water-chestnut
Chataîgne de mer -*[oursin]*- ⇒ sea-urchin
Château -*[vignoble]*- ⇒ vineyard estate in Bordeaux area
Château-Ausone ⇒ red wine from St Emilion area

Château canon -*[Fronsac]*- ⇒ high quality red wine from Fronsac near Libourne
Château-Chalon ⇒ white wine from Jura in bottles of 62 cl
Château chasse spleen -*[Moulis]*- ⇒ red Bordeaux wine from Haut Médoc
Château cheval blanc ⇒ Bordeaux red wine from St Emilion area
Château d'yquem ⇒ Sauternes white wine
Château-grillet ⇒ Rhone valley white wine
Château-haut-brion ⇒ Graves red wine
Château-lafite ⇒ Médoc red wine
Château lafite rothschild -*[haut médoc]*- ⇒ high quality Bordeaux red wine
Château-latour-pomerol ⇒ Médoc red wine
Château-latour ⇒ Médoc red wine
Château-margaux ⇒ high quality Médoc wine, red and white
Château-mouton-Rothschild ⇒ high quality Médoc red wine
Château-pétrus ⇒ Bordeaux red wine from Pomerol
Château poujeaux theil -*[Moulis]*- ⇒ red Bordeaux wine from Haut Médoc
Châteaumeillant ⇒ red wine or rosé from Berry area
Châteauneuf du Pape ⇒ red and white wine from Avignon area
Chateaubriand grillé ⇒ chateaubriand oiled and peppered, then grilled
Chateaubriand sauté ⇒ chateaubriand sautéed in butter, plus a garnish of any vegetable
Chateaubriant -*[viande]*- ⇒ chateaubriand or fillet steak or porter house « steak »
Châtelaine *(à la ...)*
    1) Généralités
      - **plats d'oeufs** ⇒ dish of eggs with chestnuts
      - **plats de viandes** ⇒ dish of ... with artichoke hearts
    2) Grosses pièces de boucherie « garnies avec fonds d'artichauts remplis de purée de marrons, accompagnés de laitues braisées et de pommes noisettes » ⇒ ... with artichoke hearts filled of chestnut purée and browned; plus braised lettuce and little potato-balls browned in butter
      - **Petites pièces de boucherie « garnies avec fonds d'artichauts étuvés et pommes noisettes »** ⇒ ... with braised artichoke hearts and little potato-balls browned in butter
    3) Autre texte pour les fonds d'artichauts ... coupés en quartiers, sautés au beurre et accompagnés de petites tomates mondées, de coeurs de céleri braisés et de pommes château ⇒ ... with quartered artichoke hearts sautéed in butter, plus small potatoes, braised celeriac and small potatoes sautéed in butter with lardoons
Chatenay -*[carotte]*- ⇒ variety of carrot
Châtillon en diois ⇒ wines from Montélimar area
Chauchat
    - **sole** ⇒ poached sole ...
    - **barbue** ⇒ poached brill ...
    - **merlan** ⇒ poached whiting ... ... covered of béchamel sauce thickened with egg-yolks plus butter; garnished of sliced potatoes
Chaud *(fem chaude ...)* ⇒ warm or hot or heated
Chaud-froid ⇒ chaudfroid
Chaud-froid de caneton ⇒ thin slices of duckling covered with a chaudfroid sauce flavoured of orange
Chaud-froid de faisan ⇒ pheasant cooked in butter and covered of chaudfroid sauce made with the cooking juice and truffle; decorated of hard boiled egg, tarragon leaves, and truffle in jelly with Madeira

Chaud-froid de poulet à l'estragon ⇒ chaudfroid of chicken seasoned of pepper and tarragon, cooked with giblets of poultry, onions, carrots, turnip, leek and clove; served with a chaudfroid sauce made of the cooking stock, jelly, butter, flour, eau de vie, port and cream

Chaud-froid de saumon ⇒ poached slices of salmon in a court-bouillon with aromatics; covered of chaudfroid sauce made with the cooking stock, then decorated of truffle or black olives and capsicums

Chaudeau ⇒ hot soup from Landes recipe

Chaudin ⇒ bowel of pork

Chaudrée ⇒ fish-dish of skates, soles, cuttlefish, bit of eels and gurnards; cooked in muscatel wine with butter, thyme, laurel, and garlic

Chaudrée fourasine ⇒ dish of soles, skates and squids, seasoned of salt and pepper; cooked in white wine

Chaudumel ⇒ bits of eel and pike first grilled, then cooked in wine and verjuice; the sauce is flavoured with ginger and saffron, then thickened with the pikes' livers

Chaudumer ⇒ bits of eel and pike first grilled, then cooked in wine and verjuice; the sauce is flavoured with ginger and saffron, then thickened with the pikes' livers

Chaudumé ⇒ bits of eel and pike first grilled, then cooked in wine and verjuice; the sauce is flavoured with ginger and saffron, then thickened with the pikes' livers

Chaufroiter ⇒ to do a chaudfroid

Chausson ⇒ turnover

Chaussons à la cussy ⇒ turnovers filled with a forcemeat of whiting added of cream, anchovy fillets, and chopped truffle

Chausson aux pommes ⇒ apple-turnover

Chaussons aux pommes et aux pruneaux ⇒ turnovers filled with apple compote and dried plum compote

Chaussons aux écrevisses ⇒ turnovers filled with a ragout of crayfishes

Chaussons de Paul Reboux ⇒ turnovers filled with cherries, then fried

Chaussons pour petites entrées

    1) à la lyonnaise ⇒ turnovers filled with a forcemeat of pike, butter, crayfish tails, truffle and cognac

    2) à la Nantua ⇒ turnovers filled with a ragout of crayfish tails

    3) à la périgourdine ⇒ turnovers filled with a culinary stuffing of foie gras, truffle and cognac

    4) à la reine ⇒ turnovers filled with a chicken purée, truffles, and diced mushrooms

Chavignol -[Berry]- ⇒ goat's milk cheese

Chawourma (la ...) ⇒ mutton meat grilled on a skewer; served in lamellas with rice salad

Chayote ⇒ gourd or marrow

Chayotes à la martiniquaise ⇒ preparation of boiled gourds, bread steeped in milk, and onions; moistened of olive oil, and browned in the oven

Chayotes au blanc ⇒ gourds cooked in consommé, served in timbale with béchamel sauce or other sauce

Chayotes braisées au jus ⇒ gourds cooked with strips from rind of pork, carrots, onions and stock; served with the cooking juice in butter

Cheddar ⇒ cheddar cheese

Cheese burger -[hamburger]- ⇒ hamburger flavoured with chopped onion, green pepper, or cheese

Cheese cake -[Amérique du nord]- ⇒ cheese cake

Cheilly les maranges ⇒ Burgundy wine from Beaune area

Chemisé (en chemise ...) -[description des viandes ou légumes servis enveloppés ou dans leur peau]-

    - pâté ⇒ pie coated with ... or pie wrapped with ...

- **pommes de terre « cuite dans leur peau »** ⇒ potatoes cooked in their jacket ½ ou ½ jacket potatoes
Chemitré *-[Lorraine]-* ⇒ kind of waffle
Chénas ⇒ Beaujolais wine
Chénier *-[collybie]-* ⇒ spotted tough shank OR wood woolly foot
Chérimole *-[anone]-* ⇒ anona or custard-apple
Cherry ⇒ cherry brandy
Cherry brandy ⇒ cherry brandy
Chervis *-[berle]-* ⇒ skirret or water-parsnip
Cheshire *-[fromage]-* ⇒ Cheshire cheese
Chester *-[fromage]-* ⇒ Cheshire cheese or cheddar cheese
Chevaine ⇒ chub or dace < *pluriel uncountable* >
Cheval *(à ...) -[steak, hamburger, entrecôte]-* ⇒ ... topped with a fried egg
Cheval ⇒ horse-meat
Chevaler ⇒ to laid the items of a dish, either in overlapping, or in ring
Chevalier *-[tricholome]-* ⇒ firwood agaric
Chevalier jaune *-[tricholome]-* ⇒ firwood agaric
Chevalière *(à la ...)*
   1) **sole** ⇒ poached sole laid on a forcemeat of fish, plus crayfishes, surrounded by oysters, poached mushrooms and crayfish tails; thickened with a sauce made of butter, tomatoes, garlic, shallots, white wine, and cognac
   2) **œufs** ⇒ eggs served with a garnish of fish forcemeat, oysters, mushrooms and crayfish in a pastry case
Chevenne *-[Chevaine]-* ⇒ chub or dace < *pluriel uncountable* >
Cheverny *-[vin]-* ⇒ wines and sparkling wine of Blois and Chambord area
Chevesne *-[Chevaine]-* ⇒ chub or dace < *pluriel uncountable* >
Cheveux d'ange *-[soupe]-* ⇒ vermicelli for soups
Cheveux de vénus *-[nigelle]-* ⇒ nigella or love-in-the-mist
Chèvre *-[viande]-* ⇒ goat
Chèvre *-[fromage]-* ⇒ goat's milk cheese
Chevreau ⇒ kid
Chevrelle *-[hydne]-* ⇒ spreading hydnum
Chevreton ⇒ goat's milk cheese from Ambert or Viverols or Forez
Chevreton de Mâcon ⇒ small goat's milk cheese
Chevrette *-[chanterelle]-* ⇒ chanterelle
Chevrette *-[hydne]-* ⇒ spreading hydnum
Chevrettes *-[crevettes roses]-* ⇒ prawns
Chevreuil ⇒ roebuckor roe-deer or roe
Chevreuil *(en ...)*
   - **tournedos** ⇒ marinated tournedossautéed in butter; served with peppered sauce and chestnut purée
   - **agneau** ⇒ round piece of lamb sautéed in butter; served with peppered sauce and chestnut purée
   - **rôti de cheval** ⇒ horse meat studded, marinated and roasted; served with a sauce for game
   - **gigot de mouton** ⇒ leg of mutton studded, marinated and roasted; served with a sauce for game
Chevreuse
   1) **noisette d'agneau ou tournedos** ⇒ ... with a garnish of little potato-balls browned in butter, artichoke hearts filled of chopped mushrooms, then covered with Madeira
   2) **velouté chevreuse** ⇒ poultry velouté added of chervil
   3) **omelette chevreuse** ⇒ omelette stuffed with a hash of chervil and butter

4) œufs chevreuse ⇒ eggs cooked in the oven sprinkled with grated cheese and surrounded by french bean purée

Chevrier -*[flageolet]*- ⇒ flageolet or kidney bean

Chevrillard -*[chevreuil]*- ⇒ roebuck or roe-deer or roe

Chevrotin -*[fromage]*- ⇒ Chevrotin

Chevrotin des Aravis ⇒ Chevrotin

Chevrotin du Bourbonnais ⇒ Chevrotin

Chevroton -*[fromage]*- ⇒ blue cheese from a mixing of cow's and goat's milk

Chez nous-fait ⇒ home made < *adjectif* >

Chialade d'Argonne -*[crêpe]*- ⇒ pancake

Chianti ⇒ chianti

Chicha -*[alcool]*- ⇒ Chicha

Chiche-kebab ⇒ mutton macerated in olive oil and lemon juice, grilled on a skewer with lardoons; served with salad or rice flavoured of saffron, plus quartered lemons

Chichifregi ⇒ fritter shaped in roll, and covered with sugar

Chicken-pie ⇒ chicken-pie

Chicon -*[endive]*- ⇒ chicory

Chicorée -*[légume]*- ⇒ endive

Chicorée -*[comme café]*- ⇒ ground chicory

Chicorée au gratin ⇒ hash of endives added of béchamel sauce, sprinkled of grated cheese and melted butter, then browned

Chicorée braisée ⇒ hash of endives braised in a roux and stock, with pepper and nutmeg

Chicorée sauvage ⇒ chicory or succory < *uncountable* >

Chicorée étuvée ⇒ hash of endives braised in butter, and served with béchamel sauce

Chien de mer ⇒ dogfish shark or smooth hound

Chiffonnade ⇒ chiffonade

Chiffonnade d'endives à la crème ⇒ braised strips of chicory in butter, lemon juice, and cream

Chiffonnade d'oseille ⇒ sorrel chiffonade, braised in butter

Chiffonnade de laitue crue ⇒ strips of chicory in french dressing

Chiffonnade de laitue cuite ⇒ strips of chicory sautéed in butter, served with cream

Chilaquilès ⇒ fried tortilla lamellas, covered with spicy sauce, and baked

Chile -*[piment Amérique du sud]*- ⇒ red pepper < *uncountable* > or pimento < *uncountable* >

Chili -*[sauce]*- ⇒ pimento sauce

Chili con carne ⇒ chili con carné

Chimay -*[gueuze]*- ⇒ Belgian beer

Chimay (*à la ...*)

- **poularde** ⇒ fried fattened pullet, stuffed with noodles in butter and forcemeat, covered with gravy; served with noodles and asparagus tips

- **oeufs durs** ⇒ hard boiled eggs ... added of mushrooms, then browned

- **oeufs mollets** ⇒ soft boiled eggs ... added of mushrooms, then browned

Chinchard ⇒ horse mackerel < *pluriel inchangé* >

Chinois confit ⇒ preserved bitter orange

Chinon ⇒ wines from Chinon area in the Loire

Chinonnaise (*à la ...*)

- **garniture pour grosses pièces de boucherie** ⇒ ... garnished with potatoes, and braised cabbage balls stuffed with sausage meat

- **lièvre** ⇒ hare ... browned in nut oil

- **lamproie** ⇒ lamprey ... browned in nut oil

Chipeau -*[canard]*- ⇒ wild duck

Chipiron ⇒ squid or calamaro

Chipolata -*[saucisse]*- ⇒ chipolata sausage
Chipolata *(à la ...)*
    - **plat** ⇒ with a garnish of braised chestnuts, glazed onions, glazed carrots, sauté mushrooms,
        lardoons, and browned chipolatas
    - **pudding** ⇒ pudding made of pig kidneys, forcemeat and sausages
Chipolatas au risotto ⇒ chipolatas braised in butter and white wine, served with risotto
Chipolatas au risotto à la piémontaise ⇒ chipolatas braised in butter and white wine, plus truffles
    added; served with risotto and cabbage
Chipotle -*[piment]*- ⇒ red pepper or pimento < *uncountable* >
Chips ⇒ potato crisps
Chiquetaille *(en ...)* ⇒ stripped salt cod, cooked on rice and tomatoes
Chiroubles -*[Beaujolais]*- ⇒ Beaujolais wine
Chivry
    1) Beurre chivry ⇒ butter mixed with herbs
    2) Sauce chivry
        - **pour poissons** ⇒ sauce of fish stock and composed butter added of herbs
        - **pour volailles pochées ou oeufs mollets ou pochés** ⇒ sauce of poultry velouté and
        composed butter added of herbs
Chlodnik -*[Pologne]*- ⇒ soup made of beetroot, sour cream, and crayfishes
Chlorelle, Ulve -*[algues]*- ⇒ green seaweed
Chocart ⇒ large turnover filled of apple jam, flavoured with cinnamon and lemon peel
Chocarts ⇒ Yffiniac cakes eaten hot
Chocolat ⇒ chocolate
Chocolat au lait ⇒ chocolate in milk
Chocolat aux amandes ⇒ chocolate mixed with sugar, egg-yolks, butter and almond powder;
    flavoured with rum
Chocolat chaud ⇒ cup of hot chocolate
Chocolat en poudre ⇒ powdered chocolate or cocoa
Chocolat frappé ⇒ chocolate made of cocoa and sugar, then mixed with crushed ice
Chocolat liégeois ⇒ chocolate ice cream with sugared whipped cream
Chocolat mousseux ⇒ melted chocolate mixed with vanilla sugar and milk
Chocolat viennois
    a) chocolat fondu ⇒ melted chocolate mixed with sugar and milk, topped of sugared whipped
    cream
    b) glace au chocolat ⇒ chocolate ice cream, topped with sugared whipped cream
Chocolate cake -*[cake]*- ⇒ chocolate cake
Chocolatine -*[pain au chocolat]*- ⇒ pain au chocolat or small pastry filled with chocolate or puff-
    pastry with chocolate filling
Choesels ⇒ testicles of bull
Choesels à la bruxelloise ⇒ ragout of sweetbread, oxtail, kidney, onions, pork fat, cayenne pepper,
    testicles and beer
Choiseul
    - **soles pochée** ⇒ poached soles ...
    - **filets de sole** ⇒ sole fillets ..., covered with white wine sauce added of truffle in julienne
Choisir -*[verbe]*- ⇒ to choose
    - **Choisi** ⇒ chosen < *v.t adjectif bien respecter l'orthographe* >
Choisy
    1) garniture choisy pour pièces de boucherie ⇒ ... with a garnish of small potatoes sautéed
        in butter with lardoons and braised lettuce
        - **les viandes sont tournedos** ⇒ tournedos

1) **garniture choisy pour pièces de boucherie (suite)** ⇒ ... with a garnish of small potatoes sautéed in butter with lardoons and braised lettuce (follow)
  - **côte de veau** ⇒ veal's rib
  - **carré de veau** ⇒ veal's end of neck

2) **omelette choisy** ⇒ omelette stuffed with lettuce chiffonade in cream

3) **sole choisy** ⇒ poached sole, covered with white wine sauce, and garnished with a julienne of lettuce and mushrooms

4) **potage choisy** ⇒ lettuce soup

Choix ⇒ choice
  - **au choix** ⇒ one of those items

Chondrus, Ulve -*[algues]*- ⇒ green seaweed

Chons -*[boudin noir, panne]*- ⇒ bits of melted pig's fat

Chop suey ⇒ chop suey

Chope -*[ustensile]*- ⇒ mug-beer

Chope de bière ⇒ mugful of beer

Choquarts ⇒ Yffiniac cakes eaten hot

Chorba -*[Afrique du nord]*- ⇒ Algerian soup

Chorizo ⇒ sausage seasoned with pimento and garlic

Choron
  - **garniture** ⇒ ... with a garnish of potato-balls browned in butter, plus artichoke hearts stuffed with peas or asparagus tips in butter
  - **sauce** ⇒ béarnaise sauce added of tomato purée

Chou -*[légume]*- ⇒ cabbage or kale < *cuisine uncountable* >

Chou à l'anglaise ⇒ boiled cabbage served with melted butter

Chou braisé ⇒ cabbage braised in strips from rind of pork with carrots, nutmeg, onion, clove, stock, and streaky bacon

Chou caraïbe ⇒ Indian katchu

Chou chinois ⇒ Chinese cabbage

Chou chinois servi avec
  - **porc** ⇒ Chinese cabbage served braised or sautéed in lamellas with pork
  - **poisson** ⇒ ... with fish
  - **crustacés** ⇒ ... with crustaceae
  - **coeur de palmier** ⇒ heart of palm

Chou de bruxelles ⇒ Brussels-sprouts

Chou de mer ou marin ⇒ sea kale

Chou farçi ⇒ cabbage stuffed with a forcemeat of pork and cabbage leaves, braised with strips from rind of pork, carrots, onions, and stock

Chou farçi à la limousine ⇒ cabbage stuffed with bacon and chestnuts

Chou frisé d'écosse ⇒ curly kale

Chou glouglou -*[coeur de palmier]*- ⇒ heart of palm

Chou marin ⇒ sea kale

Chou navet ⇒ swede

Chou palmiste -*[coeur de palmier]*- ⇒ heart of palm

Chou pommé ⇒ common cabbage

Chou rave ⇒ kohlrabi

Chou rouge ⇒ red cabbage

Chou rouge à la flamande ⇒ red cabbage stewed with apples, sugar and vinegar; then served with boiled pork or beef

Chou rouge mariné ⇒ red cabbage marinated in salt, then preserved with pepper, garlic, laurel, and vinegar

Chou-fleur ⇒ cauliflower

Chou-fleur à l'anglaise ⇒ boiled cauliflower, served with herbs and melted butter

Chou-fleur au gratin ⇒ cauliflower au gratin ½ ou ½ cauliflower with grated cheese ½ ou ½ cauliflower cheese

Chou-fleur sauté ⇒ steamed bits of cauliflower sautéed in butter

Chou-ti-coco -[coeur de palmier]- ⇒ heart of palm

Choucroute ⇒ sauerkraut < *uncountable* >

Choucroute à l'alsacienne ⇒ sauerkraut cooked with onion, clove, garlic, small ham, smoked pork, sausage, and potatoes

Choucroute au gras pour garniture ⇒ sauerkraut cooked in stock with onion, clove, garlic and potatoes

Choucroute de navets ⇒ sauerkraut made of grated turnips, pepper, and juniper berries

Choucroute garnie ⇒ sauerkraut garnished variously

Choum ⇒ rice alcohol

Chouquette ⇒ choux pastry covered with sugar

Choux -[patisserie]- ⇒ choux-pastry

Choux à la Nantua ⇒ choux pastry garnished with crayfish mousse; then covered of béchamel sauce added of mashed crayfishes, cognac, and cayenne pepper

Choux à la crème chantilly ⇒ choux pastry shaped in swan, and filled of sugared whipped cream

Choux à la crème chiboust au café ⇒ choux pastry, topped with almonds and custard added of coffee extract in white of egg

Choux à la crème pâtissière ⇒ choux pastry covered with confectioner's custard

Choux à la crème pâtissière aux raisins ⇒ choux pastry covered with confectioner's custard added of marc and grapes

Choux à la cévenole ⇒ choux pastry covered of chestnut cream mixed with whipped cream

Choux à la mousse de foie gras ⇒ choux pastry covered of whipped cream with foie gras mousse

Choux à la normande ⇒ choux pastry covered with a preparation of custard, apple compote and calvados

Choux amandines en beignets -[petits]- ⇒ fritters of choux pastry with almonds

Choux au café ⇒ choux pastry covered with a custard flavoured of coffee extract

Choux au chocolat ⇒ choux pastry covered with a chocolate custard

Choux au fromage ⇒ choux pastry covered with a preparation of béchamel sauce, grated cheese and nutmeg

Choux brocolis ⇒ broccoli or cabbage-sprout

Choux chinois à la Sseu-tch'ouannaise ⇒ bits of cabbage braised in oil with chopped garlic, pimento, and marc

Choux chinois à la pékinoise ⇒ bits of cabbage steamed with onions and slices of ham

Choux de bruxelles à l'anglaise ⇒ boiled brussels-sprouts served with melted butter

Choux de bruxelles Mornay ⇒ brussels-sprouts covered with béchamel sauce added of egg-yolks, grated cheese, and melted butter, then browned

Choux de bruxelles au beurre ou à la crème ⇒ boiled brussels-sprouts, sautéed in butter and covered with cream

Choux de bruxelles en purée ⇒ brussels-sprout purée added of mashed potatoes, cream, and pepper

Choux de bruxelles gratinés ⇒ brussels-sprouts covered with grated cheese and melted butter, then browned

Choux de bruxelles sautés ⇒ boiled brussels-sprouts sautéed in butter

Choux montmorency ⇒ choux pastry covered with a custard flavoured of kirsch, and added of stoned cherries

Choux rouge à la limousine ⇒ strips of red cabbage braised in pork fat with chestnuts and stock

Choux vert pré ⇒ choux pastry covered with a purée of peas, beans and asparagus tips, thickened of cream

Choux-fleur à la polonaise ⇒ cauliflower sprinkled with chopped hard-boiled eggs and parsley; covered with melted butter and breadcrumbs

Chouzé ⇒ cheese from Saumur

Chouée ⇒ boiled cabbage sprinkled with melted butter

Chowder ⇒ chowder

Christmas cake ⇒ English Christmas cake

Christmas cake ⇒ Irish Christmas cake

Christmas cake ⇒ Scottish Christmas cake

Christmas pudding ⇒ Christmas pudding

Christophine -*[chayote]*- ⇒ gourd OR marrow

Chrust -*[Pologne]*- ⇒ sugared biscuit

Chrysanthème -*[fleur]*- ⇒ chrysanthemum flower

Chtchi ou Tschy ou Stschy

    1) **soupe avec viande** ⇒ soup made of sauerkraut in stock, beef, duck meat, streaky bacon, smoked sausages; served with cream, fennel and chopped parsley

    2) **soupe légumes** ⇒ soup made with vegetables as spinach, sorrel, and nettle

Chufa -*[souchet]*- ⇒ galingale or sedge

Chügelipastete -*[Suisse]*- ⇒ timbale made of rice and veal's meat

Chum -*[Sockey, Pink]*- ⇒ variety of Canadian salmon

Chuños -*[Bolivie]*- ⇒ dried potatoes

Chupes -*[Chili]*- ⇒ ragout based on tripe, vegetables, or dried meat

Churrasco -*[Argentine]*- ⇒ grilled beef meat

Churros -*[Espagne]*- ⇒ fritters

Chusclan ⇒ quality wine from Côtes du Rhone

Chutes de steak ⇒ steak and kidney

Chutney à l'ananas ⇒ seasoning made of vinegar, brown sugar, mustard seeds, clove, cinnamon, ginger, bits of pineapple, and raisins

Chutney aux onions d'Espagne ⇒ seasoning made of onions, brown sugar, raisins, white wine, vinegar, garlic, ginger, curry, and clove

Chutney aux pommes et aux mangues ⇒ seasoning made of apples, vinegar, brown sugar, pimentos, sultanas, Malaga raisins, currants, cedrate, garlic, mustard seed, ginger, and mangos

Chypre -*[vins de]*- ⇒ Cyprus wines

Ciboule ⇒ ciboule or welsh onion

Ciboulette ⇒ chives

Cider cup ⇒ drink made of calvados, maraschino, curaçao, cider, ice cube, slices of orange, Schweppes soda, and bits of fruits in season

Cidre ⇒ cider < *uncountable* >

Cidre bouché ⇒ sparkling cider or bottled cider

Cierniki -*[cyrniki]*- ⇒ croquettes made of curdled milk, eggs and flour, then fried in butter

Cigale ⇒ cicada

Cigales de mer -*[brochettes au safran]*- ⇒ mantis shrimps macerated in saffron, olive oil, lemon juice, garlic, thyme, and pepper; then grilled on a skewer

Cigarette -*[biscuit]*- ⇒ small tubular biscuit

Cigarette Russe -*[biscuit]*- ⇒ small tubular biscuit

Cigarettes au citron ⇒ rolled pastries from a dough with lemon peel; filled of butter flavoured with lemon

Cigarettes russes ⇒ rolled pastries made of butter, whipped white of eggs, flour, sugar, and vanilla

Cingalaise *(à la ...)* ⇒ with cingalese sauce

Cinghalaise *(à la ...)* ⇒ with cingalese sauce

Cinq épices ⇒ sauce made with soya sauce, star anise, clove, fennel, cinnamon, and pepper or spicy seasoning

Cinq parfums *-[Cinq épices]-* ⇒ sauce made with soya sauce, star anise, clove, fennel, cinnamon, and pepper or spicy seasoning

Cinzano cobbler ⇒ cocktail made of cinzano aperitif, curaçao, kirsch, sugar, slice of orange, bits of fruits in season

Cinzano *-[vermouth]-* ⇒ vermouth

Ciociara *(alla ...)* ⇒ macaroni served with sauté vegetables sliced thinly, smoked ham, plus slices of dry sausage

Cioppino ⇒ ragout of fish and shellfish with tomato, garlic and white wine

Ciorba ⇒ sour soup of beef and vegetables

Circassienne *(à la ...)* *-[poulet]-* ⇒ chicken served with a capsicum sauce, and nuts

Citrange *-[agrumes]-* ⇒ citrus variety

Citron ⇒ lemon

Citron de mer *-[ximénia]-* ⇒ tropical fruit

Citron pressé ⇒ fresh lemon juice

Citron vert ⇒ lime

    - jus de citron vert ⇒ lime juice

Citronnade ⇒ lemon squash

Citronnat ⇒ candied lemon

Citronnelle
    1) **plante herbacée** ⇒ wormwood leaves
    2) **liqueur** ⇒ lemon peel liqueur
    3) **plantes « auronne, verveine odorante »** ⇒ vervain

Citronelle
    1) **plante herbacée** ⇒ wormwood leaves
    2) **liqueur** ⇒ lemon peel liqueur
    3) **plantes « auronne, verveine odorante »** ⇒ vervain

Citronnée *(adj ...)* ⇒ lemon flavoured

Citrons confits ⇒ lemons macerated in salt, and preserved in olive oil

Citrons farçis ⇒ lemons hollowed out and filled with a stuffing of chopped olives and parsley, plus bits of tunny, lemon pulp and juice, egg-yolk, and garlic sauce

Citrons givrés ⇒ lemons hollowed out and filled with a lemon sorbet

Citrouillat ⇒ pie made of short pastry and pumpkin

Citrouille ⇒ pumpkin

Cive ⇒ chives

Civelles ⇒ baby-eels or young eels or elvers

Civet
    - lièvre ⇒ jugged hare
    - lapin ⇒ jugged rabbit
    - chevreuil ⇒ jugged venison

Civet de chevreuil ⇒ jugged roe-deer

Civet de homard ⇒ jugged lobster with cognac, burgundy red wine, and mushrooms

Civet de lièvre *-[Haeberlin]-* ⇒ hare marinated in onions, carrot, thyme, and red wine; simmered with the marinade, cognac, tomato purée, garlic, laurel, then served with braised mushrooms, plus smoked bacon

Civet de lièvre ⇒ jugged hare

Civet de lièvre à la flamande ⇒ marinated hare simmered with red wine, pepper, brown sugar, and onions; served with fried sippets spreaded of redcurrant jelly, and sauce

Civet de lièvre à la française ⇒ marinated hare, firstly simmered in red wine, roux and garlic; secondly cooked in the oven with lardoons, mushrooms, marinade and cooking juice, then thickened of cream, s erved accompanied with fried onions, and sippets

Civet de lièvre à la lyonnaise ⇒ marinated hare, firstly simmered in red wine, roux and garlic; secondly cooked in the oven with lardoons, chestnuts, marinade and cooking juice, then thickened of cream, served accompanied by fried onions and sippets

Civet de marcassin ⇒ jugged young wild boar

Civet de râbles de lièvre aux pâtes fraîches ⇒ fore part of hare braised with carrots, onions, shallots and garlic, in red wine and vinegar; saddles of hare fried in oil

Clafir -[*Clafoutis*]- ⇒ clafoutis

Clafoutis ⇒ clafoutis

Claire -[*parc huîtres*]- ⇒ oyster bed

Clairet ⇒ light red wine

Clairette ⇒ white wine

Clairette de die ⇒ sparkling white wine

Clam ⇒ clam

Clamart
    1) **général** ⇒ with peas
    2) **potage** ⇒ soup made of mashed peas and fried sippets
    3) **oeufs** ⇒ poached eggs on canapé with mashed peas
    4) **bouchées feuilletées** ⇒ patties filled with mashed peas
    5) **volaille ou veau** ⇒ poultry or veal with peas
    6) **garniture**
      a) **petites pièces de boucherie** ⇒ tartlets or artichoke hearts filled with peas in butter
      b) **grosses pièces de boucherie** ⇒ tartlets or artichoke hearts filled with small potatoes sautéed in butter with lardoons

Clambake -[*Clam*]- ⇒ clam

Clape -[*la clape*]- ⇒ Languedoc wines

Claquebitou ⇒ Burgundian goat's milk cheese

Clarequet ⇒ jelly of unripe grape juice and apples, or redcurrants

Claret -[*vin rouge de Bordeaux*]- ⇒ claret

Clarete -[*rioja*]- ⇒ Spanish wine from Rioja

Clava -[*Clavaire*]- ⇒ coral fungus or fairy club

Clavaire ⇒ coral fungus or fairy club

Clavaire jaune ⇒ tiny yellow hands

Clavelat -[*turbot*]- ⇒ turbot < *pluriel inchangé* >

Claytone de Cuba -[*pourpier*]- ⇒ purslane

Clémentine ⇒ clementine orange

Clitocybe ⇒ flavoured edible mushroom or clitocybe mushroom

Clitocybe en forme de coupe ⇒ clitocybe mushroom

Clitocybe geotrope ⇒ trumpet agaric

Clitocybe laqué ⇒ clitocybe mushroom

Clitocybe suave -[*anisé*]- ⇒ aniseed agaric

Clitocybe vert -[*anisé*]- ⇒ aniseed agaric

Clitophile ⇒ flavoured edible mushroom or clitocybe mushroom

Clitopile petite coquille -[*langue de carpe*]- ⇒ miller

Clitopile petite prune ⇒ meadow mushroom

Clos (*les ...*) **-[*chablis*]-** ⇒ high quality chablis wine

Clos de bèze -*[chambertin]*- ⇒ Chambertin

Clos de la boudriotte -*[Chassagne Montrachet]*- ⇒ high quality Burgundy wines from cote de Beaune

Clos de la roche -*[morey st denis]*- ⇒ Burgundy red wine from Côtes de Nuits

Clos de tart -*[morey st denis]*- ⇒ Burgundy red wine from Côtes de Nuits

Clos de Vougeot ⇒ Burgundy wine from Nuits area

Clos des mouches -*[Beaune]*- ⇒ Beaune < *uncountable* >

Clos st denis -*[morey st denis]*- ⇒ Burgundy red wine from Côtes de Nuits

Clos st jean -*[Chassagne-Montrachet]*- ⇒ high quality Burgundy wines from Côtes de Beaune

Clou de girofle ⇒ clove

Clovisse ⇒ small clam or carpet shell

Club sandwich ⇒ sandwich made of toasts, mayonnaise, lettuce leaves, slices of tomato, slice of roasted chicken, and slices of hard-boiled egg

Cobbler -*[cocktail]*- ⇒ cobbler

Coca ⇒ coca

Coca cola ⇒ coca cola

Cochenille -*[substance]*- ⇒ cochineal

Cochevis -*[alouette]*- ⇒ lark or skylark

Cochon ⇒ pig

Cochon de lait ⇒ piglet or sucking pig

Cochonnaille ⇒ sausages, etc or pork butchery

Cocido ⇒ Spanish meal made of various dishes

Cock-a-leeckie ⇒ cockaleekie

Cocktail -*[boisson]*- ⇒ cocktail or mixed drink

Cocktail -*[charcuterie, saucisse]*- ⇒ snacks for cocktail

Cocktail -*[invitation]*- ⇒ cocktail party

Cocktail à l'abricot ⇒ cocktail made of milk, stoned apricots, orange juice, sugar and crushed ice cubes

Cocktail à la cerise ⇒ cocktail made of milk, egg-yolk, stoned cherries, lemon and sugar

Cocktail Alexandra ⇒ cocktail of cream, cognac, and crème de cacao

Cocktail canasta ⇒ cocktail made of cinzano aperitif, gin, and maraschino

Cocktail casbah ⇒ infusion of tea and mint, plus sugar

Cocktail champagne ⇒ cocktail made of champagne, angostura brandy, lemon peel, and sugar

Cocktail cocabana ⇒ cocktail made of pineapple juice, milk, honey, and crushed banana

Cocktail cocabricot ⇒ cocktail made of apricot juice, milk, and honey

Cocktail Curnonsky ⇒ mixing of cognac, Cointreau and orange juice

Cocktail daïquiri ⇒ cocktail made of rum, lemon juice, and sugar-cane syrup

Cocktail de crabe ⇒ crab meat, chopped lettuce, and mayonnaise flavoured with cognac

Cocktail de crevettes ⇒ chopped lettuce, mayonnaise flavoured of cognac, quartered tomatoes, hard-boiled eggs, and shrimps

Cocktail dry ⇒ cocktail made of vermouth and gin

Cocktail evening delight ⇒ cocktail made of rye whisky, curaçao and apricot brandy

Cocktail manhattan ⇒ cocktail of whisky, vermouth, Cointreau, Angostura brandy, lemon peel and a cherry

Cocktail mint julep ⇒ cocktail of ice cubes, whisky, mint leaves and sugar

- **variantes avec champagne** ⇒ champagne
- **gin** ⇒ gin
- **jus d'orange** ⇒ orange juice

Cocktail mister callaghan ⇒ cocktail of vermouth, apricot brandy and angostura brandy

Cocktail rose ⇒ cocktail of gin, vermouth, and cherry brandy

Cocktail tom collins ⇒ Tom Collins
Cocktomate ⇒ cocktail made of tomato juice, lemon juice, and chopped parsley
Cocky-leeky ⇒ cock-a-leekie
Coco *(huile ...) -[coprah]-* ⇒ copra oil
Coco *-[boisson]-* ⇒ drink based on liquorice macerated in water and lemon juice
Cocos *-[haricots]-* ⇒ haricot beans
Cocos rosés *-[haricots]-* ⇒ haricot beans
Cocotte *(en ...)* ⇒ a casserole of ...
Cocotte *-[ustensile]-* ⇒ cast-iron casserole
Codballs *-[US]-* ⇒ codballs
Coelacanthe ⇒ coelacanth
Coeur
    - animal ⇒ heart of an animal
    - légume ⇒ heart of various vegetables
    - viande ⇒ the best cut of certain meat
Coeur *(à ...) -[camembert affinage]-* ⇒ refined right through
Coeur à la crème *-[fromage frais]-* ⇒ soft white cheese
Coeur d'Arras ⇒ Flemish cheese
Coeur d'agneau ⇒ lamb heart
Coeurs d'agneau à l'anglaise ⇒ sliced lamb's hearts fried in butter, and served with the cooking juice added of Madeira
Coeurs d'agneau sautés ⇒ sliced lamb's hearts fried in butter, served with parsley and vinegar
Coeurs d'artichaut ⇒ artichoke hearts
Coeur d'entrecôte première *(Prêt à trancher ...) -[bœuf]-* ⇒ rib eye roll
Coeur de Bray ⇒ cow's milk cheese from Normandy
Coeur de boeuf *-[anone]-* ⇒ anona or custard-apple
Coeur de boeuf *-[chou]-* ⇒ cabbage
Coeur d e boeuf ⇒ ox heart
Coeur de boeuf en matelote ⇒ matelote of marinated beef's heart cooked with diced bacon, onions, red wine, pepper, garlic, lardoons, and mushrooms
Coeur de laitue ⇒ heart of lettuce or lettuce heart
Coeur de palmier ⇒ heart of palm
Coeurs de palmier aux crevettes ⇒ hearts of palm in julienne with mayonnaise, shrimp tails, soya germs, and lettuce chiffonade
Coeurs de palmier en salade ⇒ salad made of sliced hearts of palm, diced cucumber, diced tomatoes and avocado balls; seasoned with cream, chive, vinegar, and lemon juice
Coeur de pigeon *-[cerise]-* ⇒ variety of cherry
Coeur de porc ⇒ pig heart
Coeur de veau ⇒ calf heart
Coeur de veau à l'anglaise ⇒ slices of calf heart, coated of melted butter and breadcrumbs, then grilled; served with bacon, butter, and steamed potatoes
Coeur de veau en casserole ⇒ calf heart braised in butter and seasoned with pepper
Coeur de veau en casserole à la bonne femme ⇒ calf heart braised in butter with potatoes, onions and lardoons
Coeur de veau farçi ⇒ calf heart stuffed with mushrooms, larded and braised; served with vegetables, plus the cooking juice added of butter and white wine
Coeur de veau grillé en brochettes ⇒ diced calf heart and mushrooms macerated in olive oil, lemon juice, garlic and parsley; grilled on a skewer
Coeur de veau rôti ⇒ calf heart macerated in oil, pepper and lemon juice, larded and roasted on a skewer

Coeur de veau sauté ⇒ calf heart escalopes sautéed in butter with mushrooms, sprinkled with the cooking juice added of Madeira and butter

Coeur en pain d'épices *-[Picardie]-* ⇒ gingerbread shaped in heart

Coffre *-[poisson]-* ⇒ coffer fish

Coffre composé *(épaules, poitrine, colliers et 2 carrés avec découvert ...) -[mouton]-* ⇒ fore 1/4 of lamb

Coffre de homard ⇒ lobster's frame

Coffre sans côtes *-[mouton]-* ⇒ short fore 1/4 of lamb

Coffre sans côtes *(désossé ...) -[mouton]-* ⇒ short fore 1/4 of lamb « boneless »

Coffre sans côtes *(désossé et ficelé ...) -[mouton]-* ⇒ short fore 1/4 of lamb « boned and rolled »

Cognac ⇒ cognac

Coing ⇒ quince

Coing du Japon ⇒ Japanese quince

Coings au four ⇒ quinces hollowed out, and filled with a mixing of cream and icing sugar; then baked

Cointreau *-[liqueur]-* ⇒ Cointreau

Cola *-[noix de]-* ⇒ cola or kola
   - noix de cola ⇒ cola-nut

Colares *-[Portugal]-* ⇒ Portuguese red wine

Colbert *-[sole]-* ⇒ sole covered with breadcrumbs and fried, served with composed butter

Colcannon ⇒ colcannon

Colère *(en ...) -[merlan]-* ⇒ fried whiting garnished of fried parsley and quartered lemons, served with tomato sauce

Colifichet ⇒ small decorative pastry

Colin ⇒ hake < *pluriel inchangé* >

Colin à Paris *-[Merlu]-* ⇒ salt cod < *pluriel inchangé* >

Colin à la boulangère ⇒ large bit of hake moistened with melted butter, surrounded with onions and potatoes sliced thinly; sprinkled with salt, pepper, thyme and laurel powder, then baked

Colin à la duxelles *-[tranches de]-* ⇒ slices of hake, plus chopped onions and mushrooms, moistened with white wine and fish stock, then baked; covered with cream

Colin mère Joseph ⇒ bits of hake, braised in pork fat with chopped shallots, tomato purée and cognac

Colineau ⇒ codling

Colinot ⇒ codling

Collage *-[vin]-* ⇒ clarifying of wine

Collation ⇒ collation OR light meal

Collerettes *-[pommes de terre]-* ⇒ sliced potatoes shaped in collarette and fried

Collet
   - mouton ⇒ scrag of mutton
   - veau ⇒ neck of veal or collar of veal
   - boeuf ⇒ neck of beef or collar of beef

Collet *(général ...)* ⇒ neck or collar
   - mouton ⇒ scrag

Collet d'agneau ⇒ scrag end of lamb or neck of lamb

Collet de veau ⇒ neck of veal or collar of veal

Collier
   - mouton ⇒ scrag of mutton
   - veau ⇒ neck of veal or collar of veal
   - boeuf ⇒ neck of beef collar of beef

Collier *(général ...)* ⇒ neck or collar
   - mouton ⇒ scrag

Collier avec veine grasse *-[boeuf]-* ⇒ clod
Collier de boeuf pour pot au feu ou daube ⇒ boneless fore 1/4 of beef
Collier et découverte sans épaule *-[mouton]-* ⇒ neck and middle of lamb
Collier et nuque ⇒ stickin « neck »
Collins *-[cocktail tom collins]-* ⇒ Tom Collins
Collioure ⇒ Collioure red wine
Collybie à pied velouté ⇒ velvet stemmed agaric
Collybie en fuseau ⇒ spotted tough shank or wood woolly foot
Colombette *-[coulemelle]-* ⇒ parasol mushroom
Colombine ⇒ fried croquette of semolina and parmesan, filled with a culinary stuffing or a purée
Colombines de saumon Nantua ⇒ large quenelles made of crushed salmon, bread steeped in milk, eggs, cream and grated nutmeg; poached in béchamel sauce added of mashed crayfishes, cognac, and cayenne pepper
Colombo ⇒ kind of curry-powder
 - plat ⇒ all Caribbean dish seasoned with Colombo-powder
Colonel *-[Livarot]-* ⇒ Norman cow's milk cheese with a brown crust, surrounded by reed's thongs
Colvert ⇒ mallard
Colvert au poivre vert ⇒ mallard sprinkled of oil and baked, plus baked apples; served with a sauce of white wine, armagnac, green peppercorns, stock, cream and port
Colwick *-[fromage]-* ⇒ Colwick
Colza ⇒ rape or colza or cole-seed
Combottes et Les grands murs ⇒ high quality Burgundy wine from Chambolle Musigny
Cominée ⇒ with cumin
Cominées d'amandes ⇒ poultry consommé with unripe grape juice added of almonds, ginger and cumin
Cominées de geline ⇒ boiled bits of poultry and sturgeon, added of cumin, and almonds
Commanderie *-[Chypre]-* ⇒ high quality sweet Cyprus wine, with a dead leaves' colour
Commodore *-[clam]-* ⇒ poached clams with a garnish of fish quenelles, croquettes of crayfish tails, mussels, plus a sauce with crayfish purée
Commodore
 1) **garniture pour poisson poché** ⇒ ... with a garnish made of fish quenelles, crayfish tails, croquettes of crayfish tails, mussel, plus sauce added of crayfish purée
 2) **consommé** ⇒ fish consommé thickened of arrow-root, added of poached clams, and diced tomatoes
Common *-[thé]-* ⇒ variety of tea
Communard *-[Kir]-* ⇒ aperitif made of blackcurrant liqueur and red wine
Communes *-[Argentine vins]-* ⇒ ordinary wines from Argentina
Complet ⇒ full
Composé ⇒ composed with ...
Compote ⇒ compote or stewed fruit
Compote d'abricots ⇒ compote of apricots cooked in syrup
Compote d'abricots étuvés ⇒ compote of steamed apricots cooked with sugar
Compote d'airelles ⇒ compote of bilberries cooked in a syrup of icing sugar and lemon peel; served with meringues flavoured of vanilla
Compote d'alkékenges ⇒ compote of physalis cooked in syrup added of lemon
Compote d'ananas ⇒ compote of sliced pineapple cooked in a syrup added of vanilla sugar
Compote d'anguries ⇒ compote made with Caribbean cucumber
Compote de cerises ⇒ compote made of stoned cherries, in a syrup of sugar diluted with kirsch
Compote de cerises étuvées ⇒ compote made of stoned cherries macerated in sugar
Compote de coings ⇒ compote of quinces in vanilla syrup

Compote de figues fraîches ⇒ compote of figs in syrup, flavoured with vanilla

Compote de figues sèches ⇒ dried figs with a syrup of red wine and grated lemon peel, cooked in compote

Compote de fraises ⇒ strawberries, moistened with a hot orange flavoured syrup

Compote de framboises ⇒ raspberries moistened with a hot syrup

Compote de fruits en conserve ⇒ canned fruit compote

Compote de groseilles ⇒ compote made with redcurrants and syrup

Compote de légumes ⇒ vegetable compote

Compote de marrons ⇒ compote made with chestnuts, and syrup flavoured of vanilla

Compote de mirabelles ⇒ compote of mirabelle plums cooked in a boiling syrup

Compote de myrtilles ⇒ compote made with bilberries, in a syrup of sugar and lemon peel

Compote de pêches ⇒ peach compote

Compote de poires ⇒ compote of pears flavoured with vanilla or lemon

Compote de pommes ⇒ apple compote

Compote de pruneaux ⇒ compote of dried plums cooked in water or wine with sugar, lemon juice and vanilla sugar

Compote de prunes ⇒ compote made of stoned plums and syrup, served with or without cream

Compote de quatre fruits ⇒ compote made of grape, bananas, apples and pears, cooked with lemon juice, cinnamon, sugar, and orange juice

Compote de rhubarbe ⇒ compote made of sliced rhubarb cooked in syrup

Compote du vieux vigneron ⇒ quartered apples melted with sugar, topped with a compote of pears plus stoned peaches in a syrup of sugar, red wine, clove and cinnamon; covered with raisins or grape seeds and the cooking syrup

Compote poires-pommes caramélisées ⇒ alternate layers of pear compote and apple compote, sprinkled with their caramelized syrup

Compoter -[*onions, lapin en morceaux, etc ...]*- ⇒ « nom anglais » ... stewed in compote

Compris ⇒ with no further charges

Comtesse Marie -[*Biscuit glacé*]- ⇒ pastry case made of strawberry ice cream shaped in square, and filled with whipped cream flavoured of vanilla

Comté ⇒ pressed cheese from Franche-Comté

Concassé ⇒ crushed or crumbled < *v.t adjetif* >

Concassée de tomates ⇒ diced tomato pulp

Concentré ⇒ concentrate

 - bouillon ⇒ concentrate OR stock extract

 - bouillon de bœuf concentré ⇒ beef extract

 - lait condensé ou concentré ⇒ condensed milk

 - concentré de tomates ⇒ tomato purée

Concentré de tomates ⇒ tomato purée

Conches -[*fromage*]- ⇒ cheese for râclette

Conchiglie -[*pâte*]- ⇒ variety of pasta

Conchigliettes -[*pâtes*]- ⇒ pasta for soups

Concombre ⇒ cucumber

Concombre des antilles ⇒ Caribbean cucumber

Concombres étuvés au beurre ⇒ sauté cucumbers served with butter and herbs

Concombres à la crème ⇒ sauté cucumber pulp added of cream, then browned

Concombres farçis ⇒ cucumbers stuffed with a forcemeat, laid on strips from rind of pork, plus diced braised vegetables, then baked in stock

Concombres farçis à la russe ⇒ shaped boat cucumbers stuffed with a garnish of chopped onions, slices of cucumbers, fish, and soft white cheese

Concombres farçis au crabe ⇒ cucumbers stuffed with a preparation of crab, fennel, diced ham, mayonnaise, and vinegar

Concorde -*[garniture boucherie]*- ⇒ garnish of mashed potatoes, early spring carrots and peas in butter

Condé ou à la Condé
- **apprêts salés** ⇒ red bean purée
- **glaçage** ⇒ almond icing used to coat pastries OR coated with almond icing
- **entremets** ⇒ dessert made of rice and poached fruits

Condiment ⇒ condiment or seasoning

Condrieu ⇒ Rhone valley white wine

Conejo estirado -*[Bolivie]*- ⇒ Bolivian dish of rabbit

Cône ⇒ cone

Conférence -*[poire]*- ⇒ variety of pear

Confiserie ⇒ confectionery

Confit d'oie ⇒ conserve of goose

Confit de canard ⇒ conserve of duck

Confit *(e ...)*
- **fruits** ⇒ crystallized or candied or preserved fruit
- **oie** ⇒ conserve of goose
- **canard** ⇒ conserve of duck
- **porc** ⇒ conserve of pork
- **dinde** ⇒ conserve of turkey

Confit d'oie à la béarnaise ⇒ piece of conserved goose warmed up again, plus potatoes sautéed in goose fat, then sprinkled with garlic and parsley

Confit d'oie à la landaise ⇒ onions, diced ham and peas braised in goose fat, plus a piece of conserved goose added

Confit d'oie à la sarlardaise ⇒ piece of conserved goose warmed up again, plus potatoes sautéed in goose fat with truffles

Confit d'oie au chou vert ⇒ braised cabbage and potatoes, warmed up again with a piece of conserved goose

Confit de canard aux cèpes ⇒ conserve of duck with boletus

Confit de canard pommes sautées, salade ⇒ conserve of duck with sauté potatoes, salad

Confit de poule aux girolles ⇒ conserve of poultry with edible agaric

Confiture ⇒ jam

Confiture d'alkékenge ⇒ physalis jam

Confiture d'ananas ⇒ pineapple jam

Confiture d'oranges ⇒ marmalade < *uncountable* >

Confiture de Bar-le-Duc ⇒ redcurrant jam

Confiture de cerises ⇒ cherry jam

Confiture de citrons ⇒ lemon marmalade

Confiture de figues ⇒ fig jam

Confiture de fraises ⇒ strawberry jam

Confiture de framboises ⇒ raspberry jam

Confiture de groseilles ⇒ redcurrant jam

Confiture de mangue ⇒ mango jam

Confiture de marrons ⇒ chestnut jam flavoured with vanilla

Confiture de melons ⇒ melon jam

Confiture de mirabelles ⇒ plum jam

Confiture de mûres ⇒ mulberry jam

Confiture de myrtilles ⇒ bilberry jam

Confiture de noix de coco ⇒ coconut jam
Confiture de pêches ⇒ peach jam
Confiture de raisin ⇒ grape jam
Confiture de reine claude ⇒ plum jam or greengage jam
Confiture de rhubarbe ⇒ rhubarb jam
Confiture de tomates rouges ⇒ tomato jam
Confiture de tomates vertes ⇒ unripe tomato jam
Confitures d'abricots ⇒ apricot jam
Confitures d'airelles ⇒ bilberry jam
Confitures de griottes ⇒ cherry jam
Confitures de prunes ⇒ plum jam
Congelé ⇒ freezed or congealed
Congélateur ⇒ freezer or deep freeze
Congolais ⇒ petit four made of meringue mixed with grated coconut < *autre nom Rocher à la noix de coco* >
Congre ⇒ conger eel or sea eel
Conque -[*mollusque*]- ⇒ conch
Consommé ⇒ consommé
Consommé à l'amiral ⇒ fish consommé thickened of arrow-root and garnished of pike quenelles in crayfish paste, poached oysters, julienne of truffles cooked in Madeira, and chervil
Consommé à l'essence d'estragon ⇒ consommé flavoured with tarragon
Consommé à l'essence de céleri ⇒ consommé with celeriac added
Consommé à l'essence de truffe ⇒ consommé added of strips from rind of truffle, plus port or xeres
Consommé à l'impériale ⇒ consommé made of stock, plus cockscombs, poultry kidneys, rice, and diced pancakes
Consommé à l'infante ⇒ consommé thickened of arrow-root, and served with foie gras profiteroles
Consommé à l'orge perlé ⇒ consommé made of stock and barley; flavoured with celery
Consommé à la basquaise ⇒ soup of rice and capsicums cooked in consommé, plus diced tomato and chervil
Consommé à la bouchère ⇒ cabbage consommé, served with slices of poached bone-marrow
Consommé à la cancalaise ⇒ fish consommé thickened of tapioca and garnished with poached oysters; sometimes added of sole fillet lamellas or pike quenelles
Consommé à la Madrilène ⇒ chicken consommé added of tomato pulp, and diced capsicums
Consommé à la moscovite ⇒ consommé of sturgeon and cucumber, garnished with a julienne of mushrooms, plus sturgeon bone-marrow
Consommé à la parisienne ⇒ consommé made of braised diced vegetables, slices of moulded custard, and chervil
Consommé à la reine ⇒ poultry consommé thickened of tapioca, added of diced moulded custard, plus diced poultry meat
Consommé à la royale ⇒ meat or poultry consommé garnished with diced moulded custard
Consommé à la strasbourgeoise ⇒ consommé flavoured with juniper berries and thickened of fecula; garnished with a julienne of red cabbage, sliced Strasbourg sausage, and served with grated horse-radish
Consommé alexandra ⇒ poultry consommé
Consommé au fumet de gibier ⇒ game consommé added of Madeira
Consommé au riz ou à la semoule ⇒ consommé added of rice or semolina, served with grated cheese
Consommé au tapioca ⇒ consommé thickened with tapioca
Consommé au vin ⇒ consommé added of Madeira or port
Consommé aurore ⇒ consommé added of tomato purée

Consommé aux ailerons de volaille ⇒ consommé added of poached poultry pinions

Consommé aux cerises ⇒ chicken consommé thickened of tapioca, and served with stoned cherries

Consommé aux diablotins ⇒ consommé thickened of tapioca, garnished with sippets spreaded of cheese, and browned

Consommé aux nids d'hirondelles ⇒ poultry consommé cooked with bits of tern nests

Consommé aux profiteroles ⇒ consommé thickened of tapioca and chervil, served with profiteroles filled with a stuffing of meat or vegetables

Consommé Bizet ⇒ consommé added of tarragon, poached poultry quenelles and chervil

Consommé blanc clarifié ⇒ consommé made of chopped beef, diced carrots and leeks, plus white of eggs and stock

Consommé blanc simple ⇒ stock of beef and vegetables for culinary purpose

Consommé brancas ⇒ consommé added with a chiffonade of lettuce and chervil, plus julienne and vermicelli

Consommé Brillat-Savarin ⇒ consommé thickened with tapioca and garnished with chopped white meat, bits of pancake, lettuce and sorrel chiffonade, plus shredded chervil

Consommé chasseur ⇒ consommé made of julienne and mushrooms in Madeira, thickened with tapioca plus chervil

Consommé Colbert ⇒ consommé added of braised diced vegetables, poached eggs, and chervil

Consommé commodore ⇒ fish consommé with clams, diced tomatoes and arrow-root

Consommé croûte au pot ⇒ consommé; served with croutons garnished of bone-marrow, or vegetables from pot-au-feu, and browned

Consommé célestine ⇒ poultry consommé thickened with tapioca, garnished of pancakes in julienne, poached white meat, and chervil

Consommé Dalayrac ⇒ consommé thickened of tapioca and garnished with a julienne of poultry, plus mushrooms, and truffle

Consommé de gibier simple ⇒ game consommé

Consommé de poisson à la cancalaise ⇒ tapioca consommé garnished with poached oysters, sometimes added of sole fillets in julienne, or pike quenelles

Consommé de poisson simple ⇒ consommé made of pike, burbot, onions, leeks, parsley, celery, white wine and whiting; then sieved

Consommé florette ⇒ consommé added with a julienne of leeks and rice; served with cream and grated parmesan

Consommé julienne ⇒ consommé added of a julienne braised in butter, plus sorrel, peas, and chervil

Consommé Leverrier ⇒ consommé thickened of tapioca, and diced moulded custard

Consommé léopold ⇒ consommé with semolina, and sorrel chiffonade

Consommé mercédès ⇒ chicken consommé with xeres, sliced cock's kidneys, cockscombs and chervil

Consommé monaco ⇒ chicken consommé thickened with egg-yolks, and garnished with slices of bread coated of icing sugar

Consommé monte carlo ⇒ consommé served with small slices of bread, buttered and sprinkled of grated parmesan, then browned

Consommé nemrod ⇒ game consommé added of port and thickened of arrow-root; garnished with little quenelles of game and truffle

Consommé nesselrode ⇒ poultry consommé, garnished of some choux-pastries filled with chestnut purée and mashed onions, plus some other filled with chopped mushrooms

Consommé princesse ⇒ consommé added of braised asparagus and poached chicken quenelles

Consommé princesse Alice ⇒ consommé made of julienne, artichoke hearts, lettuce chiffonade and chervil

Consommé pépita ⇒ consommé added of diced moulded custard flavoured with tomato, diced capsicum, plus paprika

Consommé simple de volaille ⇒ stock of chicken, veal and vegetables for culinary purpose

Consommé St Hubert ⇒ game consommé thickened of tapioca, garnished of diced moulded custard or mushrooms braised in Madeira

Consommé villageois ⇒ leek consommé garnished with noodles

Consommé xavier ⇒ poultry consommé thickened with egg-yolks, rice cream and cream; garnished with diced chicken and butter

Constance *-[vins du lac de]-* ⇒ wines from the upper Rhine valley

Constantia *-[Afrique du sud vin]-* ⇒ Constantia

Contades *-[pâtés à la]-* ⇒ goose fat wrapped with a forcemeat of veal, and covered of pastry crust

Contender *-[haricot vert]-* ⇒ french bean

Conti ⇒ ... with lentils

- **pièces de boucherie rôties, poêlées ou braisées** ⇒ ... with a garnish of mashed lentils added of pork fat
- **garniture à la conti** ⇒ with a garnish of croquettes made of mashed lentils, and potatoes in butter
- **oeufs sur le plat à la conti** ⇒ fried eggs with mashed lentils
- **potage conti** ⇒ mashed lentils diluted in stock, and thickened of butter with sippets

Contiser ⇒ to incrust truffle lamellas or oxtongue lamellas on chicken, game or fish fillets

Contisé

- **poulet** ⇒ chicken fillets incrusted with truffle lamellas or oxtongue lamellas
- **gibier** ⇒ game fillets incrusted with truffle lamellas or oxtongue lamellas
- **poisson** ⇒ nom du poisson ... fillets incrusted with truffle lamellas or oxtongue lamellas

Contre filet *-[boeuf]-* ⇒ hind brisket of beef or sirloin steak

Conversation ⇒ puff-pastry tartlets filled with either frangipane flavoured of rum, or confectioner's custard added of almonds

Convive ⇒ guest

Cookie-leekie ⇒ cock-a-leekie

Cookies *-[Amérique du nord]-* ⇒ oat flakes' biscuits

Cooler *-[cocktail]-* ⇒ chilled cocktail

Copeaux

1) **décoration faite avec des copeaux de chocolat** ⇒ decorating made of shavings from chocolate or decorating made of chocolate vermicelli
2) **patisseries tubulaires** ⇒ small pastries shaped in tube

Copeaux de chocolat ⇒ chocolate vermicelli

Coppa *(la ...)* ⇒ shine of pork marinated in red wine and garlic, then tied up in a bowel, steamed and dried

Coprah ⇒ copra

Coprin chevelu ⇒ ink cap or horsetail fungus or maned agaric

Coprin à chevelure ⇒ ink cap or horsetail fungus or maned agaric

Coq ⇒ cock or cockerel

Coq *(à la ...)*

- **oeuf** ⇒ soft boiled egg eaten in its shell
- **article poché** ⇒ ... poached with its skin
- **avocat** ⇒ avocado eaten in its shell
- **artichaut** ⇒ artichoke eaten plain

Coque *(à la ...)*

- **oeuf** ⇒ soft boiled egg eaten in its shell
- **article poché** ⇒ ... poached with its skin
- **avocat** ⇒ avocado eaten in its shell
- **artichaut** ⇒ artichoke eaten plain

Coq à la bière ⇒ chicken braised in butter and shallots, then flamed in geneva; simmered in beer, cream and mushrooms

Coq au cidre $\Rightarrow$ cock stuffed with apples cooked with butter, shallots, apples, thyme, clove and cider; served with the cooking juice thickened of cream

Coq au vin $\Rightarrow$ cock braised in butter, lardoons and onions, plus garlic and morels; flamed in brandy and added of wine

Coq au vin de Madame Maigret $\Rightarrow$ diced cock braised with carrots, onions, leek, shallots, garlic, Riesling wine, nutmeg, and thyme; served with fresh noodles, plus the cooking juice thickened of egg-yolk, cream, lemon juice, and prunella eau de vie

Coq de bruyère $\Rightarrow$ capercaillie

Coq d'inde -*[dindon, dindonneau]*- $\Rightarrow$ turkey < *viande uncountable* >

Coq en pâte $\Rightarrow$ chicken stuffed with foie gras, truffles and cognac; covered with a paste and baked

Coque -*[fruits de mer]*- $\Rightarrow$ cockle

Coque -*[patisserie]*-
- **général** $\Rightarrow$ brioche filled with preserved fruits
- **Limoux** $\Rightarrow$ brioche filled with cedrate
- **Aveyron** $\Rightarrow$ brioche flavoured with rum and orange blossom

Coque -*[oeuf à la]*- $\Rightarrow$ boiled egg

Coquelet $\Rightarrow$ cockerel

Coquelets en crapaudine à l'américaine $\Rightarrow$ flattened chickens macerated in oil, garlic, ginger and pepper, then grilled; served with a salad

Coquelicot $\Rightarrow$ wild poppy

Coquemelle -*[coulemelle]*- $\Rightarrow$ parasol mushroom

Coqueret -*[alkékenge]*- $\Rightarrow$ physalis or winter-cherry

Coques à l'éffiloché de poireaux $\Rightarrow$ cockles with shredded leeks

Coques à la fondue de poireaux $\Rightarrow$ cockles served with leeks stewed in their own liquid

Coquetier $\Rightarrow$ egg cup

Coquillages $\Rightarrow$ shellfishes or shells

Coquille -*[preparation faite d'un salpicon, d'une purée ou d'un ragoût]*- $\Rightarrow$ shell < *... laid on a scallop shell and browned* >

Coquilles chaudes $\Rightarrow$ hot shells < *terme général dans le menu* >
- **amourettes hachées** $\Rightarrow$ chopped amourettes ...
- **cervelles avec sauce velouté** $\Rightarrow$ brains with velouté sauce ...
- **barbue avec crevettes** $\Rightarrow$ brill with shrimps ...
- **queues d'écrevisses ou foies de raie avec beurre** $\Rightarrow$ crayfish tails or skate livers in butter ...
- **laitances avec épinards** $\Rightarrow$ soft roes with spinach ...
- **huîtres avec sauce épicée** $\Rightarrow$ oysters with spicy sauce ...
- **viande sauce tomate** $\Rightarrow$ meat with tomato sauce ...
- **dés de volaille** $\Rightarrow$ diced poultry meat ...
- **moules** $\Rightarrow$ mussels ...
- **ris d'agneau** $\Rightarrow$ lamb sweetbread ...
- **morceaux de poisson sauce Mornay** $\Rightarrow$ bits of fish with béchamel sauce added of egg-yolks and gruyère ... laid on scallop shell, and browned

Coquilles froides $\Rightarrow$ cold shells < *terme général dans le menu* >
- **poisson avec mayonnaise** $\Rightarrow$ fish in mayonnaise ...
- **saumon froid** $\Rightarrow$ chilled salmon ...
- **crevettes** $\Rightarrow$ shrimps ...
- **d'escalopes de homard** $\Rightarrow$ round slices of lobster ...
- **d'huîtres ou de coquillages** $\Rightarrow$ oysters or shellfish with a sauce ...
- **decoration** $\Rightarrow$ ... decorated of mayonnaise, slices of lemon, and black olives

Coquilles aux crevetttes ⇒ shells filled with a preparation of mussels, mushrooms, béchamel sauce and crayfish tails; covered with breadcrumbs, grated parmesan and melted butter, then browned

Coquilles chaudes de homard Mornay ⇒ shells garnished of lobster poached in a court-bouillon, covered with béchamel sauce added of egg-yolks and gruyère, sprinkled of breadcrumbs, then browned

Coquilles de poisson à la Mornay ⇒ shells garnished of fish and béchamel sauce added of egg-yolks and gruyère, covered with grated cheese, then browned

Coquilles de poisson à la provençale ⇒ shells garnished of fish, sauce, and capers; covered with olive oil, and warmed up again

Coquilles de saumon victoria ⇒ shells garnished of poached salmon, braised mushrooms and truffles; covered with crayfish sauce and grated parmesan, then browned

Coquilles froides de homard ⇒ shells garnished with lettuce, lobster, mayonnaise, and hard boiled eggs

Coquille st jacques ⇒ scallop

Coquilles St jacques à la mayonnaise ⇒ scallop shells garnished with lettuce chiffonade, poached scallops in french dressing, and anchovy fillet plus capers

Coquilles St jacques à la vapeur ⇒ scallops steamed over a court-bouillon

Coquilles St jaques à la nage ⇒ scallops poached in a court-bouillon of carrots, onions, shallots, garlic, and herbs; served with the stock added of cream

Coquilles St jacques au foie gras de canard ⇒ duck's foie gras, and scallops cooked in a court-bouillon; served with a sauce made of the stock added of shallots, white wine, cream, butter and lemon juice

Coquilles st jacques au whisky ⇒ scallops cooked in whisky

Coquilles st jacques aux cèpes ⇒ scallops cooked with boletus

Coquilles St jacques crues au caviar ⇒ sliced and oiled scallops topped with caviar; served with toasts and butter

Coquilles St jacques en brochettes ⇒ scallops macerated in olive oil, garlic and lemon juice; grilled on a skewer with mushrooms, lardoons and capsicum

Coquilles St jacques en salade ⇒ shells filled with lettuce chiffonade, poached scallops, cucumber, french dressing, and quartered boiled eggs

Coquilles St jacques frites beurre colbert ⇒ scallops macerated in oil, steeped in dough and fried; served with parsley butter added of gravy and tarragon

Coquilles St jacques gratinées à la dieppoise ⇒ poached scallops, plus cooked mussels and shrimp tails, covered with a sauce made of their cooking stock, chopped mushrooms and egg-yolks; browned with breadcrumbs and melted butter

Coquilles St jacques Mornay ⇒ poached scallops covered with béchamel sauce added of egg-yolks and gruyère, sprinkled with grated cheese and melted butter, then browned

Coquillettes -[*pâtes*]- ⇒ pasta < *uncountable* >

Corail

    - **homard** ⇒ creamy lobster's meat or lobster's orangey part

    - **coquille st jacques** ⇒ yellow part from scallop OR scallop's orangey part

Corbeau ⇒ raven or crow

Corbeille ⇒ basket

Corbières ⇒ wines from Languedoc

Cordial ⇒ tonic or stimulant or invigorating liquor or cordial

Cordillon ⇒ ring of sugar paste cooked in water, coloured with saffron, then baked

Cordle ⇒ corolla

Cordon ⇒ a band of gravy or thick sauce surrounding the food on its serving dish or surrounded by ...

Coriandre ⇒ coriander

Corme ⇒ sorb-apple

Cormé ⇒ sorb-apple

Cormes -*[Limousin]*- ⇒ brioches
Cormelle -*[coulemelle]*- ⇒ parasol mushroom
Corn bread ⇒ corn bread
Corn flakes ⇒ corn flakes
Corn on the cob -*[Amérique du nord]*- ⇒ corn on the cob
Corn whiskey -*[whisky]*- ⇒ whisky
Cornas -*[vin]*- ⇒ Rhone valley red wine
Corne -*[noix]*- ⇒ variety of nut
Corne d'abondance ⇒ horn of plenty mushroom
Corne de bélier -*[pois gourmand]*- ⇒ mange-tout bean
Corne de cerf ⇒ hartshorn
Corne de gazelle ⇒ pastry shaped in crescent and made of almonds, sugar, butter, orange blossom, and dough
Corne salée -*[salicorne]*- ⇒ saltwort
Cornes -*[cornouille]*- ⇒ dogwood berry
Corned beef ⇒ corned beef
Corneille ⇒ crow or rook
Cornes de chèvre -*[Belgique]*- ⇒ potatoes
Cornet
    - **pâtisserie** ⇒ cornet
    - **cuisine** ⇒ cone-shaped slice of ham
Cornet
    - **crème glacée** ⇒ an ice-cream cone or a conical pastry filled with ice cream
    - **de frites** ⇒ cornet of chips or paper cone of chips
    - **de dragées** ⇒ cornet of sweets or paper cone of sweets
Cornet d'Anvers ⇒ fraises in whipped cream and sugar
Cornet de Murat ⇒ cornet filled with sugared whipped cream
Cornet de papier, etc ... ⇒ cornet OR paper cone
Cornets de jambon à la mousse de foie gras ⇒ slices of ham shaped in cone, filled with foie gras mousse; served with sippets and pork jelly
Cornets de saumon fumé aux œufs de poisson ⇒ slices of salmon shaped in cone, filled with caviar or salmon roes, laid on a lettuce chiffonade seasoned of french dressing; decorated of halved lemons
Cornette -*[Bourgogne]*- ⇒ corn fritter rolled in cornet
Cornflakes -*[brunch]*- ⇒ corn flakes
Cornichon ⇒ gherkin
Cornichons à la russe ⇒ macerated gherkins in salted water and fennel
Cornichons au vinaigre, à chaud ⇒ preserved gherkins in salt and vinegar, plus aromatics
Cornichons au vinaigre, à froid ⇒ preserved gherkins in salt, vinegar, onions, and aromatics
Cornioles -*[cornouille]*- ⇒ dogwood berry
Corniottes ⇒ burgundy sweets
Cornish pastry ⇒ cornish pastry
Cornouelles ⇒ Perigourdan dessert
Cornouille ⇒ dogwood berry
Cornue -*[Limousin]*- ⇒ brioches
Corosol -*[anone]*- ⇒ anona or custard-apple
Corse Calvi ⇒ Corsican wine from Balagne area
Corse Porto Vecchio ⇒ Corsican quality wine from Porto Vecchio area
Corse Sartène ⇒ Corsican red wine and rosé wine from Sartène area
Corse patrimonio ⇒ Corsican wine

Cortinaire ⇒ cortinarius mushroom
Corton-bressandes ⇒ high quality white wine from Beaune area
Corton Charlemagne ⇒ high quality white wine from Beaune area
Corton-clos-du-roi ⇒ high quality white wine from Beaune area
Corton-renardes ⇒ high quality white wine from Beaune area
Corvo di casteldaccia ⇒ Sicilian wine
Cos d'estournel -[*St estèphe*]- ⇒ high quality Médoc red wine
Cos labory -[*St estèphe*]- ⇒ high quality Médoc red wine
Cosidou ⇒ Beninese pot au feu
Costières du gard ⇒ wine from Nîmes area
Côte -[*bette*]- ⇒ chard
Côtes ⇒ vins
Côte chalonnaise -[*Bourgogne*]- ⇒ Burgundy wine
Côtes d'Auvergne ⇒ quality wines from Clermond Ferrand area
Côte de Bergerac ⇒ high quality wines from Bergerac area
Côte de beaune ⇒ Burgundy wines from Beaune area
Côte de brouilly ⇒ Beaujolais red wine
Côtes de canon Fronsac ⇒ the best red wines from Fronsac near Libourne
Côte de nuits ⇒ Burgundy red wines from Nuits-St Georges area
Côtes de Blaye ⇒ Bordeaux wines mainly red, from the Gironde right bank
Côtes de Buzet ⇒ high quality wines from Buzet sur Baïse near Agen
Côtes de Cabardès -[*Cabardès*]- ⇒ quality red and rosé wines from Carcassonne area
Côtes de Duras ⇒ quality wines from Lot et Garonne
Côtes de la Malpère ⇒ qualit y red and rosé wines from Carcassonne area
Côtes de nuits village ⇒ quality Burgundy red wines
Côtes de Provence ⇒ high quality wines from vineyards located between Marseille and Nice
Côtes de saussignac ⇒ white wines from Bergerac area
Côtes du Forez ⇒ quality red and rosé wines from Montbrisson area
Côtes du Jura ⇒ high quality wines from Jura, some sparkling
Côtes du Luberon ⇒ quality red and rosé wines from Haute Provence
Côtes du Rhône ⇒ wines from the Rhone valley, between Lions and Avignon
Côtes de Toul ⇒ quality rosé wine from Toul area
Côtes du Ventoux ⇒ high quality wine from Mont Ventoux
Côtes du Vivarais ⇒ quality wines from Rhone valley right bank
Côtes du frontonnais ⇒ high quality red and rosé wines from Montauban area
Côtes du marmandais ⇒ quality wines from Garonne banks
Côtes du roussillon ⇒ wines from Pyrenees Orientales, some classified high quality
Côte Roannaise ⇒ red wines and rosé from Roanne on the Loire
Côte rôtie ⇒ high quality red wine from the Rhone area near Vienne
Côtes ou côtelettes (*Petites pièces de boucherie ...*) -[*viande*]-
    1) **côtes de boeuf** ⇒ rib
        - **côte de veau** ⇒ cutlet
        - **côte de porc** ⇒ chop
        - **côtelette de veau** ⇒ cutlet
        - **côtelette de porc** ⇒ chop
        - **côtelette de mouton** ⇒ chop or mutton chop
        - **côtelette d'agneau** ⇒ cutlet or lamb chop or lamb cutlet
        - **côtelette ou noisette de cerf** ⇒ stag cutlet
        - **côtelette ou noisette de chevreuil** ⇒ roe-deer cutlet
        - **côte première** ⇒ 1 rib
        - **côte seconde** ⇒ 2 rib

2) Chez le boeuf
- **côte à l'os premier choix à rôtir au four** ⇒ first quality rib of beef
- **basses côtes, détaillées en tranche pour entrecôte ou traitée en rôti** ⇒ top ribs from forequarters
- **plat de côtes, pour pot au feu ou brochettes** ⇒ low ribs from forequarters

3) Chez le veau
- **côtes premières ou secondes poêlées ou grillées** ⇒ main cutlets
- **côtes découvertes poêlées** ⇒ main cutlets
- **côtes de filets, taillées dans la longe et farcies ou panées** ⇒ cutlets from the hindquarter
- **côte parisienne qui est une tranche de tendron** ⇒ slice of flank
- **carré de côte désossé pour rôtis** ⇒ boned piece of cutlets
- **haut de côtes qui est traité en blanquettes** ⇒ spare ribs

4) Chez le porc
- **côtes** ⇒ chops
- **côtes premières** ⇒ neck end chops
- **carré de côtes désossé pour brochettes et rôti** ⇒ boned loin of pork
- **plat de côtes pour potée ou petit salé** ⇒ middle chops from forequarters
- **haut de côtes ou travers** ⇒ sparerib chops

5) Chez le mouton ou l'agneau
- **carré d'agneau ou mouton** ⇒ loin of lamb or loin of mutton
- **côtes premières ou secondes avec un long manche** ⇒ mutton chops from loin
- **côtelettes découvertes** ⇒ mutton chops
- **côtelettes filets taillées dans la selle** ⇒ mutton chop fillets from the saddle
- **haut de côtelettes traité en ragoût** ⇒ mutton upper part of chops

6) Volaille
- **côtelette de volaille qui correspond à l'aile** ⇒ wing of poultry

7) Saumon
- **côtelette de saumon qui est un apprêt de la darne** ⇒ steak of salmon

8) Sanglier, marcassin
- **côtelettes mangées marinées et poêlées** ⇒ fried marinated wild boar chops

Côte de boeuf
- **Côte basse avec partie de macreuse -[boeuf]-** ⇒ steak meat
- **Côte de boeuf** ⇒ rib or rib of beef
- **Côte de boeuf dans le faux-filet** ⇒ T' bone steak

Côtes de boeuf -[*Garnitures*]-
- **a) côte de boeuf braisée avec garniture bourgeoise** ⇒ braised rib of beef served with a garnish of small onions, carrots, plus lardoons
  - **avec garniture bourguignonne** ⇒ ... with a garnish of onions, cultivated mushrooms, and lardoons
  - **avec garniture chipolata** ⇒ ... with a garnish of braised chestnuts, glazed onions, glazed carrots, sauté mushrooms, lardoons and browned chipolatas
- **b) côte de boeuf rôtie avec garniture bouquetière** ⇒ roasted rib of beef served with a garnish of vegetables laid in bunches round the large pieces of meat
  - **avec garniture bruxelloise** ⇒ ... served with a garnish of steamed brussels-sprouts, braised chicory and small potatoes sautéed in butter with lardoons
  - **avec garniture dauphine** ⇒ ... with fried small balls of mashed potatoes and choux pastry
  - **avec garniture duchesse** ⇒ ... surrounded by fried balls of mashed potatoes, eggs and butter

- **avec garniture flamande** ⇒ ... with a garnish of stuffed cabbage balls, carrots, turnips, boiled potatoes and slices of dry sausage
- **avec garniture hongroise** ⇒ ... with a garnish of potato croustades topped with cauliflower, covered of béchamel sauce, added of egg-yolks, gruyère, and paprika; plus potatoes shaped in olive and baked with butter
- **avec garniture Jardinière** ⇒ ... with vegetable salad
- **avec garniture lorraine** ⇒ ... with a garnish of red cabbage braised in red wine, plus potatoes shaped in olive and baked in butter; grated horse-radish
- **avec garniture lyonnaise** ⇒ ... with a sauce of onions braised in butter, vinegar, white wine and stock
- **avec garniture macédoine** ⇒ ... with mixed vegetable
- **avec garniture julienne** ⇒ ... served with a garnish of mushrooms, ham and oxtongue in butter, plus truffle lamellas; moistened of veal stock added of Madeira
- **avec garniture nivernaise** ⇒ ... with a garnish of shaped carrots and onions in butter, plus braised lettuce covered with the gravy
- **avec garniture parisienne** ⇒ ... with a garnish of little potato-balls browned in butter and sprinkled of chopped herbs, plus braised lettuces or artichoke hearts
- **avec garniture printanière** ⇒ ... with a garnish of early spring vegetables
- **ou bien des légumes liés au beurre ou braisés** ⇒ ... with vegetables thickened of butter or braised
- **avec des purées de légumes** ⇒ ... with mashed vegetables

Côte de boeuf braisée ⇒ large chop of beef studded of lardoons, seasoned of spices and cognac, marinated in wine with thyme, laurel and garlic; then braised

Côte de boeuf rôtie à la bouquetière ⇒ large chop of beef, sprinkled of melted butter and roasted; served with bunches of various vegetables

Côte de boeuf rôtie à la broche ⇒ rib of beef, larded and brushed with butter or oil, then roasted on a skewer

Côte de boeuf rôtie au four ⇒ rib of beef, larded and brushed with butter or oil, then roasted in the oven

Côtes de filet -[boeuf]- ⇒ ribs from the hindquarter

Côte première ⇒ loin chop

Côte de mouton ⇒ mutton chop

Côtes d'agneau ou mouton ⇒ loin chops or cutlets

Côtes de mouton découvertes ⇒ ribs partly removed of the eye muscle

Côtes de filet -[mouton]- ⇒ chump chops or mutton chop

Côtes de filet doubles -[mouton]- ⇒ crown chops « Barnsley »

Côtes de filet parées assez épaisses -[mouton]- ⇒ loin chops « trimmed »

Côtes de filet avec longes -[mouton]- ⇒ loin of lamb

Côtes de filet sans os -[mouton]-
- **parées et coupées assez épaisses** ⇒ noisettes of lamb

Côtes 1 doubles -[mouton]-
- a) **découvertes extérieur** ⇒ best end of lamb « short »
- b) **découvertes intérieur** ⇒ best end of lamb « long »

Côtes 1 manches faits, mais avec gras -[mouton]- ⇒ cutlets « French trimmed »

Côtes 1 sans os, épaisses et ouvertes en deux -[mouton]- ⇒ Valentine steaks

Côtes 2 avec manche -[mouton]- ⇒ cutlets « trimmed »

Côtes 2 doubles -[mouton]- ⇒ butterfly cutlets

Côtes nature tout venant -[mouton]- ⇒ economy chops

Côtes pas avantageuses, un peu osseuses -[mouton]- ⇒ bandsaw chops

Côte première ⇒ loin chop

Côtes de filet -[*porc*]- ⇒ chops from loin
Côte de porc ⇒ chop or chop of pork
Côtes de porc 1 épaisses ouvertes en deux ⇒ loin steaks double
Côtes de porc dans la longe sans échine ⇒ chops « rind on »
Côtes de porc parées dans la longe sans échine ⇒ chops « trimmed »
Côtes de porc sans os raccourcies ⇒ steaks of pork
Côtes de porc à l'alsacienne ⇒ braised chops of pork with sauerkraut, bacon and sausages, plus boiled potatoes
Côtes de porc à la bayonnaise ⇒ chops of pork studded with garlic, macerated in oil, pepper, thyme, laurel and vinegar; then braised and baked with mushrooms, plus potatoes
Côtes de porc à la gasconne ⇒ marinated chops of pork, sautéed in goose fat, plus garlic and stoned olives; served with the cooking juice added of white wine
Côtes de porc au pilleverjus ⇒ chops of pork sautéed in butter with chopped onions; served with a julienne of cabbage in cream, plus boiled potatoes
Côtes de porc charcutière ⇒ chops of pork, coated with breadcrumbs and butter, then grilled; served with mashed potatoes, and a sauce
Côtes de porc grillées ⇒ chops of pork brushed with butter and grilled; served with watercress and lemon
Côtes de porc sauce Robert ⇒ grilled chops of pork served with a sauce based on braised onions and white wine, plus mashed potatoes or beans
Côtes de porc sautées ⇒ sauté chops of pork, served with various vegetables
Côtes de pork aux kiwis ⇒ fried chops of pork and quartered kiwi fruits; served with the cooking juice added of pineapple juice
Côte de veau ⇒ cutlet or veal cutlet
Côte de veau Foyot ⇒ veal's chop braised in butter and covered on a side by a paste of crumbs, grated cheese and butter, topped with a tomato; served with the cooking juice added of shallot, white wine, stock, and butter
Côte de veau braisée à la custine ⇒ braised veal's chop, coated with chopped mushrooms, crumbs and eggs; served with tomato sauce
Côte de veau en casserole à la Dreux ⇒ veal's chop studded with oxtongue and truffle, then braised in butter; served with a garnish of quenelles plus mushrooms, and the cooking juice added of Madeira
Côte de veau panée Cussy en portefeuille ⇒ veal's chop which is splitted, filled with a culinary stuffing of mushrooms, carrot, ham and béchamel sauce, then coated of egg and cooked in butter; served with risotto added of truffles, plus a tomato sauce
Côte de veau pojarski ⇒ veal's chop meat, crumbs, butter and nutmeg, shaped round the veal chop bone, then cooked in butter; served with vegetable cooked in butter
Côte découverte -[*veau*]- ⇒ middle neck of veal
Côte première ⇒ loin chop of veal
Côtes 1 et secondes -[*veau*]- ⇒ best end of veal
Côtes 1 sans os parées -[*veau*]- ⇒ veal steaks
Côtes 2 avec os, natures -[*veau*]- ⇒ cutlets of veal
Côtes de filet -[*veau*]- ⇒ loin end of veal
Côtes de filet avec os -[*veau*]- ⇒ chops of veal « standard »
Côtes de filet avec os raccourcies -[*veau*]- ⇒ chops of veal « short cut »
Côtes dont les dorsales sont retirées -[*veau*]- ⇒ rack of veal
Côtes 2 dégraissées et raccourcies -[*veau*]- ⇒ cutlets of veal « larder trim »
Côtes de veau froides à la gelée ⇒ veal's chops studded of bacon and oxtongue, then braised and chilled; covered with jelly added of port or xeres
Côtes de veau à la gelée ⇒ veal's chops studded of bacon and oxtongue, then braised and chilled; covered with jelly added of port or xeres

Côtes de veal à la piémontaise ⇒ veal's chops coated with egg, crumbs and grated parmesan, then cooked in butter; served with risotto

Côtes de veau aux fines herbes ⇒ veal's chops fried in butter and covered with the gravy added of shallots, white wine, parsley, chervil, and tarragon

Côtes de veau en casserole ⇒ veal's chops cooked in butter and served with various vegetables

Côtes de veau en casserole à la bonne femme ⇒ veal's chops sautéed with lardoons, onions and potatoes

Côtes de veau en casserole à la parmentier ⇒ veal's chops baked with potatoes and sprinkled of melted butter; served with the cooking juice added of stock and white wine

Côtes de veau en casserole à la paysanne ⇒ veal's chops cooked in butter and served with a garnish of braised carrots, onions, leek, turnip, celery, potatoes and diced lardoons

Côtes de veau en chaud-froid ⇒ veal's chops cooked in butter and covered with chaudfroid sauce; served with salads in mayonnaise

Côtes de veau en papillotes ⇒ veal's chops sautéed in butter, wrapped in paper with layers of ham and chopped mushrooms, then baked

Côtes de veau grillées ⇒ veal's chops macerated in oil and tarragon, then grilled; served with a salad of mixed vegetables

Côtes de veau grillées en portefeuille ⇒ veal's chops which are splitted, filled with a culinary stuffing of mushrooms, plus béchamel sauce, then larded and grilled; served with spinach in butter

Côtes de veau grillées vert-pré ⇒ grilled veal's chops, decorated of butter; served with watercress, and a julienne of potatoes

Côtes de veau panées à la milanaise ⇒ veal's chops coated with egg, crumbs and grated parmesan, cooked in butter; served with lemon and macaroni

Côtes de veau panées à la morland ⇒ veal's chops coated with egg, crumbs and truffle, cooked in butter; served with a mushroom purée

Côtes de veau sautées à la crème ⇒ veal's chops fried in oil, covered with a sauce made of cider and cream

Côtes de veau sautées à la duxelles ⇒ veal's chops sautéed with chopped mushrooms; covered with a sauce made of cream and white wine, or Madeira

Côtes de veau sautées à la provençale ⇒ veal's chops sautéed in olive oil; served with tomatoes stuffed of chopped mushrooms, plus a sauce made of tomato purée and white wine

Côtes de veau sautées en portefeuille ⇒ veal's chops which are splitted, filled with a culinary stuffing of mushrooms, plus béchamel sauce, then larded and cooked in butter; served with braised carrots, covered with the cooking juice added of white wine, stock, and kneaded butter

Côteaux champenois ⇒ high quality wines from champagne area, but not sparkling

Côteaux d'Aix en Provence ⇒ quality wines from Aix en Provence area

Côteaux d'Ajaccio ⇒ quality wines from Ajaccio area

Côteaux d'Ancenis ⇒ wines from Loire area, near Nantes

Côteaux de l'Aubance ⇒ white wine from Anjou

Côteaux de la Loire ⇒ high quality wines from Angers area

Côteaux du Loir ⇒ quality wines from Tours area

Côteaux de Mascara ⇒ quality Algerian wine

Côteaux de Pierrevert ⇒ quality wines from Manosque area

Côteaux du giennois ⇒ quality wines from Gien area

Côteaux du languedoc ⇒ quality wines from Languedoc area

Côteaux du Tricastin ⇒ high quality wines from Rhone valley, with a taste of truffle

Côteaux du vendômois ⇒ quality wines from Vendôme area

Côtelette ⇒ chop of mutton « mouton » or chop of pork « porc » cutlet of veal « veau »

Côtelette composée ⇒ culinary stuffing of various meat or fish, shaped in cutlet and cooked in butter

Côtelette d'agneau ⇒ cutlet or cutlet of lamb

Côtelettes d'agneau à l'anversoise ⇒ cutlets of lamb sautéed in butter, plus fried sippets and a garnish of hop shoots in cream; covered with the cooking juice added of white wine

Côtelettes d'agneau à la maréchale ⇒ lamb's cutlets coated with crumbs and eggs, then fried in butter; served with asparagus tips and truffle, sautéed in butter

Côtelettes d'agneau aux figues et au miel ⇒ sautéed lamb's cutlets, served with figs sprinkled of cinnamon and nutmeg, then baked; covered with cooking juice added of honey

Côtelette d'agneau champvallon ⇒ lamb chop baked between a layer of onions and a layer of potatoes

Côtelettes d'agneau DU BARRY ⇒ sauté lamb's cutlets served with cauliflower in béchamel sauce added of egg-yolks and gruyère, then browned

Côtelettes d'agneau grillées ⇒ lamb's cutlets brushed with butter or olive oil and grilled; served with vegetables

Côtelettes d'agneau grillées à la paloise ⇒ lamb's cutlets brushed with oil and grilled; served with french beans in cream and little browned potato balls

Côtelettes d'agneau panées ⇒ lamb's cutlets coated with egg and crumbs, then sautéed in butter

Côtelettes d'agneau sautées ⇒ lamb's cutlets sautéed in butter or goose fat, served with a garnish of vegetables

Côtelettes de chevreuil sautées ⇒ roebuck's cutlets sautéed in olive oil, and served with sippets fried in butter

Côtelettes de chevreuil sautées aux cerises ⇒ sautéed roebuck's cutlets, served with a sauce made of cherry juice, port, redcurrant jelly, ginger and lemon juice

Côtelettes de chevreuil sautées à la crème ⇒ roebuck's cutlets sprinkled of paprika and sautéed in butter; served with chestnuts and a creamy sauce added of lemon juice

Côtelettes de chevreuil sautées à la mode d'Uzès ⇒ roebuck's cutlets sautéed in oil, served with croquettes and sippets; covered with the cooking juice added of orange, gherkins, and almonds

Côtelettes de chevreuil sautées au genièvre ⇒ sauté roebuck's cutlets, served with apple jam, and the gravy added of ginger

Côtelettes de chevreuil sautées aux raisins ⇒ sauté roebuck's cutlets, served with grapes in cognac, fried sippets, and peppered sauce

Côtelettes de chevreuil sautées minute ⇒ macerated roebuck's cutlet sautéed in butter, and flamed with cognac; plus sauté mushrooms, and apple compote

Côtelettes de gibier ⇒ game cutlets

Côtelettes de lièvre aux champignons ⇒ composed cutlets made of hare, crumbs, cream, and chopped mushrooms; cooked in butter

Côtelettes de marcassin aux coings ⇒ elaborated dish of pancakes covered with a forcemeat of salsify, onions and diced pears; served with cutlets of young wild boar, topped of quinces sprinkled with rum covered with a sauce based on vegetables, bones, meat, and cream

Côtelettes de mouton à la Maintenon ⇒ cutlets of mutton coated with a julienne of mushrooms, purée, and onions; then sprinkled of melted butter, and baked

Côtelettes de mouton à la Villeroi ⇒ cutlets of mutton braised first, then coated with a sauce, egg, and crumbs, then glazed in butter; served with a tomato sauce or an other

Côtelettes de mouton à la cévenole ⇒ cutlets of mutton braised with chestnuts and lardoons; served with fried chipolatas, plus sometimes braised red cabbage

Côtelettes de mouton à la fermière ⇒ cutlets of mutton sautéed in butter with peas, white wine and potatoes

Côtelettes de mouton braisées ⇒ cutlets of mutton braised with strips from rind of pork, carrot and onion, basted with stock; served with boiled brussels-bouts, and the cooking juice

Côtelettes de mouton champvallon ⇒ cutlets of mutton baked in butter with onions, garlic, thyme, sliced potatoes, stock, and pepper

Côtelettes de mouton chasseur ⇒ cutlets of mutton sautéed in butter, covered with a sauce made of the gravy added of shallots, mushrooms, white wine, tomato sauce, butter, chervil, and tarragon

Côtelettes de mouton Pompadour ⇒ cutlets of mutton, covered with purée, crumbs and egg, then browned; served with quartered lemons, and turnips in butter

Côtelettes de perdreau Romanov ⇒ composed cutlets, made with layers of rind of pork, forcemeat of poultry marinated in port and cognac, partridge, foie gras and truffle, then roasted and served with chestnut purée or boletus, plus a creamy sauce

Côtelettes de saumon ⇒ steaks of salmon cooked in butter

Côtelettes de saumon à l'anglaise ⇒ steaks of salmon coated with crumbs and egg, then cooked in butter

Côtelettes de saumon à la Bourguignonne ⇒ steaks of salmon poached in red wine, served with mushrooms

Côtelettes de saumon à la Nantua ⇒ steaks of salmon poached in a sauce added of champagne; covered with a chaudfroid added of crayfish paste

Côtelettes de saumon à la florentine ⇒ steaks of salmon cooked in stock, laid on spinach; then covered with béchamel sauce added of egg-yolks and gruyère, plus grated cheese and browned

Côtelettes de saumon à la russe ⇒ steaks of salmon poached in a court-bouillon; served on lettuce chiffonade, plus hard boiled eggs, black olives, capers, and anchovy fillets

Côtelettes de saumon aux champignons à la crème ⇒ steaks of salmon braised in butter with mushrooms; served with the cooking juice added of Madeira and cream

Côtelettes de saumon froid à la parisienne ⇒ steaks of salmon poached in a court-bouillon, served with vegetable salad, mayonnaise, asparagus tips, french beans and carrots

Côtelettes de saumon glacées à la macédoine ⇒ steaks of salmon poached in a sauce added of champagne; served with a vegetable salad in mayonnaise

Côtelettes de saumon glacées au chambertin ⇒ steaks of salmon poached in a sauce added of Chambertin wine; covered with the cooking juice jelly

Côtelettes de saumon pojarski ⇒ composed steaks made with a forcemeat of salmon, crumbs, butter and nutmeg; then browned in butter

Côtelettes de saumon au vin blanc ⇒ steaks of salmon poached in white wine with truffles and mushrooms; served with spinach, plus a sauce based on the cooking juice and white wine

Côtelettes de veau ⇒ veal cutlets

Côtelettes de volaille Helder ⇒ cutlets of poultry baked in butter; served with a culinary stuffing of artichoke hearts and mushrooms, plus a poultry and tomato velouté sauce

Cotechino ⇒ Italian dried sausage

Cotignac ⇒ quince paste

Cotriade ⇒ Brittany fish soup, cooked in butter with onions and potatoes

Cou

    - vollaille ⇒ neck of poultry

    - gibier ⇒ neck of game

Coucoulelli ⇒ small pastries in lozenges made with a dough of flour, olive oil and white wine

Coucoumelle -[amanite vaginée]- ⇒ scheathed agaric

Coudenat ⇒ large pork sausage, made with strips of rind and panada, plus eggs

Coudenou ⇒ large pork sausage, made with strips of rind and panada, plus eggs

Coudes -[pâtes alimentaires]- ⇒ pasta for dishes in gratin

Couenne ⇒ rind of pork or rind of bacon or crackling

Cougnat ⇒ small cakes filled with raisins

Cougnon ⇒ small cakes filled with raisins
Cougnous ⇒ small cakes filled with raisins
Couke -*[brioche]*- ⇒ brioche with currants
Coulas ⇒ variety of bread from Charente Maritime
Coulée-de-serrant -*[savennières]*- ⇒ high quality wines from Angers area
Coulemelle ⇒ parasol mushroom
Coulevrée -*[lépiote]*- ⇒ parasol mushroom
Coulibiac ou Koulibiac ⇒ pastry case filled with fish or meat, vegetables, rice, and hard boiled eggs
Coulirou -*[Antilles]*- ⇒ mackerel
Coulis ⇒ purée
Coulis de framboises ⇒ purée made of raspberries and sugar *or* raspberry purée
Coulis de fruits frais ⇒ purée made of several fresh fruits and sugar *or* fruit purée
Coulis de tomate -*[condiments]*- ⇒ purée made of tomato pulp, lemon juice, sugar and pepper or tomato purée
Coulis de tomate -*[sauce]*- ⇒ purée made of quartered tomatoes, carrots, onions and sugar tomato sauce
Coulommiers -*[fromage]*- ⇒ Coulommiers
Coup (*voir définitions ci-dessous ...*)
    1) coup d'avant ⇒ glass of vermouth served before the meal
    2) coup d'après ⇒ glass of wine drunk after the soup
    3) coup du milieu ⇒ glass of liquor or cognac served immediately after the roast
Coupe -*[récipient]*- ⇒ cup or glass or small bowl
Coupe bocagère -*[champignon]*- ⇒ clitocybe mushroom or flavoured edible mushroom
Coupe de fruits ⇒ fruit salad macerated in champagne
Coupe de fruits au cidre ⇒ cups filled with various fruits, sprinkled of cider laced with calvados
Coupe glacée à la cévenole ⇒ cups filled with chestnuts and kirsch; covered of vanilla ice-cream, topped of whipped cream
Coupelle ⇒ cupel
    - **en pâte** ⇒ pastry cupel
Coupes à l'ananas ⇒ cups filled with diced pineapple macerated in rum; covered with vanilla ice cream
Coupes à la cévenole ⇒ cups filled with chestnuts macerated in rum; covered with vanilla ice-cream, and topped of whipped cream
Coupes aux abricots ⇒ cups filled with a culinary stuffing of apricots macerated in eau de vie, covered with apricot ice-cream, and almonds
Coupes aux poires à la crème au caramel ⇒ cups garnished with almond milk, pears in syrup and burnt sugar custard; topped with cream
Coupes bourbon ⇒ cream with eggs, fraises, red currants and kirsch
Coupes dame blanche ⇒ cups filled with vanilla ice cream, then served with a chocolate sauce
Coupes de crème Hawaï ⇒ cups garnished with diced pineapple, strawberries, and almond milk; covered with a raspberry purée
Coupes glacées aux pêches ⇒ cups filled with a culinary stuffing of peaches and lemon juice; covered of vanilla ice-cream, topped with whipped cream
Coupes jamaïque ⇒ cups filled with diced pineapple; covered of coffee ice-cream and sprinkled with currants macerated in rum
Coupes malmaison ⇒ cups filled of vanilla ice-cream, topped with grapes and sugar
Coupiette -*[pain]*- ⇒ Corsican bread
Couque -*[brioche]*- ⇒ brioche with currants
Couque -*[pain d'épice]*- ⇒ gingerbread
Courbine -*[poisson]*- ⇒ black drum or croaker

Courge ⇒ gourd or marrow or squash

Courge au jus ⇒ bits of gourd braised in veal stock

Courges au gratin ⇒ bits of gourd browned with butter and grated cheese

Courges en purée ⇒ bits of gourd braised in butter

Courges en soufflé ⇒ purée of gourd added of sugar, vanilla and eggs

Courgette ⇒ courgette

Courgettes à l'indienne ⇒ bits of courgettes sautéed in butter with curry

Courgettes à la créole ⇒ courgettes cooked with pork fat, then seasoned

Courgettes à la mentonnaise ⇒ courgettes stuffed with courgette pulp and spinach, covered of grated parmesan, then browned

Courgettes à la niçoise ⇒ sliced courgettes, sautéed in oil with tomatoes and garlic

Courgettes à la provençale ⇒ slices of courgettes sautéed in oil, laid on rice and topped with tomatoes, plus onions sautéed in oil and garlic; sprinkled of grated cheese, then browned

Courgettes farçies ⇒ courgettes garnished with a stuffing of rice, mutton, fennel and garlic, then moistened of tomato sauce and baked

Courgettes glacées ⇒ bits of courgettes simmered first, then sautéed in butter

Courgettes sautées ⇒ sliced courgettes, floured and fried in butter or oil

Couronne -[dressage]- ⇒ ... laid in ring

Couronne ⇒ crown shaped or ring

Couronne briochée -[Rousillon]- ⇒ brioche shaped in ring

Couronne d'ananas ⇒ sponge fingers and slices of pineapple laid in ring, moistened with a cream made of white dry wine, pineapple juice, fecula and kirsch

Couronne de croûtes aux poires ⇒ slices of brioche topped with cooked lamellas of pear and apple, lemon juice, red wine, sugar, clove and cinnamon; served with the cooking juice and cream

Couronne de loup ⇒ lamellas of sea bass fillets plaited in ring and fried in butter; served with a purée of capsicums added of cream, plus broccolis in butter

Couronne de pêches à la chantilly ⇒ ring of Bavarian mousse, filled of peaches cooked in syrup; topped with sugared whipped cream, plus angelica bits

Couronne de pommes à la normande ⇒ moulded custard flavoured of calvados, filled with apples cooked in syrup, decorated of whipped cream; served with apricot sauce laced of calvados

Couronne faite avec un carré entier d'agneau ⇒ Crown of lamb

Courquinoise ⇒ browned soup made of conger eel, crab, red gurnard, gurnard, mussels, and leeks

Courraye ou Pâté de courrés -[Bretagne]- ⇒ fry galantine

Courreau -[poisson du ... « La Rochelle »]- ⇒ nom du poisson ... from local fishing boats

Cours du marché ⇒ market price

Court-bouillon ⇒ court-bouillon

Court-bouillon au citron et au vinaigre ⇒ court-bouillon made with carrots, onions, thyme, laurel, parsley, coarse salt, lemon juice, vinegar, and pepper

Court-bouillon au lait ⇒ court-bouillon made with milk, onion, thyme, salt, and pepper

Court-bouillon au vin ⇒ court-bouillon made with white wine, carrot, onion, thyme, laurel, celery, parsley, coarse salt, and pepper

Court-bouillon eau de sel ⇒ court-bouillon added of coarse salt, thyme, and laurel

Court-pendu -[pomme]- ⇒ variety of apple

Cous d'oies farçis ⇒ goose necks stuffed with a forcemeat of goose and pork, added of diced foie gras and truffle; cooked in goose fat

Cous confits de canard ⇒ conserve of duck's necks

Couscous ⇒ couscous

Couscous à la viande ⇒ couscous with mutton meat, and vegetables
Couscous au poisson ⇒ couscous with whiting fillets, and vegetables
Couscous aux légumes ⇒ couscous with various vegetables
Cousinat
    - auvergne ⇒ chestnut soup with celeriac, onions and leeks
    - côte basque ⇒ ragout of ham in pork fat, with broad beans, artichokes, carrots, and pumpkin
Cousinette ⇒ soup based on vegetable leaves, and slices of bread
Couteau -*[mollusque]*- ⇒ razor-shell or solen
Couve ⇒ flat cake flavoured with vanilla and lemon
Couvrose -*[pleurote]*- ⇒ oyster mushroom
Cox -*[pomme]*- ⇒ cox apple
Crabe ⇒ crab
Crabe à la bretonne ⇒ crab cooked in a court-bouillon, and served with mayonnaise
Crabe farçi ⇒ crab meat cooked in a court bouillon, then laid in their carapace with béchamel sauce added of egg-yolks and gruyère
Crabe mayonnaise ⇒ crab with mayonnaise
Crabes en bouillon ⇒ crabs cooked firstly in a court-bouillon, then sautéed in pork fat or oil
Crabes farçis à la martiniquaise ⇒ crab carapaces stuffed with a forcemeat of milk, crumbs, ham, shallots, garlic, crab meat, egg-yolks and rum; sprinkled of breadcrumbs, plus melted butter, and browned
Crabes farçis au gratin ⇒ crabs' meat cooked in a court bouillon, then laid in their carapace with béchamel sauce added of egg-yolks, sprinkled of grated cheese plus melted butter, and browned
Cracker -*[biscuit]*- ⇒ cracker
Crakeline -*[craquelin]*- ⇒ cracknel or water biscuit
Crambé -*[chou marin]*- ⇒ sea kale
Cramique ⇒ brioche loaf with currants
Cranberry sauce ou -*[sauce aux airelles]*- ⇒ cranberry sauce
Crapaud -*[poisson]*- ⇒ scorpion fish
Crapaudine *(en ...)* -*[volaille]*- ⇒ poultry flattened and grilled
Crapaudine *(en ...)* -*[poulet]*- ⇒ chicken flattened and grilled
Crapiau
    - Morvan ⇒ thick pancake cooked with pork fat
    - Nivernais ⇒ pancake made of a batter added with sliced apples macerated in eau de vie or rum
Crapiaux aux pommes ⇒ pancakes made of a dough prepared with flour, eggs, milk, and sliced apples macerated in rum
Craquelin -*[cracknel]*- ⇒ water biscuit
Craquelot ⇒ smoked, salted herring < *bloater* >
Craquelot ⇒ bloater < *smoked, salted herring* >
Craspois ⇒ whale fat
Craterelle ⇒ horn of plenty mushroom
Cravattine -*[pâtes alimentaires]*- ⇒ pasta for dishes au gratin
Cream sherry -*[xérès]*- ⇒ xeres
Créat -*[esturgeon]*- ⇒ sturgeon
Crécy *(à la ...)*
    1) **potage** ⇒ soup ...
        - oeufs pochés ⇒ poached eggs ...
        - omelette ⇒ omelette ...
        - filets de sole avec purée de carotte ⇒ sole fillets with mashed carrots
    2) **consommé Crécy** ⇒ consommé added of chopped carrots

3) **tournedos Crécy** ⇒ tournedos with shaped carrots
Crémant ⇒ slightly sparkling wine
Crémat -[*ail Rousillon*]- ⇒ garlic
Crème de bananes -[*liqueur*]- ⇒ crème de bananes
Crème de cacao ⇒ crème de cacao
Crème de casssis ⇒ blackcurrant liqueur
Crème de menthe ⇒ crème de menthe
Crème de mûre ⇒ crème of mulberry and armagnac
Crème de noyau ⇒ noyau
Crème -[*soupe*]- ⇒ creamy soup
Crème à la vichyssoise ⇒ leek and potato soup thickened with cream, plus chive
Crème d'artichaut ⇒ soup made of braised artichoke hearts cooked with béchamel sauce
Crème d'asperges ⇒ soup made of braised asparagus tips and béchamel sauce
Crème d'endives ⇒ soup made of braised chicory and béchamel sauce
Crème d'estragon ⇒ soup made of tarragon cooked in white wine, béchamel sauce, and butter
Crème d'orge ⇒ soup made of barley and celery cooked in consommé, added of cream
Crème de betterave ⇒ soup made of baked beetroots, béchamel sauce, consommé and cream
Crème de champignons ⇒ soup made of mushrooms cooked with béchamel sauce, plus a julienne of
       mushrooms and cream
Crème de cresson ⇒ soup made of braised watercress, and béchamel sauce
Crème de crevettes ⇒ soup made of a mixture of diced vegetables, crayfish tails, white wine, cognac,
       and béchamel sauce
Crème de céleri ⇒ soup made of celeriac cooked with béchamel sauce
Crème de laitue ⇒ soup made of lettuce cooked with béchamel sauce
Crème de poireau ⇒ soup made of braised white of leeks and béchamel sauce
Crème de riz au gras ⇒ soup made of rice cooked in consommé and added of cream, plus chervil
Crème de volaille ⇒ soup made of mashed chicken, stock, and béchamel sauce
Crème du Barry ⇒ soup made of steamed cauliflower and béchamel sauce
Crème-potage ⇒ soup made of braised vegetables and béchamel sauce
Crème violetta ⇒ soup made of baked beetroots, béchamel sauce, consommé and cream
Crème -[*patisserie*]- ⇒ custard or confectioner's custard
Crème à l'ananas ⇒ custard with kirsch and pounded pineapple
Crème à l'anglaise ⇒ egg-custard
Crème à l'orange ⇒ egg-custard added of orange peel
Crème à la banane ⇒ custard with banana purée
Crème à la vanille ⇒ custard with vanilla purée
Crème anglaise ⇒ egg-custard
Crème anglaise à la liqueur ⇒ egg-custard added of curaçao or maraschino
Crème anglaise au miroir ⇒ egg-custard glazed in the oven
Crème anglaise collée ⇒ egg-custard added of gelatine
Crème au beurre ⇒ buttered cream
Crème au beurre au café ⇒ egg-custard added of butter and coffee extract
Crème au beurre au chocolat ⇒ egg-custard added of butter, and chocolate
Crème au beurre au sirop ⇒ custard made of sugar, egg-yolks, and butter
Crème au beurre nature à l'anglaise ⇒ egg-custard added of butter
Crème au beurre nature au sucre ⇒ custard made of sugar, egg-yolks, vanilla cream and butter
Crème au beurre pralinée ⇒ buttered custard added of praline powder
Crème au café ⇒ egg-custard flavoured with coffee extract
Crème au caramel ⇒ egg-custard added of caramel

Crème au chocolat ⇒ chocolate custard
Crème au kirsch ⇒ custard with kirsch
Crème au thé ⇒ egg-custard flavoured with tea
Crème au vin blanc ⇒ custard made of lemon, white wine, cinnamon, eggs, sugar and maïzena
Crème aux abricots secs ⇒ custard with dried apricots
Crème aux citrons plus vin blanc ⇒ custard made of lemons, eggs, sugar, white wine and maïzena
Crème aux oranges ⇒ orange and lemon juice with sugar, eggs and gelatine
Crème aux pruneaux ⇒ custard with cooked dried plums
Crème aux œufs ⇒ flummery
Crème aveline ⇒ custard of milk, sugar, eggs, maïzena and nuts powder
Crème bavaroise à la vanille ⇒ cream with eggs, sugar, milk, vanilla and gelatine
Crème bavaroise au café ⇒ cream with eggs, sugar, milk, gelatine and coffee extract
Crème bavaroise au chocolat ⇒ cream with eggs, chocolate, milk and gelatine
Crème bavaroise aux fraises ⇒ cream with syrup, fraises and gelatine
Crème bavaroise aux fruits ⇒ cream with eggs, sugar, milk, vanilla, gelatine and bit of fruits <
        différentes dénominations >
    - « **pêches** » ⇒ peaches
    - « **cerises** » ⇒ cherries
    - « **fraises** » ⇒ strawberries < *dans le texte remplacer fruits par pêches, cerises ou fraises* >
Crème brûlée ⇒ crème brûlée
Crème caramel -[garniture]- ⇒ milk added of caramel
Crème caramel ⇒ crème caramel or egg custard added of burnt sugar
Crème caramel au miel ⇒ preparation made with a caramel of sugar and honey, plus a mixing of egg-yolks, honey, and milk
Crème chantilly ⇒ sugared whipped cream or crème Chantilly
Crème chiboust ⇒ confectioner's custard added of vanilla, and white of egg
Crème d'amandes ⇒ custard made of eggs, almonds, sugar, and butter
Crème de marrons ⇒ sugared chestnut jam
Crème de pruneaux ⇒ custard flavoured with dried plums
Crème de riz à la turque ⇒ custard made of rice flour, milk and sugar; garnished with preserved fruits
Crème en ramequins ⇒ custard of chocolate, milk and egg-yolks, baked in individual ramekins
Crème Eva ⇒ custard from flour, sugar, eggs and milk, flavoured with vanilla and garnished of apples cooked in syrup and red wine
Crème fouettée ⇒ whipped cream
Crème frangipane ⇒ almond-flavoured cream
Crème frite en beignets ⇒ fritters made with a custard of milk, vanilla, egg-yolks, sugar and flour
Crème frites aux fruits confits ⇒ fritters made with preserved fruits macerated in liquor, milk, vanilla, egg-yolks, sugar, and flour
Crème ganache ⇒ custard made of melted chocolate, butter, and cream
Crème glacée ⇒ ice-cream of milk, cream, sugar, and aromatics
Crème jamaïque ⇒ slices of pineapple covered with a custard made of maïzena, egg-yolks, and white wine; moistened with kirsch, then garnished of preserved cherries
Crème liégeoise ⇒ whipped eggs with sugar, kirsch and bits of pineapple
Crème marie-louise ⇒ chocolate melted in coffee with eggs
Crème pâtissière ⇒ confectioner's custard
Crème pâtissière au café ⇒ confectioner's custard added of coffee extract
Crème pâtissière au chocolat ⇒ confectioner's custard added of chocolate
Crème pâtissière au raisins ⇒ confectioner's custard flavoured with marc, and added of grapes
Crème plombières ⇒ custard made of egg-yolks, rice, milk, sugar and whipped cream

Crème renversée ⇒ cream mould
Crème renversée au chocolat ⇒ custard made of chocolate, milk, eggs, and sugar; cooked in the oven
Crème suisse ⇒ petit suisse plus sugar mixed with kirsch and whipped white of eggs
Crème laiterie et fromages
   - **Crème** ⇒ cream
   - **Crème de gruyère** ⇒ melted gruyère
   - **Crème fleurette** -[*crème pateurisée*]- ⇒ cream
   - **Crème fraîche** ⇒ cream < *uncountable* >
   - **Crème épaisse** ⇒ pasteurized cream
   - **Crémet** ⇒ curdled milk added of whipped eggs and cream; served with cream and sugar
   - **Crémets** ⇒ cream thinned with milk and mixed with white of eggs
Crenilabre ocelle -[*poisson*]- ⇒ Corkwing wrasse
Créole (*à la ...*) -[*cuisine*]- ⇒ with rice dried in the oven, capsicums, onions and tomatoes
Créole (*à la ...*) -[*dessert*]- ⇒ with rum or with pineappleor with vanilla or with banana < *rhum, ananas, vanille, banane* >
Crêpe ⇒ pancake or flapjack
Crêpe dentelle ⇒ thin pancake
Crêperie ⇒ pancake shop
Crêpes -[*Eierkçckas*]- ⇒ pancakes made of a dough added of cream, then stuffed of redcurrant jelly or raspberry jam
Crêpes à l'oeuf et au fromage ⇒ buckwheat pancakes, topped with an egg and sprinkled of grated cheese
Crêpes à la Russe ⇒ pancakes made with a dough added of cream, yeast, and sugar; served rolled and sprinkled of sugar
Crêpes à la condé ⇒ pancakes covered with rice and preserved fruits cooked in milk, plus egg-yolks
Crêpes à la confiture ⇒ pancakes spreaded of jam diluted in rum
Crêpes à la cévenole ⇒ pancakes covered with chestnut purée, sprinkled of sugar and browned
Crêpes à la frangipane ⇒ pancakes spreaded of almond-flavoured cream, sprinkled of sugar, then caramelized in the oven
Crêpes à la saucisse ⇒ pancakes served with a bit of fried sausage and butter
Crêpes au Roquefort ⇒ pancakes covered with a preparation of béchamel sauce plus Roquefort cheese; sprinkled of grated cheese and glazed
Crêpes au citron ⇒ pancakes made with a dough added of lemon peel
Crêpes aux amandes ⇒ pancakes covered with a custard flavoured of almond powder
Crêpes aux cerises ⇒ pancakes made with dough added of stoned cherries
Crêpes aux champignons ⇒ pancakes covered with chopped onions and mushrooms, sprinkled of grated cheese plus melted butter, then browned
Crêpes aux onions ⇒ buckwheat pancakes covered with braised onions, sprinkled of grated cheese plus melted butter, then browned
Crêpes aux pommes et aux noix ⇒ pancakes covered with lamellas of apple and green walnuts
Crêpes de maïs aux avocats ⇒ pancakes of cornflour, spreaded with avocado purée added of olive oil, pepper, and tarragon
Crêpes de pommes de terre ⇒ pancakes made with a dough of grated potatoes, eggs, milk and melted butter
Crêpes de sarrasin ⇒ buckwheat pancakes
Crêpes des chartreux ⇒ pancakes made with a dough added of butter, sugar, crushed meringue, chartreuse, orange peel, and cognac
Crêpes gratinées aux épinards ⇒ pancakes covered with spinach in cream, sprinkled of grated cheese plus melted butter, then browned

Crêpes mylène ⇒ pancakes garnished with lamellas of pear cooked in a syrup of butter, sugar, orange juice, lemon juice, and cognac; flamed with plum eau de vie

Crêpes normandes ⇒ pancakes made with a dough added of calvados, melted butter and fried lamellas of apple; served with cream

Crêpes suzette ⇒ pancakes flavoured with tangerine and curaçao

Crepeaux de morue ⇒ dish of salt cod from Périgord

Crépine -[veau]- ⇒ caul of veal

Crépine -[porc]- ⇒ caul of pork

Crépine d'agneau ⇒ lamb caul fat

Crépine de porc ⇒ caul of pork or pork back fat

Crépinette ⇒ faggot or crépinette or flat sausage

Crépinette de foie aux cèpes ⇒ liver's crépinette with boletus

Crépinettes de cervelle ⇒ crépinettes of calf brains, mushrooms, shallots and garlic; browned with butter

Crépinettes de lapin ⇒ rabbit stuffed with a hash of bacon, mushrooms, shallots and wrapped in a caul of pork; then sprinkled of melted butter, and browned in the oven

Crépinettes de lotte au chou ⇒ bits of angler baked with white wine, then wrapped in cabbage leaves with chopped onions and mushrooms; cooked again in butter

Crépinettes de porc ⇒ flat sausages with herbs and cognac, coated of crumbs and melted butter, then grilled; served with mashed potatoes or vegetables in butter

Crépinettes de porc Ste Ménéhould ⇒ flat sausages made with a culinary stuffing of pig trotter, truffle, and sausage meat

Crépinettes de volailles ⇒ flat sausages made with a culinary stuffing of poultry, and pork fat

Crépy ⇒ white wine from lake Geneva area

Crespet des Landes ⇒ a sweet

Cresson ⇒ watercress or cress < *tous uncountable* >

Cresson de cheval -[véronique]- ⇒ veronica

Cressonnière (*à la ...*)

    - **potage** ⇒ soup made of watercress, potatoes, egg-yolks and cream

    - **salade** ⇒ composed salad of potatoes and watercress, sprinkled with chopped egg-yolks and parsley

Crêtes de coq ⇒ cockscombs

Crêtes de coq en attereaux à la Villeroi ⇒ cockscombs covered of a sauce and put on a skewer, brushed with egg and crumbs, then cooked in butter

Cretonnée de pois ⇒ mashed peas in pork fat, added of crumbs steeped in milk, saffron and ginger, plus poultry meat; served thickened with egg-yolks and white meat

Cretons ⇒ melted fat

Cretons de la maman ⇒ preparation made with a hash of pork's shoulder, onion, garlic, crumbs, milk, parsley, and cinnamon; cooked slowly

Crevettes ⇒ shrimps or prawns

Crevettes frites ⇒ fried prawns

Crevette grise ⇒ shrimp or brown shrimp

Crevette rose ou bouquet ⇒ prawn

Crevette rouge ou gamba ⇒ large prawn

Crevettes sautées au whisky ⇒ prawns sautéed in oil and flamed with whisky

    - **variante cognac** ⇒ prawns sautéed in oil and flamed with cognac

    - **variante marc** ⇒ prawns sautéed in oil and flamed with marc

Criadillas -[animelles]- ⇒ testicles

Cribiche -[Antilles]- ⇒ large crayfish

Crimpled salmon -[saumon]- ⇒ crimpled salmon

Criots-batard-montrachet -*[chassagne-montrachet]-* ⇒ Burgundy wine either white or red

Crique -*[vivarais]-* ⇒ mashed peas in pork fat, added of crumbs steeped in milk, saffron and ginger, plus poultry meat; served thickened with egg-yolks and white meat

Criquettes -*[auvergne]-* ⇒ potato flat cakes

Cristallisé ⇒ crystallized

Criste-marine ⇒ Crithmum or rock samphire

Crithme ⇒ Crithmum or rock samphire

Crocodile ⇒ crocodile

Crocus -*[safran]-* ⇒ saffron

Croissant ⇒ croissant

Croissants au fromage ⇒ croissants filled with butter and cheese, served hot

Croissants aux amandes -*[petits]-* ⇒ croissants made with crushed almonds, white of eggs, vanilla sugar, and flour

Croissants aux crevettes ⇒ croissants filled with shrimp sauce and served hot

Croissants aux pignons ⇒ croissants coated of egg and pine-kernels

Croissants parisiens ⇒ croissants made of dough added of yeast and butter

Croissants viennois ⇒ croissants made of a dough buttered during the process

Croissants viennois à la confiture ⇒ croissants made of a dough buttered during the process, then filled of a jam

Croisillons -*[décoration]-* ⇒ lattice

Croissy -*[navet]-* ⇒ turnip

Cromesqui ⇒ floured culinary stuffing, fried in hot oil

Cromesquis à la bonne femme ⇒ balls made of boiled beef, onions, butter, and flour, then steeped in dough, and fried

Cromesquis à la florentine ⇒ rolled pancakes filled with béchamel sauce, grated parmesan and spinach, then steeped in dough and cooked

Croquant -*[adjectif]-* ⇒ crisp or crunchy

Croquante ⇒ decorative pastry

Croquants de St geniez ⇒ crisp almond and hazelnut biscuit

Croque au sel
    a) **mangé à la croque au sel** ⇒ ... eaten raw with coarse salt
    b) **sauté dans l'huile ou le beurre avec ail** ⇒ ... sautéed in oil or butter with garlic

Croque-en-bouche -*[croquembouche]-* ⇒ wedding cake glazed with a sugared syrup

Croque-madame ⇒ toasted cheese sandwich with ham and fried egg

Croque-monsieur ⇒ toasted sandwich

Croque-monsieur à la brandade ⇒ toasted sandwich filled with mashed salt cod, and sliced tomato

Croque-emmenthal ⇒ slice of ham filled with a slice of swiss cheese, steeped in dough and fried; topped with a fried egg

Croquembouche ⇒ wedding cake glazed with a sugared syrup

Croquembouche de marrons ⇒ cone pastry made of grilled chestnuts steeped in syrup

Croquet ⇒ crisp almond biscuit

Croquets aux amandes ⇒ dried biscuits based on almonds and butter, brushed with a mixing of caramel and egg, then baked

Croquets bordelais ⇒ dried biscuits based on crushed almonds, lemon or orange peel and eggs

Croquets de Bar sur Aube ⇒ dried biscuits based on almond powder and eggs

Croquets norvégiens ⇒ slices of biscuits made of flour, butter, sugar, eggs, and cream

Croquette -*[cuisine]-* ⇒ croquette

Croquette de chocolat ⇒ chocolate croquette

Croquette de poisson ⇒ fishcake

Croquettes à la viennoise ⇒ croquettes made with a culinary stuffing of lamb sweetbread, ham, mushrooms, onions, velouté sauce, and paprika

Croquettes aux abricots ⇒ croquettes filled of apricots flavoured with rum

Croquettes aux champignons ⇒ croquettes made with a culinary stuffing of sauté mushrooms, shallots, thyme and, garlic, thickened with béchamel sauce

Croquettes d'amourettes ⇒ croquettes made with a culinary stuffing of calf's marrow and mushrooms, thickened of a sauce; served with a tomato sauce

Croquettes d'épinards ⇒ croquettes made of spinach, mashed potatoes, butter, and egg

Croquettes de bœuf ⇒ croquettes made with a culinary stuffing of boiled beef and ham, thickened of béchamel sauce

Croquettes de céleri ⇒ croquettes made of a celeriac and potato purée mixed with egg-yolks, plus parsley; served with a roast

Croquettes de fromage ⇒ croquettes based on béchamel sauce, and grated cheese

Croquettes de macaroni ⇒ croquettes based on macaroni, and béchamel sauce added of grated cheese

Croquettes de marrons ⇒ croquettes made of chestnut purée added of eggs and butter

Croquettes de mimolette frites aux épices ⇒ croquettes of diced cheese, coated with egg and fried; served with a mayonnaise added of gherkins, capers, and shallot

Croquettes de morue ⇒ croquettes of salt cod, mashed potatoes, egg, and butter

Croquettes de pommes de terre ⇒ croquettes made of mashed potatoes, butter, and egg-yolks

Croquettes de riz à l'ancienne ⇒ croquettes of rice flavoured with grated parmesan and nutmeg; stuffed of chopped poultry, and fried

Croquettes de riz à l'indienne ⇒ croquettes made of rice cooked with curry, plus a culinary stuffing of onions in butter, and egg

Croquettes de riz salées ⇒ croquettes made of rice, grated parmesan, and egg

Croquettes de riz sucrées ⇒ croquettes of rice; served with a pineapple sauce

Croquettes de volaille ⇒ poultry croquettes

Croquettes montrouge ⇒ croquettes made with chopped onions, mushrooms, ham, crumbs, and egg-yolks

Croquignole ⇒ cracknels made of white of eggs, sugar, vanilla, and flour

Croquignoles parisiennes ⇒ cracknels made of white of eggs, sugar, vanilla, and flour

Crosnes ⇒ Japanese artichoke

Crosse bun -[*bun*]- ⇒ bun

Crosse de boeuf ⇒ knuckle of beef

Crosse de veau ⇒ veal ankle ½ ou ½ lower end of leg

Crostata di ricotta ⇒ kind of pie garnished with a mixing of ricotta, orange peel, lemon peel, sugar, raisins, almonds, pine kernels and egg-yolks

Crotte de chocolat ⇒ chocolate drop

Crottin de chavignol ⇒ goat's milk cheese

Crottin de Chavignol rôti en salade ⇒ grilled goat's milk cheese, served in salad

Croupe de boeuf ⇒ round or buttock or rump

Croupion ⇒ parson's nose

Crousets ⇒ quenelles made with a mixing of flour, purée, eggs and nut oil; then poached and browned

Croustade ⇒ croustade

Croustades à l'anversoise ⇒ croustades of potatoes, filled with hop shoots in cream

Croustades à la grecque ⇒ croustades of rice garnished with tomatoes cooked in their own liquid

Croustades à la langouste ⇒ croustades filled with vegetable salad in mayonnaise, and topped by a round slice of spiny lobster

Croustades à la marinière ⇒ croustades filled with mussels, covered of cream

Croustades aux cailles à la périgueux ⇒ croustades of rice, filled with stuffed quail, covered with a truffle sauce

Croustades de foie de volaille ⇒ croustades filled with sauté poultry livers, plus sauté mushrooms in Madeira sauce

Croustades de pâte feuilletée ⇒ casing in puff-pastry ½ ou ½ croustades in puff-pastry

Croustades de pain de mie ⇒ fried thick slices of bread without crusts, hollowed out in the centre and filled with a forcemeat

Croustades de pommes de terre duchesse ⇒ croustades of potatoes, filled variously

Croustades de riz ou de semoule
  - riz ⇒ croustades made of rice cooked in fat, plus eggs
  - semoule ⇒ croustades made of semolina cooked in fat, plus eggs

Croustades froides aux anchois ⇒ croustades filled with anchovies and tunny in mayonnaise; covered with anchovy paste

Croustades Montrouge ⇒ tartlets filled with mashed mushrooms added of cream; sprinkled with crumbs and browned

Croustades vert-pré ⇒ croustades of potatoes, garnished with bits of french beans, peas and asparagus tips, thickened with butter

Croustillant *(adjectif ...)* ⇒ crunchy

Croûte ⇒ crust

Croûte -*[fonds de pâte, bouchée, feuilletage, flan, tarte, timbale, vol-au-vent]*- ⇒ pastry case

Croûte à flan cuite à blanc ⇒ pastry case for flan

Croûte à timbale garnie ⇒ pastry case for timbale

Croûte à vol-au vent ⇒ puff-pastry case

Croûte feuilletée pour tarte ⇒ puff-pastry for tart

Croûte feuilletée à flan, cuite au blanc ⇒ pastry case for flan

Croûtes à la Nantua ⇒ slices of bread garnished of béchamel sauce added of crayfish paste, crayfish tails, sprinkled with grated parmesan and melted butter, then browned

Croûtes à la diable ⇒ pastry cases filled with a culinary stuffing of bacon, mushrooms, sauce, and cayenne pepper; sprinkled with crumbs and butter, then browned

Croûtes à la livonienne ⇒ slices of bread covered with mashed herring milt, béchamel sauce, plus a culinary stuffing of herring and apple, then browned

Croûtes à la lyonnaise ⇒ slices of bread covered with diced beef and onions, sprinkled of crumbs and melted butter, then browned

Croûtes à la moelle ⇒ slices of bread with a garnish of beef bone-marrow, chopped shallots in white wine, sprinkled of crumbs and melted butter, then browned

Croûtes à la reine ⇒ slices of bread covered with mashed chicken, sprinkled of crumbs and melted butter, then browned

Croûtes à la rouennaise ⇒ slices of bread garnished with a forcemeat of poultry livers, mushrooms, and sauce, then baked

Croûtes ambassadrices ⇒ slices of bread garnished of mashed chicken, truffle, and diced vegetables

Croûtes aux bananes à la maltaise ⇒ successive layers of sliced brioche and bananas, shaped in turban; garnished with an orange flavoured custard, and sprinkled of crushed macaroons

Croûtes aux champignons ⇒ pastry cases filled with mushrooms in cream, sprinkled of crumbs, and browned

Croûtes aux fruits ⇒ slices of savarin alternated with slices of pineapple, filled in the middle with a culinary stuffing of fruits, decorated of angelica and quartered apricots; covered with a sauce flavoured of rum or kirsch

Croûtes aux fruits de mer ⇒ slices of bread covered with béchamel sauce, plus mussels and oysters cooked in white wine; sprinkled with a sauce, crumbs and melted butter, then browned

Croûtes Brillat-Savarin ⇒ pastry cases filled with a culinary stuffing of veal, sauté mushrooms, plus kidneys; then thickened of Madeira sauce

Croûtes cardinal ⇒ pastry cases filled with a culinary stuffing of crawfish, truffle and béchamel sauce, sprinkled of crumbs, and browned

Croûtes Du Barry ⇒ slices of bread covered with cauliflower, béchamel sauce added of egg-yolks and grated cheese, then browned

Croûtes en couronne à la montmorency ⇒ slices of brioche laid in ring, covered with almond-flavoured cream, plus stoned cherries cooked in a vanilla syrup; decorated of angelica, and covered with redcurrant sauce flavoured of cherry brandy

Croûtes en turban à la Beauvilliers ⇒ layers of sliced brioche and bananas shaped in turban, filled with a semolina porridge thickened of vanilla, egg-yolks, and preserved fruits macerated in eau de vie; sprinkled with crushed macaroons and melted butter, then browned

Croûtes farçies à l'ancienne ⇒ crusts of bread filled with chopped vegetables, sprinkled with grated cheese and melted butter, then browned

Croûtes garnies salées ⇒ slices of bread fried in butter, covered with any garnish

Croûtes pour consommé croûte au pot ⇒ crusts of bread sprinkled of pot-au-feu fat, and glazed in the oven

Croûtons ⇒ sippets or croutons

Croûtons de gelée ⇒ jelly cut in croutons

Crozets ⇒ quenelles made with a mixing of flour, purée, eggs and nut oil; then poached and browned

Cru -[état]-
  - **adjectif** ⇒ raw
  - **v.t adjectif** ⇒ uncooked

Cru -[vin]- ⇒ vintage

Cruchades
  - **général** ⇒ porridge of maize and milk
  - **Béarn** ⇒ maize porridge chilled and fried
  - **Saintonge** ⇒ flat cake of maize, served with jam
  - **Landes** ⇒ small biscuits, fried and salted, or sugared

Crudités ⇒ salads or raw in season vegetables

Crumpets ⇒ crumpets

Crumpets au Roquefort ⇒ crumpets based on Roquefort cheese, béchamel sauce and mustard, spreaded on slices of bread, then rolled and glazed

Crusta -[cocktail; boisson]- ⇒ long drinks ... added of champagne

Crustacé -[pluriel]- ⇒ crustaceae or crustaceans

Csipetke -[goulache accompagnement]- ⇒ small quenelles of paste with eggs; poached in stock

Cube de veau sans os ⇒ diced veal

Cuchaule -[Suisse]- ⇒ brioche flavoured with saffron

Cuignots ⇒ small cakes filled with raisins

Cuillère ⇒ spoon

Cuisine
  - **cuisson** ⇒ cooking
  - **cuisine** ⇒ kitchen

Cuisine bourgeoise ⇒ plain cooking

Cuisine régionale ⇒ regional cooking

Cuisine végétarienne ⇒ vegetarian cooking

Cuisse ⇒ leg or thigh

Cuisse de grenouille ⇒ frog's leg < pluriel frogs' legs >

Cuisse de porc ⇒ leg of pork

Cuisseau ⇒ leg or haunch of veal or deer, etc

Cuisseau de chevreuil ⇒ haunch of venison

Cuisseau de veau ⇒ haunch of veal

Cuisseau désossé et roulé -[veau]- ⇒ haunch of veal « boned and rolled » or haunch of veal « boneless »

Cuisseau sans quasi -[veau]- ⇒ leg of veal

Cuisseau sans quasi, désossé et roulé -[veau]- ⇒ leg of veal « boned and rolled » or leg of veal « boneless »

Cuisses de dindon braisées ⇒ thighs of turkey cock boned, then stuffed with a poultry forcemeat, and braised

Cuisses de dindon réveillantes ⇒ thighs of turkey cock, cooked with champagne, stock, clove, diced calf sweetbread, mushrooms, anchovies, capers, and stoned olives

Cuisses de grenouille à la provençale ⇒ frogs' legs cooked and served mainly with tomatoes, olive oil, and garlic

Cuisses de grenouilles à la lyonnaise ⇒ frogs' legs sautéed in butter with chopped onions, and sprinkled of parsley

Cuisses de grenouilles à la meunière ⇒ sauté frogs' legs, sprinkled with the gravy added of lemon juice

Cuisses de grenouilles aux fines herbes ⇒ frogs' legs sautéed in butter, sprinkled of parsley and served with boiled potatoes

Cuisses de grenouilles en brochettes ⇒ frogs' legs marinated in olive oil, lemon juice and cayenne pepper, then grilled on a skewer

Cuisses de lièvre rôties ⇒ thighs of hare studded with streaky bacon, then roasted, and served with chestnut purée

Cuisson
- **temps** ⇒ cooking time
- **bouillon** ⇒ cooking stock
- **mode** ⇒ act of cooking

Cuissot ⇒ haunch of venison

Cuissot de chevreuil aux câpres ⇒ leg of roebuck marinated in red wine, olive oil, onions and shallots, studded with streaky bacon, then roasted; covered with a sauce made of the boiled marinade, added of fecula, stock, capers, and butter

Cuissot de chevreuil de 3 heures ⇒ haunch of venison studded with lardoons, braised with oil, butter, cognac, red wine, garlic, pimentos and mustard; served with the cooking juice thickened of raspberry jelly, plus chestnut purée added of cream

Cuissot de chevreuil rôti ⇒ roasted leg of roebuck, served with peppered sauce, chestnut purée and baked apples

Cuit ⇒ cooked < v.t adjectif >
- **l'opposé de cru** ⇒ cooked
- **cuit à point** ⇒ well cooked or done or done to a turn
- **trop cuit** ⇒ overdone
- **pas assez cuit** ⇒ underdone
- **bleu viande** ⇒ underdone
- **bleu steack** ⇒ very rare or underdone steak
- **saignant** ⇒ rare

Cuit sous la cendre ⇒ ... cooked in the embers

Cuit très dur ⇒ hard-baked

Cujassous de Dubjac ⇒ cheeses from the Périgord

Cul de veau -[quasi]- ⇒ veal's thick end of loin

Cul de veau à l'angevine ⇒ veal's thick end of loin garnished with mashed onions and rice, seasoned of pepper and sugar

Cul de veau aux mousserons ⇒ veal's thick end of loin, cooked with meadow mushrooms

Cul vert -*[champignon]*- ⇒ greenish russula
Cul rouge -*[champignon]*- ⇒ russula
Culotte
- **boeuf** ⇒ rump of beef
- **veau** ⇒ veal's thick of loin
- **mouton** ⇒ saddle of mutton
Culotte de boeuf aux poireaux à la bière ⇒ sliced leeks, plus diced rump of beef simmered in beer and butter
Cultivateur ⇒ soup made of vegetables and pork fat, served with slices of bread
Cumberland -*[sauce]*- ⇒ cumberland sauce
Cumin ⇒ cumin or cummin or caraway
Cumin des montagnes, des prés -*[carvi]*- ⇒ caraway
Cumin noir -*[nigelle]*- ⇒ nigella or love in the mist
Cup -*[boisson]*- ⇒ chilled drink of ...
Cup aux pêches ⇒ sliced peaches macerated in sugar, and apple juice; added of white wine, curaçao and soda water
Cup -*[cider]*- ⇒ drink made of calvados, maraschino, curaçao, ice cube, slices of orange, Schweppes soda, and bits of fruits in season
Cup -*[St James]*- ⇒ drink made of sugar in water, half a litre of cognac, half a litre of rum, curaçao, one litre of chilled tea, crushed ice, and one bottle of sparkling cider
Cup -*[Sauternes]*- ⇒ drink made of slices of lemon, curaçao, cognac, cherries in eau de vie, Sauternes wine, and soda water
Curaçao ⇒ curaçao
Curcuma ⇒ turmeric
Curé ou Fromage du curé -*[Nantais]*- ⇒ pressed cow's milk cheese shaped in square
Cussy -*[garniture]*- ⇒ ... with a garnish of artichoke hearts filled with mashed mushrooms, topped of cocks' kidneys and truffle, covered with a port or Madeira sauce
Custard powder ⇒ custard powder
Cwènes di gattes ⇒ potatoes
Cyanophycée -*[algues bleues]*- ⇒ blue seaweed
Cygne ⇒ swan
Cygne en chocolat -*[bonbon]*- ⇒ sweet in chocolate
Cynorrhodon -*[églantier]*- ⇒ eglantine fruit
Cyprin ⇒ crucian carp
Cyprin doré ⇒ goldfish
Cyrniki ⇒ croquettes made of curdled milk, eggs and flour, then fried in butter
Czernina *(tchemina ...)* ⇒ rice consommé with pasta, added of poultry blood; thickened with mashed poultry livers

D

Dacquoise ⇒ gatea u made with alternate discs of meringue and custard, covered of icing sugar

Dacquoise au café ⇒ gateau made with discs of eggs and almond powder, on alternate layers with a custard of sugar, butter and coffee extract

Dadou -[*soja*]- ⇒ soya or soya bean or soy or soy bean

Dagh kebab ⇒ cubes of veal, and onions grilled on a skewer, sprinkled of thyme; served with pilaf, or green salad, or okras or shish kebab

Dai-co ⇒ Japanese radish

Daïkon ⇒ japanese radish

Dail -[*pholade à Royan*]- ⇒ pholas or stone borer

Daim ⇒ fallow deer < *pluriel inchangé* >

Daiquiri -[*cocktail*]- ⇒ daiquiri

Daisy longhorn -[*cheddar*]- ⇒ cheddar cheese

Daizu -[*soja*]- ⇒ soya or soya bean or soy or soy bean

Dal ⇒ Indian vegetable
  - **mung dal** ⇒ bean
  - **l'urid dal** ⇒ black beans for porridge or black beans for pancake
  - **maisur dal** ⇒ lentil for fritters

Dalle -[*darne*]-
  - **morue** ⇒ steak of cod
  - **saumon** ⇒ steak of salmon

Dame-blanche -[*pâtisserie*]- ⇒ gateau made of Genoese sponge stuffed of cream and preserved fruits; covered with meringue, or egg custard, or almond ice cream

Dame-jeanne ⇒ demijohn

Damier ⇒ gateau made of Genoese sponge flavoured with rum, stuffed of custard, sprinkled with almonds and decorated in draught

Dampfnoudeln ⇒ fritters made of flour, sugar, butter, milk, and yeast; cooked in pork fat

Dampfnudeln ⇒ small discs of dough made with leaven, butter, eggs, sugar and flour, then baked

Damson cheese -[*dessert*]- ⇒ Damson cheese

Danablu ⇒ Danish cheese with a spicy taste

Danicheff
  1) salade ⇒ salad made of artichoke hearts in julienne, mushrooms, celeriac, sliced potatoes and asparagus bits; seasoned with mayonnaise sauce and decorated of egg-yolks, truffle and crayfish tails
  2) gâteau ⇒ gateau with praline paste, coffee and rum
  3) parfait ⇒ parfait with praline paste, coffee and rum

Danish blue -[*fromage*]- ⇒ Danish blue

Dão ⇒ Portuguese red wine

Dariole -[*objet*]- ⇒ dariole
  - **crème** ⇒ baked custard

Darioles au fromage ⇒ moulded custard of milk, grated cheese and eggs; covered of tomato purée, mixed with chopped mushrooms and béchamel sauce

Darioles aux amandes ⇒ moulded puff-pastry, filled with almond flavoured cream

Darjeeling -[*thé*]- ⇒ tea < *uncountable* >

Darne ⇒ steak of cod « morue » or of salmon « saumon » or of hake « colin »

Darne de colin au curry ⇒ steak of hake seasoned with curry

Darne de saumon à la vapeur de safran aux pâtes fraîches ⇒ steak of salmon steamed with saffron; served with fresh noodles

Darnes de saumon à l'américaine ⇒ dish made of halved carapace of crawfish filled with a culinary stuffing of cooked crawfish and mushrooms added of tarragon and chervil; covered with grated parmesan and butter, then browned plus two steaks of salmon braised in butter with mixed vegetables, and baked

Darnes de saumon à la meunière ⇒ floured steaks of salmon, fried in butter and served with the cooking juice plus lemon

Darnes de saumon à la Nantua ⇒ steaks of salmon poached in fish stock, served with crayfishes and a sauce added of crayfish tails

Darnes de saumon en bellevue ⇒ steaks of salmon cooked in jelly; served decorated in the jelly

Darnes de saumon frites ⇒ fried steaks of salmon served with lemons

Darnes de saumon grillées ⇒ grilled steaks of salmon, served with butter or a sauce

Darnes de saumon pochées ⇒ steaks of salmon poached in a court-bouillon, served with butter

Darnes de saumon princesse ⇒ poached steaks of salmon decorated with truffle, garnished of asparagus tips thickened with butter

Darphin
- **garniture pour filet de boeuf** ⇒ beef fillet ...
- **garniture pour tournedos** ⇒ tournedos ...
- **poêlés avec sauce madère** ⇒ fried ... with Madeira sauce ...
- **sauce Périgueux** ⇒ with Madeira sauce added of chopped truffles ... served with a garnish of potato sticks first fried, then baked shaped in flat cake

DARTOIS ou à la d'artois
1) **garniture grosses pièces de boucherie** ⇒ ... with a garnish of carrots, turnips, braised celeriac and fried potatoes
2) **potage DARTOIS** ⇒ soup made of mashed beans and julienne
3) **baron d'agneau d'ARTOIS** ⇒ saddle of lamb, plus potato croustades and Madeira sauce

Dartois *-[pâtisserie ou hors d'œuvre chauds]-*
a) **salés « appelés également Sausselis »** ⇒ puff pastry lamella filled with anchovy, or sardine, or crayfish, or foie gras
b) **sucrés** ⇒ puff pastry lamella filled with confectioner's custard, or almond custard, or jam

Dartois à la confiture d'abricots ⇒ puff-pastry filled with apricot jam and baked

Dartois à la frangipane ⇒ puff-pastry filled with almond flavoured cream and baked

Dartois aux anchois ⇒ puff-pastry filled with a forcemeat of fish, added with anchovy fillets

Dartois aux fruits de mer ⇒ puff-pastry filled with Norway lobsters, scallops and shrimps, poached and flamed in calvados

Dartois Laguipière ⇒ puff-pastry filled with a culinary stuffing of braised sweetbread, truffle and chopped vegetables, thickened of velouté sauce

Dartois pommes framboises ⇒ puff-pastry squares filled with apple compote added of raspberry jam

Dashi ⇒ Japanese stock based on seaweed

Datte ⇒ date

Dattes fourrées ⇒ stoned dates, stuffed of almond paste flavoured with kirsch

Daube *(en ...)* ⇒ braised or stewed in tightly closed saucepan

Daube
- **nom de la viande** ⇒ braised ...
- **servir une daube** ⇒ to served a dish of braised meat

Daube de boeuf à la béarnaise ⇒ pieces of beef marinated in cognac, red wine and herbs, then cooked in layers of ham, onions and carrots

Daube de boeuf à la provençale ⇒ diced beef studded of lardoons, baked in white wine with calf trotter, olives, mushrooms, onions, tomatoes and herbs

Daube de dindonneau à la bourgeoise ⇒ Turkey-chick braised with carrots, onions, and pork fat

Daube de pieds de porc ⇒ trotters and tails of pork first boiled, then baked with carrots, onions, celery, garlic, tomatoes, white wine, herbs and cumin seeds

Daumont *(à la ...)*
- **garniture pour alose** ⇒ shad ...
- **garniture pour saumon** ⇒ salmon
- **garniture pour turbot** ⇒ turbot ... with a garnish of fish quenelles, truffle lamellas, crayfish tails, mushrooms and sauté soft roes; served with a creamy sauce
- **garniture pour poisson simplifiée** ⇒ fish ...
- **garniture pour œufs mollets** ⇒ soft boiled eggs ...
- **garniture pour œufs pochés** ⇒ poached eggs ... with crayfishes and mushrooms

Dauphin *-[fromage]-* ⇒ cow's milk cheese variously shaped

Dauphine *(à la ...)*
- **légumes** ⇒ fried small balls of mashed celeriac or aubergines and choux-pastry
- **gibier ou boucherie** ⇒ with fried small balls of mashed potatoes and choux pastry

Dauphinoise *(à la ...)* ⇒ ... with sliced potatoes covered with cream and browned

Daurade ⇒ dorado or sea bream

Daurade à la meunière ⇒ floured dorado, fried in butter and sprinkled of lemon juice

Daurade au citron confit ⇒ dorado baked with slices of preserved lemon, coriander seeds, lemon juice and olive oil

Daurade farçie au fenouil ⇒ dorado filleted and stuffed with a forcemeat of milk, bread, fennel, pastis, lemon juice and thyme; then baked in white wine, sprinkled of olive oil

Daurade royale braisée aux pommes ⇒ dorado baked on a layer of fennel, onion, garlic, fish stock, olive oil and rum; with quartered apples

Daussade *-[Picardie]-* ⇒ soft white cheese flavoured with vinegar and herbs

De ⇒ of

Décaféiné ⇒ decaffeinated

Décalotter ⇒ to uncap

Décoction ⇒ decoction

Décoquiller ⇒ to shell

Décoration ⇒ decoration

Décorer ⇒ to decorate

Décortiqué ⇒ decorticated

Découpage ⇒ carving

Découper ⇒ to carve

Découverte sans collier *-[mouton]-* ⇒ middle neck

Défarde ⇒ lamb's feet and tripe, stewed with carrots, onions, leeks, laurel and clove; then baked in white wine, plus tomato purée

Deffarde ⇒ lamb's feet and tripe, stewed with carrots, onions, leeks, laurel and clove; then baked in white wine, plus tomato purée

Déglacer ⇒ to deglaze
- **sucs de cuisson mélangés à du vin pour obtenir la sauce** ⇒ thickened with ... nom anglais du vin

Déhanché sans tête de filet, à 8 côtes *-[bœuf]-* ⇒ loin and rib

Déjeuner ⇒ lunch

Délayer
- **poudre** ⇒ to mix
- **sauce** ⇒ to thin down

Délice *-[pâtisserie]-* ⇒ fancy pastry

Délice au citron ⇒ gateau flavoured with lemon, then filled of a custard made with butter, sugar, egg-yolks and lemon peel

Délices aux fraises ⇒ tartlets filled with butter added of strawberries macerated in sugar

Délices aux noix ⇒ tartlets covered with almond paste, topped by a custard of sugar, butter, egg-yolks and coffee extract, plus green walnut

Délicieux ⇒ pastry custard from flour, sugar, eggs, milk and butter, flavoured with rum, plus sultanas; garnished with chestnut jam and chopped hazelnuts

Délicieux aux pommes ⇒ kind of soufflé made of mashed apples, eggs, sugar and crumbs

Délicieux surprise ⇒ slices of brioche covered with pear lamellas, whipped cream and chocolate sauce

Demi -*[bière]-* ⇒ a glass of beer 25 cl

Demi -*[moitié]-* ⇒ half a ... plus nom anglais

Demi-bête -*[bœuf]-* ⇒ side of beef

Demi bouteille ⇒ half bottle of wine, containing roughly 35 to 37 centilitres or bottle of 35 centilitres

Demi carapace ⇒ half-shell

Demi-deuil

    a) volaille pochée ⇒ poached poultry ...

        - ris de veau ⇒ sweetbread of veal ...

        - oeufs pochés ⇒ poached eggs decorated with truffle lamellas, and covered of supreme sauce

    b) poularde ⇒ stuffed fattened pullet, studded of truffle lamellas and poached; served with vegetables

Demidof ⇒ voir poularde demidof et poulet sauté demidof

Demi-glace ⇒ reduced stock

Demi macreuse -*[boeuf]-* ⇒ braising steak

Demi mouton ⇒ side of mutton

Demi mouton roulé et ficelé ⇒ rolled side of mutton « boneless »

Demi porc avec tête entière ⇒ side of pork

Demi porc sans poitrine, ni échine, ni épaule ⇒ leg and short loin

Demi porc sans poitrine, pour hachage ⇒ leg and long loin

Demi porc sans tête ⇒ side of pork « ex head »

Demi-saison ⇒ preparation from flour, sugar, eggs, sultanas, rum and butter; garnished with a compote made of apples, pears and apricots

Demi-sel -*[fromage]-* ⇒ demi-sel cheese

Demi-sel ⇒ lightly salted

    - fromage ⇒ demi-sel cheese

Demi veau ⇒ side of veal

Démouler ⇒ to remove from mould or to turn out ... cakes, etc

Dende -*[huile de palme]-* ⇒ palm oil

Denominação de origem -*[Portugal vin]-* ⇒ quality wine

Dénoyauter -*[fruit]-* ⇒ to stone

Dénoyauté -*[fruit]-* ⇒ stoned < v.t adjectif >

Dent de lion ⇒ dandelion

Dent de loup

    - garniture ⇒ fried triangular sippet

    - biscuits ⇒ biscuits flavoured with eau de vie or cumin or aniseed

Denté à gros yeux ⇒ large eyed dentex or dog's teeth

Denté charpentier ⇒ silverfish

Denté du cap ⇒ red steenbras

Denté maculé ⇒ seventy four

Denté ⇒ large eyed dentex

Denti ⇒ large eyed dentex

Denti ⇒ large eyed dentex
Dépecé ⇒ carved up < *v.t adjectif* >
Derby -*[fromage]*- ⇒ derby cheese or sage derby
Dérobé
   - **fèves** ⇒ shelled
   - **pommes de terre** ⇒ peeled
Derval -*[garniture]*- ⇒ ... with a garnish of quartered artichokes sautéed in butter
Dés ⇒ small cubes
   - **en dés** ⇒ diced ingredients or diced ...
Descar -*[garniture pour grosses pièces de boucherie]*- ⇒ ... with a garnish made of artichoke
      hearts braised in butter, diced white of meat and potato croquettes
Désossé
   - **viande** ⇒ boned < *adjectif* >
   - **poisson** ⇒ filleted < *adjectif* >
Dessert ⇒ dessert or sweet course
Dessert de mangues et fruits de la passion au rhum vieux ⇒ parts of Genoese sponge covered
      with a sorbet of passion fruits, mango pulp, a zabaglione of rum and egg-yolks; then
      decorated with physalis
Dessous de tranche -*[Tende de tranche]*- ⇒ topside of beef
Devilled sauce ⇒ devilled sauce
Diable *(à la ...)* ⇒ devilled dishes either of meat, fish or crustaceans
Diable de mer
   - **lotte** ⇒ angler
   - **rascasse** ⇒ scorpion fish
   - **chabot** ⇒ bullhead
Diablotin ⇒ slice of bread spreaded with béchamel sauce and grated cheese, then browned; served in
      soup
   - **préparé avec du Roquefort** ⇒ slice of bread spreaded with béchamel sauce and Roquefort
      cheese, then browned < *c'est un amuse-gueule* >
Diablotin ⇒ small round piece of bread with a garnish for soups or consommé
Diablotins au fromage ⇒ small round pieces of bread, buttered and sprinkled of grated cheese, then
      browned
Diablotins aux noix et au Roquefort ⇒ small round pieces of bread, spreaded with a preparation of
      butter, Roquefort cheese and chopped green walnut
Diabolo
   - **menthe** ⇒ drink made of lemonade and mint syrup
   - **grenadine** ⇒ drink made of lemonade and pomegranate syrup
Diadragam -*[bonbon]*- ⇒ sweet
Diamant -*[courgette]*- ⇒ variety of courgette
Diane *(à la ...)*
   1) **venaison** ⇒ with a peppery sauce added of whipped cream and truffles; served with chestnut
      purée, and sippets spreaded of a game forcemeat
   2) **oeufs mollets** ⇒ soft boiled eggs, laid on crusts with game purée and a sauce
   3) **barquettes de champignons** ⇒ pastry boats filled with game purée, mushrooms and sauce
      chasseur
   4) **potage** ⇒ consommé of game purée, flavoured with port
   5) **cailles** ⇒ quail in cast-iron casserole simmered with tomato, garnished of quenelles plus
      braised lettuce

Dieppoise *(à la ...)*
    1) **général** ⇒ fishes cooked in white wine and garnished with mussels, shrimps and a white wine
        sauce
    2) **maquereaux** ⇒ mackerel ...
        - **lisettes** ⇒ mackerel ...
        - **harengs** ⇒ herrings ... marinated in white wine
Digestif ⇒ liqueur or brandy
Dijonnaise *(à la ...)*
    - **mets sucrés** ⇒ with blackcurrant liquor
    - **mets salés** ⇒ with mustard
Dill *-[aneth]-* ⇒ dill
Dinde ⇒ turkey *< uncountable >*
Dinde aux canneberges ⇒ turkey with cranberry sauce
Dinde étoffée grand duc ⇒ turkey stuffed with a forcemeat of fattened pullet, cream, foie gras
    poached in port, truffles cooked in marc, and hearts of fattened pullet macerated in
    Malaga wine; then covered with slices of ham plus pastry dough, and baked
Dindon ⇒ turkey-cock *< uncountable >*
Dindonneau ⇒ turkey-chick or turkey-poult *< all uncountable >*
Dindonneau en daube à la bourgeoise ⇒ turkey-chick braised with carrots, onions and pork fat
Dindonneau farçi aux pommes de reinettes ⇒ turkey-chick stuffed with a forcemeat of foie gras,
    butter, port and sliced apples, then roasted
Dindonneau poché vinaigrette ⇒ turkey-chick cooked with carrots, turnips, leeks and celeriac;
    served with cauliflower and french dressing added of chervil
Dindonneau rôti ⇒ roasted turkey-chick served with watercress
Dindonneau rôti à l'anglaise ⇒ turkey-chick stuffed with onions, chopped sage, crumbs in milk plus
    veal fat; then roasted and served with bread sauce
Dindonneau rôti farçi aux marrons ⇒ turkey-chick stuffed with chestnuts in a caul of pork, and
    roasted
Dindonneau truffé ⇒ turkey-chick stuffed with a forcemeat of pork, foie gras, truffles, thyme, laurel
    and cognac; then studded with truffle lamellas and roasted
Dîner ⇒ dinner
Diot ⇒ small dry sausage
Dioul *-[Algérie]-* ⇒ puff pastry
Diplomate *(à la ...)*
    1) **cuisine** ⇒ with a culinary stuffing of truffles and lobster
    2) **sauce** ⇒ sauce made of lobster butter and diced truffle
Diplomate ⇒ sponge-fingers with preserved fruits and rum
Diplomate à l'anglaise ⇒ trifle
Diplomate au bavarois ⇒ trifle of Bavarian mousse added with sultanas, covered with apricot sauce
Diplomate aux pruneaux ⇒ trifle added of dried plums and a custard flavoured with kirsch; served
    with a egg-custard
Diplomates aux fruits confits *(petits ...)* ⇒ small trifles garnished with a custard added of sultanas
    and preserved fruits, then covered with apricot jam
Dips *-[Amérique du nord]-* ⇒ thick sausages filled variously with soft white cheese, clams, tunny,
    celeriac or avocado
Dirty rice *-[Amérique du nord]-* ⇒ dirty rice
Distingué *-[bière]-* ⇒ beer mug of half a litre
Distingué *-[vin]-* ⇒ wine of high quality in all aspects
Distributeur automatique ⇒ vending machine
Ditalini *-[minestrone]-* ⇒ pasta for minestrone

Dixired -[*pêche*]- ⇒ variety of peach
Djeruk purnt -[*Indonésie*]- ⇒ aromatic small lemon
Doboschtorte -[*chocolat*]- ⇒ gateau made of caramel and chocolate
Dobostorta -[*Hongrie*]- ⇒ seven layers of biscuit based on whipped white of eggs and vanilla,
      thickened with chocolate custard; covered with caramel
Docteur jules guyot -[*poire*]- ⇒ variety of pear
Dodine
   1) ballotine ⇒ galantine ...
      - de viande ⇒ ... of meat
      - de volaille ⇒ ... of poultry
      - de gibier ⇒ ... of game
      - de poisson ⇒ ... of fish or nom anglais du poisson
   2) sauce
   a) dodine blanche ⇒ sauce of milk, ginger, egg-yolks and sugar
   b) dodine rouge ⇒ sauce of bread steeped in red wine, fried onions, pork fat, cinnamon, nutmeg,
      clove and sugar
   c) dodine au verjus ⇒ sauce of egg-yolks, verjuice, poultry livers, ginger, parsley, and stock
      - préparation de grande cuisine ⇒ voir canard et pintade
Dodine de canard ⇒ forcemeat of duck, cognac, pork fat, veal, mushrooms, almond powder, truffle
      and egg; wrapped in the duck's skin and a caul of pork, then moistened of white wine
      and baked
Doigt de gant -[*champignon*]- ⇒ cup fungi
Doisy-Daëne -[*Barsac*]- ⇒ Sauternes white wine
Doisy-Védrines -[*Barsac*]- ⇒ Sauternes white wine
Dolcelate -[*fromage*]- ⇒ Dolcelatte
Dôle -[*Suisse vin*]- ⇒ red and rosé wine from Valais
Dolic ou Dolique ⇒ bean
Dolma ⇒ vine leaf garnished with rice and mutton, then braised in olive oil
Dolmades ⇒ vine leaf garnished with rice and mutton, then braised in olive oil
Domyoji age ⇒ shrimps wrapped in rice and fried, plus pimentos, aubergines and lemon
Dôme ⇒ dome
Donax -[*olive de mer*]- ⇒ wedge shell
Döner kebab ⇒ layers of meat and fat, grilled on a skewer
Dop -[*Cameroun*]- ⇒ dish of bananas in paste, or in croquettes, or sautéed
Dorade ⇒ dorado
Dorade grise -[*poisson*]- ⇒ black sea bream
Dorer -[*cuisine*]- ⇒ to glaze or to brown
Dorer ⇒ to glaze
Doré ⇒ browned < *v.t adjectif* >
Dorée ⇒ glazed or browned < *v.t adjectif* >
Doreye ⇒ rice tart stuffed with macaroons
Doria ⇒ with white truffles
Dorine ⇒ tartlet filled with chestnut purée and custard, then sprinkled of almonds
Dornecy -[*fromage de*]- ⇒ cheese from Nevers area
Dorset blue -[*fromage*]- ⇒ Dorset blue
Dortmunder Pilsen ⇒ high quality beer
Dorure ⇒ glaze
Dou louf -[*Tchad*]- ⇒ legs of beef cooked with ketmias
Double ⇒ double

Double viande -*[culotte]*- ⇒ rump of beef
Double Gloucester -*[fromage]*- ⇒ double Gloucester
Double aloyau -*[bœuf]*- ⇒ baron of beef
Double arôme -*[rhum]*- ⇒ concentrated rum
Double bock ⇒ very strong Bavarian beer
Double-crème
    - **fromage** ⇒ cream cheese
    - **crème** ⇒ cream
    - **Excelsior** ⇒ Norman cream cheese
Double faux-filet et filet avec os ⇒ baron « double sirloin »
Double magnum -*[bouteille]*- ⇒ double magnum
Douce Provence -*[pois]*- ⇒ variety of peas
Douce ou Doux ⇒ sweet or fresh or mild or soft < *tous adjectif* >
Doucette ⇒ corn-salad or lamb's lettuce
Douceur -*[bonbon]*- ⇒ sweet
Doufu -*[tofu]*- ⇒ soya cheese
Doughnuts ⇒ doughnuts
Douillet -*[cochon au père]*- ⇒ quartered pig, simmered in white wine and aromatics
Douillon ⇒ pear hollowed out and filled with butter; wrapped in pastry, and baked
Doum ⇒ doum palm
    - **fruit** ⇒ doum palm fruit
Dourga -*[aubergine]*- ⇒ variety of aubergine
Dourian -*[durian]*- ⇒ durian
Doyenné de comice ⇒ variety of pear
Drachenblut -*[sang de dragon]*- ⇒ red Riesling wine
Dragée ⇒ dragée
Dragées de Flavigny ⇒ dragées flavoured with aniseed
Draine -*[grive]*- ⇒ thrush
Drambuie ⇒ drambuie liqueur
Dresdner stollen ⇒ brioche with preserved fruits
Dresser ⇒ to lay, laid, laid
Dromadaire -*[chameau]*- ⇒ camel
Drop -*[pastille]*- ⇒ sweet
Dry
    - **vermouth ou gin** ⇒ dry
    - **champagne** ⇒ sweet
Dry martini -*[vermouth]*- ⇒ vermouth
Du Barry
    1) général ⇒ ... with a garnish of cauliflower, plus a sauce of egg-yolk, cream and grated cheese
    2) garniture pour pièces de boucherie ⇒ ... with a garnish of small potatoes sautéed in butter with lardoons, plus cauliflower balls; covered with béchamel sauce added of egg-yolks and gruyère, then sprinkled of grated cheese and browned
Dubley ⇒ ... with a garnish of grilled mushrooms, and croustades filled with mashed mushrooms
Dubonnet fizz ⇒ cocktail of Dubonnet aperitif, orange juice and champagne
Duchesse *(à la ...)*
    1) oeufs pochés ⇒ poached eggs ...
        - **Tournedos** ⇒ Tournedos ...
        - **Coquilles de poisson** ⇒ Scallop-shell filled with fish ... surrounded by fried balls of mashed potatoes, eggs and butter

2) **Pâtisserie** ⇒ Pastry with almonds
Duchesse
1) **dessert avec poire** ⇒ dessert with pear
2) **poire** ⇒ variety of pear
3) **salées** ⇒ salted choux pastry garnished with a culinary stuffing

4) **entremets** ⇒ choux pastry stuffed of ...
- **chantilly** ⇒ sugared whipped cream
- **crème pâtissière** ⇒ confectioner's custard then sprinkled of ...
- **pistache** ⇒ pistachios
- **amandes** ⇒ almonds
- **cacao** ⇒ cocoa
- **petits fours** ⇒ petit fours soldered by two with custard
Duchesse -*[pommes]*- ⇒ fried balls made with mashed potatoes, eggs and butter
Dulce de leche -*[Argentine]*- ⇒ concentrated milk flavoured with sugar and aromatics
Dulce de membrillo -*[pâte de coing]*- ⇒ quince paste
Dumpling -*[garniture]*- ⇒ dumpling
Dumpling à la pomme ⇒ apple dumpling
- **autres fruits** ... ⇒ ... dumpling
Duncan -*[pamplemousse]*- ⇒ variety of grapefruit
Dundee cake -*[cake]*- ⇒ Dundee cake
Dundee marmelade -*[GB]*- ⇒ Dundee marmelade
Dunlop -*[fromage]*- ⇒ Dunlop
Dur ⇒ hard
Durian ⇒ durian
Durion ⇒ durian
Duroc
- **avec petites pièces de boucherie ou volailles sautées** ⇒ ... with a garnish of new potatoes browned in butter, topped of diced tomato pulp; covered with a sauce made of mushrooms, shallots, white wine and tomato
Duse
1) **garniture** ⇒ ... with a garnish of french beans thickened in butter, tomatoes and potatoes
2) **poisson** ⇒ poached sole fillets with rice, béchamel sauce added of egg-yolks and gruyère, plus a culinary stuffing of crayfish tails, and a hash of truffles
Dust -*[thé]*- ⇒ variety of tea
Duxelles ⇒ hash of mushrooms, onions and shallots sautéed in butter

E

EUROPE CENTRALE

a) Bulgarie
- **Ghivetch** ⇒ ragout of meat, plus simmered vegetables in spices, topped with eggs and yoghourt
- **Tarator** ⇒ cucumber mixed with yoghourt and chopped nuts
- **Tchorba** ⇒ chicken soup with lamb's offal
- **Viande séchée et salée** ⇒ pasterma
- **Kebabcha** ⇒ sausage on skewers
- **Feuilletés fourrés au fromage et aux légumes** ⇒ puff-pastry filled with cheese and vegetables
- **Sirene** ⇒ ewe cheese
- **Euxinograd** ⇒ Bulgarian wine
- **Slivovica** ⇒ plum brandy

b) Roumanie
- **Ciorba** ⇒ soup of fish and chicken
- **Purée d'aubergines à l'huile d'olive et au citron** ⇒ mashed aubergines with olive oil and lemon juice
- **Mititei** ⇒ grilled sausages served with ripe grape juice
- **Brandza ou Katshkawalj** ⇒ ewe cheese
- **Mamaliga** ⇒ maize

c) Tchécoslovaquie
- **Bière de pilsen** ⇒ pilsner beer
- **Jambon de Prague** ⇒ ham
- **Potage au mou de veau** ⇒ soup of veal's lungs
- **Filets de carpe aux champignons** ⇒ carp fillets with mushrooms
- **Veprové maso** ⇒ pot-au-feu served with a spicy sauce
- **Brambory** ⇒ potatoes
- **Livances** ⇒ pancakes with jam

d) Yougoslavie
- **Corba** ⇒ soup
- **Lipski-Silba** ⇒ cheese
- **Marastina ou Ljutomer** ⇒ white wines
- **Blatina** ⇒ red wine
- **Marasquin de zara** ⇒ maraschino

Ealired -[pêche]- ⇒ variety of peach

Earl grey -[thé]- ⇒ earl grey

Eau ⇒ water < uncountable >

Eau d'or de Dantzig ⇒ polish brandy

Eau de coco ⇒ liquid from ripe coconut

Eau de coing -[ou ratafia de coing]- ⇒ brandy made of eau de vie and quince

Eau de fleur d'oranger ⇒ bitter orange tree flower extract

Eau de noix -[Gascogne]- ⇒ nut liqueur

Eau de noyau -[noyau]- ⇒ noyau

Eau de rose ⇒ rose flower extract

Eau de réglisse à l'orange ⇒ drink based on liquorice and orange peel

Eau de seltz ⇒ soda water or seltzer

Eau de vie ⇒ eau de vie or brandy
Eau de vie de fraise ⇒ strawberry brandy or eau de vie made of strawberries
Eau de vie de framboises ⇒ raspberry brandy or eau de vie made of raspberries
Eau des carmes ⇒ tonic including balm alcohol
Eau gazeuse ⇒ soda water
Eau minérale ⇒ mineral water
Eau minérale gazeuse ⇒ sparkling mineral water
Eau minérale non gazeuse ⇒ still mineral water
Eau potable ⇒ drinking water
Eaux minérales *-[carte]-* ⇒ minerals
Eaux minérales *(titres dans le menu ...)* ⇒ minerals
Ecailler
    - **huître** ⇒ to open
    - **poisson** ⇒ to scale
Ecaillé *-[pour huitres et coquillages]-* ⇒ opened < *for oysters and shells* >
Ecaillé *-[pour poissons]-* ⇒ scaled < *English name of the fish* >
Ecarlate *(à l' ...)* ⇒ meat steeped in pickle or steeped in pickle
Ecarlate *-[viande]-* ⇒ pickled meat or salted meat
Eccles cake *-[cake]-* ⇒ Eccles cake
Echalote ⇒ shallot
Echaudé ⇒ squared cake made of flour, egg and butter
Echézeaux *-[vin]-* ⇒ burgundy red wine
Echine ⇒ chine or loin
Echine de mouton ⇒ chine of mutton or loin of lamb
Echine de porc ⇒ chine of pork
Echine de porc sans os ⇒ boneless neck of pork
Eclade ⇒ mussels cooked with pine needles
Eclair ⇒ éclair
Eclairs à la Karoly ⇒ small éclairs garnished either with cheese, or ham, or caviar, or foie gras
Eclairs au café ⇒ éclairs covered with confectioner's custard, and a fondant added of coffee extract
Eclairs au chocolat ⇒ éclairs covered with confectioner's custard added of chocolate
Eclanche ⇒ shoulder of mutton
Ecorce de melon au vinaigre ⇒ melon peel preserved in vinegar
Ecorces d'orange confites ⇒ preserved orange peel
Ecorces de citron confites ⇒ preserved lemon peel
Ecossaise *(à l' ...)*
    - **potage** ⇒ Scotch mutton broth
    - **autres plats servis avec une brunoise de légumes** ⇒ ... served with braised diced vegetables
Ecrevisse ⇒ crayfish < *pluriel crayfishes* >
Ecrevisses à l'américaine ⇒ crayfishes poached in a court-bouillon, then fried and flamed with cognac and armagnac; simmered in a sauce made of shallots, pounded garlic, tomato purée, cayenne pepper and dry white wine
Ecrevisses à la liègeoise ⇒ crayfishes cooked in a court-bouillon with cayenne pepper, covered with the cooking stock thickened of butter, then sprinkled of parsley
Ecrevisses à la marinière ⇒ crayfishes sautéed in butter, then braised in white wine with thyme and laurel
Ecrevisses à la nage ⇒ crayfishes cooked in a court-bouillon with cayenne pepper
Ecrevisses grillées au beurre d'ail ⇒ crayfishes sautéed in mashed garlic mixed with butter, and baked

Edam ⇒ Edam
Edam français en pain -*[broodkas]*- ⇒ French cheese similar to Edam
Edam jeune ⇒ Edam cheese refined during 3 months in cell
Edelpilz ⇒ Bavarian cow's milk cheese
Edelzwicker ⇒ high quality white wine, from a mixing of good varieties of vine
Edouard VII -*[gâteau]*- ⇒ pastry boat filled with rhubarb
Eel pie ⇒ eel pie
Effiler
    a) **amandes et pistaches** ⇒ almonds or pistachios cut in lamellas
    b) **blancs de volaille** ⇒ white meat cut thinly
        - **aiguillettes de canard** ⇒ slices of duck cut thinly
    c) **poireaux** ⇒ leeks reduced in thin threads
Effilée -*[poireaux]*- ⇒ leeks in thin lamellas
Egg sauce ⇒ egg sauce
Egg-nog -*[coktail]*- ⇒ eggnog
Eggs and bacon -*[GB]*- ⇒ eggs and bacon
Eglantier -*[fruit]*- ⇒ eglantine fruit
Eglantine ⇒ wild rose or dog-rose
Eglefin ou Aiglefin ⇒ haddock < *pluriel inchangé* >
Eglefin fumé (*ou aiglefin ...*) -*[haddock dans le commerce]*- ⇒ haddock
Egribikavér -*[vin]*- ⇒ quality Hungarian red wine
Egyptienne (*à l' ...*)
    - **aubergines** ⇒ aubergines stuffed with their pulp and chopped onion, served with sauté tomatoes
    - **garniture** ⇒ garnish of sauté sliced aubergines, rice and tomato purée
    - **salade composée** ⇒ salad made of rice, plus a culinary stuffing of poultry livers, ham, mushrooms, artichoke hearts, peas, tomatoes and capsicums
    - **oeufs sur le plat** ⇒ fried eggs served with halved tomatoes filled with rice
    - **potage** ⇒ soup of rice added of leeks and onions in butter, plus milk
Eierkückas ⇒ pancakes from a batter enriched of cream
Ekmek -*[Russe]*- ⇒ toasted slices of bread impregnated of honey
Elan ⇒ elk or moose
Eleusine -*[millet]*- ⇒ millet
Eliche -*[pâtes alimentaires]*- ⇒ pasta for cooking
Elixir ⇒ elixir or cordial
El Jadida -*[Maroc vins]*- ⇒ Moroccan quality rosé wine
Elzekaria -*[soupe]*- ⇒ soup of cabbage, haricot bean, onions, garlic, plus pork fat
Eléphant ⇒ elephant
Embeurrée -*[vendée]*- ⇒ thin slices of ...
    - **poireaux** ⇒ leeks cooked in a large portion of butter
    - **choux pommés** ⇒ common cabbage cooked in a large portion of butter
Emincer ⇒ to slice thinly
Emincé -*[plat de fines tranches de viande en sauce]*- ⇒ thin slice or rasher or dish of thin slices of meat in gravy
    - **émincé de bœuf** ⇒ voir texte
    - **émincé de chevreuil** ⇒ thin slices of roebuck, covered with ...
    - **sauce poivrade** ⇒ ... a sauce based on a mixture of diced vegetables and ham, cooked in vinegar and white wine, seasoned with pepper served with chestnut purée and redcurrant jelly

- **grand veneur** ⇒ ... a preparation of pepper sauce added of redcurrant jelly and cream served with chestnut purée and redcurrant jelly
- **chasseur** ⇒ sauce chasseur ... served with chestnut purée and redcurrant jelly
- **émincé de mouton** ⇒ thin slices of mutton, covered with ...
- **sauce aux champignons servi avec du riz** ⇒ ... mushroom sauce served with rice
- **sauce tomate servi avec du riz** ⇒ ... tomato sauce served with rice
- **sauce au paprika servi avec du riz** ⇒ ... a sauce flavoured of paprika served with rice
- **sauce indienne servi avec du riz** ⇒ ... a white sauce containing herbs, chopped onions braised in oil, nutmeg, chicken stock and coconut milk served with rice < *si une autre garniture, mettre le nom anglais de celle-ci* >
- **émincé de pork** ⇒ thin slices of pork, covered with ...
- **sauce piquant** ⇒ ... piquant sauce
- **sauce Robert** ⇒ ... a sauce of onions browned in pork fat, plus flour, white wine, stock, and mustard
- **sauce charcutière** ⇒ ... a sauce of chopped onions in pork fat, crumbs, white wine, stock, diced gherkins, and mustard
- **servi avec** ⇒ served with ...
- **purée de pommes de terre** ⇒ mashed potatoes
- **purée de pois cassés** ⇒ mashed peas
- **émincé de veau** ⇒ thin slices of veal, covered with ...
- **émincé de volaille** ⇒ thin slices of poultry, covered with ...
- **sauce tomate** ⇒ ... tomato sauce
- **sauce royale** ⇒ ... a sauce of poultry velouté, added of cream, butter, chopped truffles, and xeres
- **servi avec** ⇒ served with ...
- **pommes de terre sautées** ⇒ sauté potatoes
- **légumes au beurre** ⇒ vegetables in butter
- **légumes à la crème** ⇒ vegetables in cream
- **légumes braisés** ⇒ braised vegetables
- **purée** ⇒ purée
- **émincé de veau qui n'est pas de desserte mais fait avec de la noix de veau** ⇒ sauté topside of veal lamellas, moistened with the gravy, and garnished of sauté mushrooms

Eminçé de boeuf ⇒ thin slices of beef with ...
- **sauce madère** ⇒ ... Madeira sauce added of mushrooms
- **sauce bordelaise** ⇒ ... a sauce made of poached bone-marrow, shallots, red wine, thyme, laurel, and parsley
- **sauce chasseur** ⇒ ... sauce chasseur
- **sauce lyonnaise** ⇒ ... a sauce of braised onions in butter, plus vinegar, white wine and stock
- **sauce piquante** ⇒ ... piquant sauce
- **sauce Robert** ⇒ ... a sauce of onions browned in pork fat, plus flour, white wine, stock and mustard
- **sauce italienne** ⇒ brown sauce thickened of chopped mushrooms, diced ham, tarragon and tomato purée
- **garniture** ⇒ garnished of ...
- **pommes sautées** ⇒ sauté potatoes
- **légumes verts au beurre** ⇒ green vegetables in butter
- **légumes verts à la crème** ⇒ green vegetables in cream
- **légumes braisés** ⇒ braised vegetables
- **purée** ⇒ purée
- **pâtes** ⇒ pasta
- **risotto** ⇒ risotto

Emincés à l'italienne ⇒ cooked slices of meat in brown sauce, sprinkled of grated parmesan and warmed up again

Emincés d'agneau ⇒ cooked slices of lamb, sprinkled with sauce chasseur or other, and warmed up again

Emincés de boeuf aux champignons ⇒ slices of boiled beef with sauté mushrooms and Madeira sauce

Emincés de boeuf sauce bordelaise ⇒ slices of boiled beef, garnished with sauté bone-marrow and covered with a sauce based on Sauternes wine

Emincés de mouton au cari ⇒ slices of roasted mutton, covered with a curry sauce

Emincés de veau ou de volaille à blanc ⇒ slices of poached veal or poultry meat, covered with a sauce

Emmental ⇒ Emmenthal cheese

Emondé *(mondé ...)* ⇒ blanched or husked *< v.t adjectif >*

Empanada ⇒ turnover or croustade, filled with meat or fish

Empereur -*[pain]-* ⇒ individual small round bread

Emulsion ⇒ emulsion

En attente -*[esturgeon]-*
   - **servi froid** ⇒ sturgeon cooked in a court-bouillon, served chilled with parsley, mushrooms, olives, crayfish tails, shredded horse-radish, lemon and gherkins
   - **servi chaud** ⇒ sturgeon cooked in a court-bouillon, served with tomato purée added of crayfish butter

En aumônière ⇒ dessert made of fruits where the seed is replaced by sugar, then rolled in short-pastry and cooked in the oven; served with apricot hot sauce and garnished with chopped grilled almonds

En barbouille
   - **lapin** ⇒ rabbit stewed in wine and sauce thickened by its blood
   - **coq ou poulet** ⇒ cock or chicken stewed in wine and sauce thickened by its blood

En bellevue
   1) **général** -*[crustacé, poisson, volaille]-* ⇒ in jelly
   2) **homard, langouste** ⇒ thin slices of lobster or crawfish in jelly
   3) **bécasse** ⇒ woodcock ...
       - **caille** ⇒ quail ...
       - **grive** ⇒ thrus ... stuffed and poached in game stock, then chilled and covered of chaudfroid sauce plus jelly

En branche
   - **légumes servis entiers** ⇒ vegetables which are served whole
   - **asperges en branches** ⇒ whole asparagus OR asparagus spears
   - **céleri en branches** ⇒ sticks of celery

En cas ⇒ snack

En chemise *(description des viandes ou légumes servis enveloppés ou dans leur peau ...)*
   - **pâté** ⇒ pie coated with ... or wrapped with ...
   - **pommes de terre « cuite dans leur peau »** ⇒ potatoes cooked in their jacket or jacket potatoes

En colère ⇒ fried whiting garnished of fried parsley and quartered lemons, served with tomato sauce

En crapaudine
   - **volaille** ⇒ poultry flattened and grilled
   - **poulet** ⇒ chicken flattened and grilled

En croûte ⇒ cooked ... nom anglais, wrapped in a pastry case

En olive *(tourné ...)* ⇒ olive shaped

En pistache ⇒ cooked with clove of garlic

En poudre ⇒ powdered or granulated or crushed or grounded
En su tinta ⇒ squid cooked in black sauce
En sus ⇒ in addition or additional or extra charge
- **vous payez ceci en plus** ⇒ in addition you pay ... F.Fr, for ...
- **frais supplémentaires pour** ⇒ additional charges for ...
- **frais pour** ⇒ extra charge for ...
Encastré ⇒ embedded
Enchaud ⇒ pork fillet, boned and baked
Enchilada -[Mexique]- ⇒ enchilada
Encornet ⇒ squid
Endive ⇒ chicory
Endives à l'étuvée ⇒ chicory braised in butter with lemon juice
Endives à la Mornay ⇒ braised chicory, covered with béchamel sauce added of egg-yolks and gruyère, grated parmesan, melted butter and browned
Endives au beurre noisette ⇒ braised chicory, sprinkled with browned butter
Endives au gratin ⇒ braised chicory sprinkled of grated cheese and melted butter, then browned
Endives au jambon ⇒ braised chicory wrapped in ham, covered of béchamel sauce and grated cheese, then browned
Endives en fricots ⇒ braised chicory macerated in olive oil, wrapped in batter and fried
Enfiler sur brochettes ⇒ put on skewers
Enflammé ⇒ fiery
Enragé -[crabe]- ⇒ green crab
Enrober ⇒ to coat
Ensacher ⇒ to put into sacks, etc
Entier ⇒ entire or whole
Entolome ⇒ Entoloma mushroom
Entouré ⇒ surrounded
Entrammes ⇒ Port Salut
Entraygues -[cabécou]- ⇒ small cheese from a mixing of goat's milk and cow's milk
Entraygues-et-du-fel ⇒ wine from Aveyron area
Entre deux mers ⇒ Bordeaux white wine
Entrecôte (2 ou découverte, avec une partie de l'épaule ...) ⇒ middle rib of beef
Entrecôte ⇒ entrecôte or entrecôte steak or rib steak
Entrecôte à la ménagère ⇒ entrecôte steak sautéed in butter with carrots, onions and mushrooms; served with the cooking juice added of white wine and stock
Entrecôte basse « parée » ⇒ chuck steak
Entrecôte Bercy ⇒ grilled entrecôte steak covered of composed butter mixed with bone-marrow, shallots, white wine and pepper
Entrecôte grand mère ⇒ grilled entrecôte steak garnished with sautéed onions, mushrooms and lardoons, plus browned potatoes
Entrecôte grillée ⇒ entrecôte steak brushed with oil and grilled on wood fire, garnished of small sauté potatoes in butter added of lardoons, watercress and sometimes béarnaise sauce
Entrecôte grillée à la bordelaise
1) **normale** ⇒ entrecôte steak grilled on vine shoots, served with butter
2) **gastronomique** ⇒ grilled entrecôte steak garnished of bone-marrow and parsley, plus a browned sauce added of Sauternes wine
Entrecôte marchand de vin ⇒ grilled entrecôte steak, served with a butter added of shallots, red wine, consommé, parsley, and lemon juice
Entrecôte maître d'hotel ⇒ grilled entrecôte, served with parsley butter

Entrecôte mirabeau ⇒ grilled entrecôte steak covered with anchovy fillets, tarragon leaves, stoned olives and anchovy butter

Entrecôte poêlée ⇒ fried entrecôte steak served with butter or a sauce based on red wine

Entrecôte poêlée à la bourguignonne ⇒ fried entrecôte steak, covered with a sauce of red wine and gravy

Entrecôte poêlée à la fermière ⇒ fried entrecôte steak, plus vegetables cooked in their own liquid; served with a sauce of white wine, beef consommé and kneaded butter

Entrecôte poêlée à la hongroise ⇒ entrecôte steak sprinkled of paprika and fried with chopped onions; served with a velouté sauce added of white wine

Entrecôte poêlée à la lyonnaise ⇒ entrecôte steak fried with onions; served covered with a sauce of white wine, consommé and butter

Entrecôte poêlée aux champignons ⇒ fried entrecôte steak plus sautéed mushrooms; served with a sauce of white wine, gravy and butter

Entrecôte vert-pré ⇒ grilled entrecôte steak served with butter added of parsley, plus cress and fried shredded potatoes

Entrelarder ⇒ to lard

Entremets ⇒ dessert or sweet

Entremets au tapioca ⇒ dessert of tapioca cooked in milk with vanilla sugar, white of eggs and icing sugar

Entrée ⇒ first course or starter < *mais ce dernier mot est de l'argot* >

Enveloppe d'un fruit ⇒ casing

Epaule ⇒ shoulder of
- **mouton** ⇒ mutton
- **agneau** ⇒ lamb
- **porc** ⇒ pork
- **veau** ⇒ veal
- **boeuf** ⇒ beef

Epaule d'agneau ⇒ shoulder of lamb

Epaule d'agneau à l'albigeoise ⇒ meat loaf of boned lamb's shoulder, stuffed with a forcemeat of sausage meat and pork's liver; baked with goose fat, potatoes and garlic

Epaule d'agneau à la boulangère ⇒ boned lamb's shoulder, salted and peppered, then baked with potatoes and onions

Epaule d'agneau braisée et ses garnitures ⇒ shoulder of lamb braised with strips from rind of pork, onion, white wine and tomato purée; served with beans or an other garnish

Epaule d'agneau de lait grillé ⇒ lamb's shoulder brushed with melted butter and grilled

Epaule d'agneau farçie à l'albigeoise ⇒ meat loaf of boned lamb's shoulder, stuffed with a forcemeat of sausage meat and pork's liver; baked with goose fat, potatoes and garlic

Epaule d'agneau farçie à la gasconne ⇒ meat loaf of bone lamb's shoulder, stuffed with a forcemeat of bread, ham, onions, garlic and egg; braised with cabbage, diced carrots, onion, clove and potatoes

Epaule d'agneau rôtie en ballotine ⇒ meat loaf of boned lamb's shoulder, studded with garlic and roasted

Epaule de chevreuil aux olives ⇒ shoulder of roe-deer studded of lardoons and cooked with diced pork fat, olive oil and butter; served with olives cooked in the gravy thickened of arrow-root

Epaule de mouton ⇒ shoulder of mutton

Epaule de mouton désossée ⇒ boneless shoulder

Epaule de mouton désossée et ficelée ⇒ shoulder of mutton « boned and rolled »

Epaule de mouton désossée et roulée ⇒ shoulder of mutton « boneless »

Epaule de mouton en ballon *(ou en musette ...)* ⇒ boned shoulder of mutton, stuffed with a forcemeat of sausage meat, boletus, parsley, shallots, garlic, egg, thyme and pepper; shaped in ball, then baked in oli /e oil and white wine

Epaule de mouton en gelée ⇒ meat loaf of boned mutton's shoulder, stuffed with a forcemeat of diced ham and eggs, then braised and served chilled in jelly

Epaule de mouton en pistache ⇒ boned mutton's shoulder, cooked with diced ham, garlic, herbs and orange peel; served with the cooking juice and the garnish of garlic

Epaule de mouton ⇒ shoulder of mutton
- **rôtie** ⇒ roasted
- **braisée** ⇒ braised
- **et ses garnitures** ⇒ with a garnish ...
- **à la boulangère** ⇒ voir texte
- **à la chipolata** ⇒ voir texte
- **à la bourgeoise** ⇒ shoulder of mutton stuffed with carrots, onions and lardoons
- **à la bourguignonne** ⇒ shoulder of mutton braised in red wine with mushrooms, onions and lardoons
- **à la bretonne** ⇒ shoulder of mutton braised with
- **haricots** ⇒ beans
- **fèves** ⇒ broad beans
- **à la flamande** ⇒ shoulder of mutton braised in meat loaf with red cabbage
- **aux navets** ⇒ shoulder of mutton braised with turnips and onions
- **au riz** ⇒ shoulder of mutton braised and served with rice

Epaule de porc *-[palette et jambonneau]-* ⇒ shoulder and knuckle of ham

Epaule de porc aux cinq épices ⇒ shoulder of pork, cooked with pounded garlic and shallots, added of Vietnamese seasoning, plus a mixing of star anise, clove, fennel, cinnamon and pepper; served with rice and the cooking juice

Epaule de porc avec poitrine à 3 côtes ⇒ hand of pork

Epaule de porc avec poitrine à 3 côtes, sans os et roulée ⇒ hand of pork boned and rolled or hand of pork boneless

Epaule de porc avec échine ⇒ shoulder of pork

Epaule de porc avec échine, désossée et ficelée ⇒ shoulder of pork « boned and rolled » or shoulder of pork « boneless »

Epaule de veau ⇒ shoulder of veal

Epaule de veau avec os et jarret compris ⇒ shoulder of veal

Epaule de veau désossée ⇒ boneless shoulder of veal

Epaule de veau désossée et roulée ⇒ shoulder of veal boned and rolled

Epaule de veau farçie ⇒ meat loaf of veal's shoulder, stuffed with sausage meat, chopped mushrooms, garlic and herbs, then braised and served with the gravy

Epaule de veau farçie à l'anglaise ⇒ meat loaf of veal's shoulder, stuffed with a forcemeat of veal's kidney, grease of veal, eggs, crumbs and pepper, then braised or roasted; served with slices of pork fat, cabbage and potatoes boiled in water

Epaule de veau sans jarret ⇒ veal oyster

Epaule de veau sans os ⇒ shoulder of veal « boneless »

Epaule de veau sans os et ficelée ⇒ shoulder of veal « boned and rolled »

Epaule farçie à l'albigeoise ⇒ meat loaf of boned lamb's shoulder, studded with a forcemeat of sausage meat and pork's liver; baked with goose fat, potatoes and garlic

Epaule farçie à la gasconne ⇒ meat loaf of boned lamb's shoulder, stuffed with a forcemeat of bread, ham, onions, garlic and egg; braised with cabbage, diced carrots, onion, clove and potatoes

Epaule rôtie d'agneau en ballotine ⇒ meat loaf of boned lamb's shoulder, studded with garlic and roasted

Epeautre ⇒ spelt

Epée de mer -*[espadon]*- ⇒ swordfish

Eperlan -*[faux]*- ⇒ sand-smelt

Eperlan -*[mer]*- ⇒ sea-smelt or sand-smelt

Eperlan -*[rivière]*- ⇒ river smelt

Eperlans en brochettes ⇒ sea smelts fried on skewers

Eperlans frits ⇒ sea smelts steeped in milk and floured, then fried and served with quartered lemons

Eperlans grillés à l'anglaise ⇒ boned sea smelts, covered with melted butter and crumbs, then grilled; served with parsley butter

Eperlans marinés ⇒ sea smelts browned in oil and marinated with onions, pepper, clove, thyme, laurel and vinegar; served as a hors d'œuvre

Epi de maïs ⇒ maize ear

Epice ⇒ spice

Epice de chambre -*[fruits confits]*- ⇒ preserved fruits ½ ou ½ crystallized fruits

Epigrammes d'agneau ⇒ braised breast of lamb and sautéed lamb-chops, served with either vegetables or mushrooms or tomatoes or aubergines fritters

Epinard de la nouvelle Zelande -*[tetragone]*- ⇒ New Zealand spinach

Epinard de mer ⇒ sloke

Epinard géant du Mexique ⇒ Mexican leaves

Epinards ⇒ spinach < *uncountable* >

Epinards à l'anglaise ⇒ spinach served with butter

Epinards à la crème ⇒ spinach covered of cream and served with fried sippets

Epinards au beurre ⇒ sauté spinach seasoned with pepper and nutmeg, then buttered and decorated of fried sippets

Epinards au gratin ⇒ spinach covered of béchamel sauce, seasoned with nutmeg and added of grated parmesan; then browned

Epinards au jus ⇒ spinach covered with gravy of veal

Epine-vinette ⇒ berberis

Epinée-échine ⇒ backbone or spine, chine of pork < *porc* >

Epinoche ⇒ stickleback

Epoisses ⇒ cow's milk cheese from burgundy area, the crust being washed with sage and marc brandy

Equille ⇒ sand eel

Erable ⇒ maple

    - Sirop d'érable ⇒ maple syrup

Esaü

    - potage ⇒ lentils' soup thickened of consommé

    - oeufs ⇒ tartlets filled with mashed lentils and poached eggs; covered of veal's stock

Esbareich -*[fromage de brebis]*- ⇒ ewe's milk cheese or ewe cheese

Escabèche

    a) **poisson frit en marinade** ⇒ fried fish conserved in a spicy marinade

    b) **marinade pour conservation** ⇒ spicy marinade for conservation of cooked food

    c) **Berry-gougeons à la cascamèche** ⇒ fried gudgeons conserved in a spicy marinade

    d) **volaille et gibier** ⇒ ... cooked and conserved in a spicy marinade

    e) **Chili poulet** ⇒ chicken fried in oil with garlic, then covered of marinade added of aromatics; served chilled with lemons and onions

    f) **Belgique escavèche** ⇒ nom pour « escabèche »

Escabèche de sardines ⇒ sardines browned, then marinated in olive oil, vinegar, garlic, thyme, rosemary, laurel, parsley and capsicum

Escabecio -[*Escabèche*]-
    a) **poisson frit en marinade** ⇒ fried fish conserved in a spicy marinade
    b) **marinade pour conservation** ⇒ spicy marinade for conservation of cooked food
    c) **Berry gougeons à la cascamèche** ⇒ fried gudgeons conserved in a spicy marinade
    d) **volaille et gibier** ⇒ ... cooked and conserved in a spicy marinade
    e) **Chili poulet** ⇒ chicken fried in oil with garlic, then covered of marinade added of aromatics; served chilled with lemons and onions
    f) **Belgique escavèche** ⇒ nom pour « escabèche »

Escalope ⇒ escalope

Escalope à la crème ⇒ sautéed escalope in cream

Escalope de daurade au grains de moutarde ⇒ dorado escalope with mustard seeds

Escalope de merlu aux graines de moutarde ⇒ salt cod escalope with mustard seeds

Escalope de porc ⇒ pork escalope

Escalope de saumon aux gigondas ⇒ poached salmon escalope fried in butter; served with onions braised in boiled away Gigondas wine added of fish stock, diced tomato, mushroom, shallots and crayfish butter

Escalope de sole océane ⇒ sole escalope

Escalope de veau ⇒ veal escalope

Escalope panée ⇒ escalope coated with breadcrumbs

Escalope sauce béarnaise ⇒ veal escalope with béarnaise sauce

Escaloper ⇒ to cut in thin slices

Escalopes à la Brancas ⇒ veal escalopes covered with a julienne and breadcrumbs, then sautéed in butter, garnished with potato straws sautéed in butter, plus lettuce and sorrel braised in cream; a Madeira sauce is served apart

Escalopes à la Mandelieu ⇒ veal escalopes flamed in cognac, then covered with a slice of swiss cheese, sprinkled of breadcrumbs plus melted butter and browned; served with a sauce of mushrooms, tomato purée and consommé

Escalopes à la viennoise ⇒ wiener schnitzel

Escalopes aux aubergines et aux courgettes ⇒ veal escalopes sautéed in butter, garnished with sauté courgettes and aubergines; covered with the cooking juice added of white wine and chopped garlic

Escalopes Casimir ⇒ sauté veal escalopes seasoned with paprika on braised artichoke hearts, covered of julienne, plus creamy sauce

Escalopes chaudes de foie gras de canard au raisin *(ou d'oie ...)* ⇒ sauté foie gras escalopes laid on fried sippets, garnished with grape and covered with a sauce of wine liquor plus stock

Escalopes de foie gras montrouge ⇒ sautéed foie gras escalopes laid on fried sippets; served with mushroom purée, then covered with a sauce of Madeira, stock and arrow-root

Escalopes de lotte à la crème de poivron ⇒ angler escalopes, covered with breadcrumbs and grated parmesan, then browned; served with Worcestershire sauce added of mashed capsicums in butter

Escalopes de loup au poivre et à la crème de gingembre ⇒ sea bass escalopes peppered and fried in oil; served with spinach braised in butter, plus a sauce of stock, white wine, shallots, cream and ginger

Escalopes de porc dans la noix ⇒ pork escalopes

Escalopes de porc dans la noix pâtissière ⇒ leg steaks of pork

Escalopes de rouget au pissalat ⇒ red gurnard fillets fried in olive oil and butter, served with a composed butter added of a anchovy seasoning

Escalopes de saumon ⇒ fried salmon escalopes

Escalopes de saumon aux carottes ⇒ uncooked salmon escalopes, served with sliced carrots cooked in stock added of paprika and brandy; covered with stock thickened of pepper and cream

Escalopes de saumon cru aux deux poivres ⇒ uncooked salmon escalopes brushed with olive oil and peppered

Escalopes de turbot à l'embeurrée de poireaux ⇒ turbot fillets browned and cooked in fish stock plus cream; served with leeks baked in butter

Escalopes de veau à l'anversoise ⇒ veal escalopes sautéed in butter and laid on fried sippets, covered with a sauce based on white wine, beer and consommé; served with browned potatoes, plus hop shoots in cream

Escalopes de veau dans la noix, épluchées ⇒ veal escalopes « ex cushion »

Escalopes de veau dans les 3 noix ⇒ veal escalopes

Escalopes froides de foie gras de canard aux raisins et aux truffes *(ou d'oie ...)* ⇒ escalopes of cooked foie gras, covered with truffle lamellas and jelly; served chilled with grape macerated in brandy, plus jelly flavoured of port

Escargot ⇒ escargot or snail

Escargot de mer *-[bigorneau]-* ⇒ winkle

Escargots à l'alsacienne ⇒ snails stuffed with flavoured jelly, garlic paste, and aniseed

Escargots à l'arlésienne ⇒ snails cooked with diced bacon, flour, white wine, garlic and aromatics; served with a sauce of Madeira, cayenne pepper and lemon juice

Escargots à l'italienne ⇒ snails served with parsley butter, and grated parmesan

Escargots à la bourguignonne ⇒ snails cooked in white wine, garlic, onions, carrots and nutmeg

Escargots à la dijonnaise ⇒ snails served with parsley butter

Escargots à la gayouparde ⇒ snails simmered in olive oil, onions, ham, garlic, anchovies, then flamed with eau de vie; served with spinach, rusks, and nuts

Escargots à la lodévoise ⇒ snails simmered in olive oil, onions, ham, garlic, spinach, endive, parsley, chervil, and mint; served thickened with egg-yolks, and chopped nuts

Escargots à la narbonnaise ⇒ snails simmered in olive oil, and garlic; covered with a mayonnaise sauce, mixed with milk and ground almonds

Escargots à la nîmoise ⇒ snails simmered in olive oil, shallots, onion, garlic, ham, and anchovies, plus spinach, sorrel, chervil, and stock

Escargots à la poulette ⇒ shelled snails cooked in white wine, roux, onion, egg-yolks and lemon juice

Escargots à la sommiroise ⇒ snails browned in olive oil, with streaky bacon, anchovies, garlic, pepper and white wine

Escargots à la suçarelle ⇒ snails prepared with tomatoes, garlic, sausage and white wine, which are traditionally sucked, rather than picked from their shells

Escargots à la valaisanne ⇒ snails served with gravy added of garlic paste, and chives

Escargots cuits en meurette ⇒ snails cooked in red wine sauce, with mushrooms, onions, and lardoons

Escargots de Sommières ⇒ snails browned in olive oil, with streaky bacon, anchovies, garlic, pepper and white wine

Escargots grillés à la mode du languedoc ⇒ shelled snails grilled on vine shoots, seasoned with pepper, thyme and fennel, sprinkled of melted pork fat; served with country bread and local wine

Escarole ⇒ endive

Escavèche *-[escabèche]-*
   a) poisson frit en marinade ⇒ fried fish conserved in a spicy marinade
   b) marinade pour conservation ⇒ spicy marinade for conservation of cooked food
   c) Berry gougeons à la cascamèche ⇒ fried gudgeons conserved in a spicy marinade
   d) volaille et gibier ⇒ ... cooked and conserved in a spicy marinade

e) **Chili poulet** ⇒ chicken fried in oil with garlic, then covered of marinade added of aromatics; served chilled with lemons and onions

f) **Belgique escavèche** ⇒ nom pour « escabèche »

Escauton ⇒ stock prepared with ham, vegetables and aromatics

Escubac -*[scubac]*- ⇒ liquor made of spices macerated in brandy

Escuedella ⇒ pot-au-feu from Perpignan area sometimes comprising turkey meat, but always eggs and a hash of noodles, plus meat

Espadon ⇒ swordfish

Espagnole *(à l' ...)* ⇒ ... fried in oil with tomato, capsicum, onion and garlic
- **garniture petites pièces** ⇒ with stuffed tomatoes, capsicums, braised onions and Madeira sauce
- **mayonnaise** ⇒ mayonnaise added of chopped ham, mustard, garlic and red pepper
- **oeufs pochés** ⇒ poached eggs, served on cooked tomatoes filled with a culinary stuffing of capsicums; covered of tomato sauce and garnished with slices of fried onions
- **oeufs sur le plat** ⇒ fried eggs on a bed of onions, tomatoes cooked in their own liquid, diced fried capsicums, quartered tomatoes, onions and tomato sauce
- **oeufs brouillés** ⇒ scrambled eggs mixed with diced tomatoes and capsicums, plus slices of fried onions

Espic -*[lavande]*- ⇒ lavender < *uncountable* >

Espinoche -*[épinard]*- ⇒ spinach < *uncountable* >

Espresso -*[café]*- ⇒ espresso coffee

Esrom -*[fromage]*- ⇒ Esrom

Essence d'ail ⇒ garlic extract

Essence d'estragon ⇒ tarragon extract

Essence de bergamote ⇒ bergamot extract

Essence de café ⇒ coffee extract

Essence de cerfeuil ⇒ chervil extract

Essence de champignon ⇒ mushroom extract

Essence de jasmin ⇒ jasmine extract

Essence de rose ⇒ rose flower extract

Essence de tomate ⇒ tomato extract

Essence de truffe ⇒ truffle extract

Essence naturelle
- **fleur** ⇒ aromatic extract from flower
- **écorce** ⇒ aromatic extract from bark

Estaing ⇒ wine from the Aveyron area

Estoficado
- **Marseille-St Tropez** ⇒ ragout of salt cod with tomatoes, onions, garlic, olive oil and aromatics
- **Nice** ⇒ ragout of stockfish with tomatoes, onions, garlic, olive oil and aromatics

Estofinado
- **Marseille-St Tropez** ⇒ ragout of salt cod with tomatoes, onions, garlic, olive oil and aromatics
- **Nice** ⇒ ragout of stockfish with tomatoes, onions, garlic, olive oil and aromatics

Estouffade
- **général** ⇒ dish cooked in its steam
- **boeuf en sauce au vin** ⇒ beef steamed in wine sauce, with carrots and onions
- **cuisine classique bouillon** ⇒ stock for sauce made of beef, veal, pork, carrots, onion, garlic and herbs

Estouffade de boeuf ⇒ browned lardoons and bits of beef, plus quartered onions, seasoned with pepper, thyme, laurel and garlic, then baked in red wine and stock; served with sauté mushrooms and the thickened cooking juice

Estouffat
- **Languedoc** ⇒ stew of beans, pork fat, garlic, onions, and tomatoes
- **Agen** *-[lièvre]-* ⇒ stew of hare
- **Auvergne** *-[perdrix]-* ⇒ stew of partridge and lentils

Estouffat (suite)
- **Béarn** *-[porc]-* ⇒ stew of pork
- **Roussillon Auvergne** *-[boeuf]-* ⇒ stew of beef
- **Languedoc** *-[tripes]-* ⇒ stew of tripe

Estouffat de haricots à l'occitane ⇒ beans cooked with diced carrot, onions, crushed tomatoes, garlic and diced pork fat, in goose fat

Estouffat de noël ⇒ beef stewed with shallots, in wine and armagnac

Estouffat de perdrix ⇒ dish of partridge cooked with lentils

Estragon ⇒ tarragon < *uncountable* >

Estrées *-[pâtisseries]-* ⇒ pastry

Esturgeon ⇒ sturgeon

Esturgeon à la Brimont ⇒ sturgeon fillets studded with anchovies, cooked in the oven on a layer of vegetables cooked in their own liquid, plus tomatoes, mushrooms, potatoes, white wine and butter

Esturgeon à la russe
- **servi froid** ⇒ sturgeon cooked in a court-bouillon, served chilled with parsley, mushrooms, olives, crayfish tails, shredded horse-radish, lemon and gherkins
- **servi chaud** ⇒ sturgeon cooked in a court-bouillon, served with tomato purée added of crayfish butter

Esturgeon de la baltique ⇒ Baltic sturgeon

Esturgeon en attente *-[cuisson de l'esturgeon]-*
- **servi froid** ⇒ sturgeon cooked in a court-bouillon, served chilled with parsley, mushrooms, olives, crayfish tails, shredded horse-radish, lemon and gherkins
- **servi chaud** ⇒ sturgeon cooked in a court-bouillon, served with tomato purée added of crayfish butter

Et ⇒ and

Etoffé ⇒ stuffed

Etoile ⇒ star or star shaped

Etouffée *(à l' ...)* ⇒ braised

Etouffé de veau à la vapeur de légumes ⇒ bits of veal's shoulder cooked slowly in the vegetable steam from carrots, turnips, leeks and onions; the dish is added of a glass of white wine, plus cream at the end of the cooking

Etrennes *-[gaufres]-* ⇒ waffle

Etrille ⇒ small crab or swimming crab

Etuvée *(à l'étuvée ...)* ⇒ braised
- **étuver** ⇒ to steam

Etuvée *(à l' ...)* ⇒ braised

Etuvée de poissons *(ou fondue de poissons ...)* ⇒ fishes stewed in their own liquid

Etuver ⇒ to steam
- **à l'étuvée** ⇒ braised

Eucalyptus *-[miel]-* ⇒ eucalyptus honey

Euxinograd *-[vin]-* ⇒ Bulgarian wine

Evider ⇒ to hollow out

Evidé ⇒ hollowed out < *v.t adjectif* >
Ewe cheese ⇒ ewe cheese
Excelsa *-[café]-* ⇒ variety of coffee seeds
Excelsior *-[fromage]-* ⇒ cow's milk cheese from Normandy
Excelsior
   - garniture ⇒ ... with a garnish of braised lettuce and sliced potatoes cooked in butter
   - plat ⇒ sole fillets shaped in balls and poached, laid in ring round a culinary stuffing of lobster;
                covered of creamy sauce and decorated with truffle lamellas plus, crayfish tails
Exocet ⇒ flying fish
Express *-[café]-* ⇒ expresso coffee
Express ⇒ espresso coffee
Extra ⇒ best quality
Extra dry *-[champagne]-* ⇒ dry
   - champagne dry ⇒ sweet
   - champagne brut ⇒ very dry
Extra-sec ⇒ dry champagne < *le champagne vraiment sec est désigné Brut champagne extra dry* >
Extrait ⇒ extract

F

Fabada -*[Espagne]*- ⇒ Asturian vegetable soup
Façon *(à ma ...)* ⇒ home made, adjectif, or the way one does something ...
Fagelbö -*[smörgasbord]*- ⇒ smorgasbord
Fagioli -*[Italie]*- ⇒ beans cooked with herbs; eaten tepid with french dressing
Fagot ⇒ pie of fat and pig liver, cooked in pork fat
Faîne ⇒ beechnut
Faire monter des blancs en neige ⇒ to whisk up egg whites
Faisan ⇒ pheasant < *uncountable* >
Faisan à l'alsacienne ⇒ pheasant cooked in butter, plus sauerkraut in goose fat; served with sliced
cervelat and diced bacon
Faisan à la Sainte Alliance ⇒ pheasant studded with streaky bacon, stuffed with a forcemeat of
truffles, woodcock and bone-marrow, then roasted on a large slice of bread spreaded
with the woodcock's offal added of truffle, anchovy, grated streaky bacon and butter;
served with Burgundy high quality wine
Faisan à la douro ⇒ pheasant stuffed with a forcemeat of chestnuts, foie gras and truffle; cooked with
lardoons in port
Faisan à la géorgienne ⇒ larded pheasant cooked with nuts, orange juice, grapes, Madeira and tea;
served with fresh nuts
Faisan à la languedocienne ⇒ bits of pheasant browned with thyme, laurel and flour, then cooked in
the oven with red wine, stock, boletus, truffle and cognac
Faisan à la normande ⇒ pheasant cooked with sliced apples in butter; served covered with cream and
calvados
Faisan au chou ⇒ large cabbage stuffed with a pheasant; cooked with pork fat, plus dry sausage
Faisan au porto ⇒ bits of pheasant cooked with shallots, butter, port, parasol mushrooms and cream
Faisan aux noix ⇒ pheasant stuffed with green walnuts, petit suisse, grape juice, lemon juice, port and
tea, then cooked in the oven
Faisan en cocotte ⇒ pheasant cooked in a cast-iron casserole with butter and cognac; served with
celeriac purée < *voir textes pour purée de foie de veau, ou pour purée de foies de
volaille* >
Faisan en filets au jus d'orange ⇒ sautéed pheasant fillets in butter with parsley, chervil and chive;
covered with a sauce made of pheasant offal and meat, veal stock, champagne and
orange juice
Faisan grillé à l'américaine ⇒ sauté pheasant, grilled with bacon; served with tomatoes, mushrooms,
watercress, and potato crisps
Faisan périgueux ⇒ pheasant studded of truffle and fried in butter; served with a sauce of Madeira and
chopped truffles
Faisan rôti ⇒ pheasant brushed with melted butter and roasted; served on fried sippets with the gravy
Faisan sauté ⇒ bits of pheasant sautéed in butter; served with the gravy added of white wine
Faisan truffé ⇒ pheasant studded with truffle, stuffed with a forcemeat of truffle and streaky bacon,
then roasted; served on sippet, plus game quenelles with a sauce of Madeira and
chopped truffles
Faisandé -*[viande]*- ⇒ gamy or high
Falafel ⇒ salad
Falerne ⇒ Italian wine from Naples area
Falette ⇒ stuffed breast of mutton simmered in the oven with carrots and onions; served with beans
Fallue *(ou brioche coulante ou brioche améliorée ...)* ⇒ brioche made of flour, butter, cream, eggs,
sugar, syrup and yeast

Fanchette
- **petit four** ⇒ petit four garnished with confectioner's custard flavoured of hazelnuts, then glazed with fondant
- **macaron** ⇒ macaroons garnished with a butter custard, strawberry flavoured

Fanchonnette
1) **tartelette** ⇒ tartlet garnished of confectioner's custard and meringue
2) **gâteau fanchette** ⇒ tart garnished of confectioner's custard and meringue
3) **Fanchonnette ou Fanchette**
   a) **petit four** ⇒ petits fours
   b) **bonbon** ⇒ sweet candy made of almonds and walnuts
   c) **macaron** ⇒ macaroon garnished of butter, plus cream added of strawberries

Fanchonnette
   a) **tartelette** ⇒ puff-pastry tartlet filled with confectioner's custard, then topped of meringue
   b) **petit four** ⇒ petit four garnished with confectioner's custard flavoured of hazelnuts, then glazed with fondant
   - **macaron** ⇒ macaroons garnished with a butter custard, strawberry flavoured

Fanes *(général ...)* ⇒ tops
- **navets** ⇒ turnip-tops
- **carottes** ⇒ carrot-tops

Faon ⇒ fawn

Far breton ⇒ flan filled with dried plums macerated in rum

Far de verdure ⇒ hash of beets, cabbage, lettuce, sorrel, cream and herbs; wrapped in cabbage leaves
   ...
- **cuit au pot au feu** ⇒ ... and cooked in pot au feu
- **cuit au gratin** ⇒ ... and cooked au gratin

Far du Poitou
- **courant** ⇒ hash of beets, cabbage, lettuce, plus sorrel mixed with streaky bacon, cream and herbs; wrapped in cabbage leaves and cooked in pot au feu
- **au maigre** ⇒ hash of beets, cabbage, lettuce, sorrel, cream and herbs; wrapped in cabbage leaves ...
   a) **cuit au pot au feu** ⇒ ... and cooked in pot au feu
   b) **cuit au gratin** ⇒ ... and cooked au gratin

Far i kal *-[norvège]-* ⇒ Stew of mutton and cabbage with black pepper

Far manch *-[far breton]-* ⇒ flan filled with dried plums macerated in rum

Far poch *-[far breton]-* ⇒ flan filled with dried plums macerated in rum

Far sach *-[far breton]-* ⇒ flan filled with dried plums macerated in rum

Farce ⇒ stuffing or forcemeat

Farce à gratin ⇒ forcemeat made of sauté pork fat, shallots, « poultry livers », mushrooms, thyme, laurel and spices

Farce à la crème ⇒ forcemeat of whiting or pike with cream

Farce à la panade et à la crème ⇒ forcemeat of hashed meat, grated nutmeg, white of eggs, panada and chilled cream

Farce à la panade et au beurre ⇒ forcemeat of veal meat, pepper, grated nutmeg, panada and butter

Farce à ravioli
1) **à la viande et aux légumes** ⇒ forcemeat of hashed cooked beef, spinach, poached veal's brain, onion, melted butter, egg, grated parmesan, pepper and nutmeg
2) **à la viande et au fromage** ⇒ forcemeat of hashed meat, poached veal's brain, braised lettuce, soft white cheese, grated parmesan, egg, pepper and nutmeg
3) **aux foies de volaille** ⇒ forcemeat of poultry livers, shallot, garlic, spinach, anchovy fillet, butter, egg, basil, pepper and nutmeg

4) aux épinards ⇒ forcemeat of braised spinach, pepper, grated nutmeg, panada, butter, eggs and béchamel sauce

Farce au foie gras ⇒ forcemeat of pork, pork fat, foie gras and cognac

Farce aux champignons ⇒ forcemeat of shallots, mushrooms sautéed with nutmeg, plus panada added of egg-yolks

Farce d'ail ⇒ forcemeat of egg-yolks, crushed garlic and butter

Farce de brochet à la Lyonnaise ⇒ preparation of kidney grease, frangipane, white of eggs and pike

Farce de cervelle ⇒ forcemeat of poached veal's brain and béchamel sauce

Farce de crevettes ⇒ forcemeat of shrimps, butter and boiled egg-yolks

Farce de crustacés ⇒ forcemeat of crustaceae, white of eggs and cream

Farce de foie ⇒ forcemeat of sauté pork fat, livers, shallots, mushrooms and aromatics, added of egg-yolks

Farce de gibier ⇒ forcemeat of game meat, veal meat, pork fat and cognac

Farce de harengs saurs ou de sardines
- **harengs saurs** ⇒ forcemeat based on a roux added of milk and egg, plus chopped herring fillets
- **sardines** ⇒ forcemeat based on a roux added of milk and egg, plus chopped sardines

Farce de jaunes d'oeuf à chaud ⇒ forcemeat of boiled egg-yolks and béchamel sauce

Farce de jaunes d'oeufs à froid ⇒ forcemeat of boiled egg-yolks, butter and pepper

Farce de quenelles -[godiveau]- ⇒ forcemeat balls

Farce de veau ⇒ forcemeat of crushed veal meat, pepper, grated nutmeg, panada, butter, eggs and béchamel sauce

Farce de veau à la cervelle de veau ⇒ forcemeat of veal cooked in an edge-mould; served with veal's brains and mushrooms

Farce de veau à la glace ⇒ hashed veal meat and hashed kidney grease mixed with pepper, nutmeg and eggs, then chilled

Farce de veau aux amourettes ⇒ forcemeat of veal cooked in an edge-mould; served with amourettes and mushrooms

Farce de volaille ⇒ forcemeat of poultry meat, pork fat, eggs and cognac

Farce fine de porc ⇒ sausage meat finely chopped

Farce mousseline ⇒ forcemeat of mashed meat of veal or game, added of chilled cream and white of eggs

Farce mousseline pour mousses et mousselines de poisson ⇒ forcemeat of pepper, nutmeg and fish meat, added of white of eggs, then mixed with chilled cream

Farce pour poissons ⇒ forcemeat of crumbs in milk, onions, shallots, mushrooms, butter, white wine and egg-yolks

Farce pour volailles ⇒ forcemeat of sausage meat, hashed onions in butter, chopped parsley and crumbs

Farcement ⇒ cake made of grated potatoes, dried-plums, dried-pears, sultanas, eggs and flour

Farçi *(action de farçir ...)* ⇒ stuffed < *v.t adjectif* >

Farçi -[Périgord]-
   a) **chou** ⇒ hash wrapped in cabbage leave and cooked in stock
   b) **poule au pot** ⇒ poultry stuffed with a hash, and cooked in stock

Farçi au pot -[Poitou]-
- **courant** ⇒ hash of beets, cabbage, lettuce, plus sorrel mixed with streaky bacon, cream and herbs; wrapped in cabbage leaves and cooked in pot au feu
- **au maigre** ⇒ hash of beets, cabbage, lettuce, sorrel, cream and herbs; wrapped in cabbage leaves ... a
- **cuit au pot au feu** ⇒ ... and cooked in pot au feu
- **cuit au gratin** ⇒ ... and cooked au gratin

Farcidure
- **Limousin** ⇒ poached small balls of hash
- **Guéret** ⇒ poached small balls of buckwheat flour, plus a hash of sorrel, beets and cabbage
- **Poule sans os** ⇒ fried small balls of wheat flour, pork fat, and chopped sorrel
- **avec petit salé** ⇒ boiled small balls of wheat flour, salt pork, and chopped sorrel
- **aux pommes de terre** ⇒ poached small balls of mashed potatoes, herbs, garlic, onions, and lardoons

Farçon
- **dauphiné** ⇒ large saveloy
- **savoie** ⇒ dish of mashed potatoes mixed with eggs, herbs, sugar, milk and spice; then browned

Farée
- **chou farçi** ⇒ cabbage stuffed with pork fat
- **à l'oseille** ⇒ balls of cabbage stuffed with sorrel, salt pork, and crumbs

Farfalli ⇒ pasta for cooking

Farigoule -*[serpolet, thym]*- ⇒ wild thyme

Farigoulette -*[serpolet]*- ⇒ wild thyme

Farinade -*[Corse]*- ⇒ chestnut porridge served with cheese, goat's milk or chips

Farine ⇒ flour < *uncountable* >

Farine complète ⇒ wholewheat-flour or wholemeal-flour < *tous uncountable* >

Farine d'avoine ⇒ oatmeal

Farine de blé ⇒ wheat-flour < *uncountable* >

Farine de maïs ⇒ cornflour < *uncountable* >

Farine de sarrasin ⇒ buckwheat-flour < *uncountable* >

Farine de seigle ⇒ rye-flour < *uncountable* >

Farine de son ⇒ bran-flour < *uncountable* >

Farinette ⇒ pancake of flour and eggs < *autres noms. omelette enfarinée, pachade, farinade* >

Farineuse ⇒ farinaceous or starchy < *v.t adjectif* >

Farineux ⇒ farinaceous or starchy < *v.t adjectif* >

Farineux -*[légumes]*- ⇒ farinaceous vegetables

Fariné ⇒ floured or floured coated < *v.t adjectif* >

Farofa -*[feijoada]*- ⇒ grilled cassava flour with lardoons

Farot -*[vin]*- ⇒ Sicilian wine

Farsu magru -*[Sicile, Sardaigne]*- ⇒ rolled beef or veal meat, stuffed with a mixing of hard boiled eggs, aromatics and spices

Fassum ⇒ cabbage stuffed with rice, bacon, sausage-meat, beetroot leaves and onions

Fatanyeros -*[Hongrie]*- ⇒ grilling with raw vegetables

Faubonne ⇒ soup thickened of bean purée, consommé, julienne and chervil

Faugères -*[Côteaux du Languedoc]*- ⇒ quality wine from Languedoc

Fausse palourde -*[ou Lavignon]*- ⇒ false clam

Fausse soupe à la tortue ⇒ mock turtle soup

Fausse boutargue -*[cabillaud]*- ⇒ fresh cod

Fauve de Bourgogne -*[lapin]*- ⇒ breed of rabbit

Faux anis -*[carvi]*- ⇒ caraway

Faux éperlan ⇒ like sea smelt

Faux-filet à plat *(Prêt à trancher ...)* -*[boeuf]*- ⇒ striploin « standard »

Faux-filet à plat raccourci *(Prêt à trancher ...)* -*[boeuf]*- ⇒ striploin « short cut »

Faux-filet avec os, sans côtes et non raccourci -*[boeuf]*- ⇒ one bone sirloin

Faux-filet de veau paré ⇒ short striploin « special trim »

Faux-filet de veau sans os-Lombaires ⇒ short striploin « larder trim »

Faux-filet de veau sans os, raccourci, juste paré ⇒ short striploin
Faux-filet désossé, ficelé -*[boeuf]-* ⇒ sirloin « boned and rolled »
Faux-filet entièrement paré -*[boeuf]-* ⇒ striploin « larder trim »
Faux-filet et filet avec os -*[boeuf]-* ⇒ sirloin
Faux-filet et filet avec os, raccourci -*[boeuf]-* ⇒ sirloin « short cut »
Faux-filet légèrement paré -*[boeuf]-* ⇒ striploin « special trim » or sirloin steaks « special trim »
Faux-filet paré -*[boeuf]-* ⇒ sirloin « boneless-individual »
Faux-filet paré nature, et aplati -*[boeuf]-* ⇒ sirloin « boneless-shelled »
Faux-filet raccourci -*[boeuf]-* ⇒ one bone striploin « short cut »
Faux-filet raccourci, entièrement paré -*[boeuf]-* ⇒ striploin « larder trim »
Faux-filet épaisseur 7 mm -*[boeuf]-* ⇒ minute steaks
Faux-filet ⇒ sirloin steak, uncountable, or back ribs
Faux-filet braisé à la bourgeoise ⇒ sirloin steak studded with bacon, macerated in cognac, white wine, thyme, laurel and spices, then braised with onions, carrots, veal's trotter, tomato purée and stock
Faux-filet rôti ⇒ sirloin steak, boned and roasted
Faux mousseron ⇒ fairy-ring mushroom
Favart -*[apprêt]-*
    1) **garniture pour volaille ou ris de veau** ⇒ ... with a garnish of chicken quenelles, and tartlets filled with a culinary stuffing of boletus in cream; served with poultry velouté added of crayfish paste
    2) **oeufs mollets ou pochés** ⇒ poached eggs, laid on tartlets filled with a culinary stuffing of sweetbread, truffles and mushrooms, thickened of velouté
Favorite *(à la ...)*
    - **Potage** ⇒ cream of asparagus and lettuce soup, added of asparagus tips
    - **Petites pièces de boucherie** ⇒ with a garnish of asparagus tips, foie gras escalopes and the gravy thickened of Madeira
    - **Grosses pièces de boucherie** ⇒ with a garnish of sauté quartered artichoke hearts, celeriac, plus small potatoes sautéed in butter with lardoons
    - **Salade** ⇒ composed salad added of asparagus tips
Favouille ⇒ crab
Fécule ⇒ fecula or starch < *tous uncountable* >
Fedelini-pâtes ⇒ fedelini
Fédora ⇒ ... with a garnish of pastry boats filled with asparagus tips, carrots, turnips, quartered oranges and braised chestnuts
Feijoa ⇒ fruit from South América
Feijoada ⇒ stew of meat, black beans, onions, celery, garlic, pepper and laurel
Fela -*[congre]-* ⇒ conger eel or sea eel
Fenalar -*[Norvège]-* ⇒ roast leg of lamb
Fendant ⇒ swiss white wine
Fenouil ⇒ fennel < *uncountable* >
Fenouil bâtard -*[aneth]-* ⇒ dill
Fenouil braisé au gras ⇒ sauté fennel with rind of pork, onions and sliced carrots
Fenouil cru en salade ⇒ salad of hard boiled eggs, rice, onions, fennel lamellas, quartered tomatoes and french dressing
Fenugrec ⇒ fenugreek
Féouse ⇒ a quiche or flan, filled with a mixing of eggs, cream, and lardoons
Féra -*[lac léman]-* ⇒ Lake Geneva salmon
Ferchuse ⇒ preparation of liver, lungs and heart of pork, cooked in pork-fat, red wine, stock, shallots, garlic, plus sauté potatoes

Fermier -*[beurre]*- ⇒ farmhouse butter
Fermière *(à la ...)*
   1) grosses pièces de boucherie ⇒ ...
     - volailles à la casserole ⇒ poultry in casserole ...
     - petites pièces de boucherie ⇒ ...
     - poissons au four ⇒ baked « nom anglais du poisson » ... served with vegetables braised
       in butter
   2) omelette ⇒ omelette filled with vegetables braised in butter
   3) potage ⇒ soup added of sliced potatoes or haricot beans
Fernet Branca -*[bitter]*- ⇒ bitter drink
Féroce d'avocat ⇒ mashed avocado pear with pimentos and salt cod
Ferval ⇒ ... with a garnish of braised artichoke hearts and potato croquettes studded of ham
Festonner ⇒ to festoon
   - disposer en festons ⇒ make into festoons
Feta ⇒ feta
Fettucce ⇒ fedelini
Fettucine -*[pâtes]*- ⇒ fettucine
Feu de bois ⇒ wood fire
Feuille de Dreux ⇒ cow's milk cheese wrapped in chestnut leaves
Feuille de navets ⇒ turnip tops
Feuilletage ⇒ method for preparing puff pastry
Feuilleté ⇒ first course of puff-pastry filled with ...
   - fromage ⇒ cheese
   - jambon ⇒ ham
   - fruits de mer ⇒ seafood
Feuilleté de poisson ⇒ fish in puff-pastry
Feuilletés au Roquefort ⇒ puff-pastry filled with a mixing of Roquefort cheese, soft white cheese,
     cream, herbs, pepper and eggs; then baked
Feuilletés au crabe ⇒ puff-pastry filled with crab cooked in a sauce of carrot, onion, shallot, leek,
     celery, butter, cognac, white wine, tomato purée, garlic and pepper
Feuilletés au ris de veau ⇒ puff-pastries filled with sauté calf sweetbread; served with a creamy sauce
Feuilletés aux escargots ⇒ puff-pastries stuffed with a garnish of snails cooked in champagne and
     flamed in whisky, then added of cream
Feuilletés aux pommes à la normande ⇒ apples cooked in butter and sugar; served in puff pastry,
     and sprinkled of fried almonds
Feuilletés de coquilles St Jacques ⇒ scallops sautéed in butter, then cooked in shallots, cream,
     mustard, vermouth plus mushrooms; served in puff-pastry, browned in the oven
Feuilleton ⇒ flattened slices of ...
   - veau ⇒ veal ...
   - porc ⇒ pork ... coated with a stuffing, then wrapped in larding and braised; served with ...
   - garniture bourgeoise ⇒ ... a garnish of carrots, onions and lardoons
   - légumes braisés ⇒ braised ...
   - céleri ⇒ celery
   - endives ⇒ chicory
   - laitues ⇒ lettuce
Feuilleton de veau à l'ancienne ⇒ layers of larding, forcemeat of pork and mushrooms, plus sliced
     cushion of veal; cooked with strips from rind of pork, onions, carrots, white wine and
     stock

Feuilleton de veau « L' Echelle » ⇒ veal fillet incised in sheets and filled with a stuffing of mushrooms, ham, truffle plus chopped vegetables, then thickened with egg; braised in butter and garnished with browned potatoes, braised lettuce, plus the gravy added of Madeira

Fève ⇒ shell bean or broad bean

Fèves au lard ⇒ pork and beans

Fèves fraîches à la sarriette ⇒ broad beans boiled with savory, then sautéed in butter and cream

Fiadone ⇒ Corsican tartlet made of eggs, sugar, ewe cheese and lemon peel

Fiasque ⇒ flask or bottle

Ficelle -[pain]- ⇒ stick of bread

Ficelle -[lien]- ⇒ string or thread or twine

Ficelle picarde ⇒ pancakes filled with ham and mushrooms, plus cream and cheese; covered of cream and grated gruyère, then browned

Fiéla -[congre]- ⇒ conger eel or sea eel

Fifth -[bouteille]- ⇒ bottle of 75, 72 cl

Figari -[vin]- ⇒ Corsican wine

Figatelli ⇒ Corsican smoked sausage of pork meat, heart and kidney; flavoured with garlic, laurel and white wine

Figue ⇒ fig

Figue cake -[kaki]- ⇒ persimmon fruit

Figue de barbarie ⇒ prickly pear

Figue de mer -[violet]- ⇒ Mediterranean crustacean

Figues -[saucisson de]- ⇒ fig paste shaped in dry sausage

Figues a la mousse de framboise ⇒ fresh figs covered with whipped cream and raspberries, then chilled

Figues au vin rouge ⇒ figs in red wine

Figues fraîches au jambon cru ⇒ fresh figs served with raw ham

Figuette ⇒ drink based on dried figs and juniper berries

Filet -[quantité de liquide]- ⇒ a drop of ...

Filet -[viande; poisson]- ⇒ fillet

Filet américain -[Belgique]- ⇒ tartar steak

Filet d'agneau ⇒ fillet steak of lamb

Filet d'agneau à la Condé ⇒ lamb fillet studded with gherkins and anchovies, covered with a hash of mushrooms added of capers and aromatics; then roasted

Filets d'anchois à la Portugaise ⇒ anchovy fillets laid on tomatoes cooked in their own liquid; decorated with capers, parsley and slices of lemon, then lightly sprinkled with olive oil

Filets d'anchois à la Silésienne ⇒ mashed herring soft roes, topped with anchovy fillets; served with a salad of potatoes, rennet apples and diced beetroots, then sprinkled of french dressing and chopped parsley

Filets d'anchois à la Suédoise ⇒ anchovy fillets laid on rennet apples and diced beetroots, garnished with hard boiled eggs and sprinkled of french dressing

Filets d'anchois à la tartare ⇒ anchovy fillets covered of composed butter with grated horse-radish, laid on slices of beetroot and sprinkled of crushed hard boiled egg; sprinkled with french dressing

Filets d'anchois aux œufs durs ⇒ anchovy fillets garnished with black olives, hard boiled eggs, capers and olive oil

Filets d'anchois Talleyrand ⇒ anchovy fillets covered with mashed tunny and mayonnaise, laid on slices of hard boiled eggs plus lettuce chiffonade; decorated with lemon and beetroots, sprinkled of french dressing

Filets de bar ⇒ fried sea-bass fillets

- variantes à la meunière, à la portugaise, ou même recettes que pour filets de dorade, barbue ou sole ⇒ sea-bass fillets ...

Filets de bar au vert de laitue ⇒ sea bass fillets wrapped in lettuce leaves, then cooked on a layer of shallots and lettuce hearts, in white wine and vermouth; served with the cooking juice boiled away, and thickened of cream plus egg yolk

Filets de barbue à l'anglaise ⇒ brill fillets coated with crumbs and browned in butter; covered with parsley butter and slices of lemon

Filets de barbue à la créole ⇒ brill fillets floured and peppered, then fried in oil, covered with a hash of garlic, parsley and oil flavoured of aromatics; served with browned tomatoes stuffed of rice and diced capsicums

Filets de barbue à la duxelles ⇒ brill fillets fried in oil and butter, laid on chopped mushrooms thickened of tomato sauce, sprinkled of the cooking juice and decorated with lemon

Filets de barbue à la Toulonnaise ⇒ brill fillets fried in oil, and laid on tomatoes cooked in their own liquid, flavoured with garlic; plus diced aubergines sautéed in oil

Filets de barbue Véron ⇒ brill fillets coated with butter and crumbs, sprinkled of melted butter and grilled; served with a creamy sauce

Filet de boeuf ⇒ roast of beef

Filet de boeuf -[tranches grillées]- ⇒ slices of beef fillet, oiled and peppered, sprinkled of herbs, then grilled and served with parsley butter

Filet de boeuf -[tranches poêlées]- ⇒ slices of beef fillet fried in butter and served with the gravy added of Madeira

Filet de bœuf à la matignon ⇒ beef fillet studded with pickled oxtongue and truffle, covered with vegetables cooked in their own liquid, then larded and braised with Madeira in the oven; served with a garnish of artichoke hearts and the cooking juice

Filet de boeuf à la périgourdine ⇒ beef fillet studded with truffle, larded and braised in stock with Madeira; served with sauté foie gras escalopes studded of truffle, plus the cooking juice

Filet de boeuf coupé en long ⇒ long beef fillet

Filet de boeuf en brioche ⇒ cooked beef fillet, wrapped in brioche paste, then baked; served with a sauce of Madeira and chopped truffles

Filet de boeuf Frascati ⇒ roasted beef fillet; served with mushrooms and asparagus tips braised in butter, truffle in julienne added of Madeira, sauté foie gras escalopes, plus sauce with port

Filet de boeuf froid à la niçoise ⇒ chilled roasted beef fillet, garnished with tomatoes marinated in olive oil, and stuffed of truffles, plus artichoke hearts with asparagus tips; plus a bush-shaped of black olives, anchovies and jelly

Filet de boeuf froid à la russe ⇒ chilled roasted beef fillet, garnished with halved hard boiled eggs, and stuffed artichoke hearts filled with vegetables in mayonnaise, plus jelly

Filet de boeuf froid en gelée

    1) entier ⇒ chilled roasted beef fillet, covered with jelly flavoured of Madeira, or port, or xeres; served with flavoured mayonnaise and vegetables in any combination

    2) en tranches ⇒ chilled slices of roasted beef fillet, covered with jelly flavoured of Madeira, or port, or xeres; served with flavoured mayonnaise and vegetables in any combination

Filet de boeuf Oskar ⇒ beef fillet served with asparagus and béarnaise sauce

Filet de boeuf plus faux-filet avec os, sans côtes premières ⇒ sirloin « chump end »

Filet de boeuf Prince Albert ⇒ split beef fillet, filled with a whole foie gras macerated in cognac and studded of truffle, then braised in stock, aromatics, liver's marinade and port; served with a garnish of truffles braised in butter or poached in Madeira

Filet de bœuf rôti à la broche ⇒ beef fillet coated with butter and peppered; then roasted on a skewer

Filet de boeuf rôti au four ⇒ buttered beef fillet, roasted in the oven and served with the gravy

Filet de boeuf sans tête sur lombaire ⇒ loin fillet

Filets de cabillaud au concombre ⇒ fresh cod fillets poached in white wine and fish sauce; served with the cooking juice thickened of cream, tomato and cucumber

Filets de canard sauvage à la bigarade ⇒ wild duck legs moistened in pepper, parsley, thyme, shallots, lemon juice and oil, then roasted on a skewer; served in fillets with butter and a sauce added of orange peel

Filet de congre Waldorf ⇒ grilled marinated conger fillets, sprinkled with melted butter; served with little baked potatoes, plus an American mayonnaise

Filets de daurade à la julienne de légumes ⇒ sea bream fillets laid on a julienne added of leek, celery, fennel and turnips, then sprinkled of cream plus lemon juice and cooked in the oven

Filets de faisan au jus d'orange ⇒ sautéed pheasant fillets in butter with parsley, chervil and chive; covered with a sauce made of pheasant offal and meat, veal stock, champagne and orange juice

Filets de hareng à la russe ⇒ herring fillets alternated with sliced boiled potatoes, and sprinkled of french dressing flavoured with herbs

Filets de harengs à la livonienne ⇒ diced smoked herring fillets, sliced boiled potatoes and apple lamellas, sprinkled with french dressing, chervil and fennel

Filets de harengs frits à l'anglaise ⇒ herring fillets coated with breadcrumbs and fried; served with parsley butter

Filets de harengs marinés à l'huile ⇒ smoked herring fillets macerated in onion, carrot, coriander, thyme and peanut oil

Filet de julienne à la fondue de poireaux ⇒ ling fillet with leeks stewed in their own liquid

Filets de lièvre à la lucullus ⇒ hare fillets studded of oxtongue and roasted; served laid on pastry boats with a garnish of foie gras, truffle and sauce

Filets de lièvre rôtis ⇒ hare fillets baked in butter, laid on fried sippets and covered with a sauce

Filets de lotte à l'anglaise ⇒ monkfish fillets coated with flour, egg and crumbs, then fried; served with parsley butter

Filets de lotte à la crème et aux poireaux ⇒ monkfish fillets cooked with a hash of leek celery, turnips, garlic and white wine; served with the cooking sauce thickened of cream and butter

Filets de lotte braisés au vin blanc ⇒ monkfish fillets braised with butter and white wine in the oven; then covered of cream and served with spinach or broccoli purée

Filets de maquereau à la dijonnaise ⇒ mackerel fillets coated of mustard and baked with a sauce of onions, flour, fish stock and white wine; served with slices of lemon and parsley

Filets de maquereau à la lyonnaise ⇒ mackerel fillets baked with onions and white wine

Filets de maquereau à la piémontaise ⇒ mackerel fillets coated with crumbs and cooked in butter; served with risotto, quartered lemons and tomatoes cooked in their own liquid

Filets de maquereau au vin blanc ⇒ mackerel fillets cooked in the oven with white wine and stock; served covered with the cooking juice thickened of cream

Filet mignon ⇒ fillet mignon

Filets mignons au vin rouge ⇒ diced mutton fillets fried in butter, plus mushrooms sautéed in the gravy; served warmed up again in a sauce made of the cooking juice, red wine, stock and butter

Filets mignons de boeuf en chevreuil ⇒ small steaks of beef studded with pork fat, marinated and sautéed in oil; served with a purée and a sauce

Filets mignons de chevreuil ⇒ small steaks of roebuck, garnished variously with a purée or a compote

Filets mignons de veau au citron ⇒ small steaks of veal fried in butter; covered with the gravy added of butter, plus sugar cooked in white wine and lemon peel

Filets mignons de veau aux champignons ⇒ small steaks of veal fried in butter; served with mushrooms and sauté potatoes

Filets mignons grillés ⇒ small steaks of beef coated with melted butter and crumbs, then grilled; served with parsley butter or a sauce

Filets mignons poêlés ⇒ small steaks of beef fried in butter

Filets de morue maître d'hotel ⇒ sliced salt cod fillets, coated with crumbs and cooked in butter, covered with parsley butter; served with boiled potatoes

Filet de mouton ⇒ fillet steak of mutton

Filet de mouton double avec selle et rognons ⇒ saddle of lamb

Filet de mouton double avec selle, paré ⇒ short saddle of lamb « oven prepared »

Filet de mouton double avec selle, paré, désossé et ficelé ⇒ saddle of lamb « boneless » ½ ou ½ saddle of lamb « boned and rolled »

Filet de mouton double avec selle, peau et rognons enlevés ⇒ saddle of lamb « oven prepared »

Filet de mouton double décoré ⇒ dressed saddle of lamb

Filet de mouton double paré et dégraissé ⇒ short saddle of lamb « boned and rolled »

Filet de mouton double paré, dégraissé, ficelé (*Prêt à cuire ...)* ⇒ short saddle of lamb « boneless »

Filet de mouton double sans selle, non paré ⇒ short saddle of lamb

Filet de poisson (*terme général ...)* ⇒ fish fillet ou nom anglais du poisson plus « fillet » < *exemple conger eel fillet >*

Filets de poisson au cidre ⇒ fish fillets poached in a court-bouillon of cider, covered with the stock boiled down, and thickened of cream; then glazed in the oven

Filets de poisson en papillotes ⇒ buttered paper covered with cream, plus fish fillet sprinkled of lemon juice; cooked in the oven

Filet de porc ⇒ pork fillet or fillet of pork or tenderloin fillet

Filet de porc entier ⇒ fillet « tenderloin »

Filets de rascasse à l'antillaise ⇒ sliced scorpion fish fillets browned in oil; served with tomato pulp, onions, pepper, capsicum and sliced potatoes cooked in oil, plus rice

Filets de rouget Girardet ⇒ fried red gurnard fillets, served laid on a sauce of shallots, butter, rosemary, white wine, cream and lemon juice

Filets de saint pierre Palais Royal ⇒ crushed potatoes laid on a buttered dish, topped with john dory fillets poached in a mixing of wine, stock and lemon juice; then browned in the oven

Filets de saint pierre au citron ⇒ diced john dory fillets baked on buttered paper with sliced courgettes, lemon and pepper

Filets de saint pierre au melon ⇒ sauté john dory fillets; served with a julienne sautéed in butter, plus slices of melon cooked in butter

Filets de saint pierre au poivron rouge ⇒ john dory fillets braised in stock, covered with the cooking juice boiled down and added of sauce hollandaise; served with four spoons of mashed capsicum

Filets de saint pierre soufflés ⇒ steamed john dory fillets, baked with whipped white of eggs added of mustard

Filets de sandre au chou ⇒ pike perch fillets poached in a court-bouillon with aromatics and laid on boiled cabbage leaves; covered with sauce, onions and chive

Filets de saumon en aiguillettes ⇒ fried thin slices of salmon

Filets de saumon en bellevue ⇒ salmon fillets cooked in jelly; served decorated with the jelly

Filets de saumon sauce tomate (*Orly de ...)* ⇒ salmon fillets seasoned of shallots, nutmeg, lemon juice, olive oil, thyme and laurel, then coated of egg and fried; served with tomato sauce

Filet de saxe ⇒ pork fillet salted and smoked

Filet de sole ⇒ sole fillet

Filets de sole à l'anglaise ⇒ sole fillets coated with crumbs and cooked in butter; served with potatoes or other vegetables

Filets de sole à la Daumont ⇒ sole fillets garnished with a forcemeat of whiting and crayfishes, poached in fish stock, then topped of braised mushroom covered with a culinary stuffing of crayfish tails; plus a creamy sauce of fish stock and butter

Filets de sole à la bordelaise ⇒ sole fillets poached in butter, chopped onions, carrots and Bordeaux wine; covered with the cooking juice added of butter and served with braised mushrooms plus onions

Filets de sole à la cancalaise ⇒ sole fillets poached in fish stock and laid in turban, topped with poached oysters; served with decorticated crayfish tails

Filets de sole à la cantonnaise ⇒ sole fillets sprinkled of coriander, cinnamon, spices, nutmeg and chopped onion, then steamed garnished of ginger lamellas; served with a sauce based on capsicums, mushrooms, lardoons, ham, crayfish tails, crab, eggs, soya sauce, tomato purée and stock

Filets de sole à la panetière ⇒ loaf hollowed out, buttered and browned; filled with sole fillets cooked in butter, plus a ragout of mushrooms in cream

Filets de sole à la riche ⇒ sole fillets poached in stock, served with a culinary stuffing of lobster; covered with a creamy sauce added of lobster butter, truffle, cayenne pepper and cognac

Filets de sole à la vapeur au coulis de tomate ⇒ sole fillets steamed on a layer of basil; served with a sauce of browned shallots, poached egg, mustard, lemon juice, pepper, basil, olive oil, diced tomatoes and chervil

Filets de sole à la vénitienne ⇒ sole fillets poached in stock and white wine; served with fried sippets, plus the cooking juice added of Venetian sauce

Filets de sole au Chambertin ⇒ sole fillets baked on a layer of butter, diced carrots, chopped onions, thyme, laurel, mushrooms and Chambertin; served with the mushrooms and the cooking juice

Filets de sole au basilic ⇒ sole fillets baked on a layer of basil, shallots, olive oil and white wine; served with the cooking juice added of butter and lemon juice

Filets de sole au champagne ⇒ sole fillets laid on butter, shallots, and braised vegetables, moistened of fish stock and champagne, then baked; covered with the cooking juice, added of cream and butter

Filets de sole au gratin ⇒ sole fillets laid on butter and chopped mushrooms, surrounded of mushrooms; covered with a sauce of mushrooms, white wine and tomato sauce, plus fish stock, crumbs and melted butter, then baked

Filets de sole au vermouth ⇒ sole fillets poached in stock and vermouth, plus mushrooms cooked in butter; covered with a sauce based on the cooking juices thickened of cream and egg-yolks

Filets de sole aux champignons ⇒ sole fillets poached in white wine stock with mushrooms; covered with the cooking stock added of cream and boiled down, then thickened of butter

Filets de sole aux nouilles ⇒ noodles thickened of cream, topped of sole fillets poached in stock with white wine, covered of sauce hollandaise and cream; then glazed

Filets de sole aux pommes ⇒ sole fillets poached in green pepper, fish stock, cream and sliced apples; served with the cooking juice

Filets de sole Cubat ⇒ sole fillets poached in mushroom stock, browned in the oven with chopped mushrooms, béchamel sauce added of egg-yolks and gruyère, plus truffle lamellas

Filets de sole Drouant ⇒ sole fillets braised with butter, chopped shallots, white wine and mussel stock; covered with the cooking juice boiled down and added of butter, then served with shelled mussels, plus decorticated crayfishes

Filets de sole Marco Polo ⇒ sole fillets poached in butter, shallot, tomato and champagne; served with a sauce of lobster flamed in cognac, white wine, butter, egg-yolks and cream

Filets de sole Marguery ⇒ sole fillets poached in fish stock added of white wine, onion, laurel and parsley; served with shelled mussels and decorticated shrimp tails, covered with the cooking juice added of egg-yolks, butter and pepper, plus shaped puff-pastries

Filets de sole Mornay ⇒ poached sole fillets covered with béchamel sauce added of egg-yolks and gruyère, sprinkled of grated parmesan and melted butter, then browned

Filets de sole Nantua ⇒ poached sole fillets in stock with white wine, served with a ragout of crayfish tails; covered with a sauce of mashed crayfishes, cognac and cayenne-pepper

Filets de sole Robert Courtine ⇒ sole fillets covered with a forcemeat of fish, shallots and sour cream, then folded and steamed on seaweed; served with a sauce of shallots, white wine, cream, butter and caviar, plus a garnish of ...

- **la garniture est concombres** ⇒ ... cucumbers thickened with cream

- **crêpes** ⇒ ... pancakes of potatoes, flour, cream and eggs

Filets de sole crécy ⇒ sole fillets poached in fish stock, covered with the stock boiled down and added of béchamel sauce, plus mashed carrots; served with braised carrots

Filets de sole frits en goujons ⇒ lamellas of sole fillets, floured and fried; served in bush with fried parsley and cut lemons

Filets de sole grillés ⇒ sole fillets brushed with oil and grilled; served with slices of lemon and melted butter

Filets de sole homardine ⇒ elaborated dish of sole fillets poached in fish stock added of Chablis wine, laid on mushrooms, covered with slices of lobster flamed in cognac, then baked; served with a sauce hollandaise added of creamy lobster's meat with kneaded butter, fish stock and cream

Filets de sole joinville ⇒ sole fillets poached in a stock added of mushrooms, served laid on turban with a garnish of mushrooms in butter, diced truffle and shrimps; covered with a creamy sauce added of shrimp butter

Filets de sole princesse ⇒ poached sole fillets, served in pastry boats with asparagus tips and creamy sauce

Filets de sole St Germain ⇒ sole fillets coated with melted butter and crumbs, then grilled; served with little potato balls browned in butter, plus béarnaise sauce

Filets de sole walewska ⇒ sole fillets poached in stock, topped with a slice of cooked lobster and truffle; covered with béchamel sauce added of egg-yolks, and gruyère, plus lobster butter, then glazed in the oven

Filets de turbot à la fondue de poireaux et à la moelle ⇒ steamed turbot fillets served with leeks cooked in butter, tomatoes cooked in their own liquid and slices of bone-marrow; covered with a sauce of shallot, red wine, gravy and butter

Filet de veau ⇒ veal fillet or fillet of veal

Filet de veau complet avec os et gras, rognons enlevés ⇒ loin of veal « ex kidney »

Filet de veau double, avec os, dégraissé, rognons enlevés ⇒ saddle of veal « trimmed »

Filet de veau double, rognons enlevés ⇒ saddle of veal « ex kidney »

Filet de veau nature avec gras et rognons ⇒ saddle of veal

Filets de volailles ⇒ white meat fillet

Filet double avec selle et rognons -[mouton]- ⇒ saddle of lamb

Filet double avec selle, paré -[mouton]- ⇒ short saddle of lamb « oven prepared »

Filet double avec selle, paré, désossé et ficelé -[mouton]- ⇒ saddle of lamb « boneless » ½ ou ½ saddle of lamb « boned and rolled »

Filet double avec selle, peau et rognons enlevés -[mouton]- ⇒ saddle of lamb « oven prepared »

Filet double décoré -[mouton]- ⇒ dressed saddle of lamb

Filet double paré et dégraissé -[mouton]- ⇒ short saddle of lamb « boned and rolled »

Filet double paré, dégraissé, ficelé (Prêt à cuire ...) -[mouton]- ⇒ short saddle of lamb « boneless »

Filet double sans selle, non paré -[mouton]- ⇒ short saddle of lamb

Filet entier non paré -[boeuf]- ⇒ long fillet « standard »

Filet entièrement paré -[boeuf]- ⇒ rib steaks « bone in » or long fillet « larder trim »

Filet légèrement paré -[boeuf]- ⇒ long fillet « special trim »

Filet plus faux-filet avec os, sans côtes premières -*[boeuf]*- ⇒ sirloin « chump end »

Filet sans tête sur lombaire -*[boeuf]*- ⇒ loin fillet

Filets mignons au vin rouge ⇒ diced mutton fillets fried in butter, plus mushrooms sautéed in the gravy; served warmed up again in a sauce made of the cooking juice, red wine, stock and butter

Filets mignons de boeuf en chevreuil ⇒ small steaks of beef studded with pork fat, marinated and sautéed in oil; served with a purée and a sauce

Filets mignons de chevreuil ⇒ small steaks of roebuck, garnished variously with a purée or a compote

Filets mignons de veau au citron ⇒ small steaks of veal fried in butter; covered with the gravy added of butter, plus sugar cooked in white wine and lemon peel

Filets mignons de veau aux champignons ⇒ small steaks of veal fried in butter; served with mushrooms and sauté potatoes

Filets mignons grillés ⇒ small steaks of beef coated with melted butter and crumbs, then grilled; served with parsley butter or a sauce

Filets mignons poêlés ⇒ small steaks of beef fried in butter

Fillette *(bouteille ...)* ⇒ bottle of 37, 5 cl

Fin de Bagnols -*[haricot vert]*- ⇒ french bean

Fin de Meaux -*[cornichon]*- ⇒ gherkin

Financier

    1) **petit** ⇒ small cake rectangular or oval shaped, enriched with almond powder and white of eggs

    2) **grand** ⇒ large cake decorated with sliced almonds and preserved fruits

Financiers aux amandes ⇒ small cakes made with flour, almond powder, sugar, vanilla sugar, butter and white of eggs; sometimes covered of fondant flavoured with kirsch or chocolate

Financière *(à la ...)*

    1) **pièces de boucherie** ⇒ ... served ...

        - **ris de veau** ⇒ calf sweetbread served ...

        - **volailles poêlées** ⇒ fried poultry served ...

        - **croûtes** ⇒ pastry cases filled ...

        - **timbales** ⇒ timbales filled ...

        - **bouchées** ⇒ patties filled ...

        - **vol au vent** ⇒ vol-au vent-filled ... with a ragout of cockscombs, poultry quenelles, chopped mushrooms, plus a culinary stuffing of truffles in Madeira

    2) **attereaux à la financière**

        - **viande** ⇒ pieces of « nom anglais de la viande » coated with ...

        - **poisson** ⇒ pieces of « nom anglais du poisson » coated with ...

        - **légumes** ⇒ pieces of « nom anglais des légumes » coated with ... a ragout of cockscombs, chopped mushrooms, plus a culinary stuffing of truffles in Madeira; fried on a skewer

Financière -*[sauce]*- ⇒ Madeira sauce added of truffle extract

Finanhaddock ⇒ finnan haddock

Fine -*[eau de vie]*- ⇒ liqueur brandy or fine

Fine champagne ⇒ high quality of cognac

Fine de claire ⇒ prairie oyster

Fines herbes ⇒ chopped herbs or herbs

Finnan haddock ⇒ finnan haddock

Fino -*[xérès]*- ⇒ fino

Fiore sardo -*[Sicile]*- ⇒ Sicilian grated ewe cheese

Fiorentina -*[alla]*- ⇒ ...; served with spinach, and béchamel sauce added of egg-yolks and grated gruyère

Fiouse ⇒ a quiche or flan, filled with a mixing of eggs, cream, and lardoons

Fish and chips -*[GB]*- ⇒ fish and chips
Fish ball (*croquettes ...*) -*[morue]*- ⇒ salt cod fish balls or fish balls
Fistuline hépatique -*[langue de boeuf « champignon »]*- ⇒ beefsteak fungus or oak fungus
Fitou ⇒ red wine from Languedoc area
Fix -*[cocktail long drinks]*- ⇒ soda water
Fixe -*[menu]*- ⇒ fixed price
Fixin -*[vin]*- ⇒ Burgundy red wine from Côtes de Nuits
Fizz -*[cocktail long drinks]*- ⇒ Schweppes
Flageolet ⇒ flageolet bean or kidney bean
Flamande (*à la ...*)
> a) **garniture pour grosses pièces de viande, oie braisée, petites pièces de boucherie** ⇒ ...
> with a garnish of stuffed cabbage balls, carrots, turnips, boiled potatoes and slices of
> dry sausage
> b) **purée de choux de Bruxelles** ⇒ mashed brussels-sprouts and potatoes
> c) **endives crues dans une salade composée** ⇒ composed salad added of chicory
> d) **endives cuites en chiffonnade pour garnir une omelette servie avec de la sauce**
> **crème** ⇒ omelette filled with boiled chicory; served with béchamel sauce added of
> cream
> e) **apprêt d'asperges à l'œuf dur** ⇒ dish of asparagus and hard boiled egg
Flamber des plumes de volaille ⇒ to singe
Flambé ⇒ flamed < *v.t adjectif* >
Flambée ⇒ flamed with spirit
Flamboyant -*[radis]*- ⇒ radish
Flamenca (*à la ...*) -*[Espagne]*- ⇒ eggs baked on a layer of hashed meat and spiced vegetables;
> garnished with beans, asparagus and pimentos
Flameri ⇒ porridge of semolina in white wine, added of sugar and eggs, then baked in a mould; served
> coated of mashed red fruits
Flamiche ou Flamique
> - **flamiche aux légumes** ⇒ tart filled with a mixing of braised vegetables, and egg-yolks
> - **flamiche aux poireaux ou flamiche à porions** ⇒ tart filled with a mixing of braised leeks,
> and egg-yolks
> - **flamiche à la citrouille et onions** ⇒ tart filled with a mixing of braised pumpkin onions, and
> egg-yolks
> - **flamiche au fromage** ⇒ tart filled with cheese and eggs
> - **flamiche à l'ancienne** ⇒ puff-pastry flat cake added of cheese and butter
Flamiche aux poireaux ⇒ short pastry laid in pie-dish, covered with white of leeks and egg-yolks,
> then baked
Flammenküche
> - **général** ⇒ rectangular gateau garnished with browned onions and cream, sprinkled of lardoons
> and rape oil, then baked
> - **avec fromage blanc** ⇒ rectangular gateau garnished with a mixing of soft white cheese, cream,
> egg-yolks, plus onions and lardoons; then baked
Flamri ⇒ porridge of semolina in white wine, added of sugar and eggs, then baked in a mould; served
> coated of mashed red fruits
Flamusse aux pommes ⇒ gateau made with sliced apples and a dough of flour, granulated sugar, eggs
> and milk; then baked in a pie-dish
Flan ⇒ flan
Flan -*[crème caramel]*- ⇒ caramel custard

Flan à la bordelaise ⇒ culinary stuffing of beef bone-marrow and ham, thickened of Sauternes wine, laid on a pastry case with boletus; covered with crumbs and melted butter, then browned

Flan à la florentine ⇒ pastry case filled with chopped spinach braised in butter plus Mornay sauce, sprinkled of grated cheese and melted butter, then browned

Flan au lait ⇒ pastry case filled with a custard of flour, granulated sugar, eggs, butter, vanilla sugar and milk; then baked

Flan aux carottes ⇒ pastry case filled with slices of carrots, then baked

Flan aux cerises ⇒ pastry case filled with cherries, plus a preparation of milk, vanilla, cream, eggs and sugar, then baked

Flan aux courges ⇒ flan with gourds

Flan aux fruits de mer ⇒ pastry case filled with a ragout of sea-food, thickened of creamy sauce; sprinkled with crumbs and melted butter, then browned

Flan aux mirabelles ⇒ plums covered with a dough made of eggs, sugar, milk, flour and melted butter, then baked

Flan aux pommes Grimaldi ⇒ pastry case filled with rice cooked in milk added of preserved fruits, chopped orange peel, curaçao and butter; topped with quartered apples in syrup and glazed in the oven

Flan Brillat-Savarin ⇒ pastry case filled with scrambled eggs, sliced truffles in butter, sprinkled of grated parmesan and melted butter, then browned

Flan de cerises à la danoise ⇒ short pastry laid on a pie-dish, filled with cherries macerated in sugar and cinnamon, topped with a mixing of sugar, butter, almond powder and eggs, then baked; served covered with redcurrant jelly

Flan de foie de canard aux huîtres et aux écrevises ⇒ pastry case filled with a purée of duck foie gras, milk, eggs and beef bone-marrow, then baked; served with poached oysters and crayfishes, covered with butter melted in Monbazillac white wine

Flan de fromage ⇒ pastry case filled with a custard of cream, butter, seasoning, flour, eggs and grated cheese, then baked

Flan de poireaux à la berrichonne ⇒ tart filled with chopped ham and leeks in cream

Flan de poireaux au fromage ⇒ pastry case covered of béchamel sauce added of egg-yolks and gruyère, filled with white of leeks braised in butter, sprinkled of grated parmesan and butter, then browned

Flan de volaille Chavette ⇒ pastry case filled with escalopes of poultry livers and mushrooms sautéed in butter, added of Madeira, béchamel sauce and cream; topped with scrambled eggs mixed with grated parmesan and butter, then browned

Flan ou gâteau à la bressane ⇒ flan or gateau made of poultry livers

Flan meringué au citron ⇒ pastry case filled with a preparation of flour, sugar, milk, eggs, lemon peel and juice; then covered with whipped white of eggs and browned

Flan Sagan ⇒ pastry case filled successively with a culinary stuffing of mushrooms, truffle, cream and curry, plus some escalopes of calf brain sautéed in butter and béchamel sauce added of egg-yolks, gruyère, and curry; sprinkled with grated cheese and butter, then browned

Flanc de boeuf ⇒ side of beef

Flanc de mouton roulé ⇒ boneless rolled side of mutton

Flanchet
- **général** ⇒ flank
- **boeuf** ⇒ flank of beef or forerib

Flanchet de veau ⇒ flank of veal

Flanchet désossé *(boeuf ...)* ⇒ forerib boneless

Flandre ⇒ certains plats traduits

1) **soupes flamandres**
   a) soupe à la biére
   b) soupe verte
   c) soupe de betterave rouge
2) **poissons**
   a) craquelots de Dunkerque
   b) le wam (poisson séché)
   c) les maquereaux
   d) les cabillauds à la flamande
   e) la salade de harengs saurs
   f) les anguilles à la bière
3) **viandes**
   a) langues fumées de valenciennes
   b) andouillettes de Cambrai et d'Armentières
   c) hochepot
   d) carbonades
   e) potjevfleisch
   f) lapin à la flamande
   g) coq à la bière
   h) poule au blanc
4) **légumes**
   a) flamiches
   b) chou rouge à la lilloise
   c) chou rouge à la flamande
5) **les fromages**
   a) bergues
   b) cœur d'Arras
   c) dauphin
   d) maroilles
6) **omelettes**
   a) omelette ou flamiche au maroilles
   b) goyère de valenciennes
7) **pâtisseries**
   a) les pâtés de pommes d'Avesnes
   b) tarte aux prunes rouges
   c) craquelins de Roubaix
   d) carrés de lannoy
   e) les galopins (pain brioché trempé dans du lait, mélangé à des œufs et frit à la poêle
   f) les couques
   g) les bêtisses de cambrai
8) **boissons**
   - **bière**
   - **alcool de betterave parfumé au genièvre**
   - **alcool de céréales parfumé au genièvre**

Flaugnarde ⇒ clafoutis with apples, or pears, or dried-plums, flavoured of vanilla, cinnamon, lemon-peel, orange blossom and eau de vie

Flaunes ⇒ dough of flour, eggs, grated ewe's cheese and blossom flower; shaped in small discs and baked

Flauzonnes ⇒ dough of flour, eggs, grated ewe's cheese and blossom flower; shaped in small discs and baked

Flaveur ⇒ flavour

Flèche-cuisine ⇒ flitch of bacon

Flet -*[poisson]*- ⇒ flounder
Flétan ⇒ halibut < *pluriel inchangé* >
Fleur
  - **fleurs de sauge** ⇒ sage flowers
  - **fleurs de thym** ⇒ thyme flowers
  - **fleurs de menthe** ⇒ mint flowers
  - **eau de rose** ⇒ rose water
  - **gelée de roses** ⇒ rose jelly
  - **confiture de roses** ⇒ rose jam
  - **pétales cristallisées** ⇒ crystallized petals
  - **violettes candies** ⇒ candied violets
  - **mimosa** ⇒ mimosa flowers
  - **myosotis** ⇒ Myosotis flowers
  - **primevère** ⇒ primrose flowers
  - **fleurs d'oranger pralinées** ⇒ orange blossoms coated with praline
  - **bourrache** ⇒ infusion of borage
  - **tilleul** ⇒ infusion of lime-tree flowers
Fleur confite -*[Nice]*- ⇒ preserved flowers
Fleur cristallisée ⇒ flower dried and pounded
Fleurs d'acacia ⇒ acacia flowers
Fleurs d'oranger ⇒ orange blossom
Fleur d'oranger *(eau de ...)* ⇒ orange blossom water
Fleurs de lys ⇒ lily flower
Fleurs de courges en beignets ⇒ marrow-flowers steeped in batter and fried
Fleur de la passion -*[fruit de la passion]*- ⇒ passion fruit flower
Fleurette -*[crème]*- ⇒ pasteurized cream
FLeuri -*[pruneau]*- ⇒ dried plum
Fleurie -*[Beaujolais]*- ⇒ Beaujolais red wine
Fleuriste *(à la. ..)*
  - **petites pièces de boucherie sautées** ⇒ sauté ... nom anglais, garnished of small potatoes sautéed in butter with lardoons, braised tomatoes hollowed out and filled with vegetables in julienne
Fleuron ⇒ shaped puff pastry, for decorating purpose
Flion -*[olive de mer]*- ⇒ wedge shell
Flip ⇒ flip
  - **Porto flip** ⇒ cocktail made of port, egg, sugar, nutmeg and aromatics
Floc -*[Ratafia]*- ⇒ ratafia
Floc de gascogne ⇒ aperitif made of fermented must and armagnac
Flocon ⇒ flake
Flocons de maïs ⇒ cornflakes
Flocons d'avoine ⇒ oat flakes
Flognarde ⇒ clafoutis with apples, or pears, or dried-plums, flavoured of vanilla, cinnamon, lemon-peel, orange blossom and eau de vie
Flône
  a) Rouergue ⇒ tartlet garnished with a custard of eggs and ewe whey, flavoured with blossom flower

  b) Languedoc à Lodève
    - **Florentine** *(à la ...)* ⇒ ...; served with spinach, and!béchamel sauce added of egg-yolks and grated gruyère

- **Florian** ⇒ garnish of braised lettuce, browned onions, glazed carrots, plus potatoes shaped in olive and braised in butter
- **Flougnarde** ⇒ clafoutis with apples, or pears, or dried-plums, flavoured of vanilla, cinnamon, lemon-peel, orange blossom and eau de vie

Flowery pekoé -[*thé*]- ⇒ Ceylonese tea

Flûte

- **verre** ⇒ tall champagne glass
- **pain** ⇒ long thin stick of bread

Foglidi musica ⇒ Sicilian bread similar to pancakes

Fogoche du lac balaton ⇒ fish similar to pike perch < *cuisiné grillé ou poché au vin blanc* >

- **grillé** ⇒ kind of grilled pike perch

Foie ⇒ liver

Foie d'agneau ⇒ lamb liver

Foie d'agneau à l'ail ⇒ slices of lamb's liver fried in butter, served with a hash of garlic and vinegar in butter

Foie de boeuf ⇒ ox liver

Foie de porc ⇒ pig liver

Foie de porc à la moutarde ⇒ pork's liver brushed with mustard and sprinkled of chopped garlic, then braised in butter; served with the gravy added of mustard and vinegar

Foies de raie au vinaigre de cidre ⇒ ray livers cooked in a court-bouillon; served with sliced apples fried in butter, then sprinkled of cider vinegar and chives

Foie de veau ⇒ calf liver

Foie de veau à l'anglaise ⇒ sauté calf liver and bacon, sprinkled with parsley, lemon juice and melted butter; served with boiled potatoes

Foie de veau à l'espagnole ⇒ slices of calf liver sautéed in oil, laid on tomatoes braised in olive oil with garlic; garnished with slices of onion and parsley

Foie de veau à la bercy ⇒ grilled slices of calf liver; served with a composed butter added of bone-marrow, shallots, white wine and pepper

Foie de veau à la bordelaise ⇒ sauté slices of calf liver in butter, plus fried slices of ham; covered with a sauce made of brown sauce, bone-marrow, red wine, thyme, laurel, arrow-root and butter

Foie de veau à la bourgeoise ⇒ larded calf liver, braised in red wine and stock; served with sauté mushrooms and onions, covered with the liver gravy boiled down

Foie de veau à la bourguignonne ⇒ sauté slices of calf liver in butter, sprinkled with the gravy added of red wine and stock; served with mushrooms, onions and lardoons cooked in red wine

Foie de veau à la créole ⇒ slices of calf liver, studded with lardoons, macerated in oil, lemon and pepper, then fried in pork fat; served with the gravy added of chopped onions, parsley, crumbs, pepper, tomato purée and white wine

Foie de veau à la lyonnaise ⇒ thin slices of calf liver sautéed in butter; covered with sliced onions cooked in butter and brown sauce, then sprinkled of vinegar and served with french beans flavoured of tomato purée

Foie de veau à la Saulieu ⇒ calf liver marinated in white wine and aromatics, then braised in butter and the marinade added of Madeira; garnished with croustades filled of cockscombs and cock kidneys, then covered with a sauce of Madeira and chopped truffles

Foie de veau au bacon ⇒ sliced calf liver, floured and fried; served with fried slices of bacon and lemon juice

Foie de veau sauté à la florentine ⇒ thin slices of calf liver sautéed in butter, served on a layer of braised spinach; covered with the gravy added of white wine and garnished with sliced onions fried in batter

Foie de volaille ⇒ poultry liver

Foie gras ⇒ foie gras

Foie gras à la financière ⇒ foie gras macerated in spices and high quality cognac, then wrapped in a caul of pork and braised in Madeira; served with a ragout of cockscombs, cocks' kidneys, quenelles, olives, mushrooms, truffles and Madeira sauce

Foie gras Souvarov ⇒ foie gras macerated in high quality cognac; baked in a terrine with brown sauce added of truffle

Foie gras au four ⇒ salted foie gras marinated in paprika, spices and armagnac; baked in a terrine with goose fat

Foie gras aux raisins ⇒ foie gras simmered in a roux added of liver fat, white wine, crushed tomato, plus sultanas steeped in Madeira; served with sippets fried in goose fat

Foie gras de canard à la purée de bananes truffée ⇒ foie gras escalopes sautéed in butter, served with a banana purée, sauce hollandaise and truffles

Foie gras de canard à la vapeur au fumet de Sauternes ⇒ duck foie gras steamed with Sauternes white wine, carrots, turnip, celery and white of leek

Foie gras de canard au pacherenc ⇒ duck foie gras cooked in the oven with white wine from Adour area

Foie gras de canard au poivre blanc et au vert de poireau ⇒ moulded leek purée with cream, topped with a foie gras salted and peppered, then baked

Foie gras de canard au raisin ⇒ foie gras escalopes sautéed in butter; served with the gravy added of Sauternes white wine and grapes

Foie gras de canard aux huîtres et aux écrevisses ⇒ crushed duck foie gras, mixed with milk, cooked beef bone-marrow and eggs, baked in moulds; served with poached oysters, crayfishes and butter added of Monbazillac white wine

Foie gras de canard dans le potiron ⇒ pumpkin hollowed out of its seeds, then stuffed with pepper, chive, hyssop and a foie gras macerated in whisky, then baked

Foie gras de canard glacé ⇒ duck stuffed with a foie gras marinated in spices and port, then braised in the oven with the marinade and a jelly of giblets; served with cooked dried plums flavoured of ginger, cherries cooked in red wine, quartered apples cooked in butter, plus green olives stuffed of foie gras and decorated of quartered oranges

Foie gras du Gers ⇒ foie gras cooked in a consommé of salted giblets

Foie gras en brioche *(chaud ...)* ⇒ foie gras macerated in spices and high quality cognac, then poached; wrapped in a caul of pork, plus a brioche paste and baked

Foie gras en cocotte ou en casserole ⇒ foie gras studded of truffle and macerated in spices and Madeira; then baked in stock plus Madeira

Foie gras truffé au madère ⇒ foie gras studded with truffle and macerated in cognac, then wrapped in a caul of pork and braised with strips from rind of pork, onions, carrots and Madeira

Fond *-[bouillon]-* ⇒ cooking stock for sauces

Fond à succès ⇒ disc of crushed almonds, sugar and whipped white of eggs, baked quickly

Fond blanc de volaille ⇒ stock made of veal's shoulder, knuckle of veal, giblets of poultry, chicken, carrots, onions, white of leeks, celery and pepper

Fond blanc ordinaire ⇒ stock made of veal's shoulder, knuckle of veal, giblets of poultry, carrots, onions, white of leeks, celery and pepper

Fond brun clair ⇒ stock made of rind of pork, ham, beef, knuckle of veal, carrots, onions, garlic and coarse salt

Fond brun de veau ⇒ stock made of shoulder of veal, knuckle of veal, carrots and onions

Fond de gibier ⇒ stock made of roebuck meat, partridge, pheasant, carrots, onions, hare, sage, juniper berries and clove

Fond de veau lié ⇒ stock made of shoulder of veal, knuckle of veal, carrots, onions and arrow-root

Fond de veau tomaté ⇒ stock made of shoulder of veal, knuckle of veal, carrots, onions and tomato purée

Fonds ⇒ cooking stock for sauces

Fonds de noix ou noisettes ⇒ small pastries made of crushed hazelnuts, granulated sugar, egg-yolks, butter and fecula, then baked

Fonds napolitains ⇒ pastry discs for garnish, made of butter, flour, granulated sugar, almond powder and egg-yolks, then baked

Fond perlé ⇒ pastry case made of eggs, almond powder and sugar, then baked

Fonds sablés ⇒ shortbread made of flour, butter, eggs, granulated sugar, vanilla sugar; then baked

Fond d'artichaut ⇒ artichoke heart

Fonds d'artichauts à la cévenole ⇒ braised artichoke hearts stuffed with chestnut purée, sprinkled of grated parmesan and melted butter, then browned

Fonds d'artichauts à la duxelles ⇒ braised artichoke hearts stuffed with chopped mushrooms, sprinkled of grated parmesan and melted butter, then browned

Fonds d'artichauts à la florentine ⇒ braised artichoke hearts stuffed with braised spinach; covered with béchamel sauce added of egg-yolks and gruyère, sprinkled of grated cheese and browned

Fonds d'artichauts à la niçoise ⇒ artichoke hearts braised in olive oil, garnished with tomato purée; sprinkled of crumbs and olive oil, then browned

Fonds d'artichauts à la piémontaise ⇒ braised artichoke hearts garnished of risotto, sprinkled of grated parmesan and melted butter, then browned

Fonds d'artichauts à la portugaise ⇒ artichoke hearts braised in oil and chopped onion, with crushed tomatoes, grated garlic and parsley

Fonds d'artichauts Soubise ⇒ artichoke hearts braised in butter, garnished with a purée of onions and rice, seasoned of pepper and sugar

Fonds d'artichauts aux fines herbes ⇒ artichoke hearts sautéed in butter and sprinkled with chervil, plus parsley

Fonds d'artichauts congelés ⇒ boiled artichoke hearts preserved in the freezer

Fonds d'artichauts garnis pour plats chauds ⇒ braised artichoke hearts, garnished variously

Fonds d'artichauts garnis pour plats froids ⇒ braised artichoke hearts, garnished either with composed butter, or eggs and vegetables

Fonds d'artichauts étuvés au beurre ou à la crème ⇒ artichoke hearts braised in butter and covered with cream

Fondant ⇒ fondant

Fondants au parmesan ⇒ dough made of flour, butter, parmesan cheese and egg; cooked in the oven

Fondre
- **liquéfier** ⇒ to melt
- **liquéfié** ⇒ melted butter, etc ...
- **cuisson sans eau de légumes, poissons, etc ... appelée fondue** ⇒ ... coked in their own liquid

Fondu
- **adjectif** ⇒ ... melted or ... cooked until melted
- **légumes** ⇒ vegetables reduced to pulp by slow cooking

Fondu creusois ⇒ cow's milk cheese melted with water, milk, butter, egg-yolks, salt, and pepper; served with chips or poured on mashed potatoes and browned

Fondue (*Bourguignonne ou autre et non le mode de cuisson ...)* ⇒ fondue

Fondue au fromage ⇒ fondue

Fondue bourguignonne ⇒ fondue
Fondue -*[Brillat-Savarin]-* ⇒ dish of eggs, grated cheese and butter, melted together
Fondue au chocolat ⇒ sweet of melted chocolate, where the guests steep some biscuit or preserved fruit
Fondue chinoise ⇒ meat lamellas cooked in chicken stock; served with chopped vegetables, plus soya sauce
Fondue de légumes ⇒ vegetables stewed in their own liquid
Fondue de poissons et de fruits de mer ⇒ fishes and seafood stewed in their own liquid
Fondue de tomate ⇒ paste of melted tomatoes with onions, garlic, thyme and butter
Fondue du Valais ⇒ diced swiss cheese melted in white wine and seasoned with pepper and kirsch; served usually with meat
Fondue piémontaise -*[antipasto]-* ⇒ Italian hors d'œuvre
Fonio -*[millet]-* ⇒ millet
Fontainebleau -*[fromage]-* ⇒ cheese made of whipped cream and curdled milk
Fontainebleau *(garniture ...)* -*[tournedos]-* ⇒ sauté tournedos ...
    - noisettes d'agneau ⇒ sauté noisettes of lamb ... ... garnished of diced vegetables laid on pastry boats made of mashed potatoes, eggs and butter
Fontal -*[Fontina]-* ⇒ Italian cow's milk cheese
Fontina ⇒ Italian cow's milk cheese
Fool -*[entremets G B]-* ⇒ fool
Fool ⇒ fool
Forêt noire ⇒ gateau made with a mousse of granulated sugar, eggs, flour, cacao and melted butter, then moistened with a kirsch flavoured syrup; covered with whipped cream, decorated of cherries in brandy and sprinkled of chocolate's shavings
Forestière *(à la ...)*
    1) Petites ou grosses pièces de boucherie ⇒ ... with a garnish of mushrooms sautéed in butter, browned potatoes and browned lardoons; served with the gravy
    2) oeufs ou légumes ⇒ ... with mushrooms sautéed in butter
Forestine -*[berry]-* ⇒ sweet with hazelnuts from Bourges
Formidable -*[bière]-* ⇒ a 3 litres beer mug
Fort ⇒ strong or intense or concentrated
Fouace ⇒ rustic cakes cooked in the oven and flavoured
Fouassou -*[Quercy]-* ⇒ brioches with eggs and butter, glazed of icing sugar
Fouée
    - Anjou ⇒ flat cake spreaded of butter
    - Tours ⇒ variety of bread
    - Poitou ⇒ cake of bread dough, cream and butter
Fouée tourangelle ⇒ flat round bread from Tours
Fouetté au chocolat ⇒ chocolate cooked with sugar and water, then mixed with cream
Fouettée ⇒ whisked or whipped
    - fouetté ⇒ whipped up < *oeufs, crème, etc ...* >
Foufou -*[foutou]-* ⇒ African dish based on manioc and bananas, plus a spicy sauce
Fougasse ⇒ rustic cakes cooked in the oven and flavoured
Fougassette -*[fouace; Provence]-* ⇒ small cake flavoured with orange blossom and saffron
Fougeru -*[coulommiers]-* ⇒ Coulommiers cheese wrapped in fern leave
Foul -*[Liban]-* ⇒ broad beans served hot in salad
Foul medames -*[Egypte]-* ⇒ labiates
Four ⇒ oven
    - au four ⇒ baked or roasted in the oven
    - à four vif ⇒ baked in hot oven

- à four doux ⇒ baked in slow oven
- à four moyen ⇒ baked in medium heat
Fourchaume -*[chablis]*- ⇒ high quality Chablis wine
Fourchette ⇒ fork
Fourme ⇒ blue cow's milk cheese or type of cheese from Auvergne
Fourme d'ambert ⇒ blue cow's milk cheese ½ ou ½ type of cheese from Auvergne
Fourme de Laguiole -*[Laguiole d'aubrac]*- ⇒ cow's milk cheese from Rouergue area
Fourré ⇒ stuffed
Foutou ⇒ African dish based on manioc and bananas, plus a spicy sauce
Fowery pekoé -*[thé]*- ⇒ Ceylonese tea
Fragaria ⇒ rectangular pastry, made with layers of Genoese sponge flavoured of egg-custard added of
    butter and strawberries
Fraîche ⇒ fresh or cool or refreshing
Frais ⇒ fresh or cool or refreshing
Fraisalia ⇒ rectangular pastry, made with layers of Genoese sponge flavoured of egg-custard added of
    butter and strawberries
Fraise -*[fruit]*- ⇒ strawberry or fraise
Fraises à la crème ⇒ fraises in whipped cream and sugar
Fraises à la maltaise ⇒ halved oranges hollowed out; filled with strawberries added of orange juice,
    sugar and curaçao
Fraises cardinal ⇒ cups filled with strawberries, covered with raspberry purée and sprinkled of
    chopped almonds
Fraises condé ⇒ ring of rice cooked in milk with vanilla and egg-yolks, garnished of strawberries;
    served with a purée of raspberries, strawberries, lemon juice and granulated sugar
Fraise d'agneau ⇒ lamb's caul
Fraise de chevreau ⇒ dish made of membrane of kid's intestine
Fraise de veau ⇒ dish made with membrane of calf's intestine
Fraise de veau à l'indienne ⇒ diced poached membrane of calf's intestine, simmered in a sauce
    enriched of onion, nutmeg and coconut milk; garnished with rice
Fraise de veau au blanc ⇒ dish made of beef grease, water, vinegar, onion, clove and membrane of
    calf's intestine
Fraise de veau frite ⇒ diced membrane of calf's intestine, coated with egg and crumbs, then fried
Fraise des bois ⇒ wild strawberry
Fraisier ⇒ rectangular pastry, made with layers of Genoese sponge flavoured of egg-custard added of
    butter and strawberries
Framboise ⇒ raspberry
Française (*à la ...*)
    1) Grosses pièces de boucherie ⇒ with bunches of asparagus tips, braised lettuce, cauliflower
        covered of sauce hollandaise, and fried potato croustades filled with vegetables salad
        in butter; served with a sauce
    2) Petits pois ⇒ peas cooked with sauté bacon, consommé, butter and flour
Francfort -*[saucisse de]*- ⇒ frankfurter
Franc français ⇒ F.F
Frangipane
    - général ⇒ frangipane or almond paste
    - gâteau fourré à la frangipane ⇒ frangipane pastry
Frangy ⇒ white wine with a taste of honey
Franquette (*la ...*) ⇒ variety of nut
Frappé ⇒ iced or chilled
Frascati -*[vin]*- ⇒ Italian white wine

Fréchure ou Lévadou ⇒ pig's lung stew
Fremgeye lorrain ⇒ soft white cheese salted and peppered, then fermented in jar

French dressing -*[vinaigrette]*- ⇒ french dressing
French mustard ⇒ mustard < *uncountable* >
French plantain -*[banane]*- ⇒ large banana for cooking
French toast -*[brunch]*- ⇒ French toast
Frêne ⇒ ash tree
  - **feuilles** ⇒ ash leaves
Frénette ⇒ drink based on ash leaves, orange peel, sugar, yeast and burnt sugar
Freneuse ⇒ soup made of turnips and mashed potatoes, added of consommé
Fressure ⇒ fry or pluck
Fressure vendéen ⇒ fry of pork stewed with the blood and rind
Fretin ⇒ fry or young fish
Friand
  - **viande** ⇒ meat pastry
  - **pâtisserie** ⇒ small almond cake
Friand à la viande ⇒ meat pastry stuffed with a hash of veal, pork, mushrooms, cream and pepper
Friand de st flour ⇒ pie meat
Friandise ⇒ sweet or titbit or dainty
Fribourg -*[fromage]*- ⇒ swiss cheese
Fricadelle ⇒ small ball or quoit made with a forcemeat; served with tomato sauce flavoured of paprika or curry, pasta, rice, or mashed vegetables
Fricandeau ⇒ fricandeau or braised veal
Fricandeau d'esturgeon à la hongroise ⇒ thick slices of sturgeon studded of streaky bacon, braised with paprika, white wine and velouté sauce; served with the gravy and potatoes or a capsicum purée
Fricandeau de veau à l'oseille ⇒ slice of cushion of veal studded with streaky bacon, braised with diced carrots and onions, plus veal's trotter, wine, tomato purée and stock; served with braised sorrel and the gravy
Fricassée ⇒ fricassee
Fricassée d'agneau ⇒ fricassee made of diced lamb's meat, mushrooms and onions; served with the gravy thickened of egg-yolks
Fricassée d'anguilles ⇒ fricassee of eels, onions and mushrooms in white wine; served with fried sippets
Fricassée de langoustines ⇒ scampi
Fricassée de mer au sabayon de Bellet ⇒ fricassee of young turbot, john dory, monkfish, red gurnards, Norway lobsters, Bellet white wine, plus a zabaglione added of Bellet white wine
Fricassée de pieds de mouton aux pieds de mouton (*ou hydnes sinués ...*) ⇒ fricassee of mutton trotters and spreading hydnum, with onion, garlic, clove, lemon and other herbs; served with a sauce made of a roux, cream and the cooking juice
Fricassée de poulet à l'angevine ⇒ fricassee of chicken with onions, mushrooms, Anjou white wine and cream; served with steamed potatoes or carrots and turnips
Fricassée de poulet à la berrichonne ⇒ fricassee of chicken and carrots; served with the gravy added of egg-yolks, cream and vinegar
Fricassée de poulet à la minute ⇒ fricassee of chicken in butter, flour, pepper, grated nutmeg, onions and mushrooms; served with the gravy thickened of egg-yolks and lemon juice
Fricassée de poulet cardinal La Balue ⇒ fricassee of chicken, served with crayfish tails cooked in a court-bouillon; covered with a sauce of mashed crayfishes and cream

Fricassée de turbot en aumônière et son coulis de langoustine au cidre doux ⇒ apples in syrup shaped in corolla, topped of pancakes filled with poached turbot fillets and Norway lobster tails, plus a garnish of steamed spinach leaves and Norway lobster tails; covered with Norway lobster purée plus crushed tomatoes, then flamed in calvados and added of mustard, cider and cream

Fricassée du marin -*[assortiment de poissons]*- ⇒ various fishes in fricassee

Fricassée Perigourdine
- **général** ⇒ fricassee made of pot-au-feu vegetables braised in goose fat and stock
- **pour garniture de potage** ⇒ fricassee of garlic, onion, shallot, welsh onion, parsley, carrot, turnips, pumpkin, white of leek, celery, plus diced ham; served as a garnish for soups

Fricassin ⇒ membrane of kid's intestine boiled with onions, laurel, thyme and parsley; then fried and simmered with cream

Fricasson ⇒ offal of kid, blood, bits of head, tongue and brain, simmered in butter and cream

Fried bread sauce ⇒ fried bread sauce

Fried chicken ⇒ fried chicken

Frikadeller -*[Danemark]*- ⇒ balls made of pork and veal hashed with onion, then thickened of eggs

Fripe -*[tartine]*- ⇒ any ingredient spreaded on bread ½ ou ½ bread spreaded with ...

Frisée -*[chicorée]*- ⇒ curly endive

Fritada de mariscos -*[Brésil]*- ⇒ mussels, oysters and crab bits, wrapped in fritter dough, then fried

Friteau
- **beignet salé d'un morceau d'aliment tels que cuisse de grenouille** ⇒ frog leg
- **huître** ⇒ oyster ...
- **moule** ⇒ mussel ...
- **saumon en dé** ⇒ diced salmon ...
- **abats** ⇒ offal ...
- **légume** ⇒ Bit of vegetable steeped in batter and fried; served with fried parsley and quartered lemon, plus a spicy sauce

Fritelle
- **chataîgne** ⇒ Corsican chestnut-flour fritter, flavoured with fennel seeds
- **autre** ⇒ fritter of dough with egg-yolks and oil, stuffed with vegetables or sausage or cheese

Frites ⇒ fried potatoes or chips

Friton
- **rillettes** ⇒ kind of rillettes made with pork fat, tongue, heart and kidneys
- **grattons** ⇒ cooked goose fat

Fritot
- **beignet salé d'un morceau d'aliment tels que cuisse de grenouille** ⇒ frog leg
- **huître** ⇒ oyster ...
- **moule** ⇒ mussel ...
- **saumon en dé** ⇒ diced salmon ...
- **abats** ⇒ offal ...
- **légume** ⇒ bit of vegetable steeped in batter and fried; served with fried parsley and quartered lemon, plus a spicy sauce

Fritots d'abattis de volaille ⇒ giblets of poultry cooked in a court-bouillon, steeped in batter and fried; served with tomato sauce

Fritot d'eperlans ⇒ deep-fried fritter made with small pieces of sea smelts

Fritots d'huîtres ⇒ shelled oysters marinated in oil, garlic, parsley, lemon juice and pepper, then steeped in batter and fried; served with a sauce based on brown sauce, chopped mushrooms, diced ham, tarragon and tomato purée

Fritots de grenouilles ⇒ frogs' legs marinated in oil, garlic, parsley, lemon juice and pepper, then steeped in batter and fried; served with quartered lemons and a sauce

Fritots de moules ⇒ shelled cooked mussels, steeped in batter and fried; served with a sauce based on brown sauce, chopped mushrooms, diced ham, tarragon and tomato purée

Fritots de saumon ⇒ bits of salmon marinated in oil, lemon juice, parsley and pepper; served with quartered lemons and a sauce

Fritots de sole ⇒ bits of sole fillets marinated in oil, garlic, parsley, lemon juice and pepper, then steeped in batter and fried; served with a mayonnaise sauce

Fritots de viande ou de volaille ⇒ bits of poached meat or poultry macerated in oil, cognac, parsley and pepper, then steeped in batter and fried; served with quartered lemons and a sauce

Fritto misto ⇒ fritto misto

Friture
- **mets** ⇒ friture
- **en friture** ⇒ in deep frying
- **graisse de cuisson** ⇒ frying

Friture de la loire ⇒ tiny fish, deep-fried and served with lemon

Friture d'éperlans ⇒ friture of sea smelts

Frizzante -*[valpolicella]*- ⇒ Italian red wine

Froid ⇒ cold or cool or chilled

Fromage ⇒ cheese < *uncountable* >

Fromage à l'écarlate ⇒ composed butter with crayfish

Fromage à la crème ⇒ cream cheese

Fromage à pâte dure ⇒ hard cheese

Fromage à pâte molle ⇒ soft cheese

Fromage à tartiner ⇒ cheese spread

Fromage au lait de renne ⇒ reindeer's cheese

Fromage bavarois au parfait amour ⇒ Bavarian mousse made of cedrate peel, milk, clove, sugar, gelatine, cochineal seeds, plus soft white cheese

Fromage bavarois aux roses ⇒ Bavarian mousse made of rose petals, cochineal seeds, plus syrup of sugar, then chilled and added of soft white cheese

Fromage blanc ⇒ soft white cheese

Fromage blanc aux herbes ⇒ soft white cheese mixed with parsley, chervil, tarragon, chive and pepper; served with rye bread and jacket potatoes

Fromage bleu ⇒ Danish blue

Fromage de brebis ⇒ ewe's milk cheese or ewe cheese

Fromage de chèvre Bourguignon ⇒ goat's milk cheese preserved in marc

Fromage de soja -*[tõfu]*- ⇒ soya cheese

Fromage de tête ⇒ pork brawn

Frontage de vache ⇒ cow's milk cheese

Fromage du curé ⇒ pressed cow's milk cheese shaped in square

Fromage fondu ⇒ cheese spread

Fromage fort ⇒ grated cheese mixed with oil or wine or alcohol, and fermented

Fromage frais ⇒ soft white cheese

Fromage glacé ⇒ ice cream

Fromage gras ⇒ full-fat cheese

Fromage maigre ⇒ low-fat cheese

Fromage râpé ⇒ grated cheese

Fromagée ⇒ grated cheese mixed with oil or wine or alcohol and fermented

Froment ⇒ wheat or wheat-flour

Fromentée ⇒ wheat flour porridge

Fronsac -*[Côtes de canon-fronsac]*- ⇒ the best red wines from Fronsac near Libourne

Frontignan ⇒ sweet wine from Languedoc coast

Fronton -*[côtes du frontonnais]-* ⇒ high quality red and rosé wines from Montauban area
Fruit
  - **fruits au sirop** ⇒ preserved fruits
  - **fruits confits** ⇒ candied fruits or crystallized fruits
  - **fruit de la passion** ⇒ passion fruit
  - **fruits exotiques** ⇒ exotic fruits
  - **fruits rafraîchis** ⇒ fruit salad
  - **fruit sec** ⇒ dried fruit
Fruit de la passion ⇒ passion fruit
Fruit à pain ou Pain bois ⇒ breadfruit
Fruit en conserve ⇒ tinned fruit
Fruit givré ⇒ dessert made of fruit hollowed out, and filled with a sorbet
Fruit glacé au sucre ⇒ fruit covered with icing sugar
Fruit pressé ⇒ fruit juice
Fruits à l'alcool ⇒ fruits preserved in eau de vie
Fruits au vinaigre ⇒ small fruits preserved in vinegar
Fruits confits ⇒ candied fruits or crystallized fruits
Fruits de mer ⇒ seafood
Fruits déguisés ⇒ petits fours made of fruits, either glazed in caramel or stuffed with almond paste
Fruits exotiques ⇒ exotic fruits
Fruits meringués au riz ⇒ sweet made with layers of rice cooked in milk, apricots in syrup, whipped white of eggs and meringue, then baked; covered with apricot jam and redcurrant jelly
Fruits rafraîchis ⇒ fruit salad
Fruits rafraîchis à l'occitanienne ⇒ cups filled with slices of pears, figs and grapes, sprinkled of sugar, Limoux sweet wine and cognac; served chilled and covered of whipped cream
Fruits rafraîchis à la maltaise ⇒ chilled bits of bananas, pineapple and stoned cherries, macerated in curaçao and granulated sugar; served with orange ice-cream or orange juice
Fruits rafraîchis à la normande ⇒ chilled bits of pineapple, bananas and apples, macerated in calvados and granulated sugar; covered with cream
Fruits rafraîchis au kirsch et au marasquin ⇒ cups filled with bits of peaches, pears, apples, bananas, apricots, strawberries and grapes, macerated in kirsch and maraschino
Fruit sec ⇒ dried fruit
Fucus, Laminaires -*[algues brunes]-* ⇒ sea cabbage
Fudge ⇒ fudge
Fugu ou Diodon ⇒ Japanese fish
Fumé ⇒ smoked < *v.t adjectif* >
Fumée -*[bière]-* ⇒ beer from Bamberg
Fumée de moules ⇒ mussels cooked with pine needles
Fumet -*[cuisine]-*
  - **arome** ⇒ aroma
  - **fumet de champignons** ⇒ mushroom stock
  - **fumet de poisson** ⇒ fish stock
  - **vin** ⇒ bouquet or aroma
Fumet de champignons ⇒ stock based on butter, lemon juice and mushrooms
Fumet de poissons ⇒ stock based on fishes, onions, shallots, mushrooms, lemon, herbs and wine
Fumet de légumes ⇒ vegetable stock
Fütyülös -*[barack]-* ⇒ half a litre bottle for Barack brandy
Fynbo -*[fromage]-* ⇒ Fynbo

G

Gâche
  1) **normandie** ⇒ Flat cake of bread dough
  2) **bretagne** ⇒ Flat cake from bread dough, added of sugar and butter
  3) **vendée** ⇒ Kind of brioche, sometimes shaped in twisted cord
Gâche améliorée ⇒ brioche made of flour, butter, cream, eggs, sugar, syrup and yeast
Gâche vendéenne ⇒ bread paste enriched of butter, eggs and sugar; flavoured with orange blossom
Gade ⇒ gadoid
Gaillac
  1) **ordinaires** ⇒ wines from Gaillac area
  2) **mousseux** ⇒ Sparkling wine from Gaillac area
Galabart ⇒ large black pudding of offal
Galanga ⇒ spice from a rhizome
Galantine *(plus le nom ...)* ⇒ galantine of ...
Galantine -[Edam français]- ⇒ French cheese similar to Edam
Galantine de volaille ⇒ elaborated galantine made of poultry, hash, egg, cognac, Madeira, plus jelly
Galathée ⇒ squat lobster < *cuisine uncountable* >
Galet -[dragée]- ⇒ dragée
Galet des Alpes au poivre ⇒ dry sausage flavoured with pepper
Galette *(énumérations ...)*
  1) **Petits biscuits**
    - **Galette corrézienne -[aux noix et au châtaignes]-** ⇒ voir texte
    - **Roussillon -[aux fruits confits]-** ⇒ flat cake filled with preserved fruits
    - **Nivernais -[galette massepinée aux amandes]-** ⇒ flat cake filled with almonds
    - **Jura -[galette au fromage blanc]-** ⇒ flat cake filled with soft white cheese
    - **Normande -[galette feuilletée, fourrée de confiture et de crème fraîche]-** ⇒ puff-pastry filled with jam and cream
    - **Galettes de Pérouges -[briochée, parfumée au zeste de citron, garnie de beurre et de sucre]-** ⇒ flat cake flavoured with lemon peel, and garnished with butter and sugar
    - **Galette feuilletée des rois** ⇒ voir texte
    - **Galettes de pommes de terre** ⇒ voir texte
    - **Galettes de céréales** ⇒ flat cake of maize or millet or oat < *maïs, millet ou avoine* >
  2) **Crêpes**
    - **bretagne, normandie, vendée; les galettes sont des « crêpes de sarrasin garnies de »** ⇒ buckwheat pancakes, garnished of ...
    - **garnitures au choix fromage** ⇒ cheese
    - **œuf** ⇒ egg
    - **saucisse** ⇒ sausage
    - **sardines grillées** ⇒ grilled sardines < *voir texte* >
  3) **Biscuit sablé**
    - **Galette -[biscuit sablé au beurre]-** ⇒ small flat cake of buttered short pastry
    - **Petits biscuits secs et ronds** ⇒ various small dry flat cakes
Galette
  - **galette ou crêpe** ⇒ buckwheat pancake
  - **gâteau** ⇒ flat cake
Galette à la corézienne ⇒ flat cake filled with nuts and chestnuts

Galettes au fromage ⇒ flat cakes made of flour, butter, grated swiss cheese and egg-yolk
Galettes au vin blanc ⇒ flat cakes made of flour, butter, sugar and white wine
Galette de blé noir ⇒ buckwheat-flour pancake
Galette de plomb ⇒ short-pastry flat cake, added of cream and butter
Galette de pommes de terre ⇒ flat cake made of potatoes, egg-yolks and butter
Galette de sarrasin ⇒ buckwheat pancake
Galette des rois ⇒ twelfth-night flat cake
Galette fondante ⇒ puff-pastry flat cake, buttered and glazed with icing sugar
Galette lyonnaise ⇒ cake of mashed potatoes and onions
Galettes nantaises ⇒ flat cakes made of flour, butter, egg-yolks, almonds and sugar
Galettes orangines *(petites ...)* ⇒ small flat cakes enriched with butter, orange peel and egg-yolks
Galettes salées ⇒ flat cake made of flour, butter, salt and milk or cream
Galicien ⇒ Genoese sponge filled with pistachio cream, and coated of chopped pistachios
Galimafrée ⇒ slices of chicken or meat, fried in pork fat, then moistened with verjuice, and spiced with ginger
Galingale *-[Galanga]-* ⇒ spice from a rhizome
Gallinette *-[clavaire]-* ⇒ tiny yellow hands
Galouchka ⇒ small gnocchis of flour or noodles, salted or sugared
Galutres *-[Trescat]-* ⇒ mutton tripe cooked with egg-yolks
Gamay *(cépage ...)* ⇒ variety of vine
Gamba ⇒ large prawn
Gambas flambés ⇒ large prawns flamed with cognac or armagnac
Game chips *-[GB]-* ⇒ game chips
Game pie *-[pie]-* ⇒ game pie
Gammelost *-[fromage]-* ⇒ Gammelost
Ganache *-[crème]-* ⇒ custard based on chocolate, butter and cream
Gancia *-[Vermouth]-* ⇒ vermouth
Gandule *-[pois d'Angola]-* ⇒ Angola peas
Gape ⇒ small cow's milk cheese shaped in ball
Gaperon ⇒ small cow's milk cheese shaped in ball
Gapron ⇒ small cow's milk cheese shaped in ball
Gar *-[gomme]-* ⇒ gum
Garbure
    - plat ⇒ stew of conserved goose and cabbage in vegetable stock
    - variante appelée « Briscat » ⇒ stew of conserved goose and maize, in vegetable stock
Gardèches en omelette *-[Périgord]-* ⇒ fish omelette in local recipe
Gardon ⇒ roach < *pluriel inchangé* >
Gardon rouge *-[rotengle]-* ⇒ roach < *pluriel inchangé* >
Garenne *-[lapin]-* ⇒ wild rabbit
Gargouillau *-[entremets]-* ⇒ sweet, made of a pancake dough, added of pears and baked
Gargouillou *-[cuisine]-* ⇒ vegetable ragout
Gari ⇒ African dish based on manioc and bananas, plus a spicy sauce
Garingal ⇒ spice from a rhizome
Garni ⇒ garnished with ...
Garniture ⇒ garnish
    - garni avec ⇒ served with a garnish of ... 1 or garnished with ... 2 or covered with ... 3
    - énumérations ⇒ description du plat plus 1, 2, 3 ou rien et description de la garniture
    - choron ⇒ potato-balls and artichoke hearts stuffed with peas or asparagus tips
    - foyot ⇒ covered with béarnaise sauce added of the gravy

Garniture ⇒ garnish (suite)
- **laguipière** ⇒ covered with a sauce, and sprinkled with a julienne of truffle macerated in Madeira
- **cavour** ⇒ large mushrooms stuffed with mashed chicken's livers and sliced truffle < 2 >
- **condé** ⇒ mashed red beans < 1 >
- **du Barry** ⇒ cauliflower in a sauce of cream, egg-yolk and grated cheese < 2 >
- **meyerbeer** ⇒ fried eggs < 2 >
- **rossini** ⇒ truffles and sliced foie gras < 1 >
- **anversoise** ⇒ hop stalks in cream or butter < 2 >
- **argenteuil** ⇒ asparagus in purée or in tips < 2 >
- **nantua** ⇒ crayfishes < 2 >
- **clamart** ⇒ voir texte < 2 >
- **périgueux** ⇒ truffles and sometimes foie gras < 2 >
- **bordelaise poissons ou viandes blanches** ⇒ white wine sauce < 3 >
- **viandes rouges** ⇒ red wine sauce < 3 >
- **grand veneur** ⇒ covered with a peppery sauce added of redcurrant jelly and cream, plus chestnut purée < 3 >
- **batelière** ⇒ poached mushrooms, fried eggs, crayfishes and fried onions < 2 >
- **commodore** ⇒ fish quenelles, croquettes of crayfish tails, mussels, plus a sauce thickened of crayfish purée < 2 >
- **bouquetière** ⇒ vegetables laid in bunches < 1 >
- **jardinière, ne pas utiliser l'en tête garni avec** ⇒ ... cooked with vegetables

Garniture aromatique ⇒ garnish for flavouring or seasoning, based on garlic, carrots, celery, onions, clove, leeks, parsley, juniper berries, always drawn back from the finished meal

Garniture à la bourgeoise
- **viandes braisées** ⇒ braised ...
- **paleron** ⇒ chuck ...
- **macreuse** ⇒ shoulder of beef ...
- **gîte à la noix** ⇒ topside of beef ...
- **jarret de veau** ⇒ knuckle of veal ...
- **fricandeau** ⇒ fricandeau or braised veal ...
- **tendrons de veau** ⇒ tendrons of veal ...
- **foie de veau** ⇒ calf liver ...
- **gigot** ⇒ leg of mutton ... with a garnish of small onions, carrots, plus lardoons

Garniture bourguignonne ⇒ ... with a garnish of mushrooms, onions and lardoons cooked in red wine

Garniture camérani ⇒ with a garnish of tartlets filled of mashed foie gras, truffle lamellas, oxtongue and noodles, thickened with supreme sauce

Garniture de la côte de boeuf
1) **avec côte de boeuf braisée** ⇒ braised rib of beef; served ... < *plus garniture bourgeoise, bourguignonne ou chipolata, voir texte* >
2) **avec côte de boeuf rôtie** ⇒ roasted rib of beef; served ... < *plus garniture bouquetière, bruxelloise, dauphine, duchesse, flamande, hongroise, jardinière lorraine, lyonnaise, macédoine, milanaise, nivernaise, parisienne, printanière VOIR TEXTE* >
   - **ou bien des légumes liés au beurre ou braisés** ⇒ ... with vegetables thickened of butter or braised
   - **ou des purées de légumes** ⇒ ... with mashed vegetables

Garniture de l'épaule d'agneau braisée ⇒ braised shoulder of lamb ...
- **haricots** ⇒ ... with a garnish of beans
- **purée de légumes** ⇒ ... with mashed vegetables

- **fonds d'artichauts** ⇒ ... with artichoke hearts
- **purée d'oignons à la bretonne** ⇒ ... with onions mashed in pork fat, white wine, stock and pepper
- **cèpes à la bordelaise** ⇒ ... with boletus sautéed in oil and lemon juice, plus the gravy added of red wine, shallots, thyme and laurel

Garniture de l'épaule de mouton ⇒ mutton shoulder ...
- **à la boulangère** ⇒ voir texte
- **à la chipolata** ⇒ voir texte
- **à la bourgeoise** ⇒ ... boned and stuffed with carrots, onions and lardoons
- **à la bourguignonne** ⇒ ... boned and stuffed, then braised in red wine with mushrooms, onions and lardoons
- **à la bretonne** ⇒ ... braised and garnished with beans or flageolets
- **à la flamande** ⇒ ... braised, then served in meat loaf with red cabbage
- **aux navets** ⇒ ... braised with shaped turnips and onions
- **au riz** ⇒ ... boned, rolled and braised; served with Creole rice

Garniture de rognons de coqs ⇒ garnish of cock kidneys

Garniture de suprême de volaille ⇒ chicken served in supreme sauce with a garnish of ...
- **dés d'aubergines sautées au beurre** ⇒ ... diced aubergines sautéed in butter
- **laitue ou chicorée braisée** ⇒ ... braised lettuce or braised endive
- **gousses de concombre étuvées au beurre** ⇒ ... braised cucumbers
- **fonds d'artichaut braisés ou sautés au beurre** ⇒ ... artichoke hearts braised or sautéed in butter
- **haricots verts ou macédoine de légumes au beurre** ⇒ ... french beans in butter vegetable salad in butter
- **petits pois à la française** ⇒ ... young peas in butter, with lettuce, parsley, chervil, and baby onions
- **pointes d'asperges au beurre ou à la crème** ⇒ ... asparagus tips in butter or cream
- **purée de légumes** ⇒ ... mashed vegetables

Garniture du carré de porc rôti ⇒ Roasted loin of pork, served with ...
- **pommes de terre boulangère** ⇒ voir texte
- **pommes de terre dauphine** ⇒ voir texte
- **en purée** ⇒ mashed potatoes
- **purée de légumes** ⇒ mashed ...
- **céleri** ⇒ celery
- **navets** ⇒ turnips
- **lentilles** ⇒ lentils
- **chicorée** ⇒ endives
- **chou** ⇒ cabbage
- **choux de Bruxelles** ⇒ brussels-sprouts
- **légumes braisés** ⇒ braised ...
- **céleri** ⇒ celery
- **fonds d'artichaut** ⇒ artichoke hearts
- **chicorée** ⇒ endives
- **chou** ⇒ cabbage
- **choux de Bruxelles** ⇒ brussels-sprouts
- **fruits** ⇒ fruits
- **pommes** ⇒ apples
- **poires** ⇒ pears
- **ananas** ⇒ pineapple
- **jus de cuisson** ⇒ gravy added with ...

Garniture du carré de porc rôti ⇒ Roasted loin of pork, served with ...(suite)
- **sauce charcutière** ⇒ voir texte
- **sauce Robert** ⇒ voir texte
- **sauce tomate** ⇒ tomato sauce

Garniture financière
1) **pièces de boucherie** ⇒ ... served ...
    - **ris de veau** ⇒ calf sweetbread served ...
    - **volailles poêlées** ⇒ fried poultry served ...
    - **croûtes** ⇒ pastry cases filled ...
    - **timbales** ⇒ timbale filled ...
    - **bouchées** ⇒ patties filled ...
    - **vol au vent** ⇒ vol-au-vent filled ... with a ragout of cockscombs, poultry quenelles, chopped mushrooms, plus a culinary stuffing of truffles in Madeira
2) **attereaux à la financière**
    - **viande** ⇒ pieces of « nom anglais de la viande » coated with ...
    - **poisson** ⇒ pieces of « nom anglais du poisson » coated with ...
    - **légumes** ⇒ pieces of « nom anglais des légumes » coated with ... a ragout of cockscombs, chopped mushrooms, plus a culinary stuffing of truffles in Madeira; fried on a skewer

Garniture Joinville
- **poisson poché** ⇒ poached ... nom du poisson
- **barquette** ⇒ pastry boat filled ...
- **tartelettes** ⇒ tartlets filled ...
- **bouchées** ⇒ patties filled ...
- **garniture** ⇒ ... with a garnish of shrimp tails, mushrooms and truffles

Garniture macaire *-[garniture pour pièces de boucherie rôties ou poêlées]-* ⇒ served with potato flat cakes

Garniture montmorency *-[garniture pour petites et grosses pièces de boucherie]-* ⇒ ... garnished of artichoke hearts filled with shaped carrots, and little potato balls browned in butter

Garniture St Mandé *-[garnitures pour petites pièces de boucherie sautées]-* ⇒ ... garnish of peas or french beans in butter, plus flat cakes of mashed potatoes

Garum ⇒ Garum

Gascogne *(énumération ...) -[Gers]-*
- **garbure** ⇒ voir texte
- **tourin** ⇒ onion soup prepared with goose fat

Gascogne *(énumération ...) -[Landes et divers]-*
- **le chaudeau ou bouillon chaud** ⇒ voir texte
- **bouillon d'abattis d'oie** ⇒ soup made with giblets of goose
- **Hossegor, soupe aux poissons** ⇒ fish soup in local recipe from Hossegor
- **jambons crus de Dax et St Sever** ⇒ dry ham from Dax or St Sever
- **saucisson de Masseube** ⇒ dry sausage from Masseube
- **foie gras aux raisins** ⇒ voir texte
- **pâtés ou terrines de foie gras** ⇒ voir texte
- **confits de canard** ⇒ voir texte
- **confits d'oie** ⇒ voir texte
- **abignade** *-[boyaux d'oie cuits avec oignons, ail, sang et vin]-* ⇒ voir texte
- **alicuit** *-[abattis de canard ou d'oie]-* ⇒ voir texte
- **estouffat** ⇒ stew of pork and haricot beans
- **daubes de boeuf ou d'oie d'Auch ou de Condom** ⇒ stew of beef or goose from Auch or Condom

- **gras-double à la landaise** ⇒ veal tripe cooked in goose fat
- **civets de lièvre à l'armagnac** ⇒ jugged hare flavoured with armagnac
- **poule farçie** ⇒ hen stuffed with a forcemeat of sausage meat, parsley, onions and crumbs; then roasted
- **gigots à la gasconnade** ⇒ voir texte
- **agneaux rôtis des Landes** ⇒ voir texte
- **palombes** ⇒ wild pigeon
- **alouettes** ⇒ larks
- **bécasses** ⇒ woodcock
- **en salmis** ⇒ in salmi
- **rôties** ⇒ roasted ...
- **ortolans de Chalosse gavés à l'armagnac** ⇒ ortolans flavoured with armagnac
- **matelotes de lamproies** ⇒ lampreys in matelote
- **matelote d'anguilles** ⇒ voir texte
- **fritures de pibales** ⇒ baby eels in friture
- **aillades** ⇒ voir texte
- **cruchade** ⇒ voir texte
- **pastis gascons** ⇒ voir texte
- **feuillantines du Gers** ⇒ voir texte
- **madeleines de Dax** ⇒ kind of sponge cakes from Dax
- **chocolats de Lourdes** ⇒ chocolates
- **pâtes de fruits à l'armagnac de Condom** ⇒ fruit paste flavoured with armagnac
- **pruneaux et fruits à l'armagnac** ⇒ dried plums and fruits, preserved in armagnac
- **vins** ⇒ Madiran wine

Gaspacho ⇒ gazpacho

Gaspacho de homard ⇒ lobster's escalopes, covered with a purée of tomatoes, capsicums, cucumber, garlic and cream; decorated with a julienne of leek, celery, plus chervil

Gaspacho de Séville ⇒ Seville gazpacho

Gastrique ⇒ vinegar added of sugar, and boiled down

Gastronome (à la ...) ⇒ fried stuffed poultry or fried calf sweetbread, garnished with poached truffles, chestnuts and morels in butter, plus cockscombs and cock's kidneys; served with the gravy added of champagne

- **autre appellation pommes de terre sautées** ⇒ sauté potatoes with truffles

Gastropode ⇒ gastropod or gasteropod

Gâtais -[brioche]- ⇒ large brioche for a wedding party

Gâteau
- **cake** ⇒ gateau or tart or disc or round piece
- **dessert** ⇒ pastry

Gâteau « le prélat » ⇒ gateau made from alternate layers of sponge fingers moistened with coffee added of rum, plus a custard based on sugar, eggs and cream; covered with melted chocolate kneaded with butter

Gâteau à l'orange ⇒ gateau made of sugar, eggs, butter, flour and yeast; then sliced in two for addition of marmalade

Gâteau à la basquaise ⇒ gateau filled with custard or fruit

Gâteau à la bressane ⇒ flan or gateau made of poultry livers

Gâteau à la broche ⇒ gateau made of dough flavoured with rum or blossom flowers; cooked slowly on a wood skewer

Gâteau à la mandarine ⇒ tart filled with a preparation of pounded almonds, eggs, and a hash of tangerine peel, laid on tangerine compote; covered with tangerine compote and sprinkled of sliced almonds

Gâteau à la noix de coco ⇒ cake from a dough mixed with grated coconut, eggs and sugar; cooked in the oven

Gâteau à la parisienne ⇒ cake of almond-flavoured cream and preserved fruits, covered with meringue

Gâteau alcazar ⇒ gateau of almond paste and apricot compote

Gâteau Alexandra ⇒ cake made of chocolate, egg, granulated sugar, almond powder, fecula and butter; covered with a compote of apricots, then glazed with a chocolate syrup

Gâteau au chocolat ⇒ gateau made of butter, chocolate, sugar, rice and eggs

Gâteau au chocolat et au café ⇒ gateau made of milk, chocolate, eggs and rice; accompanied by a custard flavoured with coffee

Gâteau auvergnat ⇒ gateau made of flour, sugar, rum, cream, eggs and yeast

Gâteau aux amandes ⇒ almond cake

Gâteau aux noisettes ⇒ gateau made of sugar, eggs, hazelnut powder, fecula, yeast and rum

Gâteau aux noix ⇒ gateau made of butter, granulated sugar, eggs, almond powder, pounded walnuts, rum and flour; decorated with walnuts

Gâteau aux prunes ⇒ plum cake

Gâteau breton ⇒ cake made of preserved fruits macerated in rum, flour and eggs

Gâteau champigny ⇒ puff pastry cake, filled of apricots cooked with sugar and brandy

Gâteau chartrain ⇒ gâteau made of milk, tapioca, sugar, chocolate and semolina

Gâteau college ⇒ gateau made of sugar, flour, almond powder, butter, eggs, rum and yeast

Gâteau candle ⇒ small rectangle of puff-pastry, covered with almond icing and sugar; then baked

Gâteau de cerises ⇒ preparation of butter, salt, crushed almonds, brioche steeped in milk, eggs and cherries; moistened with kirsch when cooked

Gâteau de foies blonds de volaille ⇒ gateau made with poultry livers, bone-marrow, flour, eggs, cream, milk, nutmeg and pounded garlic; covered with tomato purée, plus port and cream icing

Gâteau de haddock ⇒ gateau made of potatoes, leeks, smoked haddock and mushroom lamellas

Gâteau de la forêt noire ⇒ gateau made with a mousse of granulated sugar, eggs, flour, cacao and melted butter, then moistened with a kirsch flavoured syrup; covered with whipped cream, decorated of cherries in brandy and sprinkled of chocolate's shavings

Gâteau de milan ⇒ gateau made of sugar, flour, butter, and eggs

Gâteau de morilles ⇒ braised mixing of courgettes in butter, morels, shallot, white wine and cognac, plus duck's gizzards, eggs and cream, cooked in dariole; served turned out on a dish covered with a sauce of shallot, white wine, plus crushed tomatoes, topped with mint

Gâteau de patates douces ⇒ gateau made of sweet potatoes, vanilla sugar, flour, eggs, plus Malaga raisins steeped in rum; served with egg-custard

Gâteau de pithiviers ⇒ puff pastry filled with preserved fruits, and covered with almond custard

Gâteau de riz ⇒ chilled dessert based on rice cooked in milk, added of sugar and eggs; served with egg-custard or fruit purée

Gâteau de riz au caramel ⇒ rice cooked in milk and added of eggs; baked in a mould coated with caramel

Gâteau de sablé ⇒ gateau made of sugar, butter, cream, fecula, flour, salt, vanilla and eggs

Gâteau de savoie ⇒ gateau made of sugar, fecula, whipped white of eggs, flour and vanilla

Gâteau des rois ⇒ twelfth-night cake

Gâteau des Rois de Bordeaux ⇒ rings made of flour, leaven, eggs, lemon peel, sugar and butter; decorated with slices of cedrate and crushed sugar

Gâteau electra ⇒ gateau from a dough made of flour, butter, sugar, eggs, yeast and lemon peel Before it is cooked, apricot jam is added in the middle

Gâteau esmeralda ⇒ sponge fingers moistened with coffee and rum; accompanied by a custard of butter, sugar and eggs, covered with a chocolate custard

Gâteau fourré à la frangipane ⇒ frangipane pastry

Gâteau grenoblois ⇒ walnut cake

Gâteau joinville ⇒ puff-pastry stuffed with raspberry jam

Gâteau le parisien ⇒ circular pastry filled with almond flavoured cream and preserved fruits; covered with meringue, then sprinkled of icing sugar and browned

Gâteau lorrain ⇒ gateau made of fecula, flour, eggs, sugar, butter and yeast; covered with sliced almonds and chopped angelica

Gâteau manqué ⇒ moulded sponge cake with almonds, topped of hazelnuts, or preserved fruits

Gâteau marbré ⇒ two parts of a paste from butter, sugar, eggs, flour and yeast; then added of cacao for one part, and moulded in alternate layers before baking

Gâteau moka ⇒ mocha cake, uncountable, or coffee cream cake

Gâteau montmorency

    a) avec sirop au kirsch ⇒ Genoese sponge covered with a syrup added of kirsch and red colouring; decorated with cherries and angelica

    b) avec crème au beurre ⇒ Genoese sponge sliced in two discs, moistened of kirsch, then stuffed with buttered cream added of cherries in brandy

Gâteau Montpensier ⇒ gateau made of flour, butter, eggs, granulated sugar, almond powder, plus preserved fruits and sultanas steeped in rum; covered with apricot jam

Gâteau moscovite ⇒ gateau made of chocolate, sugar, butter and eggs; served with custard and kirsch

Gâteau nantais ⇒ gateau made of butter, flour, egg-yolks, rum and preserved angelica; sprinkled with sliced almonds

Gâteau noisette ⇒ gateau made of sugar, eggs, hazelnut powder, fecula, yeast and rum

Gâteau parisien ⇒ cake of almond-flavoured cream and preserved fruits, covered with meringue

Gâteau petit duc ⇒ gateau made of whipped white of eggs, sugar, flour, butter and lemon peel

Gâteau polka ⇒ gateau made from a disc of sugared paste, topped with a ring of choux pastry; then filled with confectioner's custard

Gâteau sec au gingembre ⇒ ginger nut or gingersnap

Gâtis ⇒ brioche filled with Roquefort cheese and Cantal cheese, then baked

Gaudebillaux ⇒ tripe of beef

Gaudes ⇒ maize porridge

Gaufre ⇒ waffle

Gaufres bordelaises ⇒ waffles from a dough added of sugar, butter, yeast, oil, milk, egg and salt

Gaufres fines ⇒ thin waffles made with eggs, sugar, butter, kirsch, oil and milk

Gaufres fourrées ⇒ sliced waffles, stuffed with a paste of butter, icing sugar and pounded grilled almonds

Gaufres hollandaises ⇒ waffles made with milk, sugar, salt, butter, eggs and yeast

Gaufres liègeoises ⇒ waffles made of flour, yeast, granulated sugar, scrambled eggs and butter

Gaufrettes -[pommes de terre]- ⇒ chips shaped in wafers

Gaufrettes ⇒ wafers made with sugar, cinnamon, eggs, butter and yeast

Gauloise (à la ...)

    1) consommé ⇒ poultry consommé thickened of tapioca, garnished with cockscombs and poached cocks' kidneys

    2) oeufs mollets ⇒ soft-boiled eggs laid on sippets, with a culinary stuffing of ham and tomato sauce, plus fried cockscombs and cock's kidneys

    3) tartelettes ⇒ tartlets filled with a garnish made of cockscombs and cock's kidneys added with a culinary stuffing of truffles and mushrooms; thickened with supreme sauce added of Madeira

    4) poissons garniture ⇒ served with pastry boats filled of a culinary stuffing of truffles, mushrooms and cream, plus poached crayfishes

Gaulthéria -[ronce]- ⇒ blackberry

Gavottes ⇒ small biscuits

Gayette ⇒ flat sausage made of liver, pork fat, garlic and parsley; cooked in the oven, moistened with olive oil

Gazelle ⇒ gazelle

Gazpacho ⇒ gazpacho

Géant d'Hedelfingen -[*cerise*]- ⇒ variety of cherry

Géant du Bouscat -[*lapin*]- ⇒ breed of rabbit

Gelati -[*Italie*]- ⇒ Italian ice cream

Gelatine ⇒ gelatine

Gélatineux ⇒ gelatinous

Gelée ⇒ jelly or aspic < *tous uncountable* >

Gelée à la framboise ⇒ raspberry and redcurrant jelly

Gelée d'abricot ⇒ apricot jelly

Gelée d'airelles ⇒ bilberry and redcurrant jelly

Gelée d'entremets ⇒ dessert based on fruits, wine, sugar and gelatine; ...

    - **à la liqueur** ⇒ ... added of liquor

    - **au vin** ⇒ ... added of ...

    - **champagne** ⇒ champagne

    - **ou madère** ⇒ Madeira

    - **ou marsala** ⇒ marsala

    - **ou porto** ⇒ port

    - **ou xérès** ⇒ xérès

    - **aux fruits rouges** ⇒ added of ...

    - **cerises** ⇒ cherries

    - **ou fraises** ⇒ strawberries

    - **ou framboises** ⇒ raspberries

    - **ou groseilles** ⇒ redcurrants

    - **aux fruits aqueux** ⇒ added of ...

    - **citrons** ⇒ lemons

    - **ou oranges** ⇒ oranges

    - **ou mandarines** ⇒ tangerines

    - **ou ananas** ⇒ pineapple

    - **ou raisins secs** ⇒ raisins

    - **aux fruits à noyaux** ⇒ added of ...

    - **abricots** ⇒ added of apricots

    - **ou brugnions** ⇒ nectarines

    - **ou pêches** ⇒ peaches

    - **ou prunes** ⇒ plums

    - **les fonds de gelées de fruits sont parfumés avec du kirsch** ⇒ flavoured with kirsch

    - **ou du marasquin** ⇒ flavoured with maraschino

    - **ou tout autre liqueur** ⇒ flavoured with liquor

Gelée d'orange ⇒ jelly made with apples and oranges

Gelée de bigarade ⇒ jelly of bitter orange peel, lemon juice, sugar and gelatine

Gelée de cassis à chaud ⇒ blackcurrant jelly

Gelée de cassis à froid ⇒ blackcurrant jelly

Gelée de cuisine ⇒ jelly left by the cooking process, sometime coloured with caramel, flavoured with port or Madeira

Gelée de fruit ⇒ fruit jelly

Gelée de groseilles ⇒ redcurrant jelly

Gelée de groseilles à maquereau ⇒ gooseberry jelly

Gelée de poisson ⇒ fish jelly
Gelée de pomme ⇒ apple jelly added of lemon juice
Gelée de viande ⇒ meat jelly
Géline ⇒ wild chicken
Gelinotte ⇒ hazel grouse
Gendarme
   - **poisson** ⇒ red herring
   - **saucisse** ⇒ kind of hard flat sausage
Gendarme -[bolet]- ⇒ edible black boletus
Genever -[genièvre; gin]- ⇒ gin
Genevoise (à la ...) -[poisson]- ⇒ ... served with a sauce made of fish stock, a mixture of diced
      vegetables and ham, red wine and butter
Genevrette -[vin de fruits]- ⇒ genevrette
Genièvre ⇒ juniper berry or gin < *uncountable* >
Génisse ⇒ heifer
Génoise ⇒ Genoese sponge
Génépi ⇒ wormwood liquor
Gérardmer ⇒ cow's milk cheese from Lorraine area
Géromé ⇒ cow's milk cheese from Gerardmer
Gésier ⇒ gizzard
Genoise à l'abricot ⇒ gateau made with layers of Genoese sponge, plus apricot compote flavoured
      with rum; decorated of grilled almonds or preserved fruits
Genoise à la normande ⇒ Genoese sponge stuffed with a mixing of apple compote, confectioner's
      custard and calvados; covered with apricot jam, and decorated of apple lamellas,
      sliced almonds, plus angelica bits
Genoise au chocolat ⇒ gateau made with Genoese sponge chocolate flavoured, plus egg-custard
      added of butter and chocolate; sprinkled with chopped grilled almonds
Genoise aux fruits confits ⇒ Genoese sponge added of preserved fruits; moistened with a syrup
      flavoured of rum
Genoise fourrée au café ⇒ gateau made of Genoese sponge, plus egg-custard added of butter and
      coffee extract; decorated with grilled almonds
Gentiane ⇒ gentian
Georgette
   - **Pommes georgette** ⇒ baked potatoes hollowed out, and filled with a ragout of crayfish tails
      and truffle
   - **Oeufs pochés ou brouillés georgette** ⇒ poached eggs or scrambled eggs, served with
      potatoes and a ragout of crayfish tails
Gérardmer ⇒ Cow's milk cheese from Lorraine area
Germe ⇒ germ
Germe de soja ⇒ soya bean germ
Germiny -[potage]- ⇒ soup of braised sorrel, consommé, egg-yolks, and cream, added of shredded
      chervil
Germon ⇒ tunny
Geschnetzeltes -[Suisse]- ⇒ slices of poached veal covered with white wine and cream
Gevrey Chambertin ⇒ Chambertin
Gewurztraminer ⇒ spicy high quality white wine, from « traminer » variety of vine
Ghee ⇒ ghee
Ghivetch (E C ...) ⇒ stew of meat and vegetables, simmered with spices and topped of eggs and
      yoghourt
Ghomi (Russe ...) ⇒ maize porridge

Ghurdjurni *(Russe ...)* ⇒ Georgian white wine
Gibassier ⇒ large brioche flavoured with aniseed, orange peel or blossom flowers
Gibelotte ⇒ rabbit ragout in white wine
Gibier ⇒ game < *uncountable* >
Gibier à plume ⇒ wildfowl < *viande uncountable* >
Gibier à poil
   - cerf, chevreuil ⇒ venison
   - lapin ⇒ rabbit
   - lièvres ⇒ hares
   - gibier en général ⇒ game-animals
Gigolette de dinde ⇒ turkey's thigh
Gigondas ⇒ red wine or rosé from Rhone valley
Gigorit ⇒ pig's offal stewed in blood and red wine
Gigot
   - d'agneau ⇒ leg of lamb
   - de mouton ⇒ leg of mutton
   - de cheval ⇒ hind leg of horse
Gigot à la bordelaise ⇒ boned leg of mutton stuffed with ham and anchovy fillets, cooked with carrots, onions, basil and a bottle of Bordeaux red wine; served with the cooking stock added of sautéed garlic
Gigot à la boulangère ⇒ leg of mutton studded of garlic, baked with sliced potatoes and onions
Gigot à la broche persillé ⇒ leg of mutton coated with crumbs and parsley, roasted on a skewer; served with watercress and the cooking juice
Gigot à la ficelle ⇒ leg of mutton, roasted hung with a string
Gigot aux petits oignons nouveaux ⇒ leg of mutton baked with early spring onions, tomatoes and white wine; served with the onions thickened of butter
Gigot avec selle « désossé » ⇒ leg of lamb « boneless »
Gigot avec selle « désossé » ⇒ haunch of lamb « boneless »
Gigot avec selle désossé et ficelé ⇒ leg of lamb boned and rolled
Gigot avec selle désossé et manche fait ⇒ leg of lamb « carvery cut »
Gigot bouilli à l'anglaise ⇒ leg of mutton boiled in a court bouillon with vegetables; served with the vegetables in purée, or boiled potatoes, plus a sauce made of the cooking stock added of butter and capers
Gigot bouilli en Normandie *(Yvetot ...)* ⇒ leg of mutton, boiled in stock flavoured of calvados with vegetables; served with a white sauce added of capers
Gigot bouilli en Provence ⇒ leg of mutton boiled with vegetables; served with mayonnaise and vegetables
Gigot brayaude ⇒ leg of lamb or mutton studded with garlic; braised in white wine with potatoes
   - si d'autres légumes, remplacer « potatoes » par chou ⇒ cabbage
   - haricots rouges ⇒ red beans
   - lentilles ⇒ lentils
   - purée de lentilles ⇒ mashed lentils
Gigot d'agneau ⇒ roast leg of lamb
Gigot d'agneau entier avec selle ⇒ haunch of lamb
Gigot de chevreuil de 3 heures ⇒ haunch of venison studded with lardoons, braised with oil, butter, cognac, red wine, garlic, pimentos and mustard; served with the cooking juice thickened of raspberry jelly, plus chestnut purée added of cream
Gigot de mouton entier, désossé ⇒ boneless haunch of mutton
Gigot de mouton entier, raccourci ⇒ leg of mutton
Gigot de mouton entier, roulé et désossé ⇒ boned and rolled haunch of mutton

Gigot de mouton raccourci, désossé ⇒ boned leg of mutton
Gigot de mouton raccourci, roulé, désossé ⇒ boned and rolled leg of mutton or lamb
Gigot entier ⇒ haunch of lamb
Gigot entier désossé et ficelé ⇒ haunch of lamb « boned and rolled »
Gigot rôti aux quarante gousses d'ail ⇒ leg of mutton seasoned with garlic, and rosemary powder,
    then roasted on a skewer; served with forty boiled cloves of garlic, plus watercress
    and the gravy
Gigot rôti en chevreuil ⇒ leg of mutton marinated, then roasted; served with ...
    - sauce chevreuil ⇒ ... roebuck sauce
    - sauce poivrade ⇒ ... a sauce based on a mixture of diced vegetables and ham cooked in vinegar
    plus white wine, then seasoned of pepper
Gigot rôti Léa ⇒ leg of mutton marinated in anchovy fillets, olive oil, mustard, sage, basil and
    rosemary, then roasted; served with the marinade thickened of butter, and added of
    half a bottle of champagne
Gigot sans selle ⇒ leg of lamb
Gigourit ⇒ pig's offal stewed in blood and red wine
Gigue ⇒ haunch of venison
Gigue de porc fraîche aux pistaches ⇒ haunch of pork marinated in Bordeaux white wine; then
    studded of pistachios, and braised with dried plums steeped in Bordeaux white wine
Gimblette ⇒ small pastry shaped in ring, and made of flour, crushed almonds, sugar, egg-yolks, yeast,
    orange or cedrate peel
Gimblettes ... ⇒ ring biscuits flavoured ...
    - à l'orange ⇒ ... with orange peel
    - au citron ⇒ ... with lemon peel
    - au cédrat ⇒ ... with cedrate peel
    - à la bigarade ⇒ ... with bitter orange peel
    - à l'anis ⇒ ... with aniseed
    - à la vanille ⇒ ... with vanilla
    - à la fleur d'oranger ⇒ ... with orange blossom
Gimlet *-[cocktail]-* ⇒ gimlet
Gin ⇒ gin < *uncountable* >
Gin tonic ⇒ gin added of tonic water
Gin-fizz ⇒ gin-fizz < *uncountable* >
Gingembre ⇒ ginger < *uncountable* >
Ginger ale ⇒ ginger ale
Ginger beer ⇒ ginger beer
    - variantes ⇒ ginger ale or ginger wine
Ginger wine ⇒ ginger wine
Gingerbread ⇒ gingerbread
Ginkgo *-[fruit]-* ⇒ ginkgo
Ginseng ⇒ root from a Korean plant
Gioddu sarde ⇒ fermented milk
Gipa *-[cuisine juive]-* ⇒ beef stomach stuffed with rice
Girado *-[pompe]-* ⇒ large brioche flavoured with aniseed, orange peel or blossom flowers
Giraumon ⇒ pumpkin < *sert à faire des ratatouilles, des ragoUts, de la confiture, ou se mange cru*
    comme les concombres >
Giraumonade *-[Antilles]-* ⇒ mashed pumpkin
Girelle *-[poisson]-* ⇒ rainbow wrasse
Giro *-[Sardaigne]-* ⇒ Sardinian sweet wine

Girofle ⇒ clove
- **clou de girofle** ⇒ clove

Girofle rouge -*[bolet orangé]*- ⇒ orange cap boletus

Girolle ⇒ chanterelle mushroom or edible agaric

Gîte -*[boeuf]*- ⇒ shin of beef

Gîte à la noix -*[boeuf]*- ⇒ topside of beef

Gîte coupé et ficelé -*[boeuf]*- ⇒ silverside « rolled »

Gîte de derrière ⇒ hindquarter shin of beef

Gîte de derrière -*[boeuf]*- ⇒ hindquarter shin of beef

Gîte de devant -*[boeuf]*- ⇒ forequarter shin of beef

Gîte et tende de tranche -*[boeuf]*- ⇒ silverside and topside « reverse »

Gîte-gîte ⇒ shin of beef

Givrer
- **un verre** ⇒ glass with a collarette of sugar and lemon juice in its edge
- **fruit** ⇒ fruit hollowed out and filled with a sorbet made of its pulp

Givry ⇒ Burgundy wine, red or white

Givrée ⇒ frosted or frosty

Givré ⇒ frost covered

Gjetost -*[fromage]*- ⇒ Gjetost

Glaçage à chaud -*[pièce de boucherie, etc ...]*- ⇒ baked, nom de la viande ... coated with its cooking juice

Glaçage au chocolat ⇒ coating made of melted chocolate, sugar, and butter

Glaçage au froid -*[glacer]*- ⇒ chilled preparation

Glaçage blanc -*[glace de sucre]*- ⇒ coating of sugar, water and lemon

Glaçage de couleur -*[glace de sucre]*- ⇒ coating of sugar, water, plus colouring

Glace (nom ...) ⇒ ice
- **dessert** ⇒ ice-cream
- **glaces à la crème ou crème glacée** ⇒ ice-creams of milk, sugar, and aromatics
- **glaces aux œufs** ⇒ ice-creams of egg-yolks, milk, sugar and flavouring
- **glaces au sirop** ⇒ ice-creams of sugar, and flavouring

Glace à l'abricot ⇒ sorbet made of apricot purée, syrup and lemon juice

Glace à l'ananas ⇒ sorbet made of pineapple pulp, syrup and rum

Glace à la banane ⇒ sorbet made of bananas, syrup, lemon juice and rum

Glace à la liqueur (n'importe laquelle ...) ⇒ sorbet made of syrup, lemon juice and a liquor

Glace à la mangue ⇒ sorbet made of mashed mangos, lemon juice and syrup

Glace à la vanille ⇒ ice cream of egg-custard flavoured with vanilla; served ...
- **nature** ⇒ ... plain
- **fruits confits** ⇒ ... with preserved fruits poached in syrup
- **nappée d'une purée de fruits** ⇒ ... covered with mashed fruits
- **servie moulée en boules** ⇒ ... moulded in balls for cups
- **pour fourrer des profiteroles** ⇒ ... as stuffing for profiteroles

Glace à la vanille pour coupes glacées ⇒ vanilla ice cream for cups

Glace au café ⇒ sorbet made of egg-custard, coffee powder and whipped cream

Glace au café et à la fine champagne ⇒ sorbet made of egg-custard, coffee powder, syrup, whipped cream, and high quality of cognac

Glace au caramel ⇒ sorbet made of caramel, milk, lemon juice, and egg-yolks

Glace au chocolat ⇒ sorbet made of chocolate, egg-yolks, milk and sugar

Glace au grand marnier ⇒ sorbet made of syrup, lemon juice, plus a liquor based on orange and cognac

Glace aux cerises ⇒ sorbet made of mashed cherries, plus a syrup flavoured with kirsch
Glace aux truffes ⇒ ice cream made of chilled egg-custard, and chopped truffles cooked in milk
Glace de sucre ⇒ coating made of icing sugar and water, flavoured variously with ...
  - **avec café** ⇒ ... coffee
  - **chocolat** ⇒ ... chocolate
  - **liqueur** ⇒ ... liquor
  - **vanille** ⇒ ... vanilla
  - **zeste de citron** ⇒ ... lemon peel
  - **zeste de mandarine** ⇒ ... tangerine peel
  - **zeste d'orange** ⇒ ... orange peel
Glace de tomate *(ou Suc de tomate concentré ...)* ⇒ tomato purée
Glace de viande ⇒ concentrated meat stock
Glace plombières ⇒ ice cream made of egg-yolks, sugar, almond, and milk, plus a culinary stuffing of preserved fruits
Glace plombières aux marrons ⇒ ice cream made of egg yolks, sugar, almond milk, a culinary stuffing of preserved fruits, plus chestnut purée
Glace royale ⇒ coating made of icing sugar, white of eggs and lemon juice
Glacé *(e ...)*
  - **adj** ⇒ glazed
  - **fruit glacé** ⇒ glacé or candied fruit or crystallized fruit
  - **café glacé** ⇒ iced coffee
  - **chocolat glacé** ⇒ iced chocolate
  - **légumes glacé** ⇒ glazed ...
  - **viande glacé** ⇒ glazed ...
  - **boisson glacé** ⇒ icy ... or ice-cold ...
Glaçon ⇒ ice cube
Globe de bœuf « 3 principales pièces » ⇒ top piece of beef
Glögg ⇒ glogg
Gloria ⇒ coffee added with eau de vie
Gloucester *-[fromage]-* ⇒ Gloucester
Glouteron *-[bardane]-* ⇒ burdock
Glu du chêne *-[langue de bœuf « champignon »]-* ⇒ beefsteak fungus ½ ou ½ oak tongue
Glucose ⇒ glucose
Glutamaté ⇒ gluten extract
Gluten ⇒ gluten
Gnocchi ⇒ gnocchi < *invariable* >
Gnocchi à l'Alsacienne ⇒ gnocchi made of potatoes and flour, covered with cream and grated cheese; then browned
Gnocchi à la romaine ⇒ gnocchi of semolina, egg-yolks and cheese
Gnocchi de pommes de terre ⇒ gnocchi made from mashed potatoes
Gnocchis à la parisienne ⇒ gnocchi made of poached choux pastry, covered with béchamel sauce added of egg-yolks and gruyère, plus grated cheese; then browned
Gnôle ⇒ hooch
Gobie ⇒ goby
Gobo ⇒ burdock's root
Godaille *-[marasme d'oréade]-* ⇒ fairy ring mushroom

Godard
- **apprêt pour grosses pièces de boucherie, poulardes, ou ris de veau** ⇒ nom anglais
- **avec ris d'agneau** ⇒ ... with a garnish of quenelles, cockscombs, kidneys, braised lamb sweetbreads, truffles and mushrooms; covered with a sauce of white wine, or champagne, plus diced vegetables and ham
- **avec ris de veau** ⇒ ... with a garnish of cockscombs, kidneys, braised calf sweetbreads, truffles and mushrooms; covered with a sauce of white wine, or champagne, plus diced vegetables and ham

Godiveau ⇒ forcemeat balls

Godiveau à la crème ⇒ forcemeat balls made with cushion of veal, ox kidneys, eggs and cream

Godiveau à la graisse ⇒ hashed veal meat and hashed kidney grease mixed with pepper, nutmeg and eggs, then chilled

Godiveau aux anchoix ⇒ forcemeat balls made of anchovy and pike, wrapped in short pastry

Gogues ⇒ polony made of vegetables, pork fat, cream and blood; first poached, then sliced and fried

Gohan -[*Japon*]- ⇒ rice

Golden delicious -[*pommes*]- ⇒ Golden delicious apple

Golden syrup ⇒ golden syrup

Golmelle -[*coulemelle*]- ⇒ parasol mushroom

Golmotte -[*coulemelle*]- ⇒ parasol mushroom

Golmotte -[*amanite rougeâtre*]- ⇒ blusher

Gombo ⇒ ketmias

Gombos à la créole ⇒ ketmias braised in oil and chopped onions, plus crushed tomatoes, garlic, cayenne pepper and saffron; served with rice

Gomme ⇒ gum

Gomphide glutineux ⇒ glutinous gomphidius

Gonfler
- **pâte** ⇒ to rise
- **riz, lentilles ...** ⇒ to swell up

Gonflé ⇒ risen or swelled up

Gordon -[*bière*]- ⇒ Gordon beer

Gorella -[*fraise*]- ⇒ strawberry from Périgord

Gorenflot
- **cuisine** ⇒ ... with a garnish of saveloy, stuffed potatoes and a julienne of red cabbage
- **patisserie** ⇒ hexagonal baba

Gorge de porc ⇒ pork jowl

Gorgonzola ⇒ Gorgonzola

Gouch -[*kounafa*]- ⇒ pastry made of browned dough, crushed almonds and crushed hazelnuts; sprinkled with syrup
- **variantes Basma** ⇒ id
- **Gouch** ⇒ id
- **Lakhana** ⇒ ...; with soft white cheese

Gouda ⇒ Gouda

Gouéron
- **Nivernais, gouerre au cirage** ⇒ gateau with prunes
- **Touraine** ⇒ gateau of flour, eggs and goat's milk cheese
- **Berry** ⇒ pie with apples

Gouère
- **Nivernais, gouerre au cirage** ⇒ gateau with prunes
- **Touraine** ⇒ gateau of flour, eggs and goat's milk cheese
- **Berry** ⇒ pie with apples

Gouerre
- **Nivernais, gouerre au cirage** ⇒ gateau with prunes
- **Touraine** ⇒ Gateau of flour, eggs and goat's milk cheese
- **Berry** ⇒ pie with apples

Gouffé ⇒ sauté ... nom anglais de la viande, glazed in Madeira; garnished of fried croustades made with mashed potatoes, eggs, and butter, filled with asparagus tips in butter, and morels in cream

Gougeon de mer ⇒ goby

Gougnette ⇒ fritter

Gougère ⇒ pastry ring, made of choux paste added of cheese and pepper; then baked

Goujon ⇒ gudgeon

Goujonnettes -*[garniture]-* ⇒ garnish of fried sole lamellas

Goulache ⇒ goulash

Goulasch ⇒ goulash

Goumi ⇒ wild berry

Gourdon -*[cabécou]-* ⇒ small cheese from a mixing of goat's milk and cow's milk

Gourieva kacha -*[russe]-* ⇒ semolina pudding, filled with nuts and preserved fruits

Gourilos ⇒ endives

Gourilos étuvés au persil ⇒ braised endives sprinkled with parsley

Gourmandise noix de veau « du prince Murat » ⇒ packets made from bits of lobsters cooked in sauce, plus cushion of veal hashed and diced, browned in oil and butter; served with the cooking sauce from lobster, thickened of cream

Gourmeau -*[tarte au]-* ⇒ tart filled with scrambled eggs, sugar, milk, and cream

Gourmet -*[sauce]-* ⇒ sauce made of fish stock, a mixture of diced vegetables and ham, white wine, lobster butter, crayfish tails, quenelles and truffles

Gournay -*[fromage]-* ⇒ cow's milk cheese from Gournay en Bray

Gousse d'ail ⇒ clove of garlic

Gousse de vanille ⇒ pod of vanilla

Gousson de poitrine de boeuf ⇒ brisket of beef

Gousson de poitrine de boeuf désossé ⇒ boneless brisket beef

Goûter -*[collation]-* ⇒ collation or light meal

Goutte -*[petit verre]-* ⇒ nip

Goutte d'encre -*[coprin chevelu]-* ⇒ ink cap or horsetail fungus or maned agaric
- **mangé à la croque au sel** ⇒ ... eaten raw with coarse salt
- **sauté dans l'huile ou le beurre avec ail** ⇒ ... sautéed in oil or butter with garlic

Goutte d'or -*[prune]-* ⇒ variety of plum

Goyave ⇒ guava

Goyère ⇒ tart filled with a mixing of maroilles cheese and soft white cheese

Gozinakhi -*[Russe]-* ⇒ sweet made of nuts and honey

Gradin (*décoration ...*) ⇒ edible socle for the laying of a chilled dish

Grain ⇒ grain or berry or bean

Grain de café ⇒ coffee bean

Grain de pararadis -*[cardamome]-* ⇒ cardamom < *uncountable* >

Grain de raisin ⇒ grape

Graine de tounesol ⇒ sunflower seed

Graines de carvi ⇒ caraway seeds

Graines de cochenille ⇒ cochineal seeds

Graines de lotus ⇒ lotus seeds

Graisse
- **général** ⇒ grease or fat or cooking fat
- **de porc** ⇒ lard
- **végétale** ⇒ vegetable fat

Graisse de Cherbourg ⇒ mixture of pork, mutton and beef fat, cooked with carrots, onions, cloves, leeks, celery and chervil

Graisse de bœuf ⇒ beef fat

Graisse de mouton ⇒ mutton fat

Graisse normande ⇒ mixture of pork, mutton and beef fat, cooked with carrots, onions, cloves, leeks, celery and chervil

Gramolate ⇒ a sorbet

Gran Reserva *-[Rioja]-* ⇒ Spanish wine bottled after five years in barrel

Grana *-[Parmesan]-* ⇒ Grana

Grand ⇒ large or big or great or important

    sens des mots anglais
- **grande taille, par exemple tasse** ⇒ large
- **grand ou gros** ⇒ big
- **important** ⇒ great
- **important** ⇒ important

Grand ailloli ou aïoli ⇒ dish of poached salt cod, boiled mutton, carrots, celery, french beans, beetroot, cauliflower, hard boiled eggs and snails; served with a sauce of garlic, egg-yolks, and olive oil

Grand alexandre *-[pomme]-* ⇒ variety of apple

Grand arôme *-[rhum]-* ⇒ rum slowly fermented

Grand café ⇒ a large cup of coffee

Grand cru ⇒ a famous wine or a great wine or vintage

Grand duc ⇒ dishes based on asparagus tips and truffles
- **filets de sole** ⇒ poached sole fillets covered with béchamel sauce added of egg-yolks and gruyère; served with asparagus tips, crayfish tails and truffle lamellas
- **œufs** ⇒ poached eggs covered with béchamel sauce added of egg-yolks and gruyère, decorated with truffle lamellas and laid on fried sippets, surrounded by asparagus tips
- **viandes** ⇒ sauté meat, plus Madeira sauce added of truffle lamellas, surrounded by asparagus tips

Grand mandarin *-[thé]-* ⇒ Chinese tea flavoured with jasmine

Grand marnier ⇒ liqueur from bitter orange-peel and cognac

Grand mère
- **garniture** ⇒ ... cooked with a garnish of lardoons, onions, sauté mushrooms and fried potatoes
- **steak** ⇒ steak served with a garnish of lardoons, onions, sauté mushrooms and fried potatoes

Grand pourceau *-[capitaine poisson]-* ⇒ African sea bass < *pluriel inchangé* >

Grand Roussillon ⇒ muscat from Perpignan area

Grand tétras ⇒ capercaillie

Grand Veneur ⇒ sauté game, covered with a peppery sauce added of redcurrant jelly, and cream; served with chestnut purée

Grande Bretagne ⇒ principaux plats repris séparèment

Grande chartreuse *-[élixir]-* ⇒ chartreuse

Grande coulemelle *-[champignon]-* ⇒ parasol mushroom

Grande naine *-[banane]-* ⇒ variety of banana

Grande religieuse à l'ancienne ⇒ sugared pastry filled with choux pastry stuffed of custard, and topped with cream

Grande rousette *-[poisson]-* ⇒ greater spotted dogfish

Grande ruchotte -*[Chassagne-montrachet]*- ⇒ Burgundy wine either red or white

Grandjean -*[noix]*- ⇒ nut or walnut

Grands murs -*[Chambolle-musigny]*- ⇒ high quality Burgundy wine from Chambolle Musigny

Grands-échezeaux -*[Vosne-romanée]*- ⇒ Burgundy red wine from Côtes de Nuits

Granit aux fraises ⇒ preparation of strawberry purée, sugar, vanilla powder and whipped cream

Granit aux framboises ⇒ preparation of raspberry purée, sugar, vanilla powder and whipped cream

Granits de saumur en auxois ⇒ sweet filled or wrapped with chocolate

Granité ⇒ Italian sorbet

Granny smith -*[pomme]*- ⇒ granny smith apple

Grapefruit ou pomelo -*[pamplemousse]*- ⇒ grapefruit

Grappa ⇒ grappa

Grappe de raisin ⇒ bunch of grapes

Gras-double ⇒ tripe < *uncountable* >

Gras double à la poulette ⇒ diced tripe in butter; cooked in timbale with poultry stock, parsley, lemon juice and mushrooms

Gras double à la Voironnaise ⇒ diced cooked tripe, braised in a sauce of butter, flour and stock, plus onions, bundle of herbs, pepper and white wine

Gras double de bœuf à la bourgeoise ⇒ tripe cooked with carrots, onions and cayenne pepper

Gras-double de bœuf à la lyonnaise ⇒ ox tripe fried in pork fat with onions; served sprinkled of french dressing and parsley

Gratin

    1) **chapelure** ⇒ breadcrumbs

        - **fromage râpé** ⇒ grated cheese

        - **utilisé pour les plats gratinés** ⇒ ... used as covering for dishes to be browned under the grill

    2) **couverture de chapelure et de fromage râpé** ⇒ coating of breadcrumbs and grated cheese

    3) **plat préparé avec une couverture de chapelure et fromage râpé** ⇒ dish prepared with a coating of breadcrumbs and grated cheese

    4) **chou-fleur au gratin** ⇒ cauliflower cheese

    5) **plat** ⇒ cheese-topped dish of or gratin

    6) **croûte** ⇒ cheese topping or gratin

    7) **au gratin** ⇒ au gratin

    8) **gratin de pommes de terre** ⇒ potatoes au gratin

    9) **gratin dauphinois** ⇒ gratin Dauphinois

Gratin à la languedocienne ⇒ alternate layers of aubergines and tomatoes, sprinkled with parsley, breadcrumbs and olive oil, then baked until golden

Gratin à la savoyarde ⇒ leeks or cardoons or gourd au gratin

Gratin d'œufs brouillés à l'antiboise ⇒ layers of cooked scrambled eggs, fried sliced courgettes, and tomatoes cooked in their own liquid; topped with grated parmesan and melted butter, then browned

Gratin dauphinois ⇒ gratin Dauphinois

Gratin de bettes au verjus ⇒ dish of beets, whipped cream, unripe grape juice, egg-yolks, parsley and pepper; covered with grated cheese, then browned

Gratin de fraises au sabayon de citron ⇒ strawberries, covered with a zabaglione flavoured of lemon; then browned quickly

Gratin de pommes à la dauphinoise ⇒ sliced potatoes cooked with cream and browned or gratin Dauphinois

Gratin de pommes de terre ⇒ potatoes au gratin

Gratin de pommes de terre à la hongroise ⇒ mixing of baked potato pulp, plus chopped onions cooked in butter; sprinkled with paprika, crumbs and melted butter, then browned

Gratin de potiron à la provençale ⇒ layers of diced pumpkin and sliced onions; sprinkled with grated cheese and olive oil, then browned

Gratin de queues d'écrevisses « à la façon de maître La Planche » ⇒ ragout of seasoned crayfish tails alternated with buttered sliced truffles; sprinkled with grated cheese and browned

Gratin de queues d'écrevisses ⇒ ragout of crayfish tails, sprinkled with parmesan and melted butter; then browned

Gratin de volaille à la choucroute ⇒ elaborated dish of chicken, sauerkraut and aromatics; at last laid in goose fat, sprinkled of cream and grated cheese, then browned

Gratin provençal ⇒ dish of fried onions, sliced aubergines, courgettes, tomatoes, grated cheese and aromatics; sprinkled of crumbs and olive oil, then browned

Gratin savoyard de cuisses de grenouilles ⇒ sauté frogs' legs, covered with their juice thickened of white wine, then sprinkled of parsley and chives; coated with cream, added of gruyère and egg-yolks, then browned

Gratiner ⇒ to cook au gratin

Gratinée ou Gratiné
- **soupe** ⇒ bread crumbed
- **plat** ⇒ cooked au gratin

Gratte-cul -*[églantier]*- ⇒ eglantine fruit

Gratteron ⇒ burdock

Gratton -*[friton]*-
- **rillettes** ⇒ kind of rillettes made with pork fat, tongue, heart and kidneys
- **grattons** ⇒ cooked goose fat

Gratuit ⇒ without charge or free of charge
- **boisson gratuite** ⇒ a free drink

Gravenche ⇒ Salmonidae from the Alpine lakes

Graves -*[vin]*- ⇒ graves

Gravette -*[huître]*- ⇒ oyster from Arcachon

Gravlax -*[Suède]*- ⇒ raw salmon marinated in pepper, dill, sugar and salt

Gray sole -*[plie]*- ⇒ gray sole

Grecque *(à la ...)*
1) **Hors d'oeuvre de légumes** ⇒ hors d'oeuvre of vegetables cooked in a marinade flavoured with olive oil and lemon
2) **Pilaf** ⇒ pilaf added of sausage-meat, peas and diced capsicums
3) **Poissons** ⇒ ... covered with a white wine sauce, flavoured of celery, fennel, and coriander seeds

Grelatte -*[suisse]*- ⇒ aspic made of trotters, tail, head and ears from pork, plus small ham

Grelons -*[sucre en grains]*- ⇒ crushed sugar

Grelot -*[carotte]*- ⇒ variety of carrot

Grenade ⇒ pomegranate

Grenadier de roche -*[poisson]*- ⇒ roundnose grenadier

Grenadille ⇒ passion fruit

Grenadine ⇒ pomegranate syrup

Grenadins
- **veau** ⇒ round slices from loin of veal, studded with lard and braised in butter
- **dinde** ⇒ escalopes from duck's white of meat
- **petits grenadins de veau** ⇒ round slices from loin of veal, studded with lard and braised in butter

Grenadins de veau braisés ⇒ round slices from loin of veal, studded with lard and braised in butter, white wine and stock; served with spinach in butter

Grenadins de veau poêlés à la crème ⇒ round slices from loin of veal, studded with lard and fried in oil; covered with the sauce added of white wine or cider, plus cream

Grenaille *-[pomme de terre]-* ⇒ variety of potato

Grenobloise *(à la ...) -[poissons]-* ⇒ ... nom anglais des poissons floured and fried, then garnished of capers, plus diced lemon, and sometimes added of fried sippets

Grenouille ⇒ frog

  - cuisse de grenouille ⇒ frog's leg

Gressin ⇒ Italian small stick of bread paste and oil

Grèves ⇒ quality red wine from Beaune area

Gribenes *-[russe]-* ⇒ bits of goose skin fried with onions; served with buckwheat fritters

Gribiche *-[sauce]-* ⇒ sauce made of hard boiled egg-yolks, oil, chopped capers, and herbs

Gribouis ⇒ julienne of mushrooms

Griffe *-[viande]-* ⇒ scrag end of beef

Grignaudes

  - rillettes ⇒ kind of rillettes made with pork fat, tongue, heart and kidneys

  - grattons ⇒ cooked goose fat

Grillades

  - menu ⇒ grill or grillstones < *commun ou poétique* >

  - viande grillée ⇒ grilled meat or grilled ... nom anglais de la viande

Grillades de perdrix *-[porc]-* ⇒ sparerib chops

Grillé ⇒ grilled < *v.t adjectif* >

Grillons *-[rillons]-* ⇒ bits of pork macerated in salt, then cooked in pork fat

Grimolle ⇒ baked pancake with fruits

Griotte *-[cerise]-* ⇒ variety of cherry

Griotte du nord *-[cerise]-* ⇒ variety of cherry

Gris de lille *-[fromage]-* ⇒ cow's milk cheese from Lille area

Gris meunier *-[orléanais]-* ⇒ quality rosé wine from Orleans area

Grise du mans *-[pomme]-* ⇒ variety of apple

Grisette de provence *-[courgette]-* ⇒ courgette

Grissini *-[gressin]-* ⇒ Italian small stick of bread paste and oil

Grive ⇒ thrush

Grive à la casserole ⇒ casserole of thrush

Grive musicienne ⇒ song-thrush

Grives à la bonne femme ⇒ thrushes braised in butter with lardoons; added of fried sippets and sprinkled with cognac

Grives à la liègeoise ⇒ thrushes flamed with gin, braised in butter, plus juniper berries and diced ham; served on toasts, covered with their cooking juice

Grives à la polenta ⇒ roasted thrushes laid on polenta sprinkled with grated cheese and melted butter, then baked; served with their cooking juice added of white wine

Grives à la purée d'oignons au vinaigre de xérès ⇒ baked thrushes sprinkled with gin; covered with onions cooked in butter and added of thrush stock, cream and xeres vinegar

Grives au raisin ⇒ thrushes wrapped in vine leaves, plus pork fat and braised in butter, then added of grapes moistened in their juice; served covered with the cooking juice, thickened of cognac and stock

Grives en caisses ⇒ boned thrushes stuffed with a forcemeat, diced foie gras and truffle, then cooked in butter, onion, carrot, Madeira and game stock; served in individual small box with sauté mushrooms, covered of cooking juice

Grives en croûte à l'ardennaise ⇒ boned thrushes stuffed with a forcemeat, diced foie gras and truffle, sprinkled of melted butter and baked; then packed in a bread hollowed out, and garnished with a forcemeat, then covered with the cooking juice added of xeres and truffle lamellas

Grog ⇒ grog < *uncountable* >

Grondin ⇒ gurnard

Grondin gris ⇒ grey gurnard

Grondin perlon ⇒ yellow gurnard

Grondin rouge ⇒ red gurnard

Grondins au four ⇒ gurnards laid on a hash of onions, shallots, garlic and parsley; sprinkled of melted butter, white wine, pepper, thyme and laurel, then baked

Gros blanc ou escargot de bourgogne ou escargot des vignes ⇒ escargot ½ ou ½ snail

Gros bout -*[poitrine]*- ⇒ piece from brisket of beef

Gros bout de poitrine de veau ⇒ breast of veal

Gros damas -*[pruneau]*- ⇒ prune or dried plum

Gros lorraine -*[gérardmer]*- ⇒ cow's milk cheese from Lorraine area

Gros michel -*[banane]*- ⇒ variety of banana

Gros persil de macédoine -*[maceron]*- ⇒ alexanders OR horse-parsley

Gros pied -*[bolet]*- ⇒ boletus

Gros-plant ⇒ white wine from Nantes area

Gros sel ⇒ coarse salt

Gros souper -*[réveillon]*- ⇒ large meal for Christmas

Gros-vert -*[raisin]*- ⇒ variety of grape

Groseille ⇒ redcurrant

Groseilles à la neige ⇒ redcurrants laid on whipped white of eggs and sugar

Groseille à maquereau ⇒ gooseberry

   - pluriel ⇒ gooseberries

Groseilles de chine -*[kiwi]*- ⇒ kiwi fruit

Grouse ⇒ grouse

Gruau ⇒ high quality wheat flour

Gruau d'avoine -*[bouillie]*- ⇒ gruel

Grue -*[oiseau]*- ⇒ crane

Gruyère ⇒ gruyère

Gryphée ⇒ variety of oyster

Guacamole -*[sauce]*- ⇒ guacamole

Guai -*[hareng]*- ⇒ meagre herring

Guerbigny -*[fromage]*- ⇒ cheese from Picardie

Gueuze -*[Belgique]*- ⇒ Belgian beer

Guigne ⇒ heart-cherry

Guignes de Bordeaux ⇒ sweet filled or wrapped with chocolate

Guignette -*[bigorneau]*- ⇒ winkle

Guignolet ⇒ a cherry liqueur

Guignolette d'Auvergne ⇒ cherry paste, stuffed with a cherry preserved in kirsch

Guigue de chevreuil ⇒ haunch of venison

Guigue de porc fraîche aux pistaches ⇒ haunch of pork marinated in Bordeaux white wine; then studded of pistachios, and braised with dried plums steeped in Bordeaux white wine

Guildive -*[rhum]*- ⇒ rum

Guillaret ⇒ kind of cake

Guillaume -*[cerise]*- ⇒ variety of cherry

Guimauve ⇒ marshmallow sweet

Guinness *-[bière]-* ⇒ Guinness
Gulyas ⇒ goulash
Gumbo créole ⇒ stew of meat and shells
Gumpoldskirchener ⇒ Austrian white wine
Gunpowder *-[thé]-* ⇒ Chinese tea
Gutedel *-[Allemagne vins]-* ⇒ wine from Rhine right bank
Gymnote ⇒ electric eel
Gyrocéphale rousâtre ⇒ edible mushroom for salads
Gyromitre comestible ⇒ gyromitra

H

Hacher ⇒ to chop OR to hash OR to mince OR to cut up

Haché *(e ...)* ⇒ chopped OR minced

Haché aux aromates ⇒ mince « added TVP »

Haché avec 25% de gras ⇒ mince

Haché de porc ⇒ minced pork

Haché de veau ⇒ minced veal

Haché maigre *-[bœuf]-* ⇒ mince « lean »

Hachis ⇒ hash

Hachis de bœuf à l'indienne ⇒ rice cooked in a edge mould, filled with a hash of boiled beef mixed with a white sauce, added of braised chopped onions, nutmeg, chicken stock and coconut milk

Hachis de bœuf à l'italienne ⇒ hash of boiled beef warmed up again in a mixing of braised onion, stock, tomato purée, and crushed garlic; served with Italian ribbons of noodles added of eggs, plus the sauce

Hachis de bœuf bouilli ⇒ hash of boiled beef, added of hashed onions cooked in butter and stock

Hachis de bœuf en gratin aux aubergines ⇒ hash of boiled beef, mixed with a sauce of chopped onion braised in olive oil, plus tomato sauce; laid on sauté aubergines, then covered with grated parmesan plus crumbs, and browned

Hachis de veau à l'allemande ⇒ diced veal meat thickened of sauce; served in croustade or with spaghetti

Hachis de veau Mornay ⇒ hash of roasted veal mixed with a béchamel sauce, thickened of cream, herbs, grated gruyère; then covered with grated cheese, melted butter and browned

Hachis parmentier ⇒ shepherd's pie OR cottage pie

Hachua

   - **Palay** ⇒ sirloin steak and ham, simmered in white wine with carrots and onions

   - **autre recette** ⇒ ragout of veal and braised beef with diced ham, capsicums and onions

Haddock ⇒ haddock OR finnan OR pale cure *< pluriel inchangé >*

Haddock à l'indienne ⇒ haddock steeped in milk, then simmered with onions in butter, and curry sauce; served with rice

Haddock grillé ⇒ haddock steeped in milk and grilled; served with boiled potatoes and melted butter or spinach in butter

Haddock poché ⇒ haddock poached in milk; served with melted butter flavoured of lemon juice and parsley, plus boiled potatoes

Haggis ⇒ haggis

Hakkebiff *-[Danemark]-* ⇒ hamburger added of chopped onion, and covered with brown sauce

Halawi *-[datte]-* ⇒ date

Halévy

   - **oeufs** ⇒ poached eggs laid on tartlets, covered with a culinary stuffing of poultry, supreme sauce and tomato sauce

   - **cabillaud** *-[poisson]-* ⇒ poached fresh cod surrounded of mashed potatoes moulded and fried; covered with supreme sauce and tomato sauce

   - **turbot** *-[poisson]-* ⇒ poached turbot surrounded of mashed potatoes moulded and fried; covered with supreme sauce and tomato sauce

Halicot de mouton ⇒ mutton stew garnished with turnips, potatoes and onions OR haricot of mutton OR mutton stew

Haliotide *-[ormeau]-* ⇒ ormer OR haliotis OR sea ear

Hallah *-[cuisine juive]-* ⇒ plaited bread

Halua ⇒ cake made of semolina and milk; garnished of raisins, almonds and cardamom
Halva ⇒ halva OR halvah
Halwa ⇒ halva OR halvah
Hamburger *-[Boeuf]-* ⇒ beef burgers « pure »
Hamburger *-[terme général]-* ⇒ hamburger
Hamburger assaisonné *-[bœuf]-* ⇒ beef burgers « seasoned »
Hamburger économique ⇒ beef burgers « economy »
Hamburgers de poisson ⇒ fried hamburgers made of egg, crumbs, coalfish and onion; topped with a fried egg
Hampe ⇒ thin flank of beef
   - servi grillé ⇒ grilled thin flank of beef
   - servi sauté ⇒ sauté thin flank of beef
Hanche de venaison *-[venaison]-* ⇒ haunch of venison
Handköse *-[fromage]-* ⇒ Handkäse
Hangtown fry *-[amérique du nord]-* ⇒ oysters, plus scrambled eggs
Hard cider *-[cidre]-* ⇒ cider < *uncountable* >
Hareng ⇒ herring
Hareng de la baltique ⇒ herring marinated in vinegar and aromatics
Hareng doux ⇒ kipper
Hareng frais ⇒ fresh herring
Hareng fumé ⇒ smoked herring
Hareng pec ⇒ red herring
Hareng plein *-[bouvard]-* ⇒ herring
Hareng roulé ou Rollmpop ⇒ marinated herring fillets
Hareng salé ⇒ salted herring, either without head or filleted ½ ou ½ salted herring
Hareng saur ⇒ red herring OR smoked herring
Harengs à la boulangère ⇒ herrings surrounded by sliced potatoes and onions; sprinkled with pepper, thyme, laurel powder and melted butter, then baked
Harengs à la diable ⇒ herrings coated with mustard, crumbs and oil, then grilled; served with devilled sauce
Harengs frits ⇒ fried herrings, served with quartered lemons
Harengs grillés ⇒ grilled herrings, served with parsley butter or mustard sauce
Harengs marinés ⇒ soused herrings *or* herrings baked in white wine and vinegar with onions, carrots, pepper, clove, laurel, and thyme
Harengs sautés à la lyonnaise ⇒ fried herrings; served with sauté onions in butter, parsley and vinegar
Haricot ⇒ bean OR kidney bean OR haricot bean
Haricot beurre ⇒ butter bean
Haricot d'Espagne ⇒ Spanish variety of beans
Haricot de lima ⇒ tropical bean
Haricot de mer *-[olive de mer]-* ⇒ wedge shell
Haricot de mouton ⇒ mutton stew garnished with turnips, potatoes and onions
Haricot de soja ⇒ soya bean
Haricot en estouffat ⇒ beans stewed with pork fat, garlic, onions and tomatoes
Haricot grimpant ⇒ runner bean
Haricot mungo ⇒ Asian bean
Haricot noir ⇒ Mexican black bean
Haricot rouge ⇒ red kidney bean
Haricot sec ⇒ dry bean

Haricot sec de soja ⇒ dried soya bean
Haricots à la crème ⇒ boiled beans, dried and covered with cream and savory
Haricots à la lyonnaise ⇒ beans simmered with braised onions in butter, sprinkled of parsley
Haricots à la tomate ⇒ beans cooked with pork fat, then thickened of tomato sauce
Haricots à écosser ⇒ beans in the pod ½ ou ½ unshelled beans
Haricots au beurre ⇒ boiled beans, dried and thickened with butter
Haricots blancs ⇒ haricot beans
Haricots de soja ⇒ soya beans
Haricots rouges à la Bourguignonne ⇒ red kidney beans, cooked with pork fat in a mixing of red wine and water; then braised and thickened with kneaded butter
Haricots verts ⇒ french beans
Haricots verts à la bonne femme ⇒ diced pork fat braised in butter, simmered with boiled french beans and meat stock; served with butter and parsley
Haricots verts à la crème ⇒ boiled french beans simmered with cream, and sprinkled of parsley
Haricots verts à la crème à la normande ⇒ boiled french beans simmered with cream; then mixed with egg-yolk and butter
Haricots verts à la lyonnaise ⇒ boiled french beans, mixed with braised onions in butter, then sprinkled with vinegar
Haricots verts à la tomate ⇒ french beans braised in butter, then simmered in tomato sauce; served sprinkled with parsley or basil
Haricots verts au jus ⇒ french beans braised in butter, then moistened with meat stock
Haricots verts maître d'hôtel ⇒ boiled french beans, mixed with parsley butter
Haricots verts panachés ⇒ mixing of boiled french beans and flageolets; thickened of butter or cream, and sprinkled with herbs
Haricots verts sautés à la provençale ⇒ french beans sautéed in olive oil, then added of garlic and parsley chopped together
Harira -[*Maroc*]- ⇒ Moroccan soup
Harissa ⇒ seasoning based on capsicum purée, coriander, caraway and mint
Harle -[*canard*]- ⇒ wild duck
Harvey sauce -[*GB*]- ⇒ Harvey sauce
Hase -[*lièvre*]- ⇒ hare
Hasty pudding -[*pudding*]- ⇒ hasty pudding
Hâtelet ou Attelet ⇒ ornamental skewer
Hâtif de burlat -[*cerise*]- ⇒ variety of cherry
Hâtif colomer -[*abricot*]- ⇒ variety of apricot
Hâtive d'Argenteuil ⇒ variety of asparagus
Hâtive de Bâle ou de ceret -[*cerise*]- ⇒ variety of cherry
Haute qualité ⇒ excellent OR superior quality
Haut-bailly -[*Graves*]- ⇒ quality Graves red wine
Haut de côtelettes de mouton -[*ragoût*]- ⇒ middle of cutlets
Haut de côtes de porc -[*spare ribs*]- ⇒ spare ribs of pork
Haut-Médoc ⇒ high quality Bordeaux red wine
Haut Poitou -[*vins du*]- ⇒ wines from Poitiers area
Haute cuisine ⇒ Haute cuisine
Haute montagne -[*Beaufort*]- ⇒ trade mark for a cow's milk cheese from the Alps
Havarti -[*fromage*]- ⇒ Havarti
Hazepepper -[*Pays Bas*]- ⇒ jugged hare with pepper
Hecho -[*fromage de brebis*]- ⇒ ewe's milk cheese OR ewe cheese
Helder
    - **garniture** ⇒ garnish of little potatoes browned in butter, plus tomato purée

- côtes de volaille Helder ⇒ voir texte
Helvelle ⇒ helvella
Helvelle crépue -[*champignon*]- ⇒ helvella crispa
Henri IV -[*garniture*]-
   a) petites pièces de boucherie ou d'abats grillés ou sautés
      - grillés ⇒ grilled ... nom anglais de la viande
      - sautées ⇒ sauté ... nom anglais de la viande ... garnished with fried potatoes diced in cubes; covered of béarnaise sauce
   b) tournedos sautés Henri IV ⇒ sauté tournedos laid on watercress and fried potatoes diced in cubes; covered of béarnaise sauce
      - si fonds d'artichaut et pommes noisettes, remplacer « fried potatoes diced in cubes » par ⇒ artichoke hearts filled of potato-balls browned in butter
Henri IV -[*tournedos, pont-neuf, frites*]- ⇒ tournedos served with fried potatoes, watercress and béarnaise sauce
      - quelquefois au lieu de pommes de terre « fried potatoes » il y a artichauts ⇒ artichoke hearts
Herbe -[*aromatique*]- ⇒ herb
Herbe à âne -[*sarriette*]- ⇒ savory < *uncountable* >
Herbe aux teigneux -[*bardane*]- ⇒ burdock
Herbe à la tortue ⇒ mixing of aromatic herbs
Herbe de bison -[*vodka*]-
      - graines ⇒ grass seeds which flavoured the vodka of the brand name Zubrowka
      - vodka ⇒ vodka flavoured with grass seeds
Herbe de St Julien ⇒ savory < *uncountable* >
Herbe sacrée -[*herbes; sauge*]- ⇒ sage OR salvia < *tous uncountable* >
Herbe sacrée -[*hysope*]- ⇒ hyssop
Herbes aux femmes battues -[*tamier*]- ⇒ black bryony
Hermitage -[*vin*]- ⇒ hermitage wine
Herrgardsost -[*fromage*]- ⇒ Herrgardsost
Herve -[*fromage*]- ⇒ Herve
Hélianthe -[*escargot*]- ⇒ snail
Hélénettes ⇒ small cakes from egg-yolks, sugar flour, butter and almond powder
Hénon -[*coque*]- ⇒ cockle
Hérisson ⇒ hedgehog
Hérisson de mer -[*oursin*]- ⇒ sea-urchin
Hérisson gris -[*hydne*]- ⇒ imbricated hydnum
Héron -[*oiseau*]- ⇒ heron
Hibiscus -[*fleur*]- ⇒ hibiscus flower
Hickory -[*sel de*]- ⇒ salt mixed with hickory dust
High grown -[*thé*]- ⇒ Ceylonese tea
High tea -[*GB*]- ⇒ high tea
Hijiki -[*algues*]- ⇒ seaweed
Himmel und Erde -[*Allemagne*]- ⇒ mashed potatoes mixed with mashed apples, topped by a sausage
Hincho -[*Birmanie*]- ⇒ vegetable soup
Hindle wakes -[*GB*]- ⇒ Hindle wakes
Hippocampe ⇒ seahorse OR long nose seahorse OR short nose seahorse
Hirondelle -[*mer de chine*]- ⇒ salangane OR swift OR tern
Hirondelle ⇒ swallow

Hiversa *-[chou pommé]-* ⇒ common cabbage
Hochepot ⇒ Flemish pot au feu
Hoecake ⇒ Hoecake
Hoisin *-[sauce]-* ⇒ seasoning of spices, soya and flour
Hollandaise *(à la ...)* ⇒ served with sauce hollandaise
Hollande *(fromages de, énumération ...)*
- **édam** ⇒ Edam
- **gouda** ⇒ Gouda
- **mimolette** ⇒ Dutch cheese
Homard ⇒ lobster
Homard à l'américaine ⇒ bits of lobster sautéed in olive oil, plus onion, shallots, tomatoes, garlic, tarragon, white wine, cognac, and cayenne pepper; served with the gravy
Homard à l'armoricaine ⇒ bits of lobster sautéed in olive oil, plus onion, shallots, tomatoes, garlic, tarragon, white wine, cognac, and cayenne pepper; served with the gravy
Homard à la broche ⇒ lobster salted and peppered, sprinkled of thyme, laurel and melted butter, then roasted on a skewer; served with its cooking juice
Homard à la crème ⇒ diced lobster braised in butter, cognac, cream and cayenne pepper; served with the cooking juice added of lemon juice and butter
Homard à la nage ⇒ lobster cooked in a court bouillon
Homard à la Newburg ⇒ sauté lobster in a cream sauce
Homard à la parisienne ou escalopes de homard à la parisienne ⇒ escalopes of cold lobster covered with mayonnaise, decorated of truffle lamellas; served with a vegetable salad in mayonnaise
Homard au court-bouillon ⇒ lobster cooked in a court-bouillon with aromatics; served with mayonnaise
Homard cardinal ⇒ halve carapaces of a lobster in court-bouillon, filled with a culinary stuffing of diced lobster and lobster sauce 1, then topped with lobster's escalopes and truffle lamellas; covered with lobster sauce 1, grated cheese, melted butter and browned
- **1 description complète** ⇒ sauce made of fish stock in white wine, egg-yolks, melted butter, pepper, and lemon juice
Homard en chemise ⇒ lobster coated with oil or butter, wrapped in paper and baked; served with a sauce
Homard grillés ⇒ lobsters cut in two, then sprinkled with melted butter or oil, and grilled; served with parsley butter or sauce hollandaise
Homard Henri Duvernois ⇒ lobster braised in butter with leeks and mushrooms, plus xeres, cognac and cream; served with pilaf, and covered with the gravy
Homard sauté à l'orange ⇒ lobster sautéed in oil, garlic, cayenne pepper, shallots, onion and diced orange; covered with the cooking juice added of lobster's eggs, cream, cognac and tarragon, then browned
Homard surprise ⇒ lobster meat braised in butter, cognac and pepper, laid on a large pancake with sliced mushrooms; then folded, covered with the cooking juice, sprinkled of grated parmesan and browned
Homard thermidor ⇒ grilled or roasted lobster; served in the shell with a sauce made of stock, butter, mustard, chervil, tarragon and shallots
Homini grits ⇒ hominy grits
Hongroise *(à la ...)*
1) **Plats avec paprika** ⇒ dishes with paprika OR ... with paprika
2) **Garniture pour grosses pièces de boucherie** ⇒ ... with a garnish of potato croustades topped with cauliflower, covered of béchamel sauce, added of egg-yolks, gruyère, and paprika; plus potatoes shaped in olive and baked with butter

3) Sauce hongroise ⇒ sauce made of chopped onions braised in butter, plus pepper, paprika and white wine

4) Oeufs avec sauce ⇒ eggs with a sauce flavoured of paprika, plus béchamel sauce added of egg-yolks, and gruyère

    - Poissons ⇒ ... with a sauce flavoured of paprika, added of fish stock

    - Boucherie ⇒ ... with a sauce flavoured of paprika, added of the gravy

    - Volaille ⇒ ... with a sauce flavoured of paprika, added of supreme sauce

Honneur *(en ...)* ⇒ honoured

Hopjes *-[Pays bas]-* ⇒ caramels flavoured with coffee

Hoplostete rouge *-[poisson]-* ⇒ orange roughy

Hoplostete argenté *-[poisson]-* ⇒ roughy

Hopping john *-[Amérique du nord]-* ⇒ dish of rice, bacon and red beans

Horchata *-[Espagne]-* ⇒ drink made of barley, sugar and orange-flower water

Horn *-[banane]-* ⇒ large banana for cooking

Hors d'oeuvre ⇒ hors d'oeuvre OR starter « ce mot est de l'argot » OR first course

Hors d'oeuvre assortis ⇒ assorted hors d'oeuvres

Hors d'oeuvre au soja ⇒ composed salad made of crab meat, crayfish tails and soya germs; seasoned with chopped onions, soya sauce, mustard, cognac, vinegar, oil and cayenne pepper

Hors d'oeuvre de moule à la ravigote ⇒ mussels cooked in a hash of shallot and parsley, plus butter, thyme, laurel, white wine and vinegar; served with french dressing added of hard boiled eggs, parsley, chervil, tarragon and chopped gherkins

Hot *-[ketchup]-* ⇒ spicy ketchup

Hot cross buns *-[GB]-* ⇒ hot cross buns

Hot drink *-[cocktail]-* ⇒ cocktail served hot

    variétés de hot drinks

    - lait et oeuf ⇒ eggnogs

    - aux fruits et épices ⇒ shrubs

    - complétés avec du vin ⇒ mulls

Hot-dog ⇒ hot-dog

Hôtelière *(à l' ...)* ⇒ with parsley butter, lemon juice, chopped mushrooms and onions

Houblon ⇒ hop

Hoummos ⇒ Lebanese seasoning

Houx du paraguay *-[maté]-* ⇒ maté

    - infusion ⇒ maté tea

Hovasy maso ⇒ Czechoslovakian pot au feu

Huevos rancheros *-[tortilla]-* ⇒ fried eggs laid on tortilla, garnished with crushed tomatoes added of pimentos, plus slices of avocado

Huile ⇒ oil

    - de cuisson ⇒ cooking oil

Huile à l'estragon ⇒ olive oil flavoured with garlic, clove and tarragon

Huile à la sarriette ⇒ olive oil flavoured with savory

Huile au basilic ⇒ olive oil flavoured with basil

Huile au citron ⇒ olive oil flavoured with lemon

Huile au fenouil ⇒ olive oil flavoured with garlic, clove and fennel

Huile au romarin ⇒ olive oil flavoured with rosemary

Huile blanche *-[oeillette]-* ⇒ poppy-seed oil

Huile d'ail ⇒ oil flavoured with garlic

Huile d'amande ⇒ almond oil

Huile d'arachide ⇒ peanut oil

Huile d'olive ⇒ olive oil

Huile de carthame ⇒ bastard saffron oil

Huile de coco ⇒ copra oil
Huile de colza ⇒ rape oil
Huile de coprah ⇒ copra oil
Huile de faîne ⇒ beech-nut oil
Huile de graines de courge ⇒ gourd pip oil
Huile de maïs ⇒ corn oil
Huile de navette ⇒ rape oil
Huile de noisette ⇒ hazelnut oil
Huile de noix ⇒ walnut oil OR nut oil
Huile de palme ⇒ palm oil
Huile de pépins de citrouille ⇒ pumpkin pip oil
Huile de pépins de potiron ⇒ pumpkin pip oil
Huile de pépins de raisin ⇒ grape pip oil
Huile de phoque ⇒ seal oil
Huile de sésame ⇒ sesame oil
Huile de soja ⇒ soya oil
Huile de tournesol ⇒ sunflower oil
Huile essentielle
  - **fleur** ⇒ aromatic extract from flower
  - **écorce** ⇒ aromatic extract from bark
Huile pimentée ⇒ olive oil flavoured with pounded cayenne pepper
Huile vierge ⇒ unrefined olive oil
Huître ⇒ oyster
Huîtres à la Brolatti ⇒ poached oysters, braised in butter; served in their shell, covered with a sauce of oyster's water, shallots, butter, white wine, pepper and lemon
Huître de claire ⇒ prairie oyster OR fattened oyster
Huître du pauvre -[*moule*]- ⇒ mussel
Huîtres à la diable ⇒ oysters poached in their own liquid, put on a skewer, then sprinkled with melted butter, cayenne pepper, crumbs, and grilled; served with Devilled sauce
Huîtres à la rhétaise ⇒ shelled oysters, covered with a sauce of their own liquid, added of shallots, garlic butter, cream, cayenne pepper, saffron and curry; then browned
Huîtres au cidre et aux bigorneaux ⇒ oysters poached in cider, served in their shell with shelled winkles cooked in a cider court-bouillon; covered with a sauce of chopped shallots cooked in cider, cream, butter, their cooking juice and lemon juice, then glazed in the oven and sprinkled with shredded chervil
Huîtres chaudes en coquilles ⇒ poached oysters, sprinkled of coarse salt and browned; ...
  - **présentées à l'américaine** ⇒ ... sprinkled with lemon juice and cayenne pepper
  - **à la florentine** ⇒ ... served au gratin with spinach, béchamel sauce added of egg-yolks and gruyère
  - **à la polonaise** ⇒ ... sprinkled with hard boiled egg-yolks, parsley, and butter lightly cooked mixed with fried crumbs
Huîtres frites Colbert ⇒ poached oysters, milked and floured, then deep fried, laid on bush with lemons and fried parsley; served with parsley butter added of meat juice and tarragon
Huîtres pochées ⇒ oysters poached in their own liquid
Huîtres Robert Courtine ⇒ oysters cooked in their own liquid; served with a sauce of their cooking juice, shallots, champagne, butter, pepper and lemon juice
Huntsman -[*fromage*]- ⇒ huntsman
Hure
  - **porc** ⇒ pig's head
  - **saumon** ⇒ head of salmon

- brochet ⇒ head of pike

Hure à la parisienne ⇒ tongues and rind of pork in jelly

Hure à la pistache ⇒ galantine made of pig's head, veal's tongues, and a mixing of pepper, nutmeg, clove, and cinnamon; plus chopped shallots, pistachios and truffle lamellas

Hure blanche ⇒ pig's head added of ham and rind of pork

Hure de brochet ⇒ jowl of pike

Hure de Francfort ⇒ pig's head added of ham and rind of pork, in jelly

Hure de sanglier *-[cuisinée]-* ⇒ cooked head of boar

Hure de sanglier *-[général]-* ⇒ boar's head

Hure de saumon ⇒ jowl of salmon

Hure rouge ⇒ pig's head in jelly

Hushallsost *-[fromage]-* ⇒ Hushallsost

Hussarde *(à la ...)* ⇒ braised piece of beef garnished of potatoes, and stuffed aubergines; covered with the gravy and served with grated horse-radish

Hutspot *-[Pays Bas]-* ⇒ stew of pork garnished with middle ribs

Hybride de Montfavet *-[tomate]-* ⇒ variety of tomato

Hydne ⇒ hydnum mushroom

Hydne imbriqué ⇒ imbricated hydnum

Hydne sinué ⇒ spreading hydnum

Hydromel ⇒ mead

Hygrophore de Mars ⇒ March mushroom

Hypholome ⇒ Sulphur tuft

Hypocras ⇒ wine flavoured with spices and fruits

Hypocras à l'angélique ⇒ aperitif made of angelica and nutmeg infused in wine, plus sugar and eau de vie

Hypocras au genièvre ⇒ aperitif made of juniper berries infused in wine, plus alcohol, vanilla powder and granulated sugar

Hysope ⇒ hyssop

I

Icaque ⇒ kind of plum
Ice cream ⇒ ice cream
Idared -*[pomme]*- ⇒ variety of apple
Igname ⇒ yam
Ikra -*[Russe]*- ⇒ caviar < *uncountable* >
Ile flottante ⇒ dessert of baked whipped white of eggs laid on egg-custard and topped with caramel or
    floating island < *cette dernière traduction tirée du dictionnaire, s'applique plutôt*
    pour les œufs en neige pour lesquels elle est également donnée >
Ile flottante aux pralines roses ⇒ baked mousse of whipped white of eggs and praline, laid on egg-
    custard
Iles *(des ...)* -*[à la créole]*-
    a) cuisine ⇒ with rice dried in the oven, capsicums, onions and tomatoes
    b) dessert avec du rhum ⇒ with rum
        - de l'ananas ⇒ with pineapple
        - de la vanille ⇒ with vanilla
        - de la banane ⇒ with banana
Imam bayildi ⇒ aubergines stuffed with their pulp, onion, tomato, spices and aromatics
Imbiber ⇒ to impregnate
Imbriquer ⇒ to imbricate
Imbrucciata
    - tarte ⇒ Corsican tart ...
    - beignet ⇒ Corsican fritter ...
    - pâtisseries ⇒ Corsican pastries ... with soft white cheese from ewe and goat
Impératrice *(à l' ...)*
    1) Consommé ⇒ poultry consommé, added of cockscombs, diced kidneys' cock, chervil
        chiffonade, and asparagus tips
    2) Volaille et Sole ⇒ ... with supreme sauce
    3) Entremets ⇒ dessert of rice cooked in milk; preserved fruits and mousse of fruits purée added
        of whipped cream
Imperial souchong ⇒ variety of tea
Impériale *(à l' ...)*
    - garniture de poissons ⇒ served with garnishes composed variously of cockscombs, truffles,
        crayfish, soft roes and foie gras
    - consommé ⇒ consommé garnished with quenelles, cockscombs and cock's kidneys
Impériale -*[prune]*- ⇒ variety of plum
Imprégné ⇒ steeped
    - être imprégné ⇒ to be impregnated
Inarbitata -*[Bastella]*- ⇒ Corsican turnover filled with beets or spinach plus meat
Inciser ⇒ to incise
Incivulata -*[Bastella]*- ⇒ Corsican turnover filled with onions and meat
Incorporer ⇒ to incorporate or to embody
Incrusté de ou Incrusté avec ⇒ incrusted with
Indica -*[riz]*- ⇒ rice
Indienne *(à l' ...)* ⇒ with rice and curry sauce
Indigotine ⇒ carmine indigo
Indik -*[Pologne]*- ⇒ turkey < *viande uncountable* >
Infuser ⇒ to infuse, to steep or to macerate

Infusion ⇒ infusion
Intestin ⇒ intestine or bowel
Involtini Milanais ⇒ small ball of ham
Inzucatta -*[Bastella]*- ⇒ Corsican turnover filled with gourd or pumpkin plus meat
Irish christmas cake ⇒ Irish Christmas cake
Irish coffee
    a) café ⇒ drink made with whiskey plus coffee, topped of chilled cream
    b) entremets ⇒ sweet made with whiskey plus coffee, topped of chilled cream
Irish stew ⇒ Irish stew
Irish whiskey ⇒ whiskey
Irouléguy -*[vin]*- ⇒ wines from Basque area
Isard ⇒ izard or chamois of the Pyrenees
Islay -*[fromage]*- ⇒ Islay
Italie -*[vins]*- ⇒ certains sont repris individuellement
Italienne *(à l' ...)*
    1) avec sauce ⇒ ... with a sauce made of chopped mushrooms, ham and herbs
    2) avec artichauts ⇒ ... with a garnish of quartered artichokes
    3) avec macaronis ⇒ ... with macaroni
Ivoire -*[sauce]*- ⇒ supreme sauce added of veal's gravy
Izard ⇒ izard or chamois of the Pyrenees
Izarra ⇒ liqueur from herbs and coriander

J

Jabugo -*[chorizo]*- ⇒ sausage seasoned with pimento and garlic
Jacque ⇒ apple pancake
Jaerla -*[Pomme de terre]*- ⇒ new potato
Jailles ⇒ ragout made of chine of pork, aromatics, seasoning, quartered apples, stale bread and vinegar
Jalousie ⇒ rectangular puff-pastry stuffed with almond paste or compote or jam
Jambalaya de poulet ⇒ mixing of diced poached chicken, sauté diced ham, rice, and cayenne pepper
Jambe de bois -*[pot au feu]*- ⇒ pot-au-feu from Lyon
Jambe de bois -*[viande]*- ⇒ thigh of beef for pot au feu
Jambon ⇒ ham < *uncountable* >
Jambon aux clous de girofles ⇒ ham studded with cloves
Jambon blanc ⇒ cooked ham or boiled ham
Jambon braisé ⇒ ham rubbed with salt added of thyme and crushed bay-laurel, then baked with braised vegetables and butter; served covered with the cooking juice thickened of Madeira and stock
Jambon braisé à l'ananas ⇒ poached ham studded of clove and sprinkled of granulated sugar, then baked; served with sliced pineapple in syrup, plus a sauce of vinegar, pepper, caramel and xeres
Jambon braisé à la bayonnaise ⇒ poached ham, baked with butter; served with pilaf added of crushed tomatoes and mushrooms in butter, plus chipolatas and the cooking juice
Jambon braisé à la crème ⇒ poached ham baked laid on a mixture of diced vegetables and ham; served with the cooking juice thickened of cream
Jambon braisé au madère ⇒ slices of braised ham; covered with their cooking juice added of Madeira and arrow-root, then warmed up again in the oven
Jambon braisé Porte-Maillot ⇒ braised ham simmered in Madeira; served with a garnish of carrots, onions, french beans and braised lettuce, plus the cooking juice
Jambon cru ⇒ smoked raw ham
Jambon cuit ⇒ ham salted and cooked in stock
Jambon cuit à l'os ⇒ thigh of pork cooked with its bone
Jambon cuit dans le foin -*[Bocuse]*- ⇒ ham cooked in hay
Jambon d'Orthez ou Peyrehorade ⇒ ham rubbed with a mixing of salt, saltpetre, sugar, pepper and aromatics; then dried during 130 days
Jambon d'york ⇒ salted ham cooked with its bone
Jambon de Artigues ou de Lussac ⇒ boiled ham, fried with garlic and vinegar
Jambon de Bayonne ⇒ dried salted ham
Jambon de Brandenham -*[GB]*- ⇒ Brandenham ham
Jambon de campagne ⇒ country ham
Jambon de gibier -*[Touraine]*- ⇒ game ham
Jambon de Lacaune, Auvergne et Lyon ⇒ salted ham, matured carefully
Jambon de marcassin ⇒ leg of wild boar
Jambon de marcassin à l'aigre-doux ⇒ braised thigh of wild boar; served with a sauce made of the cooking juice, dried plums, currants, sultanas, caramel, vinegar, preserved cherries, chocolate powder, and kneaded butter
Jambon de Mayence ⇒ pickled ham, steeped in eau de vie and smoked
Jambon de mouton -*[Australie, NZ]*- ⇒ mutton ham flavoured with clove and juniper
Jambon de Paris ⇒ cooked ham or boiled ham
Jambon de Parme ⇒ Parma ham
Jambon de pays ⇒ country ham

Jambon de porc ⇒ leg of pork
Jambon de Prague ⇒ Czechoslovakian ham, salted, dried and smoked
Jambon de San Daniele -*[Italie]-* ⇒ high quality Italian ham
Jambon de Serrano ⇒ high quality Spanish ham
Jambon de Westphalie ⇒ salted ham, smoked with odoriferous woods
Jambon des Ardennes -*[Belgique]-* ⇒ Belgian ham
Jambon désossé et ficelé ⇒ leg of pork « boneless »
Jambon désossé et sans jambonneau ⇒ leg of pork « boned and rolled »
Jambon en gelée Reine Pédauque ⇒ York's ham sliced first, then reconstructed with mashed foie
      gras and diced truffle; covered with gelatinous sauce added of port, surrounded by
      sippets in jelly
Jambon en saupiquet ⇒ thick slices of ham simmered with a roux added of white wine, plus juniper
      berries and tarragon; served with the gravy thickened of vinegar, pepper and cream
Jambon fumé -*[Artois, Picardie]-* ⇒ smoked ham or gammon
Jambons fumé -*[Alpes, Causses, Savoie, Ardennes]-* ⇒ smoked ham or gammon
Jambon glacé au caramel ⇒ poached ham, glazed in the oven with granulated sugar; served with
      spinach and Madeira sauce
Jambon glacé de Paris ⇒ boiled ham shaped in parallelepiped
Jambon landais au miel ⇒ slices of ham coated with honey, laid on butter and rice, sprinkled of
      cinnamon and baked; served seasoned with pepper
Jambon persillé de Bourgogne ⇒ cooked ham with jelly and parsley
Jambon persillé du Morvan ⇒ thigh and shoulder of pork boiled with jelly and parsley, then
      moulded
Jambon poché en pâte à l'ancienne ⇒ casing of dough filled with a mixture of diced vegetables and
      ham, added of chopped mushrooms and diced truffle, topped with a poached ham;
      then baked
Jambon salé ⇒ cured ham or gammon
Jambon sans patte ni pointe ⇒ leg of pork « carvery cut »
Jambon sans pointe ⇒ leg of pork
Jambon sec -*[Rouergue]-* ⇒ dry ham from Naucelle or Najac
Jambonneau ⇒ shoulder of pork or small ham, uncountable, or knuckle of ham
Jambonneau arrière ⇒ hindquarter shoulder of pork
Jambonneau avant ⇒ forequarter shoulder of pork
Jambonneau de volaille ⇒ thighs of poultry stuffed with a forcemeat and shaped like small hams;
      then braised and covered with the cooking juice added of cream
Jambonneau désossé ⇒ boneless hand
Jambonnette ⇒ cooked pork butchery made of shoulder of pork, plus pork fat wrapped in rind of pork
Janots (petits ...) -*[Languedoc]-* ⇒ small pastries from Languedoc
Japonaise (p la ...) ⇒ with Japanese artichoke
Japonaise -*[glace]-* ⇒ ice cream of tea and peach
Japonica -*[riz]-* ⇒ rice
Jaque ⇒ breadfruit
Jardinière ⇒ dish of cooked mixed vegetables
      - garniture de julienne ⇒ garnish of cooked mixed vegetables
      - avec une garniture ⇒ with a garnish of cooked mixed ... « énumération des légumes »
      - macédoine ⇒ vegetable salad
Jargeau -*[andouille]-* ⇒ dry sausage made with shoulder and breast of pork; cooked before to be
      eaten
Jarlsberg -*[fromage]-* ⇒ Jarlsberg

Jarret
- **veau** ⇒ knuckle of veal
- **boeuf** ⇒ shin of beef or leg of beef
- **porc** ⇒ knuckle of pork

Jarret arrière *-[boeuf]-* ⇒ leg of beef

Jarret *(arrière-avant ...)* *-[veau]-*
- **arrière** ⇒ hock
- **avant** ⇒ knuckle

Jarret arrière de veau avec souris ⇒ knuckle of veal

Jarret avant *-[boeuf]-* ⇒ shin

Jarret de bœuf ⇒ shin of beef

Jarret de porc ⇒ knuckle of pork

Jarret de veau
- **arrière** ⇒ hock of veal
- **avant** ⇒ knuckle of veal

Jarret de veau ⇒ knuckle of veal or shin of veal

Jarret de veau à l'orange ⇒ knuckle of veal, braised with orange peel and orange juice

Jarret de veau à la provençale ⇒ slices from knuckle of veal, braised in olive oil with onions, tomatoes, white wine, stock and crushed garlic

Jarret de veau braisé au cidre ⇒ knuckle of veal braised in butter, plus onions, and flamed in calvados, then simmered in bottled cider; covered with the cooking juice added of cream, mushrooms, egg-yolk, and parsley, served with browned sliced apples

Jarrets arrière désossés *(prêts à trancher ...)* *-[boeuf]-* ⇒ boneless shin

Jaseran *-[champignon]-* ⇒ orange agaric or egg-mushroom

Jasmin ⇒ jasmine or jessamine
- **essence** ⇒ jasmine extract

Jasnières ⇒ white wine from Tours area

Jaud *-[jeune coq]-* ⇒ young cock

Jaune d'œuf ⇒ egg-yolk

Jaune d'œuf *-[oronge]-* ⇒ egg-mushroom

Jaune d'or *-[radis]-* ⇒ variety of radish

Jaunet *(au ...)* *-[tripes au safran]-* ⇒ tripe seasoned with saffron in medieval recipe

Jauniotte *-[chanterelle]-* ⇒ chanterelle

Jauniré *-[chanterelle]-* ⇒ chanterelle

Jerez *-[xérès]-* ⇒ xeres

Jéroboam *-[bouteille]-* ⇒ jeroboam

Jerky *-[U S]-* ⇒ smoked meat

Jessica *(garniture et sauce ...)*
- **suprême de volaille** ⇒ chicken in supreme sauce ...
- **escalopes de veau** ⇒ veal escalope ...
- **grenadins de veau** ⇒ round slices of veal ...
- **oeufs mollets** ⇒ soft boiled eggs ...
- **oeufs pochés** ⇒ poached eggs ...
- **garniture** ⇒ ... garnished with braised artichokes in butter, stuffed with a culinary stuffing of bone marrow, and shallots, plus sauté morels laid on tartlets of sliced potatoes in butter; covered with a ...
- **sauce** ⇒ ... brown sauce added of veal stock, and flavoured of truffle extract
- **omelette** ⇒ omelette stuffed with morels and asparagus tips in cream; served surrounded with a sauce of shallots, herbs, white wine, tarragon, and cayenne pepper

Jésuite *-[dindon]-* ⇒ turkey cock < *viande uncountable* >

Jésuite -*[pâtisserie]-* ⇒ little triangular puff-pastry stuffed with frangipane

Jésus ⇒ large smoked pork-sausage

Jésus à la vigneronne ⇒ large dry sausage steamed over a court-bouillon of wine, onions, cloves, herbs, pepper and vine-branches; served with boiled potatoes or beans

Jésus de morteau ⇒ large smoked pork-sausage

Jet -*[cocktail]-* ⇒ addition of a small quantity from ...

    - liqueur ou sirop ⇒ syrup

Jet de -*[liqueur]-* ⇒ addition of a small quantity from ...

    - liqueur ou sirop ⇒ syrup

Jet de houblon ⇒ hop shoot

Jets de houblon à la crème ⇒ hop shoots simmered with cream

Jeune

    a) Edam ⇒ Edam cheese refined during 3 months in cell

    b) Vin ⇒ wine not still at its best for consumption

Jeune fille voilée -*[Danemark]-* ⇒ gateau made with crumbs of buckwheat bread, apples, chocolate and cream

Jiang yong -*[sauce]-* ⇒ soya sauce

Jijona -*[touron]-* ⇒ sweet made of honey, sugar, nuts, hazelnuts, pine-kernels, and sometimes coriander or cinnamon

Joël ou Cabot -*[Athérine]-* ⇒ silverside

Johannisberg -*[vin]-* ⇒ Johannisberger

John dory ⇒ john dory

Johnny cake -*[US]-* ⇒ johnnycake

Joinville -*[garniture et sauce]-*

    - poisson poché ⇒ poached ... nom du poisson

    - barquette ⇒ pastry boat filled ...

    - tartelettes ⇒ tartlets filled ...

    - bouchées ⇒ patties filled ...

    - garniture ⇒ ... with a garnish of shrimp tails, mushrooms and truffles

    - omelette ⇒ omelette stuffed with a garnish of shrimp tails, mushrooms, and truffles; served surrounded by fish velouté sauce added of cream and mushrooms, plus shrimp paste and cayenne pepper

    - gâteau Joinville ⇒ puff-pastry stuffed with raspberry jam

    - sauce ⇒ covered with sole consommé, cream, egg-yolks, and mushroom extract

    - sauce normande au beurre de crevettes ⇒ fish velouté sauce added of cream, mushrooms, and shrimp paste

    - sauce crevette au beurre d'écrevisse ⇒ fish velouté sauce, added of cream, mushrooms, crayfish paste, and cayenne pepper

Jolliffie -*[telfairia]-* ⇒ kind of marrow

Jonchée ⇒ dried curdled milk

Josser an -*[oronge]-* ⇒ egg-mushroom

Joubarbe ⇒ houseleek

Joue ⇒ cheek or jowl

Joue de porc ⇒ pork jowl

Joues de bœuf en daube ⇒ jowl of beef marinated in pepper, olive oil, white wine, thyme and laurel; then diced and braised with lardoons, carrots, green olives, butter, the marinade, a bottle of white wine, crushed garlic and onions

Joues de lotte ⇒ angler cheeks

Joues de morue ⇒ cod cheeks

Joyaux de bourgogne ⇒ sweet filled or wrapped with chocolate

Judic
- **garniture des pièces de boucherie, poulet sauté, ris de veau braisé** ⇒ ... garnished of braised lettuce, stuffed tomatoes, small potatoes sautéed in butter with lardoons; served with the cooking juice added of Madeira
- **tournedos Judic** ⇒ tournedos garnished with braised lettuce, a stew of truffle lamellas, cockscombs and cocks' kidneys, plus the cooking juice added of Madeira
- **sole Judic** ⇒ poached sole fillets garnished with lettuce and fish quenelles; covered with béchamel sauce added of egg-yolks and gruyère

Judru ⇒ Burgundy dry sausage, made of pork meat macerated in marc

Juhturo -[liptauer]- ⇒ Hungary cheese

Juive (à la ...)
- **carpe** ⇒ carp braised in onion, white wine and aromatics
- **artichaut** ⇒ artichokes stuffed with crumbs, chopped mint and garlic; then cooked in oil

Jujube ⇒ jujube

Julep -[cocktail]- ⇒ variety of cocktail, based on water flavoured with mint

Jules Verne
- **garniture pièces de boucherie** ⇒ ... served with braised potatoes and turnips, plus sauté mushrooms

Julhüg -[Suède]- ⇒ Swedish preparation of superposed buckwheat bread, small round wheat bread sprinkled with sugar, a short pastry shaped in heart, and a red apple

Julienne -[poisson vendu en filets]- ⇒ ling fillets

Julienne -[vendu entier]- ⇒ ling

Julienne -[légumes]- ⇒ julienne or vegetables cut in small pieces, for soup

Julienne de céleri ⇒ celeriac in julienne, braised in butter and sprinkled of herbs

Juliènas ⇒ Beaujolais wine

Jumeau ⇒ clod of beef

Jungpana -[thé]- ⇒ variety of indian tea

Jurançon ⇒ sweet white wine from Pau area

Jurasienne -[purée de bécasses, Franche Comté]- ⇒ mashed woodcocks with lapwing eggs

Jus ⇒ juice

Jus d'orange ⇒ orange juice < *uncountable* >

Jus de citron ⇒ lemon juice

Jus de coco ⇒ coconut juice

Jus de cuisson ⇒ cooking juice

Jus de datte -[condiment]- ⇒ date juice

Jus de fruit ⇒ fresh juice of any kind of fruit

Jus de légumes (souvent mélangés ...) ⇒ vegetable juice from carrot, or red cabbage, or spinach

Jus de tomate ⇒ tomato juice

Jus de tomate aux épices -[cocktail]- ⇒ cocktail of tomato juice flavoured with lemon juice, Worcestershire sauce, celery salt, grated nutmeg, and granulated sugar

Jus de viande ⇒ gravy < *uncountable* >

Jussière (garniture viande rôtie ou poêlée ...) ⇒ ... served with stuffed onions, braised lettuce, small potatoes sautéed in butter with lardoons

K

Kabanosy -[*Pologne*]- ⇒ thin sausages smoked with wood of juniper-tree
Kacha polonaise à l'orge ⇒ pudding made of barley, milk, butter, whipped eggs, and cream flavoured with lemon
Kacha russe ⇒ dough of crushed buckwheat, cooked in the oven and splitted in small pieces
Kacha russe au parmesan ⇒ dough of crushed buckwheat and parmesan, cooked in the oven
Kache -[*kacha*]- ⇒ dough of crushed buckwheat, cooked in the oven and splitted in small pieces
Kackavalj -[*yougoslavie*]- ⇒ ewe cheese
Kadaif ⇒ preparation of vermicelli, pounded nuts and a syrup
Kadgéri -[*kedgeree*]- ⇒ kedgeree
Kaimak -[*russe*]- ⇒ concentrated cream
Kaiserschmarrn -[*Autriche*]- ⇒ sugared thick pancake
Kaiserstuhl -[*Allemagne vins*]- ⇒ wine from the right bank in the Rhine valley
Kaki -[*fruit*]- ⇒ persimmon fruit
Kakis glacés à la créole ⇒ persimmon fruits flavoured with marc and pineapple, then freezed
Kakou -[*Afrique du Sud*]- ⇒ maize bread
Kalakukko -[*Finlande*]- ⇒ dish stuffed with a hash of freshwater fishes and pork's meat
Kalatch -[*Russe*]- ⇒ white bread
Kalereï ⇒ pork brawn
Kaltschale ⇒ timbale made of fruits macerated in wine, and covered with mashed red fruits
Kangaroo tail soup ⇒ kangaroo tail soup
Kapisztran -[*œufs pochés à la*]- ⇒ poached eggs, laid on carp eggs with onions, and seasoned of paprika
Kapusniack -[*Pologne*]- ⇒ soup of cabbage, celery and pork fat
Kapuziner -[*cappucino*]- ⇒ strong coffee topped with cream and chocolate powder
Kari ⇒ curry
Karité -[*beurre*]- ⇒ butter from tropical fruit
Karkadé -[*infusion*]- ⇒ hibiscus tea
Kasche -[*kacha*]- ⇒ dough of crushed buckwheat, cooked in the oven and splitted in small pieces
Kasher ⇒ kosher
Kaskaval sajt -[*Hongrie*]- ⇒ ewe cheese
Kasseri -[*Grèce*]- ⇒ fresh Greek cheese
Katchapouri -[*Russe*]- ⇒ bread flavoured with cheese
Katchu -[*taro*]- ⇒ Indian katchu
Katshkawalj ⇒ ewe cheese
Katsuobushi ⇒ dried bonito
Katzenkopf -[*édam*]- ⇒ Edam
Kebab ⇒ meat cooked on a skewer
Kebabcha -[*Bulgarie*]- ⇒ sausages grilled on a skewer
Kebbé -[*Liban*]- ⇒ small balls made with a hash of mutton, mixed with germinated wheat, onion, parsley and pine-kernels; then roasted, or grilled on a skewer
Kedgeree ⇒ kedgeree
Keemun -[*thé*]- ⇒ Chinese tea
Kéfir -[*képhir*]- ⇒ kefir
Kefalotyri -[*grèce*]- ⇒ variety of Greek cheese
Kefta -[*Afrique du nord*]- ⇒ small balls of meat
Keftedes ⇒ chopped meat added of pork fat, spices and eggs; shaped in quoits and sautéed

Keftédès -[*Grèce*]- ⇒ mutton cooked on a skewer, or in spicy small balls
Kéfyr ⇒ Kefir
Kéknyelü ⇒ Hungarian white wine
Kémia -[*Afrique du nord*]- ⇒ marinated vegetables
Kendlach's -[*Russe*]- ⇒ small ball made of flour, eggs, goose fat, and ginger; poached or fried
Képhir ⇒ Kefir
Ketchup ⇒ ketchup < *uncountable* >
Ketmié-gombo ⇒ ketmia
Khalesch -[*datte*]- ⇒ date
Kharouf machwi -[*méchoui*]- ⇒ whole roast sheep
Kharpout kioufta -[*Russe*]- ⇒ sliced ham garnished with pounded wheat, pine-kernels, onions and parsley
Khir -[*Inde; lait*]- ⇒ concentrated milk
Kholodetz ⇒ Russian dish of boiled meat in jelly; served with gherkins, plums, plus pears marinated in vinegar
Kielbasa tatrzanska -[*Pologne*]- ⇒ rumpled sausages
Kig ha fars ⇒ soup of pork meat, carrots, cabbage, leeks, onions, plus a pouch filled with a dough of eggs, milk and buckwheat flour
Kig sal rosten ⇒ roasted pork belly, studded of garlic
Kilka -[*poisson*]- ⇒ kilka
Killo -[*poisson*]- ⇒ kilka OR Killo
Killarney -[*fromage*]- ⇒ Killarney
King -[*saumon*]- ⇒ King salmon OR chinook
Kinkéliba -[*infusion*]- ⇒ African infusion
Kipper -[*hareng*]- ⇒ kippered herring OR kipper
Kir ⇒ aperitif of white wine and blackcurrant liqueur
Kir royal ⇒ aperitif made of blackcurrant liqueur and champagne
Kirsch ⇒ kirsch < *uncountable* >
Kirschenkuchen ⇒ flat puff-pastry with cherries, cooked in the oven and covered with cherry jam
Kissel
   - froid ⇒ cold dessert of moulded jelly, mixed with berries, or white wine, or coffee
   - chaud ⇒ dessert of moulded jelly, mixed with berries, or white wine, or coffee; served hot with cream
Kissel aux airelles ⇒ compote made of bilberry juice, fecula and sugar
Kiwi ⇒ kiwi fruit
Klippfisch ⇒ dried kind of whiting
Klops -[*Russe*]- ⇒ pâté made of hashed beef, veal's grease and aromatics; baked laid on onions and aromatics
Klüsse ⇒ poached small balls of purée, eggs and milk; served with melted butter and crumbs
Klösse à la viennoise ⇒ balls made of diced bread and ham, mixed with chopped onions, chervil, tarragon and eggs; then boiled
Knack ⇒ kind of sausage
Knäckebrot ⇒ rectangular flat cake made of buckwheat flour, then flavoured with sesame seeds or flax or cummin
Knackwurst ⇒ kind of sausage
Knepfle ⇒ kind of quenelle, from pasta with eggs, or mashed potatoes
Knödel ⇒ kind of quenelle sugared or salted
Knolles -[*canole*]- ⇒ small dried cake made of flour and eggs
Knusper ⇒ large short pastry covered with chopped almonds
Koecbotteram ⇒ large brioche with milk, butter and raisins

Kokkineli -*[Chypre vins]*- ⇒ rosé wine from Cyprus

Kokoretsi -*[Grèce]*- ⇒ either lamb's intestine grilled on a skewer, or sausage from offal of lambs

Kola *(noix de ...)* ⇒ cola or kola

    - **noix de kola** ⇒ cola-nut

Kolduny -*[Pologne]*- ⇒ kind of ravioli filled of hashed beef, bone-marrow and wild marjoram

Kombu -*[algue]*- ⇒ Kombu

Kopanisti -*[Grèce]*- ⇒ Greek blue cheese

Korj ⇒ white bread

Korn -*[schnaps]*- ⇒ alcohol from grain

Kosher ⇒ kosher

Kotliety pojarskie -*[pojarski]*- ⇒ small balls of beef or veal

Koubba -*[Liban]*- ⇒ small balls made with a hash of mutton, mixed with germinated wheat, onion, parsley and pine-kernels; then roasted, or grilled on a skewer

Koucke -*[couque]*- ⇒ brioche with currants

Kougelhof -*[Kouglof]*- ⇒ brioche shaped in crown, filled with currants macerated in tea, butter, yeast, flour, milk and eggs

Kouglof ⇒ brioche shaped in crown, filled with currants macerated in tea, butter, yeast, flour, milk and eggs

Kouing-aman ⇒ large flat cake of bread dough, added of butter or cream, and caramelized

Koulibiac ⇒ puff-pastry filled with a culinary stuffing of meat, or fish, or vegetables, or rice, or hard boiled eggs

Koulibiac d'anguilles ⇒ pastry case filled with eels, vegetables, rice and hard boiled eggs

Koulibiac de saumon ⇒ puff-pastry filled with a garnish of rice, shallots, mushrooms, chicken, eggs and salmon

Koulibiac de volaille ⇒ puff-pastry filled with a garnish of chicken, eggs, shallots, rice and mushrooms

Koulitch ⇒ brioche filled with raisins, preserved fruits, saffron, cardamom, mace and vanilla

Koumys ⇒ Russian cheese

Kounafa ⇒ pastry made of browned dough, crushed almonds and crushed hazelnuts; sprinkled with syrup

    - **variantes** ⇒ basma, lakhana, gouch

Kourkouri ⇒ pot au feu of pork

Kournik -*[russe]*- ⇒ croustade of chicken with rice

Kourt -*[russe]*- ⇒ ewe cheese dried in the sun

Koutia -*[russe]*- ⇒ semolina pastry filled with poppy seeds and dried fruits

Kransekage -*[danemark]*- ⇒ tiered cake decorated with preserved fruits, small flags, and embroidered with icing sugar

Krapfen ⇒ fritter made of flour, butter, eggs, yeast and milk, stuffed of jam or almond paste; served hot with egg-custard, or a sauce made of apricot pulp, syrup and brandy

Kräuterkäse -*[schabzieger]*- ⇒ Sapsago

Kreivi -*[fromage]*- ⇒ Finnish cheese

Krendiel -*[russe]*- ⇒ sugared brioche

Kreplach -*[juive]*- ⇒ pasta stuffed with meat

Kriek -*[bière]*- ⇒ Belgian beer

Kroaztbeere -*[schnaps]*- ⇒ alcohol from mulberries

Kromesqui -*[cromesqui]*- ⇒ floured culinary stuffing, fried in hot oil

Krouchenik natté -*[russe]*- ⇒ buckwheat bread

Krupnick -*[liqueur, Pologne]*- ⇒ liqueur made of honey and spices

Krupnick -*[soupe, Pologne]*- ⇒ creamy barley and vegetable soup

Krupnikas -*[russes]*- ⇒ honey liqueur

Kryddost -[*fromage*]- ⇒ Kryddost
Kuchen -[*tarte*]- ⇒ tart garnished with fruits, and sometimes topped of whipped cream
Kugel -[*juive*]- ⇒ pudding
Kugelis -[*russe*]- ⇒ gateau made with grated potatoes
Kummel ⇒ kümmel liqueur
Kumminost -[*suède*]- ⇒ Swedish cheese flavoured with cummin
Kumquat ⇒ dwarfed orange
Kun pod ⇒ garnish made of small balls of dough flavoured with Malaga raisins
Kvas -[*Kwas*]- ⇒ kvass
Kwas ⇒ kvass

L

L'étoile -*[vin du jura]*- ⇒ white wine from Jura
L'évêque -*[cortinaire]*- ⇒ cortinarius mushroom
La Bouille -*[fromage]*- ⇒ cylindrical cow's milk cheese from Normandy
La Clape -*[vin]*- ⇒ Languedoc wines
La peuplière -*[champignon]*- ⇒ tricholoma mushroom
La-tour-blanche ⇒ quality Bordeaux wine
La-tour-carnet ⇒ quality Bordeaux wine
La-tour-haut-brion ⇒ quality Bordeaux wine
La Varenne -*[pannequets]*- ⇒ dish of pancakes covered with a preparation of chopped mushrooms, added with a culinary stuffing of ham thickened of béchamel sauce; sprinkled of grated parmesan and melted butter, then browned
La Varenne -*[sauce]*- ⇒ sauce made of mayonnaise mixed with chopped mushrooms, parsley and chervil
Laboratoire (*ne pas traduire comme laboratory qui n'est pas approprié, utiliser les phrases suivantes ...)*
    1) Toutes nos pâtisseries sont faites dans notre laboratoire ⇒ all our pastries are home made
    2) Toutes nos glaces sont faites dans notre laboratoire ⇒ all our ice-creams are home made
    3) Tous nos produits sont faits dans notre laboratoire ⇒ all our products are home made
Labre vert -*[poisson]*- ⇒ rock fish or wrasse
Labskaus ⇒ dish made of a hash of beef, onion and herrings sautéed in pork fat, added of mashed potatoes flavoured with nutmeg and pepper; served with poached egg, marinated beets and gherkins
Lacaune -*[jambon]*- ⇒ salted ham, matured carefully
Lacrima-christi ⇒ white wine from Vesuvius area
Lacrymaine velouté -*[hypholome]*- ⇒ sulphur tuft
Lactaire ⇒ orange-brown lactarius or milk agaric
Lactaire délicieux -*[champignon]*- ⇒ saffron milk cap or milk agaric
Lactaires grillés à la lucifer ⇒ grilled milk agarics sprinkled with fennel, parsley, grated parmesan cheese and covered with a spicy sauce
Ladoix-serrigny -*[vin]*- ⇒ Burgundy wines from Côtes de Beaune
Lafon-rochet -*[st estèphe]*- ⇒ high quality Médoc red wine
Lagopède d'écosse -*[grouse]*- ⇒ grouse
Laguiole -*[aubrac, fromage]*- ⇒ cow's milk cheese from Rouergue area
Laguipière -*[garniture]*- ⇒ covered with a sauce, and sprinkled with a julienne of truffle macerated in Madeira
Lait ⇒ milk < *uncountable* >
Lait barraté ⇒ buttermilk
Lait battu -*[Botermelk]*- ⇒ preparation of milk, pearl barley, brown sugar, honey and dried fruits
Lait cafeté -*[café au lait]*- ⇒ coffee with hot milk
Lait caillé ⇒ curdled milk
Lait caillé liquide -*[russe]*- ⇒ curds
Lait concentré ⇒ condensed milk
Lait condensé ⇒ condensed milk
Lait cru ⇒ plain milk
Lait cuit ⇒ warmed curds eaten with buckwheat pancakes

Lait d'amande *-[pâtisserie]-* ⇒ cake shaped in disc, based on a dough of almonds, sugar and eggs; flavoured with apricot and decorated of chopped grilled almonds

Lait d'amandes pour coupes glacées ⇒ milk made of gelatine, almonds and sugar, then frozen

Lait de coco *-[afrique noire]-* ⇒ coconut milk

Lait de poule ⇒ eggflip

Lait de poule à la bière ⇒ eggflip of beer, sugar, lemon peel and egg-yolks; served with grilled bread, currants and raisins

Lait demi-écrémé ⇒ semi-skimmed milk

Lait écrémé ⇒ skimmed milk

Lait en poudre ou lait sec ⇒ powdered milk

Lait entier ⇒ unskimmed milk

Lait marri ⇒ boiled milk added of buttermilk; served sugared

Lait pasteurisé ⇒ pasteurized milk

Lait ribot ⇒ buttermilk

Lait stérilisé ⇒ sterilized milk

Laitages ⇒ milk food

Laitance ou Laite ⇒ soft roe of fish or milt < *uncountable* >

Laitances à l'anglaise ⇒ poached milt, floured and covered with eggs, breadcrumbs, plus melted butter

Laitances à la meunière ⇒ floured milt cooked in butter and sprinkled with lemon juice

Laitances au beurre de noisette ⇒ poached milt covered with capers, chopped parsley, lemon juice and butter

Laitances de hareng au verjus ⇒ soft roes of herring fried in butter and oil, sprinkled with the cooking juice thickened of verjuice and cider vinegar; served with mushrooms, apples, plus tomatoes diced and browned in butter added of capers and pepper

Laitances en coquilles à la normande ⇒ poached milt, served in a shell and topped with oyster, mushroom, shrimp tail and mussel

Laiteron ⇒ sow-thistle or hare's-lettuce

Laitier ⇒ dairy product

Laiton *-[agneau]-* ⇒ lamb

Laitue ⇒ lettuce < *cuisine uncountable* >

Laitue romaine ⇒ cos lettuce

Laitues à l'italienne ⇒ lettuce first braised, then simmered in sauce

Laitues à la crème ⇒ braised lettuce, sprinkled with cream and covered of fried sippets

Laitues braisées à la mœlle ⇒ braised lettuce, with poached beef bone-marrow

Laitues braisées au gras ⇒ braised lettuce with rind of pork, butter, stock, carrots and onions

Laitues braisées au gratin ⇒ braised lettuce, covered with creamy sauce and grated cheese; browned in the oven

Laitues braisées au maigre ⇒ braised lettuce with butter, stock, carrots and onions

Laitues colbert ⇒ lettuce braised, then fried, and covered of butter mixed with parsley and lemon juice

Laitues de dame Simone ⇒ lettuce stuffed with poultry and rice

Laitues farçies ⇒ braised lettuce stuffed with a forcemeat, plus chopped mushrooms

Lakhana *-[Kounafa]-* ⇒ pastry made of browned dough, crushed almonds and crushed hazelnuts; sprinkled with syrup

Lakka ⇒ mulberry liqueur

Lalande de pomerol *-[néac]-* ⇒ Bordeaux red wine

Lalo *-[Afrique noire]-* ⇒ baobab leaf powder

Lamb chop *-[GB]-* ⇒ lamb chop

Lamballe *-[cailles]-* ⇒ quail stuffed with a forcemeat, cooked in butter; served in shaped boat paper with a julienne of mushrooms in cream, plus the cooking juice added of port

Lamballe -[*potage*]- ⇒ thick soup made of mashed fresh peas, then thickened with tapioca consommé; garnished with shredded chervil

Lambeau -[*viande*]- ⇒ a scrap of meat ½ ou ½ a shred of meat

Lambi -[*Antilles*]- ⇒ shell

Lambic ⇒ strong Belgian beer from malt and wheat

Lambick ⇒ strong Belgian beer from malt and wheat

Lamelle ⇒ lamella

Laminaire -[*algues*]- ⇒ sea cabbage

Lamperna ⇒ barnacle

Lampreia de ovos -[*Portugal*]- ⇒ gateau of egg-yolks shaped in lamprey, and decorated with preserved fruits

Lamproie ⇒ lamprey

Lamproie à la bordelaise ⇒ lamprey cooked in red wine, onions, carrots, and garlic, then sautéed with leeks; served with the gravy added of the blood

Lamproie de mer ⇒ sea lamprey

Lamproie de rivière ⇒ river lamprey or brook lamprey

Lancashire ⇒ Lancashire cheese

Lancashire sage ⇒ Lancashire sage

Lançon ⇒ sand eel or sand lance or grig

Landaise (*à la ...*) ⇒ dish cooked with ham or goose fat or boletus < *jambon, graisse d'oie ou cèpes autres plats, pommes de terre, becfigues, foie gras d'oie ou de canard, confit, certains plats traduits* >

Landimolle -[*crêpe*]- ⇒ pancake or flapjack

Landjäger ⇒ small flat sausage made of beef and pork fat, dried and smoked

Landrace -[*porc*]- ⇒ breed of pork

Langouste ⇒ spiny lobster or rock lobster or crawfish

Langouste à la parisienne ⇒ round slices of spiny lobster in court-bouillon, diced vegetables with mayonnaise, hard-boiled eggs filled of tomato purée, plus tomatoes

Langouste à la winterthur ⇒ halved spiny lobster in court bouillon, filled with a culinary stuffing added of crayfish tails; topped with grated cheese, melted butter, and browned

Langouste demi-deuil ⇒ spiny lobster cooked in white wine, mixed with a hash of mushrooms and Madeira, covered of creamy white sauce, then glazed in the oven; topped by a garnish of truffles

Langouste des chroniqueurs ⇒ elaborated dish of spiny lobster bits cooked in butter, oil, pepper, carrots and onions; plus wine, tomato purée and cognac added

Langouste du grincheux ⇒ sauté spiny lobster in butter, oil and pepper; then cooked in an emulsion of egg-yolks and port

Langouste du père moreau ⇒ spiny lobster escalopes cooked in court-bouillon; garnished with sauté crayfishes and sauce

Langouste grillée au beurre de basilic ⇒ spiny lobster grilled in the oven with butter and chopped basil

Langoustine ⇒ scampi < *langoustines frites « nom pluriel »* >

Langoustine ⇒ Norway lobster or Dublin bay prawn

Langoustines à la marinière ⇒ sauté Norway lobsters cooked in white wine with pepper, thyme and laurel

Langoustines à la marinière ⇒ Norway lobsters sautéed in butter, then braised in white wine with laurel and thyme

Langoustines à la pékinoise ⇒ sauté Norway lobsters with onions and chopped garlic, plus a sauce made of maïzena, gluten extract, Chinese lily flower, mushrooms and tomatoes

Langoustines aux coques d'oursin ⇒ Norway lobsters cooked in oil, cognac, white wine, shallots, cream and butter; served in sea-urchin shells

Langoustines aux noix ⇒ fried scampi seasoned with white wine, ginger juice and pepper, plus fried nuts

Langoustines frites aux légumes ⇒ scampi fried in palm oil with carrots, courgettes and onions

Langoustines pochées ⇒ poached Norway lobsters

Langoustines royales aux poivrons rouges ⇒ red capsicums cooked in vinegar, orange juice and port, plus steamed Norway lobsters

Langres -*[fromage]*- ⇒ cow's milk cheese with a brown crust

Langue -*[animal]*- ⇒ tongue

Langue à la diable ⇒ slices of poached tongue, moistened with mustard, crumbs and melted butter, then grilled; served with devilled sauce

Langue à la valenciennes ou Langues fumées de Valenciennes ⇒ slices of smoked tongue, covered with mashed foie gras

Langue d'agneau ⇒ lamb tongue

Langue d'avocat -*[Bordelais, huître]*- ⇒ oyster

Langue d'avocat -*[sole]*- ⇒ small sole

Langue de boeuf -*[champignon]*- ⇒ beefsteak fungus OR oak tongue

Langue de boeuf ⇒ ox tongue

Langue de boeuf à l'alsacienne ⇒ ox tongue cooked first in stock, then simmered with sauerkraut, pork fat, potatoes and sausages

Langue de boeuf à l'écarlate ⇒ poached pickled ox tongue

Langue de boeuf à la bourgeoise ⇒ braised ox tongue, plus carrots, onions and lardoons; cooked at last in the oven

Langue de boeuf aux concombres ⇒ ox tongue cooked with cucumbers

Langue de boeuf aux cornichons ⇒ boiled ox tongue; served with a spicy sauce and gherkins

Langue de boeuf fourrée de valenciennes ⇒ smoked ox tongue with a garnish of foie gras, butter, port, chopped truffles and pepper

Langue de carpe -*[champignon]*- ⇒ miller

Langue de chat -*[biscuit]*- ⇒ finger biscuit

Langue de chat -*[hydne]*- ⇒ spreading hydnum

Langue de chat au beurre et aux oeufs entiers ⇒ finger biscuits made of flour, butter, eggs, vanilla sugar and granulated sugar

Langue de chat au sucre et aux blancs d'oeufs ⇒ finger biscuits made of granulated sugar, flour, vanilla sugar and whipped white of eggs

Langue de chat à la crème ⇒ finger biscuits made of cream, sugar, flour, lemon peel and whipped white of eggs

Langue de chêne -*[champignon]*- ⇒ beefsteak fungus OR oak tongue

Langues de morue au pistou ⇒ browned salt cod tongues, sautéed with garlic, basil, olive oil, tomato sauce and pepper

Langues de mouton à la diable ⇒ lamb tongues braised and coated with mustard, then grilled; served with devilled sauce

Langues de mouton à la vinaigrette ⇒ lamb tongues cooked in court-bouillon; served chilled with french dressing

Langues de mouton au gratin ⇒ braised lamb tongues, covered with mushroom sauce; then sprinkled of melted butter, plus crumbs, and browned

Langues de mouton en brochettes ⇒ lamellas of braised mutton tongue, mushrooms, and lardoons, put on a skewer, then steeped in marinade or melted butter and grilled; served with tomato sauce

Langues de mouton en crépinettes ⇒ braised lamb tongue wrapped in a forcemeat added of truffle and a caul of pork, then brushed with melted butter and grilled; served with Madeira sauce added of chopped truffles

Langue de porc ⇒ pig tongue

Langue de renne fumée -*[Scandinavie]*- ⇒ smoked reindeer tongue

Langue de veau ⇒ calf tongue

Langue de veau à l'italienne ⇒ calf tongue braised with crushed tomatoes, and herbs; served sprinkled with green olives

Langue de veau bouillie ⇒ calf tongue boiled in a court-bouillon added of veal's fat ...

- **vinaigrette** ⇒ ... served with french dressing
- **sauce aux câpres** ⇒ ... served with sauce hollandaise added of capers
- **fines herbes** ⇒ ... served with a sauce made of stock, plus a hash of parsley, chervil and tarragon
- **à la hongroise** ⇒ ... served with a sauce of chopped onions braised in butter, plus pepper, paprika and white wine
- **piquante** ⇒ ... served with piquant sauce
- **à la ravigote** ⇒ ... served with ravigote sauce

Langue de veau braisée ⇒ calf tongue braised with veal bone, thigh of veal, onions, carrots, rind of pork, herbs, garlic, white wine, stock and cognac

- **le vin peut être remplacé par madère** ⇒ madeira
- **cidre** ⇒ cider
- **bière** ⇒ beer

Langue écarlate ⇒ pickled ox tongue

Languedocienne *(à la ...)*

1) **Général** ⇒ dishes with tomatoes, aubergine and boletus; together or separately

2) **Oeufs frits** ⇒ fried eggs laid on slices of aubergine; covered with tomatoes and garlic cooked in their own liquid

3) **Grosses ou petites pièces de boucherie et volailles** ⇒ ... with a garnish of sauté boletus, sliced aubergines fried in oil, plus potatoes or other vegetables; served with a sauce of stock, tomato purée and garlic

4) **Autres plats** ⇒ ... cooked with garlic, boletus and olive oil or goose fat

Lanière ⇒ lamella

Lap -*[Asie du sud est]*- ⇒ raw meat, pounded and spiced

Lapereau ⇒ young rabbit

Lapereau de campagne au cidre fermier ⇒ elaborated dish of roasted young rabbit, surrounded of watercress, the sauce-boat being filled with the gravy added of cider, cream, stock, chives and chervil; served with a gateau of sliced potatoes, sliced cabbage, Emmenthal cheese, milk and scrambled eggs

Lapin ⇒ rabbit

Lapin à la havraise ⇒ rabbit, stuffed with truffles and pig's trotters

Lapin à la moutarde ⇒ diced rabbit coated with mustard added of oil and pepper, then baked; served with a sauce of white wine and cream, plus noodles

Lapin à la valenciennes ou Lapin à la flamande ⇒ rabbit stewed with raisins and dried plums

Lapin bouilli à l'anglaise ⇒ rabbit stuffed with a forcemeat and poached; served chilled with caper sauce or cold with a mayonnaise added of herbs

Lapin coquibus ⇒ bits of rabbit marinated in white wine, sautéed in butter with onions and lardoons; then moistened with white wine plus the marinade, and cooked at last with new potatoes

Lapin de garenne ⇒ wild rabbit

Lapin de garenne au vin de l'Hermitage

Lapin de garenne au vin de l'Hermitage ⇒ diced wild rabbit flamed in marc, then braised with pork fat, onions, herbs, garlic, plus hermitage wine; served with the gravy

Lapin huppé -[mâchon]- ⇒ sliced saveloy, served with french dressing

Lapin rôti en crépine ⇒ bits of rabbit wrapped in caul of pork and coated of mustard, then roasted and covered with the gravy added of white wine, plus cream; served with noodles in butter

Lapin sauté aux pruneaux ⇒ bits of rabbit sautéed in butter; served with dried plums cooked in the gravy added of white wine, plus the seasoning

Lapin sauté chasseur ⇒ bits of rabbit braised in butter and olive oil with sliced mushrooms and lardoons, covered with the gravy added of shallots, white wine, tomato sauce, marc and tarragon; served with steamed potatoes

Lapin sauté minute ⇒ bits of rabbit sautéed in butter; covered with the gravy added of white wine, shallots, stock, butter and lemon juice

Lapsang souchong -[thé]- ⇒ Indian tea

Lapskaus -[Labskaus]- ⇒ dish made of a hash of beef, onion and herrings sautéed in pork fat, added of mashed potatoes flavoured with nutmeg and pepper; served with poached egg, marinated beets and gherkins

Laquer ⇒ to lacquer

Lard ⇒ pork fat or fat of pork or streaky bacon or fat bacon

Lard de carême -[baleine]- ⇒ whale fat

Lard de poitrine ⇒ streaky bacon

Lard de poitrine fumé -[pour choucroute]- ⇒ smoked belly

Lard fumé ⇒ smoked bacon

Lard gras ⇒ fat of pig

Lard maigre -[lard; poitrine]- ⇒ streaky bacon

Lard nantais ⇒ loin of pork braised with cracklings, offal, aromatics and white wine

Lard salé ⇒ salted pork fat

Lardon ⇒ lardoon or lardon or strip of bacon for larding

Lardé ⇒ larded < v.t adjectif >

Large de Belleville -[oseille]- ⇒ variety of sorrel

Large loche ⇒ weatherfish

Large white yorkshire -[porc]- ⇒ breed of pork

Laruns -[fromage]- ⇒ ewe's milk cheese or ewe cheese

Larzac -[fromage]- ⇒ fresh ewe cheese

Las pous -[rimotte]- ⇒ maize porridge

Lasagnes ⇒ lasagne < invariable >

Laser -[silphium]- ⇒ asafoetida

Laserpitium -[silphium]- ⇒ asafoetida

Latricières-chambertin -[Gevrey chambertin]- ⇒ Chambertin

Laurier
- **botanique** ⇒ laurel
- **culinaire** ⇒ bay leaves
- **feuille de laurier** ⇒ bay leaf
- **mettre du laurier** ⇒ to put in some bay leaves < nota nous avons utilisé « laurel » dans nos textes afin de condenser, mais vous pouvez également utiliser « bay-leaves » >

Lavagnon (Charentes ...) ⇒ false clam

Lavallière (énumérations ...)
- **volailles ou ris de veau garnis d'écrevisses troussées et de truffes à la serviette** ⇒ poultry or sweetbread of veal, garnished of crayfishes, plus truffles laid on serviette

- **velouté de volaille au céleri, garni d'un salpicon de céleri et de royale, servi avec des profiterolles fourrées de mousse de volaille** ⇒ poultry velouté with celery, garnished with a culinary stuffing of celery braised in butter, béchamel sauce, consommé and egg-yolks; served with profiteroles stuffed of poultry mousse
- **filets de sole pochés, garnis d'huîtres pochées, de quenelles de poisson et de champignons, le tout nappé d'une sauce normande** ⇒ poached sole fillets, garnished with poached oysters, fish quenelles and mushrooms; covered with fish velouté sauce, added of cream and mushrooms
- **côtes d'agneau grillées, garnies de fond d'artichauts remplis de purée de pointes d'asperges, servies avec une sauce bordelaise à la mœlle** ⇒ grilled cutlets, garnished of artichoke hearts filled with mashed asparagus tips; served with a sauce made of poached bone-marrow, shallots, red wine, thyme, laurel and parsley

Lavande ⇒ lavender < *uncountable* >

Lavandin *-[miel]-* ⇒ honey with lavender flavour

Lavaret ⇒ Coregonus or freshwater herring

Lavignon *-[Charentes]-* ⇒ false clam

Lavilledieu *-[vins de]-* ⇒ wines from South West of France

Le rouget *-[champignon]-* ⇒ russula

Le violacé *-[cortinaire]-* ⇒ cortinarius mushroom

Leben *-[petit lait]-* ⇒ whey

Leberknödel ⇒ small ball of noodles, added of mashed liver

Leckerli ⇒ gingerbread biscuit, flavoured with aromatics

Lecrelet *-[Leckerli]-* ⇒ gingerbread biscuit, flavoured with aromatics

Lecso ⇒ ratatouille of capsicums, tomatoes and onions, added of lardoons

Leg *-[vanille]-* ⇒ Mexican vanilla

Leicester *-[fromage]-* ⇒ Leicester cheese

Leiden ⇒ Dutch cheese flavoured with cumin seeds and clove

Leidse Kaas ⇒ Dutch cheese flavoured with cumin seeds and clove

Lekchyna *-[Russe]-* ⇒ noodles with eggs, plus spinach or nuts

Lemon chiffon pie *-[U S]-* ⇒ lemon chiffon pie

Lemon curd ⇒ lemon curd

Lentilles ⇒ lentils

Letchi ⇒ litchi or lychee

Levain ⇒ leaven

Levraut ⇒ leveret

Levroux *-[fromage]-* ⇒ goat's milk cheese from Berry

Levure ⇒ yeast

Leyde ⇒ Dutch cheese flavoured with cumin seeds and clove

Léanyka *-[Hongrie vins]-* ⇒ Hungarian white wine

Légumes ⇒ vegetables

Légumes à la grecque ⇒ bits of aubergines, cardoons, mushrooms, cauliflower, courgettes, fennel, artichoke hearts, firstly browned in oil; then simmered in a court-bouillon of olive oil, lemon juice, herbs, coriander seeds, and pepper seeds

Légumes braisés ⇒ braised vegetables

Légumes chop suey ⇒ vegetables in julienne, sautéed with soya bean sprouts, onion, garlic, pepper and soya sauce

Légumes en purée ⇒ mashed vegetables

Légumes secs ⇒ dry vegetables

Légumes verts ⇒ green vegetables

Légumineuses *-[fèves]-* ⇒ leguminous seeds

Lépidope -*[sabre]*- ⇒ silvered Mediterranean fish
Lépiote -*[coulemelle]*- ⇒ parasol mushroom
Lépiotes à la suprême ⇒ parasol mushrooms braised in butter, with onions, paprika, grated nutmeg,
    basil and tarragon; served with supreme sauce
Lépiote déguenillée ⇒ parasol mushroom
Lépiote pudique ⇒ parasol mushroom
Lépiote exoriée ⇒ parasol mushroom
Lèche ⇒ a thin slice of bread or a thin slice of meat
Liaison -*[ingrédient pour épaissir]*-
    - **sauce** ⇒ sauce ... thickened with ...
    - **soupe** ⇒ soup ... thickened with ...
Liant *(un ...)* ⇒ binder or a binder
Liard -*[pommes en; chips]*- ⇒ potato crisps
Liberica ⇒ variety of coffee
Lichouneries -*[Berry]*- ⇒ sweets
Lie ⇒ lees or dregs
Lié ⇒ thickened with < *v.t adjectif* >
Liebfraumilch -*[Allemagne vins]*- ⇒ average quality wine from Rhone valley left bank
Liègeoise *(à la ...)*
    1) **Général** ⇒ cooked with juniper berries and gin
    2) **Rognons à la liégeoise** ⇒ kidneys cooked in cast-iron casserole with crushed juniper berries,
        potatoes and lardoons; served with the gravy added of gin and white wine
    3) **Petits oiseaux à la liégeoise** ⇒ birds flamed in gin; cooked with juniper berries and ham
Lierre ⇒ ivy
Lieu jaune ⇒ pollack
Lieu noir ⇒ saithe or coalfish
Lièvre ⇒ hare
Lièvre à la royale ⇒ hare cooked in goose fat with onions, garlic, shallot, wine vinegar, and Burgundy
    wine; served with the gravy added of cognac
Lièvre au chocolat ⇒ saddle of hare cooked in butter, then covered with a sauce of marinade based on
    red wine, vegetables, aromatics and offal of the hare, added of butter plus chocolate
    powder; served with pears sautéed in butter, and spiced
Lièvre aux cerises ⇒ bits of hare browned in olive oil, then cooked added of onion, shallot, carrot, half
    a bottle of Burgundy red wine, garlic, clove, and pepper; served with the cooking
    juice, surrounded by stoned cherries in syrup
Lièvre en cabessal ⇒ hare marinated in red wine, oil, carrots, onions, shallots, thyme, laurel, clove and
    pepper, stuffed with a forcemeat of veal, ham, pork and egg; then braised in goose fat,
    with lardoons, eau de vie, and a bottle of quality wine; Served with the sauce and
    sippets fried in goose fat
Lièvre rôti en saugrenée ⇒ hare marinated in cider, olive oil, onion, carrot and juniper berries, then
    roasted laid on pork fat; served with a bunch of celery braised in butter and stock,
    covered with the cooking juice flavoured of calvados
Ligueil -*[fromage]*- ⇒ cheese from Saumur area
Ligurienne *(à la ...)*
    - **grosses pièces de boucherie** ⇒ nom anglais ... garnished with stuffed tomatoes, risotto added
    of saffron, and small sauté potatoes with lardoons
Limaçon ⇒ snail
Limande ⇒ dab
Limande sloop ou Limande salope ⇒ megrim
Limande sole ⇒ lemon sole

Limbourg -*[fromage]*- ⇒ Limburg or Limburger
Limburger -*[Limbourg]*- ⇒ Limburg or Limburger
Lime -*[fruit]*- ⇒ lime-tree « citrus »
Limette -*[agrumes]*- ⇒ name for a variety of ...
  - **orange** ⇒ orange
  - **citron** ⇒ lemon
Limonade ⇒ lemonade
Limonade au suc de grenade ⇒ lemonade made with juice of pomegranate seeds, lemon juice, orange juice, lemon peel, orange peel, sugar and water
Limousine (*à la ...*)
  1) Garniture pour grosses pièces de boucherie ou de porc rôties ⇒ with a garnish of red cabbage in julienne, cooked in pork-fat and vinegar; added of grated apple, plus crushed chestnuts
  2) Volaille à la limousine ⇒ poultry stuffed with sausage-meat and sauté mushrooms, then cooked; served with the gravy added of veal stock, lardoons and poached chestnuts
  3) Omelette ⇒ omelette stuffed with diced ham and sauté potatoes
Limoux (*blanquette de ...*) ⇒ effervescent white wine from Limoux
Limoux nature ⇒ dry white wine, « not sparkling », from Limoux area
Limule ⇒ king crab or horseshoe crab
Lin ⇒ flax
  - **graines de lin** ⇒ flax seeds
Linge -*[pour cuisson ou autre]*- ⇒ linen
Lingot -*[foie gras]*- ⇒ foie gras
Lingot -*[haricot à écosser]*- ⇒ beans in the pod or unshelled beans
Lingue ⇒ ling
Linguine -*[pâtes alimentaires]*- ⇒ small grains of pasta for soup
Linzertorte ⇒ tart made with a paste of flour, lemon, almond powder, granulated sugar, egg, cinnamon and butter; covered with raspberry jam and decorated in lattice with lamellas of the paste
Liptauer ⇒ Hungary cheese
Liptovsky sir -*[Liptauer]*- ⇒ Hungary cheese
Liptoï -*[Liptauer]*- ⇒ Hungary cheese
Liqueur ⇒ liquor or liqueur
Liqueur au fenouil ⇒ fennel liquor
Liqueur d'abricot ⇒ apricot liqueur or liqueur made with stoned apricots, white wine, sugar, cinnamon, and eau de vie
Liqueur d'angélique ⇒ angelica liqueur or liqueur of angelica macerated with sugar, eau de vie, cinnamon, clove and grated nutmeg
Liqueur d'anis ⇒ aniseed liqueur or infusion of aniseed, cinnamon, coriander, eau de vie and sugar
Liqueur d'évêque ⇒ drink made of wine, citrus and spices
  - **Liqueur d'évêque** ⇒ drink made of Bordeaux wine, citrus and spices
  - **Liqueur de cardinal** ⇒ drink made of white wine, citrus and spices
  - **Bichof classique** -*[ou Bishop à l'anglaise]*- ⇒ bishop or drink made of sugar in syrup, orange and lemon peel, cinnamon, clove, plus Bordeaux wine
Liqueur d'herbes ⇒ elixir or herbs macerated in alcohol
Liqueur d'orange ⇒ orange liqueur or orange juice and orange peel macerated with sugar, cinnamon, coriander powder, plus cognac
Liqueur de cardinal ⇒ drink made of wine, citrus and spices
  - **Liqueur d'évêque** ⇒ drink made of Bordeaux wine, citrus and spices
  - **Liqueur de cardinal** ⇒ drink made of white wine, citrus and spices
  - **Bichof classique** -*[ou Bishop à l'anglaise]*- ⇒ bishop or drink made of sugar in syrup, orange and lemon peel, cinnamon, clove, plus Bordeaux wine

Liqueur de cassis ⇒ blackcurrant liqueur

Liqueur de cerise ⇒ cherry liqueur or crushed cherries macerated in sugar and alcohol, then filtered and bottled

Liqueur de citrons ⇒ lemon liqueur or lemon juice and lemon peel macerated with sugar, cinnamon, coriander powder, plus cognac

Liqueur de fleur d'oranger ⇒ orange blossom liqueur or orange blossom macerated with alcohol, cinnamon, clove and sugared syrup

Liqueur de fraise ⇒ strawberry liqueur or strawberries infused in alcohol, then sugared

Liqueur de fraises des bois ⇒ wild-strawberry liqueur

Liqueur de framboise ⇒ raspberry liqueur or raspberries infused in alcohol, then sugared

Liqueur de génépi ⇒ Alpine wormwood liqueur or Alpine mugwort liqueur

Liqueur de mandarines ⇒ tangerine liqueur or tangerine juice and tangerine peel macerated with sugar, cinnamon, coriander powder, plus cognac

Liqueur de myrthe ⇒ myrtle liquor

Liqueur de myrtilles ⇒ bilberry liqueur

Liqueur de noyau ⇒ noyau

Liqueur de poire ⇒ pear liqueur

Liqueur des villageois ⇒ liqueur made with the juice of baked grapes, added with a maceration of eau de vie, pink petals, clove and cinnamon

Liqueur de Voiron *-[Dauphiné]-*
- **liqueur** ⇒ chartreuse

Liqueur du pape *-[bichof]-* ⇒ drink made of wine, citrus and spices
- **Liqueur d'évêque** ⇒ drink made of Bordeaux wine, citrus and spices
- **Liqueur de cardinal** ⇒ drink made of white wine, citrus and spices
- **Bichof classique** *-[ou Bishop à l'anglaise]-* ⇒ bishop or drink made of sugar in syrup, orange and lemon peel, cinnamon, clove, plus Bordeaux wine

Liqueur verte *-[Chartreuse]-*
- **liqueur** ⇒ chartreuse

Liquoreux *(de vin ...)* ⇒ sweet or liqueur like

Liquoroso *-[Sicile, Sardaigne]-* ⇒ Sardinian wine liqueur

Lirac ⇒ wine from Roquemaure area « Côtes du Rhone »

Lisettes *-[petits maquereaux]-* ⇒ small mackerel

Listao ⇒ bonito

Listel *-[vin rosé]-* ⇒ high quality fruity rosé wine from Languedoc area

Listrac ⇒ Médoc red wine

Lit *-[cuisine, pâtisserie]-* ⇒ a bed of ... or a layer of ...

Litchi ⇒ litchi or lychee

Litorne *-[grive]-* ⇒ fieldfare

Littorine *-[bigorneau]-* ⇒ winkle

Livadia *-[URSS vins]-* ⇒ Ukrainian red wine or muscatel

Lival *-[raisin]-* ⇒ variety of grape

Livances *-[Tchécoslovaquie]-* ⇒ pancakes with jam

Livarot ⇒ Norman cow's milk cheese with a brown crust, surrounded by reed's thongs

Livèche ⇒ lovage

Livernon *-[cabécou]-* ⇒ small cheese from a mixing of goat's milk and cow's milk

Ljutomer *-[Yougoslavie]-* ⇒ Yugoslavian white wine

Lobscouse *-[Liverpool]-* ⇒ stew of mutton or beef, with peas, potatoes and barley

Loche ⇒ loach

Loches *-[fromage de Touraine]-* ⇒ cheese from Saumur

Locorotondo *-[vin de Pouilles]-* ⇒ Italian dry white wine

Loganberry -[*framboise*]- ⇒ raspberry
Loir ⇒ dormouse
Loki -[*saumon cru Finlande*]- ⇒ raw salmon
Lokshen -[*cuisine juive*]- ⇒ boiled noodles
Lompe ou Lomp -[*lump*]- ⇒ lumpfish
    - **oeufs** ⇒ lumpfish eggs
Longane ⇒ Indian fruit
Longaniza ⇒ spicy dried sausage
Longchamp -[*potage*]- ⇒ soup of mashed peas, sorrel chiffonade braised in butter, consommé and
        vermicelli; served sprinkled with shredded chervil
Long drink ⇒ cocktail added of ...
    - **toddy** ⇒ ... water
    - **fix** ⇒ ... soda water
    - **fizz** ⇒ ... Schweppes
    - **sangaree** ⇒ ... beer
    - **cup** ⇒ ... wine
    - **crusta** ⇒ ... champagne
    - **juleps** ⇒ ... water and flavoured with mint
Longe
    - **veau** ⇒ loin of veal
    - **porc** ⇒ loin of pork
    - **agneau** ⇒ loin of lamb
    - **bœuf** ⇒ loin of beef
Longe de porc avec palette et échine, découennée ⇒ long hogmeat
Longe de porc désossée et ficelée ⇒ short loin of pork « boneless » or long hogmeat « boned and
        rolled »
Longe de porc entière ⇒ long loin of pork
Longe de porc entière désossée et ficelée ⇒ long loin of pork boneless
Longe de porc entière désossée et roulée ⇒ long loin of pork « boned and rolled »
Longe de porc ou rein ⇒ short loin of pork « boned and rolled »
Longe de porc ou rein avec la peau ⇒ short hogmeat « boned and rolled »
Longe de porc sans échine ⇒ short loin of pork
Longe de porc sans échine avec la peau ⇒ short hogmeat
Longe de veau ⇒ loin of veal
Longe de veau dégraissée, filet en moins et ficelée ⇒ loin of veal « boned and rolled »
Longe de veau désossée ⇒ loin of veal « boneless »
Longe de veau désossée ⇒ long striploin
Longe de veau désossée et parée ⇒ long striploin « special trim »
Longe de veau désossée, dégraissée et parée ⇒ long striploin « larder trim »
Longeole ⇒ braised fresh sausage preserved in oil
Longuet ⇒ bread-stick
Lonzo ⇒ boned pork fillet rubbed with saltpetre, washed in red wine, sprinkled of pimento powder; then
        dried in gut dressing
Loquat -[*nèfle du Japon*]- ⇒ Japanese medlar
Lord Sandy's sauce ⇒ Lord Sandy's sauce
Lorette
    1) **garniture grosses pièces de boucheries rôties** ⇒ nom anglais ... served with chicken
        croquettes, asparagus tips and truffle lamellas; covered with the cooking juice plus
        Madeira

Lorette
  2) **garniture petites pièces de boucherie sautées** ⇒ nom anglais ... served with chicken
      croquettes, asparagus tips and truffle lamellas; covered with the cooking juice
Lorgnette -*[merlans frits]*- ⇒ whiting fillets, rolled and fried; served with parsley and slices of
      lemon
Loring -*[pêche]*- ⇒ variety of peach
Lormes -*[fromage de]*- ⇒ cheese from Nevers area
Lorraine -*[fromage de Gérardmer]*- ⇒ cow's milk cheese from Lorraine area
Lorraine (*à la ...*)
    - **Grosses pièces de boucherie braisées** ⇒ braised « nom anglais de la viande » ... with a
        garnish of red cabbage braised in red wine, plus potatoes shaped in olive and baked in
        butter; served with the gravy and grated horse-radish
    - **Autres potées** ⇒ stew ...
    - **quiches** ⇒ quiches ...
    - **œufs** ⇒ eggs ... with smoked bacon and gruyère
Losange ⇒ lozenge
Lote -*[lotte de rivière]*- ⇒ burbot or eel pout
Lotier ou Mélilot ⇒ melilot or bird's-foot trefoil
Lotte ⇒ angler or conger eel
Lotte à l'américaine ⇒ elaborated dish of sliced angler, cooked in a sauce of Norway lobsters,
      tomatoes, shallots, garlic, tarragon, cognac and white wine; served with rice
Lotte de rivière ⇒ burbot or eel pout
Lotte des lacs ⇒ burbot or eel pout
Lotte pochée ⇒ angler poached in a white wine court-bouillon; served with quartered lemons and
      melted butter, or an other sauce
Lotte rôtie ⇒ roasted angler, surrounded by sauté mushrooms; served with tomatoes cooked in their
      own liquid
Lotus ⇒ lotus
Lou Moussu -*[cochon en périgord]*- ⇒ pork
Loubine -*[bar sur la côte atlantique]*- ⇒ sea bass « pluriel inchangé »
Lou sard ⇒ kind of red sea bream
Louise-bonne -*[poire]*- ⇒ variety of pear
Louisiane ⇒ poultry stuffed of maize in cream and diced capsicum, cooked in the oven with aromatics,
      and moistened with the cooking juice added of Madeira; served with maize in cream,
      moulded rice, and sliced fried bananas
Loukoum (*ou rahat loukoum ...*) ⇒ sweet based on sugar, honey, syrup, flour and aromatics
Loup -*[bar]*- ⇒ sea bass or sea perch or sea dace < *tous pluriel inchangé* >
Loup braisé au Graves rouge ⇒ sea bass fillets browned in butter, then simmered with sauté
      mushrooms, onions, Graves red wine and stock; served with the cooking juice
      thickened of butter and sauce hollandaise, garnished with fried sippets
Loupiac ⇒ Bordeaux white wine from Barsac area
Louquenka ⇒ small sausage flavoured with capsicum and garlic, from Basque area
Louviers -*[chou pommé]*- ⇒ common cabbage
Lucullus ⇒ ... garnished with truffle, foie gras, cockscombs, Madeira
Luizet -*[abricot]*- ⇒ variety of apricot
Luma -*[escargot]*- ⇒ snail
Lumache -*[pâtes alimentaires]*- ⇒ pasta shaped in shell
Lump ⇒ lumpfish
Luncheon meat ⇒ luncheon meat or German sausage
Lunel ⇒ muscat from Nîmes area

Lusignan -*[fromage frais]*- ⇒ goat's milk cheese
Lustré ⇒ glazed < *v.t adjectif* >
Luzerne -*[miel]*- ⇒ honey from lucern flowers or lucern honey
Lychee ⇒ litchi OR lychee
Lycoperdon ⇒ puff-ball
Lycoperdon géant -*[champignon]*- ⇒ giant puff-ball
Lymeswold -*[fromage]*- ⇒ Lymeswold
Lyonnaise *(à la ...)*
   - **plats sautés** ⇒ ... sautéed in chopped onions, butter and parsley
   - **plats avec sauce lyonnaise** ⇒ with a sauce of onions braised in butter, vinegar, white wine and
       stock
Lyonnaise -*[sauce]*- ⇒ sauce of onions braised in butter, plus vinegar, white wine and stock
Lys -*[fleur de]*- ⇒ lily

M

Macadam *-[Antilles]-* ⇒ salt cod browned in a roux, then simmered in a sauce

Macaire *(garniture pour pièces de boucherie rôties ou poêlées ...)* ⇒ ... served with potato flat cakes

Macaron ⇒ macaroon

Macarons à la crème *(variante servie avec une crème ...)* ⇒ macaroons, served with a custard, made of milk, rum, sugar, egg-yolks and maïzena

Macarons à la crème ⇒ macaroons, in vanilla flavoured cream

Macarons à la neige ⇒ macaroons cooked in custard of whipped white of eggs, butter, sugar and rum; then covered with redcurrant jam

Macarons aux noisettes ⇒ macaroons made of pounded hazelnuts, icing sugar, vanilla sugar and white of eggs

Macarons classiques ⇒ macaroons made of granulated sugar, almond powder and white of eggs; flavoured with orange paste or chocolate powder

Macarons mœlleux ⇒ macaroons made of pounded hazelnuts, icing sugar, vanilla sugar and white of eggs

Macaroni ⇒ macaroni < *uncountable* >

Macaronis à l'anglaise ⇒ macaroni boiled al dente, served with butter

Macaronis à l'italienne

   a) aux fromage ⇒ boiled macaroni mixed with grated gruyère, grated parmesan, grated nutmeg and butter

   b) avec foies de volaille cuits ⇒ boiled macaroni mixed with poultry livers, grated nutmeg and butter

   c) avec truffe ⇒ boiled macaroni mixed with truffle lamellas, grated nutmeg and butter

   d) avec fondue de tomates ⇒ boiled macaroni mixed with tomatoes cooked in their own liquid, grated nutmeg and butter

Macaronis à la créole ⇒ boiled macaroni, added of grated cheese, plus a mixing of sauté capsicums, courgettes, tomatoes, crushed garlic and pepper

Macaronis à la crème ⇒ boiled macaroni, simmered with cream and grated nutmeg; served with butter

Macaronis à la mirepoix ⇒ mixture of diced vegetables and ham, added with boiled macaroni; then sprinkled with grated cheese, plus melted butter, and browned

Macaronis à la moutarde ⇒ dish of boiled macaroni, covered with a sauce made of cream, egg-yolk, mustard, and grated parmesan; then browned

Macaronis à la sicilienne ⇒ macaroni, cooked slowly with small balls of meat, Mozzarella, and fried aubergines

Macaronis all'arrabbiata ⇒ macaroni cooked with pimentos or with mozzarella, mushrooms, peas and giblets of poultry

Macaronis au jus ⇒ boiled macaroni, simmered in meat juice

Macaronis aux fruits de mer ⇒ ragout of seafood, mixed with boiled macaroni

Macaronis en croquettes ⇒ croquettes made of macaroni, béchamel sauce and grated gruyère; served with tomatoes cooked in their own liquid

Macaronis Lucullus ⇒ timbale filled with layers of macaroni, plus a culinary stuffing of truffle, foie gras and Madeira sauce; topped with truffle lamellas

Maceron ⇒ alexanders or horse-parsley

Macis ⇒ mace of nutmeg < *uncountable* >

Macquée

   - fromage ⇒ kind of soft white cheese

- **tarte** ⇒ tart made with soft white cheese, egg-yolks and dough
Macre ⇒ water-caldron or water-chestnut
Macreuse -[*oiseau*]- ⇒ scoter or widgeon
Macreuse -[*viande*]- ⇒ shoulder of beef or part of shoulder of beef
Macvin ⇒ wine liquor based on grape juice, aromatics and marc
Macédoine
     - **fruit** ⇒ fruit salad
     - **légumes** ⇒ vegetable salad
Macédoine de légumes au beurre ou à la crème
     a) **au beurre** ⇒ vegetable salad added of butter
     b) **à la crème** ⇒ vegetable salad added of cream
Macéré ⇒ macerated < *Vt adjectif* >
Mâche ⇒ corn-salad or lamb's lettuce
Mâchon -[*Lyon*]- ⇒ kind of lunch in Lyon
Mâcon ⇒ Burgundy wine from Mâcon area
Mâcon supérieur ⇒ Burgundy wine from Mâcon area
Mâcon villages ⇒ quality Burgundy white wine
Mâconnaise (*à la ...*)
     - **poisson tronçonné** ⇒ bits of « nom anglais du poisson » cooked in red wine and herbs; laid on
                 onions, sauté mushrooms, sippets and crayfishes
Mâconnet -[*Bouton de culotte*]- ⇒ small goat's milk cheese
Madeleines ⇒ small sponge cakes
Madeleines de Commercy ⇒ kind of sponge cakes, flavoured with orange blossom
Madeleineau -[*saumon*]- ⇒ salmon or Atlantic salmon < *tous uncountable* >
Madère ⇒ Madeira
Madère -[*taro*]- ⇒ Indian katchu
Madérisé ⇒ oxidised
Madi -[*macre*]- ⇒ water-caltrop or water chestnut
Madiran ⇒ red wine from Armagnac area
Madrilène (*à la ...*) ⇒ chicken consommé with tomato pulp
Mafé -[*Afrique occidentale*]- ⇒ beef cooked with natural peanuts and millet
Magayante -[*liqueur*]- ⇒ fennel liquor
Magistère
     - **épais** ⇒ consommé based on poultry, and beef
     - **lèger** ⇒ consommé based on shin of veal, pigeon, crayfishes and watercress
Magnolia -[*fleur*]- ⇒ magnolia flower
Magnum ⇒ magnum
Magret ⇒ meat fillet from the breast of duck
Magret de canard ⇒ breast fillet of duck
Magrets de canard -[*André Daguin*]- ⇒ browned breast fillets of duck; served with a sauce of
                 shallots, Madeira wine, cream and butter
Magrets de canard au poivre vert ⇒ browned breast fillets of duck, simmered in stock, green
                 pepper and cream; served with pancakes made of rice, boletus and béchamel sauce
Mahura -[*aeglé*]- ⇒ Indian grapefruit
Maid of honour ⇒ almonds and lemon tartlet
Maigre -[*poisson*]- ⇒ meagre
Maigre ⇒ low-fat
     - **viande** ⇒ lean meat
     - **jus** ⇒ thin gravy

Maigret de la Mayenne -*[pain]-* ⇒ bread for soup
Maillot ou porte maillot (*garniture pour grosses pièces de boucherie ...)* ⇒ garnished with a
    mixing of carrots, turnips, onions and french beans
Main provençale -*[pain]-* ⇒ bread < *uncountable* >
Maingaux ⇒ mousse of whipped cream; served with fraises, mulberries or raspberries
Mainotte -*[clavaire]-* ⇒ tiny yellow hand
Maintenon
    - **garniture pour viande** ⇒ ... garnished of mushrooms, onions and béchamel sauce
    - **omelette fourrée** ⇒ omelette stuffed ...
    - **oeufs pochés** ⇒ poached eggs served ...
    - **pommes de terre farçies** ⇒ potatoes stuffed ... with mushrooms, onions and béchamel sauce
Maison ⇒ home made
    - **« Home made » est un adjectif vous devez le placer avant le nom exemple soupe de**
        poisson maison ⇒ home made fish soup
    - **exception pour phrase avec le verbe « to be » exemple Tous nos produits sont faits**
        maison ou dans notre laboratoire ⇒ all our products are home made
Maisur dal ⇒ kind of lentils
Maïa -*[araignée de mer]-* ⇒ spider crab < *cuisine uncountable* >
Maïs ⇒ maize or corn < *tous uncountable* >
Maïs bouilli ⇒ hominy
Maïs en soso aux abattis de poulet ⇒ diced giblets of poultry cooked with tomato purée, mashed
    maize, and chopped onions
Maïs frais à la béchamel ⇒ boiled maize thickened with béchamel sauce
Maïs frais au naturel ⇒ boiled maize served with butter
Maïs frais grillé ⇒ grilled maize served with butter
Maïzena ⇒ cornflour
Maître d'hôtel -*[beurre]-* ⇒ composed butter added of parsley and lemon juice
Makowiek -*[Pologne]-* ⇒ rolled pastry in jelly, stuffed with poppy seeds
Malaga ⇒ Malaga wine
Malagueta -*[piment]-* ⇒ red pepper or pimento < *uncountable* >
Malakoff
    1) **meringue** ⇒ gateau made with alternate discs of meringue and coffee mousse; covered of
        icing sugar and garnished of almonds
    2) **pâte à choux** ⇒ ring of choux pastry filled with a custard or ice cream
Malanga -*[racine]-* ⇒ edible root
Malaxé ⇒ kneaded
Malibu -*[liqueur]-* ⇒ Malibu
Malmsey -*[madère]-* ⇒ Madeira
Malossol -*[cornichon à la russe]-* ⇒ macerated gherkins in salted water and fennel
Malsat
    - **sud ouest** ⇒ white pudding based on pork belly, panada, eggs and aromatics
    - **Albi** ⇒ white pudding based on chopped spleen and eggs; served fried
Malt ⇒ malt
Malt whisky ⇒ whisky
Maltais ⇒ petit four made of preserved orange and almond powder, glazed with fondant
Maltaise (*à la ...)*
    a) **général** ⇒ preparation added of blood orange
    b) **sauce d'accompagnement avec poissons pochés** ⇒ poached ...
        - **asperges** ⇒ asparagus ...

- **bettes** ⇒ beets ...
- **cardons** ⇒ cardoons ... covered with sauce hollandaise, mixed with the peel and juice of blood oranges
c) **bombe glacée à la maltaise** ⇒ ice pudding, coated with orange ice cream, and filled of whipped cream flavoured with tangerine

Maltaise ⇒ Maltese orange

Malvasia -*[malvoisie]*- ⇒ malmsey wine

Malvoisie ⇒ malmsey wine

Mamaliga -*[Roumanie]*- ⇒ maize porridge

Mamelle ⇒ udder

Mamertino -*[Sicile, Sardaigne]*- ⇒ heady wine

Manbollen -*[édam]*- ⇒ Edam

Mancelle *(à la ...)*
- **général** ⇒ poultry or rillettes
- **omelette** ⇒ omelette stuffed with artichoke hearts and diced potatoes

Munch à gigot ⇒ leg of mutton holder

Munch de gigot ⇒ knuckle-bone from leg of mutton

Manchego ⇒ Spanish cheese

Manchette ⇒ paper frill for ...
- **gigot** ⇒ ... knuckle-bone from leg of mutton
- **jambon** ⇒ ... bone of ham
- **cuissot de chevreuil** ⇒ ... haunch of roebuck
- **cotelettes** ⇒ ... cutlets

Manchon ⇒ petit four made of a tubular biscuit filled with a custard

Mandarine ⇒ mandarin orange or tangerine

Mandarines en surprise ⇒ tangerine peel, filled with a sorbet of tangerine juice, plus a soufflé flavoured of tangerine; then sprinkled of icing sugar and browned

Mandarines givrées ⇒ sorbet of tangerine juice, wrapped in the tangerine peel and frozen

Mandelkritzler ⇒ small fried cakes, made of butter, sugar, almond powder, flour, orange flower and cinnamon

Mange mêle -*[Antilles]*- ⇒ vegetables cooked with pork fat

Mange-tout
- **pois** ⇒ mange-tout beans
- **haricots** ⇒ runner bean or french bean

Mangoustan ⇒ mangosteen

Mangouste -*[mangoustan]*- ⇒ mangosteen

Mangue ⇒ mango
- **pluriel** ⇒ mangos or mangoes

Manhattan -*[cocktail]*- ⇒ cocktail of whisky, vermouth, Cointreau, Angostura brandy, lemon peel and a cherry

Manicamp -*[Picardie]*- ⇒ Picardie cheese

Manicotti -*[pâtes]*- ⇒ variety of canneloni

Manié ⇒ kneaded

Manille -*[café]*- ⇒ coffee

Manioc ⇒ manioc or cassava < *tous uncountable* >

Mänella -*[pain]*- ⇒ bread

Manouls
- **Languedoc** ⇒ veal tripe stuffed with ham, garlic and parsley
- **Rouergue** ⇒ lamb tripe simmered with aromatics

Manqué ⇒ moulded sponge cake with almonds, topped of hazelnuts, or preserved fruits

Manqué à l'ananas ⇒ moulded sponge-cake flavoured with preserved pineapple; glazed with fondant added of rum, decorated with bits of pineapple and preserved cherries

Manqué au citron ⇒ moulded sponge-cake, flavoured with cedrate and lemon peel; covered with a preparation of white of eggs, lemon juice, and icing sugar, then decorated with bits of pineapple and preserved cherries

Manvi ⇒ freshwater fish

Manzanilla ⇒ manzanilla

Maple syrup ⇒ maple syrup

Maquereau ⇒ mackerel < *pluriel inchangé* >

Maquereaux à l'oseille ⇒ mackerel roasted in butter; served with sorrel cooked and mashed in their cooking juice, thickened of eggs

Maquereaux à la boulonnaise ⇒ poached mackerel in court-bouillon; plus mussels with butter sauce

Maquereaux à la nage ⇒ mackerel baked in a preparation of red wine, garlic, shallots, cayenne pepper, clove, cinnamon, herbs, carrots, fennel, celery, and leeks

Maquereaux au beurre noisette ⇒ poached bits of mackerel, sprinkled with vinegar; served covered with butter, added of capers, and parsley

Maquereaux au cidre Pierre Traiteur ⇒ mackerel fillets cooked with onions, apples, cider and vinegar; served with quartered apples browned in butter, and the cooking juice

Maquereaux aux deux moutardes ⇒ mackerel sprinkled of pepper and white wine, then baked; covered with a sauce of mustard, the cooking juice, and butter; accompanied by rice

Maquereaux du pêcheur quimperois ⇒ poached mackerel fillets, coated with a sauce made of egg-yolks, mustard, vinegar, butter and herbs; served with boiled potatoes

Maragnan -*[cacao]*- ⇒ cacao or cocoa < *tous uncountable* >

Maraîchère (*à la ...*)
   1) **Grosses pièces de boucherie rôties ou braisées** ⇒ ... with a garnish of shaped carrots, small onions, bits of braised cucumbers and braised quartered artichoke hearts; served with the gravy
   2) **Autre garniture « choux de bruxelles, salsifis et pommes château »** ⇒ with a garnish of brussels-sprouts, salsify and small potatoes sautéed in butter with lardoons; served with the gravy

Marasme d'oréade ⇒ fairy ring mushroom

Marasquin ⇒ maraschino

Marastina -*[Yougoslavie]*- ⇒ Yugoslavian white wine

Marbot -*[noix]*- ⇒ nut

Marbrade ⇒ preparation of moulded pork butchery, made of jelly and pork head

Marc ⇒ marc brandy

Marcassin ⇒ young wild boar

Marcelin ⇒ gateau made with a disc of dough, covered of raspberry jam, plus a mixing of eggs and almond powder

Marchand de vin
   - **en général** ⇒ ... cooked with red wine and shallots
   - **viandes grillées** ⇒ ... covered with composed butter added of red wine and shallots
   - **poissons merlan** ⇒ whiting ... poached in red wine and shallots
   - **sole** ⇒ sole ... poached in red wine and shallots

Marcillac ⇒ red wine or rosé from the South West of France

Marconnets -*[Beaune]*- ⇒ quality red wine from Beaune area

Maréchale (*à la ...*)
   1) **Petites pièces de boucherie**
         - **côtes d'agneau** ⇒ lamb chops ...

- **noisettes d'agneau** ⇒ noisettes of lamb ...
- **escalopes de veau** ⇒ veal escalopes ...
- **côtes de veau** ⇒ veal chops ...
- **ris de veau** ⇒ calf sweetbread ...
- **suprême de volaille** ⇒ chicken in supreme sauce ... coated with scrambled eggs and flour, then sautéed; served with a garnish of asparagus tips in bunches and truffle lamella, plus a sauce or parsley butter

2) **Poissons** ⇒ ... poached in white wine and fish stock, plus mushrooms and crushed tomatoes; served with the cooking juice added of butter

Marengo
- **poulet** ⇒ sauté chicken garnished with mushrooms, onions and fried sippets
- **veau** ⇒ sauté veal garnished with mushrooms, onions and fried sippets

Marenne -*[huître]-* ⇒ Marenne oyster

Marestel -*[Savoie vins]-* ⇒ Savoy white wine

Marette -*[pain pour bouillabaisse]-* ⇒ bread

Marga ⇒ sauce for couscous

Margarine ⇒ margarine

Margarita -*[cocktail]-* ⇒ cocktail made of tequila, lemon juice, sugar and curaçao

Margate -*[seiche]-* ⇒ cuttlefish

Margaux ⇒ Médoc red wines

Marguery -*[tournedos]-* ⇒ sauté tournedos laid on artichoke hearts

Marie Brizard -*[anisette]-* ⇒ anisette

Marie-Louise
- **garniture** ⇒ garnished with little potato balls browned in butter, artichoke hearts filled of chopped mushrooms and mashed onions; served with the cooking juice
- **variante** -*[tartelettes]-* ⇒ tartlets filled with peas, carrots and turnips

Marignan -*[gâteau]-* ⇒ gateau made with a paste for savarin cake, covered with apricot jam, topped of meringue and decorated with angelica

Marigny
1) **garniture petites pièces de boucherie sautées** ⇒ sauté ... nom anglais
   a) **avec pommes de terre** ⇒ ... garnished with potatoes in butter, peas, french beans, thickened with butter and laid in tartlets
   b) **avec fonds d'artichauts** ⇒ ... served with artichoke hearts filled of maize seeds in cream and hazelnuts
2) **potage** ⇒ soup based on peas and french beans

Marinade ⇒ marinade or pickle

Marinade crue pour grosses viandes de boucherie et de gibier
- **grosses viandes de boucherie** ⇒ large piece of ... or nom ...
- **gibier** ⇒ large piece of game, ... or large piece of nom ... peppered, salted, and sprinkled of fennel-flower; then marinated in onion, shallots, carrot, crushed garlic, parsley, thyme, laurel, clove, wine and cognac

Marinade crue pour petites pièces de boucherie, volaille et poissons
   a) **petites pièces de boucherie** ⇒ nom anglais ...
   b) **volaille** ⇒ nom anglais ... or poultry ...
   c) **poisson** ⇒ nom anglais ... salted, peppered and sprinkled with a mixing of onion, shallots, carrot, thyme, laurel, parsley, garlic, clove, and black pepper seeds; moistened with lemon juice and olive oil

Marinade crue pour éléments de pâté et de terrine
- **pâté** ⇒ pâté ...
- **terrine** ⇒ terrine ... salted, peppered, sprinkled of fennel-flower, crushed thyme and bay laurel; then moistened of cognac or armagnac

Marinade cuite pour viandes de boucherie et venaison
- **marinade** ⇒ marinade from a cooked mixing of aromatics, wine, and vinegar
- **viande marinée** ⇒ nom anglais de la viande ... salted and peppered, then marinated in a cooked mixing of aromatics, wine and vinegar

Marinade de pigeons au citron -*[Menon]*- ⇒ pigeon marinated in lemon juice

Marinades pour viandes en chevreuil -*[recettes en chevreuil]*- ⇒ ... marinated in a mixture of onions, carrots, shallots, celery, garlic, parsley, thyme, clove, pepper, white wine and vinegar, cooked slowly

Mariné *(e ...)* ⇒ marinated or pickled or soused < *v.t adjectif* >

Marinette ⇒ short-pastry tartlet, garnished with vanilla flavoured apple jam, raisins and lemon peel; covered of fondant flavoured with rum

Marinière *(à la ...)*
- **poissons, crustacés, coquillages, langoustines, écrevisses, grenouilles** ⇒ cooked in white wine, onions and shallots
- **garniture** ⇒ garnished with mussels and sometimes crayfish tails

Marinière de grenouilles à la coque ⇒ preparation of decorticated mussels and boned frog's legs, cooked in butter, shallots, white wine, cream, plus chives; served in egg shells, topped with a disc of puff-pastry

Marivaux
- **garniture pour grosses pièces de boucherie rôties** ⇒ Roasted ... with a garnish of french beans in butter, plus croustades of potatoes filled with carrots, celery, artichoke hearts and mushrooms braised in butter and thickened of béchamel sauce; then browned with grated cheese

Marjolaine ⇒ sweet marjoram

Markknödel ⇒ kind of quenelles added of bone-marrow

Marmande -*[tomate]*- ⇒ variety of tomato

Marmelade ⇒ compote or jam or jelly < *uncountable* >

Marmelade d'abricots ⇒ compote of apricots

Marmelade d'oranges ⇒ marmalade

Marmelade de cerises ⇒ cherry compote

Marmelade de citron vert ⇒ compote of lime

Marmelade de framboises ⇒ raspberry compote

Marmelade de jasmin ⇒ compote of jasmine

Marmelade de pêches ⇒ compote of peaches

Marmelade de pommes ⇒ compote of apples

Marmelade de prunes ⇒ compote of plums

Marmite bressane ⇒ stew of chicken

Marmite dieppoise ⇒ fish soup of sole, turbot and angler, cooked in white wine and vegetables; garnished with mussels, shrimps, and scallops, thickened of cream

Marocaine *(à la ...)*
- **Noisettes de mouton sautées** ⇒ sauté small round pieces of mutton ...
- **Noisettes d'agneau sautées** ⇒ sauté noisettes of lamb ... laid on pilaf and covered with their gravy added of tomato purée; served with sauté courgettes and sometimes capsicums stuffed of chicken

Maroilles ⇒ cheese made at Maroilles

Marquise
- **dessert** ⇒ sweet
- **boisson** ⇒ drink of white wine or champagne added of soda water; served chilled with slices of lemon
- **granité** ⇒ ice-cream of either fraise, pineapple, or kirsch, plus sugared whipped cream
- **génoise** ⇒ Genoese sponge stuffed with confectioner's custard, added of chocolate

Marquise au chocolat ⇒ cake made of chocolate, sugar, butter and eggs; covered with vanilla custard

Marri -*[caillé]-* ⇒ boiled milk added of buttermilk; served sugared

Marron ⇒ chestnut

Marron glacé ⇒ marron glacé

Marrons bouillis ⇒ boiled chestnuts served with butter

Marrons braisés ⇒ chestnuts braised with butter, aromatics and stock; served with meat

Marrons grillés ⇒ grilled chestnuts

Marrons étuvés ⇒ chestnuts simmered with butter, water and celery

Marsala ⇒ Marsala

Marseillaise -*[figue]-* ⇒ variety of fresh fig

Marsh -*[pamplemousse]-* ⇒ variety of grapefruit

Marsh-mallow -*[guimauve]-* ⇒ marshmallow sweet

Marsouin ⇒ porpoise

Martinafranca -*[Pouille vins]-* ⇒ Italian wine

Martini ⇒ martini

Mascara ⇒ Algerian red wine

Mascarpone ⇒ soft white cheese

Massacanat ⇒ large omelette garnished with diced meat

Massalé -*[Réunion]-* ⇒ young goat cooked with curry

Massandra -*[URSS vins]-* ⇒ Ukrainian wine

Masséna ⇒ cake made of discs, one in sugared dough, the other in Genoese sponge; plus chestnut purée, meringue, chocolate and coffee

Massenet
- **garniture pour grosses et petites pièces de boucherie** ⇒ nom anglais ... ... with a garnish of potatoes, little artichokes filled with a culinary stuffing of bone-marrow and french beans in butter; served with the gravy
- **apprêts d'œufs** ⇒ eggs ... garnished with asparagus tips, and artichoke hearts

Massepain ⇒ marzipan or almond paste confectionery

Massillon ⇒ petit four of sugared pastry boat, filled with almond paste and flavoured of vanilla

Mastic -*[épices]-* ⇒ mastic

Mastika ⇒ eau de vie added of mastic

Matafan
- **Bourgogne, Bresse** ⇒ thick pancake from a dough added of dried fruits
- **Lyonnais, Savoie, Dauphiné** ⇒ thick pancake from a dough added of spinach, or potatoes, or lardoons

Matafans bisontins ⇒ pancake made of milk, flour, eggs, sugar and beech-nut oil; flavoured with kirsch

Matahambre -*[matafan]-*
- **Bourgogne, Bresse** ⇒ thick pancake from a dough added of dried fruits
- **Lyonnais, Savoie, Dauphiné** ⇒ thick pancake from a dough added of spinach, or potatoes, or lardoons

Matambre -*[Argentine]-* ⇒ dish of marinated beef, stuffed with vegetables and hard boiled eggs; then roasted and boiled

Maté ⇒ maté
- **infusion** ⇒ maté tea

Matefaim savoyard ⇒ thick pancake of flour, milk, eggs, grated nutmeg and melted butter; sprinkled of grated gruyère and browned

Matelote ⇒ matelote
Matelote *(énumération; terme général traduit en anglais ...)* ⇒ matelote
- **étuvée de poissons préparée au vin rouge ou au vin blanc avec des aromates** ⇒ matelote
- **matelote de carpe** ⇒ carp in matelote
- **matelote de brochetons** ⇒ pikelet in matelote
- **matelote de truites** ⇒ trout in matelote
- **matelote d'alose** ⇒ shad in matelote
- **matelote de barbeaux** ⇒ barbels in matelote
- **Hendaye** *-[matelote d'anguilles aux champignons, à l'armagnac et au vin rouge]-* ⇒ matelote of eels with mushrooms, stewed in armagnac and red wine
- **garnitures des matelotes oignons, champignons, lardons** ⇒ ... served with a garnish of onions, mushrooms and lardoons
- **écrevisses au court-bouillon** ⇒ ... served with crayfishes cooked in court-bouillon
- **croutons frits** ⇒ ... served with fried croutons
Matelote à la canotière ⇒ matelote made of butter, onions, river fish, white wine, cognac and mushrooms; garnished with fried gudgeons, plus sometimes crayfishes
Matelote Charles Vanel ⇒ bits of eels, cooked in a mixture of diced vegetables and ham, plus two litres of red wine; served with onions, lardoons and mushrooms, braised in butter and anchovy fillets
Matelote d'anguilles ⇒ matelote made of eels, mushrooms, armagnac and red wine
Matelote du littoral normand ⇒ matelote of turbot, gurnard, conger eel, brill and other fishes, flamed in calvados; then cooked in cider, thickened of butter and added of shrimps, mussels or oysters
Mateus *-[Portugal vins]-* ⇒ rosé wine
Mateus Rosé ⇒ Mateus rosé
Mathusalem *-[bouteille]-* ⇒ Methuselah
Matignon
1) **fondue de légumes** ⇒ vegetables cooked in their own liquid
2) **garniture pour petites pièces de boucherie** ⇒ ... with a garnish of artichoke hearts stuffed with vegetables cooked in their own liquid
Matino *-[Pouilles vins de]-* ⇒ Italian wine, either red or rosé
Matonabour *-[Russe]-* ⇒ soup based on yoghourt
Matsutaké *-[Japon]-* ⇒ mushroom marinated in soya sauce and sake; then cooked with chicken, fish and ginkgo nuts
Matton *-[caillé]-* ⇒ curds or curdled milk
Mattonou brocq *-[caillé]-* ⇒ curds or curdled milk
Mattyé ⇒ dish of poultry cooked in stock; served with a sauce of grape and vinegar
Matzoun *-[Russe]-* ⇒ yoghourt < *uncountable* >
Maultaschen ⇒ ravioli stuffed with meat, nutmeg, spinach, sweet marjoram and onion; poached in stock
Maury *-[Roussillon vin]-* ⇒ sweet wine from Roussillon area
Maury ou Maury-rancio ⇒ sweet wine from Roussillon area
Mauve ⇒ mallow
Mauve musquée *-[musc]-* ⇒ musk
Mauviette *-[alouette]-* ⇒ lark or skylark
Mauvis *-[grive]-* ⇒ redwing
Mavrodaphne *-[Grèce vins]-* ⇒ sweet white wine
Mayette *-[noix]-* ⇒ nut
Mayonnaise ⇒ mayonnaise < *uncountable* >

Mayonnaise à la russe ⇒ mayonnaise added of jelly and vinegar
Mayonnaise au caviar ⇒ mayonnaise added of pounded caviar
Mayonnaise au cresson ⇒ mayonnaise added of chopped watercress
Mayonnaise aux anchois ⇒ mayonnaise added of anchovy extract
Mayonnaise aux crevettes ⇒ mayonnaise added of crushed shrimps
Mayonnaise classique ⇒ mayonnaise
Mayonnaise collée ⇒ mayonnaise added of meat jelly
Mayonnaise de homard *-[salade]-* ⇒ salad of lobster, oil, vinegar, aromatics, mayonnaise sauce, lettuce, hard boiled eggs, anchovy fillets, olives and capers
Mayonnaise de laitances *-[salade]-* ⇒ salad of lettuce, soft roes, mayonnaise added of anchovy extract, hard boiled eggs, anchovy fillets and capers
Mayonnaise de saumon *-[salade]-* ⇒ composed salad of lettuce, salmon, oil, vinegar, lemon juice, capers, anchovies, black olives and hard boiled eggs
Mazagran *-[cuisine]-* ⇒ tartlets of mashed potatoes, eggs and butter; filled with a hash
Mazarin ⇒ sponge cake with a layer of mousse flavoured with praline
Mazarine *(à la ...)*
  - **garniture petites pièces de boucherie** ⇒ ... garnished of rice, cultivated mushrooms, plus artichoke hearts filled with braised vegetables in butter
Mazis-chambertin *-[gevrey chambertin]-* ⇒ Chambertin
Mazoyères-chambertin *-[gevrey chambertin]-* ⇒ Chambertin
Mazurek *-[Pologne]-* ⇒ kind of tart sometimes topped with meringue
Mazzah *-[azyme]-* ⇒ unleavened cake
Mazzot *-[azyme]-* ⇒ unleavened cake
Mead *-[hydromel]-* ⇒ mead
Meat tea *-[thé repas]-* ⇒ meat tea
Méchoui ⇒ whole roast sheep
Médaillon ⇒ thin round slice of meat ... or médaillon
Médaillons de lotte au beurre de poivron rouge ⇒ round slices of angler baked in a preparation of vinegar, carrot, onion, aromatics, plus capsicum cooked in olive oil, shallot and cream; served covered with the gravy
Médaillons de lotte aux herbes ⇒ round slices of angler cooked in butter, white wine from Loire Valley, shallot and pepper; served laid on the gravy mixed with watercress, sorrel, chervil, and lettuce, then covered of diced tomatoes, sprinkled of chives and pepper
Médaillons de veau Alexandre ⇒ round slices of veal sautéed in butter and decorated of truffle lamellas, surrounded by browned artichoke hearts and morels in cream; covered with the gravy thickened of cognac and Marsala
Médaillons de volaille à l'égyptienne ⇒ round slices of poultry and sliced aubergines, sautéed in olive oil, laid in turban; served with pilaf, plus on the sauce-boat the gravy, thickened of tomatoes cooked in their own liquid
Médaillon de volaiile Beauharnais ⇒ round slices of poultry sautéed in butter, laid on fried sippets, then topped of braised artichoke hearts, filled with béarnaise sauce added of tarragon paste
Médaillons de volaille Fédora ⇒ round slices of poultry browned in butter, laid on fried sippets; served in ring with cucumbers braised in butter, plus a sauce made of the gravy, wine and cream
Médicis
  - **viandes** ⇒ covered with béarnaise sauce and surrounded by the gravy added of Madeira; garnished with little potato balls browned in butter, plus braised artichoke hearts filled with peas, carrots and turnips
Médoc ⇒ Médoc
Méduse *-[Chine]-* ⇒ dried jelly-fish, sliced in lamellas for salad

Mei kuei lu ⇒ alcohol of sorghum and roses
Mélange ⇒ mixture or blend or mixing
  - **mélangé** ⇒ blended or mixed
Mélasse ⇒ molasses or treacle
Melba
  a) **pêche Melba** ⇒ vanilla ice-cream topped with halved peaches poached in syrup; covered with raspberry purée
    - **autres nappages groseilles** ⇒ covered with redcurrant jelly flavoured of kirsch
    - **poires** ⇒ pears
    - **abricot** ⇒ apricot
    - **fraises** ⇒ fraise
  b) **garniture pour petites pièces de boucherie** ⇒ ... with a garnish of little stuffed tomatoes
Melbat -*[noisettes d'agneau]*- ⇒ sautéed noisettes of lamb laid on fried sippets, covered with the gravy added of stock, arrow-root, Madeira and butter; garnished of tomatoes stuffed with a culinary stuffing of poultry, truffle, mushrooms and velouté sauce
Melet -*[Martigues]*- ⇒ seasoning from Martigues
Melette ⇒ mutton's testicles
Melilot ⇒ melilot or sweet-clover
Melimelum ⇒ jam made of honey and apples or honey and apple jam
Mélisse ⇒ balm or balm-mint
  - **eau de Mélisse** ⇒ extract of balm or melissa cordial
Mélochie ⇒ Egyptian plant similar to mallow
Melon ⇒ melon
Melon au porto ⇒ melon with a hole made in the peduncle, where the seeds are replaced by port
Melon d'Arbois ⇒ melon
Melon d'eau ⇒ watermelon
Melon d'hiver ⇒ melon
Melon en surprise à la parisienne ⇒ melon's husk filled with cubes of its pulp, fruits in season, grape seeds, plums, fraises and raspberries, then sprinkled of granulated sugar and a sweet wine; served chilled, presented on a layer of crushed ice
Melon frappé ⇒ melon's husk, filled with its diced pulp added of port and chilled, plus melon granita; presented on a layer of crushed ice
Melon glacé ⇒ melon's husk, filled with a sorbet made of its pulp, and frozen; presented on a layer of crushed ice
Melon sucrin ⇒ sweet melon
Melon surprise ⇒ mixture of melon pulp, fraises, sugar and kirsch; laid in the melon husk
Melrose -*[pomme de terre]*- ⇒ variety of potato
Melsat
  - **sud ouest** ⇒ white pudding based on pork belly, panada, eggs and aromatics
  - **Albi** ⇒ white pudding based on chopped spleen and eggs; served fried
Melted butter sauce ⇒ melted butter sauce
Melva -*[thon]*- ⇒ bonito
Mendiants ⇒ dessert of almonds, figs, hazelnuts and raisins
Mendole -*[poisson]*- ⇒ mendole or cackerel
Menenas -*[Egypte]*- ⇒ ball of almond paste and orange blossom, stuffed with dates, almonds, pistachios, and cinnamon; then baked
Menetou-salon ⇒ Berry wines
Ménétru ⇒ white wine from Franche Comté
Mengrokom -*[Gabon]*- ⇒ alcohol of maize and cassava
Menotte -*[clavaire]*- ⇒ tiny yellow hands

Menthe ⇒ mint < *uncountable* >
Menthe à l'eau (*une ...*) ⇒ a glass of peppermint cordial
Menthe aquatique ⇒ watermint
Menthe bergamote ⇒ mint with a taste of fruit
Menthe citronnée ⇒ mint with a taste of fruit
Menthe coq ⇒ tansy
Menthe de chat ⇒ catmint
Menthe poivrée ⇒ peppermint
Menthe pouliot ⇒ pennyroyal
Menthe verte ou douce ⇒ spearmint or garden mint
Menthol ⇒ menthol
Mentholé ⇒ mentholated
Mentonnaise (*à la ...*)
    1) **Poissons** ⇒ ... with tomatoes, black olives and garlic
    2) **Petites pièces de boucherie** ⇒ ... with a garnish of courgettes stuffed of rice, braised
        artichokes and small potatoes sautéed in butter with lardoons
    3) **Courgettes farçies** ⇒ courgettes stuffed with spinach
Menu à prix fixe ⇒ fixed price menu or set menu
Menu droit ⇒ grilled lamellas of poultry fillet
Menus (*boyaux ...*) ⇒ small intestines of an animal or small intestines of ...
Mercédès
    - **garniture pour grosses pièces de boucherie** ⇒ nom ... served with a garnish of grilled
        mushrooms, braised lettuce, tomatoes, and potato croquettes
    - **consommé** ⇒ voir consommé Mercédès
Mercurey ⇒ Burgundy red wine
Merguez ⇒ sausage made of beef and mutton meat
Merienda ⇒ Spanish light meal
Meringue ⇒ meringue
Meringue à l'italienne ⇒ Italian meringue
Meringuer ⇒ to give a covering of meringue to ...
Meringues Suisses ⇒ small masses of meringue, flavoured with vanilla sugar; decorated of preserved
    fruits, or various coloured sugar
Meringues cuites ⇒ small masses of meringue, flavoured with coffee extract or something else; then
    baked
Meringues vanillées à la chantilly ⇒ small meringues flavoured with vanilla sugar; soldered two by
    two, with whipped cream
Merise ⇒ wild cherry
Merlan -*[viande]*- ⇒ steak taken from near the topside
Merlan -*[poisson]*- ⇒ whiting < *pluriel inchangé* >
Merlan frit en colère ⇒ fried whiting served with parsley, lemons, and tartare sauce
Merlans farçis au cidre ⇒ whiting stuffed with a julienne, and baked with olive oil, cider and fish
    stock; covered with the cooking juice thickened of cream, and sprinkled of chives
Merlans frits en lorgnette ⇒ whiting fillets, rolled and fried; served with parsley and slices of lemon
Merlan hermitage ⇒ whiting stuffed with a mixing of crumbs, butter in paste, shallot, egg, herbs and
    cayenne pepper, then baked; covered with the cooking juice thickened of butter,
    cream and pepper
Merlan pané à l'anglaise ⇒ whiting salted and floured, coated with whipped egg and oil, then fried in
    butter; served with parsley butter and boiled potatoes
Merlan pané à l'espagnole ⇒ whiting coated with whipped egg and oil, then fried in oil; served on
    tomatoes cooked in their own liquid with garlic, plus a garnish of fried onions

Merlan poché au beurre fondu ⇒ poached whiting, sprinkled of melted butter and parsley; served with a garnish of ...
- **pomme de terre vapeur** ⇒ ... steamed potatoes
- **riz** ⇒ ... rice
- **concombre au beurre** ⇒ ... cucumbers braised in butter
- **courgettes sautées** ⇒ ... courgettes sautéed in oil
- **aubergines sautées** ⇒ ... aubergines sautéed in oil
- **épinards au beurre** ⇒ ... spinach braised in butter
- **poireaux au beurre** ⇒ ... leeks braised in butter

Merlans au vin blanc ⇒ whiting laid on butter, chopped onion and shallot, then moistened of white wine, plus stock, and baked; covered with the cooking juice thickened of cream, then browned

Merlans en paupiette ⇒ whiting fillets, covered with a mousse of whiting and rolled, then baked with stock; served with the cooking juice, thickened of kneaded butter

Merle ⇒ blackbird

Merlu ⇒ hake < *pluriel inchangé* >

Merlu cosquera ⇒ slices of salt cod cooked in olive oil, with clams and pepper; sprinkled of chopped garlic and parsley

Merluche ⇒ hake, pluriel inchangé, or stockfish

Merluchon ⇒ small hake

Merlus ⇒ hake, pluriel inchangé or stockfish

Merluza salsa verde ⇒ fish covered with a garnish of fresh beans, asparagus and parsley

Mérou ⇒ grouper

Mérou sauce Corcellet ⇒ poached grouper, decorated with tarragon leaves, and tomato lamella; served with tomato purée added of mustard flavoured with aniseed

Merril gemfree -*[pêche]*- ⇒ variety of peach

Merveille de Kelvédon -*[petit pois]*- ⇒ variety of green peas

Merveille de Versailles -*[épinard]*- ⇒ variety of spinach

Merveilles ⇒ small fried cakes, from dough made with flour, egg-yolks, butter, sugar and rum

Mescal ⇒ Mexican alcohol from agave

Mescladisse ⇒ mixing of endive, lettuce, corn salad, chicory, endive, dandelion, and herbs

Mesclun ⇒ mixing of endive, lettuce, corn salad, chicory, endive, dandelion, and herbs

Mesfouf -*[couscous]*- ⇒ couscous made with broad beans, and raisins

Messicani ⇒ stuffed veal escalope, sautéed in butter; covered with the gravy thickened of white wine and Marsala

Met -*[hydromel]*- ⇒ mead

Méteil ⇒ mixing of wheat and rye for country bread

Mets endiablés ⇒ diabolical dishes

Metton ⇒ cow's milk cheese of hazelnut's size

Mettwurst -*[saucisse]*- ⇒ sausage

Méture
- **bouillie** ⇒ maize-flour porridge with ham and eggs
- **pain** ⇒ corn bread
- **Normandie** ⇒ voir Méteil

Meuille (*ou mulet ...*) ⇒ grey-mullet

Meunier -*[Alsace vins]*- ⇒ vin ordinaire

Meunier -*[champignon]*- ⇒ button mushroom

Meunière (*à la ...*)
- **poisson** ⇒ ... floured lightly and fried in butter, then served sprinkled with parsley, lemon juice and butter

- **peuvent être préparées avec la même traduction grenouilles** ⇒ frogs
- **coquilles St Jacques** ⇒ scallops
- **cervelles** ⇒ brains
- **laitances** ⇒ milt or soft roes

Meurette
- **poisson** ⇒ matelote of freshwater fish in red wine, plus lardoon, onions, and mushrooms
- **veau** ⇒ matelote of veal in red wine, plus lardoon, onions, and mushrooms
- **poulet** ⇒ matelote of chicken in red wine, plus lardoon, onions, and mushrooms

Meurette de poisson ⇒ matelote of fresh water fishes, flamed in Burgundy marc, cooked with garlic, carrot, onion and herbs, in Burgundy red wine

Meurette *(en ...) -[préparations « à la bourguignonne » ou « en meurette »]-*
- **escargots cuits en meurette** ⇒ snails cooked in red wine sauce with mushrooms, onions an lardoons
- **fromage de chèvre bourguignon** ⇒ goat's milk cheese preserved in marc
- **st florentin** ⇒ burgundy cheese
- **soumaintrain** ⇒ burgundy cheese
- **flan aux courges** ⇒ flan with gourds
- **corniottes** ⇒ burgundy sweets

Meursault ⇒ Burgundy wine from Côtes de Beaune

Meursault blagny ⇒ high quality white wine from cote de Beaune

Meursault premier cru ⇒ high quality white wine from côte de Beaune

Meursault-perrières ⇒ high quality wine from cote de Beaune

Mexicaine *(à la ...)*
1) **grosses pieces de boucherie** ⇒ nom ... braised or roasted, garnished with grilled mushrooms filled of crushed tomatoes, capsicums and aubergines; served with a sauce of tomato and capsicum
2) **paupiettes de poisson** ⇒ rolled thin slices of fish, poached and garnished of grilled mushrooms filled with crushed tomatoes; served with a sauce of white wine, tomato and capsicum

Meyerbeer ⇒ fried eggs

Michelini *-[pêche]-* ⇒ variety of peach

Michette *-[pain]-* ⇒ bread

Mi-chèvre ⇒ cheese from goat's milk and cow's milk

Mie de pain ⇒ crumb

Miel ⇒ honey *< tous uncountable >*
- **miel d'acacia** ⇒ acacia honey
- **miel d'ajoncs** ⇒ gorse honey
- **miel de bourdaine** ⇒ buckthorn honey
- **miel de bruyère** ⇒ heather honey
- **miel de fleurs** ⇒ flower honey
- **miel de lavande** ⇒ lavender honey
- **miel de luzerne** ⇒ lucerne honey
- **miel d'oranger** ⇒ orange honey
- **miel de romarin** ⇒ rosemary honey
- **miel rosat** ⇒ rose honey
- **miel de sainfoin** ⇒ sainfoin honey
- **miel de sapin** ⇒ pine honey
- **miel de sarrasin** ⇒ buckwheat honey
- **miel de thym** ⇒ thyme honey
- **miel de tilleul** ⇒ lime-tree honey
- **miel de trèfle** ⇒ clover honey

Miel d'orange ⇒ honey from orange blossom or orange honey
Miel des Vosges *-[confiserie]-* ⇒ a sweet
Miettes de thon ⇒ tiny pieces of tunny
Migaine ⇒ garnish of eggs and cream
Migé *-[soupe au vin froide]-* ⇒ chilled wine soup
Mignardise ⇒ sweet or dainty or titbit
Mignon ⇒ kind of biscuit shaped in disc, soldered with meringue
Mignonnette *-[poivre]-* ⇒ ground pepper
Mignonnette *(énumération ...)*
  - **d'agneau** ⇒ noisettes of lamb
  - **de volaille** ⇒ white of meat in supreme sauce
  - **filet mignon** ⇒ fillet mignon
  - **pommes de terre** ⇒ fried potato sticks
Mignonnette de caille Rachel ⇒ quail served with a garnish of artichoke hearts and bone-marrow lamellas, plus ...
  - **sauce bordelaise** ⇒ ... brown sauce added of garlic, tarragon, lemon pulp, clove and Sauternes wine
  - **sauce à la moelle** ⇒ ... a sauce made of shallots, white wine, meat stock, poached bone-marrow and butter
Mignonnette de mouton ⇒ small and round piece of mutton
Mignonnette d'agneau ⇒ noisettes of lamb
Mignonnettes d'agneau de lait ⇒ small round pieces of lamb marinated in thyme, rosemary and grape pip oil; then coated with mustard and cooked in a sauce of chopped shallots, wine vinegar, white wine, beef stock and cream
Mignonnettes sablées ⇒ pastries from Péronne
Migourée ou Migourée de Matata ⇒ matelote of hake, angler, ray, weever, grey-mullet, conger eel, cuttlefish, gurnard, john dory, in a court-bouillon of white wine, onion, shallot, parsley, tarragon and spices
Mijoter ⇒ to simmer
Mikado
  a) **escalopes de veau** ⇒ veal escalopes ...
    - **escalopes de volaille** ⇒ poultry escalopes ... laid on croquettes of rice, cooked in curry and soya sauce; served with tartlets filled of soya bean sprouts in cream
  b) **tournedos** ⇒ tournedos ...
    - **noisettes** ⇒ noisettes of lamb ... laid on halved grilled tomatoes; covered with crushed tomatoes added of tomato sauce, plus Japanese artichokes braised in butter
Mikong *-[pain d'épice]-* ⇒ gingerbread
Mil *-[millet]-* ⇒ millet
Milan *-[chou pommé]-* ⇒ cabbage
Milanais *-[pâtisserie]-*
  a) **petits fours** ⇒ petit four from almond paste, flavoured with lemon or orange; decorated with almonds or preserved fruits
  b) **petites galettes avec raisins secs** ⇒ small flat cakes flavoured with rum, and stuffed of raisins; covered with apricot jam
  c) **sablé ovale** ⇒ shortcake stuffed with jam, and sprinkled of icing sugar
Milanaise *(à la ...)*
  1) **viande escalopes de veau** ⇒ veal escalopes ...
    - **côtes de veau** ⇒ veal chops ... coated with egg and crumbs, then fried in butter
  2) **garniture risotto** ⇒ risotto ...

    - macaronis ⇒ macaroni ... served with a garnish of mushrooms, ham and oxtongue in julienne, plus truffle lamellas; moistened of veal stock added with Madeira

    3) plots gratinés ⇒ dishes or ... browned with grated parmesan

    4) macaronis au beurre ⇒ macaroni in butter; served with grated cheese and tomato sauce

Milandre *-[chien de mer]-* ⇒ dogfish or smooth hound

Mild *-[bière]-* ⇒ mild

Milk bar ⇒ milk bar

Milk shake *-[cocktail]-* ⇒ milk shake

Milk stout *-[stout]-* ⇒ milk stout

Millas ⇒ fried maize-flour porridge lamellas, served sugared or salted

Millas aux fruits

    1) début ⇒ maize porridge, flavoured with kirsch or cognac, laid on a dish and stuffed with ...

    2) milieu cerises ⇒ ... cherries cooked in a syrup flavoured of rum; ...

        - abricots ⇒ apricots ...

        - pêches ⇒ peaches ...

        - poires ⇒ pears ...

        - pommes ⇒ apples ...

        - pruneaux ⇒ dry plums ...

        - ananas ⇒ sliced pineapple ... cooked in a syrup flavour of rum; ... then sprinkled of crushed macaroons and melted butter, then browned

Millas en bouillie ⇒ maize porridge, flavoured with orange-blossom and lemon peel

Millasse ⇒ fried maize-flour porridge lamellas, served sugared or salted

Mille-feuille *-[dessert]-* ⇒ mille-feuille pastry

Mille-feuille *-[hors d'œuvre]-* ⇒ puff pastries stuffed with fish, or crustaceae

Mille-feuille rond ⇒ discs of millefeuille pastry, soldered and covered with confectioner's custard flavoured of rum; sprinkled with grilled almonds and icing sugar

Mille-feuilles de saumon frais au beurre rose ⇒ slices of salmon, cream and tarragon, baked between two rectangles of mille-feuille-pastry; covered with butter added of cream and compote of bilberries

Mille-feuilles de st jacques aux poivrons ⇒ scallops sautéed in butter, capsicums cooked in olive oil, and garlic cooked with cream and butter, inserted between two rectangles of mille-feuille-pastry; served with boletus sautéed in butter, plus a vinegar added of shallots and butter

Millésime *-[vin]-* ⇒ year or vintage

Millet ⇒ millet

Millias ⇒ fried maize-flour porridge lamellas, served sugared or salted

Milliasse ⇒ fried maize-flour porridge lamellas, served sugared or salted

Milliassous ⇒ almond pastry

Milliassous *-[Bordelais]-* ⇒ pastry with bitter almonds

Millière

    - riz ⇒ rice porridge

    - maïs ⇒ maize porridge

    - millet ⇒ millet porridge

Mimolette ⇒ Dutch cheese

Mimosa *-[cuisine]-*

    - garniture hors d'oeuvre ⇒ ... with a preparation of egg-yolks mixed with mayonnaise, and stuffed hard boiled eggs

    - salade ⇒ composed salad, sprinkled with chopped hard boiled egg-yolks

Mimosa *-[fleur]-* ⇒ mimosa flower

Mincemeat ⇒ mincemeat

Mincepie ⇒ mince-pie
Minérale ⇒ mineral water
Minerve ⇒ pastry from Nîmes or Uzès
Minervois ⇒ red wine from Languedoc
Minestra ⇒ vegetable soup
Minestrina ⇒ light soup
Minestrone ⇒ minestrone < *uncountable* >
Mingaux ⇒ mousse of whipped cream; served with fraises, mulberries or raspberries
Mingots ⇒ mousse of whipped cream; served with fraises, mulberries or raspberries
Mint Julep -[*cocktail*]- ⇒ cocktail of ice cubes, whisky, mint leaves and sugar
    - **variantes avec champagne** ⇒ champagne
    - **gin** ⇒ gin
    - **jus d'orange** ⇒ orange juice
Mint sauce -[*menthe*]- ⇒ mint sauce
Minutes de saumon à l'aigrelette ⇒ salmon escalopes baked in butter; covered with a sauce of mayonnaise, fish stock, pepper, chives, and tarragon
Mique
    1) **mique d'accompagnement pour les plats en sauce, le pot au feu** ⇒ pot au feu ...
      - **le petit salé aux choux** ⇒ texte
      - **la soupe** ⇒ soup ...
      - **le civet** ⇒ texte ... served with balls of flour, pork fat, goose fat, plus sometimes yeast, milk, and eggs, then poached in stock
    2) **miques potées** ⇒ balls of flour, pork fat, goose fat, plus sometimes yeast, milk, and eggs, then poached in stock; served fried with jam or sugar
    3) **miques coupées en tranches** ⇒ balls of flour, pork fat, goose fat, plus sometimes yeast, milk, and eggs, then poached in stock; served sliced, browned in goose fat, accompanied with grilled streaky bacon
    4) **Béarn, Pays Basque « miques noires ou pourrous negres »** ⇒ balls of cornflour and wheat flour, poached in polony cooking water, then grilled
Mique à la sarladaise ⇒ ball of leaven dough, added of eggs, and goose fat; cooked with a stew of pork, carrots, turnips, leeks, potatoes, cabbage, garlic, onions, and aromatics
Mique levée du Périgord noir ⇒ ball made of flour, eggs, yeast and butter; cooked in a pot au feu, and served sliced with it
Mirabeau (*à la ...*)
    - **Viandes de boucherie grillées** ⇒ grilled meat of ...
    - **Filets de sole** ⇒ sole fillets ...
    - **Oeufs sur le plat** ⇒ fried eggs ... garnished with anchovy fillets, stoned olives, tarragon leaves and anchovy butter
Mirabelle -[*eau de vie*]- ⇒ mirabelle
Mirabelle -[*prune*]- ⇒ mirabelle or mirabelle plum
Mirabelle hâtive ⇒ variety of mirabelle plum
Miraud -[*pain*]- ⇒ bread
Mireille -[*poularde*]- ⇒ bits of fattened pullet browned in butter, then cooked with white wine, morels, and cream; served with the cooking juice thickened of egg-yolk
Mirepoix au gras ⇒ mixing of diced carrots, onions, celery and ham, plus thyme and laurel, simmered in butter
Mirepoix au maigre ⇒ mixing of diced carrots, onions and celery, plus thyme and laurel, simmered in butter
Mirin -[*saké*]- ⇒ sake
Mirlirot -[*lotier*]- ⇒ melilot or sweet-clover

Mirlitons
  a) **tartelettes** ⇒ puff-pastry tartlets garnished with almond custard
  b) **petits fours** ⇒ dry petit fours flavoured with orange blossom
Mirlitons de Rouen ⇒ tartlets in puff-pastry, filled with a paste of eggs, crushed macaroons, granulated sugar and almond powder; decorated with almond
Miroirs ⇒ small cakes made of eggs, almond powder, sugar and vanilla; topped with a preparation of almonds, sugar, flour, butter, egg-yolks and rum
Miroton de bœuf ⇒ sliced boiled beef, warmed up again with onions
Mis en purée ⇒ mashed < *v.t adjectif* >
Miso ⇒ Japanese seasoning
Misseron *-[marasme d'oréade]-* ⇒ fairy ring mushroom
Mission haut brion *-[Graves]-* ⇒ Graves red wine
Mistelle ⇒ unripe grape juice added of alcohol
Mister callaghan *-[cocktail]-* ⇒ cocktail of vermouth, apricot brandy and angostura brandy
Mitan *-[saumon]-* ⇒ middle part of a salmon
Mititei *-[Roumanie]-* ⇒ small grilled sausages, served with fermented grape juice
Mixed grill ⇒ grilled meat served with green vegetables and grilled tomatoes
Mixed pickles ⇒ mixed pickles
Mochi *-[Japon]-*
  a) **mets salés** ⇒ pancakes of rice, simmered with vegetables
  b) **dessert** ⇒ pancakes of rice, simmered with red kidney beans and sugar
Mock turtle soup ⇒ mock turtle soup
Mode (*à la ...*)
  1) **cuisine régionale** ⇒ cooked according to a local recipe
  2) **grosses pièces de boeuf braisées** ⇒ braised beef added of diced veal trotters, carrots and onions
Mode de caen *-[tripes]-* ⇒ tripe à la mode de caen
Moderne (*à la ...*)
  1) **Grosses pièces de boucherie** ⇒ ... with a garnish of braised lettuce, little potato-balls browned in butter, quenelles or oxtongue; covered with thickened veal stock
  2) **Tournedos** ⇒ sauté tournedos ...
    - **Noisettes d'agneau** ⇒ sauté noisettes of lamb ... laid on grilled mushrooms, covered of the gravy added of Madeira; served with a garnish of potato-croquettes, braised lettuce, and tomatoes
Moghrabié *-[Liban]-* ⇒ couscous without vegetables, only with chicken and saffron
Moineau *-[oiseau]-* ⇒ sparrow
Moisissure ⇒ mouldiness
Mœlle ⇒ bone-marrow
Mœlle de sureau ⇒ elder-marrow
Mogette ⇒ bean
Moghrabié *-[Liban]-* ⇒ couscous without vegetables, only with chicken and saffron
Moïna ⇒ poached sole fillets, garnished of quartered braised artichokes in butter and morels in cream
Moineau *-[oiseau]-* ⇒ sparrow
Moisissure ⇒ mouldiness
Mojette ou Mojhette ⇒ haricot bean
Mojette du Poitou *-[boucheée au chocolat]-* ⇒ sweet filled or wrapped with chocolate
Moka
    - **gâteau** ⇒ mocha cake, uncountable, or coffee cream cake
    - **café** ⇒ mocha coffee < *uncountable* >
Mole poblano de guajolote ⇒ stew of turkey with Mexican sauce

Moles ⇒ Mexican sauce

Molho carioca ⇒ sauce of capsicum, vinegar, cooking juice of beans, tomatoes and chopped onions

Mollet ⇒ soft or soft boiled

Mollette ⇒ soft or soft boiled

Mollusque ⇒ mollusc

Molokhia -*[Egypte]*- ⇒ soup of onions, crushed with garlic and coriander, then browned in oil; added of beef stock, chopped mallow leaves, lemon juice and sometimes rice

Molossol -*[Russe]*- ⇒ cucumbers in cream flavoured of lemon juice, plus salt

Mombin ⇒ Caribbean fruit

Monaco
- **poisson** ⇒ poached sole fillets covered with a sauce of white wine, tomato and herbs; garnished with poached oysters and sippets
- **consommé** ⇒ poultry consommé thickened of egg-yolks, served with slices of bread sprinkled of sugar

Monaco -*[boisson]*- ⇒ glass of pomegranate syrup, lemonade, and beer

Monbazillac ⇒ sweet white wine from Bergerac area

Mondé ⇒ skinned < *v.t adjectif* >

Mondorienne -*[truite à la]*- ⇒ trout stuffed with crumbs, cream, herbs and mushrooms

Monégasque *(à la ...)* -*[tomates]*- ⇒ hors d'oeuvre of tomatoes hollowed out, seasoned with oil and vinegar, then filled with a mixing of mayonnaise, tunny, onions and herbs

Monemvasia -*[Grèce]*- ⇒ Greek wine

Monopole -*[armagnac]*- ⇒ high quality Armagnac

Monréal -*[clémentine]*- ⇒ clementine orange

Monselet *(à la ...)* ⇒ ... served with a garnish of truffles, artichoke hearts and Madeira sauce

Monstrueux de Viroflay -*[épinard]*- ⇒ spinach < *uncountable* >

Montagny ⇒ Burgundy white wine from Châlon area

Montbardoise *(à la ...)* -*[truite]*- ⇒ trout stuffed with spinach and shallots, then cooked in a court-bouillon

Montbazon -*[volaille]*- ⇒ ... garnished with fried sweetbread of lamb, quenelles, mushrooms and truffle lamellas

Montbéliard -*[saucisse de]*- ⇒ large steamed sausage

Mont-blanc ⇒ chestnut purée flavoured with vanilla, topped with a dome of whipped cream

Mont-bry -*[garniture petites pièces de boucherie]*- ⇒ ... laid on quoits of mashed spinach thickened of parmesan; covered with the gravy added of white wine, and garnish of boletus cream

Mont d'or ⇒ goat's milk cheese

Mont des cats ⇒ Flemish cheese

Mont-Dore ⇒ mashed potatoes thickened of egg-yolks and cream, added of grated cheese; then shaped in dome and browned

Monte Carlo -*[consommé]*- ⇒ consommé served with small slices of bread, buttered and sprinkled of grated parmesan, then browned

Montée de tonnerre -*[Chablis]*- ⇒ high quality Chablis wine

Monter au beurre ⇒ to whisk up with butter

Monter des blancs en neige ⇒ to whisk up egg whites

Monterminod -*[Savoie vins]*- ⇒ Savoy white wine

Montglas
- **preparation** ⇒ culinary stuffing of oxtongue, poached mushrooms, foie gras and truffle; thickened of Madeira sauce
- **côtes d'agneau** ⇒ lamb chops garnished with a rich culinary stuffing thickened of Madeira sauce and browned

- **ris de veau ou de volaille** ⇒ braised sweetbread, covered with the cooking juice added of a rich culinary stuffing thickened with Madeira sauce
- **bouchées feuilletées Montglas** ⇒ patties garnished with a rich culinary stuffing thickened of Madeira sauce; topped with foie gras and truffle

Monthélie ⇒ Burgundy wines from Côtes de Beaune

Monthoux -[*Savoie vins*]- ⇒ Savoy white wine

Montilla ⇒ Spanish wine from Córdoba area

Montlouis ⇒ white wine from Montlouis near Tours

Montmain -[*Chablis*]- ⇒ high quality Chablis wine

Montmorency
1) **cuisine; garniture pour petites et grosses pièces de boucherie** ⇒ ... garnished of artichoke hearts filled with shaped carrots, and little potato balls browned in butter
2) **glaces** ⇒ ice creams ...
    - **bombe glacée** ⇒ ice-pudding ...
    - **mousse glacée** ⇒ chilled mousse ...
    - **croûtes** ⇒ pastry cases ...
    - **tartes** ⇒ tarts ...
    - **tartelettes** ⇒ tartlets ... filled with cherries
3) **pâtisserie** ⇒ Genoese sponge filled with cherries in syrup, and coated of meringue

Montmorency -[*gâteau*]-
a) **avec sirop au kirsch** ⇒ Genoese sponge covered with a syrup added of kirsch and red colouring; decorated with cherries and angelica
b) **avec crème au beurre** ⇒ Genoese sponge sliced in two discs, moistened of kirsch, then stuffed with buttered cream added of cherries in brandy

Montmorillon -[*macarons de*]- ⇒ macaroon

Montoire -[*fromage*]- ⇒ goat's milk cheese

Montoire -[*orléanais*]- ⇒ goat's milk cheese

Montpensier -[*tournedos; petites pièces de boucherie; escalopes de volaille*]- ⇒ ...; served with a garnish of asparagus tips and truffles in julienne

Montpensier -[*gâteau*]- ⇒ gateau made of flour, butter, eggs, granulated sugar, almond powder, plus preserved fruits and sultanas steeped in rum; covered with apricot jam

Montpeyroux -[*côteaux du Languedoc*]- ⇒ quality wines from Languedoc area

Montrachet ⇒ high quality Burgundy white wine

Montravel ⇒ sweet white wine from Dordogne right bank

Montreuil
- **garniture tournedos ou petites pièces de boucherie** ⇒ garnished with braised artichoke hearts in butter, peas and carrots
- **poissons pochés** ⇒ covered with a white wine sauce, and garnished of boiled potatoes covered of shrimp purée

Montrose -[*St Estèphe*]- ⇒ high quality Médoc red wine

Montrouge ⇒ with mushrooms

Moques -[*pâtisserie*]- ⇒ pastry of dough added with browned sugar and clove

Moque -[*récipient*]- ⇒ mug

Morbier ⇒ disc of cow's milk cheese with a grey crust

Morceau ⇒ morsel or piece or tiny bit or crumb or a portion

Morceau du boucher
- **Merlan** -[*viande*]- ⇒ steak taken from near the topside
- **Tende de tranche** ⇒ topside of beef

Morceaux de boeuf à braiser ⇒ diced chuck steak

Morceaux de boeuf coupés pour daube ⇒ pie meat

Morceaux de mouton maigres -*[pour brochettes]-* ⇒ diced lamb « for kebabs »
Morceaux de mouton maigres et gras -*[pour ragoût]-* ⇒ diced lamb « for stewing »
Morceaux de poitrine de porc ⇒ sliced belly
Morceaux de porc à braiser ⇒ diced pork
Morceaux de steak coupés ⇒ chuck steak « diced »
Morceaux ou cubes de porc maigre ⇒ diced pork
Moré -*[vins de fruits]-* ⇒ fruit wine flavoured with aromatics
Moreau -*[cerise]-* ⇒ variety of cherry
Morey-St Denis ⇒ Burgundy red wine from Côtes de Nuits
Morgon ⇒ Beaujolais wine
Morille ⇒ morel mushroom
Morilles -*[gâteau]-* ⇒ mixing of courgettes in butter, morels, shallot, white wine and cognac, braised
    in butter, plus duck's gizzards, eggs and cream, cooked in dariole; served turned out
    on a dish covered with a sauce of shallot, white wine, plus crushed tomatoes, topped
    with mint
Morilles à la crème ⇒ morels braised in butter, with lemon juice, chopped shallots and cream
Morille à pied ridé ⇒ morel
Morille conique ⇒ delicious morel
Morilles farçies au ris d'agneau ⇒ morels covered with a mixing of chopped lamb sweetbreads
    braised in port, aromatics, chervil, and egg-yolk; then sautéed in butter and baked
Morillon -*[gyromitre]-* ⇒ gyromitra
Mornay -*[sauce]-* ⇒ sauce composed of béchamel sauce, egg-yolks, and grated gruyère
Moro -*[orange]-* ⇒ variety of orange
Mort subite -*[bière]-* ⇒ high quality Belgian beer
Mortadelle ⇒ mortadella or Bologna sausage or polony
Morteau -*[Jésus de]-* ⇒ large smoked pork sausage
Mortier -*[Mourtayrol]-*
    - **rouergue** ⇒ soup made of poultry stock and saffron
    - **auvergne** ⇒ pot-au-feu of beef, ham, poultry, vegetables and saffron
Morue ⇒ salt cod < *uncountable* >
Morue à l'anglaise ⇒ poached salt cod, and boiled vegetables; served with ...
    - **beurre fondu** ⇒ ... melted butter added of lemon juice, chopped hard boiled egg, and parsley
    - **sauce bâtarde** ⇒ ... butter sauce added of flour, egg-yolk and lemon juice
    - **sauce crème** ⇒ ... béchamel sauce added of cream
    - **sauce hollandaise** ⇒ ... sauce hollandaise
    - **sauce aux câpres** ⇒ ... caper sauce
    - **sauce aux fines herbes** ⇒ ... a sauce made of stock, plus a hash of parsley, chervil and
        tarragon
    - **sauce au cari** ⇒ ... curry sauce
    - **sauce à la moutarde** ⇒ ... mustard sauce
    - **avec mayonnaise** ⇒ ... mayonnaise
Morue à la bénédictine ⇒ pounded salt cod and mashed potatoes added of olive oil and milk,
    sprinkled of melted butter and browned
Morue à la créole ⇒ salt cod laid on tomatoes, oil, onion and garlic cooked in their own liquid; topped
    with quartered tomatoes and capsicums, then baked
Morue à la florentine ⇒ poached salt cod, laid on braised spinach; covered with béchamel sauce,
    added of gruyère, grated parmesan, plus melted butter, then browned
Morue à la languedocienne ⇒ bits of poached salt cod, cooked with potatoes, crushed garlic, herbs,
    stock and pepper; then sprinkled of parsley, plus olive oil, and browned

Morue à la lyonnaise ⇒ boiled salt cod, sautéed in butter and sliced onion; seasoned with pepper, grated nutmeg and lemon juice

Morue à la parisienne ⇒ poached salt cod, sprinkled of chopped hard boiled eggs and chopped parsley; served covered with crumbs fried in butter

Morue à la provençale ⇒ poached salt cod, simmered in tomatoes braised in olive oil with garlic; served sprinkled of parsley

Morue aux flageolets ⇒ salt cod dish, covered of flageolets boiled with onion, clove, aromatics and garlic; then covered with cream and baked, sprinkled of chervil

Morue d'eau douce ⇒ burbot

Morue en bamboche ⇒ fried salt cod lamellas, laid on vegetable salad thickened with butter, or cream

Morue frite ⇒ fried salt cod lamellas, served with quartered lemons

Moruette -*[cabillaud]*- ⇒ small fresh cod

Morvandelle *(à la ...)* ⇒ with raw ham from Morvan area

Mosaïque
- **charcuterie** ⇒ decoration on terrine of pork butchery
- **pâtisserie** ⇒ disc of Genoese sponge stuffed with a buttered custard; covered with a fondant, plus apricot jam in alternate lines

Mosaïque de légumes truffés -*[Troigros]*- ⇒ vegetable mosaic with truffles

Moscatel ⇒ muscat

Moscatel de Setubal -*[Portugal vins]*- ⇒ muscatel wine

Moscatello -*[Asti]*- ⇒ Italian wine

Moscato -*[Sicile, Sardaigne]*- ⇒ Sardinian sweet wine

Moscato di trani -*[Pouilles vins de]*- ⇒ Italian sweet wine, with a strong flavour

Moscovite *(à la ...)*
- **a) saumon à la moscovite** ⇒ poached salmon covered of mayonnaise, decorated with truffle, hard boiled eggs and tarragon leaves; garnished with artichoke hearts in salad and halved hard boiled eggs filled with caviar
- **b) sauce à la moscovite** ⇒ peppered sauce added of pine kernels, sultanas and juniper berries
- **c) consommé à la moscovite** ⇒ consommé of sturgeon and cucumber, garnished with a julienne of mushrooms, plus sturgeon bone-marrow
- **d) oeufs à la moscovite servis froids** ⇒ poached eggs served with vegetable salad in mayonnaise
  - **oeufs à la moscovite servis chauds** ⇒ poached eggs served with sauerkraut

Moscovite
- **bavarois** ⇒ Bavarian mousse flavoured with fruits
- **glace plombières** ⇒ voir texte
- **biscuit glacé** ⇒ biscuit moistened of kirsch and topped with chilled custard

Moselle -*[vins de]*- ⇒ Moselle
- **Allemagne** ⇒ high quality white wine from Moselle valley
- **Lorraine** ⇒ quality wine named « vins de la Moselle »

Mostèle ⇒ rockling

Motelle ⇒ rockling

Mou *(de n'importe quel animal ...)* ⇒ lungs

Mouclade ⇒ mussels, cooked in white wine, shallots and parsley; covered with their cooking juice added of cream thickened with butter and egg-yolks

Mouclade des boucholeurs ⇒ mussels served with a sauce made of their cooking juice, plus garlic, parsley, butter, saffron, pepper and cream

Mouflon ⇒ moufflon or wild sheep

Mougette ⇒ haricot bean

Mouiller
- **ajouter un liquide** ⇒ to add a liquid
- **mouiller** ⇒ to moist

Mouillette ⇒ sippet or finger of bread « for dipping »
Mouillé ⇒ moistened < *v.t adjectif* >
Moujetos ⇒ beans
Moule *-[coquillage]-* ⇒ mussel
Moule à bordure ⇒ edge mould
Moulé *(e ...)* ⇒ shaped or moulded or cooked in a mould
Moules à la bordelaise ⇒ mussels cooked in white wine, shallots and aromatics; covered with the cooking juice, added of diced vegetables and ham, plus velouté sauce, tomato sauce, lemon juice and butter
Moules à la crème ⇒ mussels cooked in white wine, shallots and aromatics; covered with the cooking juice, added of béchamel sauce thickened of cream
Moules à la poulette ⇒ mussels cooked in white wine, shallots and aromatics; covered with the cooking juice, added of white sauce mixed with egg-yolk, lemon juice and butter
Moules farçies ⇒ mussels cooked in white wine, shallots and aromatics; stuffed with composed butter added of chopped shallots, parsley and garlic, then sprinkled with crumbs and browned
Moules frites ⇒ mussels cooked in white wine, shallots and aromatics, then marinated in olive oil, lemon juice and parsley; steeped in butter and fried
Moules marinière ⇒ mussels cooked in a hash of shallot and parsley, plus butter, thyme, laurel, white wine and vinegar
Moulin à vent ⇒ high quality Beaujolais wine
Moulis ⇒ Médoc red wine
Mouloureija *-[molokhia]-* ⇒ soup of onions, crushed with garlic and coriander, then browned in oil; added of beef stock, chopped mallow leaves, lemon juice and sometimes rice
Moulu *(e ...)* ⇒ ground or powdered < *tous adjectif* >
Mounjetado ⇒ dish of beans and rind of pork
Mounjetos ⇒ beans
Mouraillons *-[salade de]-* ⇒ dandelion salad with lardoons, seasoned of cream
Mourtaïrol
    - rouergue ⇒ soup made of poultry stock and saffron
    - auvergne ⇒ pot-au-feu of beef, ham, poultry, vegetables and saffron
Mourtayrol
    - rouergue ⇒ soup made of poultry stock and saffron
    - auvergne ⇒ pot-au-feu of beef, ham, poultry, vegetables and saffron
Mouse-trap *-[fromage]-* ⇒ mouse-trap
Moussaka ⇒ moussaka
Mousse
    - patisserie ⇒ mousse
    - général ⇒ foam
Mousse à l'orange ⇒ mousse made of sugar, orange and eggs
Mousse à la confiture ⇒ mousse made of whipped white of eggs, plus raspberry or redcurrant jelly
Mousse à la crème chantilly ⇒ whipped cream and white of eggs, flavoured with vanilla or chocolate or coffee
Mousse au café ⇒ mousse made of sugar, whipped white of eggs and coffee extract
Mousse au chocolat ⇒ mousse made of chocolate and whipped white of eggs
Mousse au chocolat et aux fraises confites ⇒ cups filled with a mousse of chocolate, eggs and cream; topped with preserved strawberries
Mousse au citron ⇒ mousse made of sugar, lemon and eggs
Mousse au fraises ⇒ mousse made of crushed strawberries and whipped white of eggs
Mousse aux fruits ⇒ mousse of fruit pulp, cream and syrup

Mousse aux fruits confits ⇒ preserved cherries macerated in kirsch, mixed with whipped cream and white of eggs

Mousse d'écrevisse ⇒ preparation of crayfishes cooked in diced vegetables and ham, added of jelly, plus cream; then moulded and chilled, garnished with truffle lamellas

Mousse d'écrevisse à la Nantua ⇒ preparation of fish meat, culinary stuffing of crayfishes cooked in white wine, vegetables and spices, plus cream, moulded in dariole; served ...

- **servi directement** ⇒ ... directly, covered with béchamel sauce added of mashed crayfishes, cognac and cayenne-pepper

- **en croûtes feuilletées** ⇒ ... in puff-pastry casings, covered with béchamel sauce added of mashed crayfishes, cognac and cayenne pepper

- **en pâtes à foncer** ⇒ ... in pastry casings, covered with béchamel sauce added of mashed crayfishes, cognac and cayenne pepper

Mousse de canard rouennais ⇒ poached mousse prepared with a forcemeat of duck, spices, cognac, and foie gras

Mousse de Ceylan ou du Japon ⇒ jelly

Mousse de crevette ⇒ mashed crayfishes cooked in white wine, vegetables, ham and spices; mixed with fish velouté and fish jelly, then moulded and chilled

Mousse de foie gras de canard ou d'oie ⇒ mousse of mashed foie gras, melted jelly, poultry velouté and cream, then moulded and chilled; decorated with truffle lamellas and slices of hard boiled egg

Mousse de homard ⇒ mashed lobster cooked in white wine, vegetables, ham and spices; mixed with fish velouté and fish jelly, then moulded and chilled

Mousse de lièvre ⇒ mousse of hare meat, pepper, white of eggs and cream, then baked in dariole; served with Madeira sauce added of truffles

Mousse de navets ⇒ mousse of mashed turnips, added with white of eggs, cream, fecula and pepper, then baked in dariole; served with béchamel sauce, added of cream and chives

Mousse de poisson ⇒ forcemeat of fish, added of pepper, white of eggs and cream; then baked, and served with a sauce

Mousse de volaille ⇒ forcemeat of poached poultry, added of pepper, curry, white of eggs and cream; then baked

Mousse du chat -[au chocolat]- ⇒ mousse made of chocolate, granulated sugar, butter, and eggs; moulded in finger biscuits, and served with a custard added of coffee extract

Mousse froide de jambon ⇒ hashed ham added of velouté sauce, melted jelly and cream; then moulded and chilled

Mousse froide de tomate ⇒ tomato pulp braised in butter, added of gelatine, velouté sauce, pepper and lemon juice; then chilled

Mousse glacée à la crème ⇒ egg-custard added of cream and flavoured with ... then chilled

- **vanille** ⇒ vanilla

- **zeste d'orange** ⇒ ... orange peel ...

- **zeste de citron** ⇒ ... lemon peel ...

- **liqueur** ⇒ ... liqueur ... < *« liqueur » est le terme général, aussi pour une dénomination particulière remplacer « liqueur » par le nom anglais de la liqueur; exemple kummel « kümmel liqueur » >*

- **purée de fruits** ⇒ ... fruit purée ... < *« fruit purée » est le terme général, aussi pour une dénomination particulière remplacer « fruit » par le nom anglais du fruit; exemple mandarine « tangerine purée » >*

Mousse glacée à la fraise ⇒ syrup of sugar added of strawberry purée, and whipped cream; then chilled

Mousse glacée à la framboise ⇒ syrup of sugar added of raspberry purée, and whipped cream; then chilled

Mousse glacée à la liqueur ⇒ chilled mousse of granulated sugar, egg-yolks, liqueur, cream and milk < « *liqueur* » *est le terme général, aussi pour une dénomination particulière remplacer* « *liqueur* » *par le nom anglais de la liqueur; exemple kummel* « *kümmel liqueur* » >

Mousse glacée aux fruits ⇒ chilled mousse of meringue, cream, milk and fruit purée < « *fruit purée* » *est le terme général, aussi pour une dénomination particulière remplacer* « *fruit* » *par le nom anglais du fruit; exemple mandarine* « *tangerine purée* » >

Mousseline
- **pommes de terre** ⇒ creamed potatoes
- **mousse salée ou sucrée** ⇒ mousse moulded in small portions

Mousseline de canard rouennais ⇒ poached mousse prepared with a forcemeat of duck, spices, cognac, and foie gras

Mousseline de fumet de moules aux huîtres de Zélande ⇒ Zealand oysters, covered with sauce hollandaise, thickened of mussel cooking juice and cream; then browned

Mousseline de pommes de terre ⇒ creamed potatoes

Mousseline de reinettes aux noix ⇒ compote made of rennet apples, some braised in butter with sugar, vanilla sugar and lemon peel, some poached in a syrup, thickened of cream, eggs and crushed green walnuts, then moulded and baked; covered with a sauce of the syrup, added of butter and cream, plus stone liqueur

Mousseron ou meunier ⇒ button-mushroom

Mousseron à pied dur ⇒ fairy ring mushroom

Mousseron d'automne ⇒ fairy ring mushroom

Mousseron gris ⇒ miller or plum agaric

Mousseux *(se ...)*
- **général** ⇒ frothy or foamy
- **vin** ⇒ sparkling wine

Moût
- **de raisin** ⇒ must
- **de bière** ⇒ wort

Moutarde ⇒ mustard < *uncountable* >

Moutarde d'Orléans ⇒ mustard thickened with vinegar

Moutarde de Bordeaux -[*moût de raisin*]- ⇒ mustard thickened with must

Moutarde de Dijon ⇒ mustard or mustard seeds thickened with verjuice, and white wine

Moutarde de Vérone ⇒ fruit mustard

Mouton ⇒ sheep or mutton

Mouton -[*hydne*]- ⇒ spreading hydnum

Mouton à la catalane ⇒ sauté lamb, garnished with quartered tomatoes sautéed in butter, poached chestnuts, chipolatas and stoned olives

Mouton de pré salé
- **mouton** ⇒ salt marsh sheep
- **viande** ⇒ salt marsh lamb

Mouton en pistache ⇒ voir mouton à la catalane

Mouton entier ⇒ carcase

Mouton entier désossé et roulé ⇒ rolled lightweight lamb carcase « boneless »

Mouton haché ⇒ minced lamb

Moutonne -[*Chablis*]- ⇒ high quality Chablis wine

Moyeu -[*fouace; œuf*]- ⇒ egg-yolk

Mozart -[*garniture petites pièces de boucherie*]- ⇒ garnished of braised artichoke hearts in butter, filled with a celery purée, potato lamellas and chips

Mozzarella ⇒ mozzarella

Muësli -*[Bichermuësli]*- ⇒ mixing of cereals, dried fruits and fresh fruits, sprinkled with milk
Muffin ⇒ muffin
Mufle -*[cerf]*- ⇒ stew of deer muffle
Muge ⇒ thick-lipped mullet
Mulard -*[canard]*- ⇒ breed of duck
Mulet -*[viande]*- ⇒ mule meat or he-mule meat
Mulet -*[poisson]*- ⇒ grey mullet or mullet or thick-lipped mullet or thin-lipped mullet
Mull -*[cocktail]*- ⇒ cocktail added of wine
Müller thurgau -*[Allemagne vins]*- ⇒ variety of white wine
Mulligatawny ⇒ mulligatawny
Mung dal ⇒ kind of bean
Mungo -*[soja germes]*- ⇒ soya bean germ
Munich -*[bière]*- ⇒ German beer
Munkacsy -*[Hongrie]*- ⇒ eggs in jelly, laid on vegetable salad, with remoulade and dill
Munster ⇒ Munster
Mûrançon -*[apéritif]*- ⇒ aperitif of dry white wine from Jurançon, plus crème of mulberry and Armagnac
Murat ⇒ sole fillets floured and fried, laid on timbales with potatoes, plus sauté diced artichoke hearts; decorated with slices of tomato, sprinkled of lemon juice and butter
Mûre ⇒ mulberry
Mûre sauvage ⇒ wild mulberry
Mûres du Dauphiné -*[pâtes de fruits]*- ⇒ mulberry paste
Murène ⇒ moray eel or Muraena or sea lamprey
Murfatlar ⇒ sweet wine from Rumania or Rumanian dessert wine
Murhi biryani ⇒ rice with chicken marinated in spices, yoghourt, and flavoured of nutmeg flowers; accompanied of vegetables
Murhi tandouri ⇒ bits of chicken marinated in capsicum and spices, coated of saffron and grilled; served with salads or raw vegetables
Muria -*[saumure de thon]*- ⇒ tunny brine
Murol ⇒ cow's milk cheese with a red crust
Murolait -*[murol]*- ⇒ cow's milk cheese with a red crust
Musc ⇒ musk
Muscade ⇒ nutmeg < *uncountable* >
Muscadet ⇒ muscatel wine or muscadet wine
Muscadet des côteaux de Loire ⇒ muscatel wine or muscadet wine
Muscadet de Sèvre et Maine ⇒ muscatel wine or muscadet wine
Muscadier ⇒ nutmeg-tree
Muscadine -*[truffe au chocolat]*- ⇒ chocolate truffles, coated with icing sugar
Muscat
    - **raisin** ⇒ muscat grape
    - **vin** ⇒ muscatel wine
Muscat blanc -*[raisin]*- ⇒ variety of grape
Muscat de Frontignan -*[Frontignan]*- ⇒ sweet wine from Languedoc coast
Muscat de Hambourg -*[raisin]*- ⇒ variety of grape
Muscat de Rivesaltes -*[Roussillon]*- ⇒ sweet wine from Rivesaltes area
Muscat de Samos -*[Grèce vins]*- ⇒ Greek muscatel wine
Museau
    - **boeuf** ⇒ muzzle
    - **porc** ⇒ snout
    - **cuisine** ⇒ brawn

Museau de boeuf ⇒ boiled muzzle of beef; served sliced with french dressing, chopped shallots or onions, plus herbs

Mushroom ketchup ⇒ mushroom ketchup

Musigny ⇒ Burgundy wine from Côtes de Nuits

Muskat Sylvaner -*[sauvignon cépage]*- ⇒ variety of vine

Mussel broth -*[moule]*- ⇒ mussel broth

Mustard sauce ⇒ mustard sauce

Mustelle ⇒ rockling

Mutton broth ⇒ mutton broth

Mutton chop -*[côte ou côtelette de mouton]*- ⇒ mutton chop

Mye ⇒ soft clam

Myocastor -*[castor]*- ⇒ coypu

Myrat -*[Barsac]*- ⇒ Sauternes white wine

Myrte ⇒ myrtle

Myrtille ⇒ bilberry or whortleberry

Myshako riesling -*[URSS vins]*- ⇒ Georgian white wine

Mysost -*[fromage]*- ⇒ Mysost

N

Nabemono -[*Japon*]- ⇒ dish cooked on the table with grill
Nabuchodonosor -[*bouteille*]- ⇒ nebuchadnezzar
Nage (*à la ...*)
- « **petits homards ou langoustes ou écrevisses ou coquilles st jacques** » ⇒ small lobsters or spiny lobsters or crayfishes or scallops, cooked in a court-bouillon; served in their cooking stock added of cream or seasoned
Nageoires -[*ébarber*]- ⇒ to pare
Nageoires de tortue à l'américaine ⇒ turtle flippers cooked in stock, then braised in white wine; simmered in ...
- **sauce américaine** ⇒ ... a sauce made of shallots, pounded garlic, tomato purée, cayenne pepper and dry white wine
- **sauce au cari** ⇒ ... curry sauce
Nairac -[*Barsac*]- ⇒ Sauternes white wine
Nakypliak -[*Russe*]- ⇒ cabbage's soufflé
Nalesniki -[*Pologne*]- ⇒ pancakes stuffed of soft white cheese
Nalizniki -[*Russe*]- ⇒ pancakes stuffed with soft white cheese
Nanette
- **côtelettes d'agneau** ⇒ cutlets ...
- **escalopes de veau** ⇒ veal escalopes ...
- **ris de veau** ⇒ calf sweetbread ... garnished of artichoke-hearts stuffed with lettuce chiffonade in cream, plus mushrooms filled with truffles; served with the gravy added of Marsala, poultry velouté and cream
Nantais -[*fromage*]- ⇒ pressed cow's milk cheese
Nantais -[*gâteau*]- ⇒ shortcake enriched of almond or preserved fruits; flavoured with kirsch or rum
Nantaise (*à la ...*)
1) **avec sauce** ⇒ with a white wine and butter sauce
2) **coquilles st jacques** ⇒ poached scallops, warmed up again in white wine with oysters and mussels, then served in their shell
3) **poissons grillés** ⇒ grilled ..., served with a sauce of white wine shallots and butter
4) **viandes rôties** ⇒ roasted ...
- **viandes braisées** ⇒ braised ... served with a garnish of turnips, peas and mashed potatoes
Nantua
a) **beurre composé** ⇒ ... served with crayfish in composed butter, and sometimes added of truffle
b) **purée** ⇒ ... served with crayfish in, nom anglais, ... purée, and sometimes added of truffle
Napoléon -[*armagnac; calvados; cognac*]-
- **Armagnac** ⇒ Armagnac more then five years old
- **Calvados** ⇒ Calvados more then five years old
- **Cognac** ⇒ Cognac more then seven years old
Napoléon -[*cerise*]- ⇒ variety of cherry
Napolitain
- **gâteau** ⇒ large almond-pastry cake layered with apricot jam, or redcurrant jelly
- **chocolat** ⇒ small bar of chocolate
Napolitaine (*à la ...*)
- **hors d'oeuvres ou garnitures de petites pièces de boucherie** ⇒ ... with buttered spaghetti or macaroni, ... plus « sauce tomate » tomato sauce or ... plus « tomates concassées » crushed tomatoes, and grated cheese
- **sauce Napolitaine** ⇒ voir texte

Nappage ⇒ jelly based on apricot jam
Napper
- **cuisine** ⇒ to cover
- **nappé** ⇒ covered with ... < *v.t adjectif* >
Nappé avec ⇒ covered with < *v.t adjectif* >
Nard ⇒ spikenard
- **nard sauvage** ⇒ asarabacca
Nasco *-[vin de Sicile, Sardaigne]-* ⇒ Sardinian sweet wine
Nasi goreng ⇒ Indonesian dish of rice, chicken, onion, capsicum, tomato and lobster; served with grated coconut, grilled peanuts, and fried onion
National *-[radis]-* ⇒ variety of radish
Native *-[huître]-* ⇒ oyster
Natte *-[pain]-* ⇒ loaf of bread with poppy seeds
Natto *-[soja]-* ⇒ fermented soya beans
Nature ⇒ natural or plain or without garnish
- **omelette nature** ⇒ plain omelette
- **viande** ⇒ ... without garnish
- **café nature** ⇒ black coffee
- **eau nature** ⇒ plain water
- **thé nature** ⇒ tea without milk
- **boire le whisky nature** ⇒ to drink whisky neat
- **manger les fraises ou autres fruits nature** ⇒ to eat « strawberries » ... etc, without anything on them
Naturel *(au ...)*
- **thon** ⇒ bits of tunny, pickled and sterilized
- **homard** ⇒ lobster grilled without butter
Naturel ⇒ natural
Navarin ⇒ navarin lamb or mutton stew
Navarin de mouton printanière ⇒ mutton stew, onions, carrots, new potatoes, peas and french beans
Navarrenx *-[croquignole]-* ⇒ cracknels
Navel *-[orange]-* ⇒ variety of orange
Navet ⇒ turnip
Navets au gratin ⇒ slices of turnips braised in butter, covered with béchamel sauce added of egg-yolks and gruyère, then sprinkled of grated cheese, and browned
Navets farçis à la duxelles ⇒ boiled turnips hollowed out, then stuffed with chopped mushrooms, added of turnip pulp; covered of stock, sprinkled with crumbs, plus melted butter, and baked
Navets farçis à la piémontaise ⇒ boiled turnips hollowed out, then stuffed with risotto, added of turnip pulp; covered of stock, sprinkled of grated parmesan, and baked
Navets farçis braisés au cidre ⇒ turnips hollowed out, browned and baked in cider plus stock; stuffed with turnip pulp, added of sausage meat, basil, rosemary and thyme-flowers, then covered with the cooking juice
Navette *-[gâteau]-* ⇒ dried gateau shaped in boat
Navette ⇒ rape
- **huile de navette** ⇒ rape oil
N'dole *-[Afrique noire]-* ⇒ African leaves
Néac ⇒ Bordeaux red wine
Nectar ⇒ fruit juice added of water
Nectarine ⇒ nectarine
Nèfle ⇒ medlar

Nèfle d'Amérique ⇒ sapodilla
Nèfle du japon ⇒ Japanese medlar
Nègre ⇒ gateau made of eggs, sugar, cream, flour and cacao; stuffed with a chocolate custard
Nègre en chemise ⇒ chilled sweet with chocolate, covered of whipped cream
Négrillonne *-[cocktail]-* ⇒ cocktail of milk, chocolate powder, vanilla, sugar and ice cubes
Negru de purkar *-[URSS vins]-* ⇒ red wine from Moldavia
Neige
    - **oeufs** ⇒ floating islands
    - **sorbet** ⇒ sorbet made of red fruits added of sugar
    - **neige de Florence** ⇒ flakes of noodles
Neige de Florence
    - **oeufs** ⇒ floating islands
    - **sorbet** ⇒ sorbet made of red fruits added of sugar
    - **neige de Florence** ⇒ flakes of noodles
Nélusko
    - **cerise** ⇒ cherry stoned and filled with redcurrant jam, flavoured with cherry brandy
    - **bombe glacée** ⇒ ice cream with chocolate, praline and curaçao
    - **potage** ⇒ soup with sugar, coconut, arrow-root and almonds
Nem *-[Asie du sud est]-* ⇒ rice pancakes, stuffed and fried
Nemours
    - **garniture** ⇒ ... with a garnish of mashed potatoes moulded and fried, peas in butter, plus carrots
    - **sole** ⇒ poached sole fillets covered with shrimp sauce, topped of truffle lamellas and garnished with mushrooms thickened of a creamy sauce
    - **potage** ⇒ mashed potatoes added of consommé and thickened of cream, egg-yolk and tapioca
Nemrod
    - **garniture** ⇒ ... with a garnish of bilberry compote, croquettes, grilled mushrooms filled with chestnut purée
    - **consommé** ⇒ game consommé added of port, arrow-root, and quenelles enriched with chopped truffle
    - **attereaux nemrod** ⇒ quenelles stuffed with game and ham, plus mushrooms and hard-boiled eggs of lapwing
Néroli ⇒ orange-blossom oil
Nerto *-[liqueur]-* ⇒ liqueur made of myrtle extract
Nerveux de gîte *-[bifteck; gîte à la noix]-* ⇒ bleeding steak
Nesselrode
    - **ris de veau** ⇒ braised calf sweetbread covered with peppered sauce, garnished of chestnut purée
    - **noisette de chevreuil** ⇒ sauté small round pieces of roebuck covered with peppered sauce, garnished of chestnut purée
    - **profiterolles** ⇒ profiteroles garnished with chestnut purée
    - **consommé** ⇒ voir consommé Nesselrode
    - **pudding glacé Nesselrode** ⇒ pudding made with egg-custard added of chestnut purée, preserved fruits, raisins and whipped cream
    - **bombe glacée Nesselrode** ⇒ ice cream made with a paste of chestnut purée flavoured with kirsch, covered of vanilla ice cream
Neufchâtel *-[fromage]-* ⇒ Neufchâtel
Newburg
    - **homard** ⇒ lobster sautéed in cream
    - **sauce** ⇒ sauce of lobster, cream, and fish stock
Nez de chat *-[coulemelle]-* ⇒ parasol mushroom

Niçoise *(à la ...)*
 1) **général** ⇒ with garlic, anchovies, tomatoes, olives and french beans
 2) **poissons grillés rouget** ⇒ grilled red mullet ...
  - **sole** ⇒ grilled sole ...
  - **merlan** ⇒ grilled whiting ... served with crushed tomatoes, anchovy fillets, olives and sometimes anchovy paste
 3) **grosses pièces de boucherie et volaille** ⇒ ... with a garnish of tomatoes braised in oil and seasoned with garlic, ... 1 or 2 ...
  - **1 soit haricots verts au beurre** ⇒ french beans in butter ...
  - **2 soit courgettes et artichauts** ⇒ courgettes and braised artichokes, plus small potatoes sautéed in butter with lardoons
 4) **salade** ⇒ composed salad of tomatoes, cucumbers, fresh shell beans or small artichokes, capsicums, fresh onions, hard boiled eggs, anchovy fillets or tunny, black olives, olive oil, garlic and basil
Nid *(au ...)* ⇒ small birds roasted in nests of fried shredded potatoes
Nids d'hirondelle ou salangane *(utilisés dans les soupes, garnitures, ragoûts ...)* ⇒ bits of tern nests
Nids de pommes paille ou pommes gaufrettes ⇒ thin sticks or wafers of potatoes, fried shaped in nests
Nieule ⇒ small cakes shaped in disc, made of flour, milk, butter, eggs and sugar
Niflette ⇒ puff-pastry filled with almond flavoured cream
Nigelle ⇒ nigella or love-in-the-mist
Niglo à la gitane *-[hérisson]-* ⇒ stew of hedgehog, served with mashed potatoes cooked in red wine and lardoons
Nimono *-[Japon]-* ⇒ meal boiled in a liquid flavoured with aromatics
Ninon *(Petites pièces de boucherie sautées, accompagnées de sauce mœlle ...)*
 a) **croustades** ⇒ sauté ..., plus a sauce made of shallots, white wine, meat stock, poached bone-marrow and butter; garnished with small croustades of mashed potatoes, egg, and butter, filled with a culinary stuffing of cockscombs, cock's kidneys in velouté sauce, plus asparagus tips in butter
 b) **socle de pommes Anna** ⇒ sauté ..., laid on a socle of sliced potatoes baked in butter, covered with a sauce of Madeira and gravy; topped with a croustade filled of asparagus tips in butter, sprinkled with a julienne of truffle
  - **canapés** ⇒ canapés garnished with a culinary stuffing of cockscombs, cock's kidneys, added of asparagus tips in butter; covered with a sauce made of shallots, white wine, meat stock, poached bone-marrow and butter
  - **salade** ⇒ composed salad of lettuce, and slices of orange; seasoned with orange juice, lemon, and oil
Niolin *-[niolo]-* ⇒ Corsican ewe's milk cheese
Niolo ⇒ Corsican ewe's milk cheese
Nivernaise *(à la ...) -[grosses pièces de boucherie rôties ou braisées, canard braisé]-*
  - **rôties** ⇒ roasted ... nom anglais de la viande ...
  - **braisées** ⇒ braised ... nom anglais de la viande ... with a garnish of shaped carrots and onions in butter, plus braised lettuce covered with the gravy
Nkui *-[Cameroun]-* ⇒ salad of ketmias and maize
Nocciata ⇒ sweet of honey and nuts
Noces ⇒ oat's porridge
Nockerln *-[Autriche]-*
  - **gnocchis** ⇒ gnocchi
  - **soufflé de Salzbourg** ⇒ sugared soufflé
Nœud *-[merveille]-* ⇒ small fritter shaped in knot

Noilly Prat -*[vermouth]*- ⇒ vermouth
Noir de Bourgogne -*[cassis fruit]*- ⇒ variety of blackcurrant
Noire -*[bête; gibier]*- ⇒ wild boar
Noisette
   - **fruit** ⇒ hazelnut
   - **cuisine** ⇒ small round
   - **d'agneau** ⇒ noisettes of lamb
   - **de mouton** ⇒ noisettes of lamb
   - **de beurre** ⇒ knob of butter
Noisette -*[pomme de terre]*- ⇒ little balls of potato pulp, browned in butter
Noisette d'agneau ⇒ noisettes of lamb
Noisettes d'agneau à la turque ⇒ noisettes of lamb fried in butter, topped with pilaf and diced aubergines sautéed in oil; covered with the gravy, thickened of stock and tomato sauce
Noisettes d'agneau Melba ⇒ sauté noisettes of lamb laid on fried sippets, covered with the gravy added of stock, arrow-root, Madeira and butter; garnished of tomatoes stuffed with a culinary stuffing of poultry, truffle, mushrooms and velouté sauce
Noisettes d'agneau Montpensier ⇒ sauté noisettes of lamb laid on fried sippets, topped with a julienne of truffle; covered with the cooking juice thickened of arrow-root and stock, then decorated of asparagus tips
Noisette de beurre ⇒ knob of butter
Noisettes de chevreuil sautées nesselrode ⇒ sautéed small round pieces of roebuck covered with peppered sauce, garnished of chestnut purée
Noisettes des Tournelles ⇒ noisettes of lamb sautéed in butter, topped with purée from onions and rice, seasoned with pepper and sugar; presented with the gravy, added of vermouth, xeres, stock and butter, in the sauce-boat
Noisettes à la torque ⇒ noisettes of lamb sautéed in olive oil, garnished of pilaf and sautéed diced aubergines; covered with the gravy, added of veal stock and tomato
Noisettes Beauharnais ⇒ a dish of artichoke hearts braised in butter and covered of béchamel sauce, noisettes of lamb sautéed in butter and laid on fried sippets, with the gravy added of truffle; plus little potato-balls browned in butter
Noisettes chasseur ⇒ noisettes of lamb sautéed in oil and butter; served with sauté mushrooms, and covered with the gravy, added of chopped shallots, white wine, veal stock, plus tomato sauce
Noisettes Rivoli ⇒ noisettes of lamb sautéed in butter, laid on sliced potatoes baked in butter; covered with the gravy, added of Madeira and diced truffle
Noix ⇒ nut or walnut
Noix d'acajou -*[Noix de cajou]*- ⇒ cashew-nut
Noix de cajou ⇒ cashew-nut
Noix de coco ⇒ coconut
Noix de cola ⇒ cola-nut
Noix de côtelette ⇒ eye or cutlet meat
Noix de ginkgo ⇒ ginkgo-nut
Noix de grenoble ⇒ nut or walnut
Noix de jambon -*[porc]*- ⇒ meagre ham
Noix de longe de porc enveloppée dans de la poitrine et ficelée ⇒ loin and belly of pork « special trim »
Noix de macadam ⇒ Queensland-tree nut
Noix de muscade ⇒ nutmeg < *uncountable* >
Noix de pacane ⇒ American nut

Noix de porc ⇒ leg boneless of pork
Noix de ris de veau ⇒ calf sweetbreads
Noix de veau ⇒ topside of veal
Noix de veau -*[terme général]*- ⇒ cushion of veal
Noix de veau Brillat-Savarin ⇒ rolled cushion of veal, stuffed with a forcemeat added of shallots, morels and foie gras, then braised on a mixture of diced vegetables and ham, plus wine, beef stock, and crushed tomatoes; served with the gravy, a garnish of spinach, plus morels in cream
Noix de veau entièrement épluchée ⇒ cushion of veal
Noix de veau pâtissière ⇒ thick flank of veal ½ ou ½ toprump of veal
Noix de veau rôtie ⇒ cushion of veal, studded with pork fat, then roasted in butter
Noix du Brésil ⇒ Brazil nut
Noix en pickles ⇒ nuts preserved in vinegar, spices, and herbs
Noix en surprise ⇒ petit four made of granulated sugar and almond powder, encrusted with a green walnut
Noix muguette -*[épices]*- ⇒ a spice
Noix muscade -*[macis; muscade; beurre]*- ⇒ nutmeg < *uncountable* >
Noix patissière -*[boucherie]*- ⇒ topside of veal
Nökkelost -*[Scandinavie; fromage]*- ⇒ Norwegian cheese
None -*[Russe]*- ⇒ bread added of onions
Nonnat ⇒ nonnat
Nonnette ⇒ small gingerbread covered with icing
Nonpareille
   - câpre ⇒ caper preserved in vinegar
   - dragée ⇒ coloured dragée
Noque ⇒ poached small quenelles of flour, egg and butter
Noques à l'Alsacienne ⇒ poached small balls of butter, grated nutmeg, eggs and flour, sprinkled of grated parmesan ...
   - servies en entrées ⇒ ... served as an hors d'œuvre
   - servies avec consommé ⇒ ... added in a consommé
Noques à l'allemande
   1) au foie de porc ⇒ quenelles of flour, added of pork liver ...
   2) au maigre de veau ⇒ quenelles of choux pastry, added of lean meat ...
      - servies avec viande, nom de la viande ⇒ served with ...
      - servies avec un potage ⇒ ... served in a soup
Noques à la viennoise ⇒ small balls of butter, semolina, eggs, and cream, poached in milk flavoured with vanilla; served covered of egg-custard
Nori -*[algue]*- ⇒ nori or hoshi-nori or kuronori
Normande (*à la ...*)
   1) général ⇒ with butter, cream, sea food, apples, cider and calvados
   2) petites pièces de boucherie et poulet sauté ⇒ sauté ... covered with the gravy added of cider, then basted of cream and calvados
   3) perdreau à la normande ⇒ young partridge cooked with apples and cream
   4) boudin noir ⇒ polony served with apples
   5) croûtes, crêpes, galettes à la normande ⇒ with apples
   6) haricots verts ⇒ french beans in cream
   7) matelote à la normande ⇒ matelote of fishes flamed in calvados and moistened of cider
Norvégienne (*à la ...*)
   1) poissons froids ⇒ fishes or crustaceae in jelly, served with cucumber stuffed of salmon purée, halved hard boiled eggs filled with shrimps, hearts of lettuce and tomatoes

2) poissons chauds, soufflé ⇒ soufflé dish with haddock and anchovy
   - dariole ⇒ puff-pastry stuffed with fish and anchovy paste, decorated with anchovy fillets
  3) omelette norvégienne ⇒ voir texte
Nos -[morues]- ⇒ salt cod tripe
Noues -[morues]- ⇒ salt cod tripe
Nouet ⇒ muslin
Nougat ⇒ nougat
Nougat aux amandes ⇒ nougat added of chopped almonds
Nougat aux noisettes -[Russe]- ⇒ nougat added of hazelnuts
Nougat aux pignons ⇒ nougat added of pine-kernels
Nougat aux pistaches ⇒ nougat added of pistachios
Nougat blanc ⇒ nougat flavoured with honey, bitter orange blossom extract, and chopped almonds
Nougat chinois ⇒ Chinese nougat
Nougat de dattes ⇒ nougat made with dates, sugar, almonds, pepper, ginger seeds and sesame
Nougatine ⇒ sweet of caramel, almond and hazelnut
Nouilles (général ...) ⇒ pasta < uncountable > or noodles < toujours pluriel > or ribbon vermicelli < uncountable > or nouilles < toujours pluriel >
Nouilles à la lyonnaise ⇒ timbales of noodles in butter, topped with browned onion; sprinkled with hot vinegar
Nouilles au beurre à l'alsacienne ⇒ boiled noodles, sautéed in butter and served in timbales
Nouilles au fromage ⇒ pasta with cheese or macaroni cheese
Nouilles au gratin ⇒ noodles in butter, added of grated gruyère, sprinkled of melted butter and browned or noodles au gratin
Nouilles fraîches ⇒ fresh noodles
Nouillettes ⇒ small noodles
Nouillettes au foie gras et à la truffe ⇒ noodles mixed with cream, grated nutmeg, truffle juice, and foie gras sautéed in butter; served sprinkled of grated parmesan and browned, then covered with a sauce made of egg-yolks, butter, plus truffle cooked in Madeira and stock
Nouveau (elle ...)
  - général ⇒ new
  - vin ⇒ new wine
  - pommes de terre ⇒ new potatoes
  - carottes ⇒ spring carrots
Nouveau -[vin]- ⇒ new wine
Nouzillards -[Anjou]- ⇒ chestnuts cooked in milk
Noyau ⇒ stone
Noyau -[liqueur]- ⇒ noyau
Noyau de Poissy ⇒ liqueur from cherry stones
Nœuds ⇒ small fritters shaped in knots
Nudln -[Autriche]- ⇒ ravioli
Nuits St Georges ⇒ Burgundy wines from Côtes de Nuits
Nulles ⇒ custard of egg-yolks, sugar, and cream; flavoured with musk or ambergris
Nuoc-mâm ⇒ Vietnamese seasoning
Nyons -[olive]- ⇒ variety of olive

O

Oatcakes -[*GB*]- ⇒ oatcakes

Obéron -[*petit pois*]- ⇒ variety of pea

Obus de verdun -[*dragées*]- ⇒ shell in chocolate, filled of dragées, and fitted with a device for party
   novelties

Oeil de dragon -[*longane*]- ⇒ Indian fruit

Oeil de perdrix du Valais -[*Suisse*]- ⇒ swiss red and rosé wine from « gamay » or « pinot noir »
   varieties of vine

Oeillet -[*ratafia d'*]- ⇒ ratafia from pink

Oeillette ⇒ oil poppy or white poppy

   - **huile d'oeillette** ⇒ poppy-seed oil

Oeuf ⇒ egg

Oeuf à la coque ⇒ soft-boiled egg

Oeuf à la poêle ⇒ fried egg

Oeuf au bacon -[*brunch*]- ⇒ bacon and eggs

Oeuf au plat ⇒ fried egg

Oeuf Céline -[*nouvelle cuisine*]- ⇒ egg added of caviar, and a small quantity of vodka

Oeuf du jour ⇒ new laid egg or fresh egg

Oeuf dur ⇒ hard boiled egg

Oeuf dur Gargantua ⇒ a large hard-boiled egg made of twelve white of eggs, and twelve egg-yolks;
   served in slices, sprinkled of vinegar, or browned with béchamel sauce

Oeuf en caissette ⇒ egg baked in an individual ceramic pot with cream, or a purée

Oeuf en cassolette ⇒ egg baked in an individual ceramic pot with cream, or a purée

Oeuf en cocotte ⇒ egg baked in an individual ceramic pot with cream, or a purée

Oeuf frais ⇒ new laid egg or fresh egg

Oeuf frit ⇒ fried egg

Oeuf frits à l'italienne ⇒ slices of ham in butter, plus eggs fried in oil; covered with brown sauce
   added of chopped mushrooms, diced ham and tarragon, plus stock with tomato purée

Oeuf mayonnaise ⇒ hard-boiled egg with mayonnaise

Oeuf mollet ⇒ soft boiled egg

Oeuf poché ⇒ poached egg

Oeuf sur le plat ⇒ fried egg

Oeuf sur le plat à l'anglaise ⇒ grilled slice of bacon topped with eggs, then baked

Oeufs à l'antiboise ⇒ scrambled eggs, with sauté courgettes and tomatoes braised in oil; au gratin

Oeufs à l'infante ⇒ poached eggs; covered with a sauce made of high quality wine from champagne
   area, orange, garlic and shallot

Oeufs à la Bercy ⇒ fried eggs or scrambled eggs, garnished with chipolata sausages; surrounded by
   tomato sauce

Oeufs à la bruxelloise ⇒ pastry cases filled with chicory chiffonade, topped with a poached egg, then
   covered of béchamel sauce added of cream

Oeufs à la causalade ⇒ eggs fried with slices of ham

Oeufs à la chevalière ⇒ pastry cases filled with poached egg, plus a stew of mushrooms, cockscombs,
   and cock's kidneys; covered of supreme sauce, cockscombs coated with breadcrumbs,
   and truffle lamellas

Oeufs à la coque à la truffe ⇒ soft-boiled egg, served with diced truffle in butter

Oeufs à la liqueur -[*dragées*]- ⇒ dragées flavoured with liqueur

Oeufs à la neige ⇒ whipped white of eggs poached in milk and laid on egg-custard

Oeufs au bacon ⇒ bacon and eggs

Oeufs au lait ⇒ dessert of milk, whipped eggs and a flavouring

Oeufs au miroir ⇒ eggs fried or baked in butter

Oeufs aux feuilles de thé ⇒ hard-boiled eggs cooked in water, flavoured with salt, soya sauce, aniseed and tea; served halved with roasted pork lamellas, soya bean shoots and mushrooms, seasoned of French dressing mixed with soya sauce

Oeufs Bernis froids ⇒ poached eggs wrapped in chaudfroid sauce, decorated with truffles and laid on mousse of poultry; served with bunches of asparagus tips, and covered of jelly

Oeufs Bernis mollets ⇒ croustades filled with mousse of poultry, topped with poached eggs, then covered of supreme sauce; served with asparagus tips, thickened of butter

Oeufs Bernis pochés ⇒ croustades filled with mousse of poultry, topped with poached eggs, then covered of supreme sauce; served with asparagus tips, thickened of butter

Oeufs braisés -[Chine]- ⇒ hard boiled eggs, simmered with onions and consommé

Oeufs brouillés ⇒ scrambled eggs

Oeufs brouillés à l'américaine ⇒ timbales of scrambled eggs, added of smoked pork belly diced and browned; garnished with grilled slices of bacon, plus halved grilled tomatoes

Oeufs brouillés à l'ancienne ⇒ pastry case filled with scrambled eggs, mixed with diced mushrooms and diced truffles, browned in butter; garnished with cock's kidneys thickened of velouté, added of cream and xeres, then surrounded by fried cockscombs, plus supreme sauce in xeres

Oeufs brouillés à l'arlésienne ⇒ cooked scrambled eggs, added of diced courgettes and tomatoes cooked with garlic in their own liquid; served with halved courgettes filled with the same preparation, sprinkled of grated parmesan, plus olive oil, and browned

Oeufs brouillés à la normande ⇒ pastry cases filled with a mixing of fish velouté sauce added of cream and mushrooms, plus poached oysters, mussels cooked in white wine, shrimp tails, and mushrooms braised in butter; topped with scrambled eggs, then decorated of poached oysters, fried sippets, and truffle lamellas

Oeufs brouillés à la reine ⇒ pastry cases filled with mashed poultry and scrambled eggs; served with supreme sauce

Oeufs brouillés à la romaine ⇒ dish of spinach braised in butter, added of diced anchovy fillets; covered with scrambled eggs and grated parmesan, then browned

Oeufs brouillés au saumon fumé ⇒ timbales filled with scrambled eggs, and smoked salmon lamellas; decorated with sippets fried in butter

Oeufs brouillés aux « cèpes » ⇒ timbale of scrambled eggs, plus boletus sautéed in butter or oil, seasoned with butter or garlic; covered with sippets fried in butter

- **aux girolles** ⇒ edible agarics
- **aux mousserons** ⇒ button mushrooms
- **aux trompettes de la mort** ⇒ horn of plenty mushrooms
- **aux champignons de Paris** ⇒ cultivated mushrooms

Oeufs brouillés aux artichauts ⇒ scrambled eggs, garnished with artichoke hearts sautéed in butter, plus sippets fried in butter; decorated with thickened veal stock

Oeufs brouillés aux crevettes ⇒ timbale of scrambled eggs, plus decorticated shrimps in butter; decorated with sippets fried in butter, and shrimp sauce

Oeufs brouillés aux foies de volailles ⇒ timbales of scrambled eggs, garnished with poultry livers sautéed in butter, and thickened of brown sauce with Madeira; sprinkled of parsley

Oeufs brouillés aux queues d'écrevisses ⇒ timbale of scrambled eggs, and crayfish tails; decorated with sippets fried in butter, plus béchamel sauce added of mashed crayfishes, cognac, and cayenne pepper

Oeufs brouillés Argenteuil ⇒ scrambled eggs, added of asparagus tips braised in butter, surrounded by fried sippets; served with a béchamel sauce added of cream

Oeufs brouillés Georgette ⇒ poached eggs or scrambled eggs, served with potatoes and a ragout of crayfish tails

---

Oeufs brouillés princesse ⇒ timbale filled with scrambled eggs, asparagus tips braised in butter, julienne from white of meat thickened with supreme sauce, plus truffle lamellas in butter

Oeufs brouillés Rossini ⇒ timbales filled with scrambled eggs, sauté foie gras escalopes in butter, and truffle lamellas; covered with brown sauce in Madeira

Oeufs brouillés Sagan ⇒ timbales filled with scrambled eggs, added of grated parmesan, calf brain escalopes and truffles lamellas; served with melted butter added of lemon juice

Oeufs cocotte à la rouennaise ⇒ small casseroles filled with a forcemeat of duck livers, topped of eggs and butter, then baked; served with a sauce based on diced vegetables, butter, red wine, garlic, mushroom peel, anchovy extract and cayenne pepper

Oeufs de brochet ⇒ pike eggs

Oeufs de caille aux oursins ⇒ opened sea urchins, topped with a quail egg, and baked; covered with seasoned cream

Oeufs de cent ans ⇒ preserved Chinese duck's eggs

Oeufs de lotte ⇒ angler eggs

Oeufs de lump ⇒ lumpfish eggs

Oeufs de pâques ⇒ easter eggs

Oeufs de poisson ⇒ roes or spawn

Oeufs demi-deuil ⇒ puff-pastry croustades, filled with mushrooms in cream, and a poached egg; covered of supreme sauce, and truffle lamella

Oeufs durs à l'aurore ⇒ hard boiled eggs, served with tomato sauce

Oeufs durs à l'oseille ⇒ hard-boiled eggs, covered with sorrel cooked in its own liquid with butter, added of milk, cream and pepper

Oeufs durs à la Chimay ⇒ halved hard boiled eggs, filled with their egg-yolks mixed with chopped mushrooms; covered with béchamel sauce added of egg-yolks and gruyère, grated parmesan, and melted butter, then browned

Oeufs durs à la Soubise ⇒ hard-boiled eggs, laid on mashed onions and rice, seasoned with pepper and sugar; covered with béchamel sauce added of cream

Oeufs durs à la cressonnière

a) **avec purée de cresson** ⇒ mashed watercress, topped with hard-boiled eggs, and covered with a sauce made of chopped watercress, a hash of hard-boiled eggs, pepper, oil and vinegar

b) **sur cresson** ⇒ soft boiled eggs, laid on watercress; covered of mayonnaise mixed with a paste of pounded tarragon, watercress, parsley, spinach and chervil

Oeufs durs à la macédoine ⇒ hard-boiled eggs, stuffed with mayonnaise added of their egg-yolks, and tomato sauce; laid on vegetable salad in mayonnaise

Oeufs durs Elisabeth ⇒ hard boiled eggs stuffed with their egg-yolks, mashed artichokes and chopped truffles; laid on artichoke hearts, covered of béchamel sauce added of egg-yolks and gruyère, grated cheese, melted butter, then browned

Oeufs durs en tripe

1) **général** ⇒ preparation of sliced hard-boiled eggs, covered with béchamel sauce added of braised onions

2) **Berry** ⇒ eggs poached in a sauce of white wine, onions and aromatics

Oeufs durs en côtelettes ⇒ composed cutlets made of diced hard boiled eggs and béchamel sauce, coated with crumbs and fried in butter; served with tomato sauce, and possibly a garnish of vegetables or rice

Oeufs durs farçis aurore ⇒ halved hard-boiled eggs, stuffed with their egg-yolks, chopped herbs and velouté sauce added of tomato purée and butter; laid on a dish, sprinkled of grated parmesan and melted butter, then browned

Oeufs durs farçis aux anchois ⇒ halved hard-boiled eggs, garnished with crushed anchovy fillets, mixed with egg-yolks and mayonnaise; topped with anchovy fillet and black olive

Oeufs durs panés ⇒ layer of watercress, topped of toast browned with grated cheese; garnished with hard-boiled eggs, coated of grated cheese and crumbs, then browned in oil

Oeufs durs Verdier ⇒ sliced onions braised in butter, and thickened of béchamel sauce, topped with halved hard-boiled eggs, filled with their egg-yolks added of foie gras; covered of béchamel sauce added with julienne, sprinkled of grated parmesan and browned

Oeufs en cocotte ⇒ broken eggs cooked in ramekins

Oeufs en cocotte à l'estragon

   a) **classique, oeuf et fond de veau** ⇒ ramekins filled with egg and veal stock flavoured of tarragon leaves, and baked

   b) **sur estragon haché** ⇒ ramekins filled with chopped tarragon, egg and veal stock flavoured of tarragon; decorated with tarragon leaves, and baked

   c) **avec crème** ⇒ ramekins filled with egg, and cream flavoured with tarragon; decorated with tarragon leaves, and baked

Oeufs en cocotte à la Bérangère ⇒ ramekins filled with a forcemeat of poultry added of truffle, plus egg, and baked; garnished with a stew of cockscombs and cock's kidneys, thickened of supreme sauce

Oeufs en cocotte à la crème

   a) **avec beurre** ⇒ ramekins filled with hot cream, plus egg and butter, then baked and peppered

   b) **parmesan et beurre** ⇒ ramekins filled with hot cream, egg, sprinkled of grated parmesan and melted butter; then baked

Oeufs en cocotte à la duxelles ⇒ ramekins filled with chopped onions and mushrooms, egg, cream, and pepper; then baked

Oeufs en cocotte à la périgourdine ⇒ small casseroles filled with mashed foie gras, egg and butter, then baked; served with Madeira sauce added of chopped truffles

Oeufs en cocotte à la rouennaise ⇒ small casseroles filled with a forcemeat of duck livers, topped of eggs and butter, then baked; served with a sauce based on diced vegetables, butter, red wine, garlic, mushroom peel, anchovy extract and cayenne pepper

Oeufs en cocotte à la tartare ⇒ ramekins filled with hashed beef meat, chives and pepper; topped with eggs and cream, then baked

Oeufs en cocotte ambassadrice ⇒ ramekins filled with mashed foie gras, chopped truffle and an egg, then baked; covered with supreme sauce in xeres, plus asparagus tips

Oeufs en cocotte Bachaumont ⇒ ramekins filled with a mixture of diced vegetables and ham, plus egg, and baked; peppered, and garnished with sauté diced mushrooms

Oeufs en cocotte Brillat-Savarin ⇒ small casseroles, garnished with noodles sautéed in butter, plus egg, and baked; covered with asparagus tips in butter, and Madeira sauce

Oeufs en cocotte Jeannette ⇒ ramekins filled with a forcemeat of poultry, plus egg, and baked; garnished with asparagus tips in butter, and velouté sauce

Oeufs en meurette ⇒ eggs poached in a sauce of diced pork fat in butter, mushrooms, red wine and stock; served with the sauce, plus sippets and lardoons fried in butter

Oeufs en neige ⇒ oeufs à la neige or floating islands

Oeufs en ramequin à la gelée ⇒ ramekins filled with ham, and poached egg; plus a jelly of veal, tomato and aromatics

Oeufs en tasse à la hollandaise ⇒ cups filled with layers of butter, diced ham, grated cheese, and whipped eggs, then baked; served with spiced tomato sauce

Oeufs farçis à la russe ⇒ stuffed eggs

Oeufs filés ⇒ eggs, poached shaped in shoe-strings

Oeufs frits à l'alsacienne ⇒ eggs fried in goose fat, laid on sauerkraut with slices of ham; surrounded of brown sauce made of meat stock, vegetables and Madeira

Oeufs frits à l'américaine ⇒ fried eggs, garnished with slices of bacon, and grilled halved tomatoes

Oeufs frits à l'andalouse ⇒ fried eggs, garnished with ...

   - **avec tomates** ⇒ ... grilled tomatoes, braised capsicums and fried slices of onion

   - **avec aubergines** ⇒ ... sliced aubergines, braised capsicums, and fried slices of onion

Oeufs frits à l'italienne ⇒ slices of ham in butter, plus eggs fried in oil; covered with brown sauce added of chopped mushrooms, diced ham and tarragon, plus stock with tomato purée

Oeufs frits à la bayonnaise ⇒ fried eggs laid on fried sippets, plus browned slices of ham salted and dried; garnished with sauté boletus

Oeufs frits à la bordelaise ⇒ fried eggs laid on fried sippets, garnished with boletus sautéed in oil plus lemon juice, and sprinkled of chopped parsley

Oeufs frits à la charcutière ⇒ dish of fried eggs and grilled crépinettes, garnished of fried parsley; served with a sauce of chopped onions in pork fat, crumbs, white wine, stock, diced gherkins and mustard

Oeufs frits à la créole ⇒ grilled halved courgette, garnished with rice and fried eggs

Oeufs frits à la milanaise ⇒ fried eggs laid on crunchy macaroni; surrounded by tomato sauce

Oeufs frits aux anchois ⇒ sippets fried in butter, topped with anchovy fillets and fried egg

Oeufs frits en bamboche ⇒ ring of vegetable salad, thickened of cream, garnished with fried salt cod lamellas and fried eggs

Oeufs mollets à l'alsacienne ⇒ timbales filled with braised sauerkraut, lardoons and soft boiled eggs; covered with brown sauce made of meat stock, vegetables and Madeira

Oeufs mollets à l'américaine ⇒ fried sippets, garnished with soft boiled eggs and lobster escalopes; covered with a sauce made of shallots, pounded garlic, tomato purée, cayenne pepper and dry white wine

Oeufs mollets à l'ancienne ⇒ soft boiled eggs laid on rice cooked in pork fat; covered with velouté sauce, and separated by truffle in julienne, thickened of Madeira sauce

Oeufs mollets à l'espagnole
- œufs mollets ⇒ grilled toasts spreaded with butter added of mustard, topped with soft boiled eggs decorated of jelly, onion and chopped parsley; surrounded of tomatoes macerated in french dressing, and filled with diced capsicums

Oeufs mollets à l'écossaise ⇒ croustades filled with a purée of salmon and béchamel sauce, topped with soft boiled egg; covered with shrimp sauce

Oeufs mollets à la Beauharnais ⇒ soft boiled eggs, laid on artichoke hearts braised in butter; garnished with Béarnaise sauce added of tarragon

Oeufs mollets à la bénédictine ⇒ soft boiled eggs, laid on pounded salt cod and mashed potatoes, browned in the oven; covered with béchamel sauce, added of cream

Oeufs mollets à la bohémienne ⇒ poached eggs on foie gras croustade, covered of velouté sauce and topped with a julienne of ham in Madeira

Oeufs mollets à la bouchère ⇒ soft boiled eggs served with slices of poached bone marrow

Oeufs mollets à la châtelaine ⇒ tartlets filled with a mixing of chestnut purée, béchamel sauce and mashed onions; topped with soft boiled egg, covered of poultry velouté

Oeufs mollets à la chivry ⇒ soft boiled eggs, covered of poultry velouté added of composed butter mixed with herbs

Oeufs mollets à la Daumont
- garniture pour œufs mollets ⇒ soft boiled eggs with crayfishes and mushrooms
- garniture pour œufs pochés ⇒ poached eggs ... with crayfishes and mushrooms

Oeufs mollets à la Florentine ⇒ braised spinach in butter, topped with poached eggs; covered with Mornay sauce and grated cheese, then browned

Oeufs mollets à la forestière ⇒ croustades, garnished with mushrooms and lardoons sautéed in butter, topped with poached egg; covered with melted butter added of lemon juice, pepper and parsley

Oeufs mollets à la provençale ⇒ dish of halved tomatoes fried in olive oil, topped with a poached egg, covered with tomatoes cooked in their own liquid; garnished with sliced aubergines and courgettes, fried in olive oil

Oeufs mollets à la reine ⇒ tartlets filled with mashed poultry, topped with a poached egg; covered of béchamel sauce

Oeufs mollets à la zingara ⇒ sippets garnished of ham lamellas, topped with a poached egg; covered with a sauce of stock, tomato sauce, plus a julienne of ham, pickled ox tongue, and braised mushrooms

Oeufs mollets Aladin ⇒ dish of rice flavoured with saffron, plus capsicums and onions braised in oil; topped with soft boiled eggs, covered of tomato sauce

Oeufs mollets ambassadrice ⇒ croustades filled with a culinary stuffing of truffles and foie gras, thickened of brown sauce flavoured with xeres, and topped with soft boiled eggs; served with a garnish of asparagus tips, and covered of supreme sauce

Oeufs mollets Amélie ⇒ croustades filled with diced vegetables and ham braised in butter, plus Madeira, topped with soft boiled egg; covered with béchamel sauce added of cream, and garnished of morels in cream

Oeufs mollets Argenteuil ⇒ soft boiled eggs laid on fried sippets, covered of mashed asparagus; garnished with asparagus tips braised in butter

Oeufs mollets aurore ⇒ soft boiled eggs laid on fried sippets, covered with velouté sauce, plus tomato purée and butter; sprinkled of chopped hard-boiled egg-yolk, and surrounded of tomato sauce

Oeufs mollets aux anchois ⇒ croustades filled with a soft boiled egg; covered with béchamel sauce added of anchovy paste, then decorated with anchovy fillet

Oeufs mollets Berlioz ⇒ croustades made of mashed potatoes, egg and butter, filled with a culinary stuffing of truffles and mushrooms, thickened of Madeira sauce; topped with soft boiled eggs, covered of supreme sauce

Oeufs mollets Bonvalet ⇒ soft boiled eggs laid on sippets fried in butter, and covered of velouté sauce; surrounded of béarnaise sauce, and decorated with truffle lamella

Oeufs mollets Brillat Savarin ⇒ pastry case garnished with morels sautéed in butter, soft boiled eggs, and asparagus tips in butter; covered with Madeira sauce or xeres sauce

Oeufs mollets Brimont ⇒ croustade of puff-pastry, garnished with soft boiled eggs, mushrooms in cream, and poultry croquettes; covered with velouté sauce, added of Madeira, plus cream

Oeufs mollets Béranger ⇒ pastry case filled with a purée of onions and rice, peppered and sugared, topped with soft boiled eggs, covered of béchamel sauce added of egg-yolks and gruyère; then sprinkled of grated cheese and melted butter, then browned

Oeufs mollets Carême ⇒ soft boiled eggs, laid on artichoke hearts braised in butter, then garnished with a ragout of lamb sweetbreads, truffles and mushrooms; covered with Madeira sauce added of cream

Oeufs mollets chénier ⇒ ramekins filled with pilaf in saffron; topped with a soft boiled egg, surrounded of sliced aubergines fried in oil, and covered with tomato sauce

Oeufs mollets Massenet

    a) avec haricots ⇒ potato croustade filled with french beans in butter, topped with a soft-boiled egg, or a poached egg; covered with a sauce of shallots, white wine, meat stock, poached bone-marrow and butter

    b) avec fonds d'artichauts ⇒ potato croustade filled with artichoke heart, and asparagus tips, topped with a soft-boiled egg, or poached egg; covered with a sauce of shallots, white wine, meat stock, poached bone-marrow and butter

Oeufs mollets grand duc ⇒ poached eggs or soft-boiled eggs, covered of béchamel sauce added of egg-yolks and gruyère; served au gratin laid on croustades with truffle lamellas, and asparagus tips in butter

Oeufs moulés

    - en général ⇒ moulded eggs with a hash of parsley, ham and truffle

    - autre recette ⇒ moulded eggs with a hash of parsley, ham and truffle

Oeufs moulés bagration ⇒ moulded macaroni topped with an egg, and laid on croustade; covered with béchamel sauce added of cream, decorated of truffle lamella

Oeufs moulés bizet ⇒ moulded hash of ox tongue, truffle and eggs, laid on braised artichoke hearts; covered with Madeira sauce added of truffle

Oeufs moulés cardinal ⇒ moulded creamy lobster's meat, plus egg, laid on tartlet; covered with white cream added of mashed lobster and cayenne pepper

Oeufs moulés carême ⇒ moulded diced ox tongue, truffle and egg, laid on artichoke heart; covered with Madeira sauce added of cream, and decorated with a slice of pickled ox tongue

Oeufs moulés en chartreuse ⇒ moulded mixing of vegetables, butter, egg and pepper; served laid on braised cabbage

Oeufs moulés polignac ⇒ moulded egg with truffle lamella, laid on buttered sippet; covered with meat stock, added of parsley butter

Oeuf poché ⇒ poached egg

Oeufs pochés à l'alsacienne ⇒ timbales filled with braised sauerkraut, lardoons and soft boiled eggs; covered with brown sauce made of meat stock, vegetables and Madeira

Oeufs pochés à l'américaine ⇒ fried sippets, garnished with soft boiled eggs and lobster escalopes; covered with a sauce made of shallots, pounded garlic, tomato purée, cayenne pepper and dry white wine

Oeufs pochés à l'ancienne ⇒ soft boiled eggs laid on rice cooked in pork fat; covered with velouté sauce, and separated by truffle in julienne, thickened of Madeira sauce

Oeufs pochés à l'écossaise ⇒ croustades filled with a purée of salmon and béchamel sauce, topped with soft boiled egg; covered with shrimp sauce

Oeufs pochés à l'espagnole ⇒ tomatoes cooked in oil, garnished with a poached egg and a culinary stuffing of capsicum; served with fried onions, and covered of tomato sauce

Oeufs pochés à la Beauharnais ⇒ soft boiled eggs, laid on artichoke hearts braised in butter; garnished with Béarnaise sauce added of tarragon

Oeufs pochés à la bohémienne ⇒ poached eggs on foie gras croustade, covered of velouté sauce and topped with a julienne of ham in Madeira

Oeufs pochés à la bénédictine ⇒ soft boiled eggs, laid on pounded salt cod and mashed potatoes, browned in the oven; covered with béchamel sauce, added of cream

Oeufs pochés à la châtelaine ⇒ tartlets filled with a mixing of chestnut purée béchamel sauce and mashed onions; topped with soft boiled egg, covered of poultry velouté

Oeufs pochés à la chivry ⇒ soft boiled eggs, covered of poultry velouté added of composed butter mixed with herbs

Oeufs pochés à la florentine ⇒ braised spinach in butter, topped with poached eggs; covered with béchamel sauce added of egg-yolks and grated cheese, then browned

Oeufs pochés à la forestière ⇒ croustades, garnished with mushrooms and lardoons sautéed in butter, topped with poached egg; covered with melted butter added of lemon juice, pepper and parsley

Oeufs pochés à la provençale ⇒ dish of halved tomatoes fried in olive oil, topped with a poached egg, covered with tomatoes cooked in their own liquid; garnished with sliced aubergines and courgettes, fried in olive oil

Oeufs pochés à la reine ⇒ tartlets filled with mashed poultry, topped with a poached egg; covered of béchamel sauce

Oeufs pochés à la Zingara ⇒ sippets garnished of ham lamellas, topped with a poached egg; covered with a sauce of stock, tomato sauce, plus a julienne of ham, pickled ox tongue, and braised mushrooms

Oeufs pochés aux anchois ⇒ croustades filled with a soft boiled egg; covered with béchamel sauce added of anchovy paste, then decorated with anchovy fillet

Oeufs pochés ambassadrice ⇒ croustades filled with a culinary stuffing of truffles and foie gras, thickened of brown sauce flavoured with xeres, and topped with soft boiled eggs; served with a garnish of asparagus tips, and covered of supreme sauce

Oeufs pochés Argenteuil ⇒ soft boiled eggs laid on fried sippets, covered of mashed asparagus; garnished with asparagus tips braised in butter

Oeufs pochés aurore ⇒ soft boiled eggs laid on fried sippets, covered with velouté sauce, plus tomato purée and butter; sprinkled of chopped hard-boiled egg-yolk, and surrounded of tomato sauce

Oeufs pochés Brillat Savarin ⇒ pastry case garnished with morels sautéed in butter, soft boiled eggs, and asparagus tips in butter; covered with Madeira sauce or xeres sauce

Oeufs pochés Brimont ⇒ croustade of puff-pastry, garnished with soft boiled eggs, mushrooms in cream, and poultry croquettes; covered with velouté sauce, added of Madeira, plus cream

Oeufs pochés Carême ⇒ soft boiled eggs, laid on artichoke hearts braised in butter, then garnished with a ragout of lamb sweetbreads, truffles and mushrooms; covered with Madeira sauce added of cream

Oeufs pochés Colbert ⇒ croustades filled with vegetable salad, thickened of béchamel sauce; topped with soft boiled egg, and garnished of parsley butter mixed with meat juice, plus tarragon

Oeufs pochés Edouard VII ⇒ soft boiled eggs, laid on risotto mixed with diced truffle, and pickled ox tongue lamellas

Oeufs pochés Georgette ⇒ poached eggs, served with potatoes and a ragout of crayfish tails

Oeufs pochés grand duc ⇒ poached eggs, covered of béchamel sauce added of egg-yolks and gruyère; served au gratin laid on croustades with truffle lamellas, and asparagus tips in butter

Oeufs pochés Lucullus ⇒ poached eggs laid on artichoke hearts stuffed with a culinary stuffing of sweetbread, cockscombs, cock's kidneys and truffle

Oeufs pochés Massenet

a) avec haricots ⇒ potato croustade filled with french beans in butter, topped with a a poached egg; covered with a sauce of shallots, white wine, meat stock, poached bone-marrow and butter

b) avec fonds d'artichauts ⇒ potato croustade filled with artichoke heart, and asparagus tips, topped with a poached egg; covered with a sauce of shallots, white wine, meat stock, poached bone-marrow and butter

Oeufs pochés masqués Almavira ⇒ braised artichoke hearts, garnished with crushed foie gras, and a poached egg; covered with Mornay sauce, and sprinkled of chopped truffle

Oeufs pochés Monselet ⇒ braised artichoke hearts, topped with a poached egg; covered with a sauce made of poultry velouté, veal stock, cream and xeres, then decorated with slices of truffle

Oeufs pochés Mornay ⇒ sippets garnished with poached eggs, covered with béchamel sauce added of egg-yolks and gruyère, grated parmesan and melted butter; then browned

Oeufs pochés princesse ⇒ poached eggs laid on sippets, covered with supreme sauce, and decorated of truffle lamellas; garnished with asparagus tips braised in butter, plus chopped white of meat thickened with supreme sauce

Oeufs pochés Rachel ⇒ fried sippets garnished with a poached egg, and covered with a sauce made of shallots, white wine, meat stock, poached bone-marrow and butter; topped with a slice of bone-marrow

Oeufs pochés Rossini ⇒ foie gras escalope sautéed in butter, topped with a poached egg; covered with Madeira sauce, and decorated of truffle lamellas

Oeufs poêlés à la catalane ⇒ fried eggs, served on a layer of tomatoes and aubergines cooked in olive oil, added of crushed garlic, plus chopped parsley

Oeufs poêlés à la ménagère ⇒ sauté vegetables from pot-au-feu, garnished with fried eggs; surrounded by tomato sauce

Oeufs poêlés à la provençale ⇒ dish of halved tomatoes fried in olive oil and topped with a poached egg; served with fried aubergines, then covered with tomatoes and garlic cooked in their own liquid

Oeufs sur le plat à l'agenaise ⇒ eggs fried on chopped onions and goose fat, sprinkled of garlic and parsley; garnished with sliced aubergines sautéed in goose fat

Oeufs sur le plat à l'antiboise ⇒ transparent gobies fried in olive oil, diced gruyère and garlic, plus four eggs

Oeufs sur le plat à l'orientale ⇒ eggs cooked on a layer of onions braised in butter; served garnished of grilled capsicums, stewed with onions, garlic, consommé and pepper, plus rice cooked in butter and beef stock

Oeufs sur le plat à l'écarlate ⇒ eggs laid on tomato sauce, sprinkled of diced pickled ox tongue; then fried in butter

Oeufs sur le plat à la bretonne

  1) **oeufs seuls** ⇒ fried eggs, surrounded with a sauce of vegetables, mushrooms, white wine and cream

  2) **oeuf cuit avec purée de haricots** ⇒ egg baked on a layer of mashed haricot beans, surrounded with a sauce of vegetables, mushrooms, white wine and cream

Oeufs sur le plat à la Chaville ⇒ eggs cooked on a layer of culinary stuffing from mushrooms in butter; garnished with tomatoes cooked in their own liquid added of tarragon

Oeufs sur le plat à la chipolata ⇒ eggs baked in butter; garnished with braised chestnuts, chipolatas, diced pork, little glazed onions

Oeufs sur le plat à la conti ⇒ fried eggs with mashed lentils

Oeufs sur le plat à la cressonnière ⇒ eggs surrounded by mashed watercress and cream; then baked

Oeufs sur le plat à la lorraine ⇒ grilled slices of smoked pork belly, plus slices of gruyère; topped with eggs surrounded of cream, and baked

Oeufs sur le plat à la maraîchère ⇒ eggs surrounded by lettuce chiffonade, sorrel, and chervil braised in butter, then baked; served with slices of smoked bacon

Oeufs sur le plat archiduc ⇒ eggs fried on a layer of onions braised in butter, and flavoured with paprika; garnished with diced truffle in butter, and surrounded by supreme sauce flavoured of paprika

Oeufs sur le plat au bacon ⇒ eggs and bacon

Oeufs sur le plat Carmen ⇒ fried sippets garnished with a slice of ham, and topped with a fried egg; covered with tomato sauce

Oeufs sur le plat chasseur ⇒ fried eggs garnished with sautéed poultry livers and mushrooms; sprinkled ith parsley and surrounded with sauce chasseur

Oeufs sur le plat Condé ⇒ dish of braised slices of bacon, surrounded by mashed red beans, topped with two eggs; then baked

Oeufs sur le plat Crécy ⇒ eggs fried on a layer of mashed carrots; surrounded by béchamel sauce added of cream

Oeufs sur le plat Jockey Club ⇒ dish of fried sippets, covered with mashed foie gras, and topped with a fried egg decorated of truffle lamella; plus veal kidneys sautéed in Madeira

Oeufs sur le plat Louis Oliver ⇒ fried liver covered with poultry velouté, plus fried eggs surrounded of Madeira sauce added of chopped truffle

Oeufs sur le plat Meyerbeer ⇒ fried eggs; garnished with a grilled lamb kidney and surrounded by Madeira sauce added of chopped truffles

Oeufs sur le plat Montrouge ⇒ eggs baked surrounded by chopped mushrooms, plus cream lining the egg-yolks

Oeufs sur le plat Opéra ⇒ fried eggs with sautéed poultry livers and asparagus tips

Oeufs sur le plat Rothomago ⇒ eggs fried on slices of ham; garnished with grilled chipolatas, and tomato sauce

Oeufs surprise ⇒ halved apricots in syrup, served with sponge fingers moistened of kirsch, plus whipped cream flavoured of vanilla and sugar

Oie ⇒ goose < *viande uncountable* >

Oie à l'alsacienne ⇒ dish of roasted goose, stuffed of sausage meat, laid on sauerkraut braised with streaky bacon, plus poached sausages; served with the gravy, added of white wine and stock

Oie à l'anglaise ⇒ goose stuffed with a forcemeat of onions, crumbs in milk, pepper, grated nutmeg, and sage; served with apple compote

Oie à l'instar de Visé ⇒ bits of poached goose, simmered in goose fat; served with velouté sauce, egg-yolks, and mashed garlic

Oie à la bourguignonne ⇒ goose braised with diced pork fat, onions, mushrooms, red wine, and aromatics

Oie au pot ⇒ goose stuffed with a forcemeat of liver, apples, and anchovy fillets, then poached in stock added of garlic, herbs, onion, and clove; served with a compote of rennet apples, plus ringed pastries made of choux pastry mixed with gruyère and pepper

Oie braisée à la flamande ⇒ braised goose, served with a garnish of green cabbage stuffed and braised, shaped carrots and turnips, boiled potatoes, salted breast of pork lamellas, plus poached slices of dry sausage; covered with the gravy

Oie de Toulouse -*[animal]*- ⇒ breed of goose

Oie en daube Capitole ⇒ goose stuffed with sausage meat, foie gras, and diced truffle; braised with mushrooms, stoned olives, and chipolatas

Oie rôtie aux fruits ⇒ dish of roasted stuffed goose, quartered apples hollowed out and filled with redcurrant jelly, plus quartered apples poached in syrup; served with the gravy

Oignon ⇒ onion

Oignon vert ⇒ green onion

Oignonade ⇒ hash of onions

Oignons farçis ⇒ onions hollowed out and stuffed with a hash of onion pulp and meat, baked in butter and stock; sprinkled of crumbs, or grated parmesan, plus melted butter, then browned

Oignons frits ⇒ sliced onions, fried in oil

Oignons hachés ⇒ diced onions or chopped onions

Oille à la française ⇒ stew of poultry, pigeons, slices of beef, shin of veal, and vegetables

Oiseau ⇒ bird

Oiseau sans tête

    - **veau** ⇒ veal olive stuffed with a forcemeat

    - **boeuf** ⇒ small ball of beef stuffed with a forcemeat

    - **mouton** ⇒ small ball of mutton ... stuffed with a forcemeat

    - **servis en sauce; ajouter** ⇒ ... simmered in sauce

    - **braisés; ajouter** ⇒ ... and braised

Oiseaux à la vigneronne ⇒ birds braised with grape

Oiseaux sans tête Raymond Oliver ⇒ small balls of mutton shoulder, laid on mushrooms fried in olive oil and butter; then baked and moistened with cream added of curry

Okra -*[fruit]*- ⇒ okra

Okrochka ⇒ soup made of beer and vegetables, served with quartered hard-boiled eggs, herbs and cucumbers, plus a garnish

Olive ⇒ olive

Olive à la picholine ⇒ stoned green olives preserved in salted water added of laurel, fennel, orange peel, and coriander

Olive de mer ⇒ wedge shell

Olive noire ⇒ black olive

Olive verte ⇒ green olive

Olives cassées ⇒ opened green olives preserved in salted water, laurel, fennel, orange peel, and coriander seeds, during eight days

Olives farçies pour hors d'œuvre ⇒ stoned olives stuffed with a paste of anchovy and butter

Olives farcies pour garniture
  1) **accompagnement du lapin sauté** ⇒ sauté rabbit ...
  2) **accompagnement d'un canard** ⇒ duck ...
  3) **accompagnement d'un poulet** ⇒ chicken ...
  4) **accompagnement de boeuf braisé** ⇒ braised beef ... garnished either of stoned olives stuffed with a forcemeat added of herbs, either with bits of anchovy fillets in oil
Olivet ⇒ cow's milk cheese with a blue crust
Olivet bleu -*[fromage]*- ⇒ cow's milk cheese with a blue crust
Olivet cendré -*[fromage]*- ⇒ cow's milk cheese refined in vine-shoot ashes
Olivette -*[tomate]*- ⇒ variety of tomato or tomato
Olivette -*[œillette]*- ⇒ oil poppy or white poppy
  - **huile d'œillette** ⇒ poppy-seed oil
Ollapodrida ⇒ olla-podrida
Ollebrod -*[Danemark]*- ⇒ beer soup added of rye bread
Oloron -*[fromage de brebis]*- ⇒ ewe cheese or ewe's milk cheese
Oloroso -*[xeres]*- ⇒ Oloroso
Omar-Khayyàm -*[Egypte]*- ⇒ Egyptian red wine
Omble-chevalier ⇒ char or hill-trout or grayling
Omble-chevalier rôti à la mode de Bugey ⇒ char stuffed with a forcemeat of whiting, cream, truffle and butter; grilled on a skewer and sprinkled with cream, served garnished of crayfish tails and truffles
Ombre ⇒ grayling
Ombrine -*[poisson]*- ⇒ corb
Omelette ⇒ omelette or omelet
Omelette à l'orange ⇒ omelette filled with tomato purée, cayenne pepper, and lemon peel
Omelette à l'oseille ⇒ omelette filled with braised sorrel chiffonade
Omelette à l'oursin ⇒ omelette of eggs, lemon juice, and sea urchins
Omelette à la basquaise ⇒ omelette filled with tomato, capsicum, garlic, and ham
Omelette à la Bercy ⇒ omelette with herbs, stuffed of grilled chipolatas; surrounded by tomato sauce
Omelette à la bigourdane ⇒ omelette filled with truffle lamellas, and diced foie gras; surrounded of Madeira sauce
Omelette à la bouchère ⇒ omelette garnished with small cubes of beef bone-marrow
Omelette à la châtelaine ⇒ omelette stuffed with a mixing of chestnuts and onions braised in butter; surrounded by béchamel sauce added of cream
Omelettte à la célestine ⇒ omelette garnished with a julienne of white of meat, cream sauce, and chervil; then topped with an other omelette
Omelette à la Nantua ⇒ omelette stuffed with a ragout of crayfish tails, garnished of truffle lamellas; served with béchamel sauce added of mashed crayfishes, cognac and cayenne pepper
Omelette à la dijonnaise ⇒ two omelettes of eggs, sugar, crushed macaroons, and cream; soldered with confectioner's custard added of almond powder, and flavoured of blackcurrant jelly; Served covered of whipped white of eggs, and glazed with sugar; surrounded by blackcurrant jam
Omelette à la farine d'avoine ⇒ omelette of eggs and oatmeal, sprinkled with sugar
Omelette à la fermière ⇒ omelette of eggs, braised vegetables in butter, and diced ham fried in butter
Omelette à la grecque ⇒ two omelettes of eggs, chopped onions, and diced capsicums, soldered with a hash of braised mutton; surrounded by tomato sauce, and sprinkled of parsley, plus butter lightly cooked
Omelette à la hongroise ⇒ omelette of eggs, braised diced ham, fried onions, and paprika; served surrounded with a sauce of chopped onions braised in butter, plus pepper, paprika and white wine

Omelette à la lorraine ⇒ omelette of eggs, lardoons sautéed in butter, shavings of gruyère, and chopped chives

Omelette à la lyonnaise ⇒ omelette filled with browned onions and parsley

Omelette à la mère poulard ⇒ omelette of eggs and cream

Omelette à la morvandelle ⇒ omelette filled with diced ham, and garnished of sliced ham in butter

Omelette à la Nantua ⇒ omelette stuffed with a ragout of crayfish tails, garnished of truffle lamellas; served with béchamel sauce added of mashed crayfishes, cognac and cayenne pepper

Omelette à la niçoise ⇒ omelette filled with tomato, parsley and garlic, cooked in their own liquid, decorated with anchovy fillets

Omelette à la parisienne ⇒ omelette of eggs, chopped onions, and chopped mushrooms; covered with grilled chipolatas

Omelette à la paysanne ⇒ potato, sorrel and herb omelette

Omelette à la romaine ⇒ two omelettes soldered with spinach braised in butter, added of anchovy fillets; covered with béchamel sauce added of egg-yolks and gruyère, grated parmesan and melted butter, then browned

Omelette à la rouennaise ⇒ omelette stuffed with mashed duckling livers; surrounded with a sauce based on diced vegetables, butter, red wine, garlic, mushroom peel, anchovy extract and cayenne pepper

Omelette à la St Flour ⇒ two omelettes added of onions and lardoons browned in pork fat, soldered with braised chopped cabbage; surrounded by tomato sauce

Omelette à la verdurière ⇒ omelette filled with lettuce, and sorrel braised in butter, plus a hash of tarragon, chervil and parsley

Omelette Albina ⇒ omelette filled of diced truffle, and garnished with mashed poultry in cream

Omelette alsacienne ⇒ fried dough made of flour, salt, kirsch, eggs and milk

Omelette André Theuriet ⇒ omelette stuffed with morels in cream, garnished with asparagus tips in butter; topped by truffle lamellas in butter, and surrounded of supreme sauce

Omelette Argenteuil ⇒ omelette stuffed with asparagus tips in butter, surrounded by béchamel sauce added of cream

Omelette au bacon ⇒ bacon omelette

Omelette au boudin ⇒ omelette garnished with a hash of grilled polony

Omelette au foie gras ⇒ omelette filled with small cubes of peppered foie gras

Omelette au fromage ⇒ cheese omelette

Omelette au joli coeur -[Menon]- ⇒ Omelette stuffed with spinach, anchovies, and crayfish tails

Omelette au rhum ⇒ omelette flamed with rum

Omelette au sucre ⇒ omelette of eggs, lemon peel, salt and cream; sprinkled with sugar

Omelette au thon -[dite « du curé »]- ⇒ omelette of eggs, plus a hash of carp soft roes, tunny, and shallots sautéed in butter; laid on melted butter, added of parsley, chives and lemon juice

Omelette aux abricots ⇒ omelette of eggs, salt, apricot jam, kirsch and sugar

Omelette aux anchois ⇒ omelette filled with anchovy fillets, decorated with a lattice of anchovy lamellas

Omelette aux artichauts ⇒ omelette filled with sauté artichoke hearts

Omelette aux aubergines ⇒ omelette filled with sauté diced aubergines

Omelette aux cèpes ⇒ omelette filled with boletus sautéed in butter or oil, and chopped parsley

Omelette aux cerises ⇒ fried dough made of flour, salt, kirsch, eggs, milk and cherries

Omelette aux champignons ⇒ mushroom omelette

Omelette aux clitocybes verts ⇒ omelette filled with curry, butter, and aniseed agarics cooked in olive oil; served with green salad seasoned of nut oil, and anisette

Omelette aux confitures ⇒ omelette filled with jam, then caramelized

Omelette aux courgettes ⇒ omelette filled with sliced sauté courgettes

Omelette aux croûtons ⇒ omelette filled with fried sippets; surrounded by tomatoes cooked in their own liquid, and sprinkled of herbs

Omelette aux épinards ⇒ omelette filled with spinach braised in butter

Omelette aux fines herbes ⇒ omelette with herbs

Omelette aux foies de volaille ⇒ omelette stuffed with sauté poultry livers thickened of brown sauce; decorated of brown sauce added of Madeira

Omelette aux fruits de mer ⇒ two omelettes, soldered by a ragout of seafood, fish velouté sauce added of cream and mushrooms, plus shrimp paste and cayenne pepper; covered with béchamel sauce added of cream, and shrimp paste

Omelette aux pêches ⇒ omelette garnished with cooked slices of peaches, then flamed with rum

Omelette aux pignons ⇒ omelette filled with pine-kernels sautéed in oil and butter

Omelette aux rognons ⇒ omelette stuffed with diced kidneys sautéed in butter, plus brown sauce flavoured with Madeira

Omelette aux salsifis et aux choux de Bruxelles ⇒ omelette stuffed with diced salsify braised in butter and thickened of velouté sauce; served with little potato balls browned in butter, plus brussels sprouts sautéed in butter, then surrounded of brown sauce added of butter

Omelette brayaude ⇒ omelette filled with browned ham, and potato, sprinkled of diced tomato and cream

Omelette chasseur ⇒ omelette stuffed with poultry livers, and sauté mushrooms; surrounded of sauce chasseur

Omelette chevreuse ⇒ omelette stuffed with a hash of chervil and butter

Omelette Choisy ⇒ omelette stuffed with lettuce chiffonade in cream

Omelette Diane ⇒ mushroom omelette, stuffed with a culinary stuffing of game, truffles, and game stock; topped with truffle lamellas in butter, surrounded of brown sauce added of Madeira

Omelette du curé ⇒ omelette filled with soft roes of carp and tunny

Omelette en portefeuille ⇒ folded omelette

Omelette enfarinée ⇒ pancake of flour and eggs

Omelette farçie à l'espagnole ⇒ omelette filled with diced capsicums braised in olive oil, plus diced tomatoes, garlic, and chopped parsley; served with tomato sauce

Omelette Feydeau ⇒ mushroom omelette, topped of poached eggs; covered with béchamel sauce added of egg-yolks and gruyère, plus chopped truffle, sprinkled of grated parmesan, then browned

Omelette flambée ⇒ sugared omelette, sprinkled of sugar and rum; then flamed < *rhum, rum peut être remplacé* >

- **armagnac** ⇒ armagnac
- **calvados** ⇒ calvados
- **cognac** ⇒ cognac
- **whisky** ⇒ whisky
- **un alcool de fruit** ⇒ fruit brandy

Omelette fourrée à la duxelles ⇒ omelette stuffed with chopped onions, and mushrooms in cream; studded of fried sippets, and served with a sauce based on chopped mushrooms, white wine, tomato purée and parsley

Omelette fourrée à la japonaise ⇒ omelette stuffed with Japanese artichokes braised in butter; served with béchamel sauce added of cream

Omelette fourrée à la Maintenon ⇒ omelette filled with a culinary stuffing of chicken, mushrooms, and truffle; covered with béchamel sauce added of mashed onions, then sprinkled with cheese plus melted butter, and browned

Omelette fourrée à la portugaise ⇒ omelette stuffed with tomatoes cooked in their own liquid

Omelette fourrée aux crevettes ⇒ omelette stuffed with shrimp tails, fish velouté sauce added of cream and mushrooms, plus shrimp paste and cayenne pepper

Omelette garnie à la parisienne ⇒ omelette of eggs, chopped onions, and chopped mushrooms; covered with grilled chipolatas

Omelette garnie aux fines herbes ⇒ omelette with herbs

Omelette jurassienne ⇒ omelette filled with lardoons, onion, tomato, potatoes, grated gruyère, and chives

Omelette Mistral ⇒ omelette of diced aubergines sautéed in oil, eggs, diced tomatoes, parsley and garlic

Omelette Mont-Bry ⇒ two omelettes, soldered with braised celeriac mixed with béchamel sauce added of cream; covered with béchamel sauce added of egg-yolks and gruyère, grated parmesan, sprinkled of melted butter, then browned

Omelette mousseline ⇒ omelette of eggs and cream

Omelette nature ⇒ omelette or plain omelette

Omelette normande ⇒ omelette of eggs and milk, added of sliced potatoes fried in butter

Omelette norvégienne ⇒ pastry of biscuit and vanilla ice cream, flavoured with liquor; coated of meringue and browned, then flamed with the flavouring liquor

Omelette Parmentier ⇒ omelette of eggs, sauté diced potatoes, and chopped parsley

Omelette plate à la diplomate ⇒ two omelettes soldered with a culinary stuffing of lobster, truffle, cognac, and béchamel sauce; covered with béchamel sauce added of cream, grated cheese and lobster paste, then sprinkled of melted butter and browned

Omelette plate à la jardinière ⇒ dish of cooked mixed vegetables, added of cooked peas and cooked bits of cauliflower, then browned in butter and incorporated with the eggs in omelette; served garnished with asparagus tips, and covered with béchamel sauce added of cream

Omelette plate à la lorraine ⇒ omelette of eggs, lardoons sautéed in butter, shavings of gruyère, and chopped chives

Omelette plate à la ménagère ⇒ omelette filled with diced beef and diced onions browned in butter, plus chopped parsley

Omelette plate à la savoyarde ⇒ omelette filled with sauté potatoes and shredded gruyère

Omelette plate Du Barry ⇒ omelette with cauliflower bunches browned in butter, and chopped chervil

Omelette Reine Pédauque ⇒ two omelettes filled with sugar, powdered almonds, and cream; soldered with a mixing of apple compote, and rum

Omelette Rossini
   a) **avec salpicon** ⇒ omelette filled with a culinary stuffing of foie gras and truffle
   b) **garnie d'escalopes de foie gras** ⇒ omelette garnished with foie gras escalopes sautéed in butter, plus truffle lamellas in butter; surrounded with brown sauce added of Madeira

Omelette soufflée ⇒ omelette of eggs, sugar, salt and vanilla

Omelette soufflée aux fraises des bois ⇒ omelette made with the egg-yolks and white of eggs whipped separately; then added of wild strawberries macerated in vanilla sugar, and raspberry brandy, during the cooking process

Omelette St Hubert ⇒ omelette stuffed with mashed game, thickened of brown sauce flavoured with game stock; topped by chopped mushrooms sautéed in butter

Omelette sucrée à la compote de fruits ⇒ sugared omelette stuffed with compote of ...
   - **pêches** ⇒ peaches, flavoured with vanilla and thickened of peach jam flavoured with liquor
   - **prunes** ⇒ plums, flavoured with vanilla and thickened of plum jam flavoured with liquor
   - **pommes** ⇒ apples, flavoured with vanilla and thickened of apple jam flavoured with liquor
   - **abricots** ⇒ apricots, flavoured with vanilla and thickened of apricot jam flavoured with liquor

Omelette sucrée à la normande ⇒ omelette of eggs, sugar and cream; stuffed with sliced rennet apples cooked in butter and granulated sugar, then flavoured with calvados

Omelette surprise ⇒ pastry of biscuit and vanilla ice cream, flavoured with liquor; coated of meringue and browned, then flamed with the same flavouring liquor

Omelette Talleyrand ⇒ omelette filled of braised onions seasoned with curry powder; served with sauté calf sweetbreads, surrounded of béchamel sauce added of cream

Omelette Trucha ⇒ omelette filled with spinach and beets; served with tomato purée

Omelette Victoria ⇒ omelette filled with a culinary stuffing of lobster and truffle

Omelette viveur ⇒ omelette filled with sauté diced beef, celeriac and artichoke hearts

Omoplate de porc ⇒ shoulder bone of pork

Oncomynchus -[saumon]- ⇒ pink salmon

Onglet -[boeuf]- ⇒ body thick skirt of beef

Onglet grillé ⇒ body thick skirt of beef, oiled and peppered, then grilled

Onglet poêlé à l'échalote ⇒ body thick skirt of beef fried in butter, covered with the gravy added of vinegar and chopped shallots

Oolong -[thé]- ⇒ Taiwanese tea
- **qualité de oolong** ⇒ grand oolong fancy
- **huit autres qualités** ⇒ choicest to common

Opéra
1) **garniture pour noisettes d'agneau** ⇒ noisettes of lamb ...
   - **garniture pour tournedos sautés** ⇒ sauté tournedos ... with a garnish of poultry livers in Madeira laid on tartlets, plus asparagus tips; served with a Madeira sauce
2) **oeufs sur le plat opéra** ⇒ fried eggs with sautéed poultry livers and asparagus tips
3) **crème renversée opéra** ⇒ caramelized custard, garnished with whipped cream, crushed meringue and strawberries in kirsch

Operne ⇒ barnacle

Oppordagni -[ritjstaffel]- ⇒ thin slices of fried beef, seasoned with coconut; served with spiced rice

Opsonium ⇒ opsonium

Orange ⇒ orange

Orange à l'andalouse ⇒ gateau made of milk, sugar, orange peel, egg-yolks, whipped cream and semolina; garnished with pieces of orange

Orange amère ⇒ bitter orange

Orange douce ⇒ sweet orange

Oranges givrées ⇒ oranges uncaped and hollowed out first, then filled with an orange sorbet, and reconstituted; served very icy

Orange pekoe -[thé]- ⇒ Ceylonese tea

Orange pippers -[pomme]- ⇒ variety of apple

Orange pressée ⇒ orange juice

Orange sanguine ⇒ blood orange

Orangeade ⇒ orangeade - **boisson faite de jus d'orange** ⇒ orange juice < *uncountable* >

Orangeat- gâteau ⇒ petit four made of almond paste mixed with orange peel
- **bonbon** ⇒ sweet made of orange peel and sugar

Oranges à la liqueur ⇒ peeled oranges, moistened with curaçao liquor, then sprinkled of sugar

Oranges surprise ⇒ orange husks garnished with orange pulp, slices of apple, pear, bananas, plus raisins, cherries, sugar and rum

Oranges tahitiennes ⇒ slices of pineapple, topped by peeled oranges, covered by redcurrant jelly and a garnish of preserved fruits

Orangette -[vin de fruits]- ⇒ fruit wine flavoured with aromatics

Orangette ou écorce d'orange -[zeste]-- orange ⇒ orange peel < *uncountable* >
- **citron** ⇒ lemon peel < *uncountable* >
- **en cuisine** ⇒ zest or peel < *uncountable* >
- **avec un zeste de citron** ⇒ with a piece of lemon peel

Orangé de provence ou polonais -*[abricot]*- ⇒ variety of apricot
Orangina ⇒ bottled orangeade
Orangine ⇒ gateau made of three slices of Genoese sponge moistened with a syrup flavoured of
        curaçao, then soldered by a confectioner's custard, added of whipped cream and
        curaçao; glazed with a fondant, and decorated of preserved orange peel, plus angelica
Oreandea -*[URSS vin]*- ⇒ dry Ukrainian white wine
Oreille -*[boucherie]*-1) **veau** ⇒ ear of veal
                  2) **porc** ⇒ ear of pork
Oreille -*[cerf]*- ⇒ stew of deer ear
Oreille -*[pezize]*- ⇒ cup fungi
Oreille de chardon -*[pleurote]*-
   - **pleurote en coquille** ⇒ oyster cap
   - **pleurote du panicaut** ⇒ gloomy mushroom
Oreille de chat -*[pezize]*- ⇒ cup fungi
Oreille de l'orme -*[pleurote]*-
   - **pleurote en coquille** ⇒ oyster cap
   - **pleurote du panicaut** ⇒ gloomy mushroom
Oreille de lièvre -*[mâche]*- ⇒ corn salad
Oreille de mer ⇒ ormer or abalone or sea-ear
Oreille de morille -*[pezize]*- ⇒ cup fungi
Oreille de noiret ⇒ oyster mushroom
Oreille de porc ⇒ pig ear
Oreille de st pierre ⇒ ormer or haliotis
Oreille de St Pierre sautée à l'ail -*[ormeau]*- ⇒ ormers sautéed with garlic
Oreiller de la belle aurore ⇒ pâté in pastry case made of a forcemeat of veal, a forcemeat of games
        and truffles, plus thin slices of poultry, hare, partridge and calf sweetbreads
Oreilles d'Haman -*[cuisine juive]*- ⇒ Jewish pastry
Oreilles d'ours ⇒ fritter of eggs, salt, flour and lemon peel
Oreilles de crisse -*[Amérique du nord]*- ⇒ filling for salad
Oreilles de porc au cantal ⇒ boiled pig ears, laid on a dish; covered with a sauce of butter, flour,
        lemon juice, mustard and grated Cantal cheese, then browned
Oreilles de porc au gratin ⇒ braised pig ears, surrounded of mushrooms, covered with diced
        vegetables, crumbs, and melted butter; then browned
Oreilles de porc bouillies ... ⇒ boiled pig ears ...
   - **en fritots** ⇒ ... sliced, and fried wrapped in dough; ...
   - **grillées** ⇒ ... coated with butter and crumbs, then grilled; ... < *milieu de phrase* >
   - **servis avec sauce à la moutarde** ⇒ ... served with mustard sauce
   - **ou servis avec sauce au raifort** ⇒ ... served with horse-radish sauce
   - **plus une purée de pommes de terre** ⇒ plus mashed potatoes
   - **ou plus une purée de céleri-rave** ⇒ plus mashed celeriac
   - **à la lyonnaise** ⇒ ... sliced and sautéed in butter with onions
   - **froides à la vinaigrette** ⇒ ...; served with french dressing
   - **au gratin sauce blanche** ⇒ ...; covered with white sauce and browned
   - **sauce Mornay** ⇒ ...; covered with béchamel sauce added of egg-yolks and gruyère, then
        browned
Oreilles de porc braisées ⇒ pig ears braised with rind of pork, onion, carrot, white wine, and stock;
        served with a garnish of braised sticks of celery or braised cauliflower, sprinkled with
        the cooking juice

Oreilles de porc farçies et frites ⇒ braised pig ears, stuffed of poultry forcemeat, moistened with a sauce made of stock added of truffle extract and onion or tomato purée; then coated with crumbs and fried

Oreilles de St Pierre sautées à l'ail ⇒ ormers sautéed with garlic

Oreilles de veau à la diable ⇒ veal ears braised with a mixture of diced vegetables and ham, then coated with mustard, plus melted butter and grilled; served with devilled sauce

Oreilles de veau braisées à la mirepoix ⇒ veal ears braised with a mixture of diced vegetables and ham, a bunch of herbs, pepper, white wine, and veal stock; served covered with the cooking juice

Oreilles de veau farçies du Bugey ⇒ veal ears cooked in pot-au-feu, stuffed with a forcemeat of sweetbread, poultry, truffle, wild mushrooms, cream and egg-yolks; served coated with crumbs and fried, then sprinkled of parsley

Oreillettes ⇒ type of fritter from sugared paste, fried in oil

Oreillette -*[pezize]*- ⇒ cup fungi

Oreillettes de Montpellier ⇒ fritters flavoured with rum, and orange peel or lemon peel

Oreillons -*[abricots]*- ⇒ canned apricots

Orge ⇒ barley < *uncountable* >

Orge perlé ⇒ pearl barley

Orgeat ⇒ orgeat or a sweet drink made of barley or almonds, sugar, and orange-flower water

Orgnac -*[côtes du Vivarais]*- ⇒ quality wine from Mont Ventoux area on the right bank of the Rhone valley

Orientale *(à l' ...)* ⇒ cooking based on aubergines, tomatoes, rice, saffron, onions and capsicums

- **garniture pièces de boucherie** ⇒ ... with a garnish of tomatoes stuffed of rice, ketmias, capsicums and tomato sauce

Origan ⇒ origan or origanum or wild marjoram

Original -*[élan]*- ⇒ elk or moose

Orloff ⇒ saddle of veal stuffed with a purée of mushrooms and onions, covered with a béchamel sauce added of onions and nutmeg; sprinkled of grated parmesan and glazed

Orlong ⇒ spined sea scorpion

Orly

- **anguilles** ⇒ eels ...
- **brochet** ⇒ pike ...
- **merlan** ⇒ whiting ...
- **sole** ⇒ sole ...
- **éperlan de mer** ⇒ sea smelt ...
- **éperlan de rivière** ⇒ river smelt ...
- **saumon** ⇒ salmon nom poisson fillets steeped in batter and fried; served with tomato sauce

Orly de filets de saumon sauce tomate ⇒ salmon fillets seasoned of shallots, nutmeg, lemon juice, olive oil, thyme and laurel, then coated of egg and fried; served with tomato sauce

Orléanaise *(à l' ...)* -*[garniture grosses pièces de boucherie]*- ⇒ ... garnished of braised endives, and potatoes with parsley butter

Orléans

- **oeufs pochés** ⇒ poached eggs ...
- **oeufs mollets** ⇒ soft boiled eggs ...
- **oeufs sur le plat** ⇒ fried eggs ... laid on tartlets and garnished either with a culinary stuffing of bone-marrow and truffle, thickened with Madeira sauce, or diced white of meat in tomato sauce
- **filets de sole roulés** ⇒ rolls of sole fillets filled with a culinary stuffing of prawns and mushrooms; covered with a white wine sauce, and topped of a truffle lamella

Ormeau ⇒ ormer or haliotis

Ormeaux aux huîtres ⇒ ormer lamellas sautéed in oil, then simmered with oyster sauce, cornflour, cognac, and welsh onion

Ormier de jersey ⇒ ormer or haliotis

Ormiers de Jersey braisés ⇒ braised ormers

Oronge *-[fausse]-* ⇒ fly agaric < *poisonous* >

Oronge vineuse *-[golmote]-* ⇒ blusher

Oronge vraie des césars ⇒ orange milk mushroom or imperial mushroom or orange agaric or egg-mushroom

Orphie ⇒ garfish or sea-pike or sea needle or horn-fish

Orpin *-[joubarbe]-* ⇒ stonecrop

Orratza *-[congre]-* ⇒ conger eel or sea eel

Orsière *-[râclette]-* ⇒ cheese fondue

Ortie ⇒ nettle

Ortie de mer *-[Provence]-*
  - **beignets** ⇒ fritters filled with ...
  - **omelette** ⇒ omelette filled with ... sea anemones

Ortolan ⇒ ortolan

Ortolans à la Brissac ⇒ ortolans and bits of ham grilled on a skewer with melted butter; served with mushrooms sautéed in olive oil, and moistened of meat stock, plus lemon juice

Orval *-[bière]-* ⇒ beer

Oryza glaberrina *-[riz]-* ⇒ rice

Oryza sativa *-[riz]-* ⇒ rice

Os *(à l' ...)* ⇒ with the bone

Os ⇒ bone

Os à moelle ⇒ marrowbone < *uncountable* >

Os de poitrine charnu *-[porc]-* ⇒ barbecue spareribs

Os de tigre *-[Chine]-* ⇒ tiger bone

Oseille ⇒ sorrel

Oseille de guinée ⇒ hibiscus
  - **fruit** ⇒ hibiscus fruit

Osmazôme ⇒ sapid substance of meat

Ossau-Iraty ⇒ pressed ewe's milk cheese with a yellow crust

Ossetra ⇒ caviar

Osso bucco *-[viande de veau]-* ⇒ Osso Bucco

Osso-buco à la milanaise ⇒ ragout of Osso Bucco braised in white wine, onion and tomato; served with noodles or rice

Osso-buco alla gremolata ⇒ ragout of Osso Bucco braised in white wine, hash of garlic, orange peel, lemon peel, and grated nutmeg; served with noodles or rice

Ostara *-[pomme de terre]-* ⇒ early spring potato

Ostertorte ⇒ gateau stuffed with a buttered custard added of mocha; decorated with eggs in chocolate

Öt *-[piment]-* ⇒ capsicum purée, salted and oiled

Ouassou *-[Antilles]-* ⇒ large crayfish

Oublie ⇒ round wafer

Oublie à la parisienne ⇒ wafer flavoured with orange blossom or lemon juice; sometimes shaped in cone

Ouillade
  - **ariège** ⇒ soup of eggs and garlic
  - **roussillon** ⇒ dish of boiled pork and vegetables

Ouillat ⇒ soup of onions, garlic, beans, tomatoes and leeks, thickened with cheese, plus egg and vinegar

Oukrainka -*[Russe]*- ⇒ bread shaped in wheel
Oulade ⇒ soup made of cabbage, pork fat, and other vegetables
Ouliat ⇒ soup of onions, garlic, beans, tomatoes and leeks, thickened with cheese, egg and vinegar
Ours ⇒ bear
Oursin ⇒ sea urchin or sea hedgehog
Oursin -*[hydne]*- ⇒ spreading hydnum
Oursinade -*[Provence]*-
    - **sauce** ⇒ sea urchin sauce
    - **soup** ⇒ fish soup added of sea urchins
Ourteto ⇒ hash of spinach, sorrel, celery, leeks and garlic
Outarde ⇒ bustard
Ouzo ⇒ ouzo
Ovale -*[forme]*- ⇒ oval
Ovos moles -*[Portugal]*- ⇒ sweets made of sugar and egg-yolks
Oxtail ⇒ oxtail soup
Oyonnade ⇒ goose stewed in St Pourcain wine, plus its own liver and blood thinned down in eau de
        vie
Oyster pie -*[pie]*- ⇒ oyster pie
Oyster soup -*[GB]*- ⇒ oyster soup

P

Pacane pie ⇒ Brazil nut pie

Pacanier -*[Noix de pacane]*- ⇒ Brazil nut

Pachade -*[St Flour]*- ⇒ gateau or pancake made with a dough added of plums or dried plums

Pacherenc-du-vic-bilh ⇒ white wine from Adour area

Paczki -*[Pologne]*- ⇒ fritters stuffed with jam

Paddy -*[riz]*- ⇒ rice

Paëlla ⇒ paella

Pageot ou Rousseau ⇒ sea bream

Pageot rose ⇒ blackspot sea bream

Pagnottes du Forez ⇒ pastries from Forez area

Padre -*[poisson]*- ⇒ dorade or red porgy

Paillasson de pommes de terre -*[Darphin]*- ⇒ garnish of potato sticks first fried, then baked shaped in flat cake

Paille -*[pomme de terre]*- ⇒ potatoes shredded in straw and fried

Paille -*[chalumeau]*- ⇒ straw

Pailles au fromage ⇒ lamella cakes made of flour, salt, butter, eggs and cayenne pepper; covered with grated Cheshire cheese

Paillette ⇒ petit-four of puff-pastry shaped in stick, spiced, and flavoured of parmesan

Pain ⇒ bread < *uncountable* >

Pain à café -*[flûte]*- ⇒ long French loaf

Pains à l'anis ⇒ dried biscuits from eggs, sugar, flour, and aniseed

Pain à la romaine -*[pain perdu]*- ⇒ French toast or slices of brioche, steeped in milk vanilla flavoured, then coated of egg, and browned in butter

Pain au chocolat ⇒ small pastry filled with chocolate or puff pastry with chocolate filling or pain au chocolat

Pain au cumin ⇒ bread flavoured with cummin

Pain au gluten ⇒ gluten bread

Pain au lait ⇒ small bread kneaded with milk

Pain aux graines de sésame ⇒ bread filled with sesame seeds

Pains aux raisins ⇒ small pastries enriched with raisins OR currant buns

Pain aux raisins ⇒ currant bun

Pains aux six céréales ⇒ bread made with a mixing of wheat, rye, oat, barley, corn and sesame

Pain azyme ⇒ unleavened bread

Pain bis ⇒ brown bread

Pain blanc ⇒ french bread

Pain braisé ⇒ braised bread

Pain brié -*[Normandie]*- ⇒ bread with a crumb very white and thick

Pain brioché ⇒ bread made with a dough for brioche

Pain céleste -*[azyme]*- ⇒ unleavened bread

Pain coiffé ⇒ bread shaped in knotted dish-cloth

Pain complet ⇒ wholemeal bread or Graham bread

Pain crotté -*[pain perdu]*- ⇒ French toast or slices of brioche, steeped in milk vanilla flavoured, then coated of egg, and browned in butter

Pains d'amandes ⇒ almond pastries

Pains d'amandes ⇒ rolled cakes made of eggs, sugar, vanilla, salt, almond powder, butter, flour and yeast

Pains d'anis ⇒ small flat-cakes made of sugar, eggs, flour, and aniseed extract

Pain d'arachides aux crevettes *-[Antilles]-* ⇒ peanut bread filled with shrimps

Pain d'écrevisses *-[Franche comté]-* ⇒ forcemeat of crayfishes, moulded and baked

Pain d'épeautre ⇒ spelt bread

Pain d'épice ⇒ gingerbread

Pains d'épinards à la romaine ⇒ dariole filled with a mixing of boiled spinach, butter, diced anchovy fillets, and eggs; then baked

Pain de campagne ⇒ farmhouse bread or country bread

Pains de carottes ⇒ dariole filled with a mixing of béchamel sauce, mashed carrots, and eggs; then baked

Pains de Châtillon sur Chalaronne ⇒ bread made in local recipe from Châtillon sur Chalaronne

Pain de Cherbourg ⇒ bread kneaded with sea water

Pains de chou-fleur ⇒ dariole filled with a mixing of mashed cauliflower, béchamel sauce, grated gruyère, pepper, nutmeg and eggs

Pain de crustacé ⇒ forcemeat of cream, crab, eggs and pepper, cooked in a mould; covered with a cream

Pain de cuisine
    1) **général poisson** ⇒ fish loaf
       - **légumes** ⇒ vegetable loaf
    2) **pains de chère de poisson** ⇒ forcemeat of ...
       - **brochet** ⇒ pike moulded and baked
       - **carpe** ⇒ carp moulded and baked
       - **saumon** ⇒ salmon moulded and baked
       - **merlan** ⇒ whiting moulded and baked
    3) **pains de crustacés** ⇒ forcemeat of ...
       - **homard** ⇒ lobster moulded and baked
       - **crabe** ⇒ crab moulded and baked
       - **langouste** ⇒ spiny lobster moulded and baked
    4) **pains de volaille** ⇒ forcemeat of poultry moulded and baked
       - **viande blanche** ⇒ forcemeat of white of meat moulded and baked
       - **gibier** ⇒ forcemeat of game moulded and baked
       - **foie gras** ⇒ forcemeat of foie gras moulded and baked
    5) **pains de légumes** ⇒ forcemeat of ...
       - **endive** ⇒ chicorée braised and added of eggs, then moulded and baked
       - **épinards** ⇒ spinach braised and added of eggs, then moulded and baked
       - **laitue** ⇒ lettuce braised and added of eggs, then moulded and baked
       - **scarole** ⇒ escarole braised and added of eggs, then moulded and baked
       - **fonds d'artichauts** ⇒ artichoke hearts braised and added of eggs, then moulded and baked
       - **choux fleur** ⇒ cauliflower braised and added of eggs, then moulded and baked
       - **carottes** ⇒ carrots braised and added of eggs, then moulded and baked
       - **aubergines** ⇒ aubergines braised and added of eggs, then moulded and baked

Pain de fantaisie ⇒ bread sold by a loaf

Pain de ferme ⇒ farmhouse bread

Pain de froment ⇒ fine wheat bread

Pain de fruits *-[Bireweck]-* ⇒ bread added of fruits

Pain de gênes ⇒ large pastry added of butter and crushed almonds or Genoa cake

Pain de gruau ⇒ wheaten bread

Pain de La Mecque ⇒ choux-pastry decorated with granulated sugar and almonds

Pain de légume ⇒ voir pain de cuisine

Pain de Lodève ⇒ brown bread, hard-baked
Pain de luxe ou fantaisie ⇒ bread sold by a loaf
Pain de maïs ⇒ corn bread
Pain de mie ⇒ sandwich loaf
Pain de mélasse -*[Inde]-* ⇒ paste of dates
Pain de ménage ou ordinaire ⇒ large loaf of bread
Pain de mie ⇒ sandwich loaf
Pain de Morlaix ⇒ loaf of bread shaped in wallet
Pain de Nantes ⇒ small round cake flavoured with orange or lemon; coated of almonds and covered
with apricot jam, and fondant
Pains de navets ⇒ dariole filled with a mixing of béchamel sauce, mashed turnips, and eggs; then
baked
Pain de poires -*[Suisse]-* ⇒ pear loaf
Pain de poisson ⇒ fish loaf
Pain de régime ⇒ diet bread
Pain de sarrasin ⇒ buckwheat bread
Pain de seigle ⇒ rye bread
Pain de seigle noir ⇒ rye bread
Pain de son ⇒ bran bread
Pain de sucre ⇒ sugar loaf
Pain de tomate ⇒ preparation of tomato pulp, eggs, and pepper, moulded and baked; covered with
tomato sauce added of butter
Pain de viande, de gibier ou de volaille ⇒ forcemeat of poultry or white of meat or game moulded
and baked
　　- **Pain de foie gras** ⇒ forcemeat of foie gras moulded and baked
Pain des Parthes ⇒ biscuit
Pain du Picenum -*[Alica]-* ⇒ bread filled with raisins
Pain en épi ⇒ bread shaped in wheat ear
Pain fantaisie ⇒ bread sold by a loaf
Pain fendu ⇒ oblong bread with longitudinal splitting
Pain grillé ⇒ grilled bread-toast
Pain liquide -*[bière]-* ⇒ beer < *uncountable* >
Pain long -*[pain]-* ⇒ bread shaped in stick
Pain moulé ⇒ moulded bread
Pain noir ⇒ bread of rye and wheat
Pain perdu ⇒ French toast or slices of brioche, steeped in milk vanilla flavoured, then coated of egg,
and browned in butter
Pain plié -*[pain]-* ⇒ loaf of bread shaped in wallet
Pain polka ⇒ bread shaped in long stick
Pain rassis ⇒ stale bread
Pain rond ⇒ round loaf
Pain sans sel ⇒ unsalted bread
Pain spécial ⇒ fancy bread
Pain surprise ⇒ rye bread garnished with flavoured mashed potatoes, chop nuts, cheese and ham
Pain tordu ⇒ twisted bread
Pain viennois ⇒ wheaten bread
Paiousnaia ⇒ caviar pressed into bricks
Pak choï -*[chou chinois]-* ⇒ Chinese cabbage
　　- **Pak choï servi avec porc** ⇒ Chinese cabbage served braised or sautéed in lamellas with pork

Pak choï -*[chou chinois]*- ⇒ Chinese cabbage (follow)
  - **Pak choïservi avec poisson** ⇒ Chinese cabbage served braised or sautéed in lamellas with fish
  - **Pak choï servi avec crustacés** ⇒ Chinese cabbage served braised or sautéed in lamellas with crustaceae
Palais -*[boeuf, mouton]*-
  - **boeuf** ⇒ palate of beef
  - **mouton** ⇒ palate of mutton
Palais de boeuf ⇒ beef palate
Palatinat -*[vins de]*- ⇒ wines from Rhine left bank
Palatschinken -*[Autriche]*- ⇒ stuffed pancakes
Pale ale -*[bière]*- ⇒ pale ale
Paleron ⇒ shoulder blade or chuck or blade bone or shoulder cut of beef
Paleron ménagère ⇒ diced chuck of beef browned in oil, then braised with onions, flour, white wine, tomatoes, garlic, carrots, and turnips; served hot with parsley
Palet ⇒ cake shaped in quoit, enriched of butter and flavoured diversely
Palet de dames ⇒ cake shaped in quoit, filled with currants
Palets salés ⇒ cakes shaped in quoits, made of flour, butter, milk and salt
Paletot -*[oie]*- ⇒ goose carcase
Palette -*[vin]*- ⇒ Provencal wines
Palette
  - **mouton** ⇒ shoulder of mutton
  - **porc** ⇒ shoulder of pork
Palette de porc ⇒ shoulder of pork
Palette de porc à la choucroute ⇒ shoulder of pork with sauerkraut; sometimes some vegetables as potatoes, or carrots, or onions, or turnips, etc ... are added
Palette de porc aux haricots blancs ⇒ shoulder of pork cooked with haricot beans
Palette de porc et échine ⇒ neck end of pork
Palette de porc et échine, désossée et ficelée ⇒ neck end of pork « boned and rolled » ½ ou ½ neck end of pork « boneless »
Palette de porc sans os ⇒ blade bone « boneless »
Palme -*[huile]*- ⇒ palm oil
Palmier -*[gâteau]*- ⇒ puff-pastry cake, shaped in palm-leave
Palmiste -*[chou]*- ⇒ cabbage tree
Palois ⇒ gateau made with alternate discs of meringue and custard, covered of icing sugar
Paloise (à la ...)
  1) **petites pièces de boucherie grillées** ⇒ grilled ... garnished of little potato-balls browned in butter and french beans in cream
  2) **grosses pièces de boucherie grillées** ⇒ grilled ... with a garnish of carrots, turnips, and french beans in butter, bunches of cauliflower covered with sauce hollandaise, plus potato croquettes
  3) **sauce paloise** ⇒ béarnaise sauce added of mint
  4) **grillades à la paloise** ⇒ grilling or grilled covered with the or béarnaise sauce
     - **jus de la viande** ⇒ gravy
Palombe ⇒ wild pigeon or wood pigeon or ring-dove
Palomet -*[russule]*- ⇒ greenish russula
Palourde ⇒ clam or carpet shell
Palourde (fausse ...) -*[lavignon]*- ⇒ false clam
Palourdes farçies ⇒ clams cooked in white wine, shallots and aromatics; stuffed with composed butter added of chopped shallots, parsley and garlic, then sprinkled with crumbs and browned

Pamplemousse et pomélo ⇒ grapefruit

Pamplemousses aux crevettes ⇒ cups filled with a garnish of « prawn tails », lamellas of cucumber pulp, and pieces of grapefruit; plus a sauce of vinegar, peanut oil, pepper, sugar, soya sauce, ginger powder, ketchup and honey

Pamplemousses au crabe ⇒ cups filled with a garnish of cab meat, lamellas of cucumber pulp, and pieces of grapefruit; plus a sauce of vinegar, peanut oil, pepper, sugar, soya sauce, ginger powder, ketchup and honey

Pamplemousses aux queues de langoustines ⇒ cups filled with a garnish of scampi tails, lamellas of cucumber pulp, and pieces of grapefruit; plus a sauce of vinegar, peanut oil, pepper, sugar, soya sauce, ginger powder, ketchup and honey

Pamplemousses aux queues d'écrevisses ⇒ cups filled with a garnish of crayfish tails, lamellas of cucumber pulp, and pieces of grapefruit; plus a sauce of vinegar, peanut oil, pepper, sugar, soya sauce, ginger powder, ketchup and honey

Pamplemousses glacés ⇒ grapefruit uncaped and hollowed out, then filled again with grapefruit ice cream; closed with their cap and frozen

Pan bagnat ⇒ sandwich impregnated of olive oil, and filled with onions, celery, anchovies, and black olives

Pan double coupé à 5 ou 6 côtes *-[veau]-* ⇒ hind and end of veal

Pan pepato de Ferrare ⇒ brioche flavoured with cocoa, sugared with honey, and enriched of almonds plus orange peel; covered with chocolate, then decorated of sweets

Panaché
- **général** ⇒ mixed < *v.t adjectif* >
- **bière et limonade** ⇒ lemonade shandy

Panaché de volaille et de champignons à la mimolette ⇒ composed salad of diced supreme, horn of plenty mushrooms, and diced Dutch cheese; seasoned with a french dressing of white wine vinegar, and nut oil

Panade ⇒ panada or bread soup

Panade à la farine ⇒ panada of butter and flour

Panade à la frangipane ⇒ panada of flour, egg-yolks, butter, pepper, nutmeg, and milk

Panade à la pomme de terre ⇒ panada of milk, pepper, nutmeg, butter and potatoes

Panade au pain ⇒ panada of crumb and milk

Panade au riz ⇒ panada of rice and consommé, added of butter

Panais ⇒ parsnip

Panasserie *-[viennoiserie]-*
- **a) pain viennois** ⇒ voir texte
- **b) pain au gluten** ⇒ voir texte
- **c) pain au gruau** ⇒ voir texte
- **d) pain de mie** ⇒ voir texte
- **e) pain brioché** ⇒ voir texte

Pancake *-[Amérique du nord]-* ⇒ pancake

Pancréas ⇒ pancreas

Paner ⇒ to coat with breadcrumbs
- **pané** ⇒ coated with breadcrumbs and fried or hard-up with breadcrumbs

Pané ⇒ nom anglais fried in breadcrumbs or ... coated with breadcrumbs

Panetière *(à la ...)* ⇒ bread hollowed out, filled with cooked food and browned < *« food » peut être remplacé* >
- **ris d'agneau** ⇒ lamb sweetbread
- **foies de volaille** ⇒ poultry livers
- **salpicon de ...** ⇒ culinary stuffing of ...
- **ragoût de ...** ⇒ ragout of ...

Panetière *(à la ...)* ⇒ (suite)
- **oeufs brouillés** ⇒ scramble eggs
- **petits oiseaux** ⇒ nom anglais des oiseaux ...
- **filets de poisson en sauce** ⇒ nom poisson ... fillets in a sauce of ... nom sauce

Panettone ⇒ Italian gateau made of leaven past, egg-yolks, raisins and orange peel

Panicot *-[pleurote]-* ⇒ oyster mushroom

Panier de crudités ⇒ basket filled with quartered artichokes, carrots, radishes, bunches of cauliflower, lengths of celery, capsicums, cucumbers, broad beans, and fennel; presented with mayonnaise added of herbs, French dressing flavoured with tarragon, béchamel sauce added of anchovy paste, plus a sauce of petit suisse, soft white cheese, Roquefort, cognac, pepper and vinegar

Panisse ⇒ rectangular cake made of chick-pea flour or maize flour, sprinkled of grated cheese, and fried in olive oil

Panizze ⇒ Corsican chestnut-flour cake or maize-flour cake

Panne ⇒ fat of pig

Panne de porc ⇒ fat of pig

Pannequet
1) **terme général servi en petites entrées-hors d'œuvre chaud** ⇒ hors d'œuvre
    - **garniture de potages** ⇒ garnish for soups
    - **entremets sucrés** ⇒ sugared sweet
    - **crêpes** ⇒ pancake stuffed with ...
    - **hachis** ⇒ a hash
    - **purée** ⇒ a purée
    - **crème** ⇒ a custard
    - **grillée ou panée et frite** ⇒ then grilled or then coated with crumbs and fried
2) **pannequets salés crêpes** ⇒ pancakes stuffed with ...
    - **anchois à la béchamel** ⇒ ... anchovies in béchamel sauce
    - **anchois à la sauce tomate** ⇒ ... anchovies in tomato sauce
    - **épinards à la sauce Mornay** ⇒ ... spinach in béchamel sauce added of egg-yolks and gruyère
    - **fromage fondu** ⇒ ... melted cheese
    - **laitances aux champignons** ⇒ ... soft roes with mushrooms
    - **champignons au paprika** ⇒ ... mushrooms seasoned with paprika
    - **champignons au jambon** ⇒ ... mushrooms with ham
    - **mouton haché aux aubergines** ⇒ ... hashed mutton, plus aubergines
    - **crevettes à la sauce aurore** ⇒ ... shrimps in velouté sauce, plus tomato purée and butter
    - **purée de gibier au fumet** ⇒ ... mashed game in stock
    - **purée de volaille à la crème** ⇒ ... mashed poultry in cream
    - **écrevisses à la sauce Nantua** ⇒ ... crayfishes in béchamel sauce, added of mashed crayfishes, cognac, and cayenne pepper
3) **pannequets sucrés crêpes** ⇒ pancakes stuffed with ...
    - **crème pâtissière additionnée de fruits confits** ⇒ confectioner's custard added of preserved fruits
    - **crème pâtissière additionnée de fruits au sirop** ⇒ confectioner's custard added of fruits in syrup
    - **crème pâtissière parfumée au pralin** ⇒ confectioner's custard flavoured of grilled almonds with vanilla sugar
    - **crème pâtissière parfumée à la liqueur** ⇒ confectioner's custard flavoured with a liquor
    - **sucre** ⇒ sugar

- **crème de marrons** ⇒ chestnut jam
- **confiture** ⇒ jam
- **ils peuvent être gratinés** ⇒ ... and browned
- **ils peuvent être flambés à la liqueur** ⇒ ... flamed with « nom anglais de la liqueur »

Pannequets à la brunoise ⇒ pancakes stuffed with diced vegetables braised in butter, thickened of béchamel sauce; then rolled, cut in lengths and fried

Pannequets à la créole ⇒ pancakes covered with a preparation of confectioner's custard, flavoured of rum, added of diced pineapple in syrup, then rolled; sprinkled with icing sugar, and browned

Pannequets à la cévenole ⇒ pancakes covered with a preparation of chestnut purée, flavoured of kirsch, added of cream, then rolled; sprinkled with icing sugar, and browned

Pannequets à la florentine ⇒ pancakes stuffed with hashed spinach, thickened of béchamel sauce, plus grated cheese; then sprinkled of crumbs and browned

Pannequets à la reine ⇒ pancakes filled with mashed poultry in cream, added with a culinary stuffing of truffle; then covered with mashed poultry in cream, sprinkled of crumbs plus grated parmesan, and browned

Pannequets à potage ⇒ ... garnished of bits of pancakes filled with ...
- **brunoise** ⇒ ... braised vegetables
- **béchamel sauce** ⇒ ... béchamel added of grated cheese
- **duxelles de champignons** ⇒ ... chopped onions and mushrooms, sautéed in butter

Pannequets au fromage ⇒ pancakes stuffed with béchamel sauce, added of grated cheese; then sprinkled with crumbs, plus grated cheese and browned

Pannequets au praliné ⇒ pancakes covered with a confectioner's custard flavoured of Cointreau or armagnac, added of grilled almonds mixed in vanilla sugar, then rolled; sprinkled with icing sugar and browned

Pannequets aux abricots ⇒ pancakes covered with a preparation of confectioner's custard, flavoured of rum, added of diced stoned apricots, and hashed almonds, then rolled; sprinkled with icing sugar, and browned

Pannequets aux anchois ⇒ pancakes stuffed with a béchamel sauce, added of anchovy purée, plus diced anchovy fillets; then sprinkled of crumbs and browned

Pannequets aux crevettes ⇒ pancakes stuffed with crayfish tails, thickened of fish velouté sauce added of cream and mushrooms, plus shrimp paste, and cayenne pepper; then rolled, and sprinkled of melted butter

Pannequets aux fruits confits ⇒ pancakes covered with a custard of egg-yolks, flour, milk, and diced preserved fruits macerated in cognac or rum, and rolled; then sprinkled of icing sugar, and caramelized in the oven

Pannequets aux laitances ⇒ pancakes stuffed with a culinary stuffing of soft roes, mixed with béchamel sauce added of chopped mushrooms; then sprinkled with crumbs, plus grated parmesan, and browned

Pannequets La Varenne ⇒ dish of pancakes covered with a preparation of chopped mushrooms, added with a culinary stuffing of ham thickened of béchamel sauce; sprinkled of grated parmesan and melted butter, then browned

Pannequets Mornay ⇒ pancakes stuffed with béchamel sauce added of egg-yolks and grated gruyère, plus a culinary stuffing of mushrooms and ham; then rolled, covered with béchamel sauce added of gruyère, sprinkled of grated parmesan, melted butter, and browned

Pannequets panés et frits
1) **général farçis** ⇒ rolled pancakes stuffed with a forcemeat, then cut in lengths; coated with crumbs and fried

2) variantes à la brunoise -*[panés et frits]*- ⇒ rolled pancakes filled with chopped vegetables braised in butter, then cut in lengths; coated with crumbs and fried

- **à la Hongroise** -*[panés et frits]*- ⇒ rolled pancakes filled with a culinary stuffing of mushrooms and onions braised in butter, added of béchamel sauce flavoured with paprika, then cut in lengths; coated with crumbs and fried

- **à l'italienne** -*[panés et frits]*- ⇒ rolled pancakes filled with a mixing of chopped mushrooms, diced ham, and tomato sauce, then cut in lengths; coated with crumbs and fried

- **à la St Hubert** -*[panés et frits]*- ⇒ rolled pancakes filled with mashed roebuck, thickened of game stock, then cut in lengths; coated with crumbs and fried

- **à la Strasbourgeoise** -*[panés et frits]*- ⇒ rolled pancakes filled with mashed foie gras, and chopped truffles, then cut in lengths; coated with crumbs and fried

Pannequets sucrés aux abricots ⇒ pancakes covered with a preparation of confectioner's custard, flavoured of rum, added of diced stoned apricots, and hashed almonds, then rolled; sprinkled with icing sugar, and browned

Pannkoogid (*Russe* ...) ⇒ thick pancakes covered with jam

Panse -*[boeuf]*- ⇒ paunch

Pansotti de Rapallo ⇒ kind of ravioli stuffed with spinach; served with a nut sauce

Panure ⇒ breadcrumbs or crumbs

Panure -*[mode]*-

- **panure au beurre** ⇒ ... brushed with melted butter, then rolled on breadcrumbs

- **panure au saindoux** ⇒ ... brushed with melted pork fat, then rolled on breadcrumbs

Panure à la milanaise -*[mode de panure]*- ⇒ ... coated with flour and egg, rolled on crumbs added of grated parmesan; then fried in oil or butter

Panure anglaise ⇒ coating of whipped eggs, oil and pepper

- **plat pané à l'anglaise** ⇒ ... coated of whipped eggs, oil, and pepper

Panzarotti ⇒ fritters of rice in milk, added of eau de vie, oil, yeast, eggs, and grated lemon peel

Paon ⇒ peacock or peafowl

Papatzul -*[tortilla]*- ⇒ omelette filled with bits of pork or hard boiled eggs; served with a sauce of pounded marrows, tomato purée, and gourd oil

Papaye -*[fruit]*- ⇒ papaya or papaw or pawpaw

Papet -*[Suisse]*- ⇒ stew of leeks, thickened of pounded potatoes

Papeton -*[Avignon]*- ⇒ mashed aubergines, added of eggs, then cooked in mould or moulded dish of mashed aubergines and eggs

Papeton d'aubergines ⇒ moulded dish of mashed aubergines and eggs

Papier à fioritures ⇒ paper frills

Papier aluminium ⇒ aluminium paper < *uncountable* >

Papier sulfurisé ⇒ greaseproof paper < *uncountable* >

Papillons -*[pâtisserie]*- ⇒ rectangles of puff-pastry, golden with egg and sprinkled of sugar

Papillote -*[friandise]*- ⇒ sweet of fondants, or paste jelly, or stuffed chocolates, or pralines

Papillote

1) décoration en papier sur le manche des côtelettes ⇒ paper frills decorating the end bones of chops, etc ...

2) cuisine morceau de viande cuit dans du papier aluminium ou du papier sulfurisé ⇒ small cut of meat baked inside a case made of aluminium paper or greaseproof paper

Papillotes à la chinoise ⇒ rectangular bits of ... fillet, marinated in rice alcohol or xeres, then wrapped in greaseproof paper with chopped ginger, and fried; served with a julienne of onions

- **filets de poissons utilisés merlan** ⇒ whiting

- **cabillaud** ⇒ fresh cod

- **daurade** ⇒ dorado

- **églefin** ⇒ haddock
Papillotes de cœurs d'oies ⇒ goose hearts, plus boletus, wrapped in aluminium paper, and grilled
Papillotes de homard et de coquilles St Jacques ⇒ slices of lobster cooked in vermouth and cream, with herbs, topped with scallops and truffle lamellas; wrapped in greaseproof paper, and baked
Pappardelle -*[pâtes alimentaires]-* ⇒ noodles shaped in nests
Paprika ⇒ paprika
Paprikache ⇒ ragout of paprika, sour cream, meat or fish, and chopped onions; garnished with tomatoes, capsicums or potatoes
Paquet -*[cuisine]-* ⇒ packet
Paraffine ⇒ paraffin or paraffin wax < *uncountable* >
Parage -*[parer]-* ⇒ trimming
Parasol -*[coulemelle]-* ⇒ parasol mushroom
Parfait -*[bière]-* ⇒ a 1 litre beer mug
Parfait ⇒ parfait
- **au café** ⇒ coffee parfait
Parfait amour -*[liqueur]-* ⇒ Dutch liquor from cedrate, clove, cinnamon, and coriander, macerated in alcohol
Parfait de foie gras
a) **parfait de foie gras d'oie** ⇒ goose foie gras
b) **parfait de foie gras de canard** ⇒ duck foie gras
Parfait glacé *(variantes suivant parfum ...)*
- **alcohol** ⇒ liquor parfait
- **café** ⇒ coffee parfait
- **chocolat** ⇒ chocolate parfait
- **praliné** ⇒ praline paste parfait
- **vanille** ⇒ vanilla parfait
Parfait praliné danicheff ⇒ praline paste and rum, parfait
Parfums -*[glaces]-* ⇒ the flavours
Parfumé -*[cuisine]-* ⇒ flavoured
Paris ail -*[saucisson de Paris]-* ⇒ dry sausage flavoured with garlic
Paris Brest ⇒ crown-shaped choux pastry stuffed with a custard, praline flavoured; sprinkled with chopped almonds
Paris Nice ⇒ crowned-shaped choux pastry, stuffed with a custard praline flavoured
Parisette -*[herbe]-* ⇒ herb Paris or true love
Parisien -*[entremets]-* ⇒ sweet made of a biscuit stuffed with lemon, plus almond paste and preserved fruits; covered of meringue and browned
Parisien -*[gâteau]-* ⇒ circular pastry filled with almond flavoured cream and preserved fruits; covered with meringue, then sprinkled of icing sugar and browned
Parisien -*[pain]-* ⇒ long bread
Parisienne *(à la ...)*
- **petites et grosses pièces de boucherie ou volaille** ⇒ ... with a garnish of little potato-balls browned in butter and sprinkled of chopped herbs, plus braised lettuce or artichoke hearts
- **poissons froids ou crustacés** ⇒ cold fishes, ou nom anglais du poisson, or crustaceae with mayonnaise and often a garnish of artichoke hearts filled with vegetable salad or hard boiled eggs and jelly
- **autres plats** ⇒ with white of meat, mushrooms, oxtongue or vegetable salad
- **potage** ⇒ soup of leeks, potatoes, milk, and bits of chervil
Parisienne -*[noix]-* ⇒ nut or walnut

Parisienne *-[brioche]-* ⇒ shaped brioche with a large part topped of a small ball
Parmentier
  a) potage ⇒ potato cream
  b) oeufs ⇒ eggs
    - **omelette** ⇒ omelette stuffed with diced fried potatoes
    - **oeufs brouillés** ⇒ scrambled eggs, mixed with cubes of sauté potatoes
  c) purée ⇒ mashed potatoes topped with eggs, and browned
  d) garniture de viande *-[agneau, veau, etc ...]-* ⇒ ... with a garnish of potatoes
  e) hachis parmentier ⇒ shepherd's pie
Parmesan ⇒ Parmesan cheese
Parmesane *(à la ...)* ⇒ with grated parmesan or with grated parmesan; au gratin
Parsemer ⇒ to sprinkle
Parson's nose *-[bonnet d'évêque]-* ⇒ parson's nose
Parthenay *-[biscuits]-* ⇒ biscuit
  - **glace** ⇒ dessert shaped in brick and made of layers from different ice creams
  - **gâteau** ⇒ gateau shaped in ring or square, made of meringue and sorbet; decorated with whipped cream, preserved fruits, and chocolate vermicelli
Partie d'épaule de boeuf et basse côte ⇒ pony
Partie d'épaule de boeuf et basse côte désossée ⇒ boneless pony
Partie de l'aloyau sans côtes premières, filet et faux-filet; désossée et ficelée *-[bœuf]-* ⇒ sirloin « chump end boned and rolled »
Partie du filet de veau le long des lombaires ⇒ veal fillet « ex loin »
Partie du filet de veau sous le quasi ⇒ veal fillet « ex rump »
Partie du jambon en rôti avec gras et couenne ⇒ silverside of pork « special trim » or whole joint of pork
Partie palette d'épaule de boeuf et basse côte ⇒ middle ribs of beef
Pascade *-[Rouergue]-* ⇒ pancake with oil-nut, sometimes added of pork fat and onions
Pascaline ou Pascaline d'agneau ⇒ whole lamb, stuffed and roasted
Pasilla *-[piment]-* ⇒ pimento
Paskha ⇒ gateau made of soft white cheese, sugar, sour cream and butter; stuffed of raisins, preserved fruits and almonds, then shaped in a pyramid
Passe-crassane *-[poire]-* ⇒ variety of pear
Passerelles de Frontignan *-[raisin sec]-* ⇒ muscat grape dried in the sun
Passito *-[vin]-* ⇒ aromatic white wine
Pasta asciutta *-[pâtes alimentaires]-* ⇒ dish of noodles
Pasta con le sarda *-[Sicile-Sardaigne]-* ⇒ dish of pasta with a stew of sardines, and tomatoes
Pasta frolla ⇒ sweet pastry, like savarin pastry
Pastarma *-[pasterma]-* ⇒ smoked mutton
Pastelas *-[juive]-* ⇒ rissoles stuffed with meat, honey and vegetables
Pasteles *-[Antilles]-* ⇒ plantain leaves, stuffed and steamed
Pastenague *-[poisson]-* ⇒ common stingray
Pastèque ⇒ watermelon
Pastèque à la provençale ⇒ uncaped watermelon, filled with rosé from Rhone valley, then frozen; served sliced with the wine
Pasterma ⇒ smoked mutton
Pastilla ⇒ puff-pastry stuffed of poultry, seafood or vegetables
Pastillage ⇒ preparation for decoration on pastries
Pastille ⇒ pastille or lozenge
Pastirma *-[Pasterma]-* ⇒ smoked mutton

Pastis *-[dessert]-*
- **Andernos** ⇒ kind of brioche
- **Béarn « pastis bourrit »** ⇒ gateau of leaven paste
- **Pastis gascon** ⇒ discs of paste moistened of goose fat, filled with apple lamellas macerated in armagnac, and baked

Pastis *-[boisson]-* ⇒ pastis

Pastis bourrit *-[Landes]-* ⇒ gateaux made of flour, leaven, melted butter, sugar, eggs, vanilla sugar, and rum, moulded and baked; ...
- **servis avec crème caramel** ⇒ ... served with crème caramel
- **grillés et servis avec foie gras** ⇒ ... served sliced and grilled, with foie gras

Pastis béarnais ⇒ gateau made of eggs, bitter orange tree flower extract, eau de vie, granulated sugar, milk, melted butter and leaven; moulded and baked

Pastourma *-[pasterma]-* ⇒ smoked mutton

Pastries *-[G.B]-* ⇒ pastries

Pasturma *-[pasterma]-* ⇒ smoked mutton

Pat-xaran ⇒ cherry liqueur

Patagos ⇒ cockles

Patata *-[pomme de terre]-* ⇒ potato

Patate douce ⇒ sweet potato
- **feuilles cuisinées comme épinards** ⇒ sweet potato leaves

Patates à l'impériale
- **viande** ⇒ ... served with a ...
- **volaille rôtie** ⇒ ... served with a ...
- **gibier** ⇒ ... served with a ...
- **garniture** ⇒ ... mixing of sweet potatoes, rennet apples, and sliced bananas, sprinkled of paprika, then browned with butter

Patay *-[fromage]-* ⇒ cow's milk cheese

Pâte *(préparation ...)* ⇒ dough or paste or batter

Pâte à baba ⇒ baba mixture

Pâte à brioche ⇒ dough added of yeast, eggs and butter or dough for brioche

Pâte à choux ⇒ choux pastry

Pâte à crêpe ⇒ pancake batter

Pâte à croissants ⇒ mixture for croissants

Pâte à gaufres ⇒ batter flavoured with vanilla or orange blossom

Pâte à génoise ⇒ batter made of eggs, sugar, flour and melted butter

Pâte à mâcher ⇒ chewing paste

Pâte à meringue ⇒ meringue mixture

Pâte à pâté ⇒ pie pastry

Pâte à savarin ⇒ savarin pastry

Pâte bâtarde ⇒ dough hydrated to 60%

Pâte brisée ⇒ short-pastry

Pâte d'abricots ⇒ apricot jelly

Pâte d'arachide ⇒ peanut butter

Pâte de cacao ⇒ cocoa paste

Pâte de coing ou Cotignac ⇒ quince paste

Pâte de fruits ⇒ fruit jelly or crystallized fruit

Pâte de guimauve ⇒ marshmallow sweet

Pâte de pomme ⇒ apple jelly

Pâte de rose ⇒ rose jelly

Pâte feuilletée ⇒ flaky-pastry or puff-pastry
Pâte filée *-[fromage]-* ⇒ curds kneaded with whey
Pâte fraîche *-[fromage]-* ⇒ drained curds
Pâte levée ⇒ leavened dough
Pâte molle *-[fromage]-* ⇒ drained curds
Pâte persillée *-[fromage]-* ⇒ curds sown with moisture
Pâte poussée ⇒ leavened dough
Pâte pressée *-[fromage]-* ⇒ curds drained by pressing
Pâte sablée ⇒ sablé pastry
Pâte sucrée ⇒ sugared pastry or pastry of sugar, eggs and butter
Pâtes ⇒ pasta uncountable or macaroni, uncountable, or noodles, pluriel invariable
Pâtes à nouilles ⇒ pasta
Pâtes à potage ⇒ noodles, pluriel invariable, or vermicelli, uncountable
Pâtes alimentaires ⇒ Italian pasta or pasta < *uncountable* >
    - pour soupes ⇒ noodles
Pâtes aromatisées *-[pâtes alimentaires]-* ⇒ flavoured pasta
Pâtes coulées ⇒ batter
Pâtes fraiches *-[fromage]-* ⇒ drained curds
Pâtes molles ⇒ batter
Pâtes pectorales ⇒ cough drops or pastilles
Pâtes sèches
    - pâte brisée ⇒ short pastry
    - pâte feuilletée ⇒ puff-pastry
    - pâte sablée ⇒ sablé pastry
Pâtisserie ⇒ pastry
Pâté *-[patisserie]-* ⇒ pastry case filled with a mixture of meat, game, fish or vegetables; baked and served cold or hot
Pâté ⇒ pâté or pie or patty
    - pâté de foie gras ⇒ pâté de foie gras or patty of goose liver fat
Pâté à la contades ⇒ goose's fat wrapped with a forcemeat of veal and covered of pastry crust
Pâté à la gênoise ⇒ Genoese cake
Pâté à tramcar *-[pâté]-* ⇒ cold pâté
Pâté chaud de bécasse à la périgourdine ⇒ pie of stuffed woodcock poached in stock added of Madeira, and baked in game forcemeat, veal forcemeat, foie gras escalopes, plus truffle lamellas
Pâté chaud de bécassines Lucullus ⇒ pie of snipe stuffed with a forcemeat added of cream, foie gras, truffle and cognac, then baked with forcemeat and streaky bacon; served completed of truffle stew, thickened with game stock and Madeira
Pâté chaud de cailles aux truffes ⇒ pie of forcemeat, quail stuffed with foie gras, and cognac; then barded and baked
Pâté d'alouette *-[Orléanais]-* ⇒ carcases of larks, filled with a forcemeat of their meat, streaky bacon, and calf liver; baked wrapped in larding and short pastry
Pâté d'alouette en terrine ⇒ pâté of skylark, goose fat, foie gras, juniper berries and pork fat
Pâté d'anguilles aux fines herbes « dit à la ménagère » ⇒ eel pie cooked with spices, pike forcemeat, and its marinade; wrapped in pastry
Pâté de bécasse *-[Artois]-* ⇒ woodcock pâté
Pâté de bécasse *-[froid en croûte]-* ⇒ pie of game forcemeat added of hashed woodcock
Pâté de bécasses en croûte de Beaugency ⇒ woodcock pie
Pâté de Bécherel *-[Bretagne]-* ⇒ garlic tart
Pâté de Belley ⇒ elaborated pâté < *voir Oreiller de la Belle Aurore* >

Pâté de campagne ⇒ farmhouse pâté
Pâté de canard ⇒ duck pâté
Pâté de canard d'Amiens ⇒ duck pâté flavoured with pimentos and aromatics
Pâté de canard froid ⇒ pâté of duck, plus forcemeat added of foie gras and truffle
Pâté de chartres ⇒ partridge pie
Pâtés de corneille -[GB]- ⇒ crow pâté
Pâté de courrés ou courraye -[Bretagne]- ⇒ fry galantine
Pâté de faisan ⇒ pheasant pâté
Pâté de faisan -[froid]- ⇒ pie of game forcemeat added of hashed pheasant
Pâté de foie ⇒ liver pâté
Pâté de foie d'oie truffé ⇒ goose foie gras pâté added of truffle
Pâté de foie de canard -[Poitou]- ⇒ duck liver pâté
Pâté de foie de porc ⇒ pork liver pâté
Pâté de foie gras ⇒ foie gras pâté
Pâté de foie gras truffé ⇒ pie of foie gras studded of truffle, macerated in cognac and Madeira, plus a forcemeat; then barded and baked
Pâté de fromage de chèvre ⇒ goat's milk cheese pâté
Pâté de gibier ⇒ game pâté
Pâté de grives ⇒ thrush pâté
Pâté de grives à la provençale ⇒ pie of thrushes, forcemeat, and foie gras; barded and baked
Pâté de grives en croûte de Gien ⇒ thrush pâté wrapped in pastry
Pâté de jambon (froid ...) ⇒ pie of ham and pork meat in Madeira, plus a forcemeat and sliced truffle
Pâté de lamproie à la bordelaise (chaud ...) ⇒ pâté of lamprey fillets, fish forcemeat added of herbs, plus leeks braised in butter
Pâté de lapin sauvage ⇒ wild rabbit pâté
Pâté de lapin vendéen ⇒ terrine of wild rabbit, streaky bacon, veal, parsley, garlic, onions, shallots, aromatics and eau de vie
Pâté de lièvre ⇒ hare pâté
Pâté de lièvre ⇒ pie of hare, spices, cognac, ham, fat of pig, truffles and game forcemeat; served cold
Pâté de lièvre et de cerf ⇒ hare and roebuck pâté
Pâté de lirons ⇒ dormouse pâté
Pâté de mouton -[Languedoc]- ⇒ pâté made of lamb kidney suet, brown sugar, plus chopped preserved cedrate
Pâté de noix de veau et de porc au fumet de gibier de Chartres ⇒ pâté made with cushion of veal, leg boneless of pork, and game stock
Pâté de Pâques ⇒ brioche stuffed with hard-boiled eggs, and poultry meat; shaped in turnover and baked
Pâté de perdreaux -[Charentes]- ⇒ young partridge pâté
Pâté de Pézenas ⇒ hash of mutton meat, mutton kidneys and fat, added of brown sugar plus lemon peel; wrapped in pastry dough and baked
Pâté de pigeon -[GB]- ⇒ pigeon pâté
Pâté de poisson ⇒ fish pâté
Pâté de porc ⇒ pork pie
Pâté de porc à la hongroise -[chaud en croûte]- ⇒ pie of chine of pork lamellas, onions and mushrooms braised in butter, paprika, plus cream; then covered with a sauce of chopped onions braised in butter, plus pepper, paprika, and white wine
Pâté de prunes ⇒ plum jelly
Pâté de prunes ⇒ plum paste

Pâté de ris d'agneau *-[chaud en croûte]-* ⇒ pie of lamb sweetbreads, mushrooms in butter, forcemeat balls made with cushion of veal, eggs and cream; sprinkled of melted butter and baked

Pâté de ris de veau *-[chaud en croûte]-* ⇒ pie of calf sweetbreads, mushrooms in butter, forcemeat balls made with cushion of veal, eggs and cream; sprinkled of melted butter and baked

Pâté de saumon ⇒ salmon pâté

Pâté de tête *-[fromage]-* ⇒ pork brawn

Pâté de veau et de jambon *-[froid en croûte]-* ⇒ pie of cushion of veal, streaky bacon, ham, Madeira, herbs, shallots and forcemeat; barded and baked

Pâté de veau et de jambon en croûte ⇒ veal and ham pâté, wrapped in pastry

Pâté de viande ⇒ meat pâté

Pâté de volaille ⇒ poultry pâté

Pâté du chef ⇒ chef's special pâté

Pâté en croûte ⇒ pork pie

Pâté en croûte de Gien ⇒ thrush pâté wrapped in pastry

Pâté en pot *-[Antilles]-* ⇒ stew of offal, breast and liver of mutton, plus vegetables

Pâté en terrine ⇒ pâté

Pâté froid d'alouettes ⇒ pie of skylark, forcemeat, truffle and foie gras; barded and baked

Pâtés *-[petits]-* ⇒ meat patty or small pork pie

Pâtés à la viande sucrée *-[Languedoc]-* ⇒ voir pâté de Pézenas et pâtés de Béziers

Patelle ⇒ limpet

Pâtisserie ⇒ pastry

Pâtisson ⇒ kind of courge

Patranque ⇒ bread steeped in milk, mixed with Cantal cheese and butter, then cooked as a large pancake

Patrenque ⇒ bread steeped in milk, mixed with Cantal cheese and butter, then cooked as a large pancake

Patrimonio *-[corse vin]-* ⇒ Corsican wine

Patron ⇒ proprietor or manager < *Ne pas utiliser le mot « patron » lequel veut dire client habituel en anglais* >

Patudo *-[thon]-* ⇒ patudo, false albacore or bigeye tuna

Paturon *-[psalliote]-* ⇒ field mushroom

Paturon blanc *-[psalliote]-* ⇒ horse mushroom

Pat-xaran *-[liqueur]-* ⇒ cherry liqueur

Patyr *-[Russe]-* ⇒ pastries with cream, added of lemon juice

Pauillac *-[vin]-* ⇒ Médoc red wines

Paupiette
- **de veau** ⇒ veal olive
- **de boeuf** ⇒ beef olive
- **autres** ⇒ small ball of ...

Paupiette de poisson ⇒ rolled thin slice of fish

Paupiette de veau ⇒ veal olive

Paupiettes d'agneau à la créole ⇒ small balls of lamb filled with a forcemeat of onions, capsicums and sausage meat, then braised in butter, onions, tomatoes, parsley, garlic, lemon peel and pepper; covered with the gravy flavoured of rum, and served with rice

Paupiettes de boeuf à la hongroise ⇒ beef olives stuffed with a forcemeat of veal, onions and paprika, then braised in butter, onions, white wine and mushrooms

Paupiettes de boeuf braisées
  a) **au vin blanc** ⇒ beef olives braised in white wine or Madeira; covered with the gravy and garnished of ...
    - **pommes noisettes** ⇒ voir texte
    - **légumes braisés** ⇒ voir texte
    - **légumes en purée** ⇒ voir texte
  b) **avec garniture bourgeoise** ⇒ beef olives braised in white wine or Madeira plus a garnish of small onions, carrots and lardoons
    - **avec garniture chipolata** ⇒ beef olives braised in white wine or Madeira plus chestnuts, chipolatas, diced pork and onions
  c) **au vin rouge** ⇒ beef olives braised in red wine; plus a garnish of onions, lardoons and mushrooms
Paupiettes de boeuf Ste Ménéhould ⇒ braised beef olives, coated of mustard, melted butter and crumbs, then grilled; served with watercress, and the gravy
Paupiettes de chou ⇒ braised small balls of cabbage leaves, stuffed with a forcemeat of cabbage and sausage meat
Paupiettes de dinde à la Crécy ⇒ turkey olives braised with carrots; served with the gravy
Paupiettes de poule au chou ⇒ small ball of cabbage leaves, filled with chicken meat, braised in goose fat with carrots and onions
Paupiettes de ris de veau braisé ⇒ calf sweetbreads braised in butter with carrots, celery and leeks, then wrapped in spinach leaves; served with the cooking juice added of kneaded butter, curry, mustard and cream
Paupiettes de sole à l'ancienne ⇒ small balls of sole fillets stuffed with a forcemeat of whiting and mushrooms, coated with crumbs and braised in butter; served with composed cutlets from whiting meat, garnished with a ragout of shrimp tails, mushrooms and truffle in Madeira
Paupiettes de sole Paillard ⇒ small ball of sole fillets stuffed with a forcemeat of fish and mushrooms, then baked in white wine; served laid on artichoke hearts, covered with the cooking juice, added of mashed mushrooms, egg-yolks and cream
Paupiettes de veau ⇒ veal olive
Paupiettes de veau aux bananes ⇒ veal olives stuffed of mashed bananas, braised in butter with carrots, herbs, and onions; served with the cooking juice added of rum and cream
Paupiettes de veau braisées à brun ⇒ veal olives stuffed with a forcemeat added of mushrooms, parsley and egg, then braised in butter, larding, onions, carrots, white wine, and veal stock; served with ...
    - **légumes liés au beurre** ⇒ ... vegetables thickened of butter
    - **légumes en purée** ⇒ ... vegetable purée
    - **légumes braisés** ⇒ ... braised vegetables
Pauvre homme *(à la ...)*
    - **viande** ⇒ meat served with a sauce of roux and stock, added of shallot, chive and parsley
    - **chevreuil** ⇒ sauté small round piece or cutlet of roebuck; covered of gravy with vinegar, and thickened of kneaded butter, then added of gherkins
Pavé *-[cuisine]-* ⇒ thick piece of steak or square or rectangular pie-dish of meat
Pavé *-[patisserie]-* ⇒ pastries made in square or rectangular moulds, often stuffed with custard
Pavé blésois *-[fromage]-* ⇒ goat's milk cheese
Pavé d'Auge ⇒ cow's milk cheese with a yellow soft paste
Pavés d'entremets *-[riz]-* ⇒ squares of rice cooked in milk
Pavés de riz frits
  a) **abricots** ⇒ squares of rice cooked in milk, soldered with « compote of apricots » added with a culinary stuffing of pineapple, then coated of crumbs and fried; served with ...
    - **sauce à la fraise** ⇒ ... strawberry sauce
    - **crème anglaise** ⇒ ... egg-custard

Pavés de riz frits (suite)
  b) à la marmelade de mirabelle ⇒ squares of rice cooked in milk, soldered with « compote of plums » added with a culinary stuffing of pineapple, then coated of crumbs and fried
  c) à la compote d'oranges ⇒ squares of rice cooked in milk, soldered with « compote of marmalade » added with a culinary stuffing of pineapple, then coated of crumbs and fried
  d) à la compote de reines claude ⇒ squares of rice cooked in milk, soldered with « compote of plums » added with a culinary stuffing of pineapple, then coated of crumbs and fried
  e) à la purée de marrons ⇒ squares of rice cooked in milk, soldered with « chestnut purée » added with a culinary stuffing of pineapple, then coated of crumbs and fried
  f) à la marmelade de pommes ⇒ squares of rice cooked in milk, soldered with « compote of apples » added with a culinary stuffing of pineapple, then coated of crumbs and fried
Pavés de riz Pompadour ⇒ squares of rice cooked in milk, soldered with confectioner's custard added of rum and preserved fruits, then coated of crumbs and fried; served with apricot sauce
Pavie -[pêche]- ⇒ variety of peach
Pavillon blanc du Chateau-margaux ⇒ very high quality Médoc white wine
Pavot ⇒ poppy
Paxille à bords enroulés ⇒ involute paxillus
Paysanne
  1) potages ⇒ soup made of diced potatoes, carrots, turnips, plus squared cabbage
  2) garnitures pour poisson, viande ⇒ garnished with ...
      - garniture pour omelette ⇒ filled with ... diced potatoes, carrots and turnips, plus squared cabbage
  3) apprêts braisés avec fondue de légumes ⇒ braised ... plus vegetables cooked in their own liquid
      - omelette ⇒ omelette filled with potatoes, sorrel and chopped herbs
Pe tsaï -[chou chinois]- ⇒ Chinese cabbage served braised or sautéed in lamellas with ...
  - servi avec porc ⇒ pork
  - poisson ⇒ fish
  - crustacés ⇒ crustaceae
Peach brandy ⇒ peach brandy
Peanut butter ⇒ peanut butter
Pear pudding ⇒ pear pudding
Peau
  - animal ⇒ skin < uncountable >
  - fruit ⇒ rind < uncountable >
  - pomme de terre ⇒ jacket
Peau -[fruits]- ⇒ rind < uncountable >
Pèbre d'aï -[banon]- ⇒ cylindrical Provencal cheese wrapped in chestnut-tree leaves, steeped in eau de vie, and flavoured with savoury
Pec hareng ⇒ newly-salted herring
Pécharmant ⇒ red wine from Bergerac area
Pêche ⇒ peach
Pêches à la bordelaise ⇒ stoned peaches, sprinkled of granulated sugar, then poached in Bordeaux wine added of sugar and cinnamon; served with slices of brioche glazed in the oven
Pêches à la crème ⇒ halved peaches poached in syrup, plus a custard of milk, egg-yolks, sugar and kirsch; covered with redcurrant jelly and crushed almonds

Pêches à la duchesse ⇒ tartlets filled with a mixture of vanilla ice cream and diced pineapple macerated in kirsch, topped with half a peach in syrup; covered by a zabaglione of sugar, egg-yolks, kirsch and maraschino, then sprinkled of grilled almonds

Pêches bourdaloue ⇒ poached peaches in syrup, laid on semolina, covered with crushed macaroons and granulated sugar; then browned in the oven

Pêches chantilly ⇒ mashed peaches mixed with whipped cream, sugar and kirsch

Pêches colombine ⇒ poached peaches, stuffed of rice and cooked in milk; covered with sugar and egg-yolks, accompanied of preserved fruits

Pêches dame blanche ⇒ cups of vanilla ice cream, slice of pineapple in kirsch and maraschino

Pêches flambées au kirsh ⇒ peaches poached in a syrup of vanilla and sugar, flamed with kirsch

Pêches Melba ⇒ vanilla ice-cream topped with halved peaches poached in syrup; covered with raspberry purée

   - **Si d'autres nappages groseille** ⇒ covered with redcurrant jelly flavoured of kirsch

   - **poires** ⇒ pear

   - **abricot** ⇒ apricot

   - **fraises** ⇒ fraise < *dans ce cas remplacer redcurrant dans le texte* >

Pêches Pénélope ⇒ cups filled with an ice cream of strawberry purée, sugar, lemon juice, vanilla sugar, meringue and whipped cream, topped with half a peach, plus raspberries; then served with a zabaglione

Pêches pochées ⇒ poached peaches, sprinkled with sugar

Pêches rafraîchies aux framboises ⇒ peaches poached in vanilla syrup, covered with raspberry purée flavoured of raspberry brandy; decorated with raspberries

Pecorino ⇒ Italian ewe cheese

   - **pecorino romano** ⇒ Italian ewe cheese of cooked paste

   - **pecorino siciliano** ⇒ Italian ewe cheese of pressed paste

   - **pecorino sardo** ⇒ Italian ewe cheese of pressed paste

Pectine ⇒ pectin

Pédoncule ⇒ peduncle

Peigne -*[coquille St Jacques]*- ⇒ scallop

Pékinoise (*à la ...*)

   a) morceaux de poisson frits ⇒ bits of fried fish; served with ...

   b) beignets de langoustines ⇒ fritters stuffed with scampi; served with ...

      - **sauce aigre douce à la chinoise** ⇒ ... a sauce made of garlic, onion, ginger, soya sauce, tomato juice, maize fecula, and mushrooms

Pékinoise -*[canard laqué à la]*- ⇒ voir canard laqué ...

Pekoe -*[thé]*- ⇒ tea leaves without the buds

Pekoe souchong -*[thé]*- ⇒ short and aged tea leaves

Pélamide ⇒ bonito

Pélardon ⇒ small goat's milk cheese from the Cevennes

Pélerine (*à la ...*) -*[turbot]*- ⇒ turbot braised on a laying of onions and butter, covered with the cooking juice added of white wine, creamed and buttered, then glazed; garnished with a bush of fried scallops

Pelmieni ⇒ kind of ravioli stuffed with hashed meat and potato purée added of cheese; served with sour cream or gravy added of lemon

Peluche ou en peluche

   - **général** ⇒ shredded

   - **cerfeuil** ⇒ shredded chervil

   - **autres** ⇒ shredded ...

Pelure d'oignon ⇒ rosé wine

Pemmican ⇒ pemmican or pemican

Penne *-[pâtes]-* ⇒ pasta shaped in feather
Pennicilium glaucum *-[bleu]-* ⇒ mushroom used in the blue cheese process
Pennini *-[pâtes]-* ⇒ noodles for soup
Pepe supi *-[Guinée]-* ⇒ soup of fish and meat
Pepper pot *-[ragoût]-* ⇒ spicy stew of mutton and onion
Peppermint ⇒ peppermint
Pepsi ⇒ cola
Péquet *-[Belge]-* ⇒ ginger brandy
Péquin *-[piment]-* ⇒ red pepper or pimento, uncountable, or capsicum
Péraldou *-[pélardon]-* ⇒ small goat's milk cheese from the Cevennes
Perce-pierre ou pousse-pierre ⇒ Crithmum or rock samphire
Perche ⇒ perch or freshwater bass *< pluriel inchangé >*
Perche de mer ⇒ sea bass *< pluriel inchangé >*
Perche marine ⇒ sea-bass *< pluriel inchangé >*
Perche noire ⇒ black sea-perch *< pluriel inchangé >*
Perchette ⇒ baby perch *< pluriel inchangé >*
Perdreau ⇒ young partridge *< uncountable >*
Perdreau à la coque ⇒ young partridge filled with foie gras, and boiled
Perdreau à la Souvarov ⇒ young partridge stuffed with foie gras, truffle and cognac; then baked with
    truffles, plus game stock added of Madeira
Perdreau à la vigneronne ⇒ young partridge cooked in butter, then braised with grapes, game stock
    and cognac
Perdreaux aux raisins ⇒ young partridge filled with grapes and petit suisse, then braised in butter;
    served with the cooking juice added of unripe grapes, armagnac, sweet natural wine
    from Banyuls, and petit suisse
Perdreau en crépine Brillat Savarin ⇒ boned young partridge splitted in two, browned in butter,
    coated with a forcemeat of foie gras and truffle, wrapped in a caul of pork and grilled;
    served with Madeira sauce
Perdreaux en croustades ⇒ croustades garnished of sauté young partridge fillets, sauté boletus, plus
    poached quenelles made of partridge meat, cream and egg; covered with a sauce of
    partridge stock, thickened of foie gras
Perdreau en pistache ⇒ young partridge stuffed with a mixing of its liver, crumbs, ham, parsley,
    garlic and egg; braised in butter, with diced ham, herbs, white wine, stock, tomato
    purée and garlic
Perdreaux en vessie ⇒ young partridge stuffed with a forcemeat of sausage meat, its liver, crumbs,
    cream, thyme, port and cognac; then wrapped in pork bladders, and cooked in veal
    pot-au-feu
Perdreaux farçis à la gelée ⇒ boned young partridge stuffed with a forcemeat of game, plus a bit of
    foie gras, a truffle, spices, and cognac; served frozen, coated in the cooking jelly
Perdreau Monselet ⇒ young partridge stuffed with a forcemeat of foie gras and truffle, braised in
    butter with artichoke hearts and a culinary stuffing of truffle; served flamed in cognac
Perdrigon *-[prune]-* ⇒ variety of plum
Perdrix ⇒ partridge *< uncountable >*
Perdrix *-[coulemelle]-* ⇒ parasol mushroom
Perdrix au chou ⇒ stew of cabbage, streaky bacon, onion, clove, stock and partridge
Perdrix rouge ⇒ red-legged partridge *< uncountable >*
Périgourdine *(à la ...)* ⇒ with ...
    - avec sauce périgourdine ⇒ voir texte, sometimes added of foie gras
    - ou avec sauce périgueux ⇒ voir texte, sometimes added of foie gras

- **autres apprêts de la cuisine du Périgord avec leur recette propre** ⇒ ... in local recipe from the Périgord

Périgueux ⇒ nom d'une sauce pour petites pièces de boucherie, volailles, gibiers, bouchées, etc, qui sont dits « Périgueux » ou « à la Périgourdine »

Péritoine de mouton ⇒ lamb caul fat

Péritoine de porc ou toilette ⇒ pig caul fat

Perles d'argent -[dragées]- ⇒ dragées

Perles de Florence -[sagou]- ⇒ sago fecula

Pernand-vergelesses -[côtes de Beaune]- ⇒ Burgundy wines from Côtes de Nuits

Pernod ⇒ Pernod

Perrier ⇒ popular brand of sparkling mineral water OR Perrier water

Perroquet -[anisette]- ⇒ anisette added of mint

Perry ⇒ perry

Persane (à la ...)

    a) **côtelettes de mouton ou d'agneau** ⇒ lamb chops garnished with sliced aubergines sautéed in oil, fried onions, tomatoes and capsicums cooked in their own liquid

      - **noisettes de mouton ou d'agneau** ⇒ noisettes of lamb garnished with sliced aubergines sautéed in oil, fried onions, tomatoes and capsicums cooked in their own liquid

    b) **pilaf** ⇒ pilaf made of diced mutton and rice simmered in stock with seasoning, moistened of melted mutton grease

Persicot ⇒ persicot

Persil ⇒ parsley < *uncountable* >

Persil arabe -[coriandre]- ⇒ coriander

Persil chinois -[coriandre]- ⇒ coriander

Persil en branche ⇒ parsley < *uncountable* >

Persil frit ⇒ fried parsley

Persil haché ⇒ chopped parsley

Persil noir -[maceron]- ⇒ alexanders or horse-parsley

Persillade

    1) **général** ⇒ ... added with a mixing of parsley and chopped garlic

    2) **carré d'agneau persillé ou tomates farçies à la provençale ou escargots de bourgogne** ⇒ ... covered with a mixing of parsley, chopped garlic and crumbs

    3) **persillées pommes de terre ou tomates sautées additionnées de persillade et de persil frais ciselé** ⇒ ... with a mixing of parsley and chopped garlic added

      - **préparation ou le persil haché entre en proportions importantes « jambon persillé »** ⇒ ... added of chopped parsley

Persillade de boeuf ⇒ sauté cold beef, served sprinkled with a hash of parsley and garlic

Persillé (e ...)

    - **assaisonnment** ⇒ seasoned with chopped parsley

    - **fromage** ⇒ green spotted

    - **viande de boeuf** ⇒ spotted with fat or marbled

Persillé -[fromage]- ⇒ veined cheese

    - **persillé des aravis ou de thones ou du grand bornand** ⇒ veined goat's milk cheese < *nom* >

    - **persillé du mont cenis** ⇒ veined goat's and cow's milk cheese < *nom* >

Persillé -[fromage-Savoie]-

    - **général** ⇒ blue cheese

    - **persillé des Aravis ou de Thones ou du Grand St Bernard** ⇒ blue goat's milk cheese

    - **persillé du Mont Cenis** ⇒ blue cheese from a mixing of cow's milk and goat's milk

Persillée -[viande]- ⇒ marbled meat

Personne *(s ...)* *-[nombre]-* ⇒ for one person or for ... persons
Pescajounes *-[Quercy]-* ⇒ wheat pancakes garnished with fruits
Pet de nonne ⇒ small choux-pastry fritter, sprinkled of icing sugar
Pétafine ⇒ preparation of cheese, leaven, milk, oil, high quality cognac, aniseed and pepper
Pétales de roses ⇒ rose petals
Petchia *-[Russe]-* ⇒ calf trotters in jelly
Peteram ⇒ stew of lamb tripe, lamb trotters, ham, calf intestine, plus pork fat, and potatoes; cooked in white wine with garlic and aromatics
Pétillant *-[vin]-* ⇒ slightly sparkling wine
Petit beurre ⇒ petit beurre biscuit or tea-biscuit made with butter and flour
Petit déjeuner ⇒ breakfast
Petit déjeuner complet ⇒ continental breakfast
Petit-duc *-[garniture pour petites pièces de boucherie]-* ⇒ ... with a garnish of tartlets, filled of mashed poultry in cream, asparagus tips and truffle lamellas
Petit-four ⇒ petit-four
Petit gris *-[escargot]-* ⇒ garden snail
Petit lait ⇒ whey *< uncountable >*
Petit lisieux *-[livarot]-* ⇒ Norman cow's milk cheese with a brown crust, surrounded by reed's thongs
Petit pain ⇒ roll
Petit pâté de béziers ⇒ forcemeat of lamb kidney suet, brown sugar, mutton meat, and cedrate; wrapped in short pastry
Petit pot de chocolat ⇒ chocolate mousse served in pot
Petit poussin *-[cuisine]-* ⇒ young chicken
Petit provençal *-[petit pois]-* ⇒ variety of pea
Petit salé ⇒ streaky bacon
Petit suisse ⇒ petit suisse
Petite huile *-[œillette]-* ⇒ poppy-seed oil
Petite joubarbe ⇒ stonecrop
Petite lingue *-[lingue]-* ⇒ ling
Petite lépiote *-[coulemelle]-* ⇒ parasol mushroom
Petite marmite ⇒ dish of beef meat, ox tail, poultry, marrow bone and vegetables, plus balls of cabbage; served with grated cheese and fried croutons
Petite marmite parisienne ⇒ individual pot-au-feu, sometimes served with grated cheese, plus sippets topped of bone marrow
Petite rascasse *-[brune]-* ⇒ scorpion fish or sea-scorpion or short-spined sea scorpion or long-spined sea scorpion
Petite roussette *-[poisson]-* ⇒ lesser spotted dogfish
Petites *-[tripous]-* ⇒ braised packets made with stomach of mutton, calf trotters, and aromatics
Petites bouchées ⇒ bits of sponge fingers steeped in custard and kirsch, then rolled in
Petites fondues à la bourguignonne ⇒ fried cheese squares, served as a first course
Petites pièces de boucherie
 - **côte d'agneau** ⇒ lamb chop or lamb cutlet
 - **noisette d'agneau** ⇒ small and round piece of lamb or noisette of lamb
 - **escalope de veau** ⇒ veal escalope
 - **côte de veau** ⇒ veal cutlet
 - **ris de veau** ⇒ calf sweetbread
 - **suprême de volaille** ⇒ chicken served in supreme sauce
Petites pièces de venaison
 - **côtes** ⇒ venison chops
 - **noisettes** ⇒ noisettes of venison

- **escalopes** ⇒ venison escalopes

Petites timbales à l'épicurienne ⇒ dariole filled with a culinary stuffing of lamb sweetbread, truffle, pickled oxtongue, and mashed mushrooms, then covered with rice cooked in fat; served turned out, with tomato sauce

Petites timbales à la piémontaise ⇒ dariole filled with a culinary stuffing of pickled oxtongue, and risotto added with white truffle

Petites timbales bagration ⇒ dariole filled with macaroni thickened of cream, plus a culinary stuffing of truffles and pickled oxtongue; overturned after baking, and covered with supreme sauce

Petites timballes beauvilliers ⇒ dariole garnished with hollowed out brioche, plus a culinary stuffing of white meat thickened with a sauce based on poultry stock; then topped of asparagus tips braised in butter

Petites timbales d'entrée ⇒ dariole filled with a culinary stuffing or a forcemeat, then baked; served overturned on fried croutons or artichoke hearts

Petites timbales St Hubert ⇒ timbale filled with pickled oxtongue, plus a culinary stuffing of game meat, truffle and mushroom; served overturned with a sauce based on a mixture of diced vegetables and ham, cooked in vinegar and white wine

Petits fours à l'ananas ⇒ petits-fours made of pineapple, kirsch and angelica

Petits fours à la pâte d'amande ⇒ petits-fours made of almond powder, sugar and white of eggs

Petits fours ananas ⇒ petits-fours made of almond paste, chopped preserved pineapple and white of egg

Petits fours artichauts ⇒ petits-fours of almond past, coloured in green

Petits fours au café ⇒ petits-fours made of almond paste, sugar, white of egg and coffee extract

Petits fours aux amandes ⇒ petits-fours made of almond powder, sugar, preserved cherries, angelica, white of eggs, vanilla and milk

Petits fours avelinettes ⇒ petits-fours made of hazelnut powder, almond powder and sugar; covered with chocolate powder

Petits fours cerisettes ⇒ petits-fours made of almond paste, chopped preserved cherries and white of egg

Petits fours duchesse ⇒ petits-fours made of butter, sugar, egg-yolks, flour and yeast; topped with preserved cherry, and sprinkled of sugar

Petits fours eugénie ⇒ petits fours made of almond paste and orange peel, coloured in pink

Petits fours massepains ⇒ petits-fours of whipped white of eggs, cream, rice, sugar and almond powder

Petits fours massillons ⇒ petit four of sugared pastry boat, filled with almond paste and flavoured of vanilla

Petits fours michettes ⇒ petits-fours made of hazelnut powder, sugar and white of egg, topped by a hazelnut

Petits fours napolitains ⇒ petits-fours made of almond paste, sugar and white of eggs; coloured green or pink

Petits fours sachas ⇒ petits-fours made of almond paste, bits of angelica and chopped almonds

Petits fours souvarov ⇒ petit-four of two small flat cakes, soldered by redcurrant jelly

Petits fours tourons ⇒ a sweet or candy of almond paste with pistachios, hazelnuts and crystallized fruit

Petits gâteaux au maïs ⇒ small flat-cakes of corn flour, wheat flour, butter and sugar

Petits gâteaux fondants ⇒ small flat-cakes of butter, sugar, almond powder, eggs, fecula, vanilla and yeast

Petits janots -[*Languedoc*]- ⇒ small pastries from Languedoc

Petits macarons ⇒ small macaroons of almond powder, sugar and white of eggs

Petits pains à l'orange ⇒ rolls pink coloured, made of almond paste, apple paste, orange peel, and egg

Petits pains aux amandes ⇒ rolls made of flour, butter, almond powder, egg, sugar, cinnamon, milk and yeast

Petits pains d'épices ronds ⇒ rolls of gingerbread

Petits pains soufflés aux amandes ⇒ rolls made of flour, butter, lemon peel, sugar, eggs and yeast; covered with chopped almonds

Petits pois ⇒ pea

- pluriel ⇒ peas

Petits pois à l'anglaise ⇒ boiled peas served apart with butter

Petits pois à la bonne femme ⇒ peas cooked in butter, with diced streaky bacon, onions and consommé

Petits pois à la crème ⇒ boiled peas moistened with cream, and sprinkled of chopped herbs

Petits pois à la fermière ⇒ peas braised in butter with carrots, onions, lettuce chiffonade, and chervil

Petits pois à la française ⇒ young peas in butter, with lettuce, parsley, chervil and baby onions

Petits pois à la menthe ⇒ peas boiled with mint leaves, then mixed of butter; served in timbales, sprinkled of mint leaves

Petits pois au beurre ⇒ boiled peas mixed with butter and herbs

Petits pois au jambon à la languedocienne ⇒ peas braised in goose fat, with onion, ham, granulated sugar, and aromatics

Petits pots corinthiens ⇒ whipped cream, plus sugar and raisins macerated in rum

Petits raviolis pour potage ⇒ ravioli stuffed with a forcemeat of poultry livers or sweetbreads

- potage ou consommé au ravioli ⇒ soup or consommé added of; ravioli stuffed with a forcemeat of poultry livers or sweetbreads

Petits sablés bicolores ⇒ small shortcake made of flour, butter, sugar, cinnamon powder, and vanilla powder

Pétoncle ⇒ variegated scallop

Petticoat tails *-[GB]-* ⇒ petticoat tails

Pézize ⇒ cup fungi

Pezizes orangées Ali-Bab ⇒ cup fungi steeped in hot milk, vanilla flavoured; served covered with a liquor of sugar, orange peel, curaçao and butter

Pfefferkuchen *-[pain d'épice]-* ⇒ peppered gingerbread

Pflutters ⇒ poached balls of mashed potatoes, eggs, flour, and nutmeg; served with butter cooked lightly

Pharaonne *-[Quercy]-* ⇒ roasted guinea fowl, laid on a canapé covered with foie gras

Philadelphia pepperhot *-[Amérique du nord]-* ⇒ spicy ragout

Pho *-[Vietnam]-* ⇒ spicy soup garnished of noodles, vegetables, and meat lamellas

Pholade ⇒ pholas or stone-borer

Pholiote ⇒ changeable agaric

Pholiote changeante ⇒ changeable agaric

Pholiote pivoulade ⇒ almond agaric

Phoque *-[huile]-* ⇒ seal oil

Physalis *-[alkékenge]-* ⇒ physalis or winter-cherry

Pibales ⇒ baby eels or young eels or elvers

Pic St Loup *-[côteaux du Languedoc]-* ⇒ quality red wine or rosé from Côteaux du Languedoc

Picanchâgne ⇒ pears wrapped in bread dough and baked

Picardie

    - pâté de canard d'Amiens ⇒ voir texte

    - colvert à la picarde « cuit en casserole et garni de pommes fruits sautées avec des dés de foie de canard » ⇒ mallard cooked in casserole, then garnished with sauté fruits, and diced duck liver

    - sarcelle ⇒ voir texte

    - grives ⇒ voir texte

    - outarde ⇒ voir texte

    - Fromages ⇒ maroilles, rollot, guerbigny, manicamp, st-winocq

- daussade « **fromage blanc au vinaigre agrémenté de fines herbes** » ⇒ soft white cheese added of vinegar and herbs
- **Pâtisserie** ⇒ rabottes, taliburs, gateau « battu », tartes au riz ou aux pruneaux, chiques de berck, mignonnettes sablées de péronne, gaillettes, briquettes et brindinettes de Douai, tuiles au chocolat

Piccalilli ⇒ piccalilli

Piccata ⇒ small veal escalopes fried in butter

Piccata de veau aux aubergines et tomates fraîches ⇒ slices of veal fillet and aubergines sautéed in butter, plus onions, and capsicums braised in butter; served with crushed tomatoes

Pickelfleisch à la juive ⇒ boneless brisket of beef kneaded with salt, and saltpetre, then steeped in pickles of brown sugar, juniper berries, pimentos, thyme and laurel, then larded and cooked with carrots; served cold with gherkins, seasoning and mustard

Pickelsteiner Fleisch -*[Allemagne]*- ⇒ ragout of beef, lamb, pork and veal

Pickles ⇒ pickles

Pickles de choux fleur et de tomate ⇒ cauliflower and tomato pickles

Picodon ⇒ goat's milk cheese with a crust coloured blue, yellow or red, according to the refining

Picoussel ⇒ buckwheat cake flavoured with herbs, and garnished of plums

Picpoul-de-pinet ⇒ white wine from Languedoc

Pie -*[tourte]*- ⇒ pie

Pie à la rhubarbe ⇒ rhubarb pie

Pie au poires ⇒ pear pie

Pie au poulet ⇒ chicken pie

Pièce de boeuf ⇒ large cut of beef from the top of the rump

Pièce de boeuf braisée ⇒ rump of beef studded with lardoons, then marinated in wine, aromatics

Pièce de boeuf braisée à l'ancienne ⇒ braised rump of beef carved in casing; filled of thin slices of beef and pickled ox tongue, thickened with the gravy added of Madeira

Pièce de boeuf braisée à la bourgeoise ⇒ rump of beef marinated in white wine, then braised with calf trotter, carrots and onions

Pièce de boeuf braisée à la bourguignonne ⇒ rump of beef marinated in eau de vie, then braised in red wine

Pièce de boeuf braisée à la mode ⇒ rump of beef marinated in red wine, then braised with calf trotter, carrots and onions

Pièce de boeuf pochée ⇒ rump of beef cooked as a pot-au-feu

Pièce montée
- **ornement** ⇒ tiered cake
- **mariage** ⇒ wedding cake

Pièces parées de tranche grasse -*[bœuf]*- ⇒ beef olives

Pied ⇒ trotter

Pied bleu -*[champignon]*- ⇒ tricholoma mushroom

Pied de cheval -*[huître]*- ⇒ oyster

Pied de cochon ⇒ pig trotter

Pied de coq -*[clavaire]*- ⇒ tiny yellow hands

Pied de mouton -*[champignon]*- ⇒ pied de mouton mushroom or hedgehog fungi or spreading hydnum

Pied de mutton -*[viande]*- ⇒ lamb trotter

Pied de porc ⇒ pig trotter

Pied de taureau ⇒ bullfoot

Pied de veau ⇒ veal's trotter or calf trotter

Pied rouge -*[golmote]*- ⇒ blusher

Pieds de cendrillon -*[crépinette]*- ⇒ small seasoned flat sausages of truffle and pork trotter

Pieds de mouton à la poulette ⇒ timbales of boned lamb trotters and mushrooms, cooked in stock; covered with a sauce of the cooking stock, thickened with cream, egg-yolks, butter, lemon juice and chopped parsley

Pieds de mouton à la rouennaise ⇒ braised lamb trotters, boned and stuffed with a hash of onions, in butter and parsley; then coated with crumbs and fried

Pieds de mouton à la Vignard ⇒ boned cooked lamb totters, marinated in wine vinegar, mustard and pepper; served with mayonnaise

Pieds de mouton à la vinaigrette ⇒ bits of boned cooked lamb totters, seasoned with french dressing added of chopped herbs; served with chopped early spring onions

Pieds de porc à la vinaigrette *-[Quercy]-* ⇒ cooked pig trotters, served with french dressing

Pieds de porc en crépine ⇒ crépinettes of pig trotter, sausage meat, spices and cognac; coated of melted butter and crumbs, then grilled

Pieds de porc grillés ⇒ cooked pig trotters, coated with pork fat and crumbs, then grilled; served with mustard, and ...

   - purée de pommes de terre ⇒ ... mashed potatoes

   - purée de céleri ⇒ ... mashed celeriac

   - frites ⇒ ... chips

Pieds de porc Ste Ménéhould *-[ou pieds de cochon]-* ⇒ pig's trotters cooked slowly with onion and herbs, then covered with breadcrumbs and grilled

Pieds de veau à la custine ⇒ kind of flat sausages made of calf trotters, chopped shallots, chopped mushrooms and lemon juice; then browned in butter

Pieds de veau à la tartare ⇒ bits of calf trotter meat, coated with flour, egg, and crumbs; then fried in oil, and served with tartare sauce

Pieds et paquets de la Pomme ⇒ bits of lamb's tripe stuffed with a hash of ham, lamb's caul, garlic and parsley; cooked slowly with lamb trotters, in lardoons, leek, onions, sliced carrot, crushed tomatoes, white wine and meat stock

Piémontaise *(à la ...)*

   1) garniture des volailles, pièces de boucherie et poissons ⇒ ... with risotto served ...

   - en darioles ⇒ in dariole

   - en timbales ⇒ in timbales

   - en croquettes ⇒ in croquettes

   2) autres plats ⇒ with polenta or ravioli or macaroni

   3) patisseries ⇒ pastries based on hazelnuts

Piérogues ou Pierogui ⇒ small pie in pastry case

Pierre sur haute *-[fourme]-* ⇒ type of cheese from Auvergne OR blue cow's milk cheese

Piétrain *-[porc]-* ⇒ breed of pork

Pieuvre ⇒ octopus

Pigeon ⇒ pigeon or dove

Pigeon grillé en crapaudine ⇒ pigeon split in two, coated with a mixing of olive oil, garlic, herbs, and pepper; then grilled

Pigeons en compote ⇒ pigeons filled with juniper berries and marc, then braised in butter with onions, lardoons, mushrooms, white wine and poultry stock; served covered with the cooking juice

Pigeons farçis aux pointes d'asperges ⇒ pigeons stuffed with a forcemeat of cushion of veal, pork fat, calf sweetbread, foie gras, truffle and egg-yolk, then cooked; served with a garnish of asparagus tips and cream, au gratin, then covered with the cooking juice thickened of vermouth

Pigeonneau ⇒ young pigeon

Pigeonneau à la minute ⇒ young pigeon split in two, sautéed in butter with chopped onions; covered with the cooking juice added of cognac, meat stock, and parsley

Pigeonneaux aux petits pois ⇒ young pigeons baked in butter, with lardoons, onions, white wine and peas

Pigeonneaux en papillottes ⇒ halved young pigeons laid on a mixing of chopped mushrooms and ham, then wrapped in greaseproof paper and baked

Pignolat *-[bonbon]-* ⇒ sweet

Pignon ⇒ pine kernel or kernel of fir-cone

Pignon *-[emploi]-* ⇒ rappel pour ordre sans traduction

   - **avec d'autres fruits secs** ⇒ texte

   - **pâtisserie** ⇒ macarons, biscuits, gâteaux secs

   - **cuisine** ⇒ texte

   - **Inde, Turquie** ⇒ avec riz, moules farçies, farces de volailles

   - **Liban** ⇒ boulettes de mouton

   - **Italie** ⇒ sauces pour les pâtes, farces de poissons, omelette, poulet sauté

   - **Provence** ⇒ charcuterie, tourte aux bettes niçoise, salade de crudités à l'huile d'olive

Piirakka *-[Finlande]-* ⇒ stuffing of rice, and fish; served with melted butter, and hard-boiled eggs

Pilaf ⇒ pilaf < *uncountable* >

Pilaf de crustacés ⇒ pilaf added of crustaceae

Pilaf de volaille ⇒ pilaf moulded in crown, and garnished with bits of chicken braised in butter, white wine, stock, tomato sauce, crushed garlic, and herbs

Pilaf garni ⇒ pilaf moulded in crown, and garnished of ...

   - **foie gras et truffe** ⇒ ... foie gras escalopes and truffles, sautéed in butter and madeira

   - **foies de volaille** ⇒ ... poultry livers and mushrooms, sautéed in butter with garlic, shallot and parsley

   - **rognons de mouton** ⇒ ... lamb kidneys sautéed in butter, sprinkled of the gravy added with white wine

   - **poisson en sauce dorade au vin blanc** ⇒ ... dorado in white wine

   - **dorade à l'américaine** ⇒ ... dorado with lobster lamellas, and lobster sauce

   - **thon en daube** ⇒ ... braised tunny

   - **lotte à l'américaine** ⇒ ... sliced angler cooked in a sauce of Norway lobsters, tomatoes, shallots, garlic, tarragon, cognac, and white wine

Pilau ⇒ pilau

Pilaw ⇒ pilau

Pilchard ⇒ tinned sardine or herring, with a sauce of oil and tomato

Pilé *(e ...)* ⇒ pounded or crushed

Pili-pili ⇒ African seasoning

Pilon *-[volaille]-* ⇒ drumstick

Pilpil ⇒ previously cooked whole-wheat seeds

Pils ⇒ beer

Pilsen ⇒ beer

Pilsener *-[bière]-* ⇒ Pilsener or Pilsner

Piment ⇒ red pepper or pimento, uncountable, or capsicum

Piment au vinaigre ⇒ capsicums preserved in vinegar

Piment de cayenne ⇒ cayenne capsicum

Piment de la Jamaïque ⇒ chilli

Piment de la Martinique ou des Antilles ⇒ chilli

Piment de La Réunion ⇒ Reunion capsicum

Piment doux ⇒ pepper, uncountable, or capsicum

Piment du Brézil ⇒ Brazilian capsicum

Piment enragé ⇒ cayenne pepper

Piment oiseau ⇒ cayenne pepper

Piment rouge ⇒ chilli pepper or hot red pepper
Piment Thaïlandais ⇒ Thai capsicum
Piment vert ⇒ green capsicum
Pimenté *(e ...)*
  - adj ⇒ hot
  - verbe ⇒ to put chillis in
Pimprenelle ⇒ burnet
Pince *-[crabe-écrevisse-homard]-* ⇒ claw
Pineau
  a) **pineau des Charentes** ⇒ unripe grape juice added of cognac
  b) **pineau de cidre** ⇒ unripe apple juice added of calvados
  c) **floc de Gascogne** ⇒ aperitif made of fermented must, and armagnac
Pineau des charentes ⇒ unripe grape juice added of cognac
Pinède *-[bolet]-* ⇒ boletus
Pink *-[saumon]-* ⇒ pink salmon
Pink marsh *-[pamplemousse et pomélo]-* ⇒ grapefruit
Pinot meunier *-[vin]-* ⇒ quality rosé wine from Orleans area
Pintade ⇒ guinea-hen or guinea fowl < *pluriel inchangé* >
Pintadeau ⇒ guinea-chick
Pintadeau farçi Jean Cocteau ⇒ guinea-chick stuffed with a forcemeat of crumbs, eggs, aromatics, gizzard and liver; then braised in butter, cognac, carrots, onions, garlic and white wine; served with grilled polony, grilled white pudding, plus sauté apples
Pintadeaux aux marrons ⇒ halved guinea-chicks braised in butter, with shallots, Burgundy red wine, herbs, and chestnuts; served with the cooking juice thickened of butter
Piochons *-[Anjou]-* ⇒ green cabbages
Piononos *-[Antilles]-* ⇒ slices of bananas, stuffed and fried
Pioularde *-[agaric]-* ⇒ honey fungus or bootlace fungus
Pipe en sucre *-[bonbon]-* ⇒ sweet
Piper nigrum *-[poivre]-* ⇒ pepper
Pipérade *-[poivrons]-* ⇒ capsicums, tomato, garlic and oil cooked in their own liquid ...
  - en omelette ⇒ ... mixed in an omelette
  - oeufs brouillés ⇒ served with scrambled eggs
  - braisés à l'huile ⇒ capsicums, tomato and garlic, braised in oil served with fried slices of ham
  - braisés à la graisse d'oie ⇒ capsicums, tomato and garlic, braised in goose fat served with fried slices of ham
Pipo crème *-[fromage]-* ⇒ Pipo crème
Piquant *(e ...)* ⇒ spicy or hot or indeed piquant
Pique-aousel *-[picoussel]-* ⇒ buckwheat cake flavoured with herbs, and garnished of plums
Piquer ⇒ to stud with
  - piqué ⇒ studded with
Piquette ⇒ low quality wine
Piranha ⇒ piranha
Pire *-[sauce, Poitou]-* ⇒ pork lung and liver, simmered with onions, shallots, red wine and aromatics
Pirogi ⇒ small pie in pastry case
Pirojki ⇒ pirozhki
Pirojki au fromage ⇒ pirozhki filled with a mixing of grated cheese, butter, nutmeg, pepper and eggs
Pirojki moscovite ⇒ pirozhki filled with a hash of fish, added of sturgeon bone-marrow, hard-boiled eggs and pepper
Pirojkis Caucasiens ⇒ pirozhkis filled with béchamel sauce, added of grated cheese and chopped mushrooms

Pirojkis feuilletés ⇒ pirozhkis in puff-pastry filled with ...
- **gibier** ⇒ ... a hash of game, added of chopped hard-boiled eggs, and rice
- **poisson** ⇒ ... a hash of fish, added of chopped hard-boiled eggs, and rice

Pirojok ⇒ small pie in pastry case
Pirot ⇒ sauté bits of kid, seasoned with garlic and sorrel
Pis -*[bovin, etc ...]*- ⇒ udder
Pis
    a) **boucherie** -*[poitrine, milieu de poitrine tendron, flanchet]*- ⇒ brisket
    b) **vache** ⇒ udder
Pisquette -*[Antilles]*- ⇒ tiny fish
Pissaladière ⇒ onion tart with a garnish of anchovy fillets plus black olives or pissaladière or pizza
Pissalat ⇒ seasoning of anchovy purée with clove, thyme, laurel and pepper, kneaded in olive oil
Pissenlit ⇒ dandelion
Pissoco -*[champignon]*- ⇒ lurid boletus
Pistache -*[apprêt, Languedoc]*-
- **pistache de mouton ou mouton en pistache, mouton mariné** ⇒ marinated lamb cooked with garlic
- **ou mouton braisé** ⇒ braised lamb cooked with garlic
- **perdreau** ⇒ young partridge cooked with garlic
- **pigeon** ⇒ pigeon cooked with garlic
- **pistache de st gaudens** ⇒ lamb stew added of garlic and haricot beans

Pistache -*[graine]*- ⇒ pistachio nut
Pistache de terre -*[arachide]*- ⇒ peanut
Pistil ⇒ pistil
Pistole -*[pruneau]*- ⇒ dried plum
Pistolet -*[pain]*- ⇒ small loaf of bread
Pistou -*[assaisonnement]*- ⇒ seasoning made of basil and garlic pounded into a paste and mixed with oil
Pistou -*[soupe]*- ⇒ soup of vegetables and vermicelli seasoned with basil and garlic paste
Pithiviers -*[fromage]*- ⇒ cow's milk cheese refined under hay
Pithiviers
- **gâteau crème d'amande** ⇒ large puff-pastry filled with a custard of eggs, almonds, sugar and butter
- **gâteau aux fruits** ⇒ large puff-pastry filled with preserved fruits, then covered of fondant
- **cuisine** ⇒ large puff-pastry filled with sweetbreads in cream, or kidneys, or poultry liver in sauce, etc ...

Pitt i panna -*[Suède]*- ⇒ diced potatoes and diced meat sautéed with onion, then sprinkled of parsley; served with egg
Pitta -*[Grèce]*- ⇒ pie of spinach and ewe cheese; served with yoghourt
Pivoularde -*[pholiote]*- ⇒ changeable agaric
Pizza ⇒ pizza
Pizza Mario ⇒ pizza garnished with a paste of mussels, chopped shallots, pounded anchovies, and crushed tomatoes; decorated with anchovy fillets and black olives
Pizzaiola (*Alla ...*)
- **boeuf** ⇒ beef sautéed in oil, then simmered with tomatoes, garlic and herbs
- **veau** ⇒ veal sautéed in oil, then simmered with tomatoes, garlic and herbs

Placali -*[Afrique noire]*- ⇒ African dish based on manioc and bananas, plus a spicy sauce
Plaisir ⇒ wafers rolled into a cone
Planetas -*[dragées]*- ⇒ Spanish dragées
Planked meat -*[Amérique du Nord]*- ⇒ planked meat

Plant du blanc *-[poire]-* ⇒ variety of pear for perry
Plant roux *-[poire]-* ⇒ variety of pear for perry
Plantain ⇒ plantain
Plante *-[liqueur]-* ⇒ plant
Plante potagère ⇒ vegetable
Planter's *-[cocktail]-* ⇒ cocktail of rum, lemon juice, orange juice
Plaque chauffante ⇒ hotplate
Plaquemine *-[kaki]-* ⇒ persimmon fruit
Plat *-[Menu]-* ⇒ dish or course
Plat de côte *-[général]-* ⇒ best rib of ... or middle rib of ...
Plat de côte couvert ⇒ middle ribs or best ribs
Plat de côte couvert *-[pot au feu]-* ⇒ top ribs
Plat de côte de porc ⇒ Barbecue spareribs
Plat de côte découvert *-[pot au feu]-* ⇒ middle or best rib
Plat de côtes découvert ⇒ back ribs
Plat de poitrine de boeuf avec partie de flanchet, désossée ⇒ boneless fore 1/4 flank
Plat de poitrine de boeuf, avec partie flanchet ⇒ fore 1/4 flank
Plat de poitrine de porc en tranches doubles ⇒ belly slices double « boneless »
Plat de poitrine de veau « flanchet » ⇒ thin flank of veal or toprump of veal
Plat de résistance ⇒ main dish
Plat du jour ⇒ the dish of the day or today's special
Plat garni ⇒ plate filled with ...
Plate *-[huître]-* ⇒ common oyster or flat oyster
Plate de Chateaurenard *-[tomate]-* ⇒ variety of tomato
Plateau ⇒ tray or platter < *US seulement, GB archaïque* >
Plateau d'huîtres ⇒ plate of oysters
Plateau de fromages
    - **sur menu** ⇒ choice of cheeses
    - **language** ⇒ cheese-board
Plateau de fruits de mer ⇒ dish of various seafood or plate of seafood
Plats de viande au choix ⇒ a choice of two meat dishes or a choice of two meat courses
Platschinken *-[Autriche]-* ⇒ stuffed pancakes
Pleurote
    - **pleurote en coquille** ⇒ oyster cap
    - **pleurote du panicaut** ⇒ gloomy mushroom
Pleurote du panicaut ⇒ gloomy mushroom
Pleurote en forme d'huître ⇒ oyster mushroom
Plie ⇒ plaice < *pluriel inchangé* >
Plie à la florentine ⇒ plaice cooked in stock and white wine, then laid on spinach; covered with béchamel sauce added of egg-yolks and gruyère, grated cheese, and melted butter, then glazed
Plie franche ⇒ plaice < *pluriel inchangé* >
Plisson ⇒ milk boiled down, and sugared
Plockwurst *-[saucisse]-* ⇒ sausage of beef and pork
Plombières ⇒ chilled dessert based on egg-custard, almond milk, whipped cream added of preserved fruits macerated in kirsch
Pluches ⇒ bits of « cerfeuil » chervil, « estragon » tarragon, « persil » parsley, etc ...
Plum *-[cake ou pudding]-*
    a) **avec raisins secs** ⇒ plum-cake

b) avec fruits secs et épices ⇒ plum-pudding
Plum-cake ⇒ baked cake made of butter, sugar, eggs, orange peel, raisins, flour and rum
Plum-pudding ⇒ plum-pudding
Plumer -*[volailles]*- ⇒ to pluck
Plus ⇒ plus
Pluvier ⇒ plover
Poche à douille ⇒ forcing-bag
Poche pez ⇒ barnacle
Poché *(e ...)* ⇒ poached < *v.t adjectif* >
Pochouse ⇒ matelote of burbot, plus other freshwater fishes in white wine and butter
Pœchon -*[poisson]*- ⇒ fish
Poêlé ⇒ fried
Poêlée -*[sarrasin]*- ⇒ buckwheat porridge
Poe meia -*[Tahiti]*- ⇒ sweet of banana, sprinkled of sugar, and moistened of cream
Pogne ⇒ brioche filled with crystallized fruits or redcurrant jelly
Pogne de Romans ⇒ brioche added of bitter orange tree extract, granulated sugar and eggs
Pognon ⇒ brioche filled with crystallized fruits or redcurrant jelly
Point *(à ...)*
    - **viande rôtie** ⇒ done to a turn
    - **steak grillé** ⇒ medium
    - **fruit** ⇒ ripe
Pointe de culotte -*[culotte]*-
    - **boeuf** ⇒ rump of beef
    - **veau** ⇒ veal's thick end of loin
    - **mouton** ⇒ saddle
Pointe de porc ⇒ pork end of loin
Pointes d'asperges au beurre ou à la crème
    a) seules ⇒ asparagus tips added of melted butter or cream
    b) avec ⇒ asparagus tips added of melted butter or cream; served with ...
       - **en garniture pour Oeufs pochés** ⇒ ... poached eggs
       - **Oeufs mollets** ⇒ ... soft-boiled eggs
       - **Oeufs brouillés** ⇒ ... scrambled eggs
       - **apprêts de poisson** ⇒ ... fish
       - **petites pièces de boucherie** ⇒ ... voir dénomination
       - **des ris de veau** ⇒ ... calf sweetbread
       - **une poularde** ⇒ ... fattened pullet
       - **un gibier** ⇒ ... game < *ou nom anglais du gibier* >
Pointes d'asperges pour garnitures froides
    a) pour garnitures ⇒ ...; with a garnish of ... < *ajouter une variante* >
    b) pour salades ⇒ ... salad added with ... < *ajouter une variante* >
    c) variantes avec vinaigrette ⇒ ... asparagus tips in french dressing
       - **avec mayonnaise** ⇒ ... asparagus tips in mayonnaise
       - **avec gelée de viande** ⇒ ... asparagus tips thickened of meat jelly
Poirat ⇒ pie garnished with pears macerated in eau de vie, plus cream
Poire -*[fruit]*- ⇒ pear
Poire -*[viande]*- ⇒ steak meat
Poires à la crème ⇒ pieces of pear cooked in a syrup of sugar and vanilla, covered with custard

Poire à la duchesse ⇒ tartlets filled with a mixture of vanilla ice cream and diced pineapple macerated in kirsch, topped with halved pears in syrup; covered by a zabaglione of sugar, egg-yolks, kirsch and maraschino, then sprinkled of grilled almonds

Poires belle-hélène ⇒ pears cooked in syrup and accompanied with vanilla ice-cream, plus melted chocolate

Poires Brillat-Savarin ⇒ pears halved and hollowed out, filled with Roquefort, covered of cream, and sprinkled of paprika

Poires condé ⇒ poached halved pear laid on rice, and apricot sauce

Poire de cydonie *-[autre nom pour le coing]-* ⇒ quince

Poire de terre *-[autre nom pour topinambour]-* ⇒ Jerusalem artichoke

Poire des Indes *-[autre nom pour la goyave]-* ⇒ guava

Poires impératrice ⇒ rice cooked in milk, garnished of poached pears, and covered by redcurrant jelly with kirsch

Poires Joinville ⇒ crown of baked custard, made with milk, vanilla, eggs and granulated sugar; garnished with pears in syrup, and decorated of sugared whipped cream; served with a sauce of apricot and kirsch or pear eau de vie

Poires séchées ⇒ dried pears

Poires sur compote de pommes ⇒ slices of pears cooked in syrup on a laying of apple compote; covered with redcurrant jelly

Poires tapées au four ⇒ pears cooked in the oven and sprinkled with sugar

Poires Wanamaker ⇒ slices of sponge cake moistened of kirsch, and covered with compote of pear added of redcurrant jelly, then topped with half a pear; served sometime with a zabaglione in kirsch

Poire william ⇒ variety of pear

Poireau ⇒ leek

Poireaux à l'anglaise ⇒ boiled leeks served ...

- **avec persil et beurre** ⇒ ... sprinkled with chopped parsley; plus butter apart
- **arrosés de beurre fondu** ⇒ ... sprinkled of melted butter, and lemon juice
- **arrosés de crème** ⇒ ... sprinkled of peppered cream

Poireaux à l'huile et au vinaigre ⇒ boiled leeks, seasoned with french dressing

Poireaux à la béchamel ⇒ leeks braised in butter, covered with béchamel sauce

Poireaux à la crème ⇒ white of leeks braised in butter, and cooked with cream

Poireaux au gratin ⇒ leeks braised in butter, sprinkled of grated parmesan and melted butter; then browned

Poireaux braisés
a) **au beurre** ⇒ lengths of leek braised in butter
b) **au gras** ⇒ lengths of leek braised in meat stock

Poiré ⇒ perry

Poirée *-[sorte de bette]-* ⇒ beet

Poirissimo *-[dessert]-*
a) **assiette** ⇒ dessert served by a plate, comprising helpings of pear compote, pear jam, pears cooked in wine and honey; plus pear tart
b) **granité** ⇒ ice cream served by a glass, made of mashed pears added of lemon juice, sugar, and pear alcohol

Pois ⇒ pea or peas or green peas

Pois à écosser *-[petit pois]-* ⇒ unshelled peas

Pois cajou ⇒ Angola pea

Pois cassés ⇒ split peas

Pois chiches ⇒ chickpeas

Pois chiches à la catalane ⇒ chick-peas cooked with carrot, onion, celery, leek, herbs, oil, plus sausage seasoned with pimento and garlic; plus streaky bacon

Pois d'ambrevade ⇒ Angola peas

Pois d'Angola ⇒ Angola peas

Pois dde bois ⇒ Angola peas

Pois gourmand ⇒ french bean

Pois mange-tout ⇒ french bean

Pois princesse ⇒ french bean

Pois secs ⇒ dried peas

Pois vert ⇒ green pea

Poisson ⇒ fish

Poisson à la daumont

   1) **garniture pour alose** ⇒ shad turbot with a garnish of fish quenelles, truffle lamellas, crayfish tails, mushrooms and sautéed soft roes; served with a creamy sauce

     - **saumon** ⇒ salmon turbot with a garnish of fish quenelles, truffle lamellas, crayfish tails, mushrooms and sautéed soft roes; served with a creamy sauce

     - **turbot** ⇒ turbot with a garnish of fish quenelles, truffle lamellas, crayfish tails, mushrooms and sautéed soft roes; served with a creamy sauce

   2) **garniture pour poisson simplifiée** ⇒ fish with crayfishes and mushrooms

     - **oeufs mollets** ⇒ soft boiled eggs with crayfishes and mushrooms

     - **oeufs pochés** ⇒ poached eggs with crayfishes and mushrooms

Poisson chat ⇒ horned pout or catfish or Danubian catfish

Poisson d'eau douce ⇒ freshwater fish

Poisson de lac ⇒ lake fish

Poisson de mer ⇒ sea fish

Poisson de rivière ⇒ river fish

Poisson de roche ⇒ rock fish

Poisson en escabèche *-[servi en hors d'oeuvre]-*

   - **Poissons tels que éperlans** ⇒ sea smelts marinated in a preparation of oil, sliced onion, carrot, vinegar, herbs, cayenne pepper, and coriander

   - **équilles** ⇒ sand eels marinated in a preparation of oil, sliced onion, carrot, vinegar, herbs, cayenne pepper, and coriander

   - **vives** ⇒ weevers marinated in a preparation of oil, sliced onion, carrot, vinegar, herbs, cayenne pepper, and coriander

Poisson épée ⇒ swordfish

Poisson lune ⇒ moonfish or opah

Poisson pilote ⇒ pilot fish

Poisson scie ⇒ sawfish

Poisson torpille ⇒ torpedo fish

Poisson volant ⇒ flying fish

Poissonnaille ⇒ small fish or fry

Poissons marinés à la grecque

   - **Poissons tels que rougets** ⇒ red mullets ...

   - **sardines** ⇒ sardines ... marinated in a preparation of onions braised in olive oil, added of white wine, lemon juice, capsicums, garlic, aromatics and pepper

Poitrine *-[boucherie]-*

   - **boeuf** ⇒ brisket of beef < *uncountable* >

   - **mouton** ⇒ breast of lamb

Poitrine -[général]-
- **veau** ⇒ breast cut of veal
- **porc** ⇒ breast cut of pork
- **agneau** ⇒ breast cut of lamb
- **mouton** ⇒ breast cutof mutton
- **boeuf** ⇒ brisket of beef < *uncountable* >

Poitrine d'agneau ⇒ breast of lamb

Poitrine d'agneau en fritots ⇒ boned breast of lamb macerated in oil, lemon juice, garlic and parsley; then sliced, steeped in batter and fried; served with green salad, plus tomatoes cooked in their own liquid with garlic

Poitrine d'agneau en épigramme ⇒ sliced breast of lamb and a lamb cutlet, coated with breadcrumbs then grilled or sauté

Poitrine d'agneau farçie ⇒ boned breast of lamb, stuffed with a forcemeat of crumbs in milk, eggs, diced ham, diced mushrooms, parsley, garlic and pepper; browned in butter with rind of pork, onions, carrots, white wine, tomatoes and garlic, then baked
- **servies avec** ⇒ Served with braised small balls, of cabbage and sausage meat; plus potatoes and the cooking juice

Poitrine de boeuf ⇒ brisket of beef < *uncountable* >

Poitrine de boeuf désossée, ficelée ⇒ boneless brisket « rolled »

Poitrine de mouton ⇒ breast of mutton

Poitrine de mouton farçie à l'ariégeoise ⇒ braised mutton breast, stuffed with ham, parsley, breadcrumbs, garlic and eggs; served with stuffed cabbages, and potatoes cooked in stock and butter

Poitrine de mouton grillée à la diable ⇒ breast of lamb cooked in stock, then sliced in bits buttered and grilled; served with devilled sauce
- **variante avec sauce poivrade** ⇒ ...; served with a sauce of stock, onions, carrots, ham, parsley, vinegar and mace

Poitrine de porc ⇒ bacon or belly

Poitrine de porc aux pois cassés ⇒ pork belly boiled with carrots, turnips, celery, leeks, onions and parsnips; served with the vegetables and a pudding of split peas

Poitrine de porc roulée, salée ⇒ pork belly rubbed with a mixing of salt and chopped garlic, then sprinkled with thyme and rolled

Poitrine de veau ⇒ breast of veal

Poitrine de veau braisée à l'alsacienne ⇒ boned breast of veal stuffed with a forcemeat of sausage meat, crumbs, parsley, garlic, onions, mushrooms, pepper and grated nutmeg; then braised with sauerkraut

Poitrine de veau farçie braisée ⇒ breast of veal stuffed with a forcemeat of crumbs, milk, garlic, mushrooms, onion, shallots; braised with calf trotter, carrot, onion, leek, rind of pork and celery, then baked

Poitrine désossée -[boeuf]- ⇒ boneless brisket

Poitrine fumée ⇒ cured bacon

Poivrade
- **sauce** ⇒ peppered sauce
- **artichaut** ⇒ small artichoke eaten raw with salt

Poivre ⇒ pepper < *uncountable* >

Poivre blanc ⇒ white pepper

Poivre d'âne -[sarriette]- ⇒ savory < *uncountable* >

Poivre de cayenne ⇒ cayenne pepper < *uncountable* >

Poivre des murailles -[sédum]- ⇒ stonecrop

Poivre en grains ⇒ peppercorns or whole pepper

Poivre giroflée -[piment de la jamaïque]- ⇒ Jamaican pimento

Poivre gris ⇒ black pepper

Poivre moulu ⇒ ground pepper

Poivre noir ⇒ black pepper
Poivre noir de Si Chouan ⇒ Chinese black pepper
Poivre rouge ⇒ red pepper
Poivre vert ⇒ green peppercorns
Poivré *(e ...)* ⇒ peppery
- **poivré** *-[action]-* ⇒ peppered < *v.t adjectif* >
Poivrette *-[nigelle]-* ⇒ nigella or love-in-the-mist
Poivron ⇒ capsicum
- **vert** ⇒ green pepper
- **rouge** ⇒ red pepper
Poivron rouge ⇒ red pepper, uncountable, or capsicum
Poivron vert ⇒ green pepper, uncountable, or capsicum
Poivrons à l'orientale ⇒ grilled capsicums, stewed with onion, garlic, consommé and pepper
Poivrons à la piémontaise ⇒ layers of risotto and grilled capsicum lamellas, sprinkled of grated parmesan, plus melted butter; then browned
Poivrons en ragoût à l'espagnole ⇒ stew of capsicums, onions, olive oil, red pepper, garlic, beef stock, and tomato purée
Poivrons farçis ⇒ green peppers stuffed with a forcemeat of sorrel, onions, tomatoes, capsicums and fennel, plus rice in fat; cooked with tomato sauce added of lemon juice, and olive oil
Poivrons farçis à la turque ⇒ capsicums garnished with a forcemeat of mutton, pilaf, garlic, and tomato; cooked in oil with onions, and tomato sauce
Poivrons farçis en fritots ⇒ green peppers macerated in olive oil, lemon juice and garlic, then garnished with a paste of onions, mushrooms, butter, tomato and garlic; steeped in batter and fried
Poivrons grillés en salade ⇒ grilled green pepper lamellas, seasoned with olive oil, parsley, lemon juice and vinegar; ...
- **servis comme hors d'oeuvre seuls** ⇒ ... served as hors d'oeuvre
- **servis en hors d'oeuvre avec des toasts tartinés de tapenade** ⇒ ... served as hors d'oeuvre with toasts spreaded of a seasoning made of capers, anchovies, stoned black olives, olive oil and aromatics
- **servis en hors d'oeuvre avec des crevettes** ⇒ served as hors d'oeuvre with shrimps
- **servis en hors d'oeuvre avec des petits poulpes en salade** ⇒ served as hors d'oeuvre with small octopus in salad
Pojarski
- **veau** ⇒ composed cutlet of veal, coated with crumbs and fried
- **volaille** ⇒ composed cutlet of white meat, coated with crumbs and fried
- **saumon** ⇒ composed cutlet of salmon, coated with crumbs and fried
Polenta ⇒ polenta
Polenta au parmesan ⇒ polenta added of grated parmesan
Polignac
- **volaille** ⇒ poultry served in supreme sauce added of truffles and mushrooms in julienne
- **poissons** ⇒ poached fish served with a white wine sauce, cream and a julienne of mushrooms
- **oeufs moulés** ⇒ moulded eggs on truffle lamellas
- **oeufs mollets** ⇒ soft boiled eggs covered with Madeira sauce added of truffles
Polka
- **gâteau** ⇒ gateau made of short-pastry, choux-pastry and egg-custard, covered with granulated sugar
- **pain** ⇒ loaf of about 2 kg
Polonais *-[bolet]-* ⇒ boletus
Polonais ou orangé de provence *-[abricot]-* ⇒ variety of apricot

Polonaise *(à la ...)*
- **légumes** ⇒ boiled ..., nom anglais du légume, sprinkled of chopped hard boiled egg-yolks, chopped herbs, and crumbs fried in butter < *autres recettes de la cuisine polonaise traduites séparèment* >

Polypore des brebis *-[champignon]-* ⇒ sheep's mushroom

Polypore groupé *-[champignon]-* ⇒ dryad's mushroom

Pombé *-[bière de mil]-* ⇒ pombe

Pomelo *-[pamplemousse]-* ⇒ grapefruit

Pomerol ⇒ Bordeaux red wine

Pomidolin *-[bonbon]-* ⇒ a sweet

Pommard ⇒ red wine from Côtes de Beaune

Pomme *-[fruit]-* ⇒ apple

Pomme à la crème au kirsch ⇒ rennet apples hollowed out, cooked in vanilla syrup; covered with whipped cream added of kirsch

Pommes à la normande ⇒ baked halved apples, covered with cream

Pomme acidulée ⇒ slightly acid apple

Pommes au beurre ⇒ slices of bread topped with buttered apples, then baked

Pommes au four *-[fruit]-* ⇒ baked apples

Pommes bonne femme ⇒ apples hollowed out and filled with butter added of sugar; then baked

Pommes châtelaine ⇒ apples cooked with sugar and vanilla, flavoured with lemon juice

Pomme clochard ⇒ variety of apple

Pomme d'api ⇒ variety of apple

Pommes de cajou ⇒ apple from the cashew-nut-tree

Pomme de curetin ⇒ variety of apple

Pomme de grillot ⇒ variety of apple

Pomme de mer ⇒ tropical fruit

Pomme de rougelet ⇒ variety of apple

Pommes de terre *-[patisserie]-* ⇒ small balls made of sugar, egg, butter, flour, fecula and yeast

Pommes en bougies ⇒ semolina gateau, garnished with candles made of carved apples topped with nuts, which are lighted

Pommes en l'air *-[fruit]-* ⇒ apple

Pommes farçies aux fruits confits ⇒ apples stuffed with currants, rum, preserved fruits and butter; then baked

Pommes flambantes ⇒ apples cooked in a syrup of sugar and vanilla; flamed with rum

Pommes flambées au calvados ⇒ apples sprinkled of sugar, plus melted butter, then baked; laid in timbales, and flamed with calvados

Pommes gratinées ⇒ apples poached in syrup and laid on compote of apples, sprinkled with a mixing of crumbs and almonds, plus melted butter; then browned

Pommes hérissons ⇒ apples cooked with sugar and vanilla, then spotted of almond bits

Pomme médique ⇒ lemon

Pomme reinette ⇒ rennet apple

Pommes reinettes au miel et au beurre salé ⇒ rennet apples laid on acacia honey, topped with salted butter and baked

Pommes soufflées ⇒ halved apples hollowed out, filled with a purée of apples, granulated sugar, eggs and cognac; then sprinkled of icing sugar and browned

Pommes tapées ⇒ apples cooked in the oven, and sprinkled with sugar

Pommes à la parisienne ⇒ browned potato-balls, added of herbs

Pommes à la sarladaise ⇒ sliced potatoes sautéed in goose fat, then sprinkled with a hash of parsley and garlic

Pommes Georgette ⇒ potatoes hollowed out, and filled with a ragout of crayfish tails and truffle

Pommes allumettes ⇒ fried potato-sticks
Pommes château ⇒ small sauté potatoes with lardoons
Pommes chatouillard ⇒ deep-fried ribbon potatoes
Pommes chips ⇒ potato crisps
Pommes dauphine ⇒ deep-fried croquettes of mashed potatoes, mixed with choux pastry
Pomme d'amour -*[tomate]*- ⇒ tomato
Pomme d'or -*[tomate]*- ⇒ tomato
Pomme de Pérou -*[tomate]*- ⇒ tomato
Pomme de mouton ⇒ lamb sweetbread
Pomme de terre -*[céleri]*- ⇒ Colombian rhizome
Pomme de terre ⇒ potato
Pommes de terre à l'anglaise ⇒ boiled potatoes
Pommes de terre à l'huile ⇒ salad of sliced boiled potatoes, added of grated garlic, french dressing and chopped herbs < *si elles sont servies avec autre chose, ajouter* >
   - **filets d'anchois** ⇒ ... plus anchovy fillets
   - **harengs à l'huile** ⇒ ... plus marinated herring fillets
   - **rondelles d'onion** ⇒ ... plus sliced onion
   - **échalotes émincées** ⇒ ... plus sliced shallots
Pommes de terre à la berrichonne ⇒ potatoes cooked with sauté onions and lardoons, plus stock; served sprinkled with parsley
Pommes de terre à la boulangère ⇒ layers of sliced potatoes and onions browned in butter; baked with stock
Pommes de terre à la crème ⇒ slices of boiled potatoes baked with cream, pepper, and nutmeg; served sprinkled with herbs
Pommes de terre à la landaise ⇒ onions and ham fried in goose fat, plus potatoes, chopped garlic and parsley
Pommes de terre à la lyonnaise ⇒ sliced boiled potatoes, fried in butter with onions
Pommes de terre à la maître d'hôtel ⇒ sliced potatoes cooked in milk or water, plus butter; served sprinkled with parsley
Pommes de terre à la normande ⇒ sliced potatoes layered with white of leeks and parsley; baked in stock, plus butter
Pommes de terre à la paysanne ⇒ layers of sliced potatoes, plus sorrel, garlic and chervil; baked in stock
Pommes de terre anna ⇒ sliced potatoes baked in butter
Pommes de terre annette ⇒ potato julienne baked in butter
Pommes de terre au basilic ⇒ new potatoes baked in butter; sprinkled with basil
Pommes de terre au four à l'ail ⇒ sliced potatoes sautéed in oil and butter, with garlic and onions; then baked, and sprinkled of chives
Pommes de terre au four au foie d'oie cru ⇒ halved jacket potatoes, served topped with a thin slice of raw goose foie gras
Pommes de terre au gratin ⇒ potatoes au gratin
Pommes de terre au jus ⇒ quartered potatoes baked in stock meat, served sprinkled with parsley
Pommes de terre au lard ⇒ diced potatoes braised in pork fat, with lardoons and onions; sprinkled with parsley and chopped garlic
Pommes de terre cocotte ⇒ shaped potatoes boiled first, secondly sautéed in butter and oil, then baked
Pommes de terre collerettes ⇒ chips shaped in collarette
Pommes de terre croquettes ⇒ potato-croquettes
Pommes de terre Cussy ⇒ shaped potatoes cooked in butter, plus truffles sautéed in butter and Madeira

Pommes de terre Darphin *-[garniture]-* ⇒ thick pancake of potato sticks fried first, then baked; ...
- **servies en garniture pour filet de bœuf** ⇒ beef fillet served with ...
- **servies en garniture pour tournedos poêlés** ⇒ fried tournedos served with ...
- **avec une sauce madère** ⇒ ... covered with Madeira sauce
- **ou avec une sauce Périgueux** ⇒ ... covered with Madeira sauce added of chopped truffles

Pommes de terre des vendangeurs de Bourgogne ⇒ layers of cured bacon, sliced potatoes, pork belly, grated gruyère, and butter; baked in terrine

Pommes de terre émiellées ⇒ thin slices of potatoes sautéed in butter, and lardoons, then mixed with eggs; served with a salad

Pommes de terre en l'air ⇒ fried potato puffs

Pommes de terre en papillotes ⇒ jacket potatoes wrapped in aluminium paper, and baked

Pommes de terre en robe des champs ⇒ jacket potatoes OR potatoes baked in their jackets

Pommes de terre et sardines à l'huile ⇒ boiled potatoes and pilchards, seasoned with french dressing

Pommes de terre farçies
1) **procédé « 1 » avec grosses pommes de terre cuites au four** ⇒ Jacket potatoes hollowed out and filled with a forcemeat of their pulp, butter, pepper, plus ...
   - **duxelles** ⇒ chopped onions and mushrooms ...
   - **fromage** ⇒ cheese ...
   - **jambon** ⇒ ham ...
   - **mirepoix** ⇒ a mixture of diced vegetables and ham ...
   - **oignon fondu** ⇒ onion braised in butter ...
   - **hachis cuit** ⇒ hash of meat ... then sprinkled of grated cheese, plus melted butter, and browned
2) **procédé « 2 » avec grosses pommes de terre taillées en cylindre** ⇒ Potatoes shaped in cylinder and hollowed out, then filled with a forcemeat and baked; served au gratin with the cooking juice

Pommes de terre farçies à la Maintenon ⇒ jacket potatoes hollowed out and filled of a culinary stuffing made with white of meat, pickled ox tongue, mushrooms, and truffle, thickened with a purée of onions and rice; then sprinkled of grated cheese, crumbs, melted butter, and browned

Pommes de terre farçies à la basquaise ⇒ baked potatoes stuffed with ham, sweet peppers, tomatoes and garlic

Pommes de terre farçies à la cantalienne *-[recette pommes de terre farçies point 1 et ajouter après « pepper »]-* ⇒ plus braised cabbage; sprinkled ...

Pommes de terre farçies à la charcutière ⇒ potatoes shaped in cylinder and hollowed out, filled with sausage meat, garlic and parsley, then baked; served au gratin with the cooking juice

Pommes de terre farçies à la ciboulette ⇒ jacket potatoes hollowed out and filled with a forcemeat of their pulp, butter, pepper, pasteurized cream and chives; then warmed up in the oven

Pommes de terre farçies à la duxelles
1) **avec grosses pommes de terre cuites au four** ⇒ jacket potatoes hollowed out and filled with a forcemeat of their pulp, butter, pepper, plus chopped onions and mushrooms; sprinkled of crumbs, grated parmesan and melted butter, then browned
2) **avec grosses pommmes de terre taillées en cylindre** ⇒ potatoes shaped in cylinder and hollowed out; then filled with chopped onions plus mushrooms, cooked in a court-bouillon and browned

Pommes de terre farçies à la florentine ⇒ jacket potatoes hollowed out and filled with a forcemeat of their pulp, butter, pepper, plus braised spinach; covered with béchamel sauce added of egg-yolks and gruyère, grated cheese and melted butter, then browned

Pommes de terre farçies à la hongroise ⇒ jacket potatoes hollowed out and filled with a forcemeat of their pulp, onions in butter, pepper, and paprika; sprinkled of crumbs, plus melted butter, and browned

Pommes de terre farçies à la provençale ⇒ potatoes shaped in cylinder and hollowed out, then filled with a forcemeat of tunny, hard boiled egg-yolks, and tomatoes cooked in their own liquid; then cooked in a court-bouillon, and served au gratin

Pommes de terre farçies à la yorkaise ⇒ jacket potatoes hollowed out and filled with a culinary stuffing of their pulp, ham, cultivated mushrooms, onions in butter, and béchamel sauce; seasoned with paprika, and served au gratin

Pommes de terre farçies Soubise ⇒ jacket potatoes hollowed out, and filled with a purée of onions and rice added of cream; then sprinkled of crumbs, plus butter, and browned

Pommes de terre farçies au fromage ⇒ jacket potatoes hollowed out and filled with a forcemeat of their pulp, butter and grated cheese; then sprinkled of grated cheese, plus melted butter, and browned

Pommes de terre farçies chasseur ⇒ jacket potatoes hollowed out and filled with a forcemeat of their pulp, butter, pepper, plus poultry livers and mushrooms in butter; sprinkled of crumbs and melted butter, then browned

Pommes de terre fondantes ⇒ potatoes shaped in olive and baked in butter

Pommes de terre frites ⇒ French fried potatoes OR chips

Pommes de terre hachées ⇒ hashed and browned potatoes, sometime added of chopped onions in butter

Pommes de terre Macaire ⇒ flat cake of mashed potato pulp, pepper and butter, browned in butter

Pommes de terre mère Carles ⇒ sauté shaped potatoes, rolled in slices of cured bacon, then baked

Pommes de terre mousseline ou purée mousseline ⇒ purée of baked potato pulp, butter, egg-yolks, white pepper, nutmeg, and whipped cream

Pommes de terre nouvelles ⇒ new potatoes

Pommes de terre rissolées ⇒ browned potatoes

Pommes de terre rôties ⇒ potatoes baked in butter, sprinkled with parsley

Pommes de terre sautées ⇒ sauté potatoes < *grammaire sauté est un emprunt français de la langue anglaise avec le même sens et est un « adjectif »; toutefois le dictionnaire donne « sauté » comme verbe transitif et le mot est souvent utilisé comme verbe dans notre ouvrage sous la forme « sautéed », mais l'adjectif « sauté » est plus usuel; en fait « sauté » est utilisé quant il désigne directement l'état de la matière et « sautéed » quand il est indiqué dans quoi ou avec quoi la matière est sautée; sautéed in butter and oil par exemple >*

Pommes de terre sautées à cru ⇒ diced potatoes fried in butter or oil

Pommes de terre sous la cendre ⇒ jacket potatoes baked in cinders

Pommes duchesse ⇒ fried balls made with mashed potatoes, eggs and butter

Pommes en liards ⇒ potato crisps

Pommmes lorette ⇒ crescents or small sticks of mashed potatoes, mixed with choux pastry, and gruyère, then fried

Pommes mont-dore ⇒ mashed potatoes thickened with egg-yolks, cream and grated cheese; then browned

Pommes noisette ⇒ little balls of potato pulp, browned in butter

Pommes paille ⇒ potatoes shredded in julienne and fried

Pommes persillade *-[Languedoc]-* ⇒ slices of boiled potatoes seasoned with french dressing, and sprinkled of parsley

Pommes pont neuf ⇒ fried potatoes diced in cubes

Pommes soufflées ⇒ sliced potatoes steeped in hot oil

Pommes vapeur ⇒ steamed potatoes or boiled potatoes

Pommée *(adjectif ...) -[laitue]-* ⇒ grown to a round head

Pommée -*[variété de laitue]*- ⇒ variety of lettuce
Pompe ⇒ pastry sugared or salted
Pompe à l'huile -*[gibassier]*- ⇒ large brioche flavoured with aniseed, orange peel or blossom flowers
Pompe aux grattons ⇒ pie made of lardoons or cracklings; served with St Pourcain red wine
Pompe aux poires ⇒ pie filled with pears
  - **avec d'autres fruits** ⇒ pie filled with ... < *nom anglais des fruits* >
Pompe aux pommes ⇒ large puff-pastry turnover, stuffed with apples
  - **à la confiture** ⇒ large puff-pastry turnover, stuffed with jam
  - **aux prunes** ⇒ large puff-pastry turnover, stuffed with plums
  - **au fromage blanc** ⇒ large puff-pastry turnover, stuffed with soft white cheese
Pompes de Noël ⇒ crowns of flour, yeast, brown sugar, olive oil, eggs, orange peel, and lemon peel; baked and moistened of orange blossom extract
Pompe provençale -*[bûche de noël]*-
  - **classique** ⇒ gateau shaped in log, filled with custard and coated of chocolate in butter
  - **glacée** ⇒ gateau shaped in log, made of various ice-creams
Pompo -*[pompe aux pommes]*- ⇒ large puff-pastry turnover, stuffed with apples
Pomponette ⇒ small rissole filled with a culinary stuffing and fried
Ponch -*[punch]*- ⇒ punch < *uncountable* >
Pont l'evêque ⇒ Pont l'eveque
Pont neuf -*[pâtisserie]*- ⇒ tartlets filled with a mixing of choux-pastry and confectioner's custard flavoured with rum; covered of apricot jam or redcurrant jelly
Pont neuf -*[pommes de terre]*- ⇒ fried potatoes diced in cubes
Pop corn -*[Amérique du nord]*- ⇒ pop corn
Popoï -*[Tahiti]*- ⇒ breadfruit paste
Popped rice -*[riz]*- ⇒ popped rice
Populage ⇒ marsh marigold
Porc ⇒ pork or pork meat < *uncountable* >
Porc -*[enchaud]*- ⇒ pork fillet, boned and baked
Porc entier ⇒ carcase of pork
Porc laqué ⇒ pork lacquered with a sauce, marinated, and roasted on a skewer; served with lettuce, leeks and gherkins
Porcelet ⇒ piglet
Porcelet étoffé à l'occitane ⇒ boneless piglet stuffed with an elaborated forcemeat, baked with vegetables, cognac, white wine, pork fat, plus pieces of polony; served with mashed celery or mashed potatoes
Porcelet rôti ⇒ piglet marinated in aromatics and cognac, then roasted on a skewer; served laid on watercress
Porcellou -*[Quercy]*- ⇒ cabbage leave stuffed of veal, pork fat, and pork meat; seasoned with herbs
Porché ⇒ dish of baked pig trotters, rind of pork and sorrel
Porée Charentaise ⇒ leeks braised in butter, then cooked in fish stock, cream, salt, and pepper, with turbot fillets, scallops, and Norway lobsters; served with the cooking juice thickened of egg-yolk and sprinkled with chervil
Porphyras -*[algues]*- ⇒ red seaweed
Porreau -*[poireau]*- ⇒ leek
Porridge ⇒ porridge
Pörkölt ⇒ Hungarian dish of meat or fish with onions, seasoned of paprika
Port-salut -*[fromage]*- ⇒ Port Salut or Port du Salut
Porte-maillot ou maillot -*[garniture pour grosses pièces de boucherie]*- ⇒ ... garnished with a mixing of carrots, turnips, onions and french beans

Portefeuille *(en ...)*
- **plié** ⇒ folded and stuffed
- **ouvert** ⇒ sliced in a side and stuffed

Portion *-[nourriture]-* ⇒ helping

Porto ⇒ port < *uncountable* >

Porto flip ⇒ cocktail of port, egg-yolk, sugar, and nutmeg

Porto-Vecchio *-[vin]-* ⇒ Corsican wine

Portugaise *(à la ...)* ⇒ with a garnish of tomatoes

Portugaise ou gryphée *-[huître]-* ⇒ Portuguese oyster

Portugal *-[vins]-* ⇒ Portugese wines
- **Dénominations d'appellation vinho de consumo** ⇒ ordinary wine
- **denominaçio de origem** ⇒ quality wine
- **Vins connus Madère** ⇒ Madeira
- **muscatel de Setubal** ⇒ muscatel wine
- **vinho verde** ⇒ vinho verde
- **dio** ⇒ quality red wine
- **colares** ⇒ quality red wine
- **bucelas** ⇒ bucellas
- **Rosados** ⇒ rosé wine
- **Mateus rosé** ⇒ Mateus rosé

Portune *-[crabe]-* ⇒ small crab

Pot au feu ⇒ pot au feu

Pot en grès ⇒ earthenware pot

Pot roast ⇒ pot roast

Pot-je-vleese ⇒ terrine of veal, pork fat and rabbit

Potage ⇒ soup

Potage à la citrouille et aux poireaux ⇒ soup of pumpkin and leeks

Potage à la crécy ⇒ soup of carrots and onions braised in butter, plus beef stock and rice; served with fried croutons

Potage à la cressonnière ⇒ soup made of watercress, potatoes, egg-yolks and cream

Pottage à la Du Barry ⇒ soup made of cauliflower, mashed potatoes, milk, cream and butter

Potage à la paysanne ⇒ soup of potatoes, sorrel, garlic and chervil braised in butter, plus cabbage and peas; served with toasted bread, butter and shredded chervil

Potage à la tortue ⇒ turtle soup

Potage à la tortue lié ⇒ turtle soup thickened with a roux or arrow-root

Potage alexandra
1) **consommé de volaille** ⇒ poultry consommé
2) **potage parmentier garni de brunoise** ⇒ potato soup added of braised diced vegetables

Potage ambassadeur ⇒ soup made of peas, lettuce, onions, chervil, semolina, sorrel, and poached rice

Potage au cerfeuil ⇒ soup of braised chervil, white sauce, and cream

Potage au mouton ⇒ mutton broth with turnips, white of leeks, celery and onions braised in butter

Potage aux grenouilles ⇒ soup of frogs' legs, poultry stock, Riesling, watercress, cream, egg-yolks, butter, and chervil

Potage aux herbes à la dauphine ⇒ soup of herbs, added of marigold flower

Potage aux huîtres ⇒ soup of oysters, white wine, crackers, cream, butter, and cayenne pepper

Potage aux oronges et aux noisettes ⇒ soup made of egg-mushrooms, lettuce, butter, knuckle of veal, milk, rice, fairy ring mushroom powder, and crushed hazelnuts; served added of egg-yolks and cream

Potage Bagration au gras ⇒ soup of veal meat, velouté, egg-yolks, cream and macaroni; served with grated cheese

Potage Bagration au maigre ⇒ soup of sole fillets, velouté, egg-yolks, cream and macaroni; served with grated cheese

Potage bonne femme ⇒ soup of leeks braised in butter, consommé and potatoes; served added of butter and chervil

Potage camérani ⇒ soup of noodles and poultry livers

Potage Célestine ⇒ poultry consommé thickened of tapioca, pancakes, white meat, and shredded chervil

Potage choisy ⇒ lettuce soup

Potage Condé ⇒ soup of mashed red kidney beans, and poultry stock; thickened of butter, and served with fried croutons

Potage conti ⇒ mashed lentils diluted in stock and thickened of butter with sippets

Potage crème aux noix ⇒ soup of chicken stock, egg-yolk, crushed nuts, and pasteurized cream

Potage cultivateur ⇒ soup of diced vegetables, consommé, and lardoons

Potage d'arrow-root ⇒ consommé thickened with arrow-root

Potage d'Artois ⇒ soup of haricot beans, added of braised diced vegetables and chervil

Potage Dartois ⇒ soup made of mashed beans and julienne

Potage Derby ⇒ soup of onion and rice, flavoured with curry; garnished of foie gras quenelles, and chopped truffle

Potage de pois cassés ⇒ soup of mashed split peas, thickened with cream

Potage de poissons à la nîmoise ⇒ fish and vegetable stock, thickened with egg-yolks and garlic sauce

Potage Crécy ⇒ soup of carrots and onions braised in butter, plus beef stock and rice; served with fried croutons

Potage crème aux noix ⇒ soup of chicken stock, egg-yolk, crushed nuts, and pasteurized cream

Potage fausse tortue ⇒ mock turtle soup

Potage fermière ⇒ soup of mixed vegetables braised in butter, plus stock, cream, haricot beans, and shredded chervil

Potage Fontanges ⇒ soup of mashed peas with sorrel, enriched of cream, egg-yolk an chervil

Potage froid au concombre ⇒ soup of cucumber, onions, and soft white cheese; served chilled with shredded chervil

Potage froid de betteraves ⇒ soup of beetroots, lemon juice, white of eggs, onions, gherkins, and cream; served chilled

Potage Georgette ⇒ soup made of tomato and carrots in purée

Potage Germiny ⇒ soup of braised sorrel, consommé, egg-yolks, and cream, added of shredded chervil

Potage julienne à la cévenole ⇒ julienne braised in butter, added of consommé, chestnut purée, and butter

Potage Lamballe ⇒ thick soup made of mashed fresh peas, then thickened with tapioca consommé; garnished with shredded chervil

Potage Longchamp ⇒ soup of mashed peas, sorrel chiffonade braised in butter, consommé and vermicelli; served sprinkled with shredded chervil

Potage Marigny ⇒ soup of mashed peas, plus braised sorrel chiffonade, and french beans; garnished with shredded chervil

Potage nemours ⇒ mashed potatoes added of consommé and thickened of cream, egg-yolk and tapioca

Potage oxtail ⇒ soup based on veal's bones, oxtail, carrots, leeks, and onions

Potage parmentier ⇒ potato cream

Potage petite marmite ⇒ soup made from the broth of pot au feu

Potage poule au pot ⇒ soup made with the broth of poultry and vegetables

Potage-purée ⇒ soup of mashed vegetables

Potage-purée de marrons ⇒ soup of mashed chestnuts and celeriac; served with croutons fried in butter

Potage-purée de tomates ⇒ soup of mashed onions, tomatoes, garlic, herbs and butter; served sprinkled of parsley or basil, plus croutons rubbed with garlic and fried in olive oil

Potage-purée soissonnais ⇒ soup of mashed haricot beans, onion, clove, herbs and pork belly; served with croutons fried in butter

Potage santé ⇒ thick soup made of mashed potatoes and leeks, added of braised sorrel chiffonade thickened of cream and egg-yolks; served with bread and shredded chervil

Potage Solférino ⇒ soup of braised leeks, carrots, plus potato balls, crushed tomatoes, garlic and stock; served added of butter and shredded chervil

Potage St Germain ⇒ soup made of peas, lettuce, onions, chervil and semolina; served with butter, herbs and sippets

Potage taillé *-[paysanne]-* ⇒ soup of potatoes, sorrel, garlic and chervil braised in butter, plus cabbage and peas; served with toasted bread, butter and shredded chervil

Potage velouté aux truffes ⇒ velouté with truffles

Potage viveur ⇒ poultry consommé, added of celery in julienne; served with small round pieces of bread paprika flavoured

Potage Xavier ⇒ poultry consommé thickened with egg-yolks, rice cream and cream; garnished with diced chicken and butter

Potato *-[pomme de terre]-* ⇒ potato

Potato crisps *-[chips]-* ⇒ potato crisps

Pote de la Broye *-[Suisse]-* ⇒ snout of pig, stuffed with a fillet mignon, and braised

Potiron ⇒ pumpkin

Potiron *-[bolet]-* ⇒ boletus

Potiron à bague *-[coulemelle]-* ⇒ parasol mushroom

Potiron au jus ⇒ slices of pumpkin sautéed in veal gravy; served sprinkled with parsley

Potiron d'arbrèche *-[pleurote]-*
  1) **pleurote en coquille** ⇒ oyster cap
  2) **pleurote du panicaut** ⇒ gloomy mushroom

Potiron en entremets ⇒ mashed pumpkins covered with caramel and kirsch

Potjevfleisch ⇒ terrine of veal, pork fat and rabbit

Potted char ⇒ tinned fish

Potée ⇒ stew of boiled beef or pork and vegetables
  - **Potée de bœuf** ⇒ stew of boiled beef and vegetables
  - **Potée de porc** ⇒ stew of pork and vegetables
  - **Potée de légumes** ⇒ stew of vegetables

Potée à la bourguignonne ⇒ stew of pork, cabbage, carrots, turnips, leeks and potatoes; plus during spring, French beans, and peas

Potée albigeoise ⇒ stew of silverside of beef, knuckle of veal, ham, conserve of goose, large sausage, carrots, turnips, celery, leeks, cabbage, and haricot beans

Potée alsacienne ⇒ stew of smoked bacon, cabbage, celery, carrots, haricot beans, and goose fat

Potée artésienne ⇒ stew of pig head, streaky bacon, breast of lamb, sausage made of chitterlings, carrots, cabbage, turnips, celery, haricot beans, and potatoes

Potée auvergnate ⇒ stew of pork, sausages, pig head, cabbage, carrots, and turnips

Potée berrichonne ⇒ stew of small ham, sausages, plus red kidney beans cooked in red wine

Potée bretonne
  1) **viande** ⇒ stew of shoulder of lamb, duck, sausages, and vegetables
  2) **congre** ⇒ stew of conger eel, butter, onion, leek, carrots, turnips, potatoes, herbs, and garlic

Potée champenoise ou « dite des vendangeurs » ⇒ stew of pork, cabbage, carrots, turnips, roots and potatoes; plus sometimes sausages, or smoked ham, or poultry

Potée dite des vendangeurs ⇒ stew of pork, cabbage, carrots, turnips, roots and potatoes; plus sometimes sausages, or smoked ham, or poultry

Potée franc-comtoise ⇒ stew of beef, pork fat, sausage, mutton bone, and vegetables

Potée lorraine ⇒ stew of pork, cabbage, carrots, french beans, haricot beans, peas, turnips, leeks, celery, and potatoes; plus sometime lentils

Potée morvandelle ⇒ stew of ham, large sausage, smoked sausages, and various vegetables

Pouce pied -[operne]- ⇒ goose barnacle

Pouding ⇒ pudding or plum pudding

Pouding à la confiture ⇒ plum-pudding made of sponge fingers, apricot jam, rum and custard

Pouding à la maïzena ⇒ plum pudding made of maïzena, milk and sugar

Pouding à la maïzena et aux pêches ⇒ baked plum pudding made of milk, eggs, maïzena and sugar; topped with peaches poached in a syrup

Pouding au citron ⇒ plum pudding made of gelatine, sugar, eggs and lemon

Pouding au moka ⇒ plum-pudding made of sponge fingers, plus custard flavoured with coffee extract

Pouding au riz ⇒ plum pudding made of rice, milk, sugar, currants and eggs

Pouding aux noisettes ⇒ plum pudding made with layers of sponge fingers, butter and hazelnut custard, plus eggs and milk custard

Pouding aux reines-claude ⇒ layers of sponge fingers moistened in rum, and plum jam; covered with custard and preserved fruits

Pouding cavarois ⇒ plum pudding made of crushed hard boiled eggs, butter and vanilla, on a laying of sponge fingers moistened with kirsch, and covered by a custard

Pouding de cochon -[Amérique du nord]- ⇒ pig pudding

Pouding maïzena et chocolat ⇒ plum pudding made of chocolate, sugar, milk and eggs

Pouding Nesselrode ⇒ mixing of egg custard, chestnut purée, preserved fruits, and currants macerated in Malaga wine, plus whipped cream flavoured of maraschino; then chilled

Pouding tapioca au caramel ⇒ plum pudding made of caramel, milk, tapioca and eggs

Poudre ⇒ powder

Poudre de cacao ⇒ cocoa powder

Poudre de zinziberine -[gingembre]- ⇒ ginger powder

Poudrer ⇒ to sprinkle with

Poudré ⇒ powdered < v.t adjectif >

Pougnons ⇒ tart with fruits or marrow or pumpkin

Pouillard -[perdreau]- ⇒ young partridge < uncountable >

Pouille -[vins de]- ⇒ Italian wines

Pouilly -[vin]- ⇒ wines from Mâcon area

Pouilly fumé -[vin de Loire]- ⇒ white wine from Pouilly sur Loire

Pouilly sur Loire ⇒ white wine from Loire valley

Pouilly-fuissé ⇒ Burgundy white wine

Poulain ⇒ foal

Poularde ⇒ fattened pullet

Poularde à l'estragon ⇒ fattened pullet cooked with tarragon, and stock; served with the cooking juice thickened of tarragon or arrow-root

Poularde à l'estragon dans sa gelée ⇒ fattened pullet cooked with tarragon, then chilled; served covered with a jelly of its stock, gelatine, lean meat of beef, and Madeira

Poularde à l'ivoire ⇒ poached fattened pullet, coated of supreme sauce added of veal stock; served with poultry quenelles, plus sauté cultivated mushrooms

Poularde à la bonne femme ⇒ fattened pullet braised in butter, with lardoons, onions and potatoes

Poularde à la bourgeoise ⇒ fattened pullet steamed in butter, with lardoons and carrots; served covered with the cooking juice added of white wine, stock and glazed onions

Poularde à la bourguignonne ⇒ fattened pullet braised in butter with lardoons, onions, mushrooms, a mixture of diced vegetables and ham, red wine and stock; served with the cooking juice added of kneaded butter

Poularde à la bressane ⇒ fattened pullet stuffed with foie gras and mushrooms, then braised

Poularde à la chantilly ⇒ fattened pullet stuffed with rice, truffle and foie gras, braised in butter; served with truffles steamed in port, plus sauté foie gras escalopes, and the cooking juice added of whipped cream

Poularde à la chevalière ⇒ chicken pieces wrapped in pastry with mushrooms and truffles

Poularde à la chimay ⇒ fried fattened pullet, stuffed with noodles in butter and forcemeat; covered of the gravy and served with noodles, plus bunches of asparagus tips

Poularde à la Chivry ⇒ poached fattened pullet, covered with a sauce of poultry velouté, and composed butter added of herbs; served with artichoke hearts garnished of asparagus tips and peas

Poularde à la Clamart ⇒ fattened pullet baked in butter with peas

Poularde à la d'albuféra ⇒ fattened pullet stuffed with rice, chopped truffle and foie gras, then poached in stock; garnished of oxtongue, sweetbread and mushrooms, covered with a supreme sauce added of butter and capsicum

Poularde à la derby ⇒ chicken stuffed of rice and foie gras, served with truffles cooked in port and foie gras escalopes sautéed in butter

Poularde à la matignon ⇒ stuffed fattened pullet, covered with vegetables braised in butter, then baked, and covered of the cooking juice added of Madeira; served with a garnish of artichoke hearts stuffed of vegetables cooked in their own liquid

Poularde à la mère filloux ⇒ poached chicken served with cream, plus tartlets filled of mushrooms, supreme sauce and truffles

Poularde à la Nantua ⇒ poached fattened pullet; served with pastry-boats filled with a ragout of crayfish tails, and supreme sauce added of crayfish paste

Poularde à la Néva ⇒ fattened pullet stuffed with sausage meat added of foie gras and poached, covered with a chaudfroid sauce; served with vegetable salad in mayonnaise

Poularde à la parisienne ⇒ fattened pullet stuffed with a forcemeat and cream, covered of chaudfroid sauce and truffles; served with a julienne in mayonnaise

Poularde à la pièmontaise ⇒ fattened pullet stuffed with risotto and truffles, then cooked in butter; served with the gravy thickened of white wine and butter, then accompanied with risotto added of parmesan

Poularde à la portugaise ⇒ fattened pullet cooked in butter with tomatoes and chopped onions; covered with the cooking juice added of white wine

Poularde à la reine ⇒ fattened pullet stuffed with seasoned panada forcemeat and poached; served with tartlets garnished of chicken purée and truffles, accompanied of supreme sauce

Poularde à la Souvarov ⇒ fattened pullet stuffed with foie gras, truffle and cognac; braised in butter, then baked with truffles, plus game stock added of Madeira

Poularde ambassadrice ⇒ fattened pullet stuffed with a culinary stuffing of lamb sweetbreads, truffles and mushrooms, braised with vegetables in pork fat; served with tartlets garnished of sauté poultry livers, plus the cooking juice added of Madeira

Poularde au blanc ⇒ fattened pullet poached in stock, covered with the cooking stock, added of velouté sauce and nutmeg; served with rice and carrots

Poularde au céleri ⇒ fattened pullet braised with celery in julienne; served with the cooking juice

Poularde au riz à la Bourbon ⇒ fattened pullet cooked in pork fat, with onion, carrots, tomato purée, herbs and poultry stock; s erved in the middle of a ring of rice cooked in stock; covered with the cooking juice

Poularde au riz sauce suprême ⇒ fattened pullet cooked in stock with rice; served with supreme sauce

Poularde Clos-Jouve ⇒ bits of fattened pullet garnished with a forcemeat of leek, horn of plenty mushrooms, foie gras, cream and egg-yolk, then braised in butter; served coated with a sauce based on a stock of leek, onion, veal trotter, thyme, laurel, port, and white wine

Poularde célestine ⇒ sauté chicken plus mushrooms and tomatoes, flamed in cognac, moistened with white wine and stock; served sprinkled with parsley and garlic

Poularde dauphinoise ⇒ fattened pullet stuffed with foie gras and truffles, plus Madeira and cognac, then cooked with giblets; served with the gravy

Poularde demi-deuil ⇒ poached chicken served with cream, plus tartlets filled of mushrooms, supreme sauce and truffles

Poularde Demidof ⇒ fattened pullet stuffed with a forcemeat and baked, then braised coated with a preparation of vegetables plus Madeira; served surrounded of artichoke hearts, topped with fried slice of onion and truffle lamella

Poularde Doria ⇒ poached fattened pullet, stuffed with mushrooms, cockscombs, and white truffles, thickened of poultry velouté; covered with poultry stock, sprinkled of grated parmesan, then browned

Poularde en casserole ⇒ fattened pullet browned and baked; served with the gravy, plus braised onions or carrots

Poularde en cocotte ⇒ fattened pullet browned and baked; served with the gravy, plus braised onions or carrots

Poularde en gelée au champagne ⇒ fattened pullet baked with diced vegetables, herbs and champagne; served chilled, covered with a jelly of its cooking juice

Poularde en vessie Marius Vettard ⇒ fattened pullet stuffed with a forcemeat of liver, truffles, egg, cognac and Madeira; then wrapped in pork bladder, and poached in stock; served with vegetables or rice, accompanied of burgundy wine

Poularde farçie à la néva ⇒ fattened pullet, stuffed and covered with a chaudfroid sauce; garnished of vegetable salad thickened with mayonnaise, and sometimes added of fish or meat

Poularde Mireille ⇒ bits of fattened pullet browned in butter, then cooked with white wine, morels, and cream; served with the cooking juice thickened of egg-yolk

Poularde pochée à l'anglaise ⇒ fattened pullet poached in stock, covered with béchamel sauce added of cooking stock; served with bunches of celery, carrots, turnips and peas

Poularde princesse ⇒ fattened pullet poached in stock, covered with poultry stock; served with pastry boats, filled of asparagus tips

Poularde Rosière ⇒ fattened pullet plus a forcemeat of whiting in cream, cooked in stock; served sliced with the forcemeat, sweetbread escalopes and mashed mushrooms

Poularde Rossini ⇒ fried fattened pullet; served with tartlets garnished of foie gras escalopes and truffle lamellas, plus the gravy added of Madeira

Poularde rôtie ⇒ fattened pullet buttered and roasted; served with the gravy

Poularde truffée à la périgourdine ⇒ fattened pullet stuffed with a forcemeat of pork fat, truffles, nutmeg and aromatics; roasted on a skewer, and served with Madeira sauce added of chopped truffles

Poule ⇒ hen or fowl

Poule -[*clavaire*]- ⇒ tiny yellow hands

Poule au pot ⇒ boiled chicken

Poule au pot à la béarnaise ⇒ hen stuffed with a forcemeat of sausage meat, ham, onions, garlic, parsley and poultry livers; then boiled with vegetables

Poule au riz ⇒ chicken and rice

Poule d'eau ⇒ moorhen

Poule d'inde -[*dinde*]- ⇒ turkey < *uncountable* >

Poule de numidie -[*dinde*]- ⇒ turkey < *uncountable* >

Poule des bois -[*pleurote*]- ⇒ oyster mushroom

Poule des bois ou des coudriers -[*v gelinotte*]- ⇒ hazel grouse

Poule faisane ⇒ hen pheasant

Poule sans os

    1) **avec lard et oseille** ⇒ fried ball of wheat flour, streaky bacon, and sorrel

2) **avec petit salé** ⇒ ball of wheat flour and salt pork, boiled in cabbage soup
3) **avec pommes de terre** ⇒ poached ball of mashed potatoes, herbs, garlic, onions and
    lardoons; fried in pork fat or goose fat
Poulet ⇒ chicken or fowl < *uncountable* >
  - **de grain** ⇒ corn-fed chicken
Poulet à la Circassienne ⇒ chicken served with a capsicum sauce, and nuts
Poulet à la créole ⇒ bits of chicken braised in oil, and flamed with rum; served with slices of
    pineapple, plus the gravy added of pineapple syrup, lime juice, and cayenne pepper
Poulet à la Lyonnaise en crapaudine *-[ou ... grillé en crapaudine]-* ⇒ chicken split in two,
    coated with mustard, and crumbs; then sprinkled of melted butter, and grilled
Poulet à la mode de Sorges ⇒ chicken stuffed with a forcemeat of its liver, crumbs, streaky bacon,
    parsley, chives, shallot, garlic, pepper, nutmeg and egg-yolk; boiled with carrots,
    turnips, leeks, celeriac, onion and beets; served with a french dressing added of
    parsley, chives, shallots, and thickened with egg
Poulet à la niçoise ⇒ sauté chicken, served with braised artichoke hearts, braised courgettes, and black
    olives; covered with the gravy
Poulet à la polonaise ⇒ chicken sautéed in butter, sprinkled with lemon juice and crumbs; served with
    braised red cabbage, or chestnuts, or celeriac
Poulet au citron ⇒ bits of chicken macerated in lemon juice, then browned in butter with thyme;
    served with the gravy added of cream
Poulet au citron confit ⇒ bits of chicken braised on a layer of onions, garlic, grated ginger, oil,
    coriander and slices of candied lemon; served with rice
Poulet au persil ⇒ chicken studded of butter and parsley, then roasted
Poulet au sang ⇒ sauté bits of chicken, flamed in cognac; served with a sauce of lardoons, onions,
    mushrooms, red wine, stock and chicken blood
Poulet au xérès ⇒ sauté chicken; covered with the gravy added of arrow-root, xeres, and cayenne
    pepper
Poulet aux coings en tajine ⇒ bits of chicken braised in olive oil with onions, paprika, ginger
    powder, coriander and poultry stock; then baked with quinces
Poulet aux noisettes ⇒ bits of chicken cooked in butter and stock; served with the gravy added of
    butter, pounded hazelnuts and cream
Poulet aux pousses de bambou ⇒ chicken boiled with Chinese mushrooms, soya sauce, pepper, and
    bamboo shoots; served with green onions fried in oil, plus soya sauce
Poulet célestine ⇒ sautéed chicken with mushrooms and skinned tomatoes, flamed in cognac; then
    moistened of white wine and sprinkled with garlic powder plus chopped parsley
Poulet chasseur ⇒ hunter's chicken
Poulet créole à l'ananas et au rhum ⇒ large chicken braised in poultry fat, with ginger powder,
    cayenne pepper, onions, and shallot; then flamed with rum, and served added of
    lemon juice, and diced pineapple in syrup
Poulet de grain ⇒ corn-fed chicken
Poulet docteur ⇒ cooked chicken, moistened with port, then simmered in veal's stock and served with
    tarragon, plus veal's lamellas
Poulet en barbouille ⇒ chicken cooked with lardoons, onions, mushrooms, red wine, garlic, herbs,
    and its blood
Poulet en capilotade ⇒ boiled chicken, boned and simmered in a sauce
Poulet en compote ⇒ chicken stew
  - **gibier** ⇒ game birds stew
Poulet en croûte de sel ⇒ chicken baked in a crust of flour and salt; served with a green salad
    flavoured of nut oil
Poulet fermier ⇒ free-range chicken

Poulet frit Maryland ⇒ bits of chicken steeped in milk, then floured and fried, covered with a sauce made of the carcase boiled in milk and stock; served with slices of fried bacon, plus maize ears

Poulet froid ⇒ chilled roasted chicken

Poulet grillé à la lyonnaise en crapaudine ⇒ chicken split in two, coated with mustard, and crumbs; then sprinkled of melted butter, and grilled

Poulet grillé à la tyrolienne ⇒ chicken split in two, coated with oil and grilled; served with sliced onions fried in oil, plus tomatoes cooked in their own liquid and butter

Poulet grillé en crapaudine ⇒ chicken split in two, coated with a mixing of olive oil, garlic, herbs and pepper; then grilled

Poulet jaune des Landes ⇒ maize-fed pullet

Poulet Marengo ⇒ sauté chicken in white wine, with mushrooms, onions and fried croutons

Poulet rôti ⇒ roasted chicken

Poulet sauté à blanc ⇒ sauté bits of chicken; served with the gravy added of stock, or cream, or something else

Poulet sauté à brun ⇒ sauté bits of chicken, added of a sauce during the cooking process

Poulet sauté à l'ancienne ⇒ sauté chicken; covered with a sauce of stock, poultry velouté, butter, truffle and port

Poulet sauté à l'artichaut ⇒ chicken sautéed with artichoke hearts; served covered with the gravy added of white wine, stock and butter

Poulet sauté à l'estragon ⇒ sauté chicken; served with the gravy added of white wine, shallot, stock, lemon juice and tarragon

Poulet sauté à l'italienne ⇒ chicken sautéed in olive oil and butter; covered with the gravy added of white wine, plus a brown sauce thickened of chopped mushrooms, diced ham, tarragon and tomato purée

Poulet sauté à la biarrote ⇒ sauté chicken, covered with the gravy added of white wine, tomato sauce, and grated garlic; served with boletus, diced potatoes, diced aubergines and sliced onion, sautéed in olive oil

Poulet sauté à la bohémienne ⇒ chicken sprinkled of paprika and sautéed in oil, cooked with capsicums, tomatoes, onion, fennel and garlic; served with the gravy thickened of white wine, stock and lemon juice, accompanied with rice

Poulet sauté à la bordelaise ⇒ sauté chicken in butter, tomato purée and garlic, plus sauté potatoes, artichoke hearts and onions

Poulet sauté à la crème ⇒ sauté chicken; served with the gravy added of cider, and cream

Poulet sauté à la fermière ⇒ sauté chicken; simmered with carrots, onions, leeks and celery, braised in butter, plus diced ham

Poulet sauté à la minute ⇒ sauté chicken; covered with the gravy and lemon juice, then sprinkled of parsley

Poulet sauté à la niçoise ⇒ sauté chicken, served with braised artichoke hearts, braised courgettes, and black olives; covered with the gravy

Poulet sauté à la zingara ⇒ bits of chicken, sautéed in oil with paprika; then simmered with a julienne of ham, pickled ox tongue, mushrooms, truffle and tarragon; covered of the cooking juice added of Madeira, tomato and stock, served with toasts topped of slices of ham

Poulet sauté Alexandra ⇒ sauté chicken covered with the gravy added of mashed onions and cream; served with asparagus tips in butter

Poulet sauté Annette ⇒ sauté bits of chicken, laid on a flat cake of potato julienne baked in butter; coated with a sauce of white wine, shallot, stock, kneaded butter, lemon juice, parsley, chervil and tarragon

Poulet sauté archiduc ⇒ bits of chicken sautéed in butter with onions and paprika; covered with the gravy added of white wine, cream, lemon juice and butter

Poulet sauté au basilic ⇒ sauté chicken covered with the gravy added of white wine, basil and butter

Poulet sauté au vinaigre ⇒ sauté chicken; simmered with a sauce of giblets, diced vegetables, aromatics, shallots, garlic, onion, white wine and vinegar

Poulet sauté au xérès ⇒ sauté chicken; covered with the gravy added of arrow-root, xeres, and cayenne pepper

Poulet sauté aux cèpes ⇒ chicken sautéed in olive oil and butter, with boletus and shallots; served with the gravy added of white wine and garlic < *Note S'il est utilisé d'autres champignons que des cèpes, remplacer boletus par le nom anglais du champignon utilisé* >

Poulet sauté aux huîtres ⇒ sauté chicken, served with poached oysters; covered with the gravy added of white wine, oyster water, poultry stock, lemon and butter

Poulet sauté aux mangues ⇒ sauté chicken, simmered in olive oil and butter, with onion, tomato, mango pulp, plus lemon juice

Poulet sauté aux plantains ⇒ chicken braised with onion, tomatoes and lardoons; then simmered with boiled large bananas

Poulet sauté Boivin ⇒ sauté chicken with artichokes, baby onions and new potatoes; covered with the gravy added of stock, and lemon juice

Poulet sauté chasseur ⇒ chicken braised in butter and oil with sliced mushrooms; served with the gravy added of shallots, white wine, tomato sauce, marc and tarragon

Poulet sauté Demidof ⇒ sauté bits of chicken, simmered with white wine, a julienne of carrots, turnip, celery, and onion, plus a slice of smoked raw ham, and diced truffle; served added of Madeira and stock

Poulet sauté Doria ⇒ chicken sautéed in olive oil and butter, with shaped cucumbers; served with the gravy added of lemon juice

Poulet sauté petit-duc ⇒ sauté chicken, covered with the gravy added of Madeira and stock; served with morels and truffle lamellas browned in butter

Poulet sauté Stanley ⇒ bits of chicken sautéed in butter with onions and mushrooms; served with the gravy thickened of cream, curry, cayenne pepper and butter

Poulet tandouri ⇒ tandoori chicken

Poulet vallée d'auge ⇒ bits of chicken braised in butter, flamed in calvados and cooked in cider; served with the cooking juice added of cream, plus braised apples in butter

Poulette ⇒ pullet

Poulette *(à la ...)*

   - **anguilles** ⇒ eels ...

   - **moules** ⇒ mussels ...

   - **pieds de mouton** *-[viande]-* ⇒ lamb trotters ...

   - **tripes** ⇒ tripe ...

   - **cervelles** ⇒ brains ...

   - **escargots** ⇒ snails ...

   - **champignons** ⇒ mushrooms ... covered with a sauce of eggs, stock and lemon juice, plus chopped parsley

Pouligny St Pierre ⇒ goat's milk cheese shaped in pyramid

Poulpe ⇒ octopus

Poulpe à la provençale ⇒ sliced octopus boiled in a court-bouillon, then simmered with tomatoes, white wine, herbs, and garlic; served in timbale

Poumon ⇒ lung

Pound cake *-[Amérique du nord]-* ⇒ pound cake

Pountari ⇒ cabbage leaves stuffed with a hash of pork-fat, onions and aromatics

Pounti ⇒ flan made of a hash based on pork-fat, onions and beets, thickened with eggs

Poupelin ⇒ large pastry garnished of whipped cream, ice cream or a mousse

Poupeton ⇒ stuffed meat made in small balls, then braised

Poupeton de dindonneau Brillat-Savarin ⇒ turkey-chick stuffed with a forcemeat of veal, lamb sweetbreads, foie gras and truffle, then rolled in a caul of pork; braised in butter, ham, carrots, onions and Madeira; ...
- **servi avec la sauce** ⇒ ... served with the cooking juice
- **ou servi froid en gelée** ⇒ ... or served chilled in jelly

Pourly ⇒ Burgundy goat's milk cheese with a blue crust

Pourpier ⇒ purslane

Pourreau -*[poireau]*- ⇒ leek

Pourrous negres -*[mique noire]*- ⇒ balls of cornflour and wheat flour, poached in polony cooking water, then grilled

Pousse café ⇒ pousse café

Pousse l'amour -*[pousse café]*- ⇒ pousse café

Pousse mousse -*[pied bleu]*- ⇒ tricholoma mushroom

Pousse pierre -*[criste marine]*- ⇒ Crithmum OR rock samphire

Pousser -*[fermentation de la pâte]*- ⇒ to leaven

Pousses de bambou ⇒ bamboo shoots

Pousses de soja ⇒ soya shoots

Poussin -*[cuisine]*- ⇒ young chicken

Poussins à la piémontaise ⇒ chickens stuffed with onions and sausage meat, then braised in butter; served with risotto, plus the gravy added of white wine, tomato purée, butter and parsley

Poussins à la sicilienne ⇒ chickens stuffed with lasagne, pistachio paste and pepper; then roasted on a skewer

Poussins à la viennoise ⇒ split chickens coated with crumbs and fried; served with fried parsley and quartered lemon

Poussins de Sydney ⇒ chickens marinated in pineapple and wine, then roasted

Poussin frit ⇒ bits of chicken marinated in oil, lemon juice, garlic and aromatics; coated with breadcrumbs and fried, then served with quartered lemon

Poussin grillé à la diable ⇒ split chicken coated of mustard and cayenne pepper, then grilled; served with halved lemon, gherkins and devilled sauce

Poutargue ⇒ flat sausage made from the dried roes of the grey mullet; served sprinkled with french dressing or lemon juice

Poutargue -*[caviar blanc]*- ⇒ mullet roes dried and pressed

Poutina ⇒ mixture of fry, mainly sardines and anchovies; served fried
- **soupe** ⇒ soup garnished with poached mixture of fry, mainly sardines and anchovies < *variantes* >
- **omelette** ⇒ omelette filled with poached mixture of fry, mainly sardines and anchovies < *variantes* >

Poutine ⇒ mixture of fry, mainly sardines and anchovies; served fried
- **soupe** ⇒ soup garnished with poached mixture of fry, mainly sardines and anchovies < *variantes* >
- **omelette** ⇒ omelette filled with poached mixture of fry, mainly sardines and anchovies < *variantes* >

Pouytrolle ⇒ hash of pork, beets, spinach and aromatics, wrapped in a bowel of pork, then poached

Poyo -*[banane]*- ⇒ variety of banana

Prairie ⇒ small clam or quahaug

Pralin ⇒ grilled almonds mixed in sugar added of vanilla; then pounded

Praline ⇒ praline or burnt almond

Praliné ⇒ chocolate almonds or praline paste

Prästost -*[fromage]*- ⇒ Prästost

Premières côtes de Blaye
   1) **terme général** ⇒ high quality wine, mainly red
   2) **autres possibilités blanc** ⇒ high quality white wine
      - **rouge** ⇒ high quality red wine
Pressed beef ⇒ pressed beef
Pressé *(e ...)* ⇒ squeezed or pressed
Pression *(une ...) -[bière]-* ⇒ a glass of draught beer
Presskopf *-[saucisse]-* ⇒ sausage of pork, veal and beef
Prêtre *-[poisson]-* ⇒ silverside
Preuses *(les ...) -[chablis]-* ⇒ high quality chablis wine
Primeurs
      - **fruits** ⇒ early fruits
      - **légumes** ⇒ early vegetables
Primevère ⇒ primrose
Primitivo di mandurio *-[Pouilles vins]-* ⇒ Italian red wine
Prince Albert ⇒ piece of beef stuffed with foie gras, then braised and moistened with port; garnished
            of whole truffles
Princesse *(à la ...)*
      - **volaille** ⇒ poultry ...
      - **darnes de saumon** ⇒ steaks of salmon ...
      - **bouchées** ⇒ patties ...
      - **tartelettes** ⇒ tartlets ...
      - **oeufs** ⇒ eggs ...
      - **ris de veau** ⇒ calf sweetbread ... ... with a garnish of truffle lamellas and asparagus tips
Princesse *-[garniture]-* ⇒ garnish of asparagus tips and truffle lamellas
Princesse *-[petit pois]-* ⇒ mange-tout bean
Printanier ⇒ spring like < *est un adjectif et se place devant le nom « potage printanier » spring like*
            vegetable soup >
Printanière *(à la ...)*
   1) **général** ⇒ with a garnish of early spring vegetables
   2) **dits « printaniers » navarin de mouton** ⇒ voir texte
      - **potage aux légumes nouveaux ou potage printanier** ⇒ spring like vegetable soup
Privat bleu *-[russule]-* ⇒ russula
Privat rouge *-[russule]-* ⇒ russula
Privat vert *-[russule]-* ⇒ russula
Prix fixe ⇒ fixed price
Prix net ⇒ net price
      - **Prix nets** ⇒ net prices
Processor *-[haricot vert]-* ⇒ french beans
Profiteroles ⇒ profiteroles
Profiterolles au chocolat ⇒ profiteroles with chocolate
Profiteroles Nesselrode ⇒ profiteroles garnished with chestnut purée
Progrès ⇒ discs of pastry
Progrès au café ⇒ pastry discs flavoured with coffee extract
Prosciutto ⇒ prosciutto
Prosciutto di parma ⇒ prosciutto
Prosciutto di san daniele ⇒ prosciutto
Prots ou Protes *-[dinde, dindon, dindonneau]-* ⇒ turkey < *viande uncountable* >

Provençale *(à la ...) (suite)*
  1) pièces de boucherie ou volaillles
    a) avec tomates braisées, champignons et ail ⇒ ... with a garnish of braised tomatoes, plus mushrooms seasoned of garlic
    b) avec tomates concassées et aillées, plus olives dénoyautées ⇒ with crushed tomatoes flavoured of garlic, and stoned olives
    c) avec des tronçons d'aubergines farçis d'une fondue de tomate, des haricots verts au beurre et des pommes château ⇒ with aubergines stuffed of tomato, french beans in butter and small potatoes sautéed in butter with lardoons
  2) légumes, œufs, volailles et poissons, nappés de sauce provençale ⇒ ... covered with a sauce of tomato purée, onion, garlic and white wine
Provolone *-[fromage]-* ⇒ Provolone
Prune ⇒ plum
Prunes *-[pâté de, Poitou]-* ⇒ plum paste
Prunes à l'eau de vie ⇒ greengages coated with syrup, then preserved in fruit alcohol
Prune acide *-[ximénia]-* ⇒ tropical plum
Prune de monsieur *-[prune]-* ⇒ variety of plum
Prune d'ente ⇒ variety of plum
Prune d'espagne ⇒ caribbean fruit
Prune de coco ⇒ kind of plum
Prune de coton ⇒ kind of plum
Prune des anses ⇒ kind of plum
Prune royale ⇒ variety of plum
Prunes flambées ⇒ stoned plums poached in vanilla syrup, flamed with plum eau de vie
Pruneau ⇒ dried plum or prune
Pruneaux au bacon ⇒ stoned prunes filled with pistachio nut, and rolled in bacon; then baked
Pruneaux au rasteau et à la crème fraîche ⇒ prunes cooked in Bordeaux red wine, plus sweet red wine from Beaune de Venise, lemon, and orange; served covered of cream
Pruneaux au roquefort ⇒ stoned prunes filled with a mixing of Roquefort, crushed hazelnuts, cream and port; served chilled
Pruneaux déguisés ⇒ stoned prunes filled with a paste of sugar, almond powder, and rum
Prunelle ⇒ prunella or sloe
Pré salé ⇒ salt marsh sheep or salt marsh mutton
Prélat *(le ...) -[gâteau]-* ⇒ gateau made from alternate layers of sponge fingers moistened with0 coffee added of rum, plus a custard based on sugar, eggs and cream; covered with melted chocolate kneaded with butter
Prétentieux *-[pied bleu]-* ⇒ tricholoma mushroom
Prêtre *-[faux éperlan]-* ⇒ atherine
Psalliote ⇒ field mushroom
Psalliote des jachères ⇒ horse mushroom
Puant macéré *-[gris de lille]-* ⇒ cow's milk cheese from Lille area
Puchero ⇒ Spanish pot-au-feu
Pudding ⇒ pudding or plum pudding
Pudding à l'américaine ⇒ plum-pudding made of breadcrumbs, flour, brown sugar, beef bone-marrow, orange peel, lemon peel, eggs, nutmeg and rum
Pudding à la chicorée ⇒ baked plum-pudding made of ground chicory infusion, crumbs in milk, sultanas in rum, orange peel, sugar and eggs; served ... a ou b
  - nature ⇒ ... plain
  - nappé d'une crème anglaise à la vanille ⇒ ... covered with vanilla flavoured egg-custard

Pudding à la chipolata ⇒ mixing of prunes macerated in red wine, bits of pork kidney flamed with rum, a forcemeat of veal and pork, macaroni, chipolatas, plus fennel flower, then wrapped in a linen and poached; served hot with a sauce of chopped onions in pork fat, crumbs, white wine, stock, diced gherkins and mustard

Pudding à la semoule ⇒ plum-pudding made of semolina, milk, sugar, butter, and eggs; served with ...

- **sauce anglaise** ⇒ ... melted butter sauce
- **sauce à l'orange** ⇒ ... orange sauce

Pudding au chocolat ⇒ baked plum-pudding made of butter, chocolate, granulated sugar, vanilla sugar, eggs, and fecula; covered with egg-custard

Pudding au pain à la française ⇒ baked plum-pudding made of crumbs, eggs, granulated sugar, milk, raisins, preserved fruits, pear lamellas, and compote of apricots; served with a sauce of syrup, blackcurrant purée, and lemon juice

Pudding au pain et aux fruits à l'allemande ⇒ baked plum-pudding of diced bread and diced apples browned in butter, milk, orange peel, almond powder, Malaga raisins, granulated sugar, and eggs; served covered with a sauce of red wine, plus compote of apricots

Pudding au riz ⇒ small baked plum-pudding of rice, milk, granulated sugar, vanilla and eggs; served with
- **crème anglaise** ⇒ ... egg-custard
- **sabayon au rhum** ⇒ ... zabaglione made with rum
- **sauce aux fruits parfumée à la liqueur** ⇒ ... a fruit sauce flavoured of liqueur

Pudding aux amandes à l'anglaise ⇒ plum-pudding made of butter, granulated sugar, almonds, bitter orange tree extract, and eggs

Pudding aux poires à l'anglaise ⇒ pear pudding

Pudding aux pommes à l'anglaise ⇒ apple pudding

Pudding aux raisins de Corinthe ⇒ spotted dick

Pudding de biscuits aux fruits confits ⇒ plum-pudding made of currants macerated in rum, plus sponge fingers, milk, granulated sugar, preserved fruits, eggs and butter

Pudding de cabinet ⇒ baked plum-pudding made with alternate layers of currants, sponge fingers, preserved fruits, plus rum, then topped of vanilla flavoured cream mould; served with ... a ou b
- **crème anglaise** ⇒ ... vanilla flavoured egg-custard
- **sauce à l'abricot** ⇒ ... a sauce of apricot pulp, syrup and brandy

Pudding du Yorkshire ⇒ Yorkshire pudding

Pudding glacé Capucine ⇒ plum-pudding from alternate layers of Genoese, chilled mousse with tangerine purée, chilled mousse with caraway seed liqueur; served decorated of sugared whipped cream, on a socle of caramel, almonds and hazelnuts

Pudding nesselrode ⇒ pudding made with egg-custard added of chestnut purée, preserved fruits, raisins and whipped cream

Pudding soufflé au citron ⇒ baked plum-pudding of butter, granulated sugar, flour, milk, eggs, and lemon peel; served with egg-custard flavoured of lemon

Pudim flan -[*Portugal*]- ⇒ Portuguese pastry enriched with eggs

Puffed rice -[*riz gonflé à la chaleur*]- ⇒ puffed rice

Puits d'amour ⇒ small flaky pastries filled with jam or confectioner's custard

Puligny-Montrachet ⇒ Burgundy high quality wines from Côtes de Beaune

Pulpe -[*fruit*]- ⇒ pulp

Pulpe de tomate fraîche ⇒ tomato pulp

Pulque ⇒ Pulque

Pultost -[*fromage*]- ⇒ Pultost

Pumpernickel ⇒ rye bread

Pumpkin -[*Amérique du nord*]- ⇒ pumpkin

Punch ⇒ punch < *uncountable* >
Punch *-[biscuits]-* ⇒ small cakes made of semolina, eggs, rum, flour and butter; flavoured with orange and lemon extract
Punch antillais ⇒ punch made of pineapple juice, orange juice, barley water, and rum
Punch au kirsch ⇒ sugared tea infusion added of rum or kirsch, then flamed
Punch au thé ⇒ tea punch
Punch glacé ⇒ chilled punch of sugar, lemon peel, sweet white wine, sliced orange and lemon, plus rum
Punch marquise ⇒ punch of Sauternes white wine, sugar and lemon peel; flamed with cognac
Pupillin *-[vin de Franche Comté]-* ⇒ quality white wine from Franche Comté
Pur
    - général ⇒ pure
    - vin ⇒ undiluted wine
    - whisky, gin ⇒ neat or straight
    - boire son vin pur ⇒ to drink one's wine without water or to drink one's wine undiluted
Pur beurre *-[croissant]-* ⇒ crescent prepared with butter
Pur chèvre *-[fromage]-* ⇒ cheese made exclusively with goat's milk
Pur fruit *-[confiture]-* ⇒ jam sugared with brown sugar
Pur jus *-[cidre]-* ⇒ undiluted cider
Pur jus de fruit ⇒ natural fruit juice
Pur malt *-[whisky]-* ⇒ whisky made with a mixing of different malts
Pur porc *-[saucisson]-* ⇒ large sausage made only of pork meat
Pure *-[huile d'olive]-* ⇒ mixing of extra olive oil and refined olive oil
Pure panne *-[panne ou saindoux]-* ⇒ pork fat
Purl *-[boisson]-* ⇒ purl
Purée ⇒ purée
Purée à la bretonne ⇒ mashed haricot beans
Purée d'ail ⇒ paste of garlic added of béchamel sauce
Purée d'anchois ⇒ anchovy purée added of butter and béchamel sauce
    - garniture pour beignets ⇒ fritters
    - bouchées ⇒ patties
    - rissoles ⇒ rissoles
Purée d'anchois chaude ⇒ anchovy purée added of hard boiled egg-yolks, béchamel sauce and herbs
    - garnitures des bouchées ⇒ patties
    - tartelettes ⇒ tartlets
    - rissoles ⇒ rissoles
Purée d'anchois froide ⇒ anchovy purée added of hard boiled egg-yolks, butter and herbs
    - sert pour farçir œufs durs ⇒ hard boiled eggs stuffed with ...
    - fonds d'artichaut ⇒ artichoke hearts garnished with ...
    - poissons tels que rougets ⇒ red gurnards stuffed with ...
Purée d'avocats ⇒ avocado purée
Purée d'endives ⇒ mashed chicory added of ...
    - avec beurre ⇒ ... butter
    - avec crème ⇒ ... cream
    - avec béchamel ⇒ ... béchamel sauce
    - servie gratinée ⇒ ...; served au gratin
Purée d'épinards ⇒ mashed spinach added of butter, ...
    - avec purée de pommes de terre ⇒ ... thickened of mashed potatoes
    - avec béchamel ⇒ ... thickened of béchamel sauce

Purée d'estragon à chaud ⇒ mashed tarragon added of mashed potatoes
- **variante avec béchamel** ⇒ mashed tarragon added of béchamel sauce

Purée d'estragon à froid ⇒ mashed tarragon added of hard boiled egg-yolks, and butter

Purée d'oseille ⇒ purée of mashed sorrel, roux, cream and butter

Purée d'oursins ⇒ mashed sea-urchins added of béchamel sauce and butter
- **garniture pour bouchées feuilletées** ⇒ patties in puff-pastry garnished with ...
- **garnitre pour tartelettes** ⇒ tartlets filled with ...
- **sur tranches de pain** ⇒ ... spreaded on slices of bread, then sprinkled of grated cheese and browned

Purée de cardons ⇒ cardoon purée added of ...
- **purée de pommes de terre** ⇒ ... mashed potatoes
- **béchamel** ⇒ ... béchamel sauce

Purée de carottes ⇒ mashed carrots

Purée de carottes à la crème ⇒ mashed carrots added of cream

Purée de carottes Crécy ⇒ purée of carrots and rice

Purée de céleri ⇒ mashed celery

Purée de cervelle ⇒ mashed ox brain added of béchamel sauce and cream
- **garniture pour bouchées** ⇒ patties stuffed with ...
- **garniture pourbarquettes** ⇒ pastry boats filled with ...
- **farçi les têtes de champignons** ⇒ mushrooms filled with ...
- **farçi les fonds d'artichau** ⇒ artichoke hearts filled with ...

Purée de champignons ⇒ mashed mushrooms added of béchamel sauce, cream, white pepper, nutmeg, and butter

Purée de chicorée ⇒ mashed endives, added of béchamel sauce, veal stock, and cream

Purée de courgettes ⇒ purée of courgettes and garlic; served sprinkled of herbs, or au gratin

Purée de cresson ⇒ mashed watercress ...
- **avec pois cassés** ⇒ ... added of mashed split peas and cream
- **avec purée de pommes de terre** ⇒ ... added of mashed potatoes and cream

Purée de crevettes ⇒ mashed shrimps added of béchamel sauce and cream
- **s'emploie pour compléter farces** ⇒ forcemeat
- **sauce** ⇒ sauce < *pour poissons et crustacés* >

Purée de fèves fraîches ⇒ mashed broad beans thickened with consommé

Purée de foie de veau ou de volaille

   a) **foie de veau** ⇒ mashed calf liver flavoured with Madeira

   b) **foies de volaille** ⇒ mashed poultry livers flavoured with Madeira < *s'emploie pour farce à gratin* >

Purée de foie gras ⇒ mashed foie gras thickened of velouté and egg-yolks
- **garniture pour bouchées** ⇒ patties garnished with ...
- **barquettes** ⇒ pastry boats filled with ...
- **tartelettes** ⇒ tartlets garnished with ...
- **brioches** ⇒ brioches filled with ...
- **fonds d'artichaut** ⇒ artichoke hearts garnished with ...
- **têtes de champignons** ⇒ mushrooms garnished with ...

Purée de foie gras nature ⇒ mashed foie gras
- **garnitures hors d'œuvre froids** ⇒ hors d'œuvre
- **œufs** ⇒ eggs

Purée de fonds d'artichaut ⇒ mashed artichoke hearts added of butter or cream
- **variante avec purée de pommes de terre** ⇒ mashed artichoke hearts, added of butter and mashed potatoes

Purée de fruits ⇒ fruit purée
Purée de gibier ⇒ mashed game meat added of rice
Purée de haricots ⇒ mashed haricot beans added of butter
Purée de haricots verts ⇒ mashed french beans added of butter
Purée de laitue ⇒ mashed braised lettuce added of béchamel sauce
Purée de lentilles ⇒ mashed lentils ...
Purée de maïs au foie gras ⇒ mashed maize mixed with foie gras; served au gratin
Purée de marrons ⇒ mashed chestnuts or chestnut purée
Purée de piment ⇒ pimento purée flavoured with onion and ginger
Purée de pois cassés ⇒ mashed split peas
Purée de pommes de terre ⇒ mashed potatoes
Purée de potiron ⇒ mashed pumpkin added of mashed potatoes
Purée de saumon ⇒ mashed salmon added of béchamel sauce and butter
    - **garniture pour barquettes** ⇒ pastry boats garnished with ...
    - **garniture pour croustades** ⇒ croustades filled with ...
    - **garniture pour oeufs durs** ⇒ hard boiled eggs stuffed with ...
Purée de saumon fumé ⇒ mashed smoked salmon added of lemon juice, egg-yolks and butter
    - **garniture pour canapés** ⇒ savouries garnished with ...
    - **garniture pour barquettes** ⇒ pastry boats filled with ...
    - **garniture pour crêpes froides** ⇒ pancakes garnished with ...
    - **garniture pour tranches de saumon fumé en cornets** ⇒ cornet of sliced smoked salmon, filled with ...
Purée de tomates ⇒ tomato purée
Purée de volaille ⇒ mashed poultry meat added of rice
    - **garniture bouchées** ⇒ patties filled with ...
    - **barquettes** ⇒ pastry boats filled with ...
    - **farçi têtes de champignons** ⇒ mushrooms garnished with ...
    - **fonds d'artichaut** ⇒ artichoke hearts garnished with ...
Purée mousseline ⇒ mashed potatoes
Purée St Germain ⇒ purée of peas, lettuce, onions, chervil, consommé and cream
Purée sur croûtons *-[pâtisserie]-* ⇒ sippets fried in butter, garnished with mashed apples and some preserved cherries
Pyramide ⇒ pyramid
Pyramide du Poitou *-[fromage]-* ⇒ goat's milk cheese
Pytt i panna *-[suède]-* ⇒ diced potatoes and diced meat sautéed with onion, then sprinkled of parsley; served with egg

Q

Qahwa -*[café]*- ⇒ coffee
Quadrillage ⇒ chequer work
Quadriller
- **cuisson au grill** ⇒ criss-crossed marks let by the grilling
- **pâtisserie quadrillage avec des bandes de pâte** ⇒ chequer work of paste lamellas
- **dessin fait avec la pointe d'une brochette** ⇒ chequer drawn made with a skewer
- **croisillons de filets d'anchois** ⇒ ... covered with a chequer work of anchovy fillets

Qakers -*[avoine]*- ⇒ oat flakes
Quark -*[Allemagne]*- ⇒ soft white cheese added of onion, paprika, or herbs
Quart ⇒ a quarter or one fourth part
Quart de maroilles ⇒ cheese made at Maroilles
Quart de vin ⇒ a quarter litre of wine
Quartenier -*[sanglier]*- ⇒ a four years old wild boar
Quartier
- **portion de boeuf** ⇒ quarter
- **quartier avant de boeuf** ⇒ foreparts or forequarters
- **quartier arrière de boeuf** ⇒ hindquarter
- **viande** ⇒ large piece or chunk
- **fruits** ⇒ piece or segment

Quartier -*[venaison]*- ⇒ haunch of deer
Quartier arrière -*[boeuf]*- ⇒ hindquarter
Quartier avant -*[boeuf]*- ⇒ forequarter of beef
Quartier avant coupé à 5 côtes « entièrement désossé » -*[boeuf]*- ⇒ boneless fore 1/4 of beef
Quartier avant coupé à 5 côtes -*[boeuf]*- ⇒ short fore 1/4 of beef
Quartier avant d'agneau ⇒ forequarter of lamb
Quartier avant de mouton ⇒ forequarter of mutton
Quartier avant désossé -*[boeuf]*- ⇒ boneless fore quarter of beef
Quarts de chaume -*[vin]*- ⇒ high quality white wine from Angers area
Quasi de veau ⇒ chump or veal's thick end of loin
- **indication pour traduction se cuisine en escalopes** ⇒ escalope
- **rôti** ⇒ roast
- **braisé** ⇒ braised
- **en blanquette** ⇒ blanquette
- **en fricandeau** ⇒ fricandeau
- **en sauté** ⇒ sauté

Quassia ⇒ quassia
Quassier ⇒ quassia
Quassine ⇒ quassia extract
Quatourze -*[vin]*- ⇒ quality wine from Languedoc area
Quatre côtes de l'aloyau sorties -*[bœuf]*- ⇒ sirloin « wing rib »
Quatre côtes de l'aloyau, désossées et ficelées -*[bœuf]*- ⇒ sirloin « wing rib, boned and rolled »
Quatre épices ⇒ mixing of pepper, nutmeg, clove and cinnamon
- **botanique** ⇒ fennel flower
- **si tiré des graines de la nigelle** ⇒ crushed nigella seeds

Quatre fruits ⇒ strawberries, cherries, redcurrant, raspberry
Quatre mendiants ⇒ dessert composed of figs, almonds, raisins and hazelnuts

Quatre-quarts ⇒ chocolate cake or pound cake
Quatre quarts à l'orange ⇒ pound cake flavoured of curaçao, and orange peel; covered with marmalade
Quatre quarts aux pommes ⇒ pound cake with apples
Quatre-quarts au chocolat ⇒ gateau made of chocolate, butter, eggs, sugar, flour and lemon juice; then baked
Qemeu (en ...) -[tarte]- ⇒ tart filled with scrambled eggs, sugar, milk, and cream
Quenelle ⇒ quenelle
   - de viande ⇒ meat ball
   - de poisson ⇒ fish-ball
Quenelle de foie gras ⇒ foie gras quenelle
Quenelles de brochet ⇒ poached quenelles of pike, panada, flour, eggs, and butter
Quenelles de brochet à la florentine ⇒ dish of pike quenelles, spinach in cream, and béchamel sauce; served au gratin
Quenelles de brochet à la lyonnaise ⇒ pike quenelles in béchamel sauce; served au gratin
Quenelles de brochet mousseline ⇒ quenelles made with a forcemeat of pike meat, nutmeg, egg and cream
Quenelles de saumon ⇒ salmon quenelles covered with ...
   - sauce Nantua ⇒ voir texte
   - sauce crème ⇒ voir texte
   - sauce crevette ⇒ voir texte
   - sauce au vin blanc ⇒ voir texte
Quenelles de veau ⇒ veal quenelles cooked with béchamel sauce
Quenelles de volaille ⇒ poultry quenelles cooked with béchamel sauce
Quernoux d'Angers ⇒ sweet filled or wrapped with chocolate
Quesadilla -[tortilla]- ⇒ tortilla stuffed with meat in sauce, or vegetables in cheese; fried in pork fat
Queso ⇒ Spanish cheese
Quetsche
   - prune ⇒ quetsch plum
   - eau de vie ⇒ quetsch
Quetsche -[eau de vie]- ⇒ quetsch
Queue ⇒ tail
Queue de boeuf ⇒ oxtail
Queue de boeuf en hochepot ⇒ pot au feu of ox tail lengths, pork trotters, ear of pork, cabbage, carrots, turnips and onions; served with grilled chipolatas, and steamed potatoes
Queue de boeuf grillées à la Ste Ménéhould ⇒ boiled lengths of ox tail, coated of mustard, butter and crumbs, then grilled; served with ...
   - sauce diable ⇒ ... devilled sauce ...
   - sauce piquante ⇒ voir texte ...
   - sauce à la moutarde ⇒ voir texte ...
   - sauce poivrade ⇒ voir texte ...
   - sauce bordelaise ⇒ voir texte ...
   - sauce Robert ⇒ voir texte ... plus mashed potatoes
Queue de cerise ⇒ cherry stalk
   - infusion ⇒ infusion of cherry stalks
Queues de crevettes ⇒ shrimp tails
Queues de filet -[bœuf]- ⇒ fillet tails
Queue de porc ⇒ pig tail
Queue de porc bouillie ⇒ boiled pig tail
Queue de porc braisée ⇒ braised pig tail

Queue de porc panée et grillée ⇒ pig tail breaded and grilled

Queue de veau ⇒ calf tail

Queue de veau Ste Ménéhould ⇒ calf tail cooked slowly with onion and herbs, then covered with breadcrumbs, and grilled

Queues d'écrevisses ⇒ crayfish tails

Queue entière -[bœuf]- ⇒ ox tail

Quiaude -[canada]- ⇒ dish with heads of salt cod

Quiche ⇒ quiche

Quiche au jambon et au fromage ⇒ quiche with ham and gruyère

Quiche aux moules ⇒ quiche with mussels; served accompanied of white wine

Quiche lorraine ⇒ quiche filled with lardoons and eggs

Quiché ⇒ slice of bread covered with anchovies and olive oil, then browned

Quillet ⇒ stuffed small cake; decorated with buttered custard, flavoured of orgeat syrup

Quincy ⇒ white wine from Berry

Quinquina ⇒ quinquina or Peruvian bark or cinchona

Quinquina maison ⇒ home made quinquina aperitif

R

Rabarbaro ⇒ rhubarb aperitif

Râble
- **lièvre** ⇒ saddle of hare
- **lapin** ⇒ saddle of rabbit

Râble à la cauchoise ⇒ saddle of rabbit marinated in white wine and aromatics, then baked, covered with the cooking juice thickened of cream and mustard; served with sauté rennet apples

Râble de lièvre à l'allemande ⇒ saddle of hare baked in a marinade of carrot, onion, shallot, celery, garlic, oil, parsley, thyme and laurel; served with a compote of apples, plus redcurrant jelly

Râble de lièvre aux airelles ⇒ saddle of hare stewed with bilberries; served surrounded of sauté potatoes

Râble de lièvre rôti ⇒ saddle of hare studded with lardoons and roasted; served with sliced lemon, and ...
- **sauce avec vin blanc** ⇒ ... the gravy added of white wine
- **sauce poivrade** ⇒ ... a sauce of vegetables cooked in vinegar and white wine, seasoned with pepper
- **sauce plus vin blanc et crème épaisse** ⇒ ... the gravy added of white wine, plus pasteurized cream

Rabote ⇒ whole apple or pear wrapped in short pastry, and baked

Rabotte ⇒ whole apple or pear wrapped in short pastry, and baked

Racahout ⇒ fecula for porridge

Race -[animal]- ⇒ breed

Rachel
1) **garniture pour**
   - **petites pièces de boucherie grillées** ⇒ grilled ... or sauté ...
   - **ris de veau braisé** ⇒ braised calf sweetbreads ...
   - **oeufs pochés** ⇒ poached eggs ...
   - **oeufs mollets** ⇒ soft boiled eggs ... garnished with artichoke hearts filled of bone-marrow lamellas and ...
   - **sauce bordelaise** ⇒ ... voir texte
   - **sauce à la moelle** ⇒ ... voir texte
2) **salade composée** ⇒ composed salad with artichoke hearts
3) **merlan** ⇒ poached whiting covered with ... sauce Nantua, and garnished with truffle in julienne
   - **turbot** ⇒ poached turbot covered with ... sauce Nantua, and garnished with truffle in julienne

Racine ⇒ root of vegetable

Raclette -[fondue]- ⇒ Raclette

Radis ⇒ radish

Radis de Satzouma -[daikon]- ⇒ Japanese radish

Radis du japon -[daikon]- ⇒ Japanese radish

Radis noir ⇒ black radish

Radis noir en hors d'œuvre ⇒ slices of black radish, served with rye bread and butter

Radis rose ⇒ radish

Radis roses à l'américaine ⇒ radishes served with butter and salt

Radisse -[Lyonnais]- ⇒ large brioches from Lyon

Rafraîchi *(e ...)* ⇒ cooled or chilled, v.t adjectif, or freshened
Rafraîchissement *-[boisson]-* ⇒ refreshment
Ragondin ou Myocastor ⇒ coypu
Ragot *-[sanglier]-* ⇒ two years old wild boar
Ragoule *-[pleurote]-* ⇒ gloomy mushroom
Ragoût
  - **viande ou poisson** ⇒ ragout or hotpot
  - **légumes** ⇒ ragout of vegetables
Ragout ⇒ ragout or stew
Ragout à la cancalaise ⇒ a ragout of poached oysters and shrimp tails, thickened with fish velouté
    sauce added of cream and mushrooms
  - **accompagne des poissons entiers** ⇒ nom anglais ... plus ...
  - **accompagne des filets de poisson** ⇒ id ... fillets plus ...
  - **sert à garnir les croustades** ⇒ croustades garnished with ...
  - **des tourtes** ⇒ pies filled with ...
  - **vol au vent** ⇒ vol-au-vent garnished with ...
Ragoût à la cévenole ⇒ ragout of braised chestnuts, onions, and diced streaky bacon; served with the
    meat, thickened of the gravy
  - **Servi avec viande braisée** ⇒ braised ... nom anglais de la viande qui remplace « the meat »
    dans le texte
Ragoût d'agneau à l'anglaise ⇒ ragout of lamb, sliced potatoes, onions and aromatics; served in
    timbale, sprinkled of parsley
Ragoût d'asperges aux petits pois ⇒ ragout of sauté onions, peas, asparagus and poultry stock
Ragoût de béatilles ⇒ ragout of lamb sweetbread, cockscombs, poultry livers, cultivated mushrooms,
    truffle lamellas and Madeira; served with a sauce of poultry stock, cream, Madeira
    and butter
Ragoût de céleri-rave ⇒ ragout of shaped celeriac, butter and pepper; thickened of béchamel sauce
    added of cream
  - **garniture pour viande blanche braisée** ⇒ braised ...
  - **garniture pour rôtie** ⇒ roasted ...
  - **veau** ⇒ veal
  - **porc** ⇒ pork
  - **lapin** ⇒ rabbit
  - **volaille** ⇒ poultry ... garnished with a ... < *texte en tête* >
Ragoût de champignons ⇒ ragout of sauté cultivated mushrooms, Madeira, and béchamel sauce
    added of cream
  - **garniture de viande blanche braisée ou rôtie, ou de poisson rôti** ⇒ ...; served with a ...
Ragoût de coquillages ⇒ stew of shellfishes in white wine, shelled and thickened of white sauce;
    served with rice
Ragoût de crustacés ⇒ ragout of crustacean, thickened with ...
  - **sauce crème** ⇒ ... béchamel sauce added of cream; served with rice
  - **ou sauce au vin blanc** ⇒ ... a sauce of fish stock in white wine, egg-yolks, butter, lemon juice,
    and mushroom peel served with rice
Ragoût de fruits de mer ⇒ ragout of mussels, Norway lobsters, scallops and shrimps; covered with
    the cooking juice, added of tomatoes, cognac, onion and cream
Ragout de légumes à la printanière ⇒ ragout of carrots, turnips, onions, lettuce, french beans, peas,
    artichoke hearts, cauliflower and poultry stock
Ragoût de mouton à la bonne femme ⇒ ragout of lamb with onion, garlic, tomato purée, onions,
    streaky bacon, and potatoes
  - **variantes; remplacer « potatoes » par céleri-rave** ⇒ celeriac

Ragoût de mouton à la bonne femme ⇒ with ... (suite)
- **choux raves** ⇒ kohlrabi
- **haricots** ⇒ haricot beans
- **pois chiches** ⇒ chick peas
- **S'il est accompagné ajouter** ⇒ served with ...
- **macédoine de légumes** ⇒ vegetable salad
- **ratatouille** ⇒ ratatouille
- **riz à l'indienne** ⇒ voir texte

Ragoût de mouton à la niçoise ⇒ ragout of lamb with onion, garlic, tomato purée, onions, streaky bacon, and potatoes; plus braised courgettes

Ragoût de mouton aux pois chiches ⇒ ragout of lamb with onion, garlic, tomato purée, onions, streaky bacon, and chick peas

Ragoût de pâtes aux géziers et aux cous de canard ⇒ ragout from conserved giblets of duck, onions, carrots, garlic, and macaroni

Ragoût de poivrons doux à l'orientale ⇒ grilled capsicums, stewed with onion, garlic, consommé and pepper

Ragoût de queues d'écrevisses à la Nantua ⇒ ragout of diced vegetables and ham, crayfishes, white wine, béchamel sauce, cream and cognac
- **si le plat est complété de champignons ou autres, ajouter** ⇒ ... plus nom anglais

Ragoût de truffes ⇒ ragout of truffles, sweet natural wine from Collioure area, red wine, butter and flour; served with croutons coated of goose fat

Ragoût des îles à la créole ⇒ ragout of shoulder of beef or scrag of mutton, onions, carrots, potatoes, tomatoes, plus chopped pimento, pepper, vinegar, peanut butter, and grilled herring meat; served with rice

Ragu -*[sauce pour pâtes]*- ⇒ bolognèse sauce enriched of chopped ham, vegetables, beef, streaky bacon, chicken livers and wine

Rahat loukoum -*[loukoum]*- ⇒ sweet based on sugar, honey, syrup, flour and aromatics

Raïb -*[lait caillé]*- ⇒ curdled milk

Raidir -*[cuisson]*- ⇒ first cooking in fat
- **si fin de la cuisson avec de la sauce blanche, ajouter** ⇒ ... before to end the process in white sauce

Raie ⇒ ray or skate

Raie au beurre noir ⇒ ray fried in browned butter added of capers, chopped parsley and vinegar

Raie au beurre noisette ⇒ poached ray, sprinkled of lemon juice and parsley, then moistened of butter cooked lightly

Raie au citron ⇒ ray poached in salted water added of lemon and grated apple; served with cream, pepper, and grated nutmeg

Raie au gratin ⇒ ray baked on a layer of shallots and parsley, moistened of white wine; sprinkled with crumbs and butter, then browned

Raie aux câpres ⇒ ray browned in butter with capers

Raie blonde et autres ⇒ blonde ray
- **Raie bouclée** ⇒ thornback ray
- **autres raies** ⇒ cuckoo ray; eagle ray; spotted ray; undulate ray; common skate; common stingray

Raie bouclée -*[poisson]*- ⇒ Thornback ray

Raie fleurie ⇒ cuckoo ray

Raie marbrée ⇒ undulate ray

Raifort ⇒ horse-radish < *uncountable* >

Raiponce ⇒ rampion

Raisin ⇒ grape

Raisin *(pépins de ...)* -*[huile]*- ⇒ grape pip oil

Raisins de corinthe ⇒ currants
Raisins de malaga ⇒ Malaga raisins
Raisins de Smyrne ⇒ sultanas
Raisins secs ⇒ raisins
Raisiné ⇒ jam without sugar made of grape juice added of fruits
Raisiné de Bourgogne ⇒ jam without sugar, made of grape juice added of pears, quinces, apples,
    melon, etc
Raitas ⇒ Indian vegetable salad, seasoned with yoghourt
Raite -*[Raïto]-* ⇒ seasoning made of onions, tomatoes, garlic, ground walnuts, laurel, thyme, parsley,
    fennel, rosemary and clove; simmered in olive oil and red wine
Raiteau -*[petite raie]-* ⇒ small ray or small skate
Raiteaux frits ⇒ small skates steeped in milk and fried; served with quartered lemons
Raïto ⇒ seasoning made of onions, tomatoes, garlic, ground walnuts, laurel, thyme, parsley, fennel,
    rosemary and clove; simmered in olive oil and red wine
Raki ⇒ Turkish aperitif
Rakija -*[slivovitz]-* ⇒ slivovitz
Rakorret ⇒ trout fermented in sugar and salt
Râle ⇒ rail
    - **Râle des genêts** ⇒ land rail or corncrake
    - **Râle d'eau** ⇒ water-rail < *se cuisine comme la caille* >
Rambollet -*[Savoie]-* ⇒ potato croquette with prunes
Ramboutan ⇒ kind of litchi
Rambure -*[pomme]-* ⇒ variety of apple
Ramequin
    - **ustensile** ⇒ ramekin
    - **plat** ⇒ ramekin
Ramequin douaisien ⇒ small bread stuffed of chopped kidney, crumbs, eggs, and herbs
Ramequin du pays de gex ⇒ gruyère and blue cheese, melted in stock, red wine, butter, garlic, and
    mustard; served as a fondue
Ramequin vaudois ⇒ cheese au gratin, served on slices of bread
Ramereau ⇒ young ring-dove
Ramerot ⇒ young ring-dove
Ramier ⇒ wood-pigeon or ring-dove
Ran ou Bulot ⇒ sea gastropod
Rance ⇒ rancid
Rancio -*[banyuls]-* ⇒ kind of Malaga wine
Râpé
    - **général** ⇒ grated < *v.t adjectif* >
    - **fromage** ⇒ grated cheese or grated ... nom anglais
Râs al hânout ⇒ mixing of clove, cinnamon and pepper
Rascasse ⇒ scorpion fish or sea-scorpion or short-spined sea scorpion or long-spined sea scorpion
Rascasse blanche -*[vive]-* ⇒ Mediterranean weever
Rasimat -*[Périgord]-* ⇒ gateau made with nuts, grape, lemon and quinces
Rasoir -*[couteau mollusque]-* ⇒ solen or razor-shell
Rassis -*[pain]-* ⇒ stale bread
Rassolnick ⇒ Russian soup of poultry stock, cucumber extract, egg-yolk, cream and poultry meat
Rasteau -*[vin]-* ⇒ sweet red wine from Beaumes de Venise
Rastegaï ⇒ Russian small pie with a forcemeat of sturgeon bone-marrow, hard boiled egg and salmon;
    served with melted butter

Rat -*[poisson; vive]*- ⇒ weever
Ratafia -*[liqueur]*- ⇒ ratafia liqueur
Ratafia bourguignon ⇒ unripe grape juice added of alcohol
Ratafia d'acacia ⇒ ratafia of acacia flowers, eau de vie and sugar
Ratafia de coing ⇒ brandy made of eau de vie and quince
Ratafia d'œillet ⇒ pink ratafia
Ratatouille ⇒ ratatouille
Ratatouille créole ⇒ Caribbean ratatouille added of okra
Ratatouille niçoise ⇒ ratatouille of tomatoes, courgettes, onions, capsicums, garlic, and aubergines
             with thyme; braised in olive oil
Rate ⇒ spleen
Raton ⇒ puff-pastry filled of soft white cheese
Ratte -*[pomme de terre]*- ⇒ variety of potato for salad
Ravaille -*[pain]*- ⇒ bread from Ariège area
Rave
       - **général** ⇒ root
       - **betterave** ⇒ beetroot
       - **chou-rave** ⇒ kohlrabi
       - **celeri-rave** ⇒ celeriac
Ravigote ⇒ ravigote sauce
Raviole
       - **cuisine niçoise** ⇒ casing in pasta, stuffed with a hash of spinach, or beet, or cheese cooked in
             water
       - **cuisine savoyarde** ⇒ poached small balls of spinach, beet, flour, cheese, and eggs; browned
             and served with tomato sauce
Ravioli ⇒ ravoli < *invariable* >
Ravioli à la niçoise ⇒ ravioli stuffed with minced meat, spinach and beet; sprinkled with grated
             Parmesan, melted butter and tomato purée, then browned
Ravioli aux herbes ⇒ ravioli stuffed with a hash of beets, spinach, parsley and edible agaric; served
             with melted butter and grated cheese
       - **s'il est accompagné de sauce tomate et ciboulette, ajouter** ⇒ Accompanied with a sauce
             of tomato pulp, chives, lemon juice and olive oil
Ravioli pour potages ⇒ ravioli stuffed with a forcemeat of poultry livers or sweetbreads
       - **potage ou consommé au ravioli** ⇒ soup or consommé added of; ravioli stuffed with a
             forcemeat of poultry livers or sweetbreads
Raviolle
       - **cuisine niçoise** ⇒ casing in pasta, stuffed with a hash of spinach, or beet, or cheese cooked in
             water
       - **cuisine savoyarde** ⇒ poached small balls of spinach, beet, flour, cheese, and eggs; browned
             and served with tomato sauce
Rayte ⇒ seasoning made of onions, tomatoes, garlic, ground walnuts, laurel, thyme, parsley, fennel,
             rosemary and clove; simmered in olive oil and red wine
Raïto ⇒ seasoning made of onions, tomatoes, garlic, ground walnuts, laurel, thyme, parsley, fennel,
             rosemary and clove; simmered in olive oil and red wine
Reblochon ⇒ pressed cow's milk cheese with a yellow or red crust
Réchauffé *(e ...)* ⇒ warmed up again
Récolte ⇒ harvest or gathering or grape-picking
Reconstituer ⇒ to reconstitute
       - **reconstitué** ⇒ reconstituted < *v.t adjectif* >
Red gauntlet -*[fraise]*- ⇒ variety of fraise

Redhaven -*[pêche]*- ⇒ variety of peach
Réduction
- **général** ⇒ reduction by boiling
- **liquide ou sauce** ⇒ ... thickened < *dans ce dernier cas le mot anglais a le sens d'épaissir* >
Réduire
- **sauce** ⇒ to reduce
- **général** ⇒ to boil down or to boil away
- **les épinards réduisent à la cuisson** ⇒ spinach shrinks when you cooked it
- **faire ou laisser réduire la sauce** ⇒ to cook or to simmer the sauce to reduce it
Redwing -*[pêche]*- ⇒ variety of peach
Red Windsor -*[fromage]*- ⇒ red Windsor
Réforme ⇒ reform sauce
- **accompagne côtelettes d'agneau** ⇒ texte
- **fourre une omelette** ⇒ omelet stuffed with reform sauce
- **accompagne côtelettes de gibier** ⇒ texte
- **accompagne petites pièces de venaison** ⇒ texte
Reform -*[sauce]*- ⇒ reform sauce
- **accompagne côtelettes d'agneau** ⇒ texte
- **fourre une omelette** ⇒ omelet stuffed with reform sauce
- **accompagne côtelettes de gibier** ⇒ texte
- **accompagne petites pièces de venaison** ⇒ texte
Refroidi ⇒ cooled < *v.t adjectif* >
Refroidir ⇒ to cool
- **refroidi** ⇒ cooled < *v.t adjectif* >
Régence -*[garniture]*-
- **de quenelles de poisson** ⇒ ... with a garnish of fish quenelles ...
- **de quenelles de volaille** ⇒ ... with a garnish of poultry quenelles ...
- **de quenelles de veau** ⇒ ... with a garnish of veal quenelles ... plus poached mushrooms and truffle lamellas
- **Si servies avec des huîtres pochées, ajouter** ⇒ served with poached oysters, covered of velouté sauce added of cream, mushrooms, and truffle extract
- **Si servies avec des escalopes de foie gras, ajouter** ⇒ served with foie gras escalopes, covered of supreme sauce
Régence -*[pain]*- ⇒ bread made of juxtaposed small balls
Reggiano -*[fromage]*- ⇒ Reggiano
Régime ⇒ diet
Régime ⇒ hand of ... or cluster of ...
- **datte** ⇒ dates
- **bananes** ⇒ bananas
Région -*[vin]*- ⇒ area
Réglisse ⇒ liquorice
Reguigneu ⇒ slices of ham steeped in scrambled eggs, and fried
Rehoboham -*[bouteille]*- ⇒ rehoboam
Rein avec gras et couenne -*[porc]*- ⇒ middle hogmeat
Rein avec gras et couenne, désossé -*[porc]*- ⇒ middle hogmeat « boned and rolled »
Rein avec rognon découenné -*[porc]*- ⇒ long hogmeat « boneless »
Rein découenné, dégraissé et désossé -*[porc]*- ⇒ short hogmeat « boneless »
Rein désossé et ficelé -*[porc]*- ⇒ middle loin of pork « boned and rolled » or middle loin of pork « boneless »

Rein entier « sans flanchet » comprenant 2 rumsteacks, 2 faux filets, 2 carrés première ⇒
   full baron
Rein sans échine avec rognon -*[porc]*- ⇒ middle loin of pork
Reine *(à la ...)* ⇒ ... with poultry, sweetbread, mushrooms, truffle and supreme sauce
Reine -*[poulet]*- ⇒ category of chicken
Reine claude ⇒ greengage
Reine de Saba ⇒ cake shaped in disc, based on chocolate and whipped white of eggs
Reine des noires -*[courgette]*- ⇒ variety of courgette
Reine des prés -*[tisane]*- ⇒ meadow-sweet
Reinette ⇒ rennet apple
Réjane
   - **garniture petites pièces de boucherie ou ris de veau braisés** ⇒ ... garnished with
      cassolettes of any meat, spinach in butter, braised quartered artichoke hearts, bone-
      marrow, plus the cooking juice added of Madeira
   - **salade** ⇒ salad of sliced potatoes, asparagus tips and truffles
   - **paupiettes de merlan** ⇒ small round balls of whiting served on moulded mashed potatoes,
      then topped with oysters, mushroom, truffle lamella and shrimp
Religieuse
   - **chou** ⇒ large cream puff flavoured with coffee or chocolate
   - **tarte** ⇒ apple and apricot jam tart
Religieuse -*[raclette]*- ⇒ crust of melted cheese from the Raclette
Religieuse à l'ancienne ⇒ sugared pastry filled with choux pastry stuffed of custard, and topped with
      cream
Religieuse au café ⇒ choux pastry, glazed with a vanilla cream added of coffee extract
Relish ⇒ relish seasoning < *assaisonne plats exotiques, steaks hachés, crudités, viandes froides* >
Rémora ⇒ remora or small headed sucker or cornish sucker or sucking fish
Remoudou ⇒ Belgian cow's milk cheese
Rémoulade ⇒ remoulade
Remuer ⇒ to stir
Renaissance *(à la ...)*
   a) **grosse pièce de boucherie braisée** ⇒ braised ...
      - **grosse pièce de boucherie rôtie** ⇒ roasted ...
   b) **poularde pochée** ⇒ poached fattened pullet ...
      - **poularde rôtie** ⇒ roasted fattened pullet ... with a garnish of alternate vegetables, as
         carrots, turnips, browned potatoes, braised lettuce, french beans, asparagus tips and
         cauliflower; covered with the gravy or suprême sauce
Renard -*[poisson]*- ⇒ thresher
Renne ⇒ reindeer
Renversé à l'ananas ⇒ upside down cake
Requin ⇒ shark
Reservados -*[Argentine vins]*- ⇒ bottled Argentinian wines
Resseto -*[pompe]*- ⇒ large brioche flavoured with aniseed, orange peel or blossom flowers
Reste -*[viande, pain, etc]*- ⇒ left over
Resy -*[pomme de terre]*- ⇒ variety of potato
Rétès ⇒ Hungarian pastry garnished with soft white cheese, added of raisins and white of eggs
Retsina ⇒ retsina
Reuilly ⇒ white wine from Berry
Réveillon
   - **Noël** ⇒ Christmas supper
   - **Jour de l'an** ⇒ New year's Eve supper or New year's Eve party

- **Réveillonner** ⇒ to have a midnight party
Reverchon *-[cerise]-* ⇒ variety of cherry
Revesset ⇒ bouillabaisse from Toulon area
Rey *-[cocido]-* ⇒ Spanish meal made of various dishes
Rhin *-[vins du]-* ⇒ Rhine wines
- **Rheingau blanc** ⇒ riesling
- **Rheingau rouge** ⇒ Assmannshauser
- **Reinhessen vin ordinaire** ⇒ ordinary wine
- **Palatinat vins rouges et blancs** ⇒ red or white wines
Rhodyménie *-[algues]-* ⇒ dulse
Rhubarbe ⇒ rhubarb < *uncountable* >
Rhum ⇒ rum
Rhum grand arôme ⇒ rum slowly fermented
Ribet *-[pêche]-* ⇒ variety of peach
Riblette *-[viande]-* ⇒ thin slice of meat
Rice flakes ⇒ rice flakes
Riche *(à la ...)*
- **bécasse** ⇒ voir texte
- **sauce** ⇒ voir texte
Richebourg *-[Vosnes romanée]-* ⇒ high quality Burgundy red wine
Richelieu *-[garniture]-*
1) **garniture pour grosses pièces de boucherie**
- **« baron de boeuf »** ⇒ baron of beef ...
- **« gigot de mouton »** ⇒ leg of mutton ... with a garnish of stuffed tomatoes, stuffed mushrooms, braised lettuce, plus ...
- **pommes rissolées** ⇒ browned potatoes
- **pommes château** ⇒ small potatoes sautéed in butter with lardoons
2) **sole** ⇒ sole coated of egg and crumbs, then cooked in butter, garnished with parsley butter and truffle lamellas
3) **filets de sole** ⇒ sole fillets coated of egg and crumbs, then cooked in butter, garnished with parsley butter and truffle lamellas
4) **boudins à la richelieu** ⇒ forcemeat of poultry added with a culinary stuffing of diced white of meat, mushrooms and truffle, plus a sauce; then moulded in ramekins
5) **sauce richelieu** ⇒ sauce made of browned onions, sugar, grated nutmeg, velouté sauce, butter and chopped chervil
Richelieu *-[pâtisserie]-* ⇒ cake of alternate layers of large almond pastry, apricot jam, and frangipane; coated with fondant, and decorated of preserved fruits
Ricotta *-[fromage frais]-* ⇒ ricotta
Riesling ⇒ riesling
Rifauts *-[radis]-* ⇒ radish
Rigadelle *-[praire]-* ⇒ clam
Rigatoni *-[pâtes]-* ⇒ pasta < *uncountable* >
Rigo Jancsi *-[gâteau hongrois]-* ⇒ gateau stuffed with a mousse made of chocolate and whipped white of eggs; glazed with chocolate
Rigodon
- **quiche** ⇒ a quiche filled with diced bacon or ham, added of fecula and baked
- **pudding** ⇒ pudding of brioche steeped in milk, nuts, hazelnut, cinnamon, and fruit purée
Rigodon au lard ⇒ kind of quiche made with lardoons, milk, fecula, eggs, aromatics and butter
Rigotte *-[fromage]-* ⇒ cheese refined in marc
Rigotte de Condrieu ⇒ cylindrical cow's milk cheese

Rigotte de Pelussin ⇒ cylindrical goat's milk cheese
Rijsttafel ⇒ meal of about twenty dishes
Rillauds ⇒ bits of pork macerated in salt, then cooked in pork fat
Rillettes ⇒ rillettes
Rillettes d'oie ⇒ rillettes of goose meat
· **Rillettes de haddock** ⇒ rillettes made of smoked haddock, eggs, butter, parsley, chives, lemon juice and olive oil; served with a sauce of tomato pulp, shallots, olive oil, lemon juice and pepper
Rillettes de lapin ⇒ rillettes of rabbit, pork fat, garlic and thyme
Rillettes de saumon ⇒ rillettes made of salmon, egg-yolk, butter and olive oil
Rillettes de Tours ⇒ rillettes of pork
Rillettes et rillons de Blois et Vendôme ⇒ bits of pork cooked in seasoned lard or rillettes
Rillons ⇒ bits of pork macerated in salt, then cooked in pork fat
Rillots ⇒ bits of pork macerated in salt, then cooked in pork fat
Rimotte ⇒ maize porridge
Rincette
  - **vin** ⇒ extra drop of wine
  - **eau de vie** ⇒ nip of eau de vie
  - **marc** ⇒ nip of marc
  - **alcool** ⇒ nip of spirit or nip of brandy
Rioja ⇒ Rioja wine
Rioler *-[pâtisserie croisillon]-* ⇒ chequer work of paste lamellas
Ris ⇒ sweetbreads
Ris d'agneau ⇒ lamb sweetbread
Ris d'agneau au coulis de champignons ⇒ sauté lamb sweetbreads, served with mashed horn of plenty mushrooms
Ris de veau ⇒ calf sweetbread
Ris de veau à l'anversoise ⇒ braised calf sweetbreads; served with hop shoots in cream, plus small potatoes browned in butter
Ris de veau à la financière ⇒ croustades filled with braised calf sweetbreads, studded of truffle and pickled ox tongue; covered with a ragout of cockscombs, poultry quenelles, chopped mushrooms, plus a culinary stuffing of truffles in Madeira
Ris de veau à la périgourdine ⇒ braised calf sweetbread studded of truffle; served with a Madeira sauce added of truffle
Ris de veau aux raisins ⇒ calf sweetbread studded with lardoons, and simmered in butter with onions and cultivated mushrooms; served with the gravy added of grape juice, grapes, Madeira and butter
Ris de veau braisé à blanc ⇒ calf sweetbreads braised with rind of pork, onions, carrots, pepper; served with ...
  - **garniture anversoise** ⇒ ... voir texte
  - **garniture Nantua** ⇒ ... voir texte
  - **garniture princesse** ⇒ ... voir texte
  - **garniture Régence** ⇒ ... voir texte
Ris de veau braisé à brun ⇒ calf sweetbreads braised with rind of pork, onions, carrots, pepper, stock and white wine; served with ...
  - **garniture Clamart** ⇒ ... voir Clamart 6
  - **garniture Périgourdine** ⇒ ... voir texte
  - **légumes braisés** ⇒ ... braised vegetables
  - **purée de légumes** ⇒ ... mashed vegetables

Ris de veau braisé à la Nantua ⇒ slices of braised calf sweetbreads laid on fried croutons, covered of béchamel sauce added of mashed crayfishes, cognac and cayenne pepper; plus pastry boats filled with a ragout of crayfish tails, topped of truffle lamellas

Ris de veau braisé nesselrode ⇒ braised sweetbread of veal covered with peppered sauce, garnished of chestnut purée

Ris de veau en escalopes au gratin ⇒ slices of braised calf sweetbread, surrounded by mushrooms covered with a sauce of chopped mushrooms, white wine, tomato purée and parsley; then sprinkled of crumbs and browned

Ris de veau escalopés à l'ancienne ⇒ puff-pastries filled with braised slices of calf sweetbread, plus mushrooms braised in butter and thickened of velouté flavoured with Madeira; topped of truffle lamella

Ris de veau grillés ⇒ grilled calf sweetbread, served with ...
- **salade verte** ⇒ ... green salad
- **légume de saison** ⇒ ... steamed vegetable added of butter
- **purée de carottes** ⇒ ... mashed carrots
- **purée de petits pois** ⇒ ... mashed peas
- **du maïs frais** ⇒ ... maize

Ris de veau panés ⇒ calf sweetbread coated with crumbs, then sautéed in butter; served with ...
- **endives braisées** ⇒ ... braised chicory
- **maïs frais** ⇒ ... maize

Ris de veau pochés ⇒ calf sweetbread poached in stock, covered with the cooking juice; served with ...
- **haricots verts au beurre** ⇒ ... french beans in butter
- **fèves nouvelles** ⇒ ... early spring broad beans
- **macédoine printanière** ⇒ ... vegetable salad

Ris de veau poêlés ⇒ fried slices of calf sweetbread ...
- **servis avec pommes anna** ⇒ ... served sprinkled of parsley, with sliced potatoes baked in butter, plus a béarnaise sauce

Ris de veau princesse ⇒ braised slices of calf sweetbread, garnished with asparagus tips and truffle lamellas in butter; served with the cooking juice

Ris de veau Régence ⇒ braised calf sweetbreads studded of truffle; served with quenelles, foie gras escalopes, decorated of truffle lamellas in butter, covered with the gravy

Ris de veau rôtis ⇒ calf sweetbreads wrapped in caul of pork, and roasted on a skewer

Ris de veau ou de volaille montglas ⇒ braised sweetbread, covered with the cooking juice added of a rich culinary stuffing thickened with Madeira sauce

Risotto ⇒ risotto

Risotto à la milanaise ⇒ risotto added of tomatoes cooked in their own liquid, plus a julienne of pickled ox tongue, cooked ham, mushrooms, and white truffle

Risotto à la pièmontaise ⇒ risotto added of grated parmesan, and butter

Risotto aux foies de volaille ⇒ risotto with a hash of onions, plus tomatoes cooked in their own liquid, sauté poultry livers, cultivated mushrooms and pepper

Risotto aux fruits de mer ⇒ crown of risotto garnished with a ragout of mussels, clams and scallops cooked in white wine, plus shrimp tails; covered with the cooking juice added of cream and butter

Rissole ⇒ rissole

Rissoles à la chalonnaise ⇒ rissoles stuffed with a culinary stuffing of braised calf sweetbread, mushrooms braised in butter, truffle, and poultry velouté

Rissoles à la dauphine ⇒ rissoles garnished with ...
- **purée de foie gras** ⇒ ... mashed foie gras
- **salpicon de homard** ⇒ ... a culinary stuffing of lobster, thickened with lobster butter

Rissoles à la fermière ⇒ rissoles garnished with a culinary stuffing of diced vegetables and ham, then thickened of Madeira sauce

Rissoles aux écrevisses ⇒ rissoles garnished with a ragout of diced vegetables and ham, crayfishes, white wine, béchamel sauce, cream and cognac

Rissole de Bugey ⇒ turnover filled with roasted turkey cock, beef and currants

Rissoles de foie gras ⇒ rissoles stuffed with a culinary stuffing of foie gras, diced truffle and cognac; served with Madeira sauce added of truffle

Rissole de poisson ⇒ fish cake

Rissoles Pompadour ⇒ rissoles filled with a culinary stuffing of pickled ox tongue, truffle, and mushrooms braised in butter, thickened with a brown sauce added of Madeira

Rissolé (e ...) ⇒ browned < *v.t adjectif* >

Rivesaltes ⇒ sweet wine from Perpignan area

Riz ⇒ rice

Riz -[gâteau de]- ⇒ chilled dessert based on rice cooked in milk, added of sugar and eggs; served with egg-custard or fruit purée

Riz à l'impératrice ⇒ crown of rice cooked in milk with vanilla, granulated sugar, and preserved fruits; then added of egg-custard, plus sugared whipped cream

Riz à l'indienne ⇒ rice cooked in water and dried

Riz à l'orientale ⇒ rice cooked in water and dried

Riz à la cantonaise ⇒ cooked rice fried with pork fat, bacon, chopped celery, shrimps and eggs

Riz à la créole ⇒ rice cooked slowly in water

Riz à la crème ⇒ rice cooked in milk mixed with whipped cream, sugar, and vanilla

Riz à la grecque ⇒ rice braised in olive oil, then boiled with raisins, pepper, herbs, and garlic

Riz au blanc ⇒ boiled rice, added of butter

Riz au cari ⇒ rice flavoured with curry

Riz au gras ⇒ rice cooked in butter and beef stock

Riz au lait simple ⇒ rice cooked in milk with vanilla, and granulated sugar then added of butter and egg-yolks

Riz au sabayon ⇒ rice cooked in milk, sugar and vanilla; served with a custard of eggs, sugar, milk and vanilla

Riz au safran à la néerlandaise ⇒ rice cooked in milk, and brown sugar, then mixed with lemon juice and tarragon powder; served with biscuits flavoured of cinnamon or ginger

Riz aux macarons ⇒ rice cooked in milk with butter, and whipped eggs; then garnished with some macaroons

Riz pilaf ⇒ pilaf < *uncountable* >

Riz smyrniote ⇒ rice cooked in milk, and mixed with sultanas macerated in rum, then sprinkled of cinnamon

Rizotto ⇒ risotto

Roast beef ⇒ roast beef

Robe de chambre (en ...) -[pommes de terre]- ⇒ jacket potatoes

Robe des champs (en ...) -[pommes de terre]- ⇒ jacket potatoes

Robert -[sauce]- ⇒ sauce made of onions browned in pork fat, plus flour, white wine, stock and mustard

Robin -[pêche]- ⇒ variety of peach

Robin dixired -[pêche]- ⇒ variety of peach

Robinier ⇒ robinia or false acacia

Rocamadour -[cabécou]- ⇒ small cheese from a mixing of goat's milk and cow's milk

Rocamadour -[fromage de brebis]- ⇒ ewe cheese or ewe's milk cheese

Rocambole ⇒ garlic

Rochambeau -*[garniture grosses pièces de boucherie braisées ou rôties]*- ⇒ with a garnish of potato croustades filled with carrots, plus stuffed lettuce, cauliflower and sliced potatoes baked in butter

Roche aux moines -*[savennières]*- ⇒ high quality wines from Angers area

Rocher -*[pâtisserie]*- ⇒ rough pastry or sweet

Rocher à la noix de coco ⇒ petit four made of meringue mixed with grated coconut

Rochers aux amandes ⇒ small cakes made of whipped white of eggs, sugar and almond powder

Rock -*[bonbon]*- ⇒ sweet which display a drawing in relief

Rocou -*[colorant alimentaire]*- ⇒ roucou

Rocquencourt -*[haricot vert]*- ⇒ variety of french bean

Roebuck sauce -*[sauce chevreuil]*- ⇒ roebuck sauce

Roedgroed ⇒ Danish sweet of fruits and fecula, in white wine

Roesti -*[rosti]*- ⇒ fried sliced potatoes added of lardoons or onions

Rognon
- **veau** ⇒ lamb kidney or calf kidney
- **boeuf** ⇒ ox kidney

Rognon avec graisse -*[mouton]*- ⇒ lamb kidney « in suet »

Rognon d'agneau ⇒ lamb kidney

Rognon d'agneau à l'anglaise ⇒ lamb kidney « ex suet » coated with melted butter and crumbs, then grilled on a skewer; served with grilled slices of bacon, boiled potatoes, cress, and parsley butter

Rognons d'agneau sautés aux champignons ⇒ sauté cultivated mushrooms, and sauté lamb kidneys; served covered with the gravy added of Madeira or champagne, arrow-root, and butter

Rognons d'agneau Turbigo ⇒ dish of sauté lamb kidneys, sauté cultivated mushrooms, and grilled chipolatas; covered with the gravy added of white wine, and brown sauce

Rognon de bœuf ⇒ ox kidney

Rognon de bœuf aux lardons ⇒ slices of ox kidney, sautéed with mushrooms, lardoons, and shallots; then simmered with pepper, Madeira and cream

Rognons de coq pour garnitures ⇒ garnish of cock kidneys

Rognon de mouton ⇒ lamb kidney

Rognons de mouton Carvalho ⇒ sauté lamb kidneys « ex suet », laid on browned croutons; covered of the gravy, mixed with Madeira and brown sauce

Rognon de mouton avec graisse ⇒ lamb kidney « in suet »

Rognons de mouton au gratin ⇒ lamb kidneys « ex suet » laid on sausage meat, topped with mushrooms; covered with chopped onions and mushrooms, sprinkled of melted butter, then served au gratin

Rognon de mouton sans graisse ⇒ lamb kidney « ex suet »

Rognon de porc ⇒ pig kidney

Rognon de veau ⇒ calf kidney

Rognons de veau Ali-Baba ⇒ browned calf kidneys « ex suet », simmered in cream, lemon peel, and pepper; covered with the cooking juice added of cognac, and butter

Rognons de veau à la Bercy ⇒ slices of calf kidneys, coated with melted butter and crumbs, then grilled; served with poached bone-marrow mixed with shallots, white wine, butter and pepper

Rognon de veau à la bonne femme ⇒ calf kidney braised in butter with streaky bacon, potatoes, and veal stock

Rognons de veau à la liégeoise ⇒ calf kidneys cooked with potatoes, juniper berries, and lardoons; served with the gravy thickened of white wine and gin

Rognon de veau avec graisse ⇒ calf kidney « in suet »

Rognons de veau aux foies de volaille ⇒ sliced calf kidneys « ex suet » plus poultry livers browned in butter, then flamed in armagnac; covered with the gravy added of port, butter, and red wine from Rhone valley

Rognons de veau Collioure ⇒ calf kidneys braised in butter plus shallots, and pounded anchovy fillets; covered with the cooking juice added of white wine

Rognon de veau dégraissé ⇒ calf kidney « ex suet »

Rognon de veau grillé ⇒ calf kidney grilled on a skewer; served with ...

    - **beurre Bercy** ⇒ ... poached bone-marrow mixed with shallots, white wine, butter and pepper

    - **beurre maître d'hôtel** ⇒ ... parsley butter

    - **beurre d'anchois** ⇒ ... anchovy paste

Rognon de veau rôti à la moutarde ⇒ calf kidney peppered and coated of mustard, then roasted; served with the gravy added of Madeira

Rognon de veau sauté à la bordelaise ⇒ sauté slices of calf kidney, mixed with the gravy added of white wine, shallots, veal stock, arrow-root, and poached bone-marrow

Rognon de veau sauté aux trois moutardes ⇒ sauté calf kidney, flamed in armagnac, then simmered with Madeira, butter and mustard; garnished of browned potatoes

Rognon sans la graisse -*[mouton]*- ⇒ lamb kidney « ex suet »

Rognonnade ⇒ calf long striploin with the kidney, rolled and roasted

Rognonnade de veau ⇒ calf long striploin with the kidney, rolled and roasted

Rogue

    - **morue** ⇒ roe of cod

    - **hareng** ⇒ roe of herring

Rohan *(à la ...)* -*[garnitures pour volailles sautées ou braisées]*- ⇒ garnished with artichoke hearts topped of foie gras escalopes and truffle lamellas, plus tartlets filled of cock's kidneys thickened with supreme sauce

Roi des cailles -*[râle]*-

    - **Râle** ⇒ rail

    - **Râle des genêts** ⇒ land rail or corncrake

    - **Râle d'eau** ⇒ water-rail < *se cuisine comme la caille* >

Roisolle -*[rissole]*- ⇒ turnover filled with various forcemeat

Roll -*[Amérique du nord]*- ⇒ roll

Rollmops ⇒ herring fillets

Rollot ⇒ cow's milk cheese with a red crust

Rolpen -*[Pays Bas]*- ⇒ sauté marinated meat, served with potatoes and pineapple

Roma -*[tomate]*- ⇒ Italian tomato

Romadour -*[remoudou]*- ⇒ Belgian cow's milk cheese

Romadur -*[fromage]*- ⇒ Romadur

Romaine *(à la ...)*

    1) **oeufs aux épinards, aux anchois et au parmesan** ⇒ eggs with spinach, anchovies and parmesan

    2) **petits oiseaux en casserole, aux petits pois et au jambon** ⇒ birds in casserole with peas and ham

    3) **pain d'épinards** ⇒ spinach bread

        - **soufflé aux épinards** ⇒ soufflé made of spinach and anchovies

    4) **sauce à la romaine pour pièces de venaison roties** ⇒ voir texte

    5) **gnocchi** ⇒ gnocchi made of semolina and grated cheese

    6) **grosses pièces de boucherie** ⇒ ... with a garnish of gnocchi, plus spinach bread and tomato sauce

Romaine -*[laitue; salade]*- ⇒ cos lettuce

Romalour -*[remoudou]*- ⇒ Belgian cow's milk cheese

Romanée -*[vin de vosne romanée]*- ⇒ Burgundy red wine from Côtes de Nuits
Romanée-Conti ⇒ Burgundy red wine from Côtes de Nuits
Romanée St vivant -*[vosne romanée]*- ⇒ Burgundy red wine from Côtes de Nuits
Romanesti -*[URSS vins d']*- ⇒ red wine from Moldavia
Romanov
- **garniture pour pièces de boucherie** ⇒ ... with a garnish of cucumber stuffed with chopped mushrooms, plus potato croustades with a culinary stuffing of mushrooms, celeriac and horse-radish
- **fraises** ⇒ fraises macerated in curaçao, laid on cups, and decorated with sugared whipped cream
Romantour -*[remoudou]*- ⇒ Belgian cow's milk cheese
Romarin ⇒ rosemary < *uncountable* >
Rombosse -*[Belgique]*- ⇒ apple baked wrapped in pastry
Rombu -*[turbot]*- ⇒ turbot < *pluriel inchangé* >
Rommegrot -*[Norvège]*- ⇒ porridge made of cream added of lemon juice, flour, and milk; served sprinkled of cinnamon, sugar, melted butter and redcurrant juice
Romsteck ou rumsteck ou rumsteak ⇒ rump-steak
Roncal -*[lait]*- ⇒ cow's milk
Ronce ⇒ blackberry-bush
Roncin
- **Franche Comté** ⇒ sweet made of bread steeped in milk, whipped eggs and fruits
- **Vosges** ⇒ preparation of soft white cheese, added of whipped eggs and flour, then cooked; served with jacket potatoes
Rond -*[viande]*- ⇒ muscle from the thigh of beef
Rond de tranche grasse de bœuf ⇒ silverside of beef
Ronde de chine -*[aubergine]*- ⇒ variety of aubergine
Ronde maraîchère -*[mâche]*- ⇒ variety of corn salad
Ronde de Valence -*[aubergine]*- ⇒ variety of aubergine
Rondo -*[pois cassé]*- ⇒ split peas
Rônier -*[borrasus]*- ⇒ Asian palm-tree
Roquefort ⇒ Roquefort cheese
Roquette -*[plante]*- ⇒ rocket
Rosbif ⇒ roast beef
Rose -*[cocktail]*- ⇒ cocktail of gin, vermouth, and cherry brandy
Rose -*[fleur]*-
a) **confiture de roses** ⇒ rose jam
b) **confits de pétales** ⇒ preserved rose petals
c) **eau de rose** ⇒ rose extract
d) **essence de rose** ⇒ rose extract
e) **thé à la rose** ⇒ tea flavoured with rose petals
Rosé -*[vin]*- ⇒ rosé
Rosé ⇒ rosé or vin rosé
Rosé d'Alsace -*[vin]*- ⇒ rosé
Rosé d'Anjou ⇒ rosé
Rosé de Californie -*[vin]*- ⇒ rosé
Rosé des ricays -*[champagne]*- ⇒ rosé wine from champagne area
Rosé du Béarn -*[vin]*- ⇒ rosé
Rosette -*[vin]*- ⇒ white wine from Bergerac area
Rosette -*[saucisson]*- ⇒ dry pork sausage from Beaujolais area
Rosette de Lyon ⇒ dry pork sausage from Beaujolais area

Roseval *-[pomme de terre]-* ⇒ variety of potato
Rosquille ⇒ aniseed cake
Rossini *-[garniture]-* ⇒ ... with a garnish of truffles and foie gras
Rossini *-[tournedos]-* ⇒ fried round sippet topped successively of a fillet steak, a foie gras escalope
    and truffles; covered with Madeira
Rossolis ⇒ Italian liquor
Rossolyie *-[salade]-* ⇒ salad of herrings and beetroots
Rösti ⇒ fried sliced potatoes added of lardoons or onions
Rotengle ⇒ roach *< pluriel inchangé >*
Rothomago ⇒ fried eggs
Rothschild ⇒ soufflé based on confectioner's custard and preserved fruits; served with strawberries
Rôti *(un ...)* ⇒ a meat roast or a roast
    - rôti ⇒ roasted *< v.t adjectif >*
Rôti dans le filet *-[bœuf]-* ⇒ roasting joint
Rôti de jambon *-[Danemark]-* ⇒ roast of pork leg with goose fat
Rôti de porc ⇒ roast of pork
Rôtie *-[canapé]-* ⇒ a slice of bread toasted or baked
Rôtisserie ⇒ grills and griddle or steak house
Rouelle *-[viande]-*
    - général ⇒ round slice
    - rouelle de veau ⇒ fillet of veal
Rouelle de veau ⇒ fillet of veal
Rouennaise *(à la; énumératoin ...)*
    - canard à la presse ⇒ voir texte
    - canard rouennais en chemise ⇒ voir texte
    - oeufs pochés avec une sauce rouennaise ⇒ poached eggs covered with a sauce of red wine,
        shallots, and poultry livers
Rougail ⇒ Caribbean seasoning
Rougail d'aubergines ⇒ paste of aubergines and Caribbean seasoning
Rougail de morue ⇒ salt cod simmered with onions, tomatoes, and Caribbean seasoning
Rougail de tomates crues ⇒ dish of crushed tomatoes, onion and Caribbean seasoning
Rouge *-[vin]-* ⇒ red wine
Rouge *-[couleur]-* ⇒ red
Rouge du Roussillon *-[abricot]-* ⇒ variety of apricot
Rouge de Sernhac *-[abricot]-* ⇒ variety of apricot
Rougeret *-[bouton de culotte]-* ⇒ small goat's milk cheese
Rouget ⇒ red mullet or red gurnard
Rouget-barbet ⇒ goatfish
Rouget camus *-[grondin lyre]-* ⇒ gurnard or piper
Rouget à la nantaise ⇒ grilled red-mullet; covered with a sauce of shallots, white wine, and red-
    mullet livers
Rougets à l'orientale ⇒ browned red-mullets, covered with tomato purée, fennel, thyme, laurel,
    coriander, garlic and parsley; then baked and sprinkled of chopped parsley
Rouget au four au fenouil ⇒ red mullet laid on a hash of shallots and fennel, then sprinkled with
    olive oil, and baked
Rouget au four et à l'échalote ⇒ red mullet baked on shallots, white wine, and butter
Rougets au four à la livournaise ⇒ red mullets covered with tomato purée, crumbs, and melted
    butter; then baked

Rougets au jasmin ⇒ red mullets stuffed with a mousse of whiting, cream and jasmine extract, then baked; covered with a sauce of fish stock in white wine, egg-yolks, butter, lemon juice, and mushroom peel

Rougets en papillotes ⇒ red mullets stuffed with a forcemeat of bread, milk, parsley, and anchovy paste; then wrapped into a casing of greaseproof paper and baked

Rougets frits ⇒ fried red mullets, served with slices of lemon

Rougets grillés ⇒ grilled red mullets, served with ...

- **sauce béarnaise** ⇒ ... béarnaise sauce

- **sauce choron** ⇒ ... voir texte

- **beurre fondu** ⇒ ... melted butter

Rougets grillés à l'italienne ⇒ grilled red mullets, laid on brown sauce thickened of chopped mushrooms, sliced ham, tarragon, and tomato purée; then browned

Rougets grillés à la Bercy ⇒ grilled red mullets, covered of melted parsley butter

Rougets grillés à la bordelaise ⇒ grilled red gurnards, served with quartered lemon and a sauce

Rougets grillés à la moelle ⇒ grilled red mullets; served with a sauce of shallots, white wine, meat stock, poached bone-marrow and butter

Rougets grillés à la niçoise ⇒ grilled red mullets, laid on tomatoes cooked in their own liquid with capers; then decorated with anchovy fillet lamellas, and black olives

Rougets grillés en caisse ⇒ small boxes in paper filled with chopped mushrooms, and grilled red mullet; then covered of chopped mushrooms mixed with white wine, stock and tomato purée

Rougets pochés à la nage au basilic ⇒ poached red mullets; served with a sauce of olive oil, basil, tarragon, parsley, tomato, and xeres vinegar

Rougillon -[champignon]- ⇒ saffron milk cap or milk agaric

Rouille ⇒ sauce made with red pepper, saffron, garlic, potato pulp, olive oil and stock

Rouilleuse -[sauce du Périgord]- ⇒ sauce based on poultry blood

Roulade ⇒ roulade or rolled portion of meat

Roulade d'anguille à l'angevine ⇒ eel stuffed with a forcemeat of pike, mushrooms and truffle, simmered in white wine with onion, carrot, leak and savory; served with mushrooms in butter, plus the cooking juice added of cream, and crayfish paste

Roulade de boeuf ⇒ beef olive

Rouleau de printemps ⇒ pancake of rice, stuffed of meat and shrimps; served with soya sauce

Roulettes de Rouen ⇒ small round breads, made with crescent paste

Rousquille ⇒ aniseed cake

Rousseau ⇒ kind of dorado

Roussette -[vin]- ⇒ white wine from Rhone Valley

Roussette -[poisson]- ⇒ dogfish

Roussettes -[pâtisserie]- ⇒ small fritters made of flour, eggs, butter, cream and brandy

Roux ⇒ roux

Roux blanc ⇒ roux of butter and flour

Roux blond ⇒ roux of butter and flour, coloured by the cooking process

Roux brun ⇒ roux of butter and flour, browned by the cooking process

Royal rouget -[orange]- ⇒ orange milk mushroom or imperial mushroom or orange agaric or egg mushroom

Royale (à la ...)

  1) **poisson à la royale**

  a) **saumon poché** ⇒ poached salmon ...

  b) **turbot poché** ⇒ poached turbot ...

  c) **truite pochée** ⇒ poached trout ... served with a garnish of quenelles, mushrooms, poached oysters, truffles, plus a sauce hollandaise added of whipped cream

2) volailles à la royale ⇒ poached poultry garnished with quenelles, mushrooms and sometimes foie gras escalopes; covered of a sauce made with poultry velouté added of cream, butter, chopped truffles and xeres

3) lièvre à la périgourdine ou à l'orléanaise ou à la royale ⇒ voir texte

4) entremets chauds ou froids ⇒ puddings, soufflés, ananas garnis, coupes glaçées

Royale
- **cuisine** -*[garniture de soupes]*- ⇒ ... garnished with moulded custards of various ingredients
- **patisserie** ⇒ mixture of white of eggs and sugar

Royale d'asperge ⇒ asparagus tips, spinach, béchamel sauce, cream and egg-yolks; baked in dariole

Royale de carotte à la Crécy ⇒ carrot, béchamel sauce, cream and egg-yolks; baked in dariole

Royale de céleri ⇒ celery, béchamel sauce, cream and egg-yolks; baked in dariole

Royale de purée de volaille ⇒ mashed white of meat, added of béchamel sauce, cream and egg-yolks; then baked

Royale de tomate ⇒ tomato purée and consommé, thickened of egg-yolks; then baked

Royale ordinaire ⇒ infusion of chervil in consommé, added of eggs and baked

Royan -*[sardine]*- ⇒ sardine from Royan

Ruby
- **Porto** ⇒ young red port, sweet and fruity
- **Pamplemousse** ⇒ grapefruit with pink pulp

Ruchote chambertin -*[Gevrey chambertin]*- ⇒ Chambertin

Rudjak -*[salade]*- ⇒ salad of pineapple, cucumbers, and green mangos

Rue -*[plante]*- ⇒ rue

Ruffec -*[terrine de perdreaux]*- ⇒ young partridge pâté

Ruifard ⇒ pie filled with sliced apples, pears and quince cooked in butter, then flavoured with Chartreuse

Rullpoesle -*[Suède]*- ⇒ pork belly, spiced and rolled

Rully ⇒ Burgundy wines from Cote Chalonnaise

Rumsteack avec os, plus tête de filet ⇒ whole rump

Rumsteack ou Quasi ⇒ chump

Rumsteack sans os, avec une partie d'aiguillette ⇒ boneless 'D'Rump

Rumsteack sans os, plus Tête de filet ⇒ boneless rump

Rumsteck ⇒ rump-steak

Ruoms -*[pélardon]*- ⇒ small goat's milk cheese from the Cevennes

Russe *(à la ...)*

1) crustacés ⇒ crustaceae in round slices ...

2) poissons
- **côtelettes** ⇒ cutlets ...
- **darnes** ⇒ steaks ... < *ou nom anglais du poisson pour les poissons entiers* >

3) lustré de gelée ⇒ ... glazed with jelly
- **masqués de sauce chaud-froid** ⇒ ... covered of chaudfroid sauce
- **masqués de mayonnaise** ⇒ ... covered of mayonnaise

4) sauce pour crudités ou poissons froids ⇒ sauce made with mayonnaise added of caviar

Russerole -*[Touraine]*- ⇒ fritter made with choux pastry

Russian stout -*[stout]*- ⇒ Russian stout

Russule ⇒ russula

Russule à feuillés inégaux ⇒ russula

Russule bleu jaunâtre ⇒ blue and yellow russula

Russule jolie ⇒ russula

Russule verdoyante ⇒ greenish russula

Ruster Ausbruck -*[vin]*- ⇒ Burgenland white wine
Rutabaga ⇒ rutabaga or swede
Rye -*[whisky]*- ⇒ rye whisky
Ryyppy -*[Finlande]*- ⇒ strong grain brandy, drink chilled

S

Sabardin ⇒ offal cooked in white wine with aromatics

Sabayon
- **dessert** ⇒ zabaglione
- **sauce** ⇒ creamy sauce made with champagne

Sabayon au parfait amour ⇒ zabaglione flavoured with cedrate liquor

Sabayon au rhum et aux marrons glacés ⇒ zabaglione of egg-yolks, granulated sugar, rum, and white wine; served in cup with marron glacé

Sableau du Poitou ⇒ goat's soft white cheese

Sabler
- **a) le champagne** ⇒ to drink champagne appreciatively
- **b) le whisky** -[*boire rapidement*]- ⇒ to toss off the whisky

Sablé ⇒ kind of shortbread

Sablés à l'orange ⇒ small flat cakes made of flour, butter, sugar, orange peel and juice, topped with peel of preserved orange, and baked

Sablés à la vanille ⇒ small round flat-cakes made of flour, salted butter, sugar, egg-yolks and vanilla, then baked

Sablés au cédrat ⇒ small flat-cakes made of flour, butter, sugar, egg, lemon peel and chopped preserved cedrate, then baked

Sablés aux amandes ⇒ small lozenges made of flour, butter, almond powder, milk, sugar, egg, lemon peel and rum, then baked

Sablés bicolores (*petits ...)* ⇒ small short-cakes made of flour, butter, sugar, cinnamon powder, and vanilla powder

Sablé de Milan ⇒ shortcake made of flour, lemon peel, butter, granulated sugar, egg-yolks, and cognac

Sablés milanais ⇒ shortcake of flour, sugar, vanilla and egg; soldered by two with redcurrant jelly, and icing sugar

Sablés nantais ⇒ small cakes made of sugar, butter, flour, egg-yolks and vanilla powder

Sablés normands ⇒ small flat-cakes made of flour, sugar, butter, egg, vanilla powder and yeast

Sablé niortais ⇒ gateau made of flour, egg, rum and sugar, then baked

Sablé sec ⇒ flat cake made of sugar, flour, salt, egg and vanilla, then baked

Sabodet ⇒ sausage made of pig head, crackling and pork meat, served hot in thick slices

Sabre ⇒ cutlassfish

Sabre argenté -[*poisson*]- ⇒ silvery scaled cutlass

Sabre ceinture -[*poisson*]- ⇒ black scabbard

Sachertorte ⇒ Sachertorte

Sacristains ⇒ stripes of puff-pastry glazed with egg, and sprinkled of sugar

Sadrée -[*sarriette*]- ⇒ savory < *uncountable* >

Safran ⇒ saffron

Safran bâtard ⇒ bastard saffron

Sagan -[*garniture*]- ⇒ ... with a garnish of risotto, mushrooms stuffed with mashed brain, plus a culinary stuffing of truffles

Sage Derby -[*fromage*]- ⇒ Sage derby

Sagou ⇒ sago fecula

Sagourne -[*Berry-Touraine*]- ⇒ slices of pancreas browned in butter, salted and peppered, then added with a seasoning made of oil, vinegar, and chopped parsley; served with lemon juice

Sahlab ⇒ salep

Saignant ⇒ rare
- **bifteck saignant** ⇒ a rare steak
Saindoux ⇒ pork fat or lard
Sainfoin -[*miel*]- ⇒ honey from sainfoin meadow or sainfoin honey
Saint Agrève -[*picodon de*]- ⇒ goat's milk cheese with a crust coloured blue, yellow or red, according to the refining
Saint Amour ⇒ Beaujolais wine
Saint Aubin -[*Côtes de Beaune*]-
  a) **rouges vendus « Côtes de Beaune » village** ⇒ high quality Burgundy red wine
  b) **blancs vendus « Saint Aubin » ou « Saint Aubin Cttes de Beaune »** ⇒ high quality Burgundy white wine
Saint chinian -[*côteaux du languedoc*]- ⇒ quality wines from Languedoc area
Saint drezery -[*côteaux du languedoc*]- ⇒ quality wines from Languedoc area
Saint Emilion -[*Bordelais*]- ⇒ Bordeaux red wine
Saint Emilion -[*Bourgogne*]- ⇒ Burgundy wines from Côtes de Beaune
Saint Estèphe ⇒ Médoc red wine
Saint Florentin -[*fromage*]- ⇒ Burgundy cheese
Saint Florentin -[*gâteau*]- ⇒ sliced square of Genoese sponge stuffed with a custard of meringue, melted butter and kirsch, added of preserved cherries
Saint germain
- **grosses pièces de boucherie** ⇒ ... served with veal stock, plus a purée of peas thickened of egg-yolks, sometimes laid in dome on artichoke hearts
- **potage** ⇒ soup made of mashed peas and a garnish
- **filets de sole** ⇒ sole fillets brill fillets coated with crumbs and butter, then grilled; served with béarnaise sauce, plus a garnish of peas and little potato-balls browned in butter
- **filets de barbue** ⇒ brill fillets coated with crumbs and butter, then grilled; served with béarnaise sauce, plus a garnish of peas and little potato-balls browned in butter
Saint honoré ⇒ round short pastry surrounded by choux pastries, then filled with confectioner's custard, added of vanilla, and white of egg < *Si avec chantilly, remplacer « confectioner's custard ... » par « sugared whipped cream »* >
Saint Hubert
- **cailles st hubert** ⇒ quail stuffed with a truffle, and braised; served with the cooking juice added of Madeira
- **garniture champignons** ⇒ mushrooms filled with a game purée, served with saddle of hare in peppered sauce
- **garniture oeufs** ⇒ hard boiled eggs or soft boiled eggs with game purée in tartlets; covered with peppered sauce
- **divers garniture de bouchées, timbales, d'omelettes, préparation d'un consommé** ⇒ with game purée
Saint James cup ⇒ drink made of sugar in water, half a litre of cognac, half a litre of rum, curaçao, one litre of chilled tea, crushed ice, and one bottle of sparkling cider
Saint Joseph ⇒ red wine from Côtes du Rhone on the right bank
Saint Joseph -[*vin*]- ⇒ high quality wine from Rhone valley, on the right bank from Ardèche area
Saint Julien ⇒ St Julien wine
Saint loup -[*Touraine*]- ⇒ cheese from Saumur
Saint mâlo -[*sauce*]- ⇒ velouté sauce added of butter, braised onions, white wine, thyme, laurel, parsley; plus a drop of Worcestershire sauce
Saint Mandé -[*garnitures pour petites pièces de boucherie sautées*]- ⇒ ... garnish of peas or french beans in butter, plus flat cakes of mashed potatoes
Saint Marcellin -[*fromage*]- ⇒ cow's milk cheese with a grey crust

Saint Montant -*[Côtes du Vivarais]*- ⇒ quality wine from Ardèche area, on the right bank of the Rhone

Saint Nectaire -*[fromage]*- ⇒ cow's milk cheese refined on a bed of rye

Saint nicolas de bourgueil -*[vin de Touraine]*- ⇒ high quality red or rosé wine, with bouquet and fruity

Saint Paulin -*[fromage]*- ⇒ Saint Paulin

Saint Péray ⇒ white wine from Côtes du Rhone on the right bank

Saint pierre -*[poisson]*- ⇒ john dory

Saint pierre -*[tomate]*- ⇒ variety of tomato

Saint pierre à la rhubarbe ⇒ john dory fillets cooked in butter; served with bits of rhubarb cooked in the gravy

Saint pierre farçi à la crème d'oursins ⇒ John dory stuffed with leeks cooked in their own liquid, plus chopped chanterelle Grise mushrooms, then baked with chopped onion, thyme, laurel, white wine and cream served with a sauce of sea-urchins, egg-yolks, cream and cayenne pepper

Saint pierre grillé aux palets d'or ⇒ grilled john dory; served with quoits of freezed butter, coated of crumbs and fried

Saint Pourçain -*[vin]*- ⇒ St Pourcain quality wines

Saint Remèzes -*[côtes du vivarais]*- ⇒ quality wine from Ardèche area, on the right bank of the Rhone

Saint Romain ⇒ Burgundy wines from Côtes de Beaune

Saint saëns -*[garniture]*- ⇒ ... with a garnish of, truffle and foie gras fritters, cock's kidneys, asparagus tips, plus supreme sauce flavoured with truffle extract

Saint saturnin -*[côteaux du languedoc]*- ⇒ quality wines from Languedoc area

Saint Saviol -*[fromage]*- ⇒ goat's milk cheese

Saint Varent -*[fromage]*- ⇒ goat's milk cheese

Saint Véran -*[vin]*- ⇒ burgundy white wine

Saint Winocq -*[fromage]*- ⇒ cheese from Picardie

Sainte Alliance (à la ...)

    a) foie gras ⇒ poached foie gras with truffles and champagne

    b) poularde ⇒ fattened pullet with truffles cooked in Madeira; served with foie gras escalopes cooked in butter, plus the cooking juice

    c) bécasse ⇒ pheasant stuffed with woodcock and roasted; served on canapé covered with a mashed woodcock

Sainte Croix du Mont ⇒ sweet Bordeaux white wine

Sainte Foix Bordeaux ⇒ wines from Dordogne left bank

Sainte Maure ⇒ goat's milk cheese with a blue crust

Saison ⇒ in season

    - ce n'est plus de saison ⇒ it is out of season

Saisonnier ⇒ seasonal

Saké ⇒ sake or fermented liquor made from rice

Salade ⇒ salad

Salade à l'allemande ⇒ salad made of potatoes, apples, mayonnaise, gherkins and herring fillets

Salade à l'alsacienne ⇒ beetroot salad seasoned with french dressing added of shallots, mustard and herbs; served topped with sliced saveloy

Salade à l'américaine ⇒ salad of diced pineapple, cucumber, corn, tomatoes and hard boiled egg; seasoned with french dressing and ketchup

Salade à l'andalouse ⇒ cooked rice seasoned with french dressing added of chopped onion and parsley, plus grated garlic; served surrounded of capsicums in julienne, and quartered tomatoes, then sprinkled of chervil

Salade à l'huile de pépins de potiron ⇒ salad seasoned with pumpkin pip oil

Salade à l'indienne ⇒ cooked vegetable salad, seasoned with french dressing added of grated garlic, chopped onion, and curry

Salade à la bouchère ⇒ composed salad of boiled beef, potatoes, tomatoes, and hard boiled eggs

Salade à la cauchoise ⇒ salad of chopped ham, celery and potato, with a dressing of cream, cider vinegar, plus chervil

Salade à la cressonnière

- **potage** ⇒ soup made of watercress, potatoes, egg-yolks and cream
- **salade** ⇒ composed salad of potatoes and watercress, sprinkled with chopped egg-yolks and parsley

Salade à la crème ⇒ green salad seasoned with cream and vinegar

Salade à la d'Albignac ⇒ salad of celeriac in julienne, white of meat, hard boiled eggs, truffles, crayfish tails, artichoke hearts, and seasoning

Salade à la favorite ⇒ crayfish tails and asparagus tips laid on a cup, and garnished with white truffle lamellas; seasoned of oil, lemon juice, and pepper, then sprinkled of chopped celery and herbs

Salade à la fourme d'Ambert ⇒ salad seasoned with crushed blue cow's milk cheese added of petit Suisse, cream, Tabasco, cognac and pepper

Salade à la japonaise

- **fruits** ⇒ salad of diced tomatoes, orange and pineapple laid on lettuce leaves; covered of cream added of lemon juice, and sprinkled with sugar
- **légumes** ⇒ salad of mussels, celery, and Japanese artichoke, plus sliced truffles

Salade à la mayonnaise ⇒ salad seasoned with ...

- **mayonnaise simple** ⇒ ... mayonnaise
- **mayonnaise avec herbes** ⇒ ... mayonnaise added of herbs
- **mayonnaise à l'ail** ⇒ ... mayonnaise flavoured with garlic

Salade à la moutarde et à la crème

1) **Salade de betterave rouge** ⇒ beetroot salad ...
   - **macédoine** ⇒ vegetable salad ...
   - **céleri rave** ⇒ celeriac salad ...
   - **pommes de terre** ⇒ potato salad ...
   - **endives** ⇒ chicory salad ...
   - **scarole** ⇒ endive salad ...

2) **à la moutarde et à la crème** ⇒ seasoned with mustard added of cream, vinegar and pepper < *avec l'une des dénominations ci-dessus* >

Salade à la parisienne ⇒ vegetable salad, plus a culinary stuffing of spiny lobster and truffles in mayonnaise; decorated with quartered hard-boiled eggs

Salade à la russe ⇒ vegetable salad in mayonnaise

Salade à la scandinave ⇒ beetroot salad seasoned with french dressing; decorated with smoked herrings, hard-boiled eggs, and onions

Salade Ali-Bab ⇒ salad of shrimps in mayonnaise, courgettes, sweet potatoes, hard boiled eggs, and tomatoes; seasoned with french dressing

Salade Argenteuil ⇒ diced jacket potatoes mixed with a mayonnaise flavoured of tarragon, then garnished of asparagus tips seasoned with oil and lemon juice; surrounded by a lettuce chiffonade, plus quartered hard-boiled eggs

Salade au lard

1) **Salade de chicorée** ⇒ endive ...
   - **chou rouge** ⇒ red cabbage ...
   - **scarole** ⇒ endive ...
   - **mâche** ⇒ corn salad ...
   - **pissenlit** ⇒ dandelion ...

Salade au lard (suite)
   2) au lard ⇒ ... salad, topped with fried streaky bacon, added of vinegar
Salade arlésienne ⇒ salad of potatoes and artichoke hearts with french dressing, sprinkled of chervil, and tarragon; plus a garnish of endives, tomatoes, anchovies and black olives
Salade au Roquefort ⇒ salad seasoned with crushed Roquefort added of petit suisse, cream, Tabasco, cognac and pepper
Salade aux anchois *-[assaisonnement des salades vertes ou simples]-* ⇒ ..., seasoned with french dressing, added of mashed anchovies and capers
Salade aux anchois à la suédoise ⇒ composed salad of slightly acid apples, and cooked beetroots, seasoned with french dressing added of mustard; decorated with anchovy fillets, hard-boiled eggs, and mushroom lamellas
Salade aux fruits secs ⇒ salad sprinkled of chopped nuts, peanuts, and hazelnuts
Salade aux herbes ⇒ salad seasoned with french dressing added of chives, chervil, parsley, tarragon and mint
Salade bressane ⇒ composed salad of lettuce, diced white of meat, capsicums, hard-boiled eggs, and asparagus tips; seasoned with french dressing, and decorated of mayonnaise added of tomato purée
Salade Bagration ⇒ salad of macaroni, celeriac in julienne, artichoke hearts and mayonnaise flavoured with tomato sauce; sprinkled with egg-yolks, plus a culinary stuffing of ox tongue and truffles
Salade Carmen ⇒ composed salad of rice, diced white of meat, capsicums and peas; seasoned with french dressing added of mustard and chopped tarragon
Salade César ⇒ composed salad of lettuce, hard-boiled eggs, croutons, anchovies, and parmesan
Salade composée ⇒ composed salad
Salade composée à la banane ⇒ composed salad of celery, tomatoes, cucumber, and bananas; seasoned with a sauce of tomato pulp, lemon juice, yoghourt, pepper and herbs
Salade d'aubergines ⇒ sliced aubergines seasoned with french dressing, sprinkled of chervil and tarragon
Salade d'avocat ⇒ avocado salad seasoned with green pepper
Salade d'avocat à la californienne ⇒ composed salad of grapefruit pulp, avocado pulp, crayfish tails, sprinkled with gin or cognac; seasoned with ketchup added of mayonnaise, and decorated with sliced lemon
Salade d'avocat Archestrate ⇒ composed salad of celery in julienne, diced artichoke hearts, tomato pulp, avocado pulp; seasoned with french dressing, sprinkled of herbs
Salade d'avocat au concombre ⇒ composed salad of cucumber and avocado; seasoned with french dressing added of mustard, then sprinkled of herbs
Salade d'avocat au crabe ⇒ mixing of avocado pulp, crab meat, tomato pulp, sliced hard-boiled eggs, pepper and ketchup; served sprinkled of herbs
Salade d'endives ⇒ chicory salad
Salade d'endives à la flamande ⇒ salad of chicory, beetroot, and quartered oranges; seasoned with french dressing, added of mustard, sprinkled of chopped hard-boiled egg-yolk and chive
Salade d'endives, de betteraves et de quartiers d'orange ⇒ salad of chicory, beetroot, and quartered oranges; seasoned with olive oil, vinegar and tarragon
Salade d'épinards
   a) cuite avec vinaigrette ⇒ salad of cooked spinach, sprinkled of chopped hard-boiled egg-yolk; seasoned with french dressing
   b) cru avec haddock ⇒ salad of raw spinach and smoked haddock
   c) cru avec coquilles St Jacques ⇒ salad of raw spinach and scallop
   d) avec pommes de terre ⇒ salad of spinach, and sliced new potatoes
Salade d'oranges ⇒ orange salad, flavoured with sugar and rum
Salade de betteraves ⇒ beetroot salad

Salade de betterave à l'alsacienne ⇒ beetroot salad seasoned with french dressing added of shallots, mustard and herbs; served topped with sliced saveloy
Salade de
    1) betterave rouge ⇒ beetroot salad
       - macédoine ⇒ vegetable salad
       - céleri rave ⇒ celeriac salad
       - pommes de terre ⇒ potato salad
       - endives ⇒ chicory salad
       - scarole ⇒ endive salad
    2) à la moutarde et à la crème ⇒ ... seasoned with mustard added of cream, vinegar and pepper < *avec l'une des dénominations ci-dessus* >
Salade de boeuf ⇒ slices of boiled beef, surrounded by slices of potatoes, with pepper, white wine, and oil, plus sliced tomatoes; decorated of sliced onion and chervil, then seasoned with french dressing, added of mustard
Salade de cardons ⇒ cardoon salad, sprinkled with chervil and parsley
Salade de carottes à l'orange ⇒ salad of grated carrots, diced orange, and sliced onion; seasoned with french dressing added of lemon juice
Salade de cervelle de veau ⇒ calf brains poached in stock with aromatics, laid halved on lettuce seasoned of french dressing, surrounded by hard-boiled eggs, and anchovy fillets; covered with mayonnaise sauce
Salade de champignons ⇒ mushroom salad, seasoned with ...
    - vinaigrette ⇒ ... french dressing added of lemon juice, and herbs
    - crème ⇒ ... a mixing of cream, lemon juice, pepper, and chives
Salade de chicorée ⇒ endive salad
Salade de
    1) chicorée ⇒ endive salad
       - chou rouge ⇒ red cabbage salad
       - scarole ⇒ endive salad
       - mâche ⇒ corn salad
       - pissenlit ⇒ dandelion salad
    2) au lard ⇒ ..., topped with fried streaky bacon, added of vinegar
Salade de chicorée aux lardons ⇒ endive salad, mixed with fried lardoons, and fried croutons
Salade de chou rouge ⇒ red cabbage salad macerated in red wine vinegar, seasoned with oil and pepper
Salade de chou vert ⇒ cabbage salad
Salade de choucroute à l'allemande ⇒ salad of braised sauerkraut, added of diced onions; served garnished with hard-boiled eggs, plus beetroot cubes
Salade de choux-fleur ⇒ salad of steamed or raw cauliflower, seasoned with ...
    - vinaigrette ⇒ ... french dressing
    - anchoyade ⇒ ... texte
    - sauce chantilly ⇒ ... texte
    - mayonnaise ⇒ ... mayonnaise
Salade de clapotons *-[mâchon]-* ⇒ salad of lamb trotters, and lamb testicles; seasoned with french dressing
Salade de concombre ⇒ cucumber salad
Salade de concombre au yaourt ⇒ cucumber salad, mixed with a sauce of yoghourt, paprika, pepper, lemon juice, chervil and chives
Salade de coques aux fèves fraîches ⇒ salad of cockles and broad beans, seasoned with french dressing added of herbs

Salade de coquilles St Jacques ⇒ lettuce, cress, and white of leeks, braised in olive oil, plus sliced steamed scallops; served sprinkled of olive oil and lemon juice

Salade de courgettes ⇒ courgette salad, seasoned with french dressing, then sprinkled of chervil and tarragon

Salade de crabe ⇒ mixing of crab meat, soya bean germs, in a sauce of ketchup and cognac

Salade de cresson ⇒ cress salad seasoned with french dressing

s'il y a une garniture, ajouter

- **noix** ⇒ garnished with green walnuts
- **cubes de gruyère** ⇒ garnished with gruyère in cubes
- **cubes de pommes** ⇒ garnished with apples in cubes
- **quartiers d'oeufs durs** ⇒ garnished with quartered hard-boiled eggs

Salade de crevettes ⇒ shrimp salad; decorated with quartered hard-boiled eggs and lettuce hearts

Salade de crudités ⇒ elaborated salad of lettuce, fennel, beetroot, celery, capsicums and tomatoes; decorated with olives, and seasoned of french dressing

Salade de fruits ⇒ fruit salad flavoured with a brandy

Salade de fruits au gin ⇒ fruit salad of grapefruit, papaw, kiwi fruits, and lychees; covered with orange juice, added of granulated sugar and gin

Salade de fruits aux kiwis ⇒ fruit salad added of kiwi fruit and brandy

Salade de fruits rafraîchis ⇒ fruit salad

Salade de girolles à la chicorée ⇒ salad of sauté edible agarics, endive, shallot and parsley; seasoned with old wine vinegar, olive oil, peanut oil, nut oil and pepper

Salade de harengs saurs ⇒ salad of smoked herrings, potatoes and beetroot

Salade de haricots ⇒ haricot bean salad and chopped onion; seasoned with french dressing, and sprinkled of herbs

Salade de haricots verts ⇒ french bean salad, added of early spring onions and french dressing

Salade de laitue ⇒ lettuce salad

Salade de langouste ⇒ elaborated salad of spiny lobster, french beans, avocado, and cucumber; seasoned with a special french dressing

Salade de lentilles au cervelas ⇒ lentil salad, decorated of sliced saveloy; seasoned with french dressing added of shallot and parsley

Salade de lentilles chaudes ⇒ lentil salad, added of browned lardoons, then seasoned with french dressing added of red wine; served hot

Salade de légumes ⇒ salad of any cooked vegetables, seasoned with french dressing, and sprinkled of parsley, plus chervil

Salade de mâche aux petits lardons ⇒ corn-salad added of browned lardoons; seasoned with french dressing

Salade de mâche panachée ⇒ composed salad of beetroot, chicory, corn-salad, and apple lamellas; seasoned with french dressing added of mustard

Salade de mayonnaise de homard ⇒ salad of lobster, oil, vinegar, aromatics, mayonnaise sauce, lettuce, hard boiled eggs, anchovy fillets, olives and capers

Salad de mayonnaise de laitances ⇒ salad of lettuce, soft roes, mayonnaise added of anchovy extract, hard boiled eggs, anchovy fillets and capers

Salade de mayonnaise de saumon ⇒ composed salad of lettuce, salmon, oil, vinegar, lemon juice, capers, anchovies, black olives and hard boiled eggs

Salade de moules ⇒ salad of diced potatoes, mussels, celery, and a hash of aromatics; seasoned with a french dressing of hot vinegar, oil, mustard and pepper

Salade de mouraillons ⇒ dandelion salad with lardoons, seasoned of cream

Salade de pamplemousse ⇒ salad of grapefruit, apples, celery and lettuce; seasoned with cream, rum, and lemon juice

Salade de perdrix au chou ⇒ salad of cabbage, plus partridge wings and livers braised with boletus and slices of pork belly; covered with the gravy added of xeres vinegar, pepper and hazelnut oil

Salade de petits navets nouveaux ⇒ salad of early spring turnips poached in poultry stock, plus smoked haddock poached in milk; seasoned with french dressing

Salade de pintadeau aux fruits ⇒ green salad topped with, sliced apple, peaches, and slices of guinea-chick meat; seasoned with a sauce of yoghourt, cider vinegar and pepper

Salade de pissenlit au lard ⇒ dandelion salad, plus browned lardoons and their gravy thickened of vinegar; seasoned with white wine, oil and pepper

Salade de pissenlits ⇒ dandelion salad

Salade de poires et de pêches aux framboises ⇒ salad of pears and peaches, macerated in lemon juice and sugar; then added of raspberries

Salade de raie ⇒ mixing of endive, lettuce, corn-salad, chicory, dandelion and herbs, seasoned with french dressing; then added of poached ray, lemon peel and crushed tomatoes

Salade de riz ⇒ rice salad

Salade de riz à l'orientale ⇒ rice cooked with saffron, added of chopped onion, and seasoned with french dressing added of paprika; garnished with capsicum lamellas, diced tomatoes, and stoned black olives

Salade de saison ⇒ salad in season

Salade de sandre aux pleurotes ⇒ baked pike-perch fillets, served with a ragout of sauté Shitake mushrooms in vinegar and cream, plus a julienne

Salade de soja ⇒ salad of sauté soya germs, with poultry lamellas and hard-boiled eggs

Salade de thon

    a) avec riz ⇒ salad of tunny, rice, raisins, fried capsicums, almonds, and french dressing with herbs

    b) au soja ⇒ salad of tunny, soya shoots, hearts of palm and raw mushrooms; seasoned with french dressing added of soya sauce

    c) avec légumes ⇒ salad of tunny, grated carrots, beetroot, apples, hard-boiled eggs, and tomatoes, laid on lettuce chiffonade; seasoned with french dressing added of herbs

Salade de tomates ⇒ tomato salad

Salade de tomates à la mozarella ⇒ salad of sliced tomatoes, and slices of mozzarella; seasoned with vinegar, olive oil and basil

Salade de topinambours ⇒ Jerusalem artichoke salad

Salade de topinambours aux noisettes ⇒ salad of Jerusalem artichokes cooked in white wine; seasoned with oil, mustard and lemon juice, then sprinkled of crushed hazelnuts

Salade trévise *-[chicorée; salade]-*

    - légume ⇒ endive

    - comme café ⇒ ground chicory

Salade de truffes ⇒ truffle salad seasoned with oil, vinegar, pepper and lemon juice

Salade de volaille à la chinoise ⇒ salad of duck meat, mushrooms, and soya germs; seasoned with a sauce of mustard, sugar, ketchup, soya sauce, vinegar, pepper, ginger, thyme, crushed bay-laurel, crushed garlic, sesame oil, and cognac

Salade Du Barry ⇒ dome of steamed cauliflower, garnished with radishes and cress; seasoned with oil and lemon juice

Salade du groin d'âne ⇒ salad of dandelion, croutons, garlic and lardoons

Salade exotique au citron vert ⇒ salad of pineapple, mangos, sliced bananas in lime juice, and granulated sugar

Salade flamande ⇒ salad of boiled potatoes, baked onions, and chicory, seasoned of french dressing; decorated with herring fillet lamellas, plus chopped parsley

Salade francillon ⇒ salad of mussels, potatoes and celery, in a french dressing with a vinegar of white wine or burgundy chablis

Salade frisée ⇒ endive
Salade japonaise ⇒ salad of mussels, Japanese artichoke and celery, in french dressing with a vinegar of burgundy chablis or white wine
Salade lorette ⇒ salad made of corn-salad, celery in julienne and cooked beets
Salade Maharadjah ⇒ salad of rice and crab meat, seasoned with french dressing added of curry; surrounded of celeriac in julienne, courgette pulp and quartered tomatoes, then sprinkled of chopped hard-boiled egg-yolk and chives
Salade mikado ⇒ salad of potatoes and shrimp tails, garnished with chrysanthemum flowers, plus a julienne of capsicum, and diced tomato
Salade mimosa ⇒ salad of potatoes, artichoke hearts and french beans; seasoned with french dressing, and sprinkled of hard-boiled egg-yolk
Salade Montfermeil ⇒ salad of diced artichoke hearts, potatoes and salsify; seasoned with a french dressing added of mustard, then sprinkled with a hash of hard-boiled egg and herbs
Salade niçoise ⇒ salad of tomatoes, hard boiled eggs, anchovies, black olives, cucumber, broad beans, onions, capsicums, artichoke hearts, olive oil, garlic and basil
Salade orientale ⇒ rice cooked with saffron, added of chopped onion, and seasoned with french dressing added of paprika; garnished with capsicum lamellas, diced tomatoes, and stoned black olives
Salade panachée Brimont ⇒ salad of potatoes, artichoke hearts, mayonnaise, stoned black olives, crayfish tails or shrimp tails, and quartered hard-boiled eggs; seasoned with french dressing of olive oil, and xeres vinegar
Salade parisienne ⇒ vegetable salad, plus a culinary stuffing of spiny lobster and truffles in mayonnaise; decorated with quartered hard-boiled eggs
Salade Port Royal ⇒ salad of apples, french beans and potatoes, seasoned with mayonnaise; served surrounded by lettuce hearts, and quartered hard boiled eggs
Salade Rachel ⇒ salad of cooked celery, artichoke hearts and potatoes, seasoned with mayonnaise; then garnished of asparagus tips
Salade Raphaël ⇒ lettuce chiffonade seasoned with paprika and mayonnaise; covered of sliced cucumbers, asparagus tips, quartered tomatoes and sliced radishes, in olive oil plus lemon juice
Salade Reine Pédauque ⇒ salad of quartered lettuce in a dressing of cream, oil, lemon juice, mustard and paprika; topped by slices of orange, and stoned cherries
Salade riche -[Troisgros]- ⇒ salad of foie gras, lobster and truffle
Salade russe ⇒ vegetable salad thickened with mayonnaise, and sometimes added of fish or meat
Salade toulousaine ⇒ salad of melon pulp, artichoke hearts, a julienne of leek and ham, seasoned with french dressing added of parsley, chives, sage and cream; served sprinkled of ginger
Salade verte ⇒ green salad
Salade waldorf ⇒ salad of rennet apples, diced celeriac, and walnuts in mayonnaise
Saladier lyonnais ⇒ lamb trotters cooked in a court-bouillon, sauté chicken livers and bits of marinated herrings; seasoned with french dressing added of mustard and shallots
Salaison (s ...)
    - action ⇒ salting or pickling
    - nom pluriel ⇒ salt provisions or goods preserved in brine
Salaisons domestiques ⇒ salt provisions or goods preserved in brine
Salamandre
    - grill ⇒ grill
    - poêle ⇒ slow combustion stove
Salamis ⇒ salami < *uncountable* >
Salamis de strasbourg ⇒ salami made from smoked pork and beef
Salammbô ⇒ choux pastry filled with confectioner's custard added of kirsch
Salangane ⇒ salangane or tern

Salé ⇒ salted, v t adjectif, or briny
Saleb ⇒ salep
Salep ⇒ salep
Salers ⇒ pressed cow's milk cheese with a brown crust
Salicorne ⇒ saltwort
Sally Lunn *-[gâteau]-* ⇒ Sally Lunn
Salmanazar *-[bouteille]-* ⇒ Salmanazar
Salmigondis ⇒ hotchpotch or salmagundi
Salmis ⇒ salmi or ragout of game
Salmis de bécasse ⇒ ragout of woodcock, white wine, cognac, mushrooms and aromatics
Salmis de pintade ⇒ ragout of guinea-fowl
Salmon pie ⇒ salmon pie
Salon de thé ⇒ tea room
Salonenque *-[olive]-* ⇒ pickled olive
Salpêtre ⇒ saltpetre
Salpicon ⇒ culinary stuffing
Salpicon à l'américaine ⇒ culinary stuffing of spiny lobster meat or lobster meat, thickened with a
    sauce of shallots, pounded garlic, tomato purée, cayenne pepper and dry white wine
Salpicon à l'écossaise ⇒ culinary stuffing of pickled ox tongue, and diced truffle; thickened with
    brown sauce added of Madeira
Salpicon à la bohémienne ⇒ culinary stuffing of foie gras, truffles, Madeira sauce, butter and paprika
    - **utilisé pour garnir bouchées** ⇒ patties
    - **croustades** ⇒ croustades
    - **œufs pochés** ⇒ poached eggs
    - **tartelettes** ⇒ tartlets < *etc* ... >
Salpicon à la cancalaise ⇒ culinary stuffing of poached oysters and mushrooms macerated in lemon
    juice; thickened of ...
    - **sauce normande** ⇒ texte
    - **velouté de poisson** ⇒ fish velouté
Salpicon à la cardinal ⇒ culinary stuffing of lobster, truffles, and mushrooms; thickened of white
    cream added of mashed lobster, and cayenne pepper
Salpicon à la cervelle ⇒ culinary stuffing of poached brains, thickened of ...
    - **sauce allemande** ⇒ texte
    - **béchamel** ⇒ béchamel sauce
    - **velouté** ⇒ velouté sauce
Salpicon à la Cussy ⇒ culinary stuffing of braised calf sweetbread, truffle, and braised mushrooms;
    thickened with Madeira sauce
Salpicon à la dieppoise ⇒ culinary stuffing of shrimp tails, mussels in white wine, and braised
    mushrooms; thickened with fish velouté sauce added of cream and mushrooms
Salpicon à la langouste ⇒ culinary stuffing of spiny lobster, thickened of ...
    - **béchamel sauce** ⇒ ... béchamel sauce
    - **sauce Nantua** ⇒ béchamel sauce added of mashed crayfishes, cognac and cayenne pepper
    - **vinaigrette** ⇒ french dressing
    - **mayonnaise** ⇒ mayonnaise
Salpicon à la périgourdine ⇒ culinary stuffing of foie gras, truffle in butter and pepper; thickened of
    Madeira sauce added of truffle
Salpicon à la reine ⇒ culinary stuffing of white meat, mushrooms, and truffles; thickened with fish
    stock
Salpicon à la royale ⇒ ... culinary stuffing of mushrooms in butter, truffle and mashed poultry meat
    - **garniture pour bouchées** ⇒ patties garnished with a ... « salpicon »
    - **garniture pour barquettes** ⇒ pastry boats filled with a ... « salpicon »

Salpicon à la St Hubert ⇒ culinary stuffing of game meat, thickened with brown sauce added of Madeira, and game stock

Salpicon à la viande ⇒ culinary stuffing of meat, thickened with ...
- **sauce blanche** ⇒ ... white sauce
- **sauce brune** ⇒ ... brown sauce

Salpicon à la volaille ⇒ culinary stuffing of white of meat, thickened with ...
- **sauce allemande** ⇒ ... sauce based on poultry stock < *chaud* >
- **béchamel** ⇒ ... béchamel sauce < *chaud* >
- **sauce crème** ⇒ ... béchamel sauce added of cream < *chaud* >
- **velouté** ⇒ ... velouté sauce < *chaud* >
- **sauce brune** ⇒ ... brown sauce < *chaud* >
- **demi-glace** ⇒ ... brown sauce added of Madeira < *chaud* >
- **fond de veau** ⇒ ... veal stock < *chaud* >
- **vinaigrette aux fines herbes** ⇒ french dressing added of herbs < *froid* >

Salpicon au foie de raie ⇒ culinary stuffing of ray livers in butter, thickened of ...
- **velouté** ⇒ velouté sauce
- **vinaigrette** ⇒ french dressing

Salpicon au foie gras ⇒ culinary stuffing of foie gras, thickened with ...
- **sauce madère** ⇒ Madeira sauce
- **sauce au porto** ⇒ port wine sauce
- **sauce au xérès** ⇒ xeres sauce
- **fumet de gibier** ⇒ game stock
- **gelée** ⇒ jelly
- **si additionné de foies de volaille sautés « ajouter in fine »** ⇒ plus sauté poultry livers

Salpicon au gibier ⇒ culinary stuffing of game; thickened with ...
- **sauce blanche** ⇒ white sauce
- **brune au fumet de gibier** ⇒ brown sauce of game stock
- **gelée** ⇒ jelly

Salpicon au homard ⇒ culinary stuffing of lobster, thickened with ...
- **béchamel** ⇒ béchamel sauce
- **Nantua** ⇒ béchamel sauce added of mashed crayfishes, cognac, and cayenne pepper
- **vinaigrette** ⇒ french dressing
- **mayonnaise** ⇒ mayonnaise

Salpicon au jambon ⇒ culinary stuffing of ham, thickened with ...
- **demi-glace** ⇒ ... brown sauce added of Madeira
- **vinaigrette** ⇒ ... french dressing
- **mayonnaise** ⇒ ... mayonnaise

Salpicon au poisson ⇒ culinary stuffing of poached fish-fillets, thickened of ...
- **béchamel** ⇒ ... béchamel sauce < *chaud* >
- **sauce Nantua** ⇒ ... béchamel sauce added of mashed crayfishes, cognac and cayenne pepper < *chaud* >
- **sauce normande** ⇒ ... fish velouté sauce, added of cream and mushrooms < *chaud* >
- **vinaigrette** ⇒ ... french dressing < *froid* >
- **mayonnaise** ⇒ ... mayonnaise < *froid* >

Salpicon
- **au ris d'agneau** ⇒ culinary stuffing of lamb sweetbread in butter, thickened with ...
- **de veau** ⇒ culinary stuffing of calf sweetbread in butter, thickened with ...
- **sauce allemande** ⇒ ... sauce based on veal stock
- **demi-glace** ⇒ ... brown sauce added of Madeira

- **sauce madère** ⇒ ... Madeira sauce
- **fond de veau** ⇒ ... veal stock
Salpicon au veau ⇒ culinary stuffing of veal meat, thickened with ...
- **sauce allemande** ⇒ ... sauce based on veal stock
- **béchamel** ⇒ ... béchamel sauce
- **demi-glace** ⇒ ... brown sauce added of Madeira
- **fond de veau** ⇒ ... veal stock
Salpicon aux anchois ⇒ diced anchovy fillets thickened of ...
- **froid** ⇒ ... french dressing flavoured with tarragon
- **chaud** ⇒ ... béchamel sauce
Salpicon aux crevettes ⇒ culinary stuffing of shrimp tails, thickened of ...
- **chaud** ⇒ béchamel sauce
- **froid** ⇒ mayonnaise
Salpicon aux moules
- **Chaud** ⇒ culinary stuffing of cooked mussels, thickened with ...
- **sauce allemande** ⇒ ... fish stock
- **sauce poulette** ⇒ ... sauce poulette
- **sauce au vin blanc** ⇒ ... a sauce of fish stock in white wine, egg-yolks, butter, lemon juice, and mushroom peel
- **Froid** ⇒ culinary stuffing of marinated mussels, thickened of ...
- **vinaigrette** ⇒ ... french dressing
- **mayonnaise** ⇒ ... mayonnaise
Salpicon aux écrevisses ⇒ culinary stuffing of crayfish tails, thickened with ...
- **béchamel** ⇒ béchamel sauce
- **Nantua** ⇒ béchamel sauce added of mashed crayfishes, cognac, and cayenne pepper
- **vinaigrette** ⇒ french dressing
- **mayonnaise** ⇒ mayonnaise
Salpicon aux œufs durs
- **Chaud** ⇒ culinary stuffing of hard-boiled eggs, thickened with ...
- **sauce allemande** ⇒ ... fish stock
- **sauce béchamel** ⇒ ... béchamel sauce
- **sauce crème** ⇒ ... béchamel sauce added of cream
- **velouté** ⇒ ... velouté sauce
- **Froid** ⇒ culinary stuffing of hard-boiled eggs, thickened with ...
- **vinaigrette** ⇒ ... french dressing
- **mayonnaise aux herbes** ⇒ ... mayonnaise added of herbs
Salpicon chasseur ⇒ culinary stuffing of sauté poultry livers and mushrooms, thickened with sauce chasseur
Salpicon chaud de légumes à la crème ⇒ culinary stuffing of ... nom anglais du ou des légumes in butter, thickened of ...
- **sauce crème** ⇒ béchamel sauce added of cream
- **velouté** ⇒ velouté sauce
Salpicon chaud de truffes à la crème ⇒ culinary stuffing of truffles braised in butter; thickened of ...
- **velouté** ⇒ velouté sauce
- **sauce crème** ⇒ béchamel sauce added of cream
Salpicon de crêtes de coq ⇒ culinary stuffing of cockscombs in Madeira; thickened of ...
- **velouté** ⇒ velouté sauce
- **sauce blanche** ⇒ white sauce
- **sauce madère** ⇒ Madeira sauce

Salpicon froid de légumes à la mayonnaise ⇒ culinary stuffing of ... nom anglais du légume thickened of mayonnaise

Salpicon froid de légumes à la vinaigrette ⇒ culinary stuffing of ... nom anglais du légume thickened of french dressing added of herbs

Salsifis ⇒ salsify < *uncountable* >

Salsifis à la béchamel ⇒ cooked salsify, simmered in the oven with béchamel sauce; then covered with cream

Salsifis à la mayonnaise ⇒ cooked salsify, added with mayonnaise, then sprinkled of herbs

Salsifis à la polonaise ⇒ cooked salsify braised in butter, sprinkled of hard-boiled egg-yolk and parsley; then covered of crumbs fried in butter

Salsifis à la vinaigrette ⇒ cooked salsify, seasoned with french dressing

Salsifis au beurre ⇒ cooked salsify, sprinkled with butter cooked lightly

Salsifis au gratin ⇒ cooked salsify, added with a preparation of shallots, butter and cream; then sprinkled of grated gruyère, and browned

Salsifis au jus ⇒ cooked salsify, simmered in gravy

Salsifis en salade aux anchois ⇒ cooked salsify seasoned with mayonnaise, and bits of anchovy fillets; then sprinkled of herbs

Salsifis Mornay ⇒ cooked salsify, covered with béchamel sauce added of egg-yolks and gruyère; then sprinkled of grated parmesan, plus melted butter, and browned

Salsifis sautés ⇒ sauté salsify, sprinkled of herbs

Salsifis sautés à la provençale ⇒ salsify sautéed in olive oil; added with ...

- **ail et persil** ⇒ ... a hash of garlic and parsley

- **fondue de tomate** ⇒ ... tomatoes cooked in their own liquid

Saltimbocca ⇒ saltimbocca

Salustiana -[*orange*]- ⇒ variety of orange

Samaritaine (*à la* ...) -[*grosses pièces de boucherie braisées*]- ⇒ ... served with a garnish of timbales filled of rice, croquettes of mashed potatoes and braised lettuce

Samau malais ⇒ rice brandy

Sambal ⇒ Indonesian seasoning

- **aussi mets assaisonné avec du sambal** ⇒ meals flavoured with Indonesian seasoning

Sambayon

- **dessert** ⇒ zabaglione

- **sauce** ⇒ creamy sauce made with champagne

Sambuca ⇒ Italian anisette

Samos ⇒ Greek muscat

Sampigny-lès-maranges ⇒ high quality burgundy wines

Samsoë ⇒ Sams

Samssa -[*cuisine russe*]- ⇒ fritter made of chopped vegetables, garlic, and chives; thickened with egg

San Daniele -[*jambon*]- ⇒ Italian ham, served in thin slices with melon or figs

Sancerre ⇒ white wine from Loire valley

Sanciau

- **crêpe** ⇒ thick pancake

- **beignet** ⇒ fritter

Sancocho -[*Vénézuela*]- ⇒ stew of meat, or tripe, or fish

Sandesh -[*Inde-Pakistan*]-

   a) avec noix de coco ⇒ dessert of casein, sugar and milk; flavoured with coconut

   b) en beignets ⇒ fritter of casein, sugar and milk

Sandre ⇒ pike-perch < *pluriel inchangé* >

Sandre rôti à la mode de Bugey ⇒ pike perch stuffed with a forcemeat of whiting, cream, truffle and butter; grilled on a skewer and sprinkled with cream, served garnished of crayfish tails and truffles

Sandwich ⇒ sandwich

Sandwich alsacien ⇒ sandwich of rye bread, butter, grated horse-radish, and slices of sausage

Sandwich au basilic ⇒ sandwich spreaded of butter kneaded with basil; garnished of chopped hard-boiled eggs, black olives, plus capsicums marinated in oil

Sandwich de langue et de jambon ⇒ ham and tongue sandwich

Sang ⇒ blood

Sangaree -*[cocktail]*- ⇒ sangaree

Sang de taureau -*[vin hongrois]*- ⇒ Hungarian red wine

Sanglier ⇒ wild boar

Sangre de toro -*[Sang de taureau]*- ⇒ Hungarian red wine

Sangria ⇒ sangria

Sangria au cognac ⇒ sangria added of cognac and cinnamon

Sangria aux pêches ⇒ sangria added of peaches in syrup, plus Cointreau, or a liquor based on orange and cognac

Sangue di guida -*[Sang de taureau]*- ⇒ Hungarian red wine

Sanguette ⇒ chicken's blood with parsley and lardoons, fried in goose fat

Sanguette ⇒ coagulated poultry blood, fried in pork fat or goose fat

Sanguète ⇒ chicken's blood with parsley and lardoons, fried in goose fat

Sanguin -*[lactaire]*- ⇒ saffron milk cap or milk agaric

Sanguine ⇒ chicken's blood with parsley and lardoons, fried in goose fat

Sanguine

    - fruit ⇒ blood orange

    - plat ⇒ chicken's blood with parsley and lardoons, fried in goose fat

Sanquet ⇒ chicken's blood with parsley and lardoons, fried in goose fat

Sanquet ⇒ chicken's blood with parsley and lardoons, fried in goose fat

Sans rivale -*[fraise]*- ⇒ variety of fraise

Sans souiro -*[salicorne]*- ⇒ saltwort

Santé -*[potage]*- ⇒ thick soup made of potatoes and leeks, added of braised sorrel chiffonade, thickened of cream and egg-yolks; served with bread, and shredded chervil

Santenay ⇒ Burgundy wines from Côtes de Beaune

Saperavi -*[Ukraine]*- ⇒ Ukrainian red wine

Sapin -*[miel]*- ⇒ honey from pine flowers or pine honey

Sapinette ⇒ fermented drink of pine flowers, sugar and yeast

Sapote ⇒ sapodilla < *autres noms; abricot de st domingue, sawo mamilla, nèfle d'amérique* >

Sapotille ⇒ sapodilla < *autres noms; abricot de st domingue, sawo mamilla, nèfle d'amérique* >

Sapsago -*[schabzieger]*- ⇒ Sapsago

Sarapatel -*[Portugal]*- ⇒ stew of lamb and kid

Sarcelle ⇒ teal < *pluriel inchangé* >

Sard ou Lou sard ⇒ kind of red sea bream

Sarde -*[coulirou]*- ⇒ mackerel

Sarde (*à la ...*) -*[petites ou grosses pièces de boucherie]*- ⇒ ...; covered with the gravy added of brown sauce, and garnished of risotto croquettes, plus ...

    - champignons et haricots ⇒ ... mushrooms and french beans in butter

    - concombre et tomate ⇒ ... lengths of cucumbers, and stuffed tomatoes

Sardine ⇒ sardine or pilchard

Sardines crues ⇒ salted raw sardines; served with toasted country bread, and slightly salted butter

Sardines farçies au vin blanc ⇒ sardines stuffed with a forcemeat of fish, seasoned with salt and pepper, then moistened with white wine and baked; covered with a sauce of fish stock in white wine, egg-yolks, butter, lemon juice, and mushroom peel

Sardines frites ⇒ sardines marinated in lemon juice; then coated with whipped eggs, oil and pepper, and fried

Sardines gratinées ⇒ alternate layers of browned aubergines, grated parmesan, and sardine fillets; covered with a tomato purée flavoured of garlic, oil, pepper, and basil, then baked

Sardines grillées ⇒ grilled sardines

Sardines soufflées à l'oseille ⇒ sardines stuffed with mashed sorrel, rolled in pancakes, and browned in butter

Sargue ⇒ sargo

Sarladaise *(à la ...)* ⇒ with sliced potatoes sautéed in goose fat and sprinkled with chopped parsley, plus garlic

Sarments ⇒ vine branch or vine-shoot or sarmentum or bine

Sarrasin ⇒ buckwheat < *uncountable* >

Sarrasine *(à la ...)* *-[Grosses pièces de boucherie]-* ⇒ with a garnish of little buckwheat cakes or rice cassolettes filled with tomato and capsicum pulp, plus sliced onion and the gravy

Sarriette ⇒ savory < *uncountable* >

Sartagnado *-[Sartagnano]-* ⇒ tiny fishes fried as a thick pancake

Sartagnano ⇒ tiny fishes fried as a thick pancake

Sashimi ⇒ Japanese dish of fishes and crustaceae

Sauce *-[terme général]-* ⇒ sauce

Sauce
- **viande en sauce** ⇒ meat cooked in a sauce
- **jus de viande** ⇒ gravy
- **salade** ⇒ dressing

Sauce à l'abricot ⇒ sauce made of apricot pulp, syrup, and brandy

Sauce à l'abricot *-[Haerbelin]-* ⇒ sauce of mashed apricots, sugar, fecula and kirsch

Sauce à l'américaine ⇒ sauce made of shallots, pounded garlic, tomato purée, cayenne pepper and dry white wine

Sauce à l'ananas ⇒ pineapple syrup, thickened of arrow-root, and flavoured with brandy

Sauce à l'anglaise *-[Carême]-* ⇒ sauce of hard boiled egg-yolks, velouté, pepper, nutmeg, lemon juice, and anchovy paste

Sauce à l'anis ⇒ sauce of sugar, vinegar, white wine, aniseed, and veal stock

Sauce à l'avocat ⇒ sauce of mashed avocado pulp, lemon juice, and whipped cream

Sauce à l'échalote ⇒ sauce made with butter, braised shallots, fish stock, white wine, velouté sauce, and parsley

Sauce à l'estragon pour petites pièces de boucherie sautées ⇒ sauce of gravy, white wine, tarragon, stock, and kneaded butter

Sauce à l'estragon pour volailles pochées ⇒ sauce of poultry stock, tarragon, and arrow-root

Sauce à l'estragon pour œufs mollets ou pochés ⇒ sauce of tarragon, white wine and stock

Sauce à l'indienne ⇒ white sauce added of chopped onions braised in oil, nutmeg, chicken stock, and coconut milk

Sauce à l'italienne ⇒ brown sauce thickened of mushrooms, diced ham, tarragon, plus tomato purée

Sauce à l'œuf à l'anglaise ⇒ egg sauce

Sauce à l'onion ⇒ onion sauce

Sauce à l'onion et à la sauge ⇒ onion and sage sauce

Sauce à l'orange ⇒ orange sauce

Sauce à l'oseille ⇒ sauce of shallots, vermouth, cream, sorrel, pepper, and lemon juice

Sauce à la bohémienne ⇒ béchamel sauce added of egg-yolks, oil, plus vinegar flavoured with tarragon

Sauce à la bordelaise ⇒ brown sauce added of garlic, tarragon, lemon pulp, laurel, clove and Sauternes wine

Sauce à la bourguignotte ⇒ sauce based on mushrooms, garlic, spices, and Burgundy red wine from Côtes de Beaune

Sauce à la bretonne -*[Carême]*- ⇒ brown sauce added of onions, butter and pepper

Sauce à la chapelure -*[Carême]*- ⇒ sauce of shallots, ham, veal stock, pepper, crumbs, consommé, and lemon juice

Sauce à la crème ⇒ cream sauce

Sauce à la d'Albuféra ⇒ supreme sauce with capsicums and butter

Sauce à la diable ⇒ devilled sauce

Sauce à la diplomate ⇒ sauce of lobster butter, truffle, and lobster meat

Sauce à la duxelles ⇒ sauce of chopped mushrooms, white wine, stock, and tomatoes cooked in their own liquid

Sauce à la fraise ⇒ strawberry sauce

Sauce à la française -*[Carême]*- ⇒ béchamel sauce added of garlic, grated nutmeg, mushroom extract, and crayfish paste

Sauce à la genevoise ou genoese -*[sauces pour poisson]*-

   a) sauce genevoise ⇒ sauce made of fish stock, a mixture of diced vegetables and ham, red wine and butter

   b) sauce genoese -*[Carême]*- ⇒ sauce made of consommé, crushed tomatoes and capsicums

Sauce à la grecque pour poissons ⇒ sauce of celery and onions braised in olive oil, added of herbs, white wine, coriander, velouté sauce, and cream

Sauce à la hongroise ⇒ sauce of chopped onions braised in butter; added of pepper, paprika and white wine

Sauce à la maltaise ⇒ sauce hollandaise added with grated tangerine peel, and tangerine juice

Sauce à la menthe ⇒ mint sauce

Sauce à la mie de pain à l'ancienne -*[Carême]*- ⇒ sauce of garlic, shallot, parsley, white wine, crumbs, ground pepper, grated nutmeg, consommé, and lemon juice

Sauce à la moelle ⇒ sauce made of shallots, white wine, meat stock, poached bone-marrow and butter

Sauce à la moscovite ⇒ peppered sauce added of pine kernels, sultanas and juniper berries

Sauce à la nantaise ⇒ with a white wine and butter sauce

Sauce à la parisienne ⇒ petit suisse, plus paprika and lemon juice; thickened of mayonnaise with oil and chervil

Sauce à la piémontaise ⇒ béchamel sauce added of chopped onions, truffles, pine-kernels, garlic, and lemon juice

Sauce à la riche

   1) velouté ⇒ velouté sauce with truffles and mushrooms; thickened of cream and egg-yolks, plus lobster butter

   2) sauce normande ⇒ creamy white sauce added of lobster butter, truffles, and cayenne pepper; flavoured with cognac

Sauce à la romaine ⇒ sauce made of boiled currants and sultanas, browned sugar, vinegar, game stock, plus grilled pine-kernels

Sauce à la russe ⇒ velouté sauce seasoned with mustard, herbs, granulated sugar, pepper, and lemon juice

Sauce à la sauge et à l'oignon ⇒ onion and sage sauce

Sauce à la truffe ⇒ sauce made with egg-yolks and butter, plus truffle cooked in Madeira and stock

Sauce aigre-douce ⇒ sweet and sour sauce

Sauce aigre douce chinoise ⇒ sauce made of garlic, chopped onion, ginger lamellas, soya sauce, tomato juice, maize fecula, and mushrooms

Sauce aillade ⇒ sauce of crushed garlic, pepper, oil, and parsley

Sauce aïoli ⇒ sauce of pounded garlic, egg-yolk, pepper, and oil

Sauce albert ⇒ creamed horseradish and egg-yolks sauce

Sauce Albufèra ⇒ supreme sauce added of mashed capsicums in butter, and veal stock

Sauce allemande ⇒ velouté sauce added of nutmeg

Sauce allemande
- **pour poissons** ⇒ sauce based on fish stock
- **pour abats, volailles pochées, légumes et œufs** ⇒ sauce based on veal or poultry stock

Sauce allemande grasse ⇒ velouté sauce added of egg-yolks, and butter

Sauce allemande maigre ⇒ fish stock and velouté sauce, added of egg-yolks and butter

Sauce américaine ⇒ sauce made of shallots, pounded garlic, tomato purée, cayenne pepper and dry white wine

Sauce andalouse ⇒ velouté sauce added of tomato extract, crushed garlic, capsicum pulp, and parsley

Sauce aromatique aux morilles ⇒ sauce of consommé and aromatics, added of lemon juice, morels and butter

Sauce au beurre ⇒ sauce of butter and flour

Sauce au beurre -*[Carême]*- ⇒ sauce of butter, flour, consommé, grated nutmeg, and lemon juice

Sauce au beurre et à la peluche de cerfeuil -*[Carême]*- ⇒ sauce of butter, flour, grated nutmeg, lemon juice, and shredded chervil

Sauce au beurre et au pain à l'anglaise -*[Carême]*- ⇒ sauce of consommé, crumbs, onion, clove, grated nutmeg, and cayenne-pepper

Sauce au caramel ⇒ sauce of caramel, milk, vanilla, and egg-yolks

Sauce au cari ⇒ curry sauce

Sauce au cassis ⇒ sauce of syrup, blackcurrant purée, and lemon juice
- **utilisée froide pour pommes au four** ⇒ texte
- **œufs à la neige** ⇒ texte
- **ananas glacé** ⇒ texte
- **salade de fruits** ⇒ texte
- **utilisée chaude pour napper un entremets au riz** ⇒ dessert of rice covered with ...
- **accompagner une charlotte de pommes** ⇒ « texte » ... accompanied with a ...
- **accompagner une mousse froide** ⇒ chilled mousse served with a ...

Sauce au céleri ⇒ sauce of mashed celery, plus béchamel sauce added of cream

Sauce au chocolat ⇒ chocolate sauce or sauce of chocolate, butter, milk and cream

Sauce au fenouil ⇒ fennel sauce

Sauce au fromage blanc ⇒ sauce of petit suisse, soft white cheese, Roquefort, cognac, pepper, and vinegar

Sauce au jus coloré ⇒ brown gravy

Sauce au porto ⇒ port wine sauce

Sauce au raifort chaude ⇒ sauce made of grated horse-radish, stock, mustard, and vinegar; thickened with egg-yolks

Sauce au raifort froide ⇒ sauce of crumbs steeped in milk, grated horse-radish, sugar, cream, and vinegar

Sauce au Roquefort ⇒ sauce made of Roquefort, petit suisse, cream, pepper and cognac

Sauce au verjus aigrelette -*[Carême]*- ⇒ brown sauce added of poultry stock, butter, grated nutmeg, pepper, and verjuice

Sauce au vin blanc ⇒ thickened sauce of fish stock and white wine, added of cream and butter

Sauce au vin rouge ⇒ sauce based on diced vegetables, butter, red wine, garlic, mushroom peel, anchovy extract and cayenne pepper

Sauce au xérès ⇒ xeres sauce

Sauce au yaourt ⇒ sauce of yoghourt, paprika, pepper, lemon juice, chervil and chives

Sauce aurore ⇒ velouté sauce, added of tomato purée, and butter

Sauce aux airelles ⇒ cranberry sauce

Sauce aux anchois ⇒ sauce of pounded anchovy fillets, oil, lemon juice, and pepper

Sauce aux aromates ⇒ sauce of consommé and aromatics, added of lemon juice

Sauce aux câpres ⇒ caper sauce

Sauce aux cerises sèches ⇒ sauce of dried cherries simmered in Burgundy wine, vinegar, sugar, coriander, and lemon peel; thickened with brown sauce, plus lemon juice

Sauce aux champignons ⇒ mushroom sauce

Sauce aux écrevisses -*[Carême]*- ⇒ crayfish stock in champagne wine, added of brown sauce, champagne, crayfish paste and butter

Sauce aux fines herbes ⇒ sauce made of stock, plus a hash of parsley, chervil and tarragon

Sauce aux fruits ⇒ fruit sauce

Sauce aux groseilles à maquereau ⇒ sauce of gooseberries cooked with sugar, then added of lemon

Sauce aux huîtres ⇒ oyster sauce

Sauce aux kiwis ⇒ sauce of kiwi fruit pulp, cream, spicy seasoning, and Worcestershire sauce

Sauce aux morilles ⇒ sauce of consommé and aromatics, added of lemon juice, morels and butter

Sauce aux moules ⇒ sauce of mussels cooked in white wine, added of egg-yolks, butter, and lemon juice

Sauce aux pêches cuites ⇒ sauce of peach pulp, lemon juice, sugar, and liquor

Sauce aux pignoles à l'italienne -*[Carême]*- ⇒ sauce of sugar, vinegar, veal stock, herbs, grated nutmeg, ground pepper, brown sauce, claret, and pine-kernel

Sauce aux pommes ⇒ apple compote, added of cinnamon or cumin

Sauce banquière ⇒ supreme sauce added of Madeira, and truffle

Sauce barbecue ⇒ barbecue sauce

Sauce bâtarde ⇒ butter sauce with flour, egg-yolk and lemon juice

Sauce Beauharnaise ⇒ béarnaise sauce added of tarragon butter

Sauce Beaumanoir ⇒ sauce of flour, butter, muscatel wine, tomato extract, and aromatics

Sauce bercy ou Sauce à l'échalote ⇒ sauce made with butter, braised shallots, fish stock, white wine, velouté sauce, and parsley

Sauce bigarade -*[Carême]*- ⇒ Seville orange peel with a brown sauce

Sauce bigarade à blanc pour caneton poêlé ou rôti ⇒ gravy added of white wine, bitter orange peel, lemon juice, consommé, and arrow-root

Sauce blanche ⇒ white sauce

Sauce bolognaise ⇒ bolognèse sauce

Sauce bolognèse ⇒ bolognèse sauce

Sauce bolonaise ⇒ bolognèse sauce

Sauce Bonnefoy ⇒ sauce of bone-marrow, chopped shallots, white wine, thyme and laurel

Sauce Bontemps ⇒ sauce of onion braised in butter, paprika, cider, and velouté sauce

Sauce bordelaise ⇒ sauce made of poached bone-marrow, shallots, red wine, thyme, laurel and parsley

Sauce bordelaise -*[Carême]*- ⇒ brown sauce added of garlic, tarragon, lemon pulp, laurel, clove and Sauternes wine

Sauce bordelaise à la moëlle ⇒ sauce made of poached bone-marrow, shallots, red wine, thyme, laurel and parsley

Sauce bourguignonne pour poissons ⇒ sauce of red wine, onion, herbs, mushroom peel, pepper, and kneaded butter

Sauce bourguignonne pour viandes et volailles ⇒ sauce made of diced pork fat in butter, mushrooms, red wine and stock

Sauce brandade à la provençale *-[Carême]-* ⇒ fish stock and velouté sauce, added of egg-yolks, butter, grated nutmeg, lemon juice, olive oil, and chervil

Sauce bretonne ⇒ sauce from white of leek, celery, and onion braised in butter; then added of mushrooms, white wine, velouté sauce, cream and butter

Sauce brune *-[espagnole]-* ⇒ brown sauce

Sauce brune à la bigarade pour caneton poêlé ou rôti ⇒ brown sauce mixed with sugar, vinegar, lemon juice, and bitter orange peel

Sauce béarnaise ⇒ béarnaise sauce

Sauce béchamel ⇒ béchamel sauce

Sauce béchamel *-[Carême]-* ⇒ béchamel sauce added of cream, and grated nutmeg

Sauce cambridge ⇒ Cambridge sauce

Sauce cameline ⇒ sauce made of bread steeped in wine, spices and vinegar

Sauce caramel ⇒ caramel sauce

Sauce cardinal ⇒ a creamy pink lobster sauce containing truffles and cayenne pepper

Sauce chambertin ⇒ sauce of braised carrots and onions in butter, herbs, mushrooms, garlic, fish, pepper, and Chambertin wine

Sauce Chambord ⇒ sauce of fish stock and vegetables, moistened with red wine

Sauce chantilly ⇒ supreme sauce added of whipped cream

Sauce charcutière ⇒ sauce of chopped onions in pork fat, crumbs, white wine, stock, diced gherkins and mustard

Sauce chasseur ⇒ sauce chasseur

Sauce chateaubriand ⇒ sauce made of shallots, herbs, white wine, hashed tarragon and cayenne pepper

Sauce chaud-froid ⇒ chaudfroid sauce

Sauce chaud-froid à la tomate ⇒ jelly added of tomato pulp

Sauce chaud-froid blanche pour abats blancs, œufs et volailles ⇒ sauce of velouté, mushroom stock, jelly and cream; flavoured with ...

- **à l'andalouse** ⇒ ... xeres, and orange peel
- **à l'aurore** ⇒ ... tomato purée
- **à la banquière** ⇒ ... Madeira and chopped truffles
- **Beauharnais** ⇒ ... tarragon purée, and chervil
- **à l'écossaise** ⇒ ... Madeira, braised diced vegetables, and truffle
- **à la Nantua** ⇒ ... crayfish purée, and truffle
- **à la royale** ⇒ ... mashed truffle added of xeres

Sauce chaud-froid blanche pour volaille ⇒ sauce of jelly from knuckle of veal, poultry, turkey, onions, leeks, celery, herbs, and pepper

Sauce chaud-froid brune ordinaire pour viande diverses ⇒ gelatinous sauce added of Madeira

Sauce chaud-froid brune pour poissons et gibiers ⇒ brown sauce added of Madeira, thickened with stock, egg-yolks, and butter

Sauce chaude à l'abricot ⇒ apricot sauce

Sauce chaude aux anchois ⇒ béchamel sauce added of anchovy paste

Sauce chevreuil ⇒ roebuck sauce

Sauce chivry
   1) **pour poissons** ⇒ sauce of fish stock and composed butter added of herbs
   2) **pour volailles pochées ou oeufs mollets ou pochés** ⇒ sauce of poultry velouté and composed butter added of herbs

Sauce Choron ⇒ béarnaise sauce added of tomato purée

Sauce cinghalaise ⇒ sauce of courgette, capsicums, tomato pulp, cucumber, egg-yolk, curry, pepper, lemon juice, oil, parsley, and chives

Sauce coco ⇒ coconut sauce

Sauce coco safranée ⇒ coconut sauce flavoured with saffron

Sauce colbert ⇒ sauce of meat juices, butter, grated nutmeg, cayenne pepper, lemon juice, chopped parsley and Madeira

Sauce Corcellet ⇒ tomato purée added of mustard flavoured with aniseed

Sauce cressonnière ⇒ sauce made of chopped watercress, a hash of hard boiled eggs, pepper, oil and vinegar

Sauce crevette à l'anglaise ⇒ shrimp sauce

Sauce crevette pour poissons ⇒ fish velouté sauce, added of cream and mushrooms, plus shrimp paste and cayenne pepper

Sauce crème ⇒ béchamel sauce added of cream

Sauce cumberland ⇒ cumberland sauce

Sauce de dessert

 a) **purée ou coulis** ⇒ fruit purée or ... nom anglais du fruit ... purée

 b) **gelée** ⇒ fruit jelly or ... nom anglais du fruit ... jelly

Sauce de pire -[poitou]- ⇒ pork lung and liver, simmered with onions, shallots, red wine and aromatics

Sauce de Sorges ⇒ seasoned french dressing, added of parsley, chives, shallots, and thickened with egg

Sauce demi-glace ⇒ brown sauce added of Madeira

Sauce diable ⇒ sauce of white wine, vinegar, shallot, thyme, laurel, pepper, plus brown sauce added of Madeira

Sauce diane ⇒ peppered french dressing, added of whipped cream and truffles

Sauce dijonnaise ⇒ sauce of hard-boiled egg-yolks, mustard, pepper, oil, and lemon juice

Sauce diplomate

 1) **velouté** ⇒ velouté sauce with truffles and mushrooms; thickened of cream and egg-yolks, plus lobster butter

 2) **sauce normande** ⇒ creamy white sauce added of lobster butter, truffles, and cayenne pepper; flavoured with cognac

Sauce dodine

 a) **dodine blanche** ⇒ sauce of milk, ginger, egg-yolks and sugar

 b) **dodine rouge** ⇒ sauce of bread steeped in red wine, fried onions, pork fat, cinnamon, nutmeg, clove and sugar

 c) **dodine au verjus** ⇒ sauce of egg-yolks, verjuice, poultry livers, ginger, parsley, and stock

Sauce duxelles ⇒ sauce of chopped mushrooms, white wine, stock, and tomatoes cooked in their own liquid

Sauce échalote ⇒ sauce of shallot and vinegar

Sauce écossaise ⇒ béchamel sauce added of cream, plus braised diced vegetables

Sauce egg sauce ⇒ egg sauce

Sauce espagnole -[Carême]- ⇒ brown sauce of veal stock, butter, laurel, clove, and mushrooms

Sauce espagnole -[Denis]- ⇒ a brown sauce made with meat stock, flour, vegetables, mushrooms and tomatoes

Sauce finançière ⇒ Madeira sauce added of truffle extract

Sauce financière -[Carême]- ⇒ sauce of ham, ground pepper, thyme, bay laurel, mushroom, truffle, Madeira, consommé, and butter

Sauce forte ⇒ sauce of capsicum purée, and stock

Sauce Foyot ⇒ béarnaise sauce added of gravy

Sauce François Raffatin ⇒ sauce of egg-yolks, mustard, white wine, and chervil

Sauce froide aux anchois ⇒ sauce of pounded anchovy fillets, oil, lemon juice, and pepper

Sauce garum ⇒ seasoning obtained by maceration of offal and fish in brine and aromatics

Sauce genevoise ⇒ sauce of lobster parings, carrot, onion, thyme, bay laurel, pepper, and Chambertin or red wine from Rhone valley

Sauce genevoise *-[Carême]-* ⇒ sauce made of fish stock, a mixture of diced vegetables and ham, red wine and butter

Sauce génoise ⇒ sauce made of consommé, crushed tomatoes and capsicums

Sauce Godart ⇒ mixture of diced vegetables and ham braised in butter, added of champagne, brown sauce with Madeira, and mushroom extract

Sauce gourmet *-[pour tronçons d'anguille cuits au court-bouillon]-* ⇒ sauce made of fish stock, a mixture of diced vegetables and ham, white wine, lobster butter, crayfish tails, quenelles and truffles

Sauce grand veneur ⇒ preparation of pepper sauce added of redcurrant jelly and cream

Sauce gribiche ⇒ sauce made of hard boiled egg-yolks, oil, chopped capers and herbs

Sauce hachée ⇒ sauce of vinegar; added of chopped mushrooms, capers, gherkins, shallots, pepper, nutmeg, anchovy paste, plus brown sauce, and consommé

Sauce harissa ⇒ seasoning of capsicums, cayenne pepper, oil, garlic, coriander, caraway seeds, mint, and verbena

Sauce hoisin ⇒ seasoning of spices, soya and flour

Sauce hollandaise ⇒ sauce hollandaise

Sauce hollandaise au suprême *-[Carême]-* ⇒ sauce of egg-yolks, brown sauce, poultry stock, butter and vinegar

Sauce homard ⇒ sauce made of fish stock in white wine, egg-yolks, melted butter, pepper, lemon juice, and lobster butter

Sauce Hussarde ⇒ brown sauce flavoured with tomato, added of shallots, onions, ham, grated horseradish, and parsley

Sauce indienne froide ⇒ mayonnaise seasoned with curry, and chives

Sauce italienne ⇒ brown sauce thickened of chopped mushrooms, diced ham, tarragon, plus tomato purée

Sauce ivoire ⇒ supreme sauce added of veal stock

Sauce Joinville

a) **avec base sauce normande** ⇒ fish velouté sauce, added of cream, mushrooms, and shrimp paste

b) **avec base sauce crevette** ⇒ fish velouté sauce, added of cream and mushrooms, plus crayfish paste, and truffle

Sauce ketchup ⇒ ketchup

Sauce la varenne ⇒ sauce made of mayonnaise mixed with chopped mushrooms, parsley and chervil

Sauce Laguipière *-[Carême]-* ⇒ sauce of melted butter, consommé, grated nutmeg, vinegar, lemon juice, and butter

Sauce Laguipière pour poissons ⇒ fish velouté sauce added of cream, chopped truffles, and Madeira

Sauce Le Doyen ⇒ mayonnaise added of herbs

Sauce lyonnaise ⇒ sauce of onions braised in butter, plus vinegar, white wine and stock

Sauce madère ⇒ Madeira sauce

Sauce Maintenon ⇒ béchamel sauce added of mashed onions and nutmeg

Sauce maltaise ⇒ sauce hollandaise mixed with grated tangerine peel, and tangerine juice

Sauce marinière ⇒ sauce made of mussel cooking juice, butter, shallots, parsley and egg-yolks

Sauce mayonnaise ⇒ mayonnaise sauce

Sauce mikado ⇒ sauce hollandaise added of tangerine juice and tangerine peel

Sauce molho carioca ⇒ sauce of capsicum, vinegar, cooking juice of beans, tomatoes and chopped onions

Sauce Mornay ⇒ sauce composed of béchamel sauce, egg-yolks and grated gruyère or béchamel sauce added of egg-yolks and grated gruyère

Sauce mousquetaire ⇒ sauce made of mayonnaise mixed with chopped shallots, white wine, gravy, and cayenne pepper

Sauce mousseline ⇒ sauce hollandaise added of whipped cream or sauce mousseline

Sauce moutarde ⇒ mustard sauce

Sauce moutarde à l'anglaise ⇒ mustard sauce

Sauce moutarde à la crème ⇒ sauce of mustard, cream, lemon juice and pepper

Sauce moutarde au beurre

    a) au beurre ⇒ melted butter sauce, added of mustard

    b) avec sauce hollandaise ⇒ sauce hollandaise, added of mustard

Sauce moutarde pour grillades ⇒ sauce of onions, butter, white wine, pepper, brown sauce, mustard, and lemon juice

Sauce moutarde pour poissons froids ⇒ sauce of cream, mustard, and lemon juice

Sauce Nantua ⇒ béchamel sauce added of mashed crayfishes, cognac and cayenne pepper

Sauce napolitaine ⇒ brown sauce flavoured with grated horseradish, ham, ground pepper, grated nutmeg, and Madeira

Sauce newburg ⇒ sauce of lobster, cream and fish stock

Sauce noisette ⇒ gravy thickened with Madeira or tomato purée or wine

Sauce normande ⇒ fish velouté sauce, added of mushroom stock

Sauce orientale ⇒ tomatoes cooked in their own liquid with saffron and capsicums; then added of mayonnaise

Sauce oursinade ⇒ sauce of butter, egg-yolks, fish stock, and sea-urchins

Sauce paloise ⇒ béarnaise sauce with mint

Sauce parisienne ⇒ petit suisse, plus paprika and lemon juice; thickened of mayonnaise with oil and chervil

Sauce pauvre homme ⇒ sauce made of stock, flour, vinegar, chopped shallots, parsley and fried breadcrumbs

Sauce Pékinoise ⇒ sauce of garlic, onion, ginger, sugar, soya sauce, and tomato juice; thickened of maize fecula, and black mushrooms

Sauce périgourdine ⇒ Madeira sauce added of truffles, and mashed foie gras

Sauce Périgueux ⇒ Madeira sauce added of chopped truffles

Sauce persil ⇒ ... served with parsley sauce

    - pour tête de veau ⇒ texte

    - pieds de veau ⇒ texte

    - langue bouillie ⇒ texte

    - émincés de boeuf ⇒ texte

Sauce persil pour poissons ⇒ roux moistened of fish stock, and flavoured with parsley or nom du poisson ... served with a ...

Sauce piquante ⇒ piquant sauce

Sauce poivrade ⇒ sauce based on a mixture of diced vegetables and ham, cooked in vinegar and oil; seasoned with pepper

Sauce poivrade -[Carême]- ⇒ sauce of onions, carrots, ham, parsley, bay-laurel, thyme, ground pepper, mace, vinegar, consommé, and brown sauce

Sauce Pompadour ⇒ sauce of butter and egg-yolks, thickened with corn flour, plus verjuice

Sauce portugaise ⇒ sauce made of browned onions in olive oil, plus tomatoes, garlic, stock and pepper; thickened of kneaded butter and parsley

Sauce poulette ⇒ sauce poulette or a kind of white sauce

Sauce printanière ⇒ veal or poultry stock, mixed with butter added of spinach juice

Sauce provençale ⇒ sauce of onions and tomatoes braised in olive oil, then added of crushed garlic, herbs, white wine, gravy and basil

Sauce raïto ⇒ preparation made of onions, tomatoes, garlic, ground walnuts, laurel, thyme, parsley, fennel, rosemary and clove; simmered in olive oil and red wine

Sauce ravigote ⇒ ravigote sauce

Sauce ravigote chaude ⇒ sauce of veal stock, white wine, vinegar, shallot, plus a hash of herbs

Sauce ravigote froide ⇒ french dressing added of mustard, tarragon, parsley, herbs, chervil, onion and capers

Sauce réforme ⇒ reform sauce

Sauce Régence ⇒ sauce of browned butter, diced ham, onions and shallot; added of Graves wine and stock

Sauce rémoulade ⇒ remoulade sauce

Sauce richelieu -[*Carême*]- ⇒ sauce made of browned onions, sugar, grated nutmeg, velouté sauce, butter and chopped chervil

Sauce Riche
  1) **velouté** ⇒ velouté sauce with truffles and mushrooms; thickened of cream and egg-yolks, plus lobster butter
  2) **sauce normande** ⇒ creamy white sauce added of lobster butter, truffles, and cayenne pepper; flavoured with cognac

Sauce Robert ⇒ sauce made of onions browned in pork fat, plus flour, white wine, stock and mustard

Sauce Rossini ⇒ sauce of olive oil, mustard, vinegar, lemon juice, pepper, and truffle

Sauce rouennaise ⇒ sauce of poached bone-marrow, herbs, red wine, shallot, and poultry liver

Sauce rougail ⇒ Caribbean seasoning

Sauce rouille -[*Raymond Oliver*]- ⇒ sauce of capsicums, garlic, scorpion-fish livers, and bouillabaisse stock

Sauce rouilleuse -[*Périgord*]- ⇒ sauce based on poultry blood

Sauce royale ⇒ sauce of poultry velouté, cream, butter, chopped truffles, and xeres

Sauce russe froide ⇒ purée of caviar and lobster, added of mayonnaise

Sauce sabayon ⇒ sauce mousseline added of champagne

Sauce St Mâlo ⇒ velouté sauce added of butter, braised onions, white wine, thyme, laurel, parsley; plus a drop of Worcestershire sauce

Sauce Ste Ménéhould ⇒ sauce of braised onions in butter, plus pepper, thyme, laurel, white wine, vinegar, brown sauce, mustard, gherkins, and parsley

Sauce salmis ⇒ brown sauce of game, added of ...
  - **pour bécasse** ⇒ ... dry white wine
  - **pour pintade** ⇒ ... port
  - **pour canard** ⇒ ... Chambertin

Sauce sarladaise ⇒ sauce of hard-boiled egg-yolks, cream, chopped truffles, olive oil, lemon juice, pepper, and cognac

Sauce saupiquet ⇒ spicy sauce with red wine, verjuice, and onion

Sauce smitane ⇒ sour cream added of mustard, spices, vinegar, and hard-boiled egg-yolks

Sauce soja ⇒ soy sauce or soya sauce

Sauce soja ⇒ soya sauce

Sauce soubise ⇒ béchamel sauce added of mashed onions

Sauce suédoise ⇒ mayonnaise added of grated horse-radish, and apple compote cooked in white wine

Sauce suprême ⇒ supreme sauce

Sauce Talleyrand ⇒ sauce of poultry velouté added of cream, Madeira, butter, chopped vegetables, truffle, and pickled oxtongue

Sauce tapenade ⇒ ... seasoning made of capers, anchovies, stoned black olives, olive oil, lemon juice and aromatics

Sauce tartare ⇒ tartare sauce

Sauce Thermidor
    a) à base de sauce Bercy ⇒ sauce of butter, shallots, fish stock, white wine, parsley, and mustard
    b) à base de sauce crème ⇒ béchamel sauce added of cream, and mustard
Sauce tomate ⇒ tomato sauce
Sauce tortue *-[sauce]-* ⇒ sauce of diced ham, onions, carrots, cooked in white wine, flavoured with basil and herbs; plus beef stock, and tomato purée
Sauce toulousaine ⇒ supreme sauce, thickened with egg-yolks, and cream
Sauce tyrolienne ⇒ béarnaise sauce added of tomato purée
Sauce Valois ⇒ Béarnaise sauce added of gravy
Sauce venaison ⇒ preparation of pepper sauce added of redcurrant jelly and cream
Sauce vénitienne *-[Carême]-* ⇒ brown sauce added of tarragon, poultry stock, butter, grated nutmeg, and vinegar
Sauce verdurette ⇒ french dressing added of chives, hard-boiled eggs, chervil, tarragon, and parsley
Sauce Véron ⇒ fish velouté sauce added of cream, mushrooms, herbs, and veal stock
Sauce verte ⇒ mayonnaise mixed with a purée of tarragon, watercress, parsley, spinach and chervil
Sauce verte Le Doyen ⇒ mayonnaise added of chopped herbs
Sauce victoria pour poisson ⇒ sauce made with a culinary stuffing of lobster and truffles, plus cayenne pepper and white wine
Sauce Victoria pour venaison ⇒ brown sauce mixed with port plus redcurrant jelly, spiced with cinnamon and clove
Sauce villageoise
    1) base béchamel ⇒ béchamel sauce added of braised onions, cooking juice, egg-yolk and butter
    2) base velouté ⇒ velouté sauce thickened of egg-yolk and cream, plus butter
Sauce Villeroi ⇒ sauce of stock added of truffle extract, tomato purée, or onion purée, or chopped mushrooms
Sauce vinaigrette ⇒ vinegar sauce or oil and vinegar dressing or French dressing
Sauce Vincent ⇒ mayonnaise added of herbs, and hard-boiled egg
Sauce waterfish chaude ⇒ sauce of white wine and julienne, moistened of stock, then added of sauce hollandaise and parsley
Sauce waterfish froide ⇒ jelly of fish stock, added of julienne, capsicum, gherkins, and capers
Sauce worcester ⇒ Worcestershire sauce
Sauce yorkshire ⇒ Yorkshire sauce
Sauce zingara ⇒ brown sauce mixed with tomato sauce, then added of ham, pickled oxtongue, and mushrooms
Sauchet *-[abusseau]-* ⇒ sand smelt
Sauciau
    - crêpe ⇒ thick pancake
    - beignet ⇒ fritter
Saucière ⇒ sauce-boat
    - pour jus de viande ⇒ gravy-boat
Saucisse ⇒ sausage
Saucisses à la catalane ⇒ sausages fried with garlic, orange peel, tomato purée and white wine
Saucisses à la languedocienne ⇒ sausages braised in goose fat, then covered with the gravy added of vinegar, stock, capers, and parsley; served with ...
    - gratin d'aubergines ⇒ ... aubergines au gratin
    - tomates farçies au riz ⇒ ... tomatoes stuffed of rice
Saucisses au bacon en brochettes ⇒ sausages and slices of bacon, grilled on skewers

Saucisses au chou ⇒ braised cabbage served with grilled sausages < *Nota Si servi avec saucisses braisées au vin blanc, remplacer « grilled sausages » par « sausages braised in white wine »* >

Saucisse au vin blanc ⇒ sausage filled with sausage meat added of white wine

Saucisse de Francfort ⇒ frankfurter

Saucisse de montbéliard ⇒ large steamed sausage

Saucisse de strasbourg ⇒ sausage

Saucisses grillées ⇒ grilled sausages, served with ...

   - **avec purée de pommes de terre** ⇒ ... mashed potatoes
   - **avec purées de légumes** ⇒ ... mashed vegetables
   - **avec purée de haricots secs** ⇒ ... mashed haricot beans

Saucisse viennoise ⇒ sausage of veal and pork meat

Saucisson ⇒ dry sausage or large sausage or sausage eaten cold and sliced

Saucisson -[pain]- ⇒ long round loaf

Saucisson à l'ail ⇒ garlic sausage

Saucisson chasseur ⇒ dry sausage of pork and beef

Saucisson d'Arles ⇒ dry sausage of horse and donkey meat

Saucisson de campagne ⇒ country made dry pork sausage

Saucisson de figues -[Provence]- ⇒ fig paste shaped in dry sausage

Saucisson de Paris ⇒ dry sausage flavoured with garlic

Saucisson en brioche à la lyonnaise ⇒ cooked dry sausage, wrapped in brioche paste, and baked; served with endive salad

Saucisson sec ⇒ dry pork and beef sausage

Sauere Sahne -[Allemagne]- ⇒ sour cream

Sauerkraut -[choucroute]- ⇒ sauerkraut

Sauge ⇒ sage or salvia < *tous uncountable* >

Saugrenée ⇒ seasoning made of butter, herbs, water and salt

Sauguet ⇒ chicken's blood with parsley and lardoons, fried in goose fat

Saumon ⇒ salmon or Atlantic salmon < *tous uncountable* >

Saumon à la moscovite ⇒ poached salmon covered of mayonnaise, decorated with truffle, hard boiled eggs and tarragon leaves; garnished with artichoke hearts in salad and halved hard boiled eggs filled with caviar

Saumon à l'anglaise ⇒ salmon poached in salted water; served with melted butter, and a salad of cucumbers, or courgettes, or white of leeks

Saumon au champagne -[darnes]- ⇒ steaks of salmon laid on butter, shallots, and braised diced vegetables, moistened of fish stock and champagne, then baked; covered with the cooking juice, added of cream and butter

Saumon au champagne -[poisson entier]- ⇒ salmon baked with butter, shallots, and champagne; served with the cooking juice added of velouté sauce, egg-yolks, and cream

Saumon blanc ⇒ coalfish or hake or saithe

Saumon de fontaine -[Omble]- ⇒ char or hill trout or grayling

Saumon en croûte ⇒ salmon wrapped in puff-pastry and baked

Saumon fumé ⇒ smoked salmon

Saumon glacé à la parisienne ⇒ salmon cooked in fish jelly; served glazed with the jelly, surrounded of vegetable salad moulded with mayonnaise, tomato stuffed of vegetable salad, and mayonnaise coloured with ketchup

Saumon glacé en bellevue ⇒ salmon cooked in jelly; served decorated with the jelly

Saumon glacé à la parisienne ⇒ salmon cooked in fish jelly; served glazed with the jelly, surrounded of vegetable salad moulded with mayonnaise, tomato stuffed of vegetable salad, and mayonnaise coloured with ketchup

Saumon grillé ⇒ grilled salmon

Saumon mariné ⇒ salmon escalopes marinated in olive oil, lemon juice, chives, chervil, and tarragon; served with a sauce of cream, pepper and mustard

Saumon ou darnes de saumon poché froid ⇒ Salmon or steaks of salmon poached in fish stock; garnished with lettuce hearts, hard-boiled eggs, or stuffed vegetables as tomatoes, cucumbers, etc ...

> **pour autres garnitures, remplacer « garnished with lettuce hearts ... etc ... » par**
> - **aspics** ⇒ garnished with aspic
> - **queues de crevettes** ⇒ garnished with shrimp tails
> - **queues d'écrevisses** ⇒ garnished with crayfish tails
> - **médaillons de homard** ⇒ garnished with round slices of lobster
> - **barquettes** ⇒ garnished with pastry boats filled of caviar, or mousse, or a culinary stuffing of seafood
> - **fonds d'artichauts** ⇒ garnished with artichoke hearts filled of caviar, or mousse, or a culinary stuffing of seafood

Saumon rose ⇒ pink salmon < *uncountable* >

Saumon rôti à la mode de Bugey ⇒ salmon stuffed with a forcemeat of whiting, cream, truffle and butter; grilled on a skewer and sprinkled with cream, served garnished of crayfish tails and truffles

Saumonette -[*roussette*]-
- **aiguillat commun** ⇒ picked dogfish
- **requin hâ** ⇒ school shark

Saumur -[*vins*]- ⇒ quality wines from Saumur area, on the left bank of the Loire valley

Saumur-Champigny -[*cabernet*]- ⇒ quality red wine from « cabernet franc » variety of vine

Saumuré ⇒ pickled or soused

Saupiquet ⇒ sharp sauce

Saupiquet de canard ⇒ grilled thin slices of duck; covered with a sauce of garlic, vinegar, white wine, soft white cheese, duck liver, and olive oil flavoured with aromatics

Saupoudrer ⇒ to sprinkle
- **saupoudré** ⇒ sprinkled with ... or sprinkled of ...

Sauquet -[*sanguette*]- ⇒ chicken's blood with parsley and lardoons, fried in goose fat

Saur
- **état** ⇒ smoked or dried
- **hareng** ⇒ smoked herring or bloater

Saurel ⇒ mackerel < *pluriel inchangé* >

Saury ⇒ mackerel

Sausseli ⇒ Russian stuffed puff-pastry

Sauter -[*verbe*]- ⇒ to sauté

Sauté -[*plat*]-
- **veau** ⇒ sauté of veal
- **mouton** ⇒ sauté of mutton
- **volaille** ⇒ sauté of poultry

Sauté (e ...) ⇒ sauté < *Ce mot de la langue anglaise est emprunté au français, avec le même sens; exemple « sauté potatoes » pour pommes de terre sautées; il est aussi un verbe transitif « voir préface et grammaire » >*

Sauté d'agneau aux artichauts (*ou de veau ...*)
- **agneau** ⇒ sauté scrag or shoulder of lamb ... served with sauté artichoke hearts, plus the gravy added of white wine
- **veau** ⇒ sauté scrag or shoulder of veal ... served with sauté artichoke hearts, plus the gravy added of white wine

Sauté d'agneau aux aubergines *(ou de veau ...)*
- **agneau** ⇒ scrag of lamb browned in oil and butter, served with aubergines; covered of the gravy added with white wine, veal stock, tomato purée, and garlic
- **veau** ⇒ shoulder of veal browned in oil and butter, served with aubergines; covered of the gravy added with white wine, veal stock, tomato purée, and garlic

Sauté d'agneau aux cèpes *(ou de veau ...)*
- **agneau** ⇒ scrag of lamb browned in oil and butter, served with sauté « boletus »; covered with the gravy added of white wine, veal stock, tomato purée, and garlic
- **veau** ⇒ shoulder of veal browned in oil and butter, served with sauté « boletus »; covered with the gravy added of white wine, veal stock, tomato purée, and garlic < *si aux morilles, remplacer « boletus » par « morels »; si aux mousserons, remplacer « boletus » par « button-mushrooms »* >

Sauté d'agneau aux morilles *(ou de veau ...)*
- **agneau** ⇒ scrag of lamb browned in oil and butter, served with sauté morels; covered with the gravy added of white wine, veal stock, tomato purée, and garlic
- **veau** ⇒ shoulder of veal browned in oil and butter, served with sauté morels; covered with the gravy added of white wine, veal stock, tomato purée, and garlic

Sauté d'agneau aux mousserons *(ou de veau ...)*
- **agneau** ⇒ scrag of lamb browned in oil and butter, served with sauté button-mushrooms; covered with the gravy added of white wine, veal stock, tomato purée, and garlic
- **veau** ⇒ shoulder of veal browned in oil and butter, served with sauté button-mushrooms; covered with the gravy added of white wine, veal stock, tomato purée, and garlic

Sauté d'agneau aux tomates *(ou de veau ...)*
- **agneau** ⇒ sauté scrag of lamb or shoulder of lamb served with sauté tomatoes, plus the gravy added of white wine
- **veau** ⇒ sauté scrag of veal or shoulder of veal served with sauté tomatoes, plus the gravy added of white wine

Sauté d'agneau chasseur *(ou de veau ...)*
- **agneau** ⇒ sauté shoulder of lamb added of shallots, stock, tomato sauce; then simmered with pepper, herbs, and mushrooms
- **veau** ⇒ sauté shoulder of veal added of shallots, stock, tomato sauce; then simmered with pepper, herbs, and mushrooms

Sauté d'agneau à l'ancienne ⇒ lamb sweetbread simmered in butter with mushrooms, scrag and shoulder of lamb, Madeira, stock, herbs, and cream

Sauté d'agneau à la minute ⇒ sauté bits of veal shoulder, sprinkled of lemon juice and parsley

Sauté d'agneau au paprika ⇒ boneless shoulder of lamb browned in butter, added of onions, flour, and paprika, then moistened of white wine, stock, and tomato purée; served with mushrooms, plus the cooking juice added of cream

Sauté de truffes du Piémont ⇒ truffles sautéed in olive oil or butter, with gravy, white pepper, and grated nutmeg

Sauté de veau à la minute ⇒ sauté shoulder of veal; served with the gravy added of white wine, lemon juice, and butter

Sauté de veau à la portugaise ⇒ sauté shoulder of veal in olive oil with onion, and garlic; then simmered with the gravy added of white wine, stock, tomato sauce, herbs, tomatoes, and parsley

Sauté de veau au vin rouge ⇒ shoulder of veal browned in butter, then braised with onion, pepper, red wine, stock and garlic; served with glazed onions, and sauté mushrooms

Sauté de veau Clamart ⇒ shoulder of veal braised in butter, with stock, white wine, peas and onions

Sauté de veau Marengo ⇒ browned shoulder of veal, simmered with onions, tomatoes, flour, white wine, herbs, garlic, pepper, and mushrooms; served decorated with glazed onions, and fried croutons

Sauterelle ⇒ grasshopper

Sauternes -[*vin*]- ⇒ Sauternes

Sauternes cup ⇒ drink made of slices of lemon, curaçao, cognac, cherries in eau de vie, Sauternes wine, and soda water

Sauvage ⇒ wild

Sauvagine -[*gibier*]- ⇒ wildfowl

Sauvagine aux alouettes ⇒ lark stuffed with lark meat, butter, Crithmum, crumbs, Malaga raisins, and juniper berries; roasted on a skewer

Sauvignon ⇒ white wine from Loire valley

Sauzé-Vaussais -[*Poitou*]- ⇒ goat's milk cheese

Savarin ⇒ savarin cake

Savarin à l'orange ⇒ savarin cake made of flour, sugar, oil, eggs, orange peel and yeast; baked and topped with pieces of oranges

Savarin à la crème pâtissière ⇒ savarin cake sprinkled with a syrup of sugar and vanilla; garnish with confectioner's custard

Savarin aux fruits ⇒ savarin cake steeped with syrup flavoured of rum, covered with apricot jam; served with fruit salad sprinkled of the same syrup

Savarin aux fruits rouges à la chantilly ⇒ savarin cake steeped with vanilla syrup, covered with cherry and raspberry purée; topped of sugared whipped cream

Savarin surfin ⇒ savarin cake made of flour, butter, sugar, currants, milk, eggs and yeast; then baked

Savaron -[*Auvergne*]- ⇒ cheese from Auvergne

Savennières -[*Anjou vins*]- ⇒ high quality wines from Angers area

Savigny lès Beaune ⇒ Burgundy red wine from Côtes de Beaune

Savoie -[*biscuit de*]- ⇒ gateau containing a large quantity of whipped white of eggs, plus sugar and vanilla

Savourée -[*sarriette*]- ⇒ savory < *uncountable* >

Savoury ⇒ savoury dish

Savoyarde (*à la ...*)
1) **gratin de pommes de terre** ⇒ potatoes au gratin
2) **oeufs pochés ou mollets dressés sur gratin de pommmes de terre nappé de sauce Mornay** ⇒ poached eggs or soft boiled eggs, laid on potatoes au gratin, covered with béchamel sauce added of egg-yolks and grated gruyère
3) **oeufs sur le plat cuits avec pommes de terre sautées, du gruyère et de la crème fraOche** ⇒ eggs fried with sauté potatoes, grated gruyère and cream
4) **Omelette avec pommes de terre sautées et du gruyère** ⇒ omelet filled with sauté potatoes and gruyère

Sawo Manilla ⇒ Sapodilla

Sbrinz ⇒ swiss cooked cow's milk cheese with a brown crust

Scabetche -[*escabèche*]- ⇒ fried fish conserved in a spicy marinade or spicy marinade for conservation of cooked food

- **Berry, gougeons à la cascamèche** ⇒ fried gudgeons conserved in a spicy marinade
- **volaille et gibier** ⇒ ... cooked and conserved in a spicy marinade
- **Chili, poulet** ⇒ chicken fried in oil with garlic, then covered of marinade added of aromatics; served chilled with lemons and onions
- **Belgique, escavèche** ⇒ Belgian name for « escabèche »

Scaloppina -[*escalope*]- ⇒ italian escalope

Scamorze ⇒ Italian cheese

Scampi ⇒ scampi

Scare -[*poisson*]- ⇒ scarus or parrot-fish

Scarole ⇒ escarole

Scavèce -*[escabèche]*- ⇒ fried fish conserved in a spicy marinade or spicy marinade for conservation
of cooked food
- **Berry, gougeons à la cascamèche** ⇒ fried gudgeons conserved in a spicy marinade
- **volaille et gibier** ⇒ ... cooked and conserved in a spicy marinade
- **Chili, poulet** ⇒ chicken fried in oil with garlic, then covered of marinade added of aromatics;
served chilled with lemons and onions
Schabzieger ⇒ sapsago
Schenkelés -*[friture]*- ⇒ small fritters made of flour, eggs, almond powder, butter, rum, sugar and
lemon peel
Schiedam -*[Hollandais]*- ⇒ schiedam
Schifela ⇒ smoked shoulder of pork
Schillerwein -*[Allemagne; vin d']*- ⇒ wine from a mixing of red and white grapes
Schinkernwurst -*[saucisse à pocher]*- ⇒ smoked sausage of beef and pork
Schlagobers -*[Autriche]*- ⇒ whipped cream
Schloss Johannisberg -*[Johannnisberg]*- ⇒ high quality Johannisberger
Schnapps ⇒ schnapps
Schnaps ⇒ schnapps
Schnitzel -*[réveillon]*- ⇒ Schnitzel
Schwarzwurst ⇒ large smoked polony added of rind of pork, pig ears, pig head, pig trotters, onions,
bacon, and beef intestine
Schweppes ⇒ Schweppes Indian tonic or Schweppes ginger ale
Sciacce ⇒ patties of potatoes, garlic, tomato purée, scrambled eggs and grated cheese
Sciappa denti -*[casse museau]*- ⇒ hard small cake from almond and cheese
Sciène ⇒ sciaena
Scombridés ⇒ scombridae or scombrids
Scone -*[breakfast]*- ⇒ scone
Scorpion -*[poissson]*- ⇒ scorpion fish
Scorsonère -*[salsifis]*- ⇒ black salsify
Scotch -*[whisky]*- ⇒ scotch
Scotch ale -*[bière]*- ⇒ scotch ale
Scotch broth ⇒ scotch broth
Scotch egg sauce ⇒ scotch egg sauce
Scotch Kale -*[chou pommé]*- ⇒ variety of cabbage
Scotch mutton broth ⇒ Scotch mutton broth
Scotch pudding ⇒ pudding of crumbs, milk, bone-marrow, currants, Malaga raisins, sultanas, and
rum; served with ...
- **sabayon** ⇒ ... zabaglione flavoured of rum
- **crème anglaise au madère** ⇒ ... egg custard flavoured of Madeira
Scotch whisky ⇒ scotch whisky
Scots broth -*[Scotch broth]*- ⇒ scotch broth
Scubac ⇒ liquor made of spices macerated in brandy
Sea kale -*[chou marin]*- ⇒ sea kale
Sébaste ⇒ redfish
Sec ou Sèche *(adjectif ...)* ⇒ dry or dried
Sèche -*[poisson]*- ⇒ cuttlefish
Séchu de Belfort ⇒ dish of dry pears or apples, with slices of streaky bacon
Sédum ⇒ stonecrop
Sedum album -*[sédum]*- ⇒ stonecrop
Seelac ⇒ whiting
Seiche -*[poisson]*- ⇒ cuttlefish

Seigle ⇒ rye
- **farine** ⇒ rye-flour
- **pain** ⇒ rye-bread

Seishu *-[saké]-* ⇒ sake

Sekt ⇒ sparkling wine

Sel ⇒ salt < *uncountable* >

Sel de céleri *-[celeri]-* ⇒ celery salt

Sel de hickory ⇒ salt mixed with hickory dust

Sel de vichy *-[bicarbonate de soude]-* ⇒ bicarbonate

Sel marin ⇒ sea salt

Sélacien ⇒ selachian

Sélection *-[Armagnac]-* ⇒ high quality Armagnac

Selibomg *-[thé]-* ⇒ variety of Indian tea

Selle ⇒ saddle
- **de mouton** ⇒ saddle of mutton
- **d'agneau** ⇒ saddle of lamb
- **de lapin** ⇒ saddle of rabbit
- **de veau** ⇒ saddle of veal

Selle d'agneau ⇒ saddle of lamb

Selle d'agneau Belle Otéro ⇒ boneless leg of lamb stuffed with a forcemeat of truffles, chopped mushrooms, shallots, pepper, grated nutmeg and foie gras, then roasted; served with bunches of asparagus tips in butter, or braised artichoke hearts

Selle d'agneau Callas ⇒ boneless leg of lamb stuffed with a julienne of mushrooms, and truffles, then roasted; served with asparagus tips, plus the gravy thickened of veal stock and xeres

Selle de chevreuil à la berrichonne ⇒ roasted leg of roebuck, garnished of pears cooked in red wine, plus celery braised in butter; served with a sauce of carrots, onions, game, shallots, celery, garlic, pepper, clove, red wine, butter, and pig blood

Selle de chevreuil grand veneur ⇒ leg of roebuck studded with lardoons marinated in cognac, parsley, pepper and oil, then roasted; served with braised chestnuts, or chestnut purée, or fried croquettes of mashed potatoes mixed with choux pastry, plus a sauce of pepper sauce, redcurrant jelly and cream

Selle de chevreuil rôtie sauce poivrade ⇒ leg of roebuck seasoned with herbs and roasted on a skewer; covered with a sauce based on a mixture of diced vegetables and ham cooked in vinegar and white wine, seasoned of pepper, served with ...
- **avec marrons glacés** ⇒ marron glacé
- **avec pommes dauphines** ⇒ fried croquettes of mashed potatoes, mixed with choux pastry
- **avec pommes sautées au beurre** ⇒ sauté potatoes
- **pommes évidées avec compote d'airelle** ⇒ potatoes hollowed out, then filled with compote of bilberries, and baked

Selle de gigot de mouton ⇒ saddle of mutton or saddle of lamb

Selle de gigot de mouton raccourcie ⇒ short saddle of mutton or short saddle of lamb

Selle de veau Orloff ⇒ sliced braised saddle of veal stuffed with a purée of mushrooms, and onions, then reconstituted; served covered with a béchamel sauce added of mashed onions and nutmeg, then browned

Selles sur Cher ⇒ conical goat's milk cheese

Seltz *-[eau de]-* ⇒ soda water or seltzer

Semoule ⇒ semolina < *uncountable* >

Semoule à la crème ⇒ gateau made of semolina, milk, sugar, preserved fruits, plus whipped eggs; topped of custard

Semoule pour entremets ⇒ dessert of milk, sugar, vanilla, semolina, and butter; cooked in the oven

Séneçon ⇒ groundsel
Sénevé -*[graine de moutarde]*- ⇒ mustard seed OR mustard
Senga sengana -*[fraise]*- ⇒ variety of fraise
Sépia -*[seiche]*- ⇒ cuttlefish
Sérac -*[fromage]*- ⇒ cheese from Dauphiné
Sercial -*[madère]*- ⇒ Madeira
Serge *(à la ...)*
    - **escalopes** ⇒ escalopes ...
    - **ris de veau** ⇒ calf sweetbread ... ... coated with a mixing of crumbs, truffle and mushrooms, then sautéed and garnished with quartered artichokes braised in butter, plus a julienne of ham in Madeira; served with the cooking juice added of truffle extract
Sérieux -*[bière]*- ⇒ a 2 litres beer mug
Serpent ⇒ snake
Serpolet ⇒ wild thyme
Serra -*[fromage de brebis]*- ⇒ ewe cheese or ewe's milk cheese
Serran chèvre -*[poisson]*- ⇒ comber
Serrano -*[jambon]*- ⇒ high quality Spanish ham
Servant -*[raisin]*- ⇒ variety of grape
Servi ⇒ served
Servi avec ⇒ served with ...
Servi nappé avec ⇒ served covered with ...
Servi nappé de ⇒ served covered of ...
Service -*[prix]*- ⇒ tip or service charge
Service compris ⇒ service included or inclusive of service
Service non compris ⇒ service not included or exclusive of service
Serviette *(à la ...)*
    a) **serviette** -*[linge]*- ⇒ towel
    b) **serviette de table** ⇒ table napkin or serviette
    c) **truffes pochées** ⇒ poached truffles presented in serviette
        - **truffes sous la cendre** ⇒ truffles cooked in the embers, and presented in serviette
    d) **pommes de terre en robe des champs** ⇒ jacket potatoes presented in serviette
    e) **asperges cuites à l'eau** ⇒ boiled asparagus presented in serviette
    f) **riz à la serviette** ⇒ rice cooked in salted water, wrapped in serviette, and dried in the oven
Sésame ⇒ sesame
Sésame -*[huile de]*- ⇒ sesame oil
Séteau ⇒ variety of small soles
Sétoise *(à la ...)* ⇒ angler cooked quickly and served with a julienne braised in olive oil and white wine; covered with mayonnaise added of the cooking juice boiled down
Sévigné ⇒ soft boiled eggs or hard boiled eggs served on braised lettuce and topped with truffle lamellas
Sève -*[érable]*- ⇒ maple syrup
Sevruga -*[caviar]*- ⇒ caviar
Seyssel ⇒ white wine from Savoy area
Sébasse ⇒ Kind of scorpion fish
Sèche -*[poisson]*- ⇒ cuttlefish
Shamouti -*[orange]*- ⇒ variety of orange
Sherry ⇒ xeres or sherry
Sherry cobbler -*[cocktail]*- ⇒ sherry cobbler
Shincha -*[Japon; thé]*- ⇒ early spring tea
Shirataki -*[Japon]*- ⇒ fecula

Shortbread -*[GB]-* ⇒ shortbread or shortcake
Short cake -*[Amérique du nord]-* ⇒ short cake
Short drink -*[cocktail]-*
- « **cocktail flip** » ⇒ cocktail added of egg
- « **cocktail sour** » ⇒ cocktail added of lemon and sugar
- « **cocktail straight** » ⇒ cocktail served in glass for cognac, without any addition
Shortening -*[biscuiterie]-* ⇒ vegetable fat
Shoyu -*[soja sauce]-* ⇒ soya sauce
Shrimp sauce ⇒ shrimp sauce
Shrub -*[cocktail]-* ⇒ shrub
Sicilienne (à la ...) -*[petites pièces de boucherie ou de volailles poêlées]-* ⇒ fried ... served with a garnish of stuffed tomatoes, plus timbales of rice and potato croquettes
Side-car -*[cocktail]-* ⇒ sidecar
Siffleur -*[canard]-* ⇒ wild duck
Sigui -*[Russe]-* ⇒ kind of sprat
Sil -*[Suisse]-* ⇒ custard of rye bread moistened with red wine, added of elder syrup, raisins, and cream
Silba -*[Yougoslavie]-* ⇒ Yugoslavian cheese
Sili more -*[congre]-* ⇒ conger eel or sea eel
Silki -*[Russe]-* ⇒ kind of sprat
Silphium ⇒ asafoetida
Silure ⇒ silurus or sheat-fish
Silure glane ⇒ silurus
Silver -*[saumon]-* ⇒ silver salmon
Simple ⇒ simple or plain or unsophisticated or not compound or straight forward
Singapour -*[gâteau]-* ⇒ large cake of Genoese stuffed of jam, and fruits in syrup; covered with apricot jam, then decorated of preserved fruits
Singe ⇒ monkey or ape
Single malt -*[whisky]-* ⇒ single malt
Sington -*[thé]-* ⇒ variety of Indian tea
Siot -*[GB]-* ⇒ slot
Siphon ⇒ siphon
Sirene -*[Bulgarie]-* ⇒ Bulgarian ewe cheese
Sirloin -*[baron de bœuf]-* ⇒ sirloin
Sirop ⇒ syrup < *uncountable* >
Sirop d'alkékenge ⇒ physalis syrup
Sirop d'oranges ⇒ orange syrup
Sirop d'orgeat ⇒ barley water
Sirop de café ⇒ syrup of coffee and sugar
Sirop de capillaire -*[Portugal]-* ⇒ capillaire
Sirop de cassis ⇒ blackcurrant syrup
Sirop de cerises ⇒ cherry syrup
Sirop de fraises ⇒ strawberry syrup
Sirop de fécule ⇒ glucose syrup
Sirop de glucose ⇒ glucose syrup
Sirop de groseilles à maquereau ⇒ gooseberry syrup
Sirop de mûres ⇒ mulberry syrup
Sirop de sucre ⇒ syrup
Sirop de sureau ⇒ elder syrup
Siroper -*[imbiber]-* ⇒ moistened with syrup

Sirtema -[*pomme de terre*]- ⇒ variety of potato
Skyr -[*lait*]- ⇒ fermented milk
Skyros -[*Grèce*]- ⇒ variety of Greek cheese
Slight ale ou Bitter -[*bière*]- ⇒ slight ale or bitter
Slivovica -[*Bulgarie*]- ⇒ plum brandy
Slivovitz ⇒ slivovitz
Sloe gin -[*cocktail*]- ⇒ sloe gin
Sloke -[*algue*]- ⇒ sloke
Slottssteck -[*Suède*]- ⇒ braised beef; served with cranberries, and potatoes
Smen ⇒ clarified butter
Smenn ⇒ clarified butter
Smeum ⇒ clarified butter
Smeun -[*Afrique du nord*]- ⇒ salted ewe's butter
Smitane -[*Russe*]- ⇒ sour cream
Smorbrod -[*Norvège*]- ⇒ smorgasbord
Smorgasbord ⇒ smorgasbord
Smyrne -[*raisin sec*]- ⇒ sultanas
Snack ⇒ light meal or snack
Snack bar ⇒ snack bar < *attention « snack » veut dire repas léger* >
Sobressada de mallorca -[*soubressade*]- ⇒ small Spanish sausage
Sobronade ⇒ soup of pork, ham, haricot beans, rapes, plus other vegetables and aromatics
Socca
    - bouillie ⇒ chick-pea flour porridge
    - tranches frites ⇒ slices of chick-pea flour porridge, fried in oil
Sockeye -[*saumon*]- ⇒ red salmon or sockeye salmon
Socle ⇒ socle for decoration purpose
Soda ⇒ soda-water or fizzy lemonade
Soda bread -[*pain*]- ⇒ soda bread
Sohleb -[*sorgho*]- ⇒ millet porridge flavoured with ginger
Soisson -[*haricots*]- ⇒ haricot beans
Soissonaise (*à la ...*) ⇒ with white kidney-beans
Soja -[*sauce*]- ⇒ soy sauce or soya sauce
Soja ⇒ soya or soy or soya bean or soy bean
Sole ⇒ sole or common sole or solenette
Sole à l'arlésienne ⇒ soles poached in fish stock, served with tomatoes cooked in butter, braised
    artichoke hearts in cream; covered with the fish stock thickened of tomato sauce,
    garlic, and butter
Sole à l'orange ⇒ sole fried in butter, and garnished with slices of orange; covered with a sauce of
    butter, cream and curaçao
Sole à la Riche -[*filets de*]- ⇒ poached sole fillets garnished with a culinary stuffing of lobster;
    covered with a creamy sauce added of lobster butter, and cayenne pepper, then
    flavoured of cognac
Sole à la Richelieu ⇒ sole fillets coated with egg and breadcrumbs, cooked in butter, then served with
    truffles and parsley butter
Sole à la diplomate ⇒ poached sole fillets with a forcemeat of whiting; served with a culinary stuffing
    of lobster, covered with a sauce of lobster butter, truffle, and lobster meat
Sole à la dugléré ⇒ sole baked with tomato pulp, onions, garlic, shallots and herbs in white wine;
    served with kneaded butter and parsley
Sole à la ménagère ⇒ sole baked on a bed of braised vegetables with red wine, glazed with the
    cooking juice added of kneaded butter

Soles à la meunière ⇒ soles peppered and floured, then browned in butter and oil; sprinkled of melted butter and lemon juice, plus parsley served with ...
- **champignons** ⇒ mushrooms
- **aubergines** ⇒ sauté aubergines
- **courgettes** ⇒ sauté courgettes
- **pommes à l'anglaise** ⇒ boiled potatoes
- **épinard au beurre** ⇒ spinach in butter
- **d'autres garnitures possibles** ⇒ voir traduction, ou la construire

Sole à la nantua ⇒ sole ...
- **beurre composé** ⇒ ... with crayfish in composed butter, and sometimes added of truffle
- **purée de ou coulis de** ⇒ ... with crayfish in nom anglais ... purée, and sometimes added of truffle

Sole à la normande ⇒ sole poached in fish stock; garnished of poached oysters, mussels in white wine, shrimp tails, mushrooms, truffles, fried freshwater gudgeons and fried sippets

Sole à la panetière -[filets de]- ⇒ voir filets de ...

Sole à la paysanne ⇒ sole poached with mixed vegetables, in the oven

Sole à la portugaise ⇒ sole laid on tomatoes cooked in their own liquid with garlic, sprinkled of olive oil, lemon juice, fish stock, and baked; then sprinkled of crumbs and browned

Sole à la walewska -[filets de]- ⇒ poached sole with truffles and lobster escalope; coated of cheese sauce with lobster butter, then browned

Sole au thym ⇒ sole browned in butter, then cooked with pepper, thyme and white wine; covered with the cooking juice added of cream, plus a slice of lemon

Sole aux légumes poêlés ⇒ sole floured and fried in butter and oil; served surrounded of fried vegetables, sprinkled of lemon juice and parsley, covered with the cooking juice

si vous utilisez un légume particulier, remplacer « fried vegetables » par
- **courgettes** ⇒ fried courgettes
- **aubergines** ⇒ fried aubergines
- **gousses de concombres** ⇒ cucumbers braised in butter
- **fonds d'artichaut** ⇒ sauté artichoke hearts
- **champignons de Paris** ⇒ sauté cultivated mushrooms
- **cèpes** ⇒ sauté boletus
- **poivrons** ⇒ capsicums braised in oil

Sole albert ⇒ sole in Maxim's recipe

Soles Armenonville ⇒ flat cake of sliced potato baked in butter, topped with soles poached in fish stock; then covered with a sauce of white wine, fish stock, and boletus in butter
- **Recette traditionnelle** ⇒ soles poached in fish stock, surrounded by fried balls made of mashed potatoes, eggs, butter, and truffle

Sole Bagatelle ⇒ sole stuffed with a culinary stuffing of lobster, mushrooms, truffle, and cream, then fried in butter; served with a sauce of shallot, white wine, fish stock, pepper, parsley, lemon juice, and kneaded butter

Sole Bercy ⇒ sole baked with shallots, parsley, white wine, lemon juice, and butter

Sole bonne femme ⇒ voir sole à la paysanne

Sole chauchat ⇒ poached sole, coated with béchamel sauce thickened of egg yolks; served surrounded with boiled potatoes

Sole choisy ⇒ poached sole, covered with white wine sauce and garnished with a julienne of lettuce and mushrooms

Sole Colbert ⇒ fried sole fillets, served with parsley butter added of gravy, and tarragon

Sole cubat -[filets de]- ⇒ sole fillets poached in mushrooms stock, browned in the oven with chopped mushrooms, Mornay sauce and truffle lamellas

---

Soles de ligne à la fondue de poireau ⇒ sole baked on a layer of seaweed; served surrounded by white of leeks braised in butter, and thickened of cream

Sole dorée ⇒ sole peppered and floured, then browned in butter; decorated with slices of lemon, and sprinkled of butter cooked lightly

Sole farçies Auberge de l'Ill ⇒ soles stuffed with a forcemeat of whiting fillet, white of egg, pepper, grated nutmeg, cream, salmon fillet, and pistachios; then baked with shallots, Riesling, and fish stock; served covered with the cooking juice added of cream, butter, and lemon juice; decorated of truffle lamellas, and shaped puff-pastries

Soles frites ⇒ soles deep-fried in oil, sprinkled of salt, then served with quartered lemons

Sole grillée ⇒ sole peppered and oiled, then grilled; served with lemon, and « a sauce » < *ou remplacer « a sauce » par la description de la sauce choisie* >

Sole grillée à la niçoise ⇒ grilled sole, surrounded of tomatoes cooked in their own liquid, with tarragon, and anchovy paste, plus capers, and stoned black olives

Sole limande ⇒ lemon sole

Soles meunière Mont Bry ⇒ soles floured and browned in butter; served with sauté noodles, plus tomatoes cooked with salt, sugar, onion and garlic

Sole nemours ⇒ poached sole fillets covered with shrimp sauce, topped of truffle lamellas and garnished with mushrooms thickened of a creamy sauce

Sole sur le plat ⇒ sole stuffed of butter, then baked with fish stock and lemon juice

Soleil de Marcillac *-[Rouergue]-* ⇒ leaven paste added of almonds

Solen ⇒ solen or razor-shell

Solette ⇒ slip

Solianka *-[Russe]-* ⇒ soup of cucumber, onion and tomato, garnished of meat or fish

Solilemme ⇒ brioche enriched of eggs, butter and cream, sliced in two parts still hot and sprinkled of salted melted butter

Solognote *(à la ...)*
- **canard poêlé** ⇒ fried duck stuffed with its liver marinated in armagnac and herbs
- **agneau rôti** ⇒ roasted lamb marinated in white wine, vinegar and herbs

Solonina *-[Russe]-* ⇒ beef rolled in pickles, then poached; garnished with sauerkraut and potatoes, plus a sauce based on grated horse-radish

Somaintrain *-[fromage]-* ⇒ Burgundy cheese

Sommelier ⇒ wine-waiter or butler or cellarman

Son ⇒ bran

Songe *-[plante; taro]-* ⇒ Indian katchu

Sopa seca *-[tortilla]-* ⇒ bits of tortillas and sauce, served hot

Sopes *-[tortilla]-* ⇒ tortilla stuffed of meat, haricot beans, and spicy sauce

Sopito *-[Antilles]-* ⇒ bouillabaisse with coconut milk

Soquarel *-[agaric]-* ⇒ honey fungus or bootlace fungus

Sorbais *-[Maroilles]-* ⇒ Maroilles cheese

Sorbe *-[corme]-* ⇒ sorb-apple

Sorbet ⇒ sorbet or sherbet

Sorbet à l'orange ⇒ sorbet of orange juice and sugar

Sorbet à la fraise ⇒ sorbet of strawberries, sugar, lemon juice, and orange juice

Sorbet à la framboise ⇒ sorbet of syrup, raspberries, and lemon juice

Sorbet à la groseille ⇒ sorbet of syrup and redcurrant juice

Sorbet à la mangue ⇒ sorbet of mango pulp, syrup, and lemon juice

Sorbet à la pêche ⇒ sorbet of syrup and peach pulp

Sorbet à la pêche avec champagne ⇒ sorbet of syrup and peach pulp; served covered with champagne

Sorbet à la poire ⇒ sorbet of pear pulp, sugar, and lemon juice

Sorbet à la tomate ⇒ sorbet of tomato juice, syrup, vodka, and whipped white of eggs
Sorbet au cacao et aux raisins ⇒ sorbet of sugar, cocoa, vanilla extract, rum, and raisins macerated in whisky
Sorbet au calvados ⇒ sorbet of syrup, lemon juice, cinnamon, white of eggs, and calvados
Sorbet au cassis ⇒ sorbet added of black currant liquor and meringue
Sorbet au citron ⇒ sorbet added of lemon
Sorbet au miel et aux pignons de pin ⇒ sorbet of orange honey, lemon juice, bitter orange tree flower extract, and grilled pine-kernels
Sorbet au thé ⇒ sorbet of tea and sugar
Sorbet aux fruits ⇒ sorbet of syrup and fruits
Sorbet aux fruits de la Passion ⇒ sorbet of syrup and Passion fruit pulp
Sorbet aux fruits exotiques ⇒ sorbet of syrup, cinnamon, vanilla sugar, plus the juice of pineapple, mangos, and bananas
Sorgho ⇒ sorghum or Indian millet
Soringue ⇒ eel simmered in a sauce made of crumbs, unripe grape juice, ginger, cinnamon, clove and saffron
Sosati -*[Afrique du sud]*- ⇒ marinated mutton, grilled on skewers
Sota -*[cocido]*- ⇒ Spanish meal made of various dishes
Sot-l'y-laisse ⇒ parson's nose
Sot-l'y-laisse aux morilles ⇒ parson's nose braised in butter, with shallot, pepper, morels, white wine from Loire valley, grated nutmeg, and cream
Sottise -*[bêtise]*- ⇒ sweet made of cooked sugar flavoured with mint
Sottises de Valenciennes ⇒ sweet, made of cooked sugar flavoured with mint
Sou fassum ⇒ cabbage stuffed with rice, bacon, sausage meat, tomatoes, beet leaves and onions
Soubise
  - **plat** ⇒ onions added in purée
  - **sauce** ⇒ béchamel sauce added of mashed onions
Soubressade ⇒ small Spanish sausage
Souchet -*[plante]*- ⇒ galingale or sedge
Souchet -*[canard]*- ⇒ wild duck
Souchette -*[collybie]*- ⇒ spotted tough shank or wood woolly foot
Souchong -*[thé]*- ⇒ variety of tea
Souci ⇒ marigold
Soufflé ⇒ soufflé or soufflé dish
Soufflé ambassadrice ⇒ soufflé of egg-custard, vanilla, crushed macaroons, almonds macerated in rum, and white of eggs
Soufflé à la cervelle ⇒ soufflé of béchamel sauce, mashed brains, pepper, grated nutmeg, and eggs
Soufflé à la cervelle « à la hongroise » ⇒ soufflé of béchamel sauce, mashed brains, pepper, grated nutmeg, eggs, onions, mushrooms, and paprika
Soufflé à la chicorée ⇒ soufflé of braised endive, béchamel sauce, nutmeg, and eggs
Soufflé à la mandarine ⇒ soufflé of syrup, tangerine, and white of eggs
Soufflé à la patate douce ⇒ soufflé of mashed sweet potatoes, cream, and eggs
Soufflé à la pomme de terre ⇒ soufflé of mashed potatoes, cream, and eggs
  - **Pour les variantes remplacer « mashed potatoes » par aux marrons** ⇒ chestnut purée
  - **à la patate douce** ⇒ mashed sweet potatoes
  - **au topinambour** ⇒ mashed Jerusalem artichokes
Soufflé à la reine ⇒ soufflé of béchamel sauce, mashed poultry, butter, and chopped truffle
Soufflé à la romaine ⇒ soufflé of braised spinach, anchovy fillets, béchamel sauce, nutmeg, and eggs
Soufflé à la tomate ⇒ soufflé of béchamel sauce, tomato purée, and grated parmesan
Soufflé à la vanille ⇒ soufflé made of milk, sugar, vanilla, flour, butter, and whipped white of eggs

Soufflé à la volaille ⇒ soufflé of béchamel sauce, mashed poultry, and butter

Soufflé au café ⇒ soufflé made of milk, egg-yolks, rice, salt, sugar, whipped white of eggs, and coffee extract

Soufflé au chocolat -[léger]- ⇒ soufflé made of milk, chocolate, flour, sugar, butter and whipped eggs

Soufflé au chocolat ⇒ soufflé made of milk, sugar, chocolate, whipped egg-yolks, and rice

Soufflé au citron ⇒ soufflé made of whipped egg-yolks, sugar, lemon juice, and whipped white of eggs

Soufflé au citron vert ⇒ soufflé of confectioner's custard added of lime juice, white of eggs, and granulated sugar; served with egg-custard added of lime peel

Soufflé au crabe ⇒ soufflé of béchamel sauce, mashed crab, and eggs

Soufflé au curaçao -[ou autre liqueur]- ⇒ soufflé of sugar, eggs, and curaçao < *Si le soufflé est fait avec une autre liqueur, remplacer « curaçao » par le nom anglais de celle-ci* >

Soufflé au fromage ⇒ cheese soufflé

Soufflé au fromage ⇒ soufflé of béchamel sauce, grated cheese, and grated nutmeg

Soufflé au fromage et aux œufs pochés ⇒ soufflé of milk, butter, eggs, and grated gruyère; baked with poached eggs

Soufflé au gibier sauce Périgueux ⇒ soufflé of mashed pheasant or partridge, béchamel sauce, and eggs; served with Madeira sauce added of truffle

Soufflé au homard ⇒ soufflé of béchamel sauce, mashed lobster, and eggs

Soufflé au jambon ⇒ soufflé of béchamel sauce, grated cheese, grated nutmeg, and chopped ham

Soufflé au saumon ⇒ soufflé made with a hash of salmon, cream, and eggs

Soufflé aux bananes ⇒ soufflé of flour, milk, granulated sugar, banana pulp, egg-yolks, butter and kirsch

Soufflé aux champignons ⇒ soufflé of mashed mushrooms, and eggs; baked in ramekins

Soufflé aux châtaignes ⇒ soufflé of chestnut purée, added with eggs; served with a sorbet of syrup and tangerine

Soufflé aux crevettes ⇒ soufflé of béchamel sauce, mashed shrimps, and eggs

Soufflé aux foies de volaille ⇒ soufflé of mashed poultry livers, shallots, parsley, and béchamel sauce

Soufflé aux fraises ou aux framboises

    a) aux fraises ⇒ soufflé of confectioner's custard, mashed strawberries, and white of eggs

    b) aux framboises ⇒ soufflé of confectioner's custard, mashed raspberries, and white of eggs

Soufflé aux fruits au sirop de sucre ⇒ soufflé of syrup, fruits, and white of eggs < *« fruits » peut être remplacé par le nom anglais du fruit* >

Soufflé aux fruits confits ⇒ vanilla soufflé, added of macerated preserved fruits

Soufflé aux légumes ⇒ soufflé of béchamel sauce, braised vegetables, eggs, nutmeg, and grated parmesan < *si un légume particulier est utilisé, remplacer « vegetables » par le nom anglais de celui-ci* >

Soufflé aux macarons ⇒ soufflé made of crushed macaroons, apricot jam, sugar, egg-yolks and whipped white of eggs

Soufflé aux marrons ⇒ soufflé made of chestnut purée, cream, egg-yolks, sugar, vanilla and whipped white of eggs; served with vanilla sauce

Soufflé aux topinambours ⇒ soufflé of mashed Jerusalem artichokes, cream, and eggs

Soufflé aux truffes à la royale ⇒ soufflé of béchamel sauce, and mashed truffles

Soufflé aux violettes ⇒ soufflé flavoured with violet extract, then added of crystallized violets

Soufflé aux épinards ⇒ soufflé of braised spinach, béchamel sauce, nutmeg, and eggs

Soufflé de bécasses aux châtaignes ⇒ soufflé of woodcock meat, carrots, onions, celery, butter, chestnut purée, cayenne-pepper, and eggs

Soufflé de canard rouennais
  1) **recette habituelle** ⇒ duck stuffed with a forcemeat of duck, spices, cognac and foie gras, then wrapped in greaseproof paper and baked; served with tartlets filled with a culinary stuffing of truffles and mushrooms, thickened of Madeira sauce; accompanied with ...
      - **sauce Périgueux** ⇒ ... Madeira sauce added of chopped truffles
      - **sauce rouennaise** ⇒ ... a sauce of red wine and shallot, enriched with poultry livers
  2) **mousses ou mousselines de canard rouennais** ⇒ poached mousse prepared with a forcemeat of duck, spices, cognac, and foie gras
  3) **soufflé de canard en timbales** ⇒ soufflé in timbales made of duck, spices, cognac, and foie gras

Soufflé de cervelle à la chanoinesse ⇒ soufflé of mashed brain, béchamel sauce, grated nutmeg, grated parmesan, truffle, and eggs

Soufflé de stockfisch aux navets ⇒ soufflé of béchamel sauce, grated gruyère, mashed cod poached in champagne, eggs, and turnip lamellas

Soufflé glacé ⇒ ice cream shaped in soufflé

Soufflé glacé aux framboises ⇒ soufflé of mashed raspberries, granulated sugar, whipped cream and whipped white of eggs, then deep-freezed; served with raspberry compote, biscuits, and champagne

Soufflé glacé aux fruits ⇒ soufflé of syrup, added of white of eggs, mashed fruits, and whipped cream; then deep-freezed

Soufflé Lapérouse ⇒ soufflé of confectioner's custard added of grilled almonds, rum, preserved fruits, and white of eggs

Soufflé Mont Bry aux marrons ⇒ soufflé of milk, sugar, flour, eggs, butter, chestnut purée, and vanilla

Soufflé Rothschild ⇒ soufflé of confectioner's custard, preserved fruits macerated in Polish brandy, and eggs

Soufflé Simone ⇒ soufflé of chocolate, milk, confectioner's custard, and eggs; served with whipped cream

Soufflé « sucre » -[*rocher*]- ⇒ cooked sugar whipped with white of eggs, and lemon juice
Soumaintrain -[*fromage*]- ⇒ Burgundy cheese
Soumbala -[*Afrique noire*]- ⇒ pounded dry fruit
Souparoun -[*Réveillon de Noël*]- ⇒ Provencal Christmas supper
Soupe ⇒ soup < *uncountable* >
Soupe à l'ail -[*Languedoc*]- ⇒ garlic soup
Soupe à l'anguille de Hambourg ⇒ soup of eels, carrots, peas, asparagus, dried plums, and dried apricots
Soupe à l'oignon ⇒ onion soup
Soupe à la bière ⇒ soup of poultry stock and beer, enriched with cream plus grated cheese
Soupe à la bonne femme ⇒ soup from white of leeks braised in butter, consommé, sliced potatoes, and shredded chervil
Soupe à la fausse tortue ⇒ mock turtle soup
Soupe à la jambe de bois ⇒ soup from leg of beef, hen, partridge, veal fillet, and vegetables
Soupe à la pie ⇒ soup made of sugar, red wine, and bread
Soupe à la poutine -[*Provence*]- ⇒ soup garnished with fried sardines, and anchovies
Soupe à la tortue ⇒ turtle soup
Soupe à la tripe -[*Artois*]- ⇒ soup of pig offal, onions, leeks, carrots, rapes, pepper, and aromatics
Soupe albigeoise ⇒ soup of top ribs from beef, calf trotter, salted pork, dry sausage, cabbage, carrots, turnips, potatoes, an garlic; garnished with thin slices of conserve of goose, browned in butter
Soupe alénoise ⇒ watercress soup
Soupe alsacienne à la farine ⇒ soup of flour, consommé, nutmeg, cream, and butter

Soupe au cantal ⇒ soup with Cantal cheese

Soupe au chou -*[Rouergue]*- ⇒ cabbage soup

Soupe au gras double à la milanaise ⇒ soup of tripe, lardoons, onion and white of leek braised in butter, cooked with stock, cabbage, tomato pulp, peas, and broccolis

Soupe au jambon fumé ⇒ soup with smoked ham

Soupe au pistou ⇒ soup made of beans, herbs, french beans, carrots, turnips, courgettes, tomato pulp, garlic, basil, grated parmesan and olive oil

Soupe au poireau -*[Artois-Picardie]*- ⇒ leek soup

Soupe au sarrasin et au lard -*[Bretagne]*- ⇒ soup of buckwheat flour, lardoons braised in pork fat, mint and nutmeg

Soupe aux abattis d'oie -*[ou de canard]*- ⇒ soup of vegetables, goose fat, giblets of goose or duck, verjuice, and browned onions; served with croutons of brown bread

Soupe aux boulettes de foie gras à la hongroise ⇒ poultry consommé; served with poached small balls made of mashed liver braised in pork fat, onions in butter, parsley, pepper, paprika, and grated nutmeg

Soupe aux cerises ⇒ soup of stoned cherries in a mixing of red wine and water; served with slices of country bread browned in butter

Soupe aux clams ⇒ soup of browned streaky bacon, onions, celery, capsicum, flour, stock, clams, and cream

Soupe aux clovisses -*[Languedoc]*- ⇒ small clam soup

Soupe aux corbeaux et aux légumes poudrée de fromage râpé ⇒ soup of crow and vegetables, sprinkled of grated cheese

Soupe aux fanes de radis ⇒ soup of radish-tops braised in butter, plus poultry stock, potatoes, pepper, cream, and chervil

Soupe aux fèves -*[Périgord]*- ⇒ soup of haricot beans and broad beans, sometimes added of streaky bacon

Soupe aux fielas -*[Provence]*- ⇒ conger eel soup

Soupe aux grenouilles ⇒ frog soup

Soupe aux légumes -*[Normandie]*- ⇒ soup of vegetables; added of a mixture of pork, mutton and beef fat with carrots, onions, cloves, leeks, celery, and chervil

Soupe aux moules -*[Provence]*- ⇒ soup of mussels cooked with onion, laurel, and tomatoes, plus cooked rice, and white of leeks braised in olive oil

Soupe aux poireaux et aux pommes de terre ⇒ soup of leeks and potatoes, plus bits of bread

Soupe aux pois cassés ⇒ split pea soup

Soupe aux pois et au jambon fumé -*[Belgique]*- ⇒ soup of peas, and smoked ham

Soupe aux pois jaunes -*[Suède]*- ⇒ soup of peas, thyme and sweet marjoram, served with a slice of pork; sometimes followed by pancakes covered with bilberry compote

Soupe aux quenelles de veau ⇒ soup of veal stock, added of veal quenelles, and herbs

Soupe bagration ⇒ veal or fish soup with macaroni and grated cheese

Soupe blanchie à l'oseille -*[Périgord]*- ⇒ soup flavoured with sorrel

Soupe brayaude ⇒ vegetable soup

Soupe d'abats hachés -*[Finlande]*- ⇒ soup of hashed offal, cooked with carrots and potatoes; thickened of blood, and garnished with barley small balls

Soupe d'épeautre ⇒ soup of lamb shoulder, dry sausage, onion, clove, carrots, turnip, leek, celery, garlic, and spelt

Soupe de betteraves rouges -*[Flandre]*- ⇒ beetroot soup

Soupe de céleri ⇒ celery soup

Soupe de chalet -*[Suisse]*- ⇒ soup of vegetables, herbs, noodles, cheese, milk, cream, and butter

Soupe de citrouille ⇒ pumpkin soup

Soupe de concombres ⇒ cucumber soup

Soupe de congre -*[Bretagne]*- ⇒ conger eel soup

Soupe de courge à la crème -*[Lyonnais]*- ⇒ soup of gourd and cream
Soupe de favouilles -*[Nice-Provence]*- ⇒ crab soup
Soupe de légumes -*[Normandie]*- ⇒ soup of vegetables; added of a mixture of pork, mutton and beef fat with carrots, onions, cloves, leeks, celery, and chervil
Soupe de mandarines ⇒ syrup of sugar, tangerine peel, and mint, poured on quartered tangerines; served chilled
Soupe de poisson ⇒ fish soup
Soupe de poisson aux moules ⇒ soup made with leeks, carrots, celery, saffron, thyme, laurel, garlic, tomatoes, brill fillets, devilfish fillets, red gurnard fillets, weever fillets, braised in olive oil; then simmered in fish stock with decorticated mussels
Soupe de poisson de Bergen -*[Norvège]*- ⇒ fish soup with vegetables, sour cream, and egg-yolks
Soupe de poisson maison ⇒ home made fish soup
Soupe de poissons à la sètoise ⇒ soup of various fishes, crustaceae, plus onions, tomatoes, garlic, and leek braised in olive oil; boiled in white wine and water, with capsicum; t he fishes are served apart
Soupe de potiron ⇒ pumpkin soup
Soupe de poulet à l'anglaise ⇒ soup of chicken, stock, onion, celery and rice, plus braised diced vegetables
Soupe de relevailles -*[Mali]*- ⇒ soup of hen and tripe
Soupe des habitants -*[Antilles]*- ⇒ soup of beef, sweet potatoes, pumpkin, celery, purslane, and french beans
Soupe glacée aux moules ⇒ chilled preparation of mashed tomatoes with Tabasco, added of mussels cooked in white wine, plus diced cucumber, capsicum, and broad beans
Soupe gratinée -*[oignon]*- ⇒ onion soup, au gratin
Soupe hollandaise ⇒ soup of onion, cheese, celery, tomatoes, African seasoning, and cream; served with croutons, and vegetables
Soupe oursinade ⇒ fish soup added of sea urchins
Soupe panade au gras ⇒ panada of onion braised in oil, with tomato pulp, then added of stock, origan powder, breadcrumbs, and herbs
Soupe panade au lait ⇒ panada with milk
   - **Soupe panade au lait sucrée** ⇒ panada with milk added of sugar
   - **Soupe panade au lait muscade** ⇒ panada with milk sprinkled of nutmeg
   - **Soupe panade au lait jaune d'oeuf et crème** ⇒ panada with milkenriched of egg-yolk and cream
Soupe savoyarde ⇒ soup of celeriac, leeks, turnips, potatoes and milk; served with fried croutons, and cheese lamellas
Soupe stracciatella ⇒ soup of crumbs, eggs, grated parmesan, and hot consommé
Soupe viennoise à la crème aigre ⇒ soup of consommé, onion, herbs, cumin powder, nutmeg, cream, and lemon juice
Souper ⇒ supper
Soupir de nonne ⇒ voir pet de nonne
Soupresse -*[galantine]*- ⇒ fish terrine
Sour -*[cocktail]*- ⇒ sour
Sour cream -*[smitane]*- ⇒ sour cream
Sourdon vert -*[coques]*- ⇒ cockle
Souris -*[gigot]*- ⇒ knuckle « of leg of mutton »
Sous la cendre ⇒ ... cooked in the embers
Sous-nix de veau ⇒ silverside of veal
Souvaroff ⇒ petit-four of two small flat cakes, soldered by redcurrant jelly

---

Souvarov *-[plats]-*
- **gibier à plume ou poularde** ⇒ ... stuffed with foie gras and truffle, then fried first and secondly cooked in a cast-iron casserole with truffle extract and Madeira
- **foie gras** ⇒ foie gras baked in terrine with truffles

Souvarov ⇒ petit-four of two small flat cakes, soldered by redcurrant jelly

Souvlakia *-[Grèce]-* ⇒ kebab of kidney, tomato, and capsicum

Souwaroff ⇒ petit-four of two small flat cakes, soldered by redcurrant jelly

Sovietski ⇒ Russian cheese from pasteurized cow's milk

Spaghetti ⇒ spaghetti < *uncountable* >

Spaghetti à la bolognèse ⇒ spaghetti alla bolognèse

Spaghetti à la ligurienne ⇒ spaghetti covered with a seasoning of olive oil, garlic, basil, and crushed Italian cheese

Spaghetti au basilic ⇒ spaghetti mixed with a paste of olive oil, pounded garlic, and basil; plus butter and stoned black olives

Spaghettini *-[pâtes alimentaires]-* ⇒ pasta < *uncountable* >

Spaghettis « alla carbonara » ⇒ spaghetti served with a sauce made of lardoons, cream, butter, grated parmesan and egg-yolks

Spalla ⇒ Italian pork butchery of pork shoulder

Sparaillon *-[sargue]-* ⇒ sargo

Sparassis crépu ⇒ cauliflower fungus

Spare ribs ⇒ ribs of pork macerated in soya sauce, ketchup, ginger and sugar, then grilled

Spätzele ⇒ small balls made of flour, eggs and cream, poached in water

Spätzle ⇒ small balls made of flour, eggs and cream, poached in water

Spätzle au beurre noisette ⇒ poached small balls made of flour, eggs and cream; served sprinkled of butter cooked slightly

Spekeskinke ⇒ ham eaten with early spring vegetables

Spetzli ⇒ small balls made of flour, eggs and cream, poached in water

Spécial ⇒ special

Spéciale *-[bière]-* ⇒ beer fermented between 18 and 25 degrés C

Spéciale *-[huître]-* ⇒ fattened oyster, bred during six months in oyster park

Spécialité ⇒ speciality

Spéculas ⇒ small flat cakes

Spéculos ⇒ small flat cakes

Spéculoos ⇒ small flat cakes

Spekeskinke *-[Norvège]-* ⇒ ham eaten with early spring vegetables

Spirali ⇒ pasta, spiral shaped < *uncountable* >

Spiritueux *-[alcool]-* ⇒ spirit or spirits

Spondias *-[mombin]-* ⇒ Caribbean fruit

Sponge cake *-[cake]-* ⇒ sponge cake

Spoom ⇒ sorbet made of fruit juice or wine, plus meringue

Spoutnik *-[cocktail]-* ⇒ cocktail of vodka, vermouth, and onion

Sprat *-[salage]-* ⇒ sprat

Sprats à la vinaigrette ⇒ sprats macerated in french dressing, with shallot and parsley; served with parsley, rye bread, plus poached bone-marrow mixed with shallots, white wine, butter and pepper

Springtime *-[pêche]-* ⇒ variety of peach

Spumone ⇒ Italian ice-cream

Spunchade ⇒ sorbet based on fruits and flavoured with kirsch

Spunchade au citron ⇒ sorbet of syrup, lemon juice, soda water, white of egg and meringue

Spunta *-[pomme de terre]-* ⇒ variety of potato

Squale -*[requin]*- ⇒ shark or dogfish
Squaw bread -*[Amérique du nord]*- ⇒ squaw bread
Squille -*[crustacé]*- ⇒ squill
Stachelbeerkuchen ⇒ gooseberry tart, covered with whipped cream
Stamp and go -*[acra]*- ⇒ edible root
Stanley
   - **plat** ⇒ dish served with onion
   - **œufs** ⇒ poached eggs laid on tartlets filled with a purée added of onion; covered with a curry
      sauce
Stargazey pie -*[GB]*- ⇒ stargazey pie
Starking delicious -*[pomme]*- ⇒ variety of apple
Stchi -*[Pologne]*- ⇒ pot au feu of beef, pig tongue and ears, flavoured with fennel
Steak ou Steack ⇒ steak or beefsteak
Steak à point ⇒ medium
Steak and kidney pie ⇒ steak and kidney pie
Steak and kidney pudding ⇒ steak and kidney pudding
Steak au poivre ⇒ steak sprinkled with crushed pepper, then sautéed in butter; served with the gravy
      thickened of white wine, cognac, veal stock and cream
Steak aux huîtres ⇒ steak sliced in a side, brushed with mustard, and browned, then flamed in cognac;
      stuffed with oysters, and covered with a sauce of oysters, Worcestershire sauce, and
      cognac
Steak bien cuit ⇒ well-done
Steak bleu ⇒ ultra-rare
Steak dans la culotte de boeuf ⇒ rump steak
Steak dans le faux-filet ⇒ sirloin steak or club steak
Steak dans un morceau à braiser ⇒ braising steak
Steaks de jambonneau ⇒ leg steaks
Steak de thon blanc haché aux algues ⇒ diced tunny mixed with tartare sauce; served with
      seaweed, seasoned of pepper, lemon juice, and olive oil
Steak diane ⇒ steak, served with peppered French dressing added of whipped cream and truffles
Steak haché -*[boeuf]*- ⇒ beef burger
Steak saignant ⇒ very rare
Steak tartare ⇒ tartare steak
Steinhäger -*[schnaps]*- ⇒ potato alcohol, flavoured with juniper berries
Stelline -*[pâtes alimentaires]*- ⇒ pasta for soup, shaped in star
Sterlet -*[esturgeon]*- ⇒ sterlet or sterliad
Stilton -*[fromage]*- ⇒ Stilton cheese
Stingo -*[GB]*- ⇒ stingo
Stoba -*[Antilles]*- ⇒ stew of goat, seasoned of cumin, capers and olives; cooked with cucumbers and
      lemon
Stocaficado -*[estofinado]*-
   - **Marseille-St Tropez** ⇒ ragout of salt cod with tomatoes, onions, garlic, olive oil and aromatics
   - **Nice** ⇒ ragout of stockfish with tomatoes, onions, garlic, olive oil and aromatics
Stockfisch ⇒ dried cod or stockfish
Stockfisch à la niçoise ⇒ dish of tomatoes cooked in their own liquid with garlic, plus diced cod,
      sliced potatoes, and stoned black olives; cooked at last with basil
Stollen -*[dresdner stollen]*- ⇒ brioche with preserved fruits
Stonsdorfer -*[schnaps]*- ⇒ schnapps
Store -*[cheddar]*- ⇒ cheddar cheese
Storzapreti ⇒ balls of spinach, Corsican ewe cheese, eggs and pepper

Stout ⇒ stout ale

Stracchino ⇒ Stracchino

Straight -*[cocktail]*-
- **bourbon** ⇒ Bourbon without mixing
- **cocktail** ⇒ short drink cocktail, served without any addition

Strasbourg -*[saucisse de]*- ⇒ sausage

Strasbourgeoise (*à la* ...)
1) **Grosses pièces de boucherie et de volailles braisées ou poAlées** ⇒ braised ... or fried ..., garnished with braised sauerkraut, streaky bacon lamellas, sauté foie gras escalopes, covered with the gravy
2) **Tournedos sautés** ⇒ sauté fillet-steak of beef, laid on foie gras escalopes, covered with the gravy added of Madeira
3) **Consommé** ⇒ consommé flavoured with juniper berries, thickened of fecula, plus a garnish of red cabbage in julienne and slices of sausage; served with grated horse-radish

Stravecchio -*[parmesan]*- ⇒ best quality of parmesan

Strawberry short cake -*[Amérique du nord]*- ⇒ strawberry short cake

Strenna -*[Corse]*- ⇒ pie with Corsican ewe cheese

Stroganov ⇒ Stroganoff

Strudel ⇒ rolled pastry stuffed with a garnish of ...
- **pommes à la cannelle et aux raisins secs** ⇒ ... apples with cinnamon and raisins
- **cerises** ⇒ stoned cherries mixed with sugar, lemon peel, and pounded almonds
- **fromage blanc** ⇒ soft white cheese mixed with egg-yolks, lemon peel, raisins, and cream
- **bœuf bouilli** ⇒ chopped boiled beef mixed with pork fat, onion, paprika, and parsley
- **chou** ⇒ chopped cabbage, baked with sugar and fat

Strudel aux pommes ⇒ cake stuffed with apples, cinnamon and raisins, then flavoured of lemon peel

Stschy
1) **soupe avec viande** ⇒ soup made of sauerkraut in stock, beef, duck meat, streaky bacon, smoked sausages; served with cream, fennel and chopped parsley
2) **soupe légumes** ⇒ soup made with vegetables as spinach, sorrel, and nettle

Stufato ⇒ Corsican ragout of meat with tomato and onions; served with noodles

Stufatu ⇒ Corsican ragout of meat with tomato and onions; served with noodles

Stunggis -*[Suisse]*- ⇒ stew of pork, vegetables, and potatoes

Suau -*[Barsac]*- ⇒ Sauterne wine

Subric ⇒ small croquette thickened with béchamel sauce, whipped eggs, flour, cream and grated cheese; sautéed in butter

Subrics d'entremets au riz ⇒ discs or squares of cooked rice, added with a culinary stuffing of preserved fruits macerated in liquor, then brushed with butter, and fried; served with jam or canned apricots

Subrics d'épinards ⇒ preparation of spinach, béchamel sauce, egg, and cream; moulded in small balls or quoits, then fried; served with béchamel sauce added of cream, and nutmeg

Subrics de foie gras ⇒ small balls of diced foie gras, thickened with flour, egg, cream, pepper, and fennel flower; fried in oil and butter, then served with Madeira sauce added of truffle

Subrics de pommes de terre ⇒ preparation of potatoes braised in butter, béchamel sauce, eggs, and nutmeg; moulded in small balls or quoits, and fried

Subrics de semoule ⇒ discs of cooked semolina, added of egg-yolks, and fried; served with redcurrant jelly, or an other jam

Suc ⇒ juice or extract or secretion

Suc de cerise ⇒ cherry juice added of alcohol

Suc de coing ⇒ quince juice added of alcohol

Suc de framboise ⇒ raspberry juice added of alcohol

Suc de groseille ⇒ redcurrant juice added of alcohol

Suc de mûre ⇒ mulberry juice added of alcohol

Suc de tomate concentré ⇒ tomato purée

Suc de viande ⇒ meat juice or meat extract

Suçarelle *(à la ...)* *-[escargot]-* ⇒ snails prepared with tomatoes, garlic, sausage and white wine, which are traditionally sucked, rather than picked from their shells

Succès ⇒ cake made of two pastry discs separated by a buttered custard added of praline

Succotash *-[Amérique du nord]-* ⇒ succotash

Sucette ⇒ lollipop

Suchenn *-[hydromel]-* ⇒ mead

Sucre ⇒ sugar < *uncountable* >

Sucre brun ⇒ brown sugar

Sucre candi ⇒ candy sugar

Sucre cristallisé ⇒ granulated sugar

Sucre d'anis ⇒ crushed aniseed added of sugar

Sucre d'orange ⇒ sugar flavoured with orange peel

Sucre d'orge à l'ancienne ⇒ barley sugar

Sucre de betterave ⇒ beet sugar

Sucre de bigarade ⇒ sugar flavoured with bitter orange peel

Sucre de canne ⇒ cane sugar

Sucre de cannelle ⇒ crushed cinnamon added of sugar

Sucre de cédrat ⇒ sugar flavoured with cedrate peel

Sucre de citron ⇒ sugar flavoured with lemon peel

Sucre de fleur d'oranger ⇒ pounded orange blossom added of sugar

Sucre de fruit ⇒ fructose

Sucre de gingembre ⇒ crushed ginger added of sugar

Sucre de girofle ⇒ pounded clove added of sugar

Sucre de lait ⇒ lactose

Sucre de mandarine ⇒ sugar flavoured with tangerine peel

Sucre de pomme ⇒ barley sugar with apple flavouring

Sucre en morceaux ⇒ cube sugar or lump sugar

Sucre en poudre ⇒ powdered sugar or caster sugar

Sucre glace ⇒ icing sugar

Sucre roux ⇒ brown sugar

Sucre semoule ⇒ granulated sugar

Sucre tourné ⇒ cooked sugar

Sucre vanillé ⇒ vanilla sugar

Sucré ⇒ sugared or sweetened < *v.t adjectif* >

Sucrerie *-[bonbon]-* ⇒ sweet

Sucrin *-[melon]-* ⇒ sweet melon

Sucuk *-[saucisson]-* ⇒ spicy dry sausage

Suédoise *(à la ...)*
- **salades** ⇒ mixing of vegetables, fruits, mushrooms, cheese and crustaceae, plus vinegar flavoured with herbs
- **mayonnaise** ⇒ mayonnaise added of grated horse-radish, plus apples cooked in white wine
- **rôti de porc** ⇒ roasted pork stuffed with dried plums; served with apples stuffed of dried plums

Suédoise *-[dessert]-* ⇒ sweet made of fruits poached in syrup and flavoured with wine or liquor; served with ...
- **chantilly** ⇒ sugared whipped cream
- **crème** ⇒ cream
- **coulis de fruits** ⇒ fruit purée

Suif ⇒ tallow or animal fat or suet
Sukiyaki ⇒ sukiyaki
Sultane *(à la ...)*
    1) **Beurre composé** ⇒ composed butter added of pistachio
    2) **Velouté de volaille** ⇒ poultry velouté, thickened with composed butter added of pistachio
    3) **Poisson** ⇒ ... served with pistachio
    4) **Glace ou entremets à base de fruits « abricots, poires, pAches »** ⇒ ... flavoured with pistachio
    5) **Suprême de volaille** ⇒ poultry served in sauce supreme, laid on poultry forcemeat; garnished with tartlets filled of mashed truffles and pistachio
    6) **Grosses pièces de boucherie** ⇒ ... with a garnish of fried crescents made of mashed potatoes, eggs and butter, plus a julienne of braised red cabbage
Sumac ⇒ sumac or sumach
Suncrest *-[pêche]-* ⇒ variety of peach
Sundae *-[Amérique du nord]-* ⇒ sundae
Sun ki *-[pousses de bambou]-* ⇒ bamboo shouts
Supion *-[calmar]-* ⇒ squid or calamaro
Supion *-[seiche]-* ⇒ cuttlefish
Suprême ⇒ supreme
    - **poulet** ⇒ chicken served in supreme sauce
    - **gibier** ⇒ game served in supreme sauce
    - **poisson** ⇒ fish served in supreme sauce
Supreme *-[sauce]-* ⇒ supreme sauce
Suprêmes de canard aux truffes ⇒ supreme of duck, laid on timbales with truffle lamellas; served with a sauce of duck carcase, brown sauce, cognac, and butter
Suprême de poisson
    - **général** ⇒ supreme
    - **poisson** ⇒ fish served in supreme sauce
Suprêmes de poulet à la Valdostana *-[Italie]-* ⇒ supreme of chicken; covered with white truffles and mozzarella sautéed in white wine
Suprême de volaille
    - **général** ⇒ supreme served in supreme sauce
    - **poulet** ⇒ chicken served in supreme sauce
    - **gibier** ⇒ game served in supreme sauce
Suprêmes de volaille à blanc ⇒ supreme of poultry cooked in butter, and lemon juice
Suprêmes de volaille à brun ⇒ sauté supreme of poultry
Suprêmes de volaille à l'anglaise ⇒ supreme of poultry coated with crumbs and fried, topped with a slice of grilled bacon; served with sliced potatoes baked in butter, and grilled tomatoes
Suprêmes de volaille à la financière ⇒ supreme of poultry cooked in butter, laid on croutons fried with butter, or wrapped in puff-pastry; covered with Madeira sauce added of truffle extract; served surrounded with a ragout of cockscombs, chopped mushrooms, plus a culinary stuffing of truffles in Madeira
Suprêmes de volaille à la florentine ⇒ supreme of chicken or turkey-chick cooked in butter and lemon juice, laid on braised spinach; covered with béchamel sauce added of egg-yolks, gruyère, and butter, then browned
Suprêmes de volaille à la périgourdine ⇒ sauté supreme of poultry, topped with slice of foie gras and truffle lamella; covered with Madeira sauce added of chopped truffle
Suprêmes de volaille Montpensier ⇒ sauté supreme of poultry, with braised asparagus tips, and diced truffle in butter; covered with slightly cooked butter

Suprêmes de volaille ambassadeur ⇒ croutons fried in butter, topped with supreme of poultry and truffle lamellas; served with mushrooms in cream, and asparagus in butter, then covered with supreme sauce

Suprêmes de volaille aux champignons ⇒ supreme of poultry cooked in butter; garnished with mushrooms braised in butter, velouté added of poultry stock and cream, plus sometimes mushroom extract and lemon juice

Suprêmes de volaille et leurs garnitures ⇒ supreme of poultry, garnished with ...
- **aubergines** ⇒ ... sauté diced aubergines
- **laitue** ⇒ ... braised lettuce
- **chicorée** ⇒ ... braised endives
- **concombre** ⇒ ... cucumbers braised in butter
- **épinards** ⇒ ... braised spinach
- **artichauts braisés** ⇒ ... braised artichoke hearts
- **artichauts sautés** ⇒ ... sauté artichoke hearts
- **haricots verts** ⇒ ... french beans in butter
- **macédoine** ⇒ ... vegetable salad in butter
- **petits pois** ⇒ ... peas
- **asperges au beurre** ⇒ ... asparagus tips in butter
- **asperges à la crème** ⇒ ... asparagus tips in cream
- **purée de légumes** ⇒ ... mashed vegetables

Surati ⇒ buffal's milk cheese

Sureau -*[fleurs]*- ⇒ elder flowers

Surgelé ⇒ frozen food or frozen ...

Surimi -*[japon]*- ⇒ surimi

Surinam -*[riz]*- ⇒ variety of rice

Sûrkrût -*[choucroute]*- ⇒ sauerkraut

Surlonge -*[boeuf]*- ⇒ chuck or chuck steak

Surmulet ⇒ surmullet

Surmulet -*[rouget de roche]*- ⇒ red mullet

Surprise (*en ...*) ⇒ with a special coating or decoration

Surprise des halles -*[fraise]*- ⇒ variety of fraise

Surströming -*[Scandinavie]*- ⇒ pickled herring, eaten with brown bread, and potatoes

Surullito -*[acra]*- ⇒ edible root

Sushi -*[Japon]*- ⇒ sushi

Suze ⇒ gentian liquor

Suzette -*[crêpes]*- ⇒ pancakes flavoured with tangerine and curaçao

Swartsoppa -*[Suède]*- ⇒ soup of goose blood

Syllabub ⇒ syllabub

Sylvaner -*[vin]*- ⇒ white wine from sylvaner variety of vine

Syngnathe ⇒ pipefish or syngnathus

Szamorodni -*[tokay]*- ⇒ Tokay wine

T

t'aam -*[couscous]*- ⇒ couscous
T' bone steak -*[Amérique du nord]*- ⇒ T' bone steak
Tabasco ⇒ Tabasco
Tabatière -*[pain]*- ⇒ bread from Jura area, shaped in hinge
Tabboulé ⇒ crushed wheat mixed with aromatics, tomatoes, onion and mint
Tabil ⇒ Arab spices
Table d'hôte ⇒ fixed priced menu
Tablette ⇒ tablet of chocolate, etc ... or bar of chocolate, etc
Tablette de chocolat ⇒ bar of chocolate or tablet of chocolate
Tablier de sapeur ⇒ bits of ox tripe coated with egg and breadcrumbs, then grilled and served with a
      ...
      - beurre d'escargot ⇒ ... composed butter added of shallots, parsley and garlic
      - sauce gribiche ⇒ ... sauce made of hard-boiled egg-yolks, oil, chopped capers, and herbs
      - sauce tartare ⇒ ... Tartare sauce
Tacaud ⇒ kind of salt cod
Taco ⇒ taco
Tadorne ⇒ sheldrake or shelduck
Tafelspitz -*[Autriche]*- ⇒ boiled meat, served with salad, and compote
Tafi -*[Argentine]*- ⇒ type of Argentinian Cantal cheese
Tafia ⇒ tafia
Tagliatelle ⇒ Italian ribbons of noodles added of eggs
Taglierini ⇒ Italian ribbons of noodles added of eggs
Tagliolini ⇒ Italian ribbons of noodles added of eggs
Tahin -*[confiserie]*- ⇒ sweet made of sesame paste
Tahina -*[confiserie]*- ⇒ sweet made of sesame paste
Tahitienne (à la ...)
      a) **filets de poissons crus** ⇒ diced fish fillets marinated in lemon juice and oil; served with
          tomato and sprinkled of grated coconut
      b) **salade composée** ⇒ salad of diced fish fillets marinated in lemon juice and oil, avocado,
          grapefruit and lettuce chiffonade; seasoned with mayonnaise added of lemon
Taillé ⇒ cut < *attributif adjectif* >
Tajine -*[cuisine]*- ⇒ ragout
Tajine de carottes ⇒ dish of carrots, onions, coriander, parsley, garlic, ginger, cumin, capsicum, ·
          saffron, and pepper, simmered in olive oil; served with black olives, and lemon juice
Tajine de courgettes ⇒ ragout of courgettes
Tajine de mouton aux pruneaux et au miel ⇒ ragout of mutton simmered with olive oil, onion,
          ginger, coriander, saffron, cinnamon, dried plums, and honey; served sprinkled of
          grilled sesame seeds
Takenoko -*[pousses de bambou]*- ⇒ bamboo shouts
Taleggio ⇒ squared Italian cow's milk cheese with a yellow paste
Talibur -*[rabotte]*- ⇒ whole apple or pear baked inside a short pastry case
Talleyrand
      1) **côtes ou ris de veau, tournedos, grosses pièces de veau et de volailles** ⇒ ... with a
          garnish of noodles, butter and cheese, plus truffles in julienne added of diced foie
          gras; covered with a truffle sauce
      2) **filets d'anchois farçis en paupiettes** ⇒ balls of stuffed anchovies
      3) **omelette au cari fourrée de ris de veau** ⇒ omelette with curry, stuffed of calf sweetbread

4) croquettes de semoule farçies d'un salpicon de volaille, langue écarlate, truffe et champignons saucés de demi-glace ⇒ semolina croquettes filled with a culinary stuffing of poultry, oxtongue, truffle and mushrooms

5) gâteau ⇒ kind of savarin cake added of chopped pineapple and covered with apricot jam

Talmouse ⇒ cheese cake

Talmouses à l'ancienne ⇒ rectangular puff-pastries garnished with a preparation of béchamel sauce, grated cheese, and grated nutmeg; topped with diced gruyère, and baked

Talmouses à la Florentine ⇒ rectangular puff-pastries garnished with a preparation of braised spinach, béchamel sauce, nutmeg, and eggs; topped with diced gruyère

Talmouses Bagration ⇒ tartlets filled with choux-pastry added of cheese, and sprinkled of diced gruyère

Talon -[boeuf]- ⇒ muscle from the neck of beef or braising steak

Talon de collier -[boeuf]- ⇒ muscle from the neck of beef or braising steak

Tamal ⇒ tamal or tamale

Tamarin ⇒ tamarind

Tamié ⇒ pressed cow's milk cheese

Tamier ⇒ black bryony

Tamis ⇒ sieve

Tamiser ⇒ to sieve

Tanaisie -[condiment ou herbe]- ⇒ tansy

Tanche -[poisson]- ⇒ tench

Tandoori chicken ⇒ tandoori chicken

Tandouri ⇒ tandoori

Tangelo ⇒ kind of citrus fruit

Tangerine ⇒ tangerine

Tango ⇒ glass of pomegranate syrup, and beer

Tanin ⇒ tannin

Tant-pour-tant ⇒ mixing of granulated sugar and almond powder

Tantimolle -[crêpe]- ⇒ pancake or flapjack

Tantouillet ⇒ head and offal of pig stewed in blood and red wine, with chicken, onions, and spices

Tantouillée ⇒ head and offal of pig stewed in blood and red wine, with chicken, onions, and spices

Tapas ⇒ hors d'œuvres served with Malaga wine or xeres

Tapenade ⇒ ... seasoning made of capers, anchovies, stoned black olives, olive oil, lemon juice and aromatics

   - se tartine sur tranches de pain grillées ⇒ toasts spreaded with a ...

   - garnit des œufs durs ⇒ hard boiled eggs garnished with a ...

   - accompagne les viandes ou un poisson grillé ⇒ ... served with a ...

Tapès -[fausse palourde]- ⇒ false clam

Tapinette orléanaise ⇒ tart filled with a mixing of soft white cheese, milk, flour and whipped eggs

Tapioca ⇒ tapioca < uncountable >

Tapioca au lait ⇒ tapioca cooked in milk with sugar, vanilla, and orange blossom extract

Tarama ⇒ taramasalata

Tarato -[soupe]- ⇒ soup of mashed aubergines, capsicums, yoghourt, and french dressing

Tarator -[Bulgarie]- ⇒ gooseberry tart, covered with whipped cream

Tard venu -[pied bleu]- ⇒ tricholoma mushroom

Tarhonya -[Hongrie]- ⇒ paste of flour browned in pork fat

Taro ⇒ a rhizome

Tarpon ⇒ tarpon

Tarragona -[vin]- ⇒ Tarragona

Tarry souchong -*[thé]*- ⇒ variety of tea
Tartare *(à la ...)* ⇒ with raw meat
Tarte ⇒ tart
Tarte à l'alsacienne ⇒ fruit and custard tart
Tarte à l'ananas ⇒ tart filled with a custard of milk, lemon juice, and pineapple syrup; then garnished
    with slices of pineapple in syrup
Tarte à la cassonade ⇒ tart covered with brown sugar
Tarte à la citrouille ⇒ tart filled with pumpkin and onion
Tarte à la crème ⇒ tart accompanied with cream
Tarte à la frangipane ⇒ tart filled with frangipane
Tarte à la mélasse ⇒ treacle tart
Tarte à la pacane ⇒ pie made with American nuts
Tarte à la rhubarbe ⇒ rhubarb tart
Tarte à la tomate ⇒ tart filled with a preparation of eggs, cream, butter, grated gruyère, and crushed
    tomatoes
Tarte au caillé ⇒ tart filled with a mixing of soft white cheese, milk, flour and whipped eggs
Tarte au chocolat ⇒ chocolate tart, covered with a custard of bitter chocolate, butter, and cream
Tarte au citron ⇒ tart covered with a custard of eggs, sugar, and lemon; decorated with slices of
    lemon poached in syrup
Tarte au citron -*[Nahmias]*- ⇒ tart covered with a custard of eggs, sugar, butter and « lemon »
    - **Tarte aux oranges** ⇒ remplacer « lemon » par « orange »
    - **Tarte aux mandarines** ⇒ remplacer « lemon » par « mandarin orange »
Tarte au fromage blanc ⇒ tart filled with a preparation of soft white cheese, cream, flour, eggs, and
    pepper
Tarte au me'gin à la mode de Metz ⇒ tart garnished with a mixing of soft white cheese, eggs,
    granulated sugar and vanilla
Tartes au muscat *(petites ...)* ⇒ tarts filled with a preparation of muscat grape juice, cream, melted
    butter, eggs, and sugar
Tarte au potiron ⇒ tart filled with pumpkin and onion
Tarte au riz ⇒ tart filled with a garnish of rice cooked in milk, added of vanilla, sugar, egg, cream, and
    preserved fruits macerated in rum
Tarte aux abricots ⇒ apricot tart
Tarte aux asperges ⇒ tart filled with mashed poultry in cream, garnished of asparagus tips, and
    covered with béchamel sauce
Tarte aux cerises ⇒ cherry tart covered with a custard of granulated sugar, eggs, milk, and flour
Tarte aux cerises à l'allemande ⇒ puff-pastry tart filled with cherries; covered of cherry compote <
    Si les cerises sont remplacées par des demi-abricots, rayer « cherries » et mettre «
    halved apricots » >
Tarte aux figues ⇒ tart filled with apricot compote added of rum, and figs macerated in lemon juice;
    then decorated of sugared whipped cream
Tarte aux fraises ⇒ strawberry tart, covered with a syrup of redcurrant jelly, lemon juice, and
    granulated sugar
Tarte aux framboises ⇒ tart filled with confectioner's custard, and raspberries; covered with
    redcurrant and raspberry jelly
Tarte aux groseilles à maquereau à l'allemande ⇒ voir texte
Tarte aux mûres ⇒ mulberry tart; served with cream or sugared whipped cream
Tarte aux myrtilles ⇒ tart filled with bilberries in syrup, covered of apricot compote; then decorated
    with sugared whipped cream
Tarte aux onions ⇒ tart filled with mashed onions added of rice ½ ou ½ onion tart

Tarte aux onions et au miel ⇒ tart filled with onions braised in butter, added of honey, cinnamon, and pepper

Tarte aux pignons ⇒ tart filled with blackcurrant jelly, confectioner's custard, almond powder, and pine-kernels

Tarte aux poireaux ⇒ leek tart

Tarte aux pommes ronde ⇒ apple tart; served with cream apart

Tarte aux pruneaux ⇒ prune tart

Tarte aux prunes ⇒ plum tart

Tarte aux prunes à l'alsacienne ⇒ tart filled with plum jam, decorated of pastry lamella; served with cream

Tarte aux prunes rouges ⇒ red plum tart

Tarte aux raisins frais ⇒ tart covered with grapes, topped of cream added of eggs, sugar and kirsch

Tarte aux raisins secs ⇒ tart filled with a custard of cream, eggs, granulated sugar, and vanilla; topped with raisins steeped in armagnac

Tarte aux épinards ⇒ puff-pastry tart filled with spinach in butter, decorated with anchovy fillets < « *anchovy fillets » peut être remplacé par « sardines » >*

Tarte basque ⇒ tart filled with quartered apples browned in butter, and sprinkled of granulated sugar

Tarte cauchoise ⇒ tart filled with left over of meat, plus a preparation of braised onions, egg, cream, pepper, and nutmeg

Tarte de pommes de terre ⇒ potato tart

Tarte en gourmeau ⇒ tart filled with scrambled eggs, sugar, milk, and cream

Tarte en quemeu ⇒ tart filled with scrambled eggs, sugar, milk, and cream

Tarte feuilletée aux pommes ⇒ puff-pastry tart filled with apple compote, and sauté apple lamellas

Tarte galette ⇒ squared or rectangular fruit tart

Tarte meringuée au citron ⇒ tart filled with a preparation of flour, maïzena, sugar, lemon, egg and butter; covered with meringue

Tarte montmorency ⇒ tarts filled with cherries

Tarte salée ⇒ salted tart

Tarte suisse au vin ⇒ tart filled with a preparation of eggs, sugar, and white wine

Tarte sèche ⇒ tart sprinkled with aniseed

Tarte tatin ⇒ apple tart, baked upside-down

Tartelette ⇒ tartlet or small tart

Tartelette Agnès Sorel ⇒ tartlet filled with mashed poultry in cream, pickled oxtongue, mushroom, and béchamel sauce added of cream

Tartelette amandine -[*Ragueneau*]- ⇒ almond tartlet

Tartelette aux mûres ⇒ mulberry tartlet; served with cream or sugared whipped cream

Tartelette aux noix et au miel ⇒ tartlet filled with crushed almonds; covered of acacia honey

Tartelettes à l'ananas ⇒ tartlets of short-pastry with a garnish of pineapple, egg, sugar, butter and kirsch

Tartelettes à l'orange ⇒ tartlets of short-pastry with egg, sugar, orange juice and butter

Tartelettes au café ⇒ tartlets filled with egg-custard added of butter, and coffee extract

Tartelettes au chocolat ⇒ tartlets filled with sugared whipped cream added of chocolate

Tartelettes au citron ⇒ tartlets of short-pastry with egg, sugar, lemon juice and butter

Tartelettes au millet ⇒ tartlets made with millet flour, granulated sugar, eggs, and lemon peel

Tartelettes au raisin ⇒ tartlets with grapes glazed in syrup, plus apricot jam

Tartelettes au rhum et pâte d'amandes ⇒ tartlets of short-pastry and a garnish of almonds flavoured with rum

Tartelettes aux marrons ⇒ tartlets garnished with chestnut purée flavoured with kirsch

Tartelettes montmorency ⇒ tartlets filled with cherries

Tartine ⇒ a slice of bread and butter

Tartine de confiture ⇒ a slice of bread and jam
Tartines marquise ⇒ slices of sandwich loaf, covered with béchamel sauce thickened of egg-yolk,
        plus grated gruyère; then fried
Tartiner ⇒ to spread with butter or to spread with jam, etc ...
Tartoufle ou Cartoufle ⇒ potato
Tartouillat ⇒ apples in cabbage leave wrapped in pancake dough; cooked in the oven
Tassau ⇒ bits of meat poached in a court-bouillon, then fried and served with boiled bananas
Tasse
        - général ⇒ cup
        - café ⇒ a coffee cup
        - thé ⇒ a tea cup
Tastevin ⇒ wine-tasting cup
Taupe -[poisson]- ⇒ porbeagle
Taureau -[bœuf]- ⇒ bull
Tavel ⇒ rosé from Rhone valley
Tawny -[Porto]- ⇒ old port
Tcherek -[cuisine russe]- ⇒ bread sprinkled of sesame seeds
Tchernina -[czernina]- ⇒ rice consommé with pastas, added of poultry blood; thickened with
        mashed poultry livers
Tcholent -[cuisine russe]- ⇒ brisket of beef cooked with onions, potatoes, and small balls of
        buckwheat
Tchorba ⇒ mutton soup
Tchoulend ⇒ Jew's ragout
Teigne (ou herbe au teigneux ...) ⇒ burdock
Teigneux -[herbe au]- ⇒ burdock
Telfairia ⇒ kind of marrow
Tende de tranche ⇒ topside of beef
Tende de tranche coupée et ficelée ⇒ topside of beef « rolled »
Tendrons de veau ⇒ tendrons of veal
Tendrons de veau aux épinards ou à l'oseille ⇒ braised tendrons of veal, served with braised ...
        - épinards ⇒ spinach
        - oseille ⇒ braised sorrel
Tendrons de veau braisés à la bourgeoise ⇒ sauté tendrons of veal; covered with mushrooms
        braised in stock, white wine, tomato sauce, and shallot
Tendrons de veau chasseur ⇒ sauté tendrons of veal; covered with mushrooms braised in stock,
        white wine, tomato sauce, and shallot
Tentation de Jansson -[smorgasbord]- ⇒ gratin of anchovies, potatoes, cream, and onions
Tequila ⇒ tequila
Tequila Sunrise ⇒ cocktail made of tequila, orange juice, and pomegranate syrup
Terfez -[truffe]- ⇒ North Africa truffle
Teriyaki -[sauce japonaise]- ⇒ sauce of sake, soya sauce, sugar, and ginger
Terrapin -[tortue]- ⇒ breed of tortoise
Terrine
        - récipient ⇒ a rectangular earthenware cooking-dish with a cover
        - plat ⇒ terrine or pie-dish
Terrine de Body ⇒ pâté of chopped veal escalope, pork belly, shallots, parsley, black pepper, and
        white wine
Terrine de brochet sauce Nantua ⇒ pâté made with a preparation of frangipane, pike, cultivated
        mushrooms, shallots, parsley, white wine, and white of eggs; served with béchamel
        sauce added of mashed crayfishes, cognac, and cayenne pepper

Terrine de caille ⇒ pâté of quail, plus pork fat macerated in fennel flower, cognac, and thyme, then added with chopped onions and mushrooms; plus pork belly, orange peel, and eggs

Terrine de caneton ⇒ pâté of duckling, plus pork fat, macerated in fennel flower, cognac, and thyme; then added of chopped onions and mushrooms, pork belly, orange peel, and eggs

Terrine de faisan ⇒ pâté of pheasant, plus pork fat macerated in fennel flower, cognac, and thyme, then added with chopped onions and mushrooms; plus pork belly, orange peel, and eggs

Terrine de foie gras -[Alsace-Gascogne]- ⇒ foie gras pâté

Terrine de foie gras aux truffes ⇒ pâté of goose foie gras macerated in spices and cognac; mixed with a forcemeat of pork, truffles, Madeira and spices

Terrine de foie gras de ... nom de la viande ⇒ nom anglais ... foie gras pâté

Terrine de fruits à la gelée de miel ⇒ pâté made with a jelly of honey, sugar, orange peel, lemon peel, and wormwood leaves, added of strawberries, raspberries, wild strawberries, quartered pears, grape, and preserved orange peel; served with raspberry purée

Terrine de grives Fernand Point ⇒ pâté of thrushes, poultry liver, pepper, ginger, and white wine

Terrine de l'océan ⇒ pâté of turbot, pike, salmon, red mullet, lobster, mussels, leeks, garlic, sorrel, eggs, fennel flower, mustard, tarragon, and scallops

Terrine de légumes Fontanieu ⇒ pâté of cream, mushrooms, spices, carrots, french beans, peas, turnips, courgettes, celeriac and tomatoes; sprinkled with a dressing of vinegar flavoured with raspberries, olive oil and pepper

Terrine de lièvre ⇒ hare pâté

Terrine de perdreau ⇒ pâté of young partridge, plus pork fat macerated in fennel flower, cognac, and thyme, then added with chopped onions and mushrooms; plus pork belly, orange peel, and eggs

Terrine de ris de veau ⇒ pâté made with calf sweetbreads, a mixture of diced vegetables, white wine, Madeira, and port; plus a forcemeat from cushion of veal, cream, egg, foie gras and pepper

Terrine de sardines crues ⇒ pâté of raw sardines marinated in olive oil, orange peel, clove, laurel, onion, and cognac; served with grilled country bread, butter, and coarse salt

Terrine de saumon ⇒ pâté of salmon marinated in white wine, plus fishes, shrimp tails, eggs, cream, and pepper; served with a mayonnaise mixed with a paste of pounded tarragon, watercress, parsley, spinach and chervil

Terrine du chef ⇒ chef's special pâté

Terrinée ⇒ rice cooked in milk with cinnamon

Test
- **homard** ⇒ carapace
- **oursin** ⇒ shell

Testicule ⇒ testicle

Tête -[animal]- ⇒ head

Tête d'ail ⇒ head of garlic

Tête de champignon ⇒ mushroom head

Tête de filet sur illion -[boeuf]- ⇒ rump fillet

Tête de maure -[édam]- ⇒ Edam

Tête de moine ⇒ cylindrical cow's milk cheese with a red paste

Tête de mort -[édam]- ⇒ Edam

Tête de mort -[lycoperdon]- ⇒ giant puff-ball

Tête de mort -[Gouda]- ⇒ Gouda

Tête de nègre -[pâtisserie]- ⇒ cake shaped in ball and covered of chocolate custard

Tête de nègre -[bolet]- ⇒ edible black boletus

Tête de porc ⇒ pig head

Tête de porc roulée ⇒ pig head « boneless », cooked and moulded; served in slices

Tête de veau ⇒ calf head

Tête de veau à l'anglaise ⇒ boiled calf head, served with a sauce of butter, flour, egg-yolk, and lemon juice

Tête de veau à l'occitane ⇒ poached bits of calf head, baked with onion, garlic, black olives, sauté tomatoes, and sliced hard-boiled eggs; then sprinkled with olive oil, and lemon juice

Tête de veau à la financière ⇒ diced boiled calf head, braised in Madeira and garnished with a ragout of cockscombs, poultry quenelles, chopped mushrooms, plus a culinary stuffing of truffles in Madeira

Tête de veau à la lyonnaise ⇒ bits of boiled calf head, laid on braised onions and parsley; then covered with a sauce of onions braised in butter, vinegar, white wine, and stock; served au gratin

Tête de veau à la piémontaise ⇒ diced boiled calf head, steeped in batter and deep fried; served with risotto and tomato sauce

Tête de veau bonne femme ⇒ boiled calf head, simmered with diced potatoes, carrots, turnips, and squared cabbage

Tête de veau Caillou ⇒ sliced boiled calf head, sautéed with chestnuts, olives, and Madeira; then moistened with a sauce of onion, ham, stock, and aromatics; served with sauté veal escalopes, and croutons fried in butter

Tête de veau chaude en sauce chaude ⇒ diced boiled calf head, served with the tongue and brain; covered with a sauce ...
- **sauce aux câpres** ⇒ texte
- **aux fines herbes** ⇒ texte
- **sauce hongroise** ⇒ texte
- **sauce ravigote** ⇒ texte
- **sauce charcutière** ⇒ texte
- **sauce diable** ⇒ texte
- **sauce piquante** ⇒ texte
- **sauce Robert** ⇒ texte
- **sauce tomate** ⇒ texte
- **sauce à la menthe** ⇒ texte < *s'il y a déja le terme « a sauce » dans le début de la description, ne pas en tenir compte* >

Tête de veau chaude en sauce froide ⇒ boiled calf head, served with slices of the tongue and brain; covered with ...
- **aioli** ⇒ texte
- **sauce aux anchois** ⇒ texte
- **sauce gribiche** ⇒ texte
- **mayonnaise** ⇒ texte
- **ravigote** ⇒ texte
- **rémoulade** ⇒ texte
- **tartare** ⇒ texte
- **Vincent** ⇒ texte
- **vinaigrette** ⇒ texte

Tête de veau en crépinettes ⇒ flat sausage filled with sausage meat, mixed with a culinary stuffing of calf head, mushrooms, truffles, and Madeira sauce; coated with pork fat and grilled; served with Madeira sauce added of truffle

Tête de veau en poupeton ⇒ meat loaf of boiled calf head, plus a stuffing for quenelles, chopped mushrooms, and eau de vie; cooked in stock of Madeira, ham, knuckle of veal, carrots, onion, and herbs; served with a garnish of braised sweetbreads, cockscombs in Madeira, olives, crayfishes, and the cooking juice

Tête de veau en ragoût ⇒ calf head boiled with lemon juice, vinegar, onions, clove, carrots, garlic, herbs, and pepper, served with a garnish of carrots, onions, sauté edible agarics, and shallots; covered with a sauce of white wine, poultry stock, sage, sweet marjoram, rosemary, basil, thyme, laurel, pepper, Madeira, and ginger

Tête de veau en tortue ⇒ boiled calf head and sweetbread, covered with a brown sauce of white wine flavoured with tomatoes and herbs, then added of braised mushrooms, green olives, and gherkins; g arnished with quenelles and croutons

Tête ou Pomme *-[chou-fleur]-* ⇒ cauliflower inflorescence

Tétine *-[pis]-* ⇒ udder

   - **Tétine braisée** ⇒ sliced udder braised with streaky bacon

   - **si elle est garnie champignons** ⇒ ... garnished with mushrooms

   - **si elle est garnie riz** ⇒ ... garnished with rice

Tétragone ⇒ New Zealand spinach

Tétras ⇒ grouse

   - **grand Tétras** ⇒ Capercaillie

Tétras lyre *-[coq de bruyère]-* ⇒ grouse

Teurgoule ou Teurt-goule *-[terrinée]-* ⇒ rice cooked in milk with cinnamon

Tfina ⇒ Arab ragout

Thé ⇒ tea < *uncountable* >

Thé à la menthe ⇒ infusion of tea and mint, added of sugar

Thé à la menthe ⇒ mint tea

Thé au citron ⇒ lemon tea

Thé au lait ⇒ tea with milk

Thé chinois ⇒ infusion of black tea

Thé de bœuf *-[beef tea]-* ⇒ beef tea

Thé de chine ⇒ china tea

Thé des jésuites *-[maté]-* ⇒ maté

   - **infusion** ⇒ maté tea

Thé du mexique *-[ambroisie]-* ⇒ infusion of ambrosia leaves, and ambrosia flowers

Thé glacé ⇒ infusion of green tea and mint; served chilled with rum

Thé grand mandarin ⇒ Chinese tea flavoured with jasmine

Thé indien au lait aux épices ⇒ infusion of tea in milk, spiced with cinnamon, clove, cardamom, and ginger

Thé nature ⇒ black tea

Thé parfumé ⇒ flavoured tea

   - **Thé parfumé au jasmin** ⇒ tea flavoured with jasmine

   - **Thé parfumé au mûre** ⇒ tea flavoured with mulberry

   - **Thé parfumé à la mangue** ⇒ tea flavoured with mango

   - **Thé parfumé au cassis** ⇒ tea flavoured with blackcurrant

   - **Thé parfumé au fruit de la passion** ⇒ tea flavoured with passion fruit

   - **Thé parfumé à à la mandarine** ⇒ tea flavoured with mandarin orange

   - **Thé parfumé à la cerise** ⇒ tea flavoured with cherry

   - **Thé parfumé à la framboise** ⇒ tea flavoured with raspberry

   - **Thé parfumé à la vanille** ⇒ tea flavoured with vanilla

   - **Thé parfumé à noix de coco** ⇒ tea flavoured with coconut

   - **Thé parfumé à la pommme** ⇒ tea flavoured with apple

   - **Thé parfumé à l'abricot** ⇒ tea flavoured with apricot

   - **Thé parfumé au gingembre** ⇒ tea flavoured with ginger

   - **Thé parfumé à la cannelle** ⇒ tea flavoured with cinnamon

   - **Thé parfumé à la rose** ⇒ tea flavoured with rose

Thé parfumé ⇒ flavoured tea (suite)
- **Thé parfumé à la bergamote** ⇒ tea flavoured with bergamot citrus
- **Thé parfumé à la fleur d'oranger** ⇒ tea flavoured with orange blossom
- **Thé parfumé au lotus** ⇒ tea flavoured with lotus < *etc* >

Thés de ceylan ⇒ Ceylon teas

Thermidor -*[homard]*- ⇒ grilled or roasted lobster; served in the shell with a sauce made of stock, butter, mustard, chervil, tarragon and shallots

Thomson -*[orange]*- ⇒ variety of orange

Thon ⇒ tuna or tunny-fish < *pluriel « tunnies » ou inchangé* >

Thon au thé ⇒ fried steak of tunny, simmered in tea, with diced pork belly, ginger, pepper, Vietnamese seasoning, and sugar

Thon blanc -*[germon]*- ⇒ albacore

Thon en daube ⇒ tunny braised with onion, tomatoes, garlic, herbs, and red wine

Thon en daube à la provençale ⇒ tunny braised with onion, tomatoes, garlic, herbs, and white wine

Thon grillé ⇒ steak of tunny marinated in olive oil, lemon juice, pepper, and garlic, then grilled; served with ...
- **beurre de poivron** ⇒ ... red pepper cooked slowly in olive oil
- **beurre d'anchois** ⇒ ... anchovy paste

Thon Max ⇒ tunny fillet cooked slowly in peanut oil with carrots, onions, pepper, paprika, herbs, tomatoes, and tomato purée; served chilled

Thonine ⇒ little tunny

Thonnine ⇒ carved up tunny roasted or fried in oil, then salted and spiced

Thouarsais -*[vins du]*- ⇒ wines from Thouars area

Thoum -*[ail]*- ⇒ garlic < *uncountable* >

Thourin ⇒ onion soup with pork fat, thickened of egg-yolks

Thym ⇒ thyme < *uncountable* >

Tian
- **ustensile** ⇒ Provencal cooking-dish
- **gratin** ⇒ dish from layers of potatoes, onion, tomatoes, thyme, and pepper; au gratin

Tian d'artichauts ⇒ dish of artichoke hearts and anchovies; au gratin

Tian d'aubergines ⇒ dish of aubergines and tomatoes; au gratin

Tian d'épinards ⇒ dish of spinach; au gratin

Tian de haricots blancs ⇒ dish of haricot beans; au gratin

Tian de morue ⇒ dish of salt cod; au gratin

Tié bou diéné ⇒ Senegalese dish of fishes

Tiède ⇒ tepid or lukewarm

Tiep dien ⇒ Senegalese dish of fishes

Tige ⇒ stalk or stem

Tignolet -*[pain Pays Basque]*- ⇒ folded loaf or bread

Tilleul ⇒ lime-tree flowers
- **infusion** ⇒ infusion of lime-tree flowers

Tilsit -*[fromage]*- ⇒ Tilsit

Timbale ⇒ timbale

Timbales à l'épicurienne (*petites* ...) ⇒ dariole filled with a culinary stuffing of lamb sweetbread, truffle, pickled oxtongue, and mashed mushrooms, then covered with rice cooked in fat; served overturned, with tomato sauce

Timbales à la fermière (*petites* ...) ⇒ dariole filled with braised diced vegetables, forcemeat for quenelles, and vegetable salad thickened of béchamel sauce; served overturned with béchamel sauce added of cream, and herbs

Timbales à la piémontaise *(petites ...)* ⇒ dariole filled with a culinary stuffing of pickled oxtongue, and risotto added with white truffle

Timbales Agnès Sorel ⇒ timbale of chopped truffle, chopped pickled oxtongue, a forcemeat of poultry added with a purée of onions and rice; plus a culinary stuffing of poultry, truffles, and Madeira sauce

Timbales Bagration *(petites ...)* ⇒ dariole filled with macaroni thickened of cream, plus a culinary stuffing of truffles and pickled oxtongue; overturned after baking, and covered with supreme sauce

Timbales Beauvilliers *(petites ...)* ⇒ dariole garnished with hollowed out brioche, plus a culinary stuffing of white meat thickened with a sauce based on poultry stock; then topped of asparagus tips braised in butter

Timbale Brillat-Savarin ⇒ brioche hollowed out, covered with apricot compote added of kirsch, then filled of confectioner's custard mixed with crushed macaroons, plus pears in syrup; served with a sauce made of apricot pulp, syrup, and brandy

Timbale d'écrevisses ⇒ pastry case filled with ragout of crayfish tails, plus Coregonus quenelles; covered with béchamel sauce added of mashed crayfishes, cognac, and cayenne-pepper

Timbales d'entrée *(petites ...)* ⇒ dariole filled with a culinary stuffing or a forcemeat, then baked; served overturned on fried croutons or artichoke hearts

Timbale de bécasse froide ⇒ pastry case covered with a forcemeat of game meat and diced truffle, then filled with woodcock stuffed of forcemeat, mashed foie gras, and cognac; served chilled coated with game jelly, flavoured of Madeira or dessert wine

Timbales de foies de volaille ⇒ timbale of macaroni mixed with poultry livers, mushrooms, Madeira sauce, and cream

Timbales de pâtes à la bolognaise ⇒ timbale of pasta, added of sauté mushrooms, a hash of garlic and shallots, ham in butter, and bolognèse sauce

Timbales Elysée ⇒ pastry boat filled of sliced Genoese moistened with kirsch, vanilla ice-cream, and fruits in season; covered with redcurrant jelly added of kirsch, surrounded of sugared whipped cream

Timbales St Hubert *(petites ...)* ⇒ timbale filled with pickled oxtongue, plus a culinary stuffing of game meat, truffle and mushroom; served overturned with a sauce based on a mixture of diced vegetables and ham, cooked in vinegar and white wine

Ti nain *-[banane]-* ⇒ large banana for cooking

Tinto barroco *-[Afrique du sud; vin]-* ⇒ variety of vine for red wines from Durbanville, Paarl, Stellenbosch, Robertson, Worcester

Tintos *-[Espagne; vin]-* ⇒ Valdepeñas red wine

Tiof *-[Afrique noire]-* ⇒ fish similar to grouper

Tioro ⇒ fish stock with white wine, crushed tomatoes and capsicums, poured boiling on fried bits of fishes; served with mussels, Norway lobsters and fried sippets

    - Biarritz ⇒ fish stock with sorrel and thickened of egg-yolk, poured boiling on fried bits of fishes

Tire *-[maple syrup]-* ⇒ maple syrup

Tiritis *-[Antilles]-* ⇒ small fishes and fry < *Nota « fry » est un nom au pluriel* >

Tisane ⇒ herbal tea

    - tisane de tilleul ⇒ lime-blossom tea

    - tisane de menthe ⇒ mint tea

Tivoli *(à la ...) -[garniture pour petites pièces de boucherie]-* ⇒ ... with a garnish of asparagus tips, plus mushrooms filled with a culinary stuffing of cockscombs thickened of supreme sauce

Tô *-[pâte de mil]-* ⇒ millet paste

Toad in the hole ⇒ toad-in-the-hole

Toast ⇒ toast < *uncountable* >
Toasts chauds aux anchois ⇒ toast garnished with anchovy fillets, then browned
Toca -*[pompe]*- ⇒ large brioche flavoured with aniseed, orange peel or blossom flowers
Toddy -*[cocktail]*- ⇒ toddy
Toffee -*[confiserie]*- ⇒ toffee
Töfu ⇒ soya cheese
Tokaji -*[tokay; vin]*- ⇒ Tokay
Tokàny ⇒ Hungarian ragout
Tokay ⇒ Tokay
Tokay aszru -*[vin]*- ⇒ Tokay
Tom Collins -*[cocktail]*- ⇒ Tom Collins
Tom pouce ⇒ small squared cakes soldered by two with a custard of butter, crushed hazelnuts, sugar, and coffee extract
Tom yam ⇒ Thai soup
Tomato ⇒ tomato
  - pluriel ⇒ tomatoes
Tomate -*[apéritif]*- ⇒ aniseed aperitif coloured with pomegranate syrup
Tomate de mer ⇒ red sea anemone
Tomate -*[purée de]*- ⇒ tomato purée
Tomate -*[sauce]*- ⇒ tomato sauce
Tomates farçies ⇒ stuffed tomatoes
Tomates farcies à la grecque ⇒ tomatoes stuffed of rice cooked in olive oil, with saffron, pepper and herbs, added of sultanas; then baked
Tomates farcies à la reine ⇒ tomatoes stuffed with a mixing of poached white meat, braised mushrooms, truffle and velouté sauce; then sprinkled of crumbs, plus melted butter, and baked
Tomates farçies chaudes à la bonne femme ⇒ tomatoes stuffed with a forcemeat of sausage meat, braised onion in butter, breadcrumbs, parsley, garlic, and pepper; then baked
Tomates farçies chaudes à la languedocienne ⇒ tomatoes stuffed with a forcemeat of sausage meat, braised onion in butter, breadcrumbs, parsley, garlic, pepper, and chopped hard-boiled egg; then baked with olive oil
Tomates farcies chaudes à la niçoise ⇒ tomatoes stuffed with a forcemeat of rice cooked in fat, diced sauté aubergines, parsley, garlic, and breadcrumbs; sprinkled of olive oil and baked
Tomates farcies chaudes à la parisienne ⇒ tomatoes stuffed with a stuffing of sausage meat, truffle, and mushrooms, then baked
Tomates farcies chaudes à la piémontaise ⇒ tomatoes stuffed with risotto, and tomatoes cooked in their own liquid, sprinkled of melted butter and baked; served sprinkled of parsley, with tomato purée
Tomates farcies chaudes en nid ⇒ tomatoes stuffed with an egg, peppered and salted, then sprinkled of melted butter and baked
Tomates farcies froides à la crème et à la ciboulette ⇒ tomatoes stuffed with a mixing of cream or soft white cheese, chive, garlic, vinegar and cayenne-pepper; served chilled
Tomates farcies froides au thon ⇒ tomatoes stuffed with a mixing of pilaf, tiny pieces of tunny, mustard, herbs, and lemon pulp; served chilled
Tomates grillées ⇒ peppered tomatoes, coated with olive oil; then grilled
Tomates sautées à la provençale ⇒ braised halved tomatoes, topped with breadcrumbs, herbs and garlic
Tomates soufflées ⇒ tomatoes filled with a preparation for soufflé, sprinkled of grated parmesan, and baked
Tomato ketchup ⇒ tomato ketchup

Tombe -*[grondin perlon]*- ⇒ tub gurnard
Tomber ou Tombée de *(avec ...)*
   - **avec une tombée d'épinards** ⇒ ... with dried spinach
   - **avec une tombée d'oseille** ⇒ ... with dried sorrel chiffonade
   - **avec une tombée d'onions émincés** ⇒ ... with dried thinly sliced onions
   - **avec le liquide de cuisson** ⇒ ... with the thickened cooking juice
Tomme ou Tome ⇒ ewe's milk or goat's milk cheese
Tomme de Planèze ⇒ Cantal cheese from Planèze
Tomme de St Marcellin ⇒ cheese from Dauphiné
Tomme de savoie ⇒ Savoy cheese, made of pressed paste, with a regular crust spotted of yellow or red
Tonic ⇒ tonic water
Tonkinois
   a) manqué ⇒ moulded sponge-cake with almonds, topped of praline; sliced and stuffed with a
      buttered custard added of praline
   b) petit four ⇒ cubic petit four made with a preparation of caramel, almonds and hazelnuts plus
      frangipane flavoured with praline; covered of chocolate, plus chopped pistachios
Tonneau ⇒ cask
Tonnine -*[Thon]*- ⇒ carved up tunny roasted or fried in oil, then salted and spiced
Tonton -*[bolet]*- ⇒ boletus
Topinambour ⇒ Jerusalem artichoke
Topinambours à l'anglaise ⇒ Jerusalem artichokes cooked in butter, then simmered in cream or
      béchamel sauce
   - **Si servi en garniture** ⇒ ...; served with ... < *plus le texte ci-dessus* >
Toque du président Adolphe Clerc ⇒ pâté made of hare, woodcock, young partridge, thrushes,
      truffles and goose fat
Torchon *(en ...)*
   a) serviette -*[linge]*- ⇒ towel
   b) serviette de table ⇒ table napkin or serviette
   c) truffes pochées ⇒ poached truffles presented in serviette
      - **truffes sous la cendre** ⇒ truffles cooked in the embers, and presented in serviette
   d) pommes de terre en robe des champs ⇒ jacket potatoes presented in serviette
   e) asperges cuites à l'eau ⇒ boiled asparagus presented in serviette
   f) riz à la serviette ⇒ rice cooked in salted water, wrapped in serviette, and dried in the oven
Torchon *(cuit au ...)* -*[jambon]*- ⇒ ham salted and cooked in stock or boiled ham
Tordu -*[pain]*- ⇒ twisted bread
Torgoule -*[terrinée]*- ⇒ rice cooked in milk with cinnamon
Torpille ⇒ torpedo or electric ray
Torpille marbrée -*[poisson]*- ⇒ marbled electric ray
Torrone -*[touron]*- ⇒ a sweet or candy of almond paste with pistachios, hazelnuts and crystallized
      fruit
Torroni -*[touron]*- ⇒ a sweet or candy of almond paste with pistachios, hazelnuts and crystallized
      fruit
Torsade ⇒ twisted cord
Torta -*[tortellini]*- ⇒ tortellini
Tort orzechowy -*[Pologne]*- ⇒ gateau added of nuts, glazed with coffee
Torta di pane -*[Suisse]*- ⇒ gateau made of stale bread
Torteil ⇒ brioche shaped in ring, flavoured with aniseed
Tortell ⇒ brioche shaped in ring, flavoured with aniseed
Tortelletti ⇒ tortellini
Tortelli ⇒ tortellini

Tortellini ⇒ tortellini
Tortelloni ⇒ tortellini
Tortilla ⇒ tortilla
Tortillon -[*gâteau*]- ⇒ ring of sugared paste cooked in water, coloured with saffron, then baked
Tortillon -[*petit four*]- ⇒ petit four with preserved fruits or almonds
Tortillon -[*brassadeau*]- ⇒ ring of sugared paste cooked in water, coloured with saffron, then baked
Tortiglioni ⇒ tortellini
Tort orzechowy -[*pâtisserie polonaise*]- ⇒ gateau added of nuts, glazed with coffee
Tortue
    - **mer** ⇒ turtle
    - **terre** ⇒ tortoise
Tortue (*en ...*) ⇒ calf head and sweetbread simmered in white wine, olives, mushrooms and gherkins; laid in timbales
Toscane (*à la ...*)
    - **en France** ⇒ dishes with parmesan and ham
    - **étranger** ⇒ grillades de bœuf, haricots, chianti
    - **macaronis** ⇒ macaroni thickened of mashed foie gras, and diced truffles sautéed in butter
Toso -[*saké*]- ⇒ sake
Totelots ⇒ salad of squared pasta with egg, added of sliced hard-boiled eggs; seasoned with a french dressing flavoured of onion, garlic, and shallots
Tôt-fait ⇒ pound cake flavoured with lemon; served with jam, or compote, or fruits poached in syrup
Touchouri -[*Russe*]- ⇒ Russian cheese
Toucy -[*Nivernais fromage*]- ⇒ cheese from Nevers area
Touffe ⇒ tuft or bunch or wisp or clump or cluster
Touffé -[*Antilles*]- ⇒ stew of marinated shark, covered with tomato sauce
Touffé de requin à la créole ⇒ bits of shark marinated in lemon juice, garlic, pepper, capsicum, Caribbean wood; then cooked with onions, shallots, tomatoes, capsicum, garlic, and herbs; served with lemon juice, parsley and grated garlic, plus rice and haricot beans
Toulia ⇒ onion soup
Toulousaine (*à la ...*)
    - **volaille pochée ou poêlée, croustade, tourte, vol-au-vent** ⇒ ... garnished with a ragout of poultry, quenelles, sweetbreads or cockscombs, cock's kidneys, mushrooms and truffles; thickened of supreme sauce added of egg-yolks and cream
    - **autres plats du sud ouest** ⇒ certains traduits
Toupin
    - **ustensile** ⇒ cooking pot
    - **fromage** ⇒ milk's cheese from savoy
Toupinel ⇒ baked potatoes hollowed out, then filled with their pulp added of cream, butter and nutmeg; covered of béchamel sauce added of egg-yolks and gruyère, topped with a poached egg
Tour eiffel -[*fromage*]- ⇒ goat's milk cheese shaped in pyramid
Tourain ⇒ onion soup with pork fat, thickened of egg-yolks
Tourangelle (*à la ...*)
    - **grosses pièces de mouton ou d'agneau rôties** ⇒ roasted ... served with the gravy, plus a garnish of french beans and flageolets thickened of butter
    - **oeufs pochés ou mollets** ⇒ poached eggs or soft boiled eggs laid on tartlets filled with flageolet purée and covered of béchamel sauce added of cream
Touri ⇒ onion soup with pork fat, thickened of egg-yolks
Tourifas ⇒ slices of bread covered with mushrooms, herbs, lamellas of ham and pork fat, then fried
Touril ⇒ onion soup with pork fat, thickened of egg-yolks

Tourin ⇒ onion soup with pork fat, thickened of egg-yolks

Tourin à l'ail -[*Quercy*]- ⇒ onion and garlic soup with pork fat, thickened of egg-yolks

Tourin à l'aoucou -[*Quercy*]- ⇒ onion soup cooked with conserve of goose thigh

Tourin de noces ⇒ soup of onions and tomatoes browned in goose fat, thickened with vermicelli and grilled croutons

Tourin périgourdin ⇒ soup of onions browned in goose fat, plus garlic, and crushed tomatoes; thickened with egg-yolks and country ham

Tourlourou -[*Antilles*]- ⇒ land crab

Tournebride -[*auberge*]- ⇒ quiet inn

Tournedos ⇒ fillet steak of beef or tournedos

Tournedos à la bordelaise ⇒ grilled tournedos topped with slice of poached bone-marrow and parsley; served with a sauce made of poached bone-marrow, shallots, red wine, thyme, laurel, and parsley

Tournedos à la béarnaise ⇒ grilled tournedos, garnished of small potatoes sautéed in butter with lardoons; served with Béarnaise sauce

Tournedos à la d'Abrantès ⇒ sauté tournedos seasoned with paprika, laid on slice of grilled aubergine; served with the gravy added of braised onion, capsicum, and tomato sauce

Tournedos à la portugaise ⇒ sauté tournedos served with stuffed tomatoes, and small potatoes sautéed in butter with lardoons; accompanied with the gravy added of white wine, tomato sauce, and kneaded butter

Tournedos à la périgourdine ⇒ sauté tournedos, laid on fried crouton, then topped of truffle lamellas in butter; served with the gravy added of Madeira

Tournedos archiduc ⇒ sauté tournedos laid on a pancake of fried balls made with mashed potatoes, eggs, and butter; garnished of calf brain croquettes and truffle lamellas, then covered with the gravy added of xeres, cream, veal stock and paprika

Tournedos au lissé fermier ⇒ tournedos cooked in butter, garnished with browned cultivated mushrooms; covered with the gravy added of calvados, soft white cheese, and cream

Tournedos aux anchois ⇒ sauté tournedos laid on fried crouton; covered with the gravy added of veal stock, white wine, and anchovy paste, topped of anchovy fillets

Tournedos aux champignons ⇒ sauté tournedos, covered with the gravy added of veal stock, and Madeira; garnished of sauté mushrooms

Tournedos Brillat-Savarin ⇒ tournedos served with morels braised in butter, and mustard thickened of cream; covered with the gravy added of port

Tournedos chasseur ⇒ sauté tournedos; covered with sauce chasseur

Tournedos Clamart ⇒ sauté tournedos, garnished of artichoke hearts filled with peas or mashed peas; served with the gravy added of veal stock, and white wine

Tournedos entièrement paré ⇒ tournedos or fillet steak « larder trim »

Tournedos grillés ⇒ grilled tournedos

Tournedos Helder ⇒ sauté tournedos, covered with Béarnaise sauce and tomatoes cooked in their own liquid; plus the gravy

Tournedos Henri IV ⇒ tournedos served with « fried potatoes », watercress and béarnaise sauce < *quelquefois au lieu de « fried potatoes », pommes de terre, il y a « artichoke hearts », artichauts* >

Tournedos légèrement paré ⇒ tournedos or fillet steak « special trim »

Tournedos Lucullus ⇒ sauté tournedos laid on a sippet, covered with a sauce of Madeira and chopped truffles, topped with a poached mushroom; garnished with cockscombs, cock's kidneys, and asparagus tips

Tournedos Marguery ⇒ braised artichoke hearts garnished with truffle in cream, and sauté morels, then topped with sauté tournedos; served with cockscombs, cock's kidneys, plus the cooking juice added of port, and cream

Tournedos Marigny ⇒ sauté tournedos, surrounded by artichoke hearts braised in butter, corn in butter, and little potato-balls browned in butter; served with the gravy added of white wine

Tournedos Masséna ⇒ sauté tournedos topped of bone-marrow lamellas, served with artichoke hearts covered of Madeira sauce added of truffle

Tournedos montpensier ⇒ tournedos served with a garnish of asparagus tips and truffles in julienne

Tournedos niçois ⇒ grilled fillet steak, served with anchovies, lettuce and olives or grilled tournedos, served with anchovies, lettuce and olives

Tournedos Rossini ⇒ fried round sippet topped successively of a fillet steak, a foie gras escalope and truffles; covered with the gravy thickened of Madeira

Tournedos sauté « garniture pour » *-[opéra]-* ⇒ sauté tournedos with a garnish of poultry livers in Madeira laid on tartlets, plus asparagus tips; served with a Madeira sauce

Tournedos sautés ⇒ sauté tournedos

Tournedos Saint Germain ⇒ sauté tournedos laid on fried crouton, then garnished with mashed peas

Tourner *-[façonner les légumes]-* ⇒ shaped ... < *plus nom anglais du légume* >

Tournesol ⇒ sunflower

Tourné *-[sucre]-* ⇒ cooked sugar

Touron ⇒ a sweet or candy of almond paste with pistachios, hazelnuts and crystallized fruit

Tourrin ⇒ onion soup with pork fat, thickened of egg-yolks

Tourte ⇒ covered pie or covered tart or pie
- **tourte à la viande** ⇒ meat pie
- **tourte au poisson** ⇒ fish pie

Tourte à la lorraine ⇒ pie filled with marinated pork and veal in cream of eggs

Tourte à la mode béarnaise ⇒ pies of butter, leaven, sugar, egg, rum, lemon peel, and flour

Tourte à la pacane ⇒ pie made with American nuts

Tourte à la viande ⇒ short pastry filled with meat

Tourte au sirop d'érable ⇒ pie filled with maple syrup added of maize fecula, and butter, plus chopped almonds

Tourte aux abricots Mont Bry ⇒ apricot pie
- **variantes ananas** ⇒ pineapple pie
- **variantes cerises** ⇒ cherry pie
- **variantes brugnons** ⇒ nectarine pie
- **variantes poires** ⇒ pear pie
- **variantes pommes** ⇒ apple pie
- **variantes prunes** ⇒ plum pie

Tourte aux feuilles de bette ⇒ pie filled with beet leaves, added of figs, crushed macaroon, sultanas, eggs, and pine-kernels

Tourte de grives à la périgourdine ⇒ pie filled with thrushes braised in Madeira, forcemeat, truffle lamellas, and the gravy added of Madeira

Tourte de saumon ⇒ short pastry filled with salmon

Tourte de truffes à la périgourdine ⇒ pie filled with foie gras, fennel-flower, cognac, truffles, Madeira, and truffle extract

Tourte de veau au parmesan ⇒ pie filled with cushion of veal and pork fat, macerated in white wine, cognac, thyme and pepper; plus calf liver, shallots, eggs, and grated parmesan

Tourte de viande ⇒ short pastry filled with meat

Tourte La Varenne ⇒ Marzipan garnished with a lemon custard, plus preserved cherries

Tourteau *-[Périgord; Quercy; Rouergue]-* ⇒ small maize pancake

Tourteau *-[crabe]-* ⇒ large crab

Tourteau *-[pâte de cacao]-* ⇒ cocoa paste

Tourteau fromagé ⇒ cake made of goat's milk cheese, flour, eggs, cream, and sugar; flavoured with cognac

Tourteau pruneau ⇒ puff-pastry tart filled with mashed prunes

Tourterelle ⇒ turtle-dove

Tourtes à la mode béarnaise ⇒ pies of butter, leaven, sugar, egg, rum, lemon peel, and flour

Tourtisseau d'Anjou ⇒ perfumed fritter

Tourton ⇒ pancake of rye

Tourtou ⇒ pancake of rye

Tout-épice ⇒ allspice or pimento

Tracy -[fromage de Nivernais]- ⇒ cheese from Nevers area

Train de côtes -[rosbif]- ⇒ seven bone rib « oven prepared »

Traiteur ⇒ caterer

Traminer -[Alsace; Allemagne vins]- ⇒ high quality wine from Alsace area, of « traminer » variety of vine

Tranche -[de pain, etc ...]- ⇒ slice

Tranche -[Boeuf]- ⇒ steak

Tranche -[viande-saumon]-
  - **boeuf** ⇒ beefsteak
  - **saumon** ⇒ salmon steak
  - **veau** ⇒ veal cutlet

Tranche d'aloyau avec os comprenant le filet et le faux-filet ⇒ T' bone steaks « standard »

Tranche d'aloyau avec os, comprenant le filet et le faux-filet, mais raccourci ⇒ 'T'bone steaks « short cut »

Tranche d'épaule de mouton ⇒ shoulder steaks of lamb

Tranche de colin à la duxelles ⇒ slices of hake, plus chopped onions and mushrooms, moistened with white wine and fish stock, then baked; covered with cream

Tranche de faux-filet nature avec gras ⇒ sirloin steaks « standard »

Tranche de faux-filet raccourci, avec gras ⇒ sirloin steaks « short cut »

Tranche de filet -[boeuf]- ⇒ fillet steak of beef

Tranches de filet de boeuf grillées ⇒ slices of beef fillet oiled and peppered, sprinkled of herbs; then grilled and served with parsley butter

Tranches de filet de boeuf à la poêle ⇒ slices of beef fillet fried in butter and served with the gravy added of Madeira

Tranche de gigot avec os ⇒ leg steaks of lamb « bone in »

Tranche de gigot de mouton ou d'agneau
  - **mouton** ⇒ leg steak of mutton or a slice off the leg of lamb
  - **agneau** ⇒ leg steak of lamb or a slice off the leg of lamb

Tranche de gigot maigre parée ⇒ leg steaks of lamb « ex topside »

Tranche de gigot sans os ⇒ leg steaks of lamb « boneless »

Tranche de gîte à griller, avec une légère couche de gras, maximum 1, 5 cm ⇒ braising steaks

Tranche de palette avec perdrix -[porc]- ⇒ neck and chops of pork

Tranche de poitrine à griller -[porc]- ⇒ sliced belly

Tranche de romsteck ⇒ piece of rump-steak

Tranche grasse -[bœuf]- ⇒ Toprump of beef or Thick flank of beef

Tranche grasse ficelée, entière ⇒ Toprump of beef or Thick flank of beef « rolled »

Tranche napolitaine ⇒ Neapolitan slice

Tranches sucrées ⇒ rectangular flat-cakes made of flour, sugar, butter and egg

Trappiste -[fromage]- ⇒ cow's milk cheese shaped in disc, containing 40% of cream

Trappiste -[bière de]- ⇒ Belgian beer

Trappiste de Bricquebec -*[Normandie]*- ⇒ cow's milk cheese shaped in disc, containing 40% of cream
Trappiste de tamié -*[Tamié]*- ⇒ cow's milk cheese shaped in disc, containing 40% of cream
Trappisten -*[fromage]*- ⇒ Austrian cheese with a yellow paste
Trappistine ⇒ liquor made of Armagnac and herbs
Trasi -*[Indonésie]*- ⇒ seasoning of fermented shrimp
Trator -*[Bulgarie]*- ⇒ raw cucumber mixed with yoghourt, and chopped nuts
Travers ⇒ spare ribs of pork
Travers de porc ⇒ spare ribs of pork
Travers de porc à la citronnelle -*[Asie du sud est]*- ⇒ spare ribs of pork, macerated with wormwood leaves, then grilled
Travers de porc pour barbecue ⇒ barbecue spareribs
Trébèche -*[trois cornes]*- ⇒ triangular cow's milk cheese
Trébucs -*[Béarn-Pays Basque]*- ⇒ bits of conserve of goose or pork
Trèfle -*[miel]*- ⇒ honey from clover flower or clover honey
Trèfle de cheval -*[lotier]*- ⇒ melilot or sweet-clover
Treize desserts *(les ...)* -*[Provence]*- ⇒ thirteen Provencal sweets for Christmas
Tremble -*[poisson torpille]*- ⇒ torpedo fish
Trémellodon gélatineux ⇒ a jelly fungus
  - pluriel ⇒ jelly fungi
Tremper ⇒ to steep
Trempé dans ⇒ steeped in < *v.t adjectif* >
Trénels ⇒ lamb tripe filled with garlic, clove and ham lamellas, simmered in rind of pork, carrots, thyme, laurel, and white wine
Trescat ⇒ mutton tripe cooked with egg-yolks
Tresses -*[pain]*- ⇒ bread from Alsace
Trévise -*[chicorée]*- ⇒ endive
Triboulet -*[turbot]*- ⇒ turbot < *pluriel inchangé* >
Tricholome -*[champignon]*- ⇒ tricholoma
Tricholome équestre ⇒ firwood agaric
Tricholome ruiné ⇒ tricholoma mushroom
Tricholome russule ⇒ russula
Tricholome de la St George ⇒ tricholoma
Tricholome travesti ⇒ tricholoma mushroom
Trids -*[Tunisie]*- ⇒ stuffed pancakes
Trigle -*[poisson]*- ⇒ gurnard or gurnet
Trimolette de perdrix -*[Salmis]*- ⇒ sweet and sour salmi
Triomphe de Farçi -*[haricot vert]*- ⇒ french bean
Tripe *(à la ...)*
  - général ⇒ preparation of sliced hard-boiled eggs, covered with béchamel sauce added of braised onions
  - Berry ⇒ eggs poached in a sauce of white wine, onions and aromatics
Tripe *(à la ...)* ⇒ sliced hard-boiled eggs covered with béchamel sauce added of mashed onions
Tripes ⇒ tripe < *uncountable* >
Tripes à la Lyonnaise ⇒ tripe à la Lyonnaise
Tripes à la mode de caen ⇒ tripe à la mode de Caen
Tripes à la nivernaise ⇒ tripe cooked with beef trotter, carrots, pepper, thyme, laurel, and white wine; served with boiled turnips
Tripes à la provençale ⇒ tripe cooked in white wine, with crushed tomatoes and garlic
Tripes au jaunet ⇒ tripe seasoned with saffron in medieval recipe

Tripes au safran ⇒ tripe seasoned with saffron in medieval recipe
Tripes d'agneau ⇒ lamb tripe
Tripes de La Ferté Macé ⇒ tripe cooked in packets on skewers
Tripes de chevreau
  - bouillies ⇒ kid tripe boiled with peas, and haricot beans
  - grillées ⇒ grilled kid tripe
  - rôties ⇒ roasted kid tripe
Tripes de morue ⇒ salt cod tripe
Tripes de thon *-[Languedoc-Palavas]-* ⇒ tripe of tunny cooked with onion, celery, herbs, white wine and rum
Tripette *-[clavaire]-* ⇒ tiny yellow hands
Tripettes à la mode corse ⇒ fried tripe with tomato sauce
Triple crème *-[fromage]-* ⇒ cheese containing 75% of cream
Tripotch ⇒ spicy black pudding made of mutton and veal
  - à Biriatou ⇒ spicy black pudding made of mutton and veal; served with apple purée
Tripotcha ⇒ spicy black pudding made of mutton and veal
  - à Biriatou ⇒ spicy black pudding made of mutton and veal; served with apple purée
Tripous ⇒ braised packets made with stomach of mutton, calf trotters, and aromatics
Tripoux ⇒ braised packets made with stomach of mutton, calf trotters, and aromatics
Trique madame *-[joubarbe; sédum]-* ⇒ stonecrop
Trockenbeerenauslese *-[Allemagne vins]-* ⇒ riesling
Trois cornes ⇒ triangular cow's milk cheese
Trois étoiles
  a) Armagnac ⇒ one year old Armagnac
  b) Calvados ⇒ two years old Calvados
  c) Cognac ⇒ two years old Cognac
Trois frères ⇒ gateau shaped in ring, made of rice flour, melted butter, whipped eggs and sugar; flavoured with vanilla and apricot jam, then decorated of angelica
Trois pommes *-[calvados]-* ⇒ two years old Calvados
Trois Quarts *-[lièvre]-* ⇒ hare from the year
Trompette de la mort ⇒ horn of plenty mushroom
Tronçon *-[général]-* ⇒ length
Tronçons de turbot à la vapeur ⇒ steamed lengths of turbot, covered with a sauce of shallots, vinegar, cream, and mashed bananas; surrounded by garlic in butter
Trôo *-[fromage]-* ⇒ goat's milk cheese
Trou normand ⇒ small glass of calvados or spirit drunk between courses meal
Trou Provençal ⇒ sorbet made with marc
Trouète *-[truite]-* ⇒ trout < *pluriel inchangé* >
Trucha ⇒ omelette filled with spinach and beets; served with tomato purée
Truchet *-[truite]-* ⇒ trout
Truffade ⇒ fried potato cake mixed with cheese
Truffado ⇒ fried potato cake mixed with cheese
Truffat
  1) avec fromage blanc ⇒ grated potatoes cooked with soft white cheese
  2) avec œufs ⇒ cake of grated potatoes, butter, whipped eggs and pepper, then baked
Truffe ⇒ truffle
Truffe blanche ⇒ white truffle
Truffe en chocolat ⇒ ball of chocolate melted with butter and flavoured of cognac, rum or whisky
Truffer ⇒ to garnish with truffles
  - truffé ⇒ garnished with truffle

Truffes à la croque au sel ⇒ sliced truffles, served with butter
Truffes au champagne ⇒ truffles cooked in a stock of ham, fillet of veal, pork fat, carrots, onions, aromatics, and champagne; served hot
Truffes au chocolat à la crème ⇒ balls made of chocolate, cocoa, coffee, and cream
Truffes au paprika ⇒ balls made of chocolate, cream, and prunes in armagnac; then rolled in cocoa powder added of paprika
Truffes en chaussons ⇒ turnovers filled with a truffle, and streaky bacon
Truffes en chocolat au beurre ⇒ balls made of chocolate, butter, eggs, cream, and icing sugar
Truffes pour garnitures ⇒ truffles braised in butter, then moistened of dessert wine
Truffes sous la cendre ⇒ truffles cooked in the embers
Truffes sous les cendres ⇒ truffles cooked in the embers
Truffette *-[truffe de chambéry]-* ⇒ ball of chocolate melted with butter and flavoured of cognac, rum or whisky
Truffiat
    1) avec fromage blanc ⇒ grated potatoes cooked with soft white cheese
    2) avec œufs ⇒ cake of grated potatoes, butter, whipped eggs and pepper, then baked
Truie *-[porc]-* ⇒ sow
Truie de mer ⇒ hog-fish
Truite ⇒ trout < *pluriel inchangé* >
Truite à la Beauvaisienne ⇒ trout sprinkled with pepper seeds, then roasted
Truite à la mondorienne ⇒ trout stuffed with crumbs, cream, herbs and mushrooms
Truite à la montbardoise *-[caprice de Buffon]-* ⇒ trout stuffed with spinach and shallots, then cooked in a court-bouillon
Truite arc en ciel ⇒ rainbow trout < *pluriel inchangé* >
Truite au bleu ⇒ trout au bleu
Truite aux poireaux ⇒ trout stuffed with a forcemeat of whiting in cream, wrapped in leek leaves, then baked with white wine and shallots; served covered with the cooking juice
Truite brune ⇒ brown trout < *pluriel inchangé* >
Truite de lac ⇒ trout < *pluriel inchangé* >
Truite de mer ⇒ sea trout < *pluriel inchangé* >
Truite de rivière ⇒ trout < *pluriel inchangé* >
Truite saumonée ⇒ salmon trout < *pluriel inchangé* >
Truite saumonée Beauharnais ⇒ salmon trout stuffed with a forcemeat of whiting in cream, plus a mixture of braised vegetables, then baked with fish stock and white wine; served with little potato-balls browned in butter, and artichoke hearts filled with béarnaise sauce
Truite saumonée Berchoux ⇒ salmon trout stuffed with a forcemeat of pike in cream, plus truffles, then baked in stock fish and white wine; served with a garnish of carp milt, croquettes made of spiny lobster and mushrooms, plus artichoke hearts filled with a culinary stuffing of truffles in cream and parmesan
Truite saumonée en salade
    - Recette ordinaire ⇒ salad of salmon trout lamellas macerated in olive oil and pepper, avocado, poached quail eggs, julienne of orange peel and ginger, poached crayfishes, lemon juice and olive oil
    - Recette d'automne ⇒ salad of salmon trout lamellas macerated in olive oil and pepper, egg-mushroom lamellas, marinated boletus, pastry boats filled with beetroot, artichoke hearts, poached quail eggs, plus a julienne of orange peel and ginger
Truite saumonée rôtie à la mode de Bugey ⇒ sea trout stuffed with a forcemeat of whiting, cream, truffle and butter; grilled on a skewer and sprinkled with cream, served garnished of crayfish tails and truffles
Truitelle *-[truite]-* ⇒ two years old trout < *pluriel inchangé* >

Truites à la bourguignonne ⇒ trout baked with mushrooms, carrot, onion, and Burgundy red wine; served with glazed onions, covered of the cooking juice added of kneaded butter

Truites à la nage Jean Giono ⇒ trout macerated in vinegar, salt and pepper; then cooked in vinegar, olive oil, carrot, leek, onion, garlic, ginger, thyme, pepper, and fennel seeds

Truites aux amandes ⇒ trout fried in butter with almonds; served with lemon juice, plus the cooking juice added of vinegar

Truites frites ⇒ fried trout, served with green salad, and slices of lemon

Tsarine *(à la ...)*

   a) **volaille pochée** ⇒ poached poultry garnished with cucumbers in butter, plus béchamel sauce added of egg-yolks, gruyère and paprika

   b) **autres** *-[énumération]-*
   - **crème de gélinotte et de céleri garnie d'une julienne de céleri** ⇒ mashed hazel grouse and celery
   - **œufs pochés dressés sur des tartelettes remplies de purée de gélinotte, nappées de sauce à la crème et aux champignons** ⇒ poached eggs, laid on tartlets filled of mashed hazel grouse; covered of béchamel sauce added of cream and mushrooms
   - **laitances pochées au vin blanc, garnies de vésiga haché et de caviar** ⇒ soft milt poached in white wine, garnished of chopped sturgeon bone-marrow, and caviar

Tschy *-[chtchi]-*
   1) **soupe avec viande** ⇒ soup made of sauerkraut in stock, beef, duck meat, streaky bacon, smoked sausages; served with cream, fennel and chopped parsley
   2) **soupe légumes** ⇒ soup made with vegetables as spinach, sorrel and nettle

Tsimes *-[russe]-* ⇒ sweet and sour hors d'œuvre of carrots or beetroot

Ttoro ⇒ fish stock with white wine, crushed tomatoes and capsicums, poured boiling on fried bits of fishes; served with mussels, Norway lobsters and fried sippets
   - **Biarritz** ⇒ fish stock with sorrel and thickened of egg-yolk, poured boiling on fried bits of fishes

Tubetti ⇒ variety of pasta

Tuile ⇒ an almond biscuit shaped like a curved roof tile or kind of biscuit

Tuile ⇒ dry petit four shaped in roman tile

Tuile aux noisettes ⇒ pastry made of egg, sugar, flour, hazelnut powder and vanilla

Tuiles ⇒ pastry made of whipped egg, flour, almonds and vanilla

Tuilé *-[vin]-* ⇒ wine with a colour of brick

Tumbler *-[cocktail; verre]-* ⇒ glass for cocktail

Turban ⇒ turban

Turban de volaille ⇒ crown of poultry escalopes, plus poultry forcemeat, culinary stuffing of poultry meat added of truffle and mushrooms, then baked; garnished in the centre with braised calf sweetbread escalopes, plus sauté morels, then covered with béchamel sauce added of cream

Turban glacé ⇒ crown of vanilla ice cream, mixed with preserved fruits macerated in rum; garnished with sugared whipped cream, added of vanilla

Turbigo ⇒ sauté lamb kidneys garnished with grilled chipolatas and sauté mushrooms; served with the cooking juice added of white wine

Turbot ⇒ turbot *< pluriel inchangé >*

Turbot à la pélerine *-[turbot]-* ⇒ turbot braised on a laying of onions and butter, covered with the cooking juice added of white wine, creamed and buttered, then glazed; garnished with a bush of fried scallops

Turbot à l'impériale ⇒ slices of turbot poached in milk, served with crayfish tails; then covered with a sauce of egg-yolks, butter, and truffle, cooked in stock, plus Madeira

Turbot aux morilles ⇒ turbot escalopes coated of morels browned in butter with shallots and cream, then baked; covered with a sauce of shallots, pounded garlic, tomato purée, cayenne pepper and dry white wine; served topped with a slice of lobster

Turbot frit Brillat-Savarin ⇒ fried turbot

Turbotin ⇒ young turbot < *pluriel inchangé* >

Turbotin aux poireaux ⇒ young turbot lamellas poached in fish stock, cream, sugar, pepper and vermouth, laid on baked leeks; covered with the cooking juice

Turin ou Turinois *-[petit four]-* ⇒ squared sugared petit four, garnished of chestnut purée and kirsch; covered with apricot jam, and chopped pistachios

Turinois ⇒ gateau made of chestnuts purée added of sugar, butter, chocolate and kirsch

Turnip tops *-[feuilles de navets]-* ⇒ turnip tops

Turque *(à la ...)*

    a) riz pilaf en couronne ⇒ pilaf shaped on crown and garnished

    - **riz en darioles** ⇒ pilaf moulded in dariole, served with ...

    - **œufs au plat** ⇒ fried eggs

    - **omelette** ⇒ omelette

    - **noisette d'agneau** ⇒ noisettes of lamb

    - **aubergines sautées** ⇒ sauté aubergines

    b) foie de volaille ⇒ sauté poultry livers, added of onion, and brown sauce with tomato

    c) aubergines ou poivrons ⇒ aubergines or capsicums stuffed with chopped mutton, rice, and chopped mushrooms; baked with onions and tomatoes cooked in their own liquid

Turron ou Turrones *-[touron]-* ⇒ sweet made of honey, sugar, nuts, hazelnuts, pine-kernels, and sometimes coriander or cinnamon

Tursan *-[vin]-* ⇒ wines from Dax area

Turtle soup ⇒ turtle soup

Tussilage ⇒ coltsfoot

Tutti frutti ⇒ tutti-frutti

Tvarog ⇒ mixing of soft white cheese, butter, whipped eggs and pepper

Twarogue ⇒ mixing of soft white cheese, butter, whipped eggs and pepper

Twin *-[cheddar]-* ⇒ cheddar cheese

Tychen *-[thé]-* ⇒ similar to gunpowder tea

Tyrolienne *(à la ...)*

    - **garniture** ⇒ ... with a garnish of fried onion and tomato fondue

    - **sauce** ⇒ béarnaise sauce added of tomato purée

Tzatziki *-[Grèce]-* ⇒ hors d'œuvre of cucumber, yoghourt, and garlic

U

Ujhazi -*[Hongrie]*- ⇒ boiled chicken
Ulluco ⇒ kind of beetroot
Ulve -*[algues]*- ⇒ seaweed
Unigento -*[fraise]*- ⇒ variety of fraise
Unkar beyendi -*[Turquie]*- ⇒ kebab of mutton and grease, served with mashed aubergines
Upside down cake -*[renversé à l'ananas]*- ⇒ upside down cake
Uranoscope -*[vive]*- ⇒ weever
Urgenta -*[pomme de terre]*- ⇒ variety of potato
Urid dal ⇒ bean powder or bean powder for pancakes and porridge
Uszka -*[Pologne]*- ⇒ small pastries stuffed with mushrooms
Uva highland -*[thé]*- ⇒ Ceylonese tea

V

Vacances romaines -*[cocktail]*- ⇒ cocktail of ice cubes, coffee and sugar
Vache
   - **général** ⇒ cow
   - **fromage** ⇒ cow's milk cheese
Vache -*[poisson Antilles]*- ⇒ nurse shark
Vache rouge -*[lactaire]*- ⇒ saffron milk cap or milk agaric
Vacherin -*[pâtisserie]*- ⇒ kind of meringue
Vacherin -*[fromage]*- ⇒ Vacherin
Vacherin d'abondance -*[fromage]*- ⇒ Vacherin
Vacherin de Fribourg -*[Suisse]*- ⇒ Vacherin from Fribourg area
Vacherin fin moka ⇒ disc of crushed almonds, sugar, and whipped white of eggs, filled of Mocha ice-cream; decorated with sugared whipped cream
Vacherin glacé ⇒ discs of meringue soldered with vanilla ice cream, decorated with a syrup added of cream
Vacherin glacé aux marrons ⇒ meringue covered of chilled chestnut purée added of rum and whipped white of eggs; decorated with sugared whipped cream
Vacherin mont d'or -*[fromage]*- ⇒ Vacherin
Vacqueyras -*[vin]*- ⇒ Provencal wine
Vaillon -*[Chablis]*- ⇒ quality Chablis wine
Vairon ⇒ minnow
Valaisanne *(à la ...)* -*[escargot]*- ⇒ snails prepared with gravy added of capsicum, garlic paste, and chive
Valdepeñas -*[Espagne vins]*- ⇒ Spanish quality wine from Cindad Real area
Valençay -*[fromage]*- ⇒ goat's milk cheese from Berry
Valençay -*[vin]*- ⇒ wines from Loire valley
Valence -*[orange]*- ⇒ Spanish orange
Valencia -*[orange]*- ⇒ late orange
Valencienne *(à la ...)* -*[« de la région de Valence »]*-
   - **noisette d'agneau** ⇒ noisettes of lamb ...
   - **tournedos sautés** ⇒ sauté tournedos ...
   - **volailles poêlées** ⇒ fried poultry ... served with the gravy, plus a garnish of rice added with a culinary stuffing of capsicums, ham and sometimes tomatoes or peas
Valenciennes *(à la ...)* -*[« région de Valenciennes »]*-
   - **lapin ou langue à la Valenciennes** ⇒ voir textes
Valérianelle potagère -*[mâche]*- ⇒ corn salad
Valesniki ⇒ pancakes covered with a mixing of soft white cheese, eggs and butter
Vallée d'Auge -*[poulet]*- ⇒ chicken braised in butter, flamed in calvados and cooked in cider; served with the cooking juice added of cream, plus braised apples in butter
Valmur -*[chablis]*- ⇒ high quality chablis wine
Valois
   a) **garniture** ⇒ ... with a garnish of sliced potatoes baked in butter; covered with the cooking juice added of white wine < *volaille, petites pièces de boucherie* >
   b) **sauce** ⇒ béarnaise sauce added with juice of meat
Valpolicella ⇒ Italian red wine
Valréas -*[picodon]*- ⇒ goat's milk cheese from comtat Venaissin
Valérianelle potagère -*[mâche]*- ⇒ corn salad
Van den hum -*[Afrique du sud]*- ⇒ South African brandy

Vandoise -[*chevaine*]- ⇒ dace < *pluriel inchangé* >
Vanille ⇒ vanilla < *uncountable* >
Vanilline ⇒ clove-tree extract
Vanillon -[*vanille*]- ⇒ vanilla < *uncountable* >
Vanneau -[*mollusque*]- ⇒ queen scallop
Vanneau -[*oiseau*]- ⇒ lapwing or peewit
Vapeur (*à la ...*) ⇒ boiled or steamed < *v.t adjectif* >
Var -[*vins*]- ⇒ wines from Toulon area
Varech ⇒ varec or seaweed
Variante -[*pickles*]- ⇒ pickles
Varié ⇒ varied
Varieniki ⇒ kind of ravioli
Varietal wines -[*Californie vins*]- ⇒ Californian wine with at least 51% of one variety of vine
Vasteddi -[*Sicile*]- ⇒ small loaf sprinkled of cumin seeds, stuffed with ricotta, fried pork meat, and smoked ham < *small loaf, pluriel small loaves* >
Vatapa -[*Brésil*]- ⇒ shrimps cooked with coconut
Vatrouchka ⇒ tart filled with soft white cheese
Vatrouchki -[*Russe*]- ⇒ small turnover filled with salted soft white cheese
Vaudésirs -[*chablis*]- ⇒ high quality chablis wine
Veau ⇒ veal < *viande uncountable* >
Veau (*queue de ...*) -[*Ste Ménéhould*]- ⇒ calf tail cooked slowly with onion and herbs, then covered with breadcrumbs, and grilled
Veau -[*tête de*]- ⇒ calf head
Veau en morceaux ⇒ diced veal
Veau entier ⇒ veal carcase
Veau haché ⇒ minced veal
Veau Marengo ⇒ veal marengo
Veau Orloff ⇒ sliced braised saddle of veal, reconstituted by soldering with a preparation of mashed onions, cream, and mushrooms; covered of béchamel sauce added of mashed onions and grated nutmeg, then browned
Veau sauté à la lyonnaise
   a) **escalopes** ⇒ sauté veal escalopes ...
   b) **côtes** ⇒ sauté veal cutlets ... ... plus braised onions; covered with the cooking juice added of vinegar, parsley, and stock
Veau thonné froid à l'italienne ⇒ cushion of veal cooked with tunny, anchovies, diced lemon, pepper, herbs, onions, white wine, and veal stock; served with the cooking juice added of mayonnaise
Veine -[*boeuf*]- ⇒ clod
Veine grasse et collier -[*bœuf*]- ⇒ clod and stickin
Velours ⇒ soup added with tapioca
Velouté -[*potage*]- ⇒ velouté
Velouté -[*sauce*]- ⇒ velouté sauce
Velouté à l'oseille ⇒ poultry velouté, added of braised sorrel
Velouté aux huîtres ⇒ fish velouté, added of poached oysters
Velouté chevreuse ⇒ poultry velouté added of chervil
Velouté d'artichaut ⇒ velouté added of braised artichoke hearts, egg-yolks, cream, and butter
Velouté d'asperges ⇒ cream of asparagus soup
Velouté d'éperlans à la dieppoise ⇒ velouté added of mashed sea-smelts braised with onions; garnished with mussels cooked in white wine, and crayfish tails

Velouté de champignons ⇒ velouté added of braised cultivated mushrooms, egg-yolks, cream, and butter

Velouté de crevettes, d'écrevisses, de homard, ou de langouste
    a) crevettes ⇒ velouté added with a mixture of diced vegetables and « shrimps », plus egg-yolks, cream and butter
    b) écrevisses ⇒ remplacer « shrimps » par « crayfishes »
    c) homard ⇒ remplacer « shrimps » par « lobster »
    d) langouste ⇒ remplacer « shrimps » par « spiny lobster »

Velouté de céleri ⇒ velouté added of braised celeriac, egg-yolks, cream, and butter

Velouté de ⇒ velouté cooked with ..., then added of egg-yolks, cream, and butter < *choisir le mot correspondant* >
    - gibier ⇒ game
    - de viande ⇒ meat
    - de volaille ⇒ poultry

Velouté de poisson ⇒ fish velouté

Velouté de viande ⇒ velouté cooked with meat, then added of egg-yolks, cream, and butter

Velouté glacé à l'avocat ⇒ chilled velouté of avocado pulp, lemon juice, cream and milk; served decorated with diced tomato, cucumber pulp, and mint leaves

Veltiner *-[gumpoldskirchener]-* ⇒ high quality Austrian white wine

Venaco ⇒ Corsican goat's milk cheese

Venaison ⇒ venison

Vendôme ⇒ soft cow's milk cheese with a blue crust

Vendôme bleu *-[bleu]-* ⇒ soft cow's milk cheese with a blue crust

Vendômois *-[fromage]-* ⇒ goat's milk cheese

Vénitienne *(à la ...)*
    1) sole ⇒ poached sole fillets sautéed in butter
    2) congre ⇒ bits of conger eel sautéed in butter
    3) volaille ⇒ poached poultry served with a boiled down sauce of vinegar and tarragon, then added of white wine, butter, plus herbs
    4) oeufs ⇒ poached eggs served with a boiled down sauce of vinegar and tarragon, then added of white wine, butter, plus herbs

Ventadour
    1) tournedos ⇒ tournedos garnished with truffle lamellas and bone-marrow; served with mashed artichoke hearts, plus boiled potatoes sautéed in butter
    2) noisette d'agneau ⇒ noisettes of lamb garnished with truffle lamellas and bone-marrow; served with mashed artichokes, plus boiled potatoes sautéed in butter

Ventre ⇒ belly or breast

Ventre tripe *-[boeuf]-* ⇒ tripe < *uncountable* >

Ventrèche *-[lard]-* ⇒ pork fat or fat pork or streaky bacon

Vénus à verrue *-[praire]-* ⇒ quahaug

Ver ⇒ worm

Verdelho *-[madère]-* ⇒ Madeira

Verdier ⇒ hard boiled eggs stuffed with foie gras, then browned in onions; covered with a béchamel sauce added of parmesan and truffle

Verdure ⇒ greenstuff

Verdurette *-[sauce]-* ⇒ french dressing added of chives, chervil, tarragon and chopped hard-boiled egg-yolks

Vergeoise ⇒ unrefined sugar

Verjus ⇒ verjuice or unripe grape juice

Vermicelle ⇒ vermicelli < *uncountable* >

Vermouth ⇒ vermouth
Vernaccia *-[vin]-* ⇒ Sardinian white wine, very alcoholic
Vernis *-[mollusque]-* ⇒ kind of clam
Vernis à la mode de Kléber Haedens ⇒ shelled venus shells simmered in butter, crumbs and shallots, then added of cream, garlic, and parsley; served browned
Vernon *-[apprêt pour petites pièces de boucherie sautées]-* ⇒ sauté ... nom anglais de la viande, garnished of artichoke hearts, topped with asparagus tips, turnips stuffed of mashed potatoes, plus apples hollowed out and filled of peas in butter
Véronique ⇒ veronica
Verre *-[boisson]-* ⇒ glass
Vert *(au ...) -[anguille]-* ⇒ eel cooked with herbs
Vert-cuit ⇒ not quite cooked
Vert de Laon *-[artichaut]-* ⇒ variety of artichoke
Vert de Massy *-[cornichon]-* ⇒ gherkin
Vert de Paris *-[cornichon]-* ⇒ gherkin
Vert de poireau ⇒ green leaves from a leek
Vert-pré
    1) viandes grillées
        - **rognons** ⇒ grilled kidneys ...
        - **steaks** ⇒ grilled steaks ...
        - **entrecôtes** ⇒ grilled entrecôtes ...
        - **côtes** ⇒ grilled chops ...
        - **noisettes d'agneau** ⇒ grilled noisettes of lamb ...
        - **tournedos** ⇒ grilled tournedos ...; served with a garnish of potatoes shredded in julienne and fried, plus parsley butter
    2) viande blanche
        - **caneton** ⇒ duckling garnished with a mixing of peas, asparagus tips and french beans, thickened of butter
        - **bouchées feuilletées** ⇒ puff-pastry patties garnished with a mixing of peas, asparagus tips and french beans, thickened of butter
    3) volaille ou poisson ⇒ ... covered with ... sauce verte
Verte *-[asperge]-* ⇒ asparagus from Rhone valley
Verte *-[lentille]-* ⇒ green lentils from Le Puy
Verte à carde blanche *-[bette]-* ⇒ common beet
Verte du Nord *-[mâche]-* ⇒ variety of corn salad
Verte frisée à carde blanche *-[bette]-* ⇒ automnal beet
Verte frisée à carde rouge *-[bette]-* ⇒ despised beet
Vertes de Marennes ⇒ prairie oysters
Vertjus *-[Moyen âge]-* ⇒ preparation of grape juice, lemon juice, herbs, and spices
Verveine ⇒ vervain or verbena
Verveine odorante *-[citronnelle]-* ⇒ saffron milk cap or milk agaric
Very Old *(V O ...)*
    - **armagnac** ⇒ armagnac at least four years old
    - **calvados** « V O » ou « **vieille réserve** » ⇒ four years old calvados
    - **cognac** ⇒ five years old cognac
V.S.O.P *(very superior old pale ...)*
    - **armagnac** ⇒ high quality armagnac
    - **calvados** ⇒ five years old calvados
    - **cognac** ⇒ five years old cognac
Vésiga ⇒ sturgeon bone-marrow

Vesse de loup -*[lycoperdon]*- ⇒ puff-ball
Vessie de porc ⇒ pork bladder
Vessies de poisson -*[Chine]*- ⇒ air bladders or swimming bladders
Vésou -*[canne à sucre]*- ⇒ sugar-cane juice
Viande ⇒ meat < *uncountable* >
Viande -*[morceau]*- ⇒ large piece or chunk
Viande blanche
- **veau** ⇒ veal
- **porc** ⇒ pork
- **lapin** ⇒ rabbit
- **volaille** ⇒ poultry
Viande de boeuf pour tourte ⇒ pie meat
Viande de mouton hachée ⇒ minced lamb
Viande de mouton pour brochettes ⇒ diced lamb for kebabs
Viande de mouton pour ragoût ⇒ diced lamb for stewing
Viande de porc hachée ⇒ minced pork
Viande des Grisons ⇒ salted beef, dried in the open air
Viande froide ⇒ cold meat
Viande hachée dégraissée -*[boeuf]*- ⇒ mince lean meat
Viande noire -*[gibier]*- ⇒ game
Viande pour tourte à la viande de boeuf et aux rognons ⇒ steak and kidney meat
Viande rouge
- **mouton** ⇒ mutton
- **agneau** ⇒ lamb
- **boeuf** ⇒ beef
- **cheval** ⇒ horse
Viande salée -*[Suisse]*- ⇒ salted meat
Viande séchée -*[Suisse]*- ⇒ salted beef, dried in the open air
Vichy -*[eau minérale]*- ⇒ Vichy water
Vichy -*[carottes]*- ⇒ slices of carrots cooked in water added of sugar; served with butter and parsley
Vichy fraise ⇒ strawberry syrup in Vichy water
Vichyssoise ⇒ vichyssoise
Vicomtesse héricart de thury ⇒ late variety of fraise
Victoire -*[haricot vert]*- ⇒ french bean
Victoria -*[fruit]*- ⇒ fruit and nut cake laced with rum
Victoria -*[turbot]*- ⇒ turbot served with a ... sauce victoria pour poisson ...
Victoria
- **barquettes** ⇒ pastry boat filled with a culinary stuffing of lobster and truffle
- **bouchées** ⇒ patties stuffed with a culinary stuffing of lobster and truffle
- **filets de sole** ⇒ sole fillets garnished with a culinary stuffing of lobster and truffle
- **oeufs pochés** ⇒ poached eggs garnished with a culinary stuffing of lobster and truffle
- **oeufs mollets** ⇒ soft boiled eggs garnished with a culinary stuffing of lobster and truffle
- **omelettes fourrées** ⇒ omelettes stuffed with a culinary stuffing of lobster and truffle
- **coquilles de poisson Victoria** ⇒ shells of ... nom anglais du poisson ... ... garnished with mushrooms and truffle; covered with béchamel sauce added of mashed crayfishes, cognac, and cayenne-pepper, decorated of truffle lamellas
- **salade composée Victoria** ⇒ composed salad of cucumbers, culinary stuffing of lobster, celeriac, artichoke hearts, potatoes, truffle in julienne; seasoned with mayonnaise coloured with crayfish paste

- **garniture pour petites pièces de boucherie sautées** ⇒ sauté ... nom anglais de la viande, garnished of tomatoes stuffed with mushroom purée, and artichoke hearts braised in butter; covered with the gravy thickened of Madeira and port
- **Sauce Victoria pour poissons** ⇒ ...
- **Sauce Victoria pour venaison** ⇒ ...
- **bombe Victoria** ⇒ ice cream made of egg-yolks, sugar, almond milk, and a culinary stuffing of preserved fruits; coated with strawberry ice-cream
- **Victoria cake** ⇒ plum cake with spices, sugar, and preserved cherries

Victoria cake ⇒ Victoria cake

Vide -[*hareng*]- ⇒ meagre herring

Vider -[*poisson, poulet, etc* ...]- ⇒ to gut or to clean out

Vieille ⇒ sea wrasse or rock fish

Vieille perlée ⇒ sea wrasse or rock fish

Vieilles aux pommes de terre ⇒ layers of streaky bacon lamellas, shallots, and potatoes; baked in pork fat with sea wrasse

Vieille réserve
- a) **armagnac** ⇒ armagnac more than five years old
- b) **calvados -[*V.O ou Vieille réserve*]-** ⇒ four years old calvados
- c) **cognac** ⇒ seven years old cognac

Viennoise (*à la* ...)
- 1) **escalopes de veau** ⇒ veal escalopes ...
  - **filets de volaille** ⇒ poultry fillets ...
  - **filets de poisson** ⇒ fish fillets ... ... coated with egg and crumbs, then sautéed and served with hard boiled eggs, fried parsley and capers; decorated with lemon, stoned olives and anchovy fillet
- 2) **poussins** ⇒ chicken bits coated with egg and crumbs, then sautéed or fried

Viennoise -[*saucisse*]- ⇒ sausage of veal and pork meat

Viennoiserie
- **croissants** ⇒ voir texte
- **brioches** ⇒ voir texte
- **pains au chocolat** ⇒ voir texte

Vierge -[*sauce*]- ⇒ sauce of butter mixed with lemon juice and pepper

Vieux -[*calvados-vin*]-
- a) **calvados** ⇒ three years old calvados
- b) **vin** ⇒ old wine

Vieux lille -[*gris de lille*]- ⇒ cow's milk cheese from Lille area

Vigneau ou Vignot -[*bigorneau*]- ⇒ winkle

Vigneronne (*à la* ...)
- 1) **salade** ⇒ composed salad of dandelions or corn-salad, plus browned lardoons, seasoned with nut oil
- 2) **petits oiseaux** ⇒ small birds cooked in cocotte with grapes
- 3) **escargots** ⇒ shelled snails sautéed in garlic and shallots, then wrapped in dough with chives, and fried

Vignoble
- **champ de vignes** ⇒ vineyard
- **appellation** ⇒ wine production area

Villageoise *(à la ...)*
1) **viande blanche ou volailles pochées accompagnées d'une sauce villageoise** ⇒ ...; served with ...
- **sauce villageoise base béchamel** ⇒ béchamel sauce added of braised onions, cooking juice, egg-yolk and butter
- **sauce villageoise base velouté** ⇒ velouté sauce thickened of egg-yolk and cream, plus butter
2) **consommé villageois** ⇒ leek consommé garnished with noodles

Villalon *-[brebis]-* ⇒ ewe cheese or ewe's milk cheese
Villanyi-burgundi *-[Hongrie vins]-* ⇒ high quality Hungarian red wine
Villaudrie *-[côtes du frontonnais]-* ⇒ high quality Hungarian red wine
Villeroi *(à la ...)* ⇒ ... coated of ... sauce Villeroi, egg and crumbs, then fried; served with ...
- **sauce tomate** ⇒ ... tomato sauce
- **sauce diable** ⇒ ... voir texte
- **sauce chasseur** ⇒ ... voir texte
- **sauce aux champignons** ⇒ ... voir texte

Vin ⇒ wine
Vin aromatisé ⇒ flavoured wine
Vin au miel *-[apéritif]-* ⇒ wine flavoured with honey
Vin aux fruits ⇒ wine flavoured with fruits
Vin blanc ⇒ white wine or vin blanc
Vin blanc cassis ⇒ blackcurrant liqueur mixed with dry white wine
Vin chaud ⇒ hot drink made of red wine, sugar and aromatics
Vin chaud à la cannelle et au girofle ⇒ hot red wine flavoured with orange, clove, and cinnamon
Vin cuit ⇒ boiled down must added of sugar, eau de vie, spices and aromatics
Vin d'honneur ⇒ drink offered in honour of ...
Vin d'oranges ⇒ orange juice added of sugar, then fermented
Vin d'un bon millésime ⇒ vintage wine
- **quel est le millésime de ce vin ?** ⇒ what is the vintage of this wine ? < *voir vin millésimé pour la réponse* >

Vin de Bordeaux ⇒ Bordeaux wine
Vin de Bordeaux rouge ⇒ Claret
Vin de Bourgogne ⇒ Burgundy wine
Vin de Cahors ⇒ red wine from cahors
Vin de Cassis ⇒ quality wine from Cassis near Marseille
Vin de carafe ⇒ cheap quality wine
Vin de cerises ⇒ wine made of fermented cherries
Vin de cerneau ⇒ rosé wine to be drunk with walnuts
Vin de datte ⇒ lightly sparkling wine from date-palm sap
Vin de dessert
- **Malaga** ⇒ Malaga wine
- **Marsala** ⇒ Marsala
- **Murtaflar** ⇒ Rumanian dessert wine
- **Porto** ⇒ port
Vin de Frontignan ⇒ sweet wine from Languedoc coast
Vin de fruits ⇒ alcoholic drink made of fermented fruits
Vin de liqueur ⇒ dessert wine
Vin de mai ⇒ alcoholic drink made of fermented fruits
Vin de malvoisie ⇒ malmsey wine

Vin de paille ⇒ wine based on dried grapes
Vin de palme ⇒ palm wine
Vin de pays ⇒ wine from a delimitate area
Vin de pouille ⇒ Italian wines
Vin de riz -*[Chine]-* ⇒ rice wine
Vin de sorgho -*[Chine]-* ⇒ sorghum wine
Vin de sureau ⇒ elder-berry wine
Vin de sureau au tilleul ⇒ wine made of macerated elder-berry flowers, lime tree flowers, sugar,
              sliced lemons, and vinegar
Vin de table ⇒ table wine or vin ordinaire
Vin de Tavel ⇒ rosé from Rhone valley
Vin doux ⇒ sweetened wine
Vin doux naturel ⇒ fortified wine added of alcohol
Vin du rhin ⇒ Rhine wine
Vin épicé ⇒ flavoured wine
Vin fou -*[Arbois]-* ⇒ sparkling wine from Jura
Vin gris ⇒ rosé wine
Vin herbé -*[apéritif]-* ⇒ flavoured wine
Vin jaune ⇒ high quality Jura wine with a yellow colour
Vin jeune ⇒ wine not still at its best for consumption
Vin maison ⇒ ordinary wine from the restaurant or wine selected by the restaurant
Vin millésimé
    - général ⇒ a vintage wine < *exemple a wine from the vintage of 1959* >
    - Bordeaux ⇒ a vintage Bordeaux or a Bordeaux wine from the vintage of ...
    - Bourgogne ⇒ a vintage Burgundy or a Burgundy wine from the vintage of ... < *Pour indiquer*
            l'année, ajouter l'année en chiffres à la fin de la deuxième traduction >
Vin mousseux ⇒ sparkling wine
Vin nouveau ⇒ new wine
Vin ordinaire ⇒ vin ordinaire
Vin perlé -*[Gaillac]-* ⇒ slightly sparkling wine from Gaillac area
Vin rosé ⇒ vin rosé or rosé
Vin rouge ⇒ red wine
Vin tuilé ⇒ wine with a colour of brick
Vin viné ⇒ fortified wine
Vinaigre ⇒ vinegar < *uncountable* >
Vinaigre à l'estragon ⇒ vinegar flavoured with tarragon
Vinaigre aux herbes ⇒ vinegar flavoured with herbs
Vinaigre d'alcool ⇒ spirit vinegar
Vinaigre de cidre ⇒ cider vinegar
Vinaigre de vin ⇒ wine vinegar
Vinaigre framboisé ⇒ vinegar flavoured with raspberry
Vinaigre rosat ⇒ vinegar flavoured with rose petals
Vinaigrette ⇒ vinegar sauce or oil and vinegar dressing or French dressing
Vincent ⇒ mayonnaise added of herbs and chopped hard boiled egg < *accompagne les crudités, les*
            viandes et les poissons froids >
Vindaye -*[Antilles]-* ⇒ pork cooked coated with ginger paste, garlic, onion, saffron, and capsicum
Vinho de consumo -*[Portugal; vins]-* ⇒ ordinary wine
Vinho verde -*[Portugal vin]-* ⇒ vinho verde
Vino corriente -*[Espagne vin]-* ⇒ ordinary wine

Vintage *-[porto]-* ⇒ a vintage port
Viola *-[pomme de terre]-* ⇒ variety of potato
Violet *-[poisson]-* ⇒ Mediterranean specie of seafood
Violet *-[artichaut]-* ⇒ autumnal variety of artichoke
Violet *-[haricot vert]-* ⇒ variety of french bean
Violette *-[asperge]-* ⇒ variety of asparagus
Violette *-[fleur]-* ⇒ violet
Violette candie *-[fleur]-* ⇒ violet flower candied in syrup
Violette cristallisée *-[Languedoc]-* ⇒ violet flower candied in syrup
Violette de Solliès *-[figue]-* ⇒ fig
Violette de Toulouse *-[aubergine]-* ⇒ variety of aubergine
Violon *-[poisson]-* ⇒ kind of skate
Viques *-[Franche comté]-* ⇒ small breads of flour, yeast, and milk
Viquotes *-[Franche comté]-* ⇒ small breads of flour, yeast, and milk
Viroflay
    1) croquettes ⇒ croquettes of mashed spinach wrapped in leaves, coated of béchamel sauce added of egg-yolks and gruyère, then browned
    2) garniture grosses pièces de boucherie ⇒ ... covered with the gravy thickened of sauté quartered artichoke hearts, and sauté potatoes in butter with lardoons; garnished with croquettes of mashed spinach
Visitandine ⇒ pastry-boat made of white of eggs, almond powder, butter and sugar
Vitello tonnato *-[Italie]-* ⇒ dish of veal, tunny and anchovies; garnished of capers
Vivaneau ⇒ snapper
Vivaneau campèche ⇒ red snapper
Vivaneau sorbe ⇒ mutton snapper
Vivaneau gazou ⇒ lane snapper
Vivaneau dentchen ⇒ schoolmaster
Vivaneau noir ⇒ black snapper
Vivaneau à queue jaune ⇒ yellowtail snapper
Vivaneau ti-yeux ⇒ vermilion snapper
Vivaneau amarante ⇒ pargo colorado
Vivaneau bourgeois ⇒ red emperor
Vivaneau queue noire ⇒ taiva
Vive ⇒ weever
Vive *-[algue]-* ⇒ seaweed
Vives grillées ⇒ weevers marinated in oil, lemon juice, pepper, parsley, and garlic, then grilled; served with ...
    - beurre fondu ⇒ ... melted butter, added of herbs
    - huile d'olive ⇒ ... mixing of olive oil, and crushed tomatoes
Viveur
    - potage ⇒ poultry consommé, added of celery in julienne; served with small round pieces of bread paprika flavoured
    - omelette viveur ⇒ voir texte
Vladimir ⇒ ... with a garnish of sauté cucumbers and courgettes, plus a sauce made of sour cream, horse radish and paprika
V.O « Very Old » *-[armagnac]-* ⇒ armagnac at least four years old
Voandzeia ⇒ African pea
Vodka ⇒ vodka < *uncountable* >
Vodka fizz ⇒ cocktail of sugar, vodka, pineapple juice, and soda water
Voiler ⇒ to cover

- **voilé** ⇒ covered with ...
Voillipäpôyta -*[smörgasbord]*- ⇒ smorgasbord
Vol-au-vent ⇒ vol-au-vent
Volaille ⇒ poultry < *nom collectif* >
Volnay ⇒ Burgundy red wine from Côte de Beaune
Volvaire soyeuse ⇒ edible mushroom
Vorshmack -*[Finlande]*- ⇒ hash of mutton, beef, and salted herring, flavoured with garlic and onion
Vosne-Romanée ⇒ Burgundy red wine from Côtes de Nuits
Vouvray ⇒ white wine from Tours area
Vrai mousseron ⇒ meadow mushroom
Vras ⇒ wrasse
Vrille de vigne ⇒ vine's tendril or tendril
V.S.O.P -*[very superior old pale]*-
   - **armagnac** ⇒ high quality armagnac
   - **calvados** ⇒ five years old calvados
   - **cognac** ⇒ five years old cognac

W

Wakame -[*algues, Japon*]- ⇒ Wakame
Waldorf -[*salade*]- ⇒ salad of apples, celeriac and nuts, seasoned with mayonnaise
Walewska (*à la ...*) ⇒ poached fish, garnished of crustaceae and truffle lamellas; covered with a béchamel sauce added of egg-yolks and gruyère, then browned
Walnut ketchup ⇒ walnut ketchup
Wam -[*Flandre*]- ⇒ dried fish
Wasabi -[*Japon*]- ⇒ seasoning of rice vinegar, sesame oil, and horse-radish mustard
Washington -[*garniture pour volailles pochées ou braisées*]- ⇒ ... with a garnish of boiled maize thickened of cream
Washinton -[*orange*]- ⇒ variety of orange
Waterfish chaude -[*sauce*]- ⇒ sauce of white wine and julienne, moistened of stock, then added of sauce hollandaise and parsley
Waterfish froide -[*sauce*]- ⇒ jelly of fish stock, added of julienne, capsicum, gherkins, and capers
Waterzooi ou Waterzol
    - poisson ⇒ sea fishes and eels cooked in court-bouillon, with aromatics, and parsley roots; served added of butter and cream
    - volaille à Gand ⇒ bits of poultry cooked in court-bouillon, with aromatics, and parsley roots; served added of butter and cream
Waterzoï de poissons ⇒ stew of freshwater fishes, leek, celery, pepper, herbs, sage, fish stock, and cream
Waterzoï de poulet ⇒ stew of chicken, leek, celery, pepper, herbs, onion, and cream
Wedding cake -[*cake*]- ⇒ wedding cake
Weisslacker ⇒ cubic German cow's milk cheese
Weisswurst -[*saucisse blanche*]- ⇒ sausage of veal, beef, and parsley
Welsh rarebit ⇒ welsh rarebit or welsh rabbit
Wensleydale -[*fromage*]- ⇒ wensleydale
Went -[*Ethiopie*]- ⇒ Ethiopian sauce
Wexford -[*fromage*]- ⇒ wexford
Whisky ⇒ whisky
Whiskey -[*whisky Irlandais*]- ⇒ whiskey
Whisky mac ⇒ whisky added of ginger wine
Whitbread -[*bière*]- ⇒ whitbread
    - brune ⇒ brown whitbread
    - blonde ⇒ pale whitbread
Whitebait -[*blanchaille*]- ⇒ whitebait
Wilking du Maroc -[*mandarine*]- ⇒ early spring mandarin orange
William -[*poire*]- ⇒ kind of sweet pear
    - boisson ⇒ pear based drink
Williamine -[*eau de vie de poire*]- ⇒ pear eau de vie
Winthertur -[*langouste*]- ⇒ spiny lobster cooked in a court-bouillon, filled with a culinary stuffing of truffles, mushrooms and shrimps
Wladimir
    1) turbot ou sole ⇒ poached turbot or sole, covered with a white wine sauce added of crushed tomatoes and poached small clams, then browned
    2) petites pièces de boucherie ⇒ sauté ... garnished with braised cucumbers, and sauté courgettes; covered of sour cream added of paprika and grated horse-radish

3) oeufs sur le plat ⇒ fried eggs sprinkled of grated parmesan and garnished with diced truffle, plus asparagus tips

Worcestershire sauce ⇒ Worcestershire sauce

Wuchteln ⇒ dessert made of leaven paste, filled with plum jam

X

Xaintray -*[Poitou fromage]*- ⇒ goat's milk cheese
Xampan -*[Espagne vin]*- ⇒ Spanish sparkling wine
Xanfaïna -*[sauce pour volaille, escalope, viande blanche ou homard]*- ⇒ sauce made of diced
onions, capsicums and vegetables cooked in hot oil with mint, parsley, cumin and
pepper
Xanfaina d'Espagne -*[sauce pour volaille, escalope, viande blanche ou homard]*- ⇒ sauce
made of diced onions, capsicums and vegetables; cooked in hot oil with mint, parsley,
cumin, and pepper
Xavier -*[potage]*- ⇒ poultry consommé thickened with egg-yolks, rice cream and cream; garnished
with diced chicken and butter
Xérès ⇒ xeres
Xiang xsin -*[champignon]*- ⇒ Chinese mushroom
Xilopia ⇒ guinea pepper
Ximénia ⇒ tropical fruit
Xinxin de galinha -*[Brésil]*- ⇒ chicken fricassée with peanut, and manioc
XO -*[armagnac]*- ⇒ high quality Armagnac

Y

Yack ⇒ yak

Yakitori ⇒ kebab of poultry steeped in a sauce of sake, soya sauce, and ginger; then grilled

Yalanci dolmas ⇒ vine leaves stuffed with rice, onions, lamb meat, and mint; then braised in olive oil, lemon juice, stock, and coriander

Yaourt ⇒ yoghourt < *uncountable* >

    - **traduire le pluriel par** ⇒ ... with some yoghourt

Yassa ⇒ Senegalese dish of mutton, chicken or fish; served with rice or millet

Yassa de poulet ⇒ chicken cooked in its marinade; served with rice

Yecla ⇒ Spanish rosé wine

Yemas de santa Teresa ⇒ pastry balls made of white of eggs, and sugar

Yerba maté -*[maté]*- ⇒ maté

    - **infusion** ⇒ maté tea

Yorkaise (*à la ...*)

    - **boeuf** ⇒ beef with York ham

    - **oeufs** ⇒ poached eggs laid on ham covered with Madeira jelly

Yorkshire pudding ⇒ Yorkshire pudding88

Yorkshire sauce ⇒ Yorkshire sauce

Youp gwad ⇒ oat's porridge added of pig blood

Yucca -*[fruit du Mexique]*- ⇒ yucca

Yunnan -*[thé]*- ⇒ high quality Chinese tea

Z

Zabaglione ⇒ zabaglione
Zabaione -*[sabayon]*-
   - **dessert** ⇒ zabaglione
   - **sauce** ⇒ creamy sauce made with champagne
Zakouski ⇒ Russian hors d'œuvres
Zampone ⇒ stuffed pig trotter
Zapparota *(alla ...)* -*[spaghetti]*- ⇒ spaghetti cooked with capsicum, and pimento
Zarzuela ⇒ ragout of fish and seafood
Zavyvaniets -*[Russe]*- ⇒ small pastry balls stuffed of fruits and nuts, then wrapped with sugar paste
Zébu
   - **lait** ⇒ zebu's milk
   - **viande** ⇒ zebu meat
Zée ou St Pierre ⇒ john dory
Zegeni -*[Erythrée]*- ⇒ mutton cooked with pimento paste and vegetables; served with flat cakes
Zephyr
   - **soufflé** ⇒ soufflé
   - **quenelles** ⇒ quenelles
   - **mousses** ⇒ mousses
   - **Zéphyr antillais** ⇒ balls of ice-cream flavoured with vanilla and rum, coated with meringue; accompanied of a zabaglione
   - **Petits gâteaux** ⇒ small cakes coated with custard flavoured of praline or coffee
Zéphyr aux fruits de mer ⇒ soufflé added of chopped mussels and crayfishes; topped with mussels, crayfishes and grated cheese, then browned
Zeste ⇒ peel or rind < *tous uncountable* >
   - **fruits orange** ⇒ orange peel < *uncountable* >
   - **citron** ⇒ lemon peel < *uncountable* >
   - **cuisine** ⇒ zest or peel < *uncountable* >
   - **avec un zeste de citron** ⇒ with a piece of lemon peel
Zeste de citron confit au vinaigre ⇒ diced lemon peel, candied in sugar and vinegar
Zewelwai ⇒ onion tart added of cream, eggs, pepper, nutmeg, and lardoons
Ziminu ⇒ Corsican bouillabaisse from Corte
Zingara -*[garniture et sauce]*- ⇒ with paprika
Zubrowka -*[vodka]*- ⇒ vodka flavoured with graminaceous
Zucchini ⇒ marrow or courgette
Zungenwurst
   1) **boudin noir** ⇒ polony added of oxtongue, or pig tongue
   2) **saucisse** ⇒ sausage of streaky bacon, blood and tongue
Zupa szczawiowa ⇒ soup added of sorrel and smoked bacon
Zuppa di cozze ⇒ soup of garlic, celery, and onion, garnished with mussels
Zuppa inglese ⇒ Genoese sponge moistened with kirsch, then stuffed of confectioner's custard, plus preserved fruits
Zwetschenknüdel -*[Autriche]*- ⇒ small pastry balls, stuffed with compote of cherries, or compote of apricots; then poached
Zwicker -*[vin]*- ⇒ wine made with secondary varieties of vine, from Alsace area
Zwieback -*[biscotte]*- ⇒ Zwieback
Zwiebelfleisch -*[Autriche]*- ⇒ beef cooked with onions and cumin

Cet ouvrage a été achevé d'imprimer en octobre 1997
dans les ateliers de Normandie Roto Impression s.a.
61250 Lonrai
N° d'impression : 972106
Dépôt légal : octobre 1997

Imprimé en France